. . . historical learning

grants men glimpses of life

completed and whole;

and such a vision should be

the chief solace of whatever is mortal

and cut off imperfectly from fulfillment."

HILAIRE BELLOC, *The Old Road*

ROSS J. S. HOFFMAN, PH.D., LL.D., LITT.D., L.H.D.
PROFESSOR OF HISTORY, FORDHAM UNIVERSITY, NEW YORK

GAETANO L. VINCITORIO, PH.D.
PROFESSOR OF HISTORY, ST. JOHN'S UNIVERSITY, NEW YORK

MORRISON V. SWIFT, M.A.
ASSISTANT PROFESSOR OF HISTORY, MANHATTAN COLLEGE, NEW YORK

DOUBLEDAY & COMPANY, INC.
CATHOLIC TEXTBOOK DIVISION
GARDEN CITY, NEW YORK

MAN AND HIS HISTORY

World History and Western Civilization

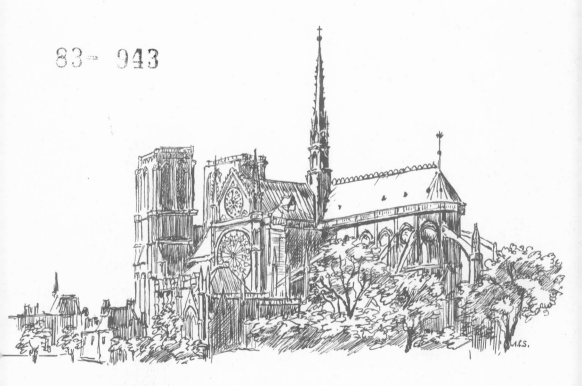

The Christian Democracy Series

A HISTORY AND SOCIAL STUDIES SERIES FOR CATHOLIC HIGH SCHOOLS

Editor-in-Chief: ROSS J. S. HOFFMAN, PH.D.
PROFESSOR OF HISTORY, FORDHAM UNIVERSITY

NIHIL OBSTAT: Martinus S. Rushford, PH.D., *Censor Librorum*

IMPRIMATUR ✠ Bryan Iosephus McEntegart, D.D., LL.D., *Episcopus Bruklyniensis*

BRUKLYNI
Die xi februarii, 1958
The Feast of Our Lady of Lourdes

DESIGNED BY JOSEPH P. ASCHERL · ILLUSTRATIONS BY DAN NOONAN
CARTOGRAPHY BY DONALD PITCHER · BINDING DESIGN BY RAFAEL PALACIOS
STUDY AIDS BY GEORGE D. WENDEL · COPYEDITED BY JEANNE POSILLICO HANSEN
INDEX BY GRACE OLSEN EGAN

Preface

The authors of MAN AND HIS HISTORY have aimed to present, intelligibly and therefore in predominantly chronological order, an account of those great human events that learned and philosophical scholars recognize as the substance of universal or world history. To do this, it was necessary to have a clear and definite concept of what is meant by the term *world history*. It does not mean the complete account of all human events, of all that human beings in all lands and all ages have thought, said, made, or done. The meaning is limited to the story of the great events or developments—the growth of civilizations and empires, the rise and spread of universal religions, major revolutions, voyages and discoveries, scientific achievements, industrial progress, world wars—that have influenced or affected the whole or greater part of human society in a recognized strongly marked manner. Moreover, it means the presentation of these events in a particular way: raising them out of their narrow regional or merely national importance to display their universal significance. For this reason much that is known about the past is left unsaid and the whole story of man is not told, but only that part which a universal aspect throws into relief. World history might be likened in geography to a large-scale map of the world that shows all the continents and major islands, the principal mountain ranges, the oceans and larger lakes and rivers, but cannot show a vast number of smaller features of the earth's surface that would appear only on maps of smaller scale.

World history, so conceived, displays form and pattern and appears as an expanding process of civilization, understanding of natural forces, institution-building, and human society's knowledge of itself. A principal feature of it has been the activity of Europeans, who may be said to have been the principal architects of the larger part of this expanding process. It was they who went out to explore the world and took the lead in knitting the ties and contacts that enabled the scattered branches of mankind to become mutually acquainted. Africans, North American Indians, and Chinese did not go out to meet the Europeans, but the Europeans went out to meet them. That is why a great part of European history and the history of so much that went into the making of European civilization displays a world-historic aspect. It is so recognized in this book.

The study of world history, as presented here, is an excellent preparation of the pupil's mind for the study of the history of the United States. It will give him his bearings, so that he will grasp where he stands on the long course of historical life; and he will come later to a course in American history equipped with intelligent perspective and a true concept of his country's relation to other nations of the past and the present.

ROSS J. S. HOFFMAN

EDITOR-IN-CHIEF, *The Christian Democracy Series*

Other books in *The Christian Democracy Series:*

MAN THE CITIZEN: *The Foundations of Civil Society*
By Rev. Joseph N. Moody, Ph.D.
and Joseph F. X. McCarthy, M.A.

CONCEIVED IN LIBERTY: *The History of the United States*
By Marshall Smelser, Ph.D.
and Harry Kirwin, Ph.D.

THE COMMON GOOD: *Christian Democracy and American National Problems*
By Thomas Neill, Ph.D.

Maps

Contents

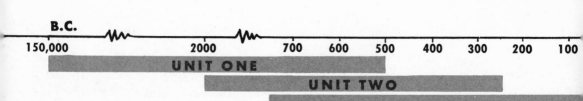

A.D.

| 1 | 50 | 100 | 150 | 200 | 250 | 300 | 350 | 400 | 450 | 500 | 550 | 600 |

UNIT THREE

| 400 | 450 | 500 | 550 | 600 | 650 | 700 | 750 | 800 | 850 | 900 | 950 | 1000 |

UNIT FOUR

UNIT THREE

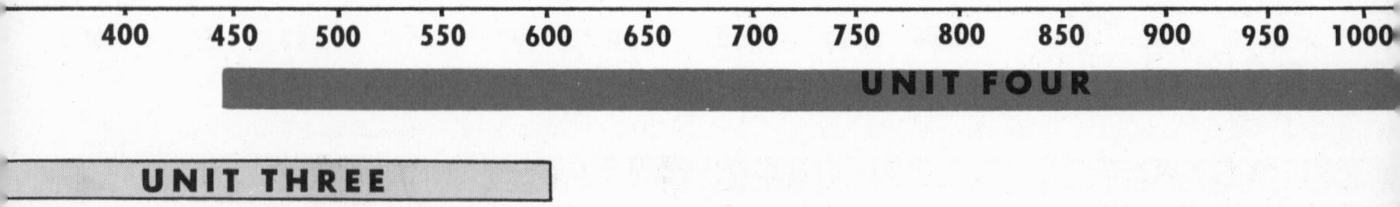

1050   1100   1150   1200   1250 1300   1350   1400   1450   1500   1550   1600   1650

UNIT FIVE

UNIT SIX

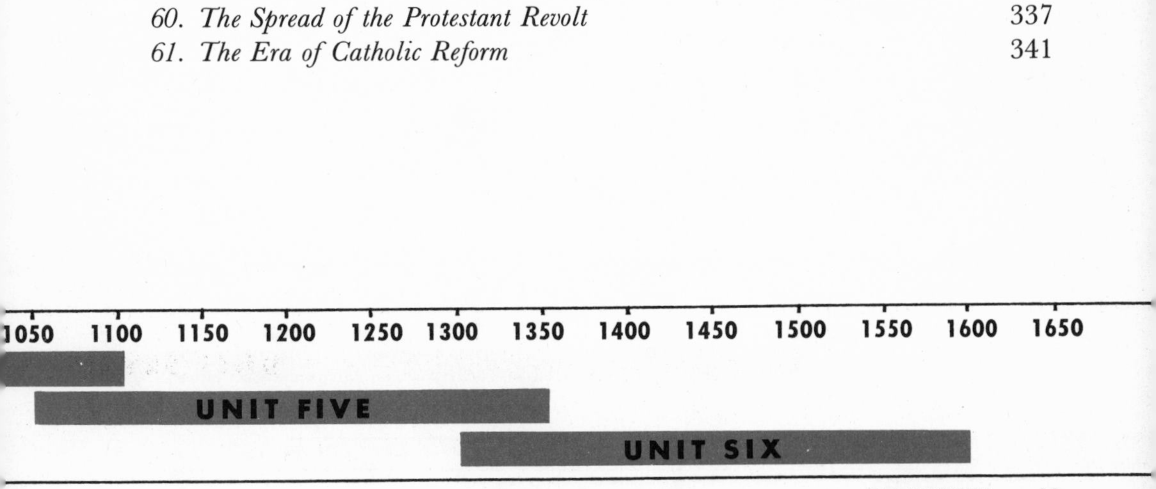

| 1400 | 1425 | 1450 | 1475 | 1500 | 1525 | 1550 | 1575 | 1600 | 1625 | 1650 |

UNIT SEVEN

UNIT SIX

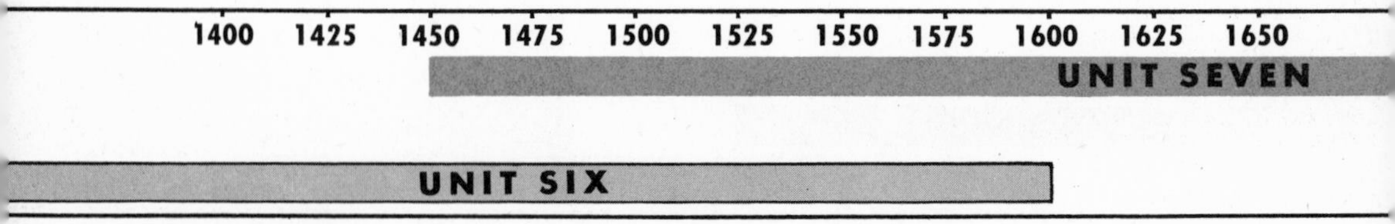

1675   1700   1725   1750   1775   1800   1825   1850   1875   1900   1925

UNIT EIGHT

UNIT NINE

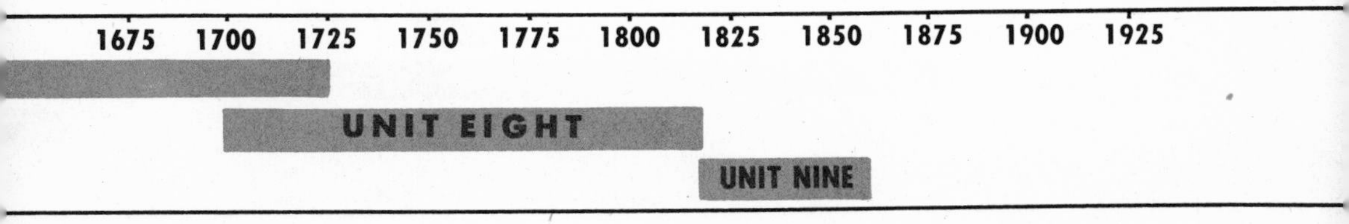

1830   1840   1850   1860   1870   1880   1890

UNIT TEN

UNIT NINE

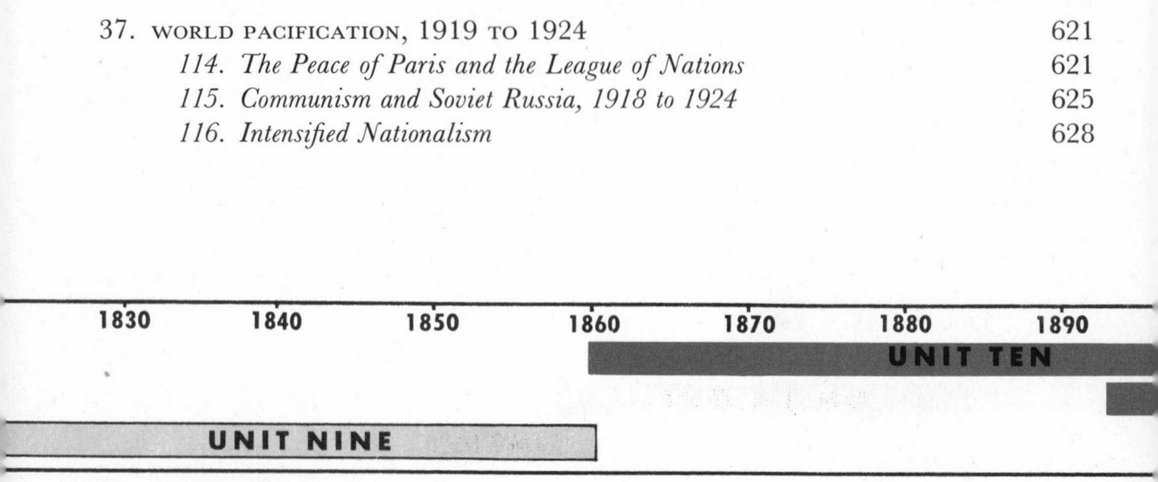

1900   1910   1920   1930   1940   1950   1958

UNIT ELEVEN

UNIT TWELVE

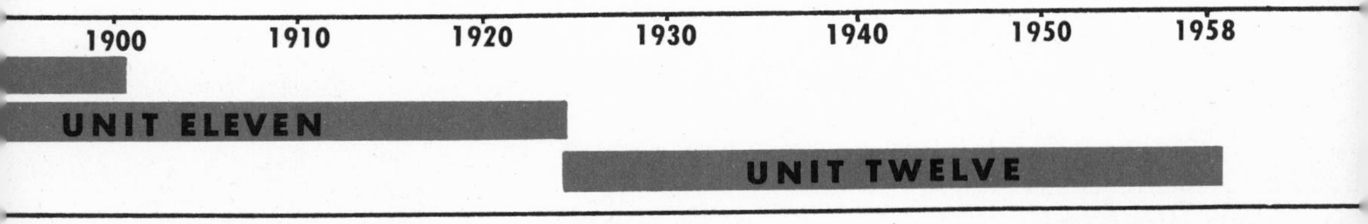

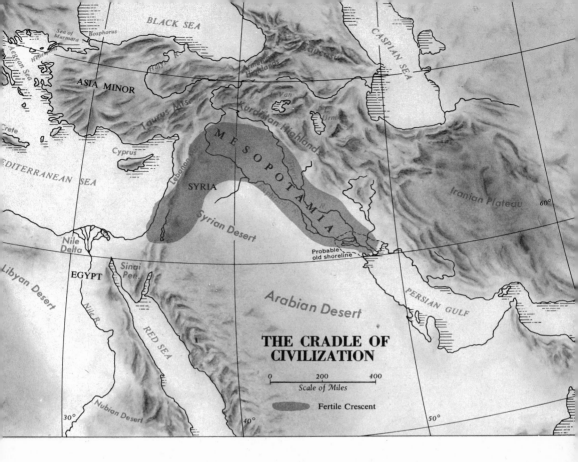

The map shows labels: BLACK SEA, Sea of Marmara, Bosphorus, ASIA MINOR, Taurus Mts., Armenian Highland, Van, Urmia, Kurdistan Highland, CASPIAN SEA, MESOPOTAMIA, Iranian Plateau, 60°, Aegean Sea, Crete, Cyprus, Lebanon, SYRIA, Syrian Desert, MEDITERRANEAN SEA, Nile Delta, EGYPT, Sinai Pen., Probable old shoreline, PERSIAN GULF, Libyan Desert, Nile R., Arabian Desert, RED SEA, Nubian Desert, 30°, 40°, 50°

THE CRADLE OF CIVILIZATION

0   200   400

Scale of Miles

▬ Fertile Crescent

UNIT ONE
The Ancient World

The Study of History · The Human Race in the Stone Age · Mesopotamia and Egypt, 4000 to 1800 B.C. · Character of the Earliest Civilizations · The Rise and Decline of the Egyptian and Hittite Empires · The International World c. 1200 to 900 B.C. · The Assyrian, Neo-Babylonian, and Persian Empires · The Rise of Universal Religious Concepts and Ideals · Civilization and Religion in Ancient India and China

Chapter 1. Our Earliest Ancestors

1. THE STUDY OF HISTORY

The word *history* is used in various ways, but always it is connected with an idea of the past. Today—this minute—we may do any one of a number of things; tomorrow they will be part of our history. Everything that exists or ever did exist has a history, because it has a past. Your country, your state, your city, your school, your family have their histories. You have your own personal history. This word may mean either the past events themselves or a written account telling when, how, and why they happened. Thus even this book, which *is* a history, *has* a history—a history of why the authors wrote it, where they learned what they have written, where and how it was printed, and why your principal or teacher came to choose it as a suitable book for you to study the history of the world.

What is world history? It is not the history of the planet Earth, although that too has a history, since it is millions or billions of years old and has passed through many great changes. To define world history we must first determine what we mean by the word *world*, which, like the word *history*, is used in various ways. If we say that the world is round, we are talking about the planet. But if we say that a young man, having finished his schooling, has gone into the world or taken his place in the world, we are talking about the society of mankind. This is exactly the meaning of the word *world* when we speak of world history. We mean the world of human relations, mankind considered socially, human society. *World* history is the history of human beings living together, working together, creating together.

The study of world history takes our minds back to times long ago about which we can say little more than that the human race then existed. Then it carries our minds forward to the times in which we live. But it is important to understand that world history does not include everything that all men and women have thought, said, and done at all times everywhere in the world. If it included so much, it would be a total account of human life, which only God knows. Vast though it is in scope, world history can take but a partial and limited view of the human world. The records that make it possible to write world history are very incomplete. Even the search for those records is far from complete. It is possible to know only a small part of the story of mankind, and world history does not even include every fact that is known about all the people of the world. It confines itself to the great and important events and developments which have affected the whole human world. It treats of the building of the cities, states, nations, and empires that have in some degree influenced the whole or the greater part of mankind. It deals with the development of laws and religions that have had more than a small local significance. It is concerned with the growth of knowledge and wisdom, of invention, discovery, and moral and material progress. It is the story of human society "on the move."

In certain parts of the earth there still are tribes of people who live just as their ancestors lived thousands of years ago. They neither discover nor invent, but keep to their ancient ways. A description of one of their days would differ hardly at all from a description of all of their days. They are part of the population of the earth and therefore part of human society. But they have taken no part in world history, although in the future they may do so. World history is the story of a social process or activity that began among peoples in certain regions of the earth and spread more and more widely. The nature of that process will be revealed as we read through this book.

Excavations help archaeologists in their study of mankind by uncovering evidences of past civilizations. The grid marks on the side of the pit aid in classifying the findings. (Geol. Survey of China, Dr. Franz Weidenreich)

Why study history? Every so often somebody asks this foolish question. In the back of such a person's mind is the notion that since the past is dead and gone forever why bother about it? But the truth is, the past is not really dead and gone. It is all around us and in us. Our laws, our schools, our religion —all our civilization—form a heritage that we have received from the past. Each of us is born into a society and material order of things that are of past formation. We may change them a little during our lives, but we did not make them. How did such an arrangement of the scene of life come about? Why this? Why that? If we have ordinary intelligence, natural curiosity moves us to ask such questions. The answers are from history. Our world would be completely incomprehensible to us if we knew no

history. Moreover, since each of us is a little different today because of what we did yesterday, yesterday made its mark on us, and the mark is there for the rest of our lives even though we may not be conscious of it. Thus we carry all our yesterdays forward with us as we move into the future. So does all human society. Time marches on, but what we and all the human race did in the past is fixed forever in the present.

History as verified experience. Of course every person who lives a normal length of time and looks about and notices what is going on in the world learns a good deal of history without doing much systematic studying of it. He observes great changes, especially if he lives through wars or revolutions, and he remembers and reflects upon them. But unless his curiosity drives

Cambridge University students are shown engaged in archaeological excavations at Yorkshire, England. At the left the findings are photographed for further study. (British Information Services)

him to investigate the world *before his own times,* his ideas about his own times will not be very profound. If we are to be wise in our rather short span of life, we must know a good deal about the experience of past generations of people. History ought to be thought of as remembered and verified human experience. If mankind were to forget its history, it would be like a man suffering from loss of memory. Such a man no longer knows his own name, or where he lives, or anything about himself. He must recover his memory, or he is handicapped in whatever he does. Moreover, just as a man gains in wisdom from reflecting on his own experience, so does the human race grow wiser by reflecting on its much larger, longer, and more varied experience. When we learn about people in past ages who lived, thought, and acted in ways very different from our own today, we obtain a much richer and deeper knowledge of the kind of race to which we belong. Therefore, we know more about ourselves and understand human nature better.

Moral wisdom. Great truths of morality are demonstrated in history, and by studying it we become more aware of the reality and activity of Divine Providence in the affairs of men. We extend our natural limits and learn more of life. We come to understand how God can draw good out of evil in the long slow process of history. As a great Catholic poet and historian has written:

It is excellent to see perpetual agony and failure perpetually breeding the only enduring things; it is excellent to see the crimes we know ground under the slow wheels whose ponderous advance we can hardly note during the flash of one human life. One may say that historical learning grants men glimpses of life completed and whole; and such a vision should be the chief solace of whatever is mortal and cut off imperfectly from fulfillment.[1]

The best things in our life have resulted from the work, thought, sacrifice, and suffering of many past generations. And the best things in the future will be due to the hard work, virtuous intentions, and sacrifices of those living today. Wise men have always had gratitude in their hearts for what they owe to those who went before them, and lived with a sense of holding a trust for the generations to come. History alone reveals how living in this spirit works for the welfare of all generations.

The best way to approach the study of history, therefore, is by realizing at the start that it is not something that has no relation to *us.* It is *our* history, the story of the race to which we belong.

Before history began. World history, as we have defined it, does not reach back to the beginning of all things. It can hardly be said to have started until about six thousand years ago. Before that there were thousands and thousands of years during which men left no records of the kind that enable a historian to reconstruct their history, although it is certain that the human race existed. And back beyond that *prehistoric* age occurred what may poetically be called the world's first morning.

Millions, perhaps billions, of years

[1] Hilaire Belloc, *The Old Road* (Philadelphia: J. B. Lippincott Co., 1911), p. 9.

Records of world history are found in libraries and museums all over the world. At the left is the Archeological Museum of Istanbul; at the right is the National Library in Vienna.

before the human race existed God created the earth and all the universe. Geologists and other natural scientists have found evidence that our spinning globe underwent many great alterations before assuming its present surface, climate, and seasons. Whole continents have been submerged by seas, and mountain ranges have been thrown up from the floors of oceans by volcanic activity. Much smaller changes on the face of the earth have taken place since *historic* men are known to have observed them; in fact, the surface of the earth is always changing in some degree. Volcanoes still erupt. Tides wash away shores and rivers flood their banks, making the land a little different each time. The great ice-covered polar caps rumble, crack, and let loose icebergs to float off in the sea. Mountains, so massive and awesome that they seem to stand motionless for eternity, are

changed by landslides and by the effects of melting and freezing on their high glacial peaks and in their valleys. Moreover, human beings change the geographic form of the earth by cutting canals or reclaiming land from the sea with dikes, or dumping earth into offshore shallows. Earth has never been still and fixed in its form. There is good reason to believe that vast sheets of ice have covered the greater part of the globe at least four times in the last million years. These were the great glacial ages, each lasting perhaps twenty-five thousand years, with still longer interglacial ages of moderate climate occurring before and after them. In such remote and unimaginable ages various forms of animal and plant life appeared and passed away. Substantial evidence shows that human beings existed in the last interglacial age, which probably lasted from 150,000 to 50,000 years ago. But when and where the first man was formed is a complete mystery, and there is no possibility that this mystery can ever be solved by *historical* investigation. Even if, as some suppose, man evolved from some lower order of animal life (which has never been proved) there could be no human record or memory of such a process or event.

Religion teaches what history cannot teach. We have only to reflect a little to see how inevitable it is that our race should have no record or remembrance of its origin. No one remembers and records his own birth or even his early infancy. We exist before we are aware of the fact and are in the world for some time before it even occurs to us to ask any questions about it. We could not know who our parents are, or where we were born, or how we acquired our names, if our parents did not tell us. So it is with the human race, which can know of its creation only what its Creator has chosen to reveal. This is why the creation of man is not a subject for *historical* study but belongs to religion. History treats of the relations between man and man. Religion has to do with the relations between man and God, and the first and fundamental of these relations is that of creature to Creator. In Genesis, the first book of the Old Testament, we may read what God has revealed about the origin of mankind: the creation of Adam and Eve, and the story of their disobedience to God and expulsion from the Garden of Paradise. But the author of Genesis did not learn of this by searching into historical records; he wrote under the direct inspiration of God. He wrote truth, but truth of a far higher order than that which is written by uninspired historians, who must trace out the story of mankind by studying the things men leave behind them—tools, weapons, utensils, writings, and so forth. The search for such records stops far short of leading back to our earliest ancestors. Only where human records begin can what is properly called history begin, because without records the historian cannot discover anything about the past.

Glacial remains in Alberta, Canada. Glaciers, which change the topography of the earth, are studied for traces of early man and for valuable information about man's changing habitats. (American Museum of Natural History)

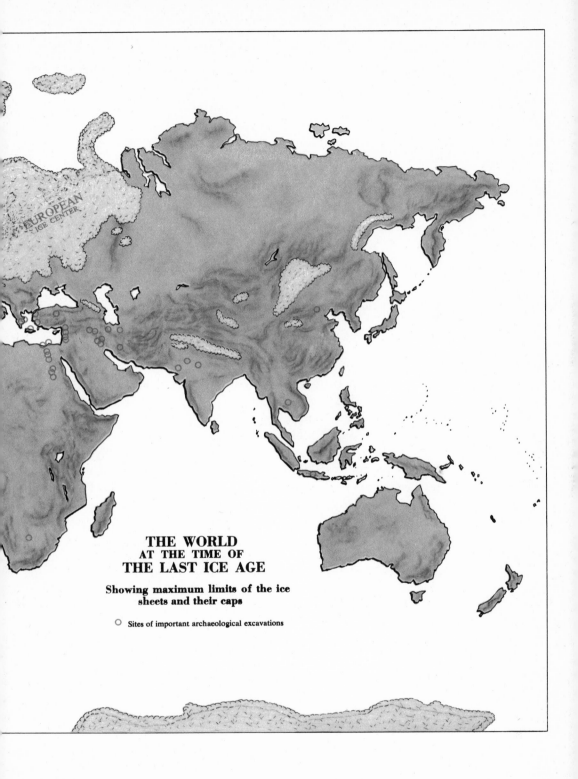

THE WORLD
AT THE TIME OF
THE LAST ICE AGE

**Showing maximum limits of the ice
sheets and their caps**

○ Sites of important archaeological excavations

2. THE HUMAN RACE IN THE STONE AGE

The Old Stone Age. The earliest evidence of the existence of the human race consists of crude stone tools and weapons. Such things have been found in caves or buried deep in the ground, under conditions that indicate they had lain there since before the last glacial age. Since making tools is a distinguishing characteristic of human beings, where such remains are found it is certain that they were made by our ancestors. Because of such stone tools and weapons, the remote times of the people who made and used them are called the Old Stone Age, or the Paleolithic Age, which means the same thing. Specialists who make it their business to study the evidence divide the Old Stone Age into the Early (or Lower) Paleolithic period, and the Later (or Upper) Paleolithic period. The former lasted probably during the period from 1,000,000 (or even farther back) to about 50,000 years ago. The later period did not end until about 10,000 years ago.

Little more can be said about Lower Paleolithic people than that they spread over much of Europe, Asia, and Africa, and lived by hunting and killing animals. No doubt they ate wild fruits, vegetables, and berries wherever they could find them, but they had no agriculture. They learned to build fires and to cook their meat. They clothed themselves in the skins of animals and probably built rude huts of branches of trees. Since speech is a necessary characteristic of human nature, there is no doubt they had language—vocal sounds to represent things and actions. Skeleton remains of Lower Paleolithic times show that many great and terrifying beasts roamed the earth. Among them was the elephant, which still exists. Others, such as the huge mammoth and terrible saber-toothed tiger, have long disappeared from the earth. Life, therefore, was very dangerous, as well as poor and hard, for our Stone Age ancestors.

After many thousands of years the climate began to grow colder and colder. The change must have been so gradual, however, that nobody then living could notice what was happening. Little by little the last Ice Age came upon the earth, bringing the reindeer to regions from which elephants, tigers, and rhinoceroses disappeared. People took to living in caves or holes in the ground. About a hundred years ago the skull of a man of this age was found in the valley of the Neander River in Germany, whence he gets his name, Neanderthal man.

In the Upper or Later Paleolithic period the climax of the ice and cold was reached and the earth began slowly to grow warmer. Men were still hunters and cave dwellers, but they had learned to chip stone a little better. Among their weapons now were the bow and arrow tipped by a sharp-pointed stone. Animal bones and horns were made into tools. From this time dates the earliest known art: crude carvings on stone and ivory. Some Upper Paleolithic peoples developed high artistic ability. They found a way to make colors for painting. On the walls of certain caves in southern France and Spain, Paleolithic paintings of great skill and beauty

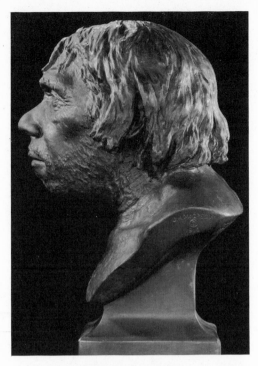

Neanderthal man lived part of the year in a cave. In some cave excavations skeletons were found buried with food and implements, which might indicate that the Neanderthal man believed in immortality. (American Museum of Natural History)

man has a sense of dependence on external powers which are conceived as mysterious and higher than man's own, there is religion, and . . . the root of worship and prayer."[2] Men never have been wholly without that sense of dependence. Sometimes it has been dulled, but it cannot be completely extinguished in human nature. Various have been its manifestations. The Paleolithic peoples, being hunters, depended for survival on killing animals for food. Some great beasts were very hard to kill with crude stone weapons; they had to be surrounded and attacked by many men acting together. Often there were human casualties in such risky undertakings. It seems likely that people felt the need for help from higher powers and believed in the existence of mighty beast-gods who ruled over and protected the beasts. Hence men had to obtain the favor of those gods in order to be allowed to kill the animals. The caves decorated with the pictures of animals may well have been temples for the

have been found in modern times. They depict great bison, wild boars, horses, and reindeer in the most natural and lifelike way; yet they undoubtedly were painted by people who lived from twenty to thirty thousand years ago. They prove that the "cave man" hunter of the Stone Age was something more than a wild savage. He was an artist.

Religion in the Old Stone Age. It is not less certain that Paleolithic people were religious, because man is religious by nature. "Wherever and whenever

[2] Christopher Dawson, *The Age of the Gods* (London: John Murray, Ltd., 1928), p. 22.

As man developed skills and invented more efficient implements, he painted colorful and lasting pictures of his surroundings on cave walls. This cave painting found in Altamira, Spain, shows a curled bison. (American Museum of Natural History)

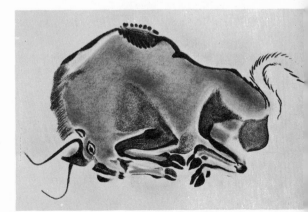

worship of the beast-gods. If so, one can but wonder what strange prayers and sacrifices took place in those caves.

Our imagination fails us when we try to see in the mind's eye the uncounted generations of Paleolithic people. We know what men have proved capable of accomplishing—their sciences and arts and great civilizations. Why, then, did they live for so long in the wilderness? It appears as if some great calamity had fallen upon human nature itself, as if some sentence of banishment and damnation had been laid on man by his Creator. Such is the answer that religion gives to this deep and mysterious question.

Examples of some of the earliest known engraving and sculpture found in Europe, representing the culture of the Later or Upper Paleolithic period. Some of these items were useful as well as decorative. (American Museum of Natural History)

The Neolithic Age. The long slow melting that put an end to the last age of ice had probably gone far enough by about ten thousand years ago for the main geographic and climatic features of the world to become nearly as we know them today. Forests and prairies, lakes and rivers appeared where all had been ice in most of the land surface of the Northern Hemisphere. Therefore, many changes took place gradually in animal life. The human race adapted itself to this immense alteration, which occurred so slowly that nobody in a single lifetime could notice what was happening. Evidence dug from the earth in very recent times shows that some progressive improvement in the conditions of life had started in certain regions by about seven thousand years ago. Men were learning now to tame and breed herds of cattle and sheep; that is, to domesticate such animals. They had domesticated also pigs and goats. (Paleolithic people probably had made helpful friends of dogs.) Herds of animals now provided a good supply of milk, meat, and skins. People learned to weave flax and make linen cloth. Stone weapons and tools were improved by means of grindstones and polished and shaped in various more useful ways. Sharp stone axes aided in cutting wood and in building crude wooden dwellings and boats. Some unknown genius conceived and made the wheel, one of the greatest inventions in human history. By means of the wheel, carts and wagons were constructed. The art of molding and baking clay into pottery was developed. Most important of all, men discovered how to plant seeds and create a food supply by growing such vegetables and fruits as were then known to be edible. Thus was agriculture started. The ground was scratched by sharp stone tools. Wheat, barley, peas, lentils, and beans were planted, harvested, and stored in clay pots and jars. Grain was ground and bread was made. All this achievement no doubt was the work of many centuries, for primitive men were fearful of new things lest they offend against old sacred ways of life ordained by their gods. Wherever evidence is found to indicate that primitive peoples had begun to make these improvements, we may say that they had moved into a new age. It is called the Neolithic Age, which means the New Stone Age.

Perhaps it was the killing off of most of the wild animals in a large region that challenged the men there to become stock breeders and farmers. Great changes in their physical environment have usually provoked people to alter their way of life and to find new methods of getting a food supply from nature. No doubt the

Neolithic pottery, important to archaeologists, is the most widespread and oldest form of art on record. Primitive people fashioned them for daily use and made them of enduring materials. (American Museum of Natural History)

presence of wild grains in particular parts of the world offered inviting opportunities for agriculture. Great rivers that spread rich soil when they flooded their banks must also have been a stimulus to agriculture in the Neolithic Age. Rivers, lakes, and the sea challenged fishermen and the builders of boats to improve their methods. As people became more dependent on agriculture they naturally moved about less. Families built permanent houses, and village communities grew up in places that afforded plentiful water, a good soil, and rich pasturage for their flocks and herds. Such communities grew to be small states ruled by "kings" who were the high priests of the local gods. But life in Neolithic times continued to be very hard and dangerous. Wars were

The manufacture of the knife, man's most basic tool, from ordinary stones was a great accomplishment. He learned after thousands of years to chip stone to a sharp-cutting edge. (American Museum of Natural History)

perpetually breaking out among the little states, and there still were wild and nomadic tribes who repeatedly attacked and plundered the village communities.

Family and State. Since man is by nature a social being, he has always lived in some sort of group or community. He cannot live a completely solitary life. The family, therefore, has existed in some form or other throughout all times. It is a natural, and therefore a divinely created, social institution. Families generate new families, who in primitive times formed themselves in blood-related clans. Then as clans multiplied they became tribes, or nations. Such developments brought a corresponding increase in social discipline, tribal customs, and organization. The members of a clan or tribe had to stick together and co-operate to defend their herds, pastures, and crops against robbers, or aggressive and jealous neighbors, or ferocious wild beasts such as wolves and hyenas. From such necessities there arose leadership and authority in society. Thus did government originate. But of course it was not until the settled Neolithic communities were formed that the *territorial* state, with more or less definite boundaries, could come into existence.

Division of Labor. As Neolithic ways of life developed, the occupations of people became more numerous and varied. Some people made tools and weapons, while others watched the herds or worked in the fields. This distribution of tasks is known as the division of labor; the more it developed, the greater became the productivity of all the people participating, and the more

skilled each person became at his special task. Hence, clothing, weapons, utensils of various kinds, and pottery were improved in usefulness and appearance. Man's natural artistic impulse was stimulated. From fragments and whole pieces of pottery found in various places it is possible to recognize a wonderful progress among Neolithic peoples in the artistic shaping and painting of bowls, jars, and vases.

Trade and commerce sprang up between Neolithic communities. Presently (nobody knows exactly where or when) men learned how to melt and mold copper. About six thousand years ago they invented the art of writing, and laid the foundation of natural science. When these things were achieved we may say that Neolithic cultures had developed civilization.

Culture and civilization. It is important to understand the meaning of these words. A culture is the sum total of a people's habits, customs, and ideas about life and the world in which they live. It includes their religious practices, morals, and folkways. Since all people have these, it is certain that the most primitive savages have a culture; and we may properly speak of Paleolithic and Neolithic cultures. Our word *civilization,* however, derives from the Latin word *civitas,* which means a city or city-state. It was when men formed the first city-states that they made a great advance in building houses and temples, developed improved mechanical devices, learned how to write, kept records and accounts, and began the development of science. This high and complex achievement is what is meant by civilization.

Stonehenge, a group of standing prehistoric stones on Salisbury Plain, England, is probably the remains of a temple connected with sun worship. Excavations in the area disclosed burial mounds of the Bronze Age. (British Information Services)

How little we know. The student should realize that very little is known about our Stone Age ancestors. The general character and conditions of their ways of life may be described with a fair measure of probability. We can be sure, too, that as agriculture was developed an enlarged food supply fostered an increase in population. But we have no knowledge of the extent of the population. Efforts to trace the movement of peoples from one part of the world to another are largely guesswork based on geographical probability. Thus it is believed that North America's earliest people were Paleolithic hunters who made their way from Asia by way of Alaska at some unknown time after the last Ice Age.

Not until the art of writing was developed did human society begin to leave behind the kind of record the historian needs to ascertain specific activities and events. Hence it is only with the beginnings of *civilization* that history takes on the character of a story about particular peoples and individual persons.

Where recorded history began. The earliest Neolithic cultures developed in the region of western Asia and northeastern Africa, which in modern times has been called the Near East, or Near and Middle East. Probably physical and climatic conditions there first became favorable for a cultural advance. Look at the map of this region that appears on p. 17 and observe its geographical features. It is bounded roughly by six seas: the Mediterranean, the Red, the Persian Gulf, the Caspian, the Black, and the Aegean seas. There is no place that is much more than five hundred miles from the sea. There are the most varied geographic forms: mountains and plateaus, narrow straits of water, peninsulas, lakes, offshore islands, deserts, and great rivers. Possibly this variety in the physical scene caused peoples to develop differing ways of life and, in mingling or colliding, to react upon one another and thus to stimulate the development of their ideas and knowledge. To the northwest you see a peninsula with many off-shore islands. The peninsula is Asia Minor, a high tableland with the Taurus Mountains rising still higher in the south. These appear as part of a great mountain system running off to the east, to the Armenian and Kurdistan highlands. Down from these mountains flow waters that form two rivers, the Tigris and Euphrates, which run in a general southeasterly direction to the salt sea of the Persian Gulf. Their way takes them through an almost flat plain, called Mesopotamia, which means "the land between the rivers." Every year the rivers flood their banks to inundate great stretches of the plain, and the water leaves behind a fertile sediment, or silt. The extreme southern part of the plain became especially rich from being actually formed by the silt carried down the rivers. This region was fashioned by nature to invite men to agriculture and the establishment of settled communities; also, it challenged

those communities to regulate the flood waters by digging irrigation ditches and constructing dikes and canals. Exposed to attack from mountain and desert marauders, the communities of the region were compelled to organize for defense. Such were some of the reasons why the earliest Asiatic civilization revealed by historical records originated in Mesopotamia.

The Fertile Crescent. The whole of this region forms part of what is sometimes called the Fertile Crescent, which extends from Palestine on the Mediterranean around northern Arabia to the Persian Gulf. South of this crescent is a high and largely desert land of immense area, Arabia, where you do not see a river. But to the west in Africa is another great river, the Nile. It flows in a general northerly direction from lakes and highlands far to the south. About a hundred miles before it empties into the Mediterranean Sea it breaks into a number of lesser streams, which form a shape like the Greek letter Δ (D), called delta. Hence the lower Nile is called the Nile Delta. Like lower Mesopotamia, the delta lands were formed by the silt of the

The Nile made Egypt the cradle of civilization and the crossroads of the ancient world by providing water transportation and promoting trade and commerce. It also provided irrigation for crops. (Egyptian State Tourist Admin.)

The Rosetta Stone, key to Egyptian hieroglyphics. The French scholar Champollion was able to translate the Egyptian by comparing it with the Greek inscription at the base of the stone. It is now in the British Museum. (British Museum)

river. From its origins (which have been discovered only in the last century) the Nile is about three thousand miles long, but the part of it that flows through ancient Egypt is only about six hundred miles in length. Until it reaches the low plain of the delta, it flows through a sort of ditch or valley in a high desert country. This valley averages about twelve miles in width, and in it are all the arable lands in the whole of Egypt. Annually the river overflows its low banks, depositing new rich soil, and this is the source of life in Egypt. It has been said that "the Nile is Egypt, and Egypt is the Nile." Rain is almost unknown in this country. Its sole supply of water is this mighty river which renews each year the fertility of the agricultural lands in the ditch through the desert. In that valley, and especially in the delta, was another natural invitation to people to organize settled agricultural communities.

It was along the banks of the Nile and in Mesopotamia that the first civilizations developed approximately at the same time. In the next chapter some account of them will be given.

REVIEW

STUDY SECTIONS IN REVIEW
1. The Study of History
A. The word *history* has various meanings, but what is meant when we refer to *world* history?

B. List some of the advantages that can be derived from the study of history.

C. How can historical study be of aid in learning moral truths?

D. Why must historical study confine itself to the last six thousand years of the world's existence?

2. The Human Race in the Stone Age
A. Describe the life of our ancestors in the early Stone Age (Paleolithic period).

B. What improvements in the condition of man's life were introduced during the Neolithic Age?

C. How did the family serve as the basis for larger social groups during this period?

D. What was the importance of the division of labor for man's material progress?

E. Distinguish between the terms *culture* and *civilization*.

F. What is the importance of the Fertile Crescent area in the history of mankind?

THE CHAPTER IN REVIEW
A. How does the study of history aid our understanding of human nature and our present civilization?

B. What evidence have we that would indicate that man has lived on earth for over 150,000 years?

c. On your textbook or classroom map, trace the so-called Fertile Crescent. What were the natural advantages of this area?

D. Discuss the following statement: "The creation of man is not a subject for historical study." If not history, what division of knowledge would treat man's earliest origins?

FOR YOUR NOTEBOOK

You will find that keeping a notebook is the best way of mastering the story of world history, for it is a complex story of many peoples and many events. Your teacher will probably want to review your notebook from time to time to see that you are keeping it up to date and that you are supplementing the story as given in the text, highlighting the most important developments, understanding the interrelationship of event to event and nation to nation, and appreciating the significance this story should have for you today. A well-kept notebook will serve like each installment of a continued story: it will keep you abreast of the story so that you will understand how the next chapter develops. As you progress in the course it would be well to review your notes from time to time to change them, add to them, and, in general, re-evaluate the history studied.

In your notebook you will want to accomplish these things: (1) keep track, perhaps by parallel-column charts, of what is happening in other countries when the text deals with only one or two countries; (2) list *causal* and *conditioning* factors to account for historical developments; (3) observe the contributions made to the development of world history by outstanding men and women; (4) outline the material of each section so that you can see the two or three principal developments and the way details fall into place; (5) select outstanding dates and events to serve as something like road markers to show where world history stands at a certain time or place.

You should begin your notebook by writing a paragraph on why history is a valuable study from both the practical and cultural points of view and what you expect to get from this course in world history. The next entries are on "prehistory": (1) a statement on the limits of what we can know about this period and what we can safely say about it; (2) a scaled line drawing (perhaps each sixteenth of an inch indicating a century) to show the small part of human life on earth that is covered by recorded history; (3) a list of the most important "discoveries" in prehistoric times, such as fire, the wheel, and the use of iron, with an approximate date for each discovery.

SELECTED READINGS

Descriptions of life and history in the "prehistorical" ages are based on "clues," such remains as pottery, instruments, and clothing, from which the archaeologist deduces how primitive men must have lived, very much as a detective reconstructs a crime from a few clues. This means that descriptions of primitive man's history must be tentative, general, and probable.

Reading almost like a detective story is Anne T. White's, *Lost Worlds: Adventures in Archaeology* (New York: Random House, 1941). The noted explorer Roy Chapman Andrews has written a more advanced but equally interesting description of the home life and environment of primitive man, *Meet Your Ancestors: A Biography of Primitive Man* (New York: The Viking Press, 1945). More detailed are the two books by Marjorie and Charles H. Quennell, *Everyday Life in the Old Stone Age* (New York: G. P. Putnam's Sons, 1955), and *Everyday Life in the New Stone, Bronze, and Early Iron Ages* (New York: G. P. Putnam's Sons, 1955).

Chapter 2. The Earliest Civilizations

3. MESOPOTAMIA AND EGYPT, 4000 TO 1800 B.C.

As people turned away from being mere hunters, to cultivate the soil, to breed stock, and to live in settled communities, their religious ideas gradually changed. The great beast-gods tended to go out of human imagination, to be replaced by other gods; or perhaps what happened was that the beast-gods took on new forms and activities, thus becoming gods from whom kings believed themselves to be descended. There arose, too, the idea of a great female deity, conceived as the mother goddess of the earth and all nature. This was natural, since men always worship what they believe to be the creative source of life.

Sumerians and Akkadians. When, therefore, historical records first tell us of people who have achieved a higher (or civilized) culture, we find them in a *sacred* way of life. They are organized in temple-states, which are little cities grown up around the religious centers with surrounding agricultural and grazing lands. The source of all authority is the temple, a sacred dwelling place of the god. The king rules with the authority of the god. The king and the priests of the temple direct the whole organization and life of the community. We know that such temple-states arose in a cluster in Mesopotamia at least six thousand years ago. The people were of the Semitic race. The name "Semitic" derives from the name of Sem, who, according to tradition, was one of the sons of Noah. History knows nothing more about their origin. Probably they were already spread widely about western Asia when a people known as the Sumerians invaded lower Mesopotamia about 4000 B.C. The Sumerians are believed to have come from the highlands east of the Persian Gulf. They subdued the Semites in the lower valleys of the Tigris and Euphrates. It is not likely that they brought a higher culture with them, but they gave their name to the country which they conquered—Sumer. They brought their gods and established numerous temple-states. To the north, in the country called Akkad, there existed at the same time numerous Semitic temple-states.

In modern times some of these ancient Sumerian and Akkadian temple-states have been excavated by archaeologists, and it has become possible to know a good deal about them because the people developed the art of writing. Probably they began by carving religious symbols on seals, then made picture-like figures (pictographs), and at length developed signs indicating vocal sounds. They wrote by making wedge-shaped (cuneiform) marks with a stylus or reed on clay tablets, which were then baked like bricks and made almost indestructible. Thousands of these clay tablets have been found, and scholars have learned how to read them. They tell much of the religion, social life, business, manufacturing, and scientific knowledge of these ancient people. They even make it possible to reconstruct some part of the ancient history of this region.

Empire of Sargon I. There were many conflicts and rivalries among the Sumerian and Akkadian states, and these were always thought of as clashes among the various gods. Sometimes the king of one temple-state rose to great power over the others and

forced them to pay tribute. About 2800 B.C. the leading king in Sumeria was Lugalzaggizi, who made campaigns far and wide, even to the Mediterranean. Rivaling him was Sargon I, the chief king among the Akkadians. In due course Sargon defeated Lugalzaggizi and united all Sumer and Akkad in an empire that lasted about two hundred years. Sargon and his successors thought of themselves as great world rulers—"kings of the East and West"—and made their power felt over all western Asia. This was one of the ways in which the cultural achievements of the Sumerians and Akkadians were spread to other peoples. Sargon I was the first "emperor" known in the history of the world.

Egypt. About the same time the basic forms of civilization were being developed in Mesopotamia, a parallel development was occurring in the Nile Valley. Small temple-states arose, each with its god and king. About 4000 B.C. two large kingdoms had arisen over the temple-states. The more advanced kingdom was in the delta region

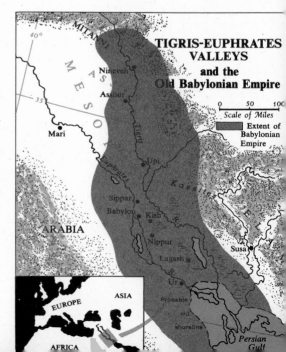

TIGRIS-EUPHRATES VALLEYS and the Old Babylonian Empire

(Lower Egypt); the other was to the south (Upper Egypt). The kings, who were called Pharaohs, ruled as divine beings descended from gods and therefore presumed to be gods. We may perhaps see the survival of the beast-gods in the fact that the pharaohs of Upper Egypt thought of themselves as descended from the falcon-god Horus. The two kingdoms were united by the Upper's conquest of the Lower about 3000 B.C. The first king of. united Egypt is said to have been the Pharaoh Menes. Thus, what is called the Old Kingdom of Egypt came into being; it lasted for about five hundred years.

Papyrus rolls. By the time of Menes, the Egyptians had learned the art of writing. We call their writing hieroglyphic, which means sacred-symbolic. Probably it began, as in Mesopotamia, by making religious symbols. Then pictographs were made and developed to convey accounts of events and ideas. Ink was manufactured, and the Egyptians learned how to press the pith of the papyrus plant to make a sort of paper. The sheets of papyrus were pasted together to make a roll, or book. Because of the extreme dryness of the Egyptian climate, many of these papyrus rolls have survived, and scholars have learned how to read them. From *papyrus* comes the word *paper*. The ancient Egyptians also carved many writings on stone, which was so abundant in their country.

Pharaohs and pyramids. In the long history of ancient Egypt there were many dynasties (hereditary lines of kings). Under the third and fourth dynasties (about 2800 to 2500 B.C.) the Old Kingdom reached its complete development. It was an absolute and sacred

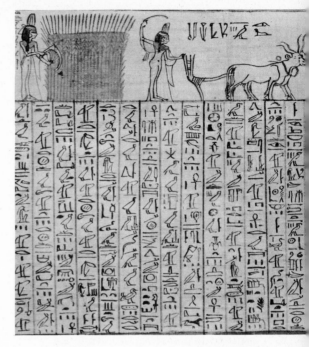

Egyptians believed that life after death was physical and material. They buried their dead with papyrus rolls depicting activities after death. Note the Princess Entiu-ny plows and reaps corn. (The Metropolitan Museum of Art)

monarchy. The whole life of the kingdom centered in the Pharaoh's palace at Memphis. He was served by priests and numerous officials. He owned all the land, and his servants directed the whole economic life of the country. All were Pharaoh's slaves. The people were taught (and they believed) that the welfare of all and even the course of natural events depended upon the sacred rites which the Pharaoh and his priests practiced. The Pharaoh was probably as much a slave of this system as anybody else.

Being a god, the Pharaoh was expected to live forever as a god. He would die, of course, as all men die, but the Egyptians believed that life would continue after death. They believed this so intensely that it was characteristic of them to direct most of their activities toward preparing for the life to come, which they imagined to be somewhat like the life they knew. For Pharaoh it seemed necessary to make the greatest preparations. Hence a vast part of the labor of the people went to building tombs for the Pharaohs of the Old Kingdom. These are the famous pyramids which cluster around Memphis and are among the wonders of the world. The city of Memphis has disappeared, but they remain. It is largely because of them that we have been able to learn a great deal about Egyptian life and history in that remote age. They were built to last forever! Connected with each pyramid tomb was a temple, and on the walls of these structures are many inscriptions that tell about the Pharaoh's life. The dead rulers' bodies were expertly embalmed (mummified), and a great many articles useful in

life were entombed with them. Among these were ships on which they might sail to heaven!

The Great Pyramid. The greatest of the pyramids is the tomb of Pharaoh Cheops (or Khufu), who lived about 2800 B.C. It consists of 2,300,000 blocks of limestone, each weighing about two and one-half tons. They were cut from quarries on the east side of the Nile and ferried on rafts across the river for fourteen miles at times when the river flooded to within two hundred yards of the base of the pyramid. Then they were carried up ramps built of bricks and lifted into place by rocking them on "cradles" elevated by wedges. Completed, the pyramid rose 482 feet, formed a perfect square at the base, and covered nearly thirteen acres. Cheops spent the greater part of his life directing its construction! The only power available was in the muscles of thousands of slaves. But perhaps they worked gladly in what they thought of as a great community religious undertaking. In 1954 archaeologists exploring around the base discovered the "solar boat" that Khufu built to carry him to heaven. It is about sixty feet long and had been placed in an underground chamber sealed with fifteen-ton blocks of stone.

The Pharaoh who built the Great Pyramid may have been a near contemporary of Sargon I.

The spread of civilization. Egyptians of the Old Kingdom were seafarers and traders and from early times were in contact with the island of Crete, where a civilization arose and was flourishing when the pyramids were being built. The Cretans acquired many arts from Egypt and, being sea traders,

ANCIENT EGYPT

Rosetta Mouth of the Nile
(Rosetta)
LOWER EGYPT (NILE DELTA) (GOSHEN)
Heliopolis
Gizeh
Memphis
(CANAAN)
SINAI PENINSULA
Mt. Sinai
(Gulf of Suez)
(Gulf of Aqaba)
UPPER EGYPT
Hermopolis
Akhetaton (Tell el Amarna)
Nile
RED SEA
GREAT OASIS
Coptos
Karnak
Luxor Thebes
First cataract
Nile
30°
30°
25°

0   100   200
Scale of Miles

▲ Location of pyramids
  Fertile areas

It is believed that the Giant Sphinx was built from rock left over after building the Great Pyramid. The head is that of the sun-god Re. The body, which is 240 feet long, is that of a lion who in Egyptian mythology was the guardian of sacred places. (Trans World Airlines)

they spread their influence to the Aegean Islands, Cyprus, and other Mediterranean lands. Because the legendary name of their kings was Minos, their civilization is often called the Minoan civilization. The Cretans may be regarded as the first bearers of the higher culture to Europe. They learned to write, but no modern scholar has learned how to read what they wrote.

Remains of brick houses, statues, painted pottery, and copper tablets were found along the Indus River about twenty-five years ago. They show that civilization had started in India as early as the age of Menes in Egypt. No doubt future explorations will discover many more evidences of the spread of civilization over western Asia in the third millennium before Christ. It is certain that during that thousand years the temple-state and the early arts of civilization extended from Crete in the west to India in the

east. But nobody knows how many such states rose and fell in what was the faint early dawn, not the broad daylight, of history.

An era of great disorder. Toward the end of the third millenium B.C. a

Examples of toilet articles used for hairdressing by the Egyptians about 4000–3400 B.C. Egyptians, who loved beauty and lived luxuriously, wore wigs and jewelry and used cosmetics. (The Metropolitan Museum of Art)

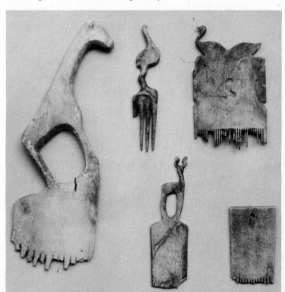

great crisis occurred in the Old Kingdom of Egypt which led to its breakup into numerous small states. We can only guess at the causes and history of this immense happening. Warlike invaders from the desert probably plundered the cities and temples. One of the writings of the age records: "Behold, strangers are come into the land. The men of Egypt are no longer found anywhere. The people of the desert take their place. The land is desolate . . . The cattle are left to stray. There is no man to herd them. When the Nile overflows, none ploughs . . . Blood is on every side. Death ceases not." Probably men now lost faith in the divine authority of Pharaoh, and his officials became rich and strong enough to usurp his powers. Egyptian civilization was dealt a heavy blow, but it was not destroyed. In 2050 B.C. a new dynasty with its capital at Thebes partially restored the power of the Pharaoh over the whole country. Thus what is known as the Middle Kingdom of Egypt arose. Troubled by invasions, it nevertheless endured for perhaps five hundred years but never attained the massive solidity and sanctified authority of the Old Kingdom.

The forces that brought chaos and disorganization in Egypt about 2200 B.C. were very widespread. About the same time the Akkadian empire of Sargon I and his successors fell apart. Thus the whole region of the Fertile Crescent became disorganized for several hundred years.

The Babylonian empire. In the closing years of the third millennium (when Egypt had come together again in the Middle Kingdom) the temple-state of Babylon in Mesopotamia grew in wealth and power. Its kings created a new empire that extended over much the same territory Sargon I had conquered. They too became "kings of the East and West." As the Babylonian empire rises, we hear no more of the Sumerians, who simply disappear from history, lost among the Semites whom they had once conquered. Babylonian rulers were Semitic. One of them, Hammurabi, is famous for establishing the earliest code of law known to history. It has been preserved almost entire, because a stele (stone tablet) on which a copy of it is engraved was found by archaeologists not many years ago. It contains about 285 laws that regulated commerce, crimes, wages, marriage, debts, and other affairs of that ancient society. On the stele Hammurabi is shown in bas-relief receiving the code from the Babylonian god Shamash. Thus the code appears as of divine origin and must have had the force of divine law. Much of the Code of Hammurabi continued to be observed in that part of the world for fifteen hundred years.

Barbarian invasions. By the early centuries of the second millenium B.C., warlike barbarians invaded and conquered both Babylonia and Egypt. Doubtless these barbarians had acquired some of the techniques of civilization, especially its weapons. They were filled with envy of the wealthy temple-states and passion to plunder them. Moreover, both the Babylonian empire and the Egyptian Middle Kingdom lacked the power to control their subject temple-states effectively and maintain a coherent government.

Hammurabi, shown receiving the code of laws from Shamash, god of the sun and justice, was the earliest lawgiver. The code invoked harsh punishments, such as "If a man kill another man's son, his son shall be put to death." (Caisse Nationale des Monuments Historiques)

About 1800 B.C. mounted warriors known as the Kassites came from the eastern highlands and conquered Babylon. Then a dynasty of Kassite kings ruled the capital of a broken empire for nearly six hundred years. The horse, which is mentioned in cuneiform writings as "the ass of the hill country," was introduced into Babylonia (Mesopotamia) by the Kassites. About the same time the Kassites conquered this homeland of civilization, mounted nomads (wandering tribes) called the Hyksos invaded Egypt from Arabia and southern Palestine. They brought the horse into the Nile Valley, where they remained to rule for about two hundred years. Thus both Egyptian and Meso-potamian civilization, now two thousand years old (older by far than European-Christian civilization), had experienced the greatest catastrophes: foreign conquests, destruction of the temples of gods, the ending of old dynasties and the founding of new ones, the dissolution and re-creation of great territorial states. Even if the historian could know all the events, what writer could vividly portray in words the immensity of the experiences through which lived the human generations of twenty centuries!

But civilization continued, and we must now look briefly at some of its features.

4. CHARACTER OF THE EARLIEST CIVILIZATIONS

Ancient society in Egypt, Mesopotamia, Crete, and the whole world of the temple-state was organized in what we may call a sacred way of life. People lived in accordance with what their gods, acting through kings and priests, decreed to be the right way to live. It did not occur to people that they should decide for themselves or have the freedom to determine their own lives. No doubt the brains and talents of many humble people contributed much to improvement in the arts; but in economic methods, in weapons of war, and building, the advance was due largely to royal and priestly direction.

In Egypt the Pharaoh and his officials decided what fields should be planted, what seeds were to be sown, and even who should do the work. They directed the construction of canals, dikes, temples and tombs, the hunting of wild animals, the mining of metals, and the quarrying of stone. Law was what the government decreed. The government regulated all trade and manufacture. All income belonged to the Pharaoh, who decided what part of it each person should have. The Old Kingdom was what we today would call a complete socialist state.

In Mesopotamia the social system was a little different, but not less sacred. The king ruled with divine authority, but he was not, as in Egypt, the sole owner of all the land. Hence he was less despotic. There were social classes of rich landowners and merchants, whose rights of inheritance were secured by sacred law. The great "kings of the East and West" never achieved the unlimited rule over human life which the Pharaohs had asserted. Hence the general rule of law, reflecting the habits and customs of the people, became characteristic of Mesopotamian society.

Economic life. Agriculture was the basis of economic life in both Egypt and Mesopotamia. It was greatly strengthened by building and maintaining networks of canals and dikes to direct the river waters through the countryside. Improved methods of cultivation were introduced, including the rotation of crops to preserve the fertility of the soil. Copper had been used as early as 4000 B.C., and it was now alloyed with tin to produce the much harder bronze. So widespread did the use of the alloy become that historians often call this period the Bronze Age. Other metals, notably gold and silver, were known and used. The ox-plow was invented. The Babylonians even devised a sort of machine for plowing and sowing seed at the same time. In countless ways mechanical skill was improved, and because of the great power of government each improvement was quickly spread through society. The division of labor became more and more complex. There were skilled potters, weavers, stonemasons, brick makers, carpenters, miners and metalworkers, sculptors, painters and jewelers, in addition to farmers and stock breeders, priests and government officials. Trade was carried on up and down the rivers, throughout the Fertile Crescent, and by vessels that traversed the eastern Mediterranean, the Red Sea, and the Persian Gulf.

Architecture and other arts. The greatest architectural works of ancient civilization were the tombs and temples of Egypt and the temples and palaces of Babylonia. There was much use of stone in Egypt, but not in Mesopotamia, where it was scarce. Hence brick prevailed there and nothing comparable to Egyptian pyramids and tombs has survived. All the main principles of architecture were known —doorways and halls, rooms, courts, pavements, and staircases were built. But the arch was not known, nor was the spire. For decoration of buildings there were many statues, paintings, colored tiles, and rich woven carpets. Chairs, couches, tables, and cabinets were constructed.

The ancient artists made beautiful vases and jars, perfect in design and proportion, from clay and copper. Jewelers worked with precious stones and gold and silver. Wood was beautifully carved. Animals and human

Egyptian mummy of Khunum-hotep. Egyptians believed in life after death and took great pains to preserve the body so that the soul could return to it. Mummification was costly, and it took days to complete the process. (The Metropolitan Museum of Art)

heads were realistically sculptured in wood and stone or modeled in clay. Most artistic work of this sort was religious in theme.

Science, which means systematic knowledge derived from the careful observation of nature, had its beginnings in Egypt and Mesopotamia. Perhaps it started by noticing the regularity in the apparent movement of the stars, the moon, sun, and planets. The first scientists were the priests of the temples, who sought to know facts that would enable them to predict the future. From watching the heavens, the calendar was made. In Egypt someone noticed that the dog star Sirius appeared on the eastern horizon with the rising sun about the time of the annual flooding of the Nile which renewed the richness of the soil. This day (our July 19) marked the beginning of the year for the Egyptians. They counted 365 days between the occurrence and recurrence of these events, and they divided the year into four seasons, twelve months of thirty days each, with twenty-four hours in a day—plus

A wooden chess game called "Hounds and Jackals," example of fine craftsmanship in the twelfth dynasty during the reign of Amenemhat IV. The playing pieces are made of ivory and ebony. (The Metropolitan Museum of Art)

The skill of the goldsmiths in Mesopotamia was the most advanced in their day. They carved gems and cast metals more than did other civilizations. Below, necklace, earrings, and seal caps made of gold. (The Metropolitan Museum of Art)

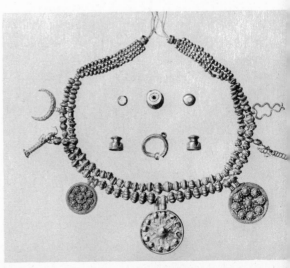

five extra days that were considered unlucky! Gradually they observed a growing divergence between the beginning of their year and the appearance of the dog star on the horizon with the rising sun. Then—over a period of 1460 years—they noted them coming together again. By such observations they made their calendar, perhaps as early as 4241 B.C., and certainly before 2700 B.C. Many other observations of natural events and forces were made and recorded in the temples.

In Mesopotamia also a calendar was made from astronomical observations. From there comes our division of the week into seven days. In the age of Babylonian power in this part of the world, a great effort was made to connect all the known facts of nature in a system from which general conclusions could be drawn. This primitive natural science (including some medical knowledge) was later transmitted to the Greeks and Romans, who led in the development of early European civilization.

Not much is known of this ancient science, but the little that is known suggests that it was extensive. Very exact mathematical calculations were needed to build the pyramids. Systems of weights and measures were devised. We may be sure that when men learned to record their observations a desire to predict or control natural events—for the honor and power of their gods—sharpened human perceptions and reasonings.

Law. No laws or codes of law in Egypt of the Old and Middle kingdoms have been discovered, but much can be known of ancient law in Mesopotamia from the Code of Hammurabi. The idea of justice and reason in law, rather than the mere arbitrary will of the gods, is shown in that code. There were courts in which evidence was heard and weighed. But justice was on the principle of an eye for an eye and a tooth for a tooth. Thus, if a man's house collapsed and killed him through a fault of the builder, the builder was put to death; if the owner's son was killed, the builder's son was executed. If a man charged another with an offense for which the penalty was death and failed to prove his case, he was liable to suffer death. The code had provisions for punishing commercial frauds and other forms of dishonesty. Harsh though the penalties for various crimes were, the code reveals an awareness of the natural moral law of justice which men always discover when they begin to reason. Although the code appears as if it had been handed down to Hammurabi by the Babylonian god Shamash, there is clear evidence that the laws actually are the product of custom and opinion in the temple-state society. That is to say, Hammurabi defined and wrote out the law already existing; he did not make it himself.

Magnitude of achievement. It would be difficult to exaggerate the marvelous advance of mankind in the temple-state society of the fourth and third millenniums B.C. One historian has summed it up in these words:

All the great achievements in which the life of civilization rests had been already reached, and there was no important addition to its material equipment until the rise of the great scientific and industrial movement in Western Europe in modern times. The most important inventions which characterise the higher culture, such as agriculture and the domestication of animals, the plough and the wheeled vehicle, irrigation and the construction of canals, the working of metals and stone architecture, navigation and sailing ships, writing and the calendar, the city state and the institution of kingship, had been already achieved by the fourth millenium, and by the third we find organised bureaucratic states, written codes of law, a highly developed commerce and industry, and the beginnings of astronomy and mathematics.[1]

We shall see in a later chapter that men had already begun to draw from the nature of human life more profound ideas of religion than those connected with the gods of this early civilization.

5. THE RISE AND DECLINE OF THE EGYPTIAN AND HITTITE EMPIRES

New peoples in history. As Egypt was passing through two centuries (1500–1600 B.C.) of turmoil, confusion, and weakness under the rule of the Hyksos, and while the Kassites held Babylon, other peoples and temple-states were beginning to make their influence felt. They entered, we may say, the scene of recorded history. We begin to hear more of the kingdom of Elam, which had often fought against the Sumerian and Akkadian temple-states. It was in the western part of present-day Iran (Persia); it was hostile to Babylon and now appeared growing in power. To the north, on the upper Tigris, the temple state of Asshur, which had been under both Akkadian and Babylonian rule, was

---

[1]Dawson, *The Age of the God,* p. 237.

growing in strength as well as independence, even establishing a colony to the north in Asia Minor. Asshur was destined to become the capital of the great Assyrian empire nearly a thousand years later. We hear, too, of a people called the Hurrians, who were important because they first developed the two-wheeled horse-drawn chariot. They came down from the highlands of Armenia to the upper waters of the Tigris and Euphrates, where they established (about 1500 B.C.) the Mitanni kingdom. A strong kingdom of the Hittites was arising in Asia Minor (modern Turkey), and we know that even before the Kassite conquest of Babylon the Hittites had raided the Babylonian empire.

The light from historical records of this time turns also upon the Semitic temple-states of the land called Phoenicia along the coast of Asia to the west of Syria. They were trading and seafaring communities and are remembered not only for their maritime and colonizing energies but for having invented the alphabet, one of the great advances of the human mind. Other Semitic peoples in Palestine and Syria are beginning to enter historical daylight; for example, the Canaanites, whose land (Palestine) would be conquered by the Israelites (as told in the Bible) a few centuries later. Again, the traders, colonizers, and pirates of Crete and the Aegean lands flourished in this age. We know of fortified towns (and leagues of such) growing up in Greece and along the coast of Asia Minor during the first half of the second millennium B.C. All these peoples (and others) had acquired the essential arts of civilization,

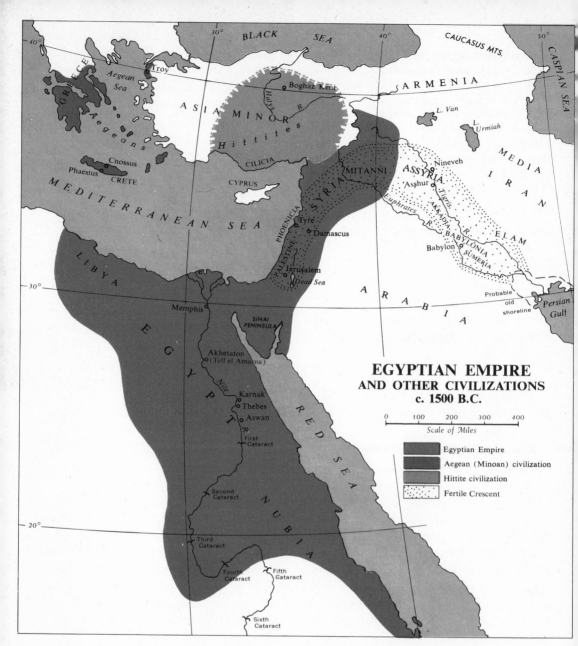

**EGYPTIAN EMPIRE
AND OTHER CIVILIZATIONS
c. 1500 B.C.**

0   100   200   300   400
Scale of Miles

Egyptian Empire
Aegean (Minoan) civilization
Hittite civilization
Fertile Crescent

which now were spread from the
Caucasus Mountains to the Persian
Gulf and from India to the Greek
mainland. But the whole scene had
become more turbulent, more characterized by war. By 1500, weapons had
been improved by the widespread use
of iron. What is sometimes called the
Iron Age had begun.

Rise of the Egyptian empire. The capacity of Egypt for resurrecting its
unity and power was brilliantly shown
when the Pharaohs of the seventeenth
and eighteenth dynasties carried to
success a long struggle to drive out or
destroy the Hyksos. These hated people were killed, or expelled, or enslaved by about 1580 B.C. Then, to

prevent another such invasion and to give release to the new political energies of Egypt, the Pharaohs set out to establish their rule far beyond Egypt. They conquered the lands of Palestine, Phoenicia, and Syria and held them under strict control. They campaigned also to the south and established their rule over Nubia (the modern Sudan). They built powerful naval vessels and made the island of Cyprus tributary. They even imposed some sort of tribute on Crete. The greatest of these Pharaoh-emperors was Thutmose III (eighteenth dynasty), who reigned for fifty-four years until 1447 B.C. His empire was more firmly controlled than any great state that had yet appeared in the world. Modern writers have called him "the Napoleon of Egypt." The story of his military conquests was carved in hieroglyphics on the walls of the temple at Karnak. One historian has described this story as "the first chapter of military and political history in the world's literature."

The Pharaoh-emperors and their officials were in political or diplomatic contact with most of the then civilized world. This was proved in modern times by the discovery at Tell el Amarna of a great number of letters

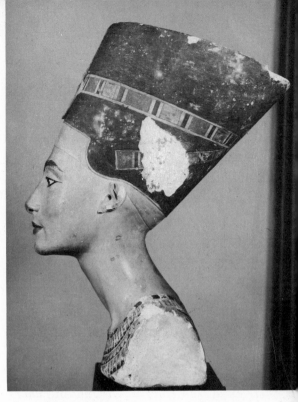

Queen Nefertiti was sculptured by artists who defied convention to bring out her natural beauty. She was the wife of Ikhnaton, who failed in his attempt to introduce the idea of one God to his people. (Berlin Museum)

from the kings of Assyria, Mitanni, and Babylon. They date from the reigns of the Pharaohs Amenhotep III and Amenhotep IV (1412–1358 B.C.). The language is like that of Sumer and

Egyptians weapons of the eighteenth dynasty. At the top is a battle-ax made of bronze and wood. Below, left, are ferrules from ends of sticks; right, arrow points made of bronze. (The Metropolitan Museum of Art)

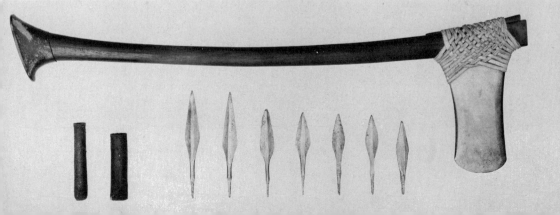

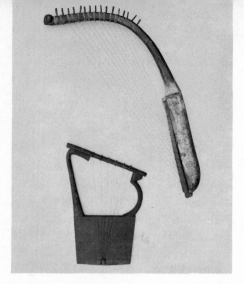

The lyre and the harp were among the instruments played as accompaniment for Egyptian dancers. Music and dancing were highly cultivated arts and were encouraged among all classes of people. (The Metropolitan Museum of Art)

Akkad—cuneiform writing on clay bricks. These letters, found in the ruined palace of Amenhotep IV, reveal to us the existence of an international state system in which ambassadors went from one country to another and treaties were made. The letters help the historian to understand how the Egyptian empire tried to maintain its strong position by preventing any combination of other kingdoms against it.

The Hittite empire. By the time of the Tell el Amarna letters the power of the Egyptian empire probably was in decline. The subject peoples in Syria, Palestine, and Phoenicia were growing restive. Moreover, great internal disorders were arising in Egypt as a result of Amenhotep IV's effort to change religion, which was opposed by the priests at Thebes. (See p. 40.) Meanwhile the power of the Hittites was expanding.

The Hittites appear to come from outside the world of the sacred temple-states. They were a federation of mountain tribes who recognized the authority of their leading chief, or king, at

Cretan craftsmen achieved high artistic skill in interior fresco decoration. This colorful fresco taken from the palace at Cnossus in Crete depicts a circus scene. (The Metropolitan Museum of Art)

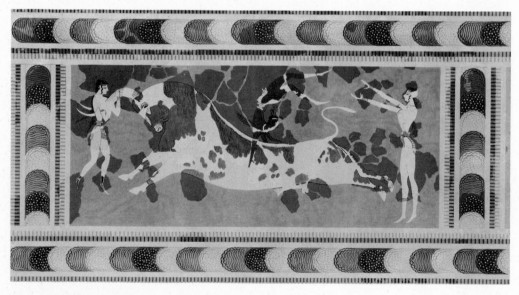

Boghaz Keui in the high country northeast of the modern capital of Turkey at Ankara. They had easy access to copper and iron mines and were of bold, warlike spirit. They were remarkable builders of fortified palaces or castles, and their disposition was to extend their control over other peoples as a ruling class. Hence they made as many kingdoms recognize their power and pay tribute to them as they could. Between 1390 and 1350 B.C. the greatest of their kings, Shubbiluliu, reduced Mitanni to vassalage and established Hittite supremacy over all Asia Minor and northern Syria. As a result the Hittites came to armed collision with the weakened Egyptian empire. The Pharaohs did not refuse the challenge. A long and bloody war, or series of wars, was fought for the control of Syria. Neither side can be said to have won, and the power of both was weakened. At length, in 1271 B.C. a treaty of peace (which still exists) was made between the Pharaoh Ramses II and the Hittite ruler, Hattushilish III. Before another century had passed, the Hittite empire came to an end and its ruling people disappeared from historical record. Their power may have been destroyed by migrating adventurers from the Aegean lands to the west.

After the long war with the Hittites the Egyptian empire sank steadily, and the subject peoples in Palestine, Syria, and Phoenicia resumed their local independence until the next great conqueror came along. He would come from the east—from Assyria, where a new "king of the East and West" was rising on the horizon of history.

The Aegeans in this age. About 1600 B.C. the center of Aegean civilization at Crete experienced a terrible disaster. The great palace cities of Cnossus and Phaestus were destroyed, perhaps by an earthquake. But they were rebuilt and Cretan life continued to flourish

Ruins of the palace at Cnossus in Crete. Art was used so extensively in the decoration of the interior of this great palace that even the pots and pans were designed. The Middle Minoan period saw the high development of various arts and skills. (Trans World Airlines)

and spread. A maritime empire headed by Crete grew up in the form of a federation of Aegean city-states which reached to the mainland of Greece. These Aegeans were spirited, lively, and fond of athletics. They cultivated olive orchards and vineyards and sailed the seas as traders and pirates; they also were bold colonizers. Their art, in spite of its having been influenced by Egypt, was not inspired by the worship of a god-king or by absorption of minds with prospective life after death. Probably the peoples of Egypt and western Asia thought of the Aegeans as wild, daring, and lawless. The Egyptian empire for a time made Crete tributary, but that was not for long. About 1400 B.C., however, the Cretan federation was broken up and the great palace-cities in the island were again destroyed. This appears to have been the action of an alliance of other city-states from the mainland of Greece. Perhaps it was the outcome of a great civil war in the Cretan federation. Immense turmoil and confusion came into the Aegean world, caused in part by people whom we shall meet later as the Mycenaean Greeks. There was a movement of Aegeans to the coasts of Asia Minor, Syria, Palestine, Phoenicia, and Egypt as the Egyptian and Hittite empires declined and dissolved.

REVIEW

STUDY SECTIONS IN REVIEW

3. Mesopotamia and Egypt, 4000 to 1800 B.C.

A. Is there evidence from early forms of government that religion played a vital role in early civilizations?

B. What contributions to culture were made by the Sumerian and Akkadian states?

c. Identify the following: Pharaoh, dynasty, pyramid, solar boat.

D. What was the role of the Cretans in the spread of early culture?

E. Explain the importance of the Code of Hammurabi.

F. What were the effects of the barbarian invasions of the Middle East (*c.* 1800 B.C.)?

4. Character of the Earliest Civilizations

A. Explain the differences between the Egyptian and Mesopotamian forms of monarchy.

B. Discuss the beginnings of science in the period under study.

c. Mention three contributions of these early civilizations which improved the economic life of the people.

D. Describe the nature of justice available to the people in these early states.

5. The Rise and Decline of the Egyptian and Hittite Empires

A. What new peoples and states enter recorded history around 1500 B.C.?

B. Explain briefly the rise of the Egyptian empire.

c. Describe the principal contributions of the Hittites to early culture.

D. Did the Egyptian and Hittite empires prosper after their peace treaty of 1271 B.C.?

THE CHAPTER IN REVIEW

A. Note the important role which religion played in the early Middle Eastern civilizations. Cite examples of religious influence in each of the following areas: nature of kingship; architecture, development of the art of writing.

B. Discuss the following statement: "The Code of Hammurabi, though harsh, reveals that man by the use of reason can become aware of the nature of justice."

c. What areas came under the domination of Egypt after 1580 B.C.? Locate these regions on your classroom or textbook map.

D. Discuss evidences of the decline of the Egyptian empire which were apparent prior to the war with the Hittites.

FOR YOUR NOTEBOOK

In our second chapter of world history we enter the period of recorded history, which covers about the last six thousand years. We now have occasional written records to tell us what people were doing and thinking in the more than two thousand years covered in this chapter. To understand the major developments in the long period covered by this chapter you should make the following entries in your notebook:

1. Draw up parallel columns for each of the peoples introduced in this chapter in order to show when each of them come on the scene of recorded history and the area in which each settled.

2. Read a digest of the Code of Hammurabi in one of the standard encyclopedias in your library. From the contents of the code write a short description of Babylonian civilization, indicating, for example, the position of women, the use of credit, the place of contracts, and other such matters.

3. From your study of geography draw up a list of contrasting conditions between the Nile and Mesopotamia areas. Show how these contrasting conditions affected the Egyptian and Babylonian religions and views on life.

4. The Nile and Mesopotamian valleys are called the "cradle of Western civilization." Summarize the accomplishments they had made in science, religious knowledge, and social and political organization which they bequeathed to history by about 1800 B.C.

SELECTED READINGS

An interesting description of the astounding accomplishments of these ancient civilizations is Edgar J. Banks, *Seven Wonders of the Ancient World* (New York: G. P. Putnam's Sons, 1916), in which the author describes such "wonders" as the walls of Babylon and the Pyramid of Khufu.

Egyptian history is interestingly and satisfactorily covered by James Baikie, *The Story of the Pharaohs* (New York: The Macmillan Co., 1908), and in story form by Louise Lamprey, *Long Ago in Egypt* (Boston: Little, Brown & Co., 1926).

Frances K. Gere writes an interesting account of what life must have been like in the Mesopotamian and Euphrates valleys in *Boy of Babylon* (New York: Longmans, Green & Co., 1941), and Edward Chiera shows how Mesopotamian history is revealed in bricks of clay in *They Wrote on Clay* (Chicago: University of Chicago Press, 1938; Phoenix Reprint, 1957).

Chapter 3. World Empires and World Religions

With the breakup of the Hittite and Egyptian empires after 1200 B.C., the subject states and peoples became free and a great historical activity became manifest among the Semitic peoples of Palestine, Syria, and Phoenicia. Much is heard of the Aramaeans, tribes of the Syrian desert who traded by caravan between the Phoenician cities and Mesopotamia. They developed a notable trading center at Palmyra and an important kingdom centering at Damascus. They traded and traveled so widely that they spread their language over much of western Asia. Between 1100 and 900, Aramaean tribes struck a crippling blow at the previously rising kingdom of Assyria. They invaded northern Mesopotamia and there established several kingdoms.

The Israelites. Of far greater historical importance than the Aramaeans were the people who established the kingdom of Israel shortly before 1000. Indeed, one may say that they were more important in history than the people of Egypt or Mesopotamia, because they were the bearers of a religious tradition that was destined to influence the whole world. According to their tradition, they descended from Abraham of Ur (in Mesopotamia), who, at the command of God, left his homeland and went to live in Canaan (Palestine). His descendants were known as Hebrews, and some of them were perhaps in Palestine when it was made part of the Egyptian empire in the middle of the second millennium B.C. From the book of Genesis in the Old Testament we have the story of how the sons of Jacob (grandson of Abraham) sold their brother Joseph into captivity. He was taken to

Egypt and became the chief official of the Pharaoh. Later, famine in Canaan caused his brothers to go to Egypt, where he received them with favor; they brought their father Jacob and all who were of his house. These Hebrews in Egypt called themselves the children of Israel, a name said to have been given by God to their father Jacob. It meant "he who strives with God." After a time there came a new Pharaoh and the Israelites in Egypt were cruelly oppressed. A great leader arose—Moses—who led them out of their captivity and toward their homeland in Canaan. We have no way of knowing how long the Israelites had been in Egypt, but it may well have been for three hundred years. The exodus from Egypt took place about 1200 B.C. Moses led them onto the Sinai peninsula, where they lived as nomadic herdsmen for forty years and grew in numbers. Eventually they moved north to the country east of the Dead Sea and the Jordan River.

Conquest of Palestine. Under the leadership of Josue, they crossed into Canaan, where they fought many wars with other peoples during the twelfth and eleventh centuries B.C. At length their twelve tribes (by tradition descended from the sons of Jacob) were consolidated in a kingdom under King Saul. There were great disorders and defeats in Saul's last years and for a short time thereafter.

David and Solomon. Under the next ruler, David, the kingdom of Israel became a formidable power that extended from the Mediterranean coast northward and eastward into the Aramaean country. David established the capital at Jerusalem. He was suc-

KINGDOM OF ISRAEL

0   50   100   150
Scale of Miles

━ ━ ━ Boundary of Kingdom of Israel

ceeded by his son Solomon, who greatly developed the royal authority and organization. Solomon built a royal palace, the famous Temple of Jerusalem, and a wall around the city. He promoted trade, developed a system of taxation, and erected many public buildings in various parts of the kingdom. On the whole, his reign was marked by peace and prosperity. As David was remembered for his heroism and courage, Solomon was remembered for his wisdom and the magnificence of his reign—also for his many wives! These got him into trouble, as might be expected, since he is said to have had seven hundred of them! In spite of his wisdom, he fell into many follies and violated the Israelite religion. Revolts and other political disorders came in his last years. After his death in 933 B.C. the kingdom broke into two parts, Israel to the north and Juda to the south. In the kingdom of Juda the heredi-

Phoenician ship of the thirteenth century B.C. *Noted shipbuilders and traders, Phoenicians spread the arts of numbers and writing throughout the Mediterranean area. (The Commercial Museum, Phila.)*

tary line of kings from David was continued.

It is possible to know the history of Israel better than that of any other people of those times because of the Old Testament. In the four books of Holies the history of Israel for about five hundred years is recorded.

The Phoenician city-states. The cities along the coast to the north of Palestine flourished greatly in the period of Israel under David and Solomon. The leading ones were Tyre, Sidon, and Byblos. They were dominated by Semitic people who traded extensively with the Aegean kingdoms and developed commercial relations with many lands of the Mediterranean, including North Africa, Spain, Sicily, Italy, and Gaul (France). They established a colony called Utica in the country we know as Tunisia. In 814 B.C. they established another near it. This was Carthage, which in time became the capital of a great empire. Later we shall read more about Carthage.

Other kingdoms. In Asia Minor the kingdom of Phrygia arose in the wake of the fallen Hittite empire. It was founded by people who came from Thrace in southeastern Europe about 1200 B.C. It endured for perhaps five hundred years, but little is known of its history. From it, however, came the well-known legend of King Midas, whose touch turned everything to gold. To the south appeared the kingdom of Lydia, where it is said the coining of money was begun. To the east of Asia Minor, in the country called Armenia, a powerful kingdom of Van existed from about 1270 to 612 B.C. We might mention other states, but this is enough to show that there was a large international state system spread wide over western Asia, northeastern Africa, and the eastern Mediterranean lands. Over it, after 900 B.C., a series of mighty empires were to rise.

7. THE ASSYRIAN, NEO-BABYLONIAN, AND PERSIAN EMPIRES

Assyria. As the Israelite kingdom after Solomon's age fell into division and chaos, the kings of Asshur (or Assyria) resumed the path of power and conquest. Situated on the upper Tigris River, Asshur had long been a sort of military outpost of Mesopotamian civilization on guard against the warlike tribes of the highlands to the north and east. It had been hard pressed by the Hittites and the Hurrians. Soon after the fall of the Hittite empire, the Assyrian king, Tiglath-pileser I (1116–1093), gained control of the main trade routes between upper Mesopotamia and Phoenicia, until the Aramaeans proved too strong for Assyria. In the ninth century, however, Assyria turned the tables on the Aramaeans. It had by this time become the most military state the world had yet known. Its soldiers developed the battering-ram for breaking through walled cities and learned how to dig tunnels under fortifications. They formed swift cavalry units and an infantry armed with swords, pikes, and bows and trained to fight in close formation. The Assyrians may be regarded as the founders of military science. This state, moreover, was characterized by what appeared to its enemies as an unusual and extreme ruthlessness. The rulers were capable of deporting or massacring whole con-

Museums and libraries provide facilities to aid scholars in their work. Here at the British Museum a scholar uses a flashlight and magnifying glass to read inscriptions on the Stele of Shalmaneser III of Assyria. (British Information Services)

Bas-relief was a favorite art of the Assyrians and decorated the walls of their palaces. The reliefs, chiseled from alabaster, depicted the daily routines of the king. Above, arms-bearer of the king. (The Metropolitan Museum of Art)

quered populations and inflicting the most dreadful tortures in order to terrorize all who dared to oppose them.

Assyrian conquests. During the years 883–810 the Assyrians fought one campaign after another. They subdued the Aramaean kingdom and laid the Phoenician cities under tribute. The shadow of Assyrian power thus fell upon the disintegrated nation of Israel. After a period (782–745) of weakness and increased danger from the kingdom of Van, the Assyrian state was reinvigorated under Tiglath-pileser III. He defeated Van, made himself king of Babylon, and laid parts of Israel under tribute. In the reign of Sargon II (722–705) the whole of Israel was conquered by Assyria and a great many of the people of that ill-fated kingdom were deported to the east, where they simply disappeared from historical records. Biblical history tells us that ten of the original

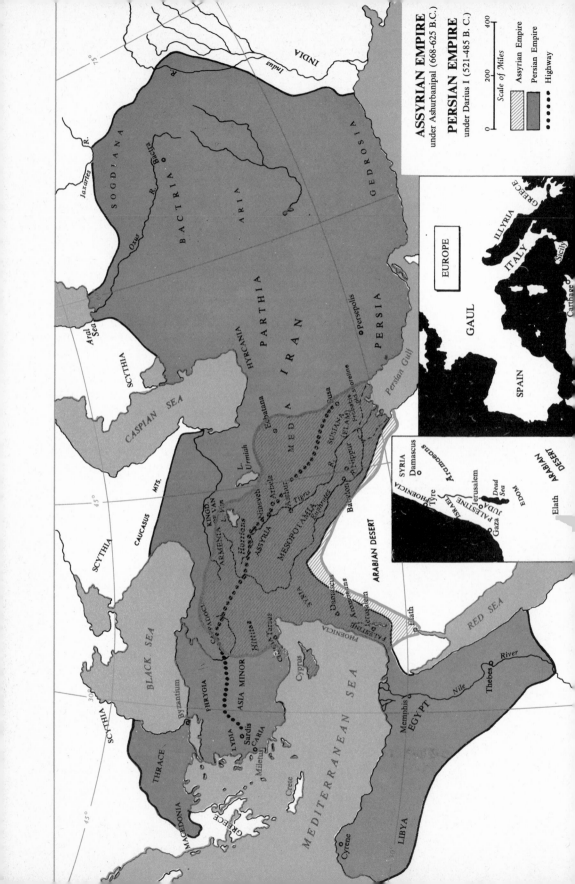

ASSYRIAN EMPIRE
under Ashurbanipal (668–625 B.C.)

PERSIAN EMPIRE
under Darius I (521–485 B.C.)

Scale of Miles

0   200   400

Assyrian Empire
Persian Empire
Highway

EUROPE

GAUL

SPAIN

ILLYRIA

GREECE

ITALY

Sicily

Carthage

SYRIA

Damascus

PHOENICIA

Tyre

PALESTINE

ISRAEL

Jerusalem

JUDA

Gaza

Dead Sea

EDOM

Elath

ARABIAN DESERT

Aram-Dammascus

INDIA

Indus R.

Jaxartes R.

Oxus R.

Bactra

Aral Sea

SOGDIANA

BACTRIA

ARIA

GEDROSIA

SCYTHIA

CASPIAN SEA

HYRCANIA

PARTHIA

IRAN

MEDIA

PERSIA

Persepolis

Persian Gulf

Probable shoreline

Ecbatana

L. Urmiah

Susa

SUSIANA (ELAM)

R. Nippur R.

Babylon

MESOPOTAMIA

Euphrates

Tigris

Arbela

Ashur

Nineveh

ASSYRIA

KINGD. of VAN

ARMENIA

Hurrians

L. Van

CAUCASUS

SCYTHIA

MTS.

45°

30°

75°

CAUCASUS MTS.

CAPPADOCIA

Hittites

Tarsus

CILICIA

Kurds

Krocleans

Damascus

SYRIA

PHOENICIA

PALESTINE

Jerusalem

Elath

RED SEA

ARABIAN DESERT

BLACK SEA

THRACE

Byzantium

PHRYGIA

ASIA MINOR

LYDIA

Sardis

CARIA

Miletus

Crete

Cyprus

MEDITERRANEAN SEA

MACEDONIA

GREECE

LIBYA

Cyrene

EGYPT

Memphis

Thebes

Nile

River

45°

twelve tribes of Israel had formed that kingdom after the division that followed the death of Solomon, and that only two tribes were in the kingdom of Juda. The Israelites who were deported by Assyria are often referred to as "the lost tribes of Israel." One fact at least is known of them: they were settled in the country of Media to the east of Assyria in what is called Iran.

The Assyrian empire. During the reign of Sargon II's successor, Sennacherib (705–681), an immense crisis shook the Assyrian empire. There was a revolt in Babylonia, and another which was aided by Egypt in Palestine and Syria. Sennacherib, however, got the better of his enemies. He destroyed the city of Babylon, defeated the Egyptians, and invaded Juda. But he failed to take Jerusalem, probably because a great plague struck his army. His successor, Essarhaddon, conquered Egypt in 671 B.C.

Thus, one great power ruled for a time over most of the civilized world. It was a world empire in the sense that it was the greatest military and territorial power in the world. It reached northward into Armenia and eastward over Iran, but it did not include Asia Minor. Its capital had been established by Sargon II at Nineveh, somewhat to the north of Asshur.

Ashurbanipal. The rule of the next Assyrian emperor, Ashurbanipal (668–625), was more distinguished for his patronizing of arts and letters than for conquests. He created at Nineveh a vast library of cuneiform writings, which was discovered by modern archaeologists. These writings, together with many other clay tablets and carved pictures and inscriptions on walls of palaces and temples in excavated cities, show that the Assyrians created little that was new except in methods of war. Rather they continued the earlier Babylonian civilization. They held their empire together by terror and tribute, not by developing an imperial system of administration. Thus the slightest diminution of their terrorizing resulted in the loss of their empire. During Ashurbanipal's reign Egypt threw off Assyrian rule, and when he died Babylonia rose against his successor. In alliance with the Medes of Iran, the revived Babylonian kingdom overthrew and destroyed the Assyrian empire.

The Neo-Babylonian empire. Media and Babylon partitioned Assyria, and now for a brief period Babylon became again a great capital of what is called the neo- (or new) Babylonian empire, which extended over the Fertile Crescent. The most famous of its rulers was

Wall slab from the palace of Sennacherib at Nineveh, showing a cavalryman fording a stream. (The Metropolitan Museum of Art)

Panel of enameled brick, depicting lion in blue, white, and yellow, from the Procession Street in Babylon. King Nebuchadnezzar built Babylon into the greatest city of the ancient world. (The Metropolitan Museum of Art)

Nebuchadnezzar (605–561), who conquered Juda, nearly destroyed the sacred city of Jerusalem, and carried off the leading part of that nation into captivity. This neo-Babylonian empire is sometimes called the Chaldean empire.

Rise of the Persian empire. On the Iranian plateau to the east of Mesopotamia, between the Caspian sea to the north and the Persian Gulf to the south, dwelt two tribal kingdoms which we have already mentioned: Elam and Media. Both had been subject to Assyria, by which the southern kingdom, Elam, was in fact destroyed. Not so the kingdom of Media, which, as we have seen, allied with Babylon to overthrow Assyria. Soon afterward a people called the Persians, who had in some way been connected with the Elamites, appeared to challenge the Medes. In 550 B.C. the king of the Persians, Cyrus, forced a union upon the Medes and became king of both peoples. Then he attacked and conquered all Babylonia. Like his empire-building predecessors, he was now a "king of the East and

West" and extended his power to the Mediterranean and over the kingdoms of Asia Minor. He was called Cyrus the Great.

Cyrus' son, Cambyses, conquered Egypt in 525 B.C., and Darius I (521–485) not only pushed the empire far to the east but attacked Greece, where he was turned back at the battle of Marathon, 490. During the next century Persian power declined somewhat, but not until 160 years later was it conquered and replaced by the empire of Alexander the Great, a Macedonian Greek. We shall hear more of him in a later chapter.

Nature of the Persian empire. It was not only the largest but the best-organized empire the world had yet seen. Before it began to decline it included almost all the peoples, temple-states, and kingdoms known in the ancient world. On the north it ran eastward from the shore of Thrace and Macedonia along the Black Sea coast to the Caucasus Mountains. Then it half encircled the Caspian Sea and went on to the Aral Sea and the Jaxartes River. It reached

Darius I and his umbrella-carriers. When the Persian empire became the greatest in the world, Darius reorganized its administration. He set up a central secret police, the "eyes and ears of the king," and a rapid postal "pony express" system. (Library of Congress)

southeast into India. On the south it skirted the Arabian Sea, the Persian Gulf, and the Arabian Desert. To the west it included the island of Cyprus, all Asia Minor, and Libya, in addition to Egypt.

How could so vast an empire be held together? Not by the Assyrian method of mere terror. The Persians indeed showed themselves comparatively tol-

erant and humane. They did not, like the Assyrians, deport and massacre peoples or annex them and force their own religion on them. They did not destroy other people's institutions of religion and government. They established a true imperial system by creating a governmental superstructure over the various states. Their idea was to hold all states and tribes in a great harmonious union. They established many provincial administrations with a military governor over each. He was called a *satrap* and was responsible to the emperor. Further, to promote unity and speed of movement for the imperial army through the empire, great military roads were built from one end of the land to the other. There were great advantages to all subject peoples in the existence of this empire. The empire facilitated trade, travel, and the spread of arts and knowledge. Even a uniform imperial coinage was created. Under Persian rule the Mediterreanean Sea was connected with the Red Sea by cutting a canal from the Nile River through the desert to the Red Sea. The emperors maintained a number of royal residences or capitals in Iran and one at Babylon.

Kingdom of Judea. The tolerant disposition of the Persian rulers was shown in many ways. The most famous was in their treatment of the people of Juda who had been taken into captivity by Nebuchadnezzar. After conquering Babylonia, Cyrus the Great allowed them to return to their homeland to rebuild the Temple of Solomon. From this time their kingdom is called Judea and the people are known as Jews. Judea, of course, was a part of the Persian empire. Cyrus saw no reason why all peoples should not be allowed to worship what gods they pleased (as long as they obeyed his satraps!). The biblical writer Esdras records that Cyrus decreed that whoever was of Judea should "go up to Jerusalem, which is in Judea, and build the house of the Lord the God of Israel: he is the God that is in Jerusalem." Probably Cyrus thought that the God of Israel was but one of the many local gods. It was not his policy to antagonize people in their religion.

Persian religious policies. The Persian rulers adopted their policy of tolerating various different religions partly because it was politically prudent and partly because of their own religion (later something of this will be related). They did not think of themselves as gods but were willing to accommodate themselves to local beliefs. Thus, because the Babylonian rulers had always professed to receive their authority from the god Marduk, the Persian rulers governed Babylon in his name. In Egypt, they simply became new Pharaohs and, in accordance with ancient Egyptian religion, allowed themselves to be worshiped as the descendant of a god. In religion they were all things to all peoples.

Historical importance of the Persian empire. So successful and long-lasting was the Persian system of imperial government that it did not even come to an end when the Persian emperors ceased to rule. Alexander the Great would take over that system and in turn bequeath it to the Roman emperors. Persia as a kingdom in Iran would later rise again to power and be a formidable enemy of the Romans, but that topic belongs to a later chapter in this book.

8. THE RISE OF UNIVERSAL RELIGIOUS CONCEPTS AND IDEALS

The ancient world of the temple-states and tribes and of the great empires that rose and declined was a world of many gods. Religion showed the greatest variety of forms, but the historian can see certain common features or principles in this variety. We have already noted the disappearance or transformation of the beast-gods and have seen that with the development of agriculture there spread wide in the human imagination the idea of a great mother goddess of the earth from which came all living and growing things. (We still speak figuratively of "Mother Nature"!) Associated with her was a lover or husband, who signified the principle of fertility. He died and was reborn each year. It seemed to men that there must be two deities regulating the cycle of the seasons, since the earth was always there but not always fruitful. In Mesopotamia the earth goddess was called Ishtar. It was imagined that she was wedded to Tammuz when nature came alive but was separated from him by death when the winter came. A somber, shadowy underworld was imagined as the place where Tammuz went. It was ruled by another god. Ishtar during the winter wandered through the land mourning her loss, and at length went down into the underworld to awaken and obtain the release of Tammuz. There were many myths about these gods and about the temple-state gods who were imagined to be related to them.

Egyptian gods. In Egypt the same two gods appeared as Isis and Osiris. Their

Osiris, seated on his throne, judges the princess who stands beside the goddess Isis. The jackal-headed Anubis weighs her heart against a feather, the symbol of truth. Above, she addresses the hawk-god. (The Metropolitan Museum of Art)

story was connected with notions surviving from the primitive beast-gods, such as Ptah (the bull), Amon (the ram), Hathor (the cow), Bast (the cat), and Horus (the falcon). The Isis-Osiris cult arose or was brought into Egypt as agricultural life succeeded the early life of the hunters. Somehow Horus, the falcon-god of the earliest kings of Egypt, came to be thought of as the son of Osiris, the god of fertility. A god called Set symbolized the desert and destructive forces of nature. He was the brother of Osiris, who was the husband of Isis, the earth goddess. Set was the murderer of Osiris, and Horus was believed to have the power to restore Osiris to life and union with Isis. In later verisions of this religious myth Horus disappears and Osiris becomes the lord of the underworld, with power to judge the dead and grant immortality to worthy souls.

It is not very important to know these ancient myths, but it is necessary to realize that it was in human nature to imagine that the world man saw roundabout him was ruled by gods.

When one man grew great and powerful and ruled over others, he seemed to be something more than a mere man and was imagined to be a god. The whole of ancient religion is to be explained by man's marveling at or standing in dread of all that gave life and imposed death, all that he could not understand or control. It was natural for men to try to weave their superstitions into some kind of related pattern, to link this with the seasons, and to spin stories of their gods. It was not less natural for men to attribute sacred powers to certain places, objects, and words, to pray to the gods to win favors from them, to make statues of their gods, and to obey what was thought to be the will of the gods.

Gradually, as it became evident that the earth and heavens formed a vast unity, there arose the concept of a god greater than all other gods, even a god who made and ruled the universe. In Egypt this great god appeared to be the sun, called Re. The sun became the supreme god, ruler of the Egyptian kingdom in the age of the pyramid-building Pharaohs, who professed to be the sons of Re. Thus the worship of Re became the state religion of Egypt, which was maintained by all the succeeding Pharaohs. That is why the Egyptian monarchy is often called the Solar Monarchy. Of course, the myths of Horus and Set and Isis and Osiris continued as parts of a complex Egyptian theology. When Amenhotep IV (1375–1358) tried to abolish the belief in all other gods but Re, there was great resistance to him and he failed.

Human experience, knowledge, and conscience gradually revealed that there is a moral order, or law of justice, which had to be respected if life was to be worth living. This idea was naturally connected with belief in one supreme Creator and Lawmaker. Outside Egypt the idea of observing the moral order was not linked with the idea of being rewarded with a happy life after death; men seemed to believe that death could lead only to a dark and misty underworld. But in Egypt it became the practice to bury with a dead person little writings on papyrus to tell the lord of the underworld of the person's moral worth so that his soul might be allowed to go and live among the gods off somewhere in the sky. Many of these writings have been found. Collected, they are called the *Book of the Dead.*

The God of Israel. It remained for the Israelites to challenge violently the whole structure of ancient religious myths. Their god was the God who created the universe and man, and He was the enemy of all other gods. God, whom the Israelites called Yahweh, had chosen them to serve and worship Him alone. They had a history of their relations with God. He had brought them out of Egypt. He had given to Moses on Mount Sinai the Ten Commandments, which forbade them to serve "strange gods" and prescribed to them the fundamental laws of right morality. He had disciplined them severely. He brought or allowed to be brought on them the greatest sufferings and disasters when they disobeyed His will. Again and again they had fallen into idolatry, worshiping "strange gods." For this they always were chastised. Their history from the time of Moses (*c.* 1200 B.C.) to the establishment of

the kingdom in Palestine ruled by David and Solomon is largely a history of wars against idolatrous peoples, and of punishments falling upon Israel for slipping into the ways of idolatrous people. Beginning with Aaron, Moses' brother, they had an official priesthood. They built temples and altars for the worship of the one true God. To Him they offered sacrifices of sheep and cattle, their chief worldly goods. They were required to obey a minutely detailed moral and civil law in their relations with one another and with God and the worship in the temple. This law is known as the Mosaic Law, because it was believed that God revealed the law through Moses. Many of the early Israelites no doubt thought Yahweh as of a tribal god, *their* tribal god who was at war with *other* tribal gods. But under the discipline of the law and by the teaching of the priests they were gradually elevated in understanding and came to know that Yahweh was the one and only God who created and ruled the universe. Then they were willing to admit other people to Israel if such people would worship the true God and forswear all other gods.

The author of the book of Wisdom (perhaps King Solomon) in the Old Testament wrote these words about the people who worshiped the old gods of human imagination:

For they went astray for a long time in the ways of error, holding those things for gods which are the most worthless among beasts, living after the manner of children without understanding. . . . But all men are vain, in whom there is not the knowledge of God, and who by these good things that are seen, could not understand him that is, neither by at-

The Dead Sea Scrolls, dating from about the second century B.C., *were found in stone jars in 1947 and in 1952 and brought new information concerning the Old Testament. Left, the cave in which the scrolls were found. Right, a page and a rolled manuscript. (Wide World)*

tending to the works have acknowledged who was the workman, but have imagined either the fire, or the wind, or the swift air, or the circle of the stars, or the great water, or the sun and moon, to be the gods that rule the world. With whose beauty, if they, being delighted, took them to be gods, let them know how much the Lord of them is more beautiful than they: for the first author of beauty made all those things.

The Prophets. The greatest of the Israelite teachers of religion were the Prophets, men who are depicted in the Old Testament as arising from time to time to make known the will of God. Professing to speak with divine inspiration, they exposed and rebuked evil, called the people and even the kings from evil ways, and often foretold things to come. Their teachings revealed an ever-deepening wisdom. Many of the Prophets foretold the coming of Jesus Christ.

Israelite and Jewish religious ideas exerted a vast influence on the ancient world. The kingdoms of Israel and Juda and the later Judea had many contacts with Egypt and the Aramaean and Mesopotamian peoples. It will be recalled that Sargon II of Assyria deported "the lost tribes of Israel" to the east and that Nebuchadnezzar of Babylon carried off the leading people of Juda into captivity.

Zoroastrianism. The great empires that arose and seemed to embrace the world probably helped to prepare men's minds to believe in one God as the Lord of the whole of creation. In the Persian empire another universal religious doctrine was spread. It is called Zoroastrianism, from Zoroaster, who lived in Iran in the period just before the conquests of Cyrus the Great. It became the Persian state religion. Zoroaster taught that there was but one god, Ahura Mazda, who was the spirit of light, truth, wisdom, and all good. He was constantly opposed by an evil force or principle called Ahriman. The conflict between them ran through all human life. It symbolized the struggle of man's higher nature—his reason, conscience, and will—against his lower animal passions. Man was held to be responsible for his actions and master of his fate. His duty was to live in accordance with the moral order. A time was to come when Ahura Mazda would triumph finally over Ahriman. Then the dead would rise and live forever. Zoroastrianism was no tribal or temple-state religion, but could be adopted by all men. It spread wide over the Persian empire and was tolerant of local religions. Perhaps there was some connection between Zoroaster's teachings and the religion of the Israelites who were deported to Iran about a century before he taught. Historians, however, have not discovered such a connection.

The Temples of Pehowa, India. Temples were built around a sacred shrine, forming a religious center with cells for priests and accommodations for pilgrims. (Government of India Tourist Office)

9. CIVILIZATION AND RELIGION IN ANCIENT INDIA AND CHINA

In the age that saw the rise of the Persian empire, the civilization of India and China had come into the full daylight of recorded history.

India. India is a large country that drops down from the highest mountains in the world, the Himalayas, to the Deccan, deep in the tropical zone. The climate of the greater part of the country is torrid and humid. Jungle prevailed over it in antiquity, and indeed it is still one-fifth jungle. There were many poisonous plants, dread reptiles, insects, and ferocious beasts. The country was not favorable; it had a harmful effect on human beings.

Another early temple-state culture, comparable to that of Mesopotamia, is known to have existed (in the third millennium B.C.) in the valley of the Indus River in western India. Its history, however, is buried in obscurity. That region was conquered (sometime before 1200 B.C.) by a people named Aryans. They came from Iran, bringing their gods and a religion fundamentally similar to other temple-state peoples. From early religious records it is evident that priests called Brahmans exerted a dominant influence. The conquerors established a class system that hardened into castes based on blood inheritance. The Aryans thrust the native Dravidian people into the lowest caste. Almost all that is known of these Aryans comes from surviving hymns to their gods. The earliest collection of them is the *Rigveda*. From these writings it is clear that the Aryans were herdsmen, farmers, artisans, and had horses and chariots. In time they moved eastward to the Ganges River Valley and into the Deccan (the great southern peninsula), crowding the early native stocks to the south. Many small kingdoms were founded by the Aryans.

Brahmanism. Brahman writings of about 800 to 500 B.C. reveal a reaction to the misery of life. There was much speculation on the mysterious and terrifying nature of life and the world. Men imagined a great world soul, the Brahma, that animated all living beings. The priests taught that all souls created by Brahma were born again and again, rising higher or sinking lower in accordance with their behavior during each incarnation. Thus a man of a low caste might be born into a higher one if he lived the right sort of life and followed the ceremonial rules of the Brahmans. Or if he lived wrongly he might sink to be a dog in his next incarnation. The goal of all striving was finally to be absorbed and identified with Brahma and not to be born again. The way lead through meditation and renunciation of all material desires. Brahmanism, often called Hinduism (religion of India), thus did not aspire to create a moral order in the world but shrank from a world of frightening appearance to the spiritual soul within. Various forms of Brahmanism continued throughout Indian history. All togther, they are often called Hinduism.

Buddhism. About 563 B.C. a great man, Siddhartha Gautama, was born. He was a prince, the son of a ruler in Himalayan country we call Nepal, and had a Brahman education. When he was about thirty he left his wife and child and went to live as a hermit, imposing upon himself the greatest austerities in his effort to become one with Brahma. But he came to a different philosophy and went about as a beggar, teaching. He was called the Buddha, which means "the enlightened one." Rejecting the old ceremonial Brahman rules, he taught that wisdom consisted in self-mastery, in putting aside all selfish and material desires, in doing no harm to a living creature, and loving all living creatures. This was the way of life that led away from cruelty, evil, and pain. He set the example and won many followers, who formed communities (monasteries) for living according to that way. Holding virtue to be superior to caste, Buddha and his followers broke through the caste system and therefore were opposed by the Brahman priests.

Buddha did not reject the doctrine of recurrent rebirth or transmigration of souls. He taught that souls were condemned to be born again and again into lives of misery until through gradual perfection they reached Nirvana, which was unconscious eternal repose —the end of misery through not being born! That such a religion could arise tells us much of the state of life in India. Its appeal, however, was not in the doctrine of Nirvana but in the moral ideals of love, justice, and self-perfection. Buddhism was destined to become one of the great enduring world religions, but it could hardly have done so if later Buddhists had not developed teachings that promised personal survival and salvation rather than Nirvana.

Buddhism was not destined to become the dominant religion of India. Brahmanism was too strong for it in

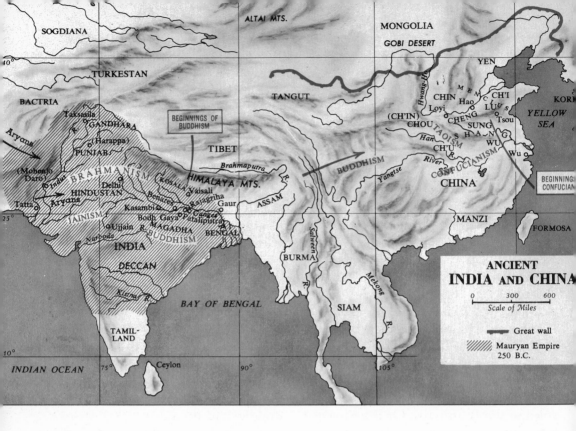

ANCIENT INDIA AND CHINA

Scale of Miles

| 0 | 300 | 600 |

    Great wall

////// Mauryan Empire 250 B.C.

the land south of the Himalayas. But in time it spread northward and eastward, assuming new forms and doctrines but retaining the monastic life as a chief characteristic.

The Buddha was contemporary with the rise of the great empire of Cyrus the Great and his successors. By this time there were numerous Aryan kingdoms, but no one great kingdom. Detailed astronomical observations had been made. Remarkable discoveries in medicine and a large knowledge of the structure and functions of the human body were features of Indian civilization. An alphabet of forty-six letters had been developed. Such advances were the accomplishments of the priestly aristocratic caste of the Brahmans. The Persian emperor, Darius I (521–485), made western India part of his empire.

China. By this time an already long-established civilization existed in China. So far as is known, it originated independently of civilization in western Asia. Probably it began in the valleys of the Yangtse and Hwang (Yellow) rivers. There is little archaeological evidence to supply accurate dates before 776 B.C. One characteristic of the Chinese was the writing of annals or historical records. The oldest writings of this kind that have survived are called the *Book of History*. According to tradition, it was put together by Kung Fu-tse, who lived from 551 to 479. Outside China he has been called Confucius. From these sources it appears credible that as early as 1000 B.C. (which was about the time of King David in Israel) there existed a unified state headed by "emperors" of the Chou dynasty. This dynasty did not cease to reign until the latter part of the third century B.C. Its long existence bequeathed to China the tradition of a great state, but during the last five hundred years of the Chou dynasty the empire had virtually dissolved into a system of independent states. Such was the condition of China in the time of Confucius, who served for a while as "minister of justice" in the principality of Lu.

From the *Book of History* and other writings attributed to Confucius it is possible to visualize a society that long before had observed the stars, developed a calendar, and invented a highly complex form of writing. There was a system of weights and measures, medicine, the cultivation of the silkworm, and manufacture of fine silken cloth. Maps of the provinces were made; a census of the people was taken periodically. Government was divided into departments presided over by *mandarins*. Examinations had to be passed for admission to public office. Great was the respect shown for education in the six arts: archery, horsemanship, writing, mathematical calculation, music, and official ceremonial. A strict etiquette ruled throughout Chinese society. There were nature gods, and one of the most striking features of religion was ancestor worship. The highest ideal of the ancient Chinese was to honor and be worthy of his ancestors. This fact tended to stabilize society and hold it unchanged from one generation to another. Thus, after developing a high civilization, the Chinese became intensely conservative.

Chinese philosophy. Numerous wars broke out among the states after the breakdown of effective imperial authority. It seemed to the Chinese that once all things had been well ordered but now there was great disorder. This led to much philosophical speculation about life and the universe. But this speculation did not, as in India, inspire a flight of the mind from the natural to the spiritual world. Rather it sought for the principles of moral order in the natural world. The earliest known Chinese philosopher was Lao-tse, who may have been contemporary with Zoroaster in Persia. He saw man as part of a harmonious universe governed by law. He urged simplicity, kindliness, self-control, humility. By these virtues men could discover the way of nature and live in harmony with it. Men, he thought, were naturaly good and did wrong only from want of knowing better. Lao-tse is said to have written the *Tao-Te-King,* which means roughly "the way of reason and virtue." *Tao* signified the whole unchanging course of nature, which seemed immortal, and also a way of living guided by reason, conscience, and virtue. Although Lao-tse was probably only an ethical philosopher, a religion called Taoism developed from his teachings.

Confucius. As a moral philosopher, Confucius had more influence than any other man on Chinese civilization. He wrote or collected works on various subjects and tried to promote political and social reforms for the sake of justice. He was sure that if people were well governed, their conduct would be good, and he was an acute reasoner.

Many disciples attached themselves to him to hear his wise words. Of his sayings that have come down through the ages, a large number still strike us as maxims of prudence and good judgment. An example is: "If you employ a man, trust him; if you don't trust a man, don't employ him." Confucius taught morality, but not religion; he probably regarded the religion of his times as mere superstition.

These Chinese ethical philosophers lived in the same general age that produced the Buddha in India, Zoroaster in Persia, and many of the prophets of Israel. All signify that there had begun a universal quest for a moral law and way of life directing men to right living, away from misery and towards happiness. Thus the old tribal and temple-state gods were losing their hold on the human imagination. We shall see presently that the same quest was beginning among the Greeks.

The Mayan civilization. How widespread was the development of the higher cultures in this age is indicated by the fact that the Mayan Indians of Central America had developed agriculture, learned to use copper, developed a 365-day calendar and a hieroglyphic form of writing. There is evidence that the Mayas, and indeed all the Indian peoples of North and South America, came from Asia in a remote age. But the advanced Mayan culture seems to have developed independently and without contact with other centers of civilization.

Race and language. The reader may have noticed that so far nothing has been said of *race*. This term signifies a part of mankind showing certain common physical characteristics, such as the color of the skin, the shape of the head, texture of the hair, or general cast of facial features. We know that such physical differences exist, or the idea of separate races would never have entered the human mind. But how such differences came to exist, and how far they may have significance in human behavior, no one can say with certainty. One thing is sure: people are more alike than they are different. They all are of a common origin and belong to the only race we can be sure is a genuine one: the human race.

Whatever may be the importance of racial differences, the peoples mentioned so far are of three general racial types: the white, the Negroid, and the Mongoloid. The Sumerians, Semites, Egyptians, Hittites, Aegeans, Persians, Aryans were all white-skinned people. In Nubia and the Deccan of India there were Negroid peoples. The Chinese were Mongoloid, and there were Mongoloid characteristics in the American Indians. Historians, however, know of no unmixed people, no "pure" race.

Similarities and differences in language have probably been more important in history than racial characteristics. Thus the word *Semitic* refers to a people speaking the same or similar languages rather than to a racial group. From earliest known times various but fundamentally similar tongues were spoken by the peoples of the Fertile Crescent, and we call these languages Semitic. On the other hand, most of the peoples who invaded that region from the north, east, and west spoke what are called Indo-European languages. Certain basic verbal uniformities have been found in the languages of the Hittites, the Persians, the Aryans (whose language was Sanskrit), and almost all the languages of Europe. This fact has suggested the early existence of a Neolithic people dwelling in central-eastern Europe from whom came waves of invaders who moved as far east as India and over the whole of Europe. This concept is in harmony with what we know of the most ancient history of western Asia and the earliest history of Europe.

It is to Europe now that we must turn our attention. By the time the Persian empire had arisen, the peoples of Europe had passed through the Bronze Age and into the Iron Age. In fact, a brilliant civilization, originating in Greece, had arisen.

REVIEW

STUDY SECTIONS IN REVIEW

6. The International World, c. 1200 to 900 B.C.

A. In what way is the history of the Israelites more significant than that of the Egyptians or Mesopotamians?

B. Indicate the significance of Moses, Josue, and Saul in Israelite history.

C. What are the principal sources of knowledge concerning Israelite history?

D. What division of the Israelites occurred after the death of Solomon?

7. The Assyrian, Neo-Babylonian, and Persian Empires

A. Why was Assyria able to embark upon such widespread conquests?

B. What were the fates of Juda and Israel under the successive Assyrian and Babylonian empires?

C. How did the Persian empire come into being?

D. Why was the Persian empire more stable than previous empires, such as that of Assyria?

E. How did the tolerance of the Persian rulers benefit the Judeans?

8. The Rise of Universal Religious Concepts and Ideals

A. What is demonstrated by the fact that certain common principles were present in most ancient religions?

B. Describe the Israelites' idea of the Supreme Being in their religion.

C. Explain the role of the Prophets in the Israelite religion.

D. What were the basic principles of Zoroastrianism, the Persian state religion?

9. Civilization and Religion in Ancient India and China

A. Did religion develop along with civilization in India? Explain.

B. What is the oldest existing source of knowledge concerning Chinese civilization?

C. Demonstrate with examples that Chinese civilization was highly developed.

D. Indicate the significance of Lao-tse and Confucius to Chinese culture.

E. In what areas did the Semitic and Indo-European languages originate?

THE CHAPTER IN REVIEW

A. The Israelites suffered many adversities in their early history. Trace chronologically these difficulties.

B. Compare the rises to power of the Assyrian and Persian empires. Contrast the manner by which each attempted to preserve its imperial possession.

C. Discuss the following statement: "Chinese philosophers such as Confucius taught morality but not religion."

D. At the time of the rise of the Persian empire, were there civilizations developing or already in existence in other parts of the world? Explain.

FOR YOUR NOTEBOOK

In this chapter you met a number of new peoples who enter the scene of world history for the first time. Some of them, such as the Chinese and the Indians, will go pretty much their own way until recent times, while others will have an important influence on our own Christian civilization. Important among these, of course, are the Israelites. To keep your notebook up to date you should do at least the following:

1. Continue the parallel columns suggested as #1 for the preceding chapter in order to introduce into the stream of world history the peoples making their appearance in this chapter.

2. Use the Old Testament to write the story of the Israelite "captivity" in Egypt and that in Babylonia in such a way as to describe conditions under which the Israelites lived and how long their captivity endured in each case.

3. Compare the religious beliefs of the various peoples treated in this chapter to show their similarity; show the uniqueness of the Israelite religion.

4. Indicate the influence on history of each of the following:

    a. Confucius
    b. Solomon
    c. Cyrus the Great
    d. Siddhartha Gautama

SELECTED READINGS

Dorothy Mills, *Book of the Ancient World* (New York: G. P. Putnam's Sons, 1923) gives good coverage to all the New Eastern civilizations. It is written for young people and is based on the most scholarly accounts of specialists. Equally well written is Frederic A. Kummer, *First Days of History* (New York: George H. Doran Co., 1925). Kummer also considers Persia, India, and China, as well as Egypt and Mesopotamia.

Helen Zimmern has edited *Epic of Kings* (New York: The Macmillan Co., 1940), which is a collection of ancient Persian tales. A good summary of Chinese history in easy-to-read form is Elizabeth Seeger's *Pageant of Chinese History* (New York: Longmans, Green & Co., 1947); an excellent, well-illustrated view of ancient Indian civilization is found in Padmini Sengupta, *Everyday Life in Ancient India* (London: Oxford University Press, 1950).

CHRONOLOGICAL REVIEW

50,000 End of Early Paleolithic Age; Neanderthal Man
25,000 *European cave art*
8000 End of Later Paleolithic Age
4000 Egyptian, Sumerian, and Akkadian temple-states
3500 *Hieroglyphic and cuneiform writing*
3000 Founding of Egyptian Old Kingdom
2900 Beginning of Cretan civilization
2800 *Beginning of the Pyramid Age*
2450 Sargon of Akkad rules Mesopotamia
2100 Rise of the Egyptian Middle Kingdom
2000 Decline of the Sumerians
1900 *The Babylonians and Hammurabi's Code Classical Age of Egyptian literature*
1800 Kassite conquest of Babylonia
1750 Hyksos conquest of Egypt
1500 Rise of the Egyptian empire
1479 Egyptian conquest of Palestine
1400 Destruction of Cretan power
1375 *Pharaoh Ikhnaton tries to impose monotheism on Egypt*
1350 Hittite rule over Asia Minor

1200 *The Hebrew exodus from Egypt*
1090 Decline of the Egyptian empire
1000 Chou dynasty reigning in China
973 *Death of King David of Israel*
933 *Death of King Solomon*
814 Phoenicians found Carthage
729 Assyrians conquer Babylonia
671 Assyrian conquest of Egypt
660 *Possible date of Zoroaster's birth*
655 Assyrian empire at its height
652 Egypt throws off Assyrian rule
650 *Renaissance of Egyptian culture*
625 Rise of the Median kingdom; Rise of the neo-Babylonian kingdom
612 Medes & Chaldeans destroy Nineveh
586 *Nebuchadnezzar captures Jerusalem; the Babylonian captivity*
550 Cyrus sets up the Persian empire
538 Cyrus conquers Babylonia and Syria
525 Cambyses conquers Egypt
516 *Persians rebuild Temple at Jerusalem*
483 *Death of the Buddha*
479 *Death of Confucius*

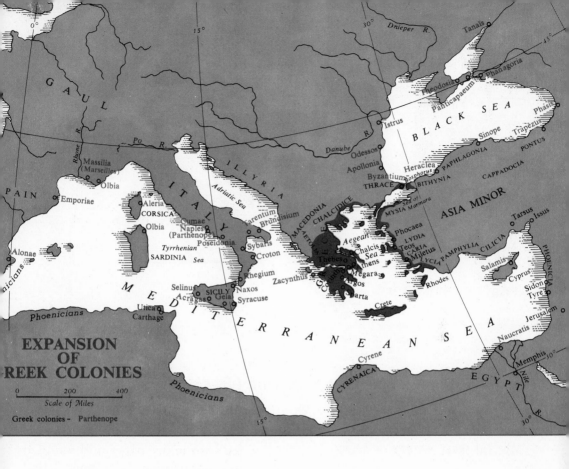

UNIT TWO
The Civilization of Greece

The Early History of Greece · Sparta and Athens · Early Greek Religion, Philosophy, and Literature · The Persian Wars and the Rise of Athens · Athenian Society in the Fifth Century B.C. · The Peloponnesian War and the Macedonian Conquest of Greece · The Philosophers: Socrates, Plato, and Aristotle · Greek Drama, Historiography, and Art · Alexander's Conquests and Empire, 336 to 323 B.C. · The Hellenistic Age, 323 to 31 B.C.

Chapter 4. The Beginnings of Greek Civilization

10. THE EARLY HISTORY OF GREECE

The Mycenaean Greeks (2000 to 1100 B.C.). Around the year 2000 B.C. barbarians from the valley of the Danube River in central Europe began migrating into the southern part of the Balkan peninsula. Their migration seems, on the whole, to have been rather peaceful, and they intermarried with the natives of the lands they occupied. The descendants of the northern barbarians and the natives were the earliest Greeks. They borrowed from the Minoan civilization of Crete and built up a civilization of their own which is called Mycenaean—from Mycenae, a great stronghold in the northeastern Peloponnesus, where many ruins of this civilization have been found.

The Mycenaean Greeks were di-vided into many tribes and founded many independent kingdoms. Tribal feeling was so strong among them that the only true citizens in a kingdom were those who belonged to the tribe of the king. Mere residence in a kingdom, even for generations, had nothing to do with citizenship. The king was the supreme priest, judge, and military commander of the tribe that he ruled. He lived in a fortified hilltop called a *polis* (fortress) and was advised by a council of nobles, who were almost as powerful as the king. If the nobles agreed among themselves, they could force the king to do their will. There was also an assembly of the common people, which was consulted in matters of great importance, such as declaring war. But this assembly could easily be overruled.

The Trojan War (1194 to 1184 B.C.). Our knowledge of these Mycenaean Greeks is very limited, for scholars have not succeeded in reading the written records which they left. The later Greeks told many stories about their Mycenaean ancestors, but these stories contain so many fantastic happenings that it is often extremely hard to separate fact from legend. Some of these later stories, however, contain valuable information, especially the two great epic poems, the *Iliad* and the *Odyssey*. According to the Greeks, the author of these two poems was a blind Greek poet named Homer, although many experts do not ascribe the *Odyssey* to him. He lived in Asia Minor about 800 B.C., several hundred years after the events which he describes took place. The *Iliad* is concerned with the famous Trojan War, while the *Odyssey* is concerned with the wanderings of Odysseus (or Ulysses, as he was known to the Romans) after the destruction of Troy by the Greeks. From the historical point of view, the *Iliad* is the more valuable of the two poems. It does not tell the story of the whole Trojan War but is concerned chiefly with the anger and the mighty

This Attic-type helmet, about sixth century B.C., *was of simple design and offered some protection for the face. (The Metropolitan Museum of Art)*

deeds of the hero Achilles in the tenth and final year of the war. We must go to other Greek legends to find out more about the war and its cause; for example, how Paris, the son of the King of Troy, carried off the Spartan queen, Helen; and how her brother-in-law, Agamemnon, King of Mycenae, organized a mighty Greek expedition to bring her back. In the *Odyssey,* Homer tells how the Greeks finally got into

The Minoan dagger blade, found in Crete, dates from 1800–1600 B.C. *Note the primitive engraving and bolts to fasten the blade to its hilt. The spearhead dates from about 500* B.C. *and shows the development in the use of bronze. (The Metropolitan Museum of Art)*

Troy by means of a wooden horse and completely destroyed the city.

The Dorian invasion (1100 B.C.). About a hundred years after the destruction of Troy the kingdoms of the Mycenaean Greeks were invaded by Greek-speaking barbarians from the north. These barbarians, called Dorians, were a very fierce people and destroyed the great Mycenaean fortresses. They caused so much destruction that Mycenaean civilization came to an end. Many Greeks abandoned their homes to escape the fury of the Dorians and settled in the islands of the Aegean Sea and on the western coast of Asia Minor. Though their own Mycenaean civilization had been ruined, these transplanted Greeks soon began to develop close contact with the great civilizations of the East. They combined their own knowledge with what they learned from the East and slowly began to build up a new

ANCIENT GREECE

Greek civilization. They did not call themselves Greeks, but Hellenes, and gave the name of Hellas to their country.

The rise of the city-state. Besides destroying Mycenaean civilization, the Dorian invasion had other important effects on Greek society. One of these was that the nobles took advantage of the confusion to deprive the kings of their power. The kingdoms were broken up, and many very small states, ruled by the nobles, were formed. Another result was the establishment of a new basis for citizenship. Before the Dorian invasion, citizenship in the various Greek kingdoms was based on membership in the ruling tribes. But the Dorians split up the tribes and scattered them far and wide. Consequently, Greeks of many different tribes now found themselves side by side. The new basis of citizenship which they established was their common worship of a particular god. Henceforth the citizens of a particular state were all those who worshiped at the temple of this god. Generally the god's temple was situated on a **polis,** which had formerly been the residence of the king. After a while the Greeks who worshiped together at a particular *polis* began to think of themselves as members or citizens of that *polis.* Thus *polis* gradually acquired the meaning of "state," while the hilltop where the god's temple was situated came to be called the *acropolis* ("high fortress"). In this new sense, *polis* is generally translated "city-state," since all the Greeks who worshiped at the god's temple considered themselves citizens of the city where the temple was situated.

The Acropolis (high fortress), which overlooks Athens, was crowned by many temples, some of the finest examples of Greek architecture. (Royal Greek Embassy)

By the eighth century B.C. hundreds of independent city-states had been formed. Many of these had a thriving industry and commerce and were becoming very prosperous. There was much discontent in these states, however. Rival factions of nobles fought bitterly for power, while at the same time the common people were struggling to gain some of the power and privileges of the nobles. There were economic problems, too, for good land was so scarce that hardly enough food could be grown to feed the ever-increasing population.

Greek colonization. Some city-states sought to solve their political and economic problems through colonization. Thus in the eighth and seventh centuries B.C., thousands of Greeks who for one reason or another were discontented settled overseas. They founded colonies, which were really independent city-states, along the shores of the Black Sea and the Black Sea straits, and along the northern shore of the Mediterranean as far west as Spain.

Most of their settlements were in uncivilized areas whose resources had not yet been tapped and where the natives were too loosely organized to oppose them. The colonists held onto their Greek language and customs and considered the new cities just as much a part of Greece as the old cities of Balkan Greece and Asia Minor. Since they made few attempts to force their culture on the neighboring natives, Greek culture never penetrated very far inland from the colonies. One result of this was that many centuries later, when the native states became better organized and more powerful, they absorbed their Greek neighbors, and consequently Greek culture disappeared in those areas. Before this happened, however, the less civilized neighbors of the Greeks, such as the Romans, were able to begin a civilized life of their own, thanks in great part to what they had learned from the Greeks.

Many colonies became far wealthier and more powerful than their mother cities. Some of them have remained prominent to the present day, though very few have retained their Greek character. In eastern Sicily the Corinthians founded Syracuse, which became the leading Greek city in the West and remained so for hundreds of years. Today it is still an important Italian city. On the coast of Italy the little city of Chalcis founded Naples, which has ever since been one of Europe's leading cities. In southern Gaul the Phocaeans founded Marseilles. Today it is France's principal port on the Mediterranean and is second only to Paris in size. On the Bosphorus near the Black Sea, Megara founded Byzantium. Of all the Greek colonies, Byzantium has had the greatest history. In the seventh century B.C. it became an important stopping-off station for ships traveling between the Black and the Aegean seas. Its position had great strategic value, for it guarded the straits connecting these two seas. In the fourth century of the Christian Era, Byzantium was renamed Constantinople and became the capital of the Roman Empire. Today it is called Istanbul and is the largest city in Turkey. Its historic role of guarding the Black Sea straits has never been greater than it is today.

Political changes in the city-states. A brisk trade developed between the old and the new Greek cities. But colonization and greater prosperity failed to solve the problems of the older cities. Instead, the problems were often made worse. The more a city developed its industry and commerce, the larger its merchant and working classes grew. These classes exerted great pressure on the ruling nobility for greater rights,

particularly for a share in the government. Often there was bitter fighting, and slowly the nobles gave way. At first the nobles admitted the wealthy merchants to a share in the government; next they admitted the citizens of more moderate means. But the loudest cries for greater rights came from the lower classes, the workers and the farmers. Often ambitious nobles took the side of these discontented citizens and used their support to seize supreme power. Nobles who seized power in this way ruled in a manner similar to that of dictators and "strong men" today. The Greeks called them *tyrants,* and their form of government *tryranny.* Many Greek city-states, especially in the seventh and sixth centuries B.C., were ruled by tyrants. But to the Greeks, tyranny did not necessarily have the bad meaning that it has to us today. Many sections of the population, especially the workers and the farmers, received political and economic advantages from the tyrants which they had never enjoyed before. Even after tyranny was abolished, the lower classes were so successful in holding their new-won advantages that they often succeeded in forcing the wealthier citizens to consent to a democratic form of government.

11. SPARTA AND ATHENS

Why Sparta became a military state. From the eighth century B.C. onward, two city-states played an ever-greater role in Greek affairs. These were Sparta and Athems, who would some-day become deadly enemies. The

Spartans were descendants of those Dorian Greeks who had come down from the north around 1100 B.C. After spreading destruction far and wide, they settled down to a peaceful existence in the southern Peloponnesus and founded the city-state of Sparta. When their growing population began to make a severe strain on their food resources in the eighth century B.C., they solved their problem by seizing the lands of the Messenians, their Greek neighbors to the west. They reduced most of the Messenians to the condition of slave-farmers, called *helots,* and made them turn over a certain amount of their produce to their Spartan masters. The Messenian helots resented the loss of their freedom and staged a great rebellion against the Spartans around 650 B.C. They very nearly succeeded in overthrowing the Spartans and were subdued only after twenty years of bitter fighting. Since there were about 250,-000 helots and only 25,000 Spartans, the Spartans realized that in order to maintain their superiority over the helots they would have to change their entire way of life. Henceforth there could be but one occupation for the Spartan—that of the soldier.

Spartan training. Sparta became one vast armed camp. At the age of seven boys were taken from their mothers and raised in the barracks. They drilled and exercised continually. They were fed a starvation diet and encouraged by their superiors to steal what food they could. Successful stealing, they were taught, was a skill that every good soldier needed. But woe to the boy who let himself be caught, for he was beaten mercilessly! Such beatings, of course, were considered part of the training. Indeed, the greatest honor that a boy could win was to endure the longest flogging at an annual religious festival. Many boys preferred to die under the lash rather than let out so much as a whimper or say that they had had enough. Spartan mothers fully approved of this system, for they wanted their sons to become, above all else, good soldiers. The greatest disgrace that could befall a Spartan mother was for her son to run away from battle. When the Spartans left for war, mothers told their sons: "Come back *with* your shield or *on* it."

Spartan government. At the age of thirty the Spartan was allowed to live at home, though he was still required to take his evening meal with his military company. He was strictly forbidden to engage in non-military work and remained in active service until he was sixty. After retirement from the army he devoted his remaining years to instructing the youths and to government. The government, consequently, was dominated by old men. Laws were passed by the Spartan *Assembly of Citizens,* which was composed of all male citizens over thirty years old. But the Assembly could pass into law only those measures which the *Council of Elders* saw fit to subit to it. Members of this Council were elected by the Assembly and had to be at least sixty years old. Executive power was exercised by the *five ephors,* also elected by the Assembly, whose general task was to see that law and order were maintained. Both the Council of Elders and the ephors acted as courts of law. Sparta also had *two kings,* who were members of two different royal families. But they enjoyed very little real power except in wartime, when they commanded the army. Even then their conduct of military affairs was closely supervised by the ephors.

The "Spartan system" was very successful. For at least three hundred years the Spartans had the best army in Greece and kept the helots firmly under control. Spartan discipline was a source of wonder to the other Greeks, who admired the Spartans but were in no hurry to imitate them. But the price which the Spartans paid for their discipline and military efficiency was a heavy one. Since they had time only for soldiering, they contributed nothing to the great literature, art, philosophy, science, and democratic achievements which were the glory of ancient Greece.

Conflict at Athens. The history of Athens is very different from that of Sparta. The city of Athens was situated on a rocky peninsula called Attica, which originally contained about twelve city-states. By the eighth century B.C. all of these city-states had joined with Athens to form one large city-state. This enlarged city-state was called Athens, after its leading city. All of its citizens were called Athenians, whether they lived in the city of Athens proper or in the most distant part of Attica. In the eighth and seventh centuries B.C., Athens had very much the same political and economic problems that troubled other Greek city-states. Like Sparta, however, she did not seek to solve her problems by colonization. Her discontented classes remained at home and improved their economic situation by concentrating heavily on industry and commerce. The Athen-

In the sixth century B.C., *Athens was well known for the manufacture of highly decorated vases, used for storing oil and wine. Horse racing was a popular sport of the period. (The Metropolitan Museum of Art)*

ians discovered that their rocky soil, which they had used mostly for growing wheat, was ideal for growing olive trees and grapevines. Thus they abandoned their wheat-growing to a great extent and concentrated on the production of olive oil and wine. They also discovered that the clay soil that lined the riverbanks was excellent for making pottery. They poured their olive oil and wine into pots and shipped them abroad for sale. The Athenian pots were in as much demand as the olive oil and wine. These pots were, in reality, beautifully ornamented vases, which Greeks and non-Greeks alike were pleased to place in their homes. Athenian olive oil and wine, shipped in these vases, brought the Athenians excellent revenues, which enabled them to buy grain and other necessities from abroad.

Not all classes shared in Athenian prosperity. The lower classes claimed that the law favored the ruling nobility, that the nobles had most of the wealth, and that the unfair competition of wealthy landowners was driving the small farmers into debt and even into slavery. So great was the pressure of the commoners for greater rights and opportunities that the nobles were compelled to surrender their privileges one by one. This process did not stop until the fifth century B.C., when Athens finally achieved almost complete democracy. Thus the early history of Athens is, to a great extent, the story of her progress toward democracy.

The reforms of Draco and Solon. The nobles began surrendering their privileges in 621 B.C., when they appointed Draco to publish the law. Hitherto the law had been recorded only in the minds of the aristocrats and had been administered by them alone. But when Draco made it possible for every citizen to know the law, the nobles could no longer interpret the law as they pleased to their own advantage. Further reforms were issued by Solon in 594 B.C. He improved the lot of the farmers by canceling debts and by forbidding enslavement for debt in the future. He helped Athenian industry by inviting foreign craftsmen to settle in Athens to teach the Athenians new skills and trades.

Solon's reform of the Athenian government. Solon issued political reforms which paved the way for democracy. Henceforth the essential features of the Athenian constitution were as follows: All magistrates were elected by the *Assembly* composed of all male citizens. This Assembly was also the supreme lawmaking body of Athens. Its freedom of action, however, was limited by the fact that it could act only on measures submitted to it by the *Council of Four Hundred,* which was composed of four hundred wealthy men chosen annually by lot from the four tribes of Athens. Besides preparing measures for the Assembly to pass into law, the Council acted as the chief executive body of Athens. The most truly democratic feature of the Athenian government was the *Supreme Court.* Its members were annually chosen by lot from the entire citizen body. The Su-

Solon's agricultural reforms included limiting the size of an individual's estate and encouraging the growth of olives, which were better suited to the soil than was grain. (Sculpture by Brenda Putmann)

preme Court had authority to hear appeals from the verdicts of the magistrates' courts and to punish outgoing magistrates guilty of wrongdoing in office.

Peisistratus rules Athens as tyrant (561 to 527 B.C.). Despite Solon's far-reaching reforms, there was still much discontent in Athens. In 561 B.C. an influential nobleman, Peisistratus, took advantage of this discontent and set up a tyranny. He never held any official position, and on the surface the government functioned legally. But the support of numerous Athenians and of an army of mercenaries (which he always kept close by) was enough to make certain that his own candidates were always elected. Peisistratus went far in carrying out his pledges to those who supported him. He confiscated the estates of his opponents and distributed them to poor farmers. He created employment for the workers through an extensive program of public works. By bringing a number of Aegean islands and several towns on the Hellespont under Athenian control, he provided Athenian merchants with new markets and a safer route to the grain markets on the Black Sea. Peisistratus' sons succeded him to the tyranny in 527 B.C. but ruled the Athenians so badly that one was killed and the other driven from power in 510 B.C.

The democratic reforms of Cleisthenes (508 B.C.). To prevent further tyranny, the Athenians appointed Cleisthenes to make reforms in the constitution that would satisfy the majority of the people. He divided the citizens into ten new tribes and reorganized the Council to include five hundred members—fifty annually chosen by lot from the *entire* citizen body of each tribe. To nip would-be tyrants in the bud, he introduced the custom of ostracism, whereby every year the citizens were given the opportunity to exile for a period of ten years any man whom they considered dangerous. Cleisthenes' reforms, however, did not achieve full democracy. Though even the poorest citizens could now serve in the powerful Council of Five Hundred, often they could not afford to do so, since Council members received no salary from the state. Moreover, the higher magistracies were still restricted to the wealthier classes. These were relatively minor obstacles to full democracy, however, and were removed in the following century.

12. EARLY GREEK RELIGION, PHILOSOPHY, AND LITERATURE

The Greeks, as we have seen, were politically disunited. They were formed into hundreds of little independent city-states which frequently made war upon one another. Nevertheless, the Greeks were quite conscious of being a single people, distinct from all other peoples, whom they called barbarians. This feeling of oneness which all Greeks had, no matter where they lived, was based on their common language, culture, and religion. Religion, in particular, was a great unifying force among the Greeks.

The Greeks gods. The Greeks were polytheists, that is, they worshiped many gods. Some Greeks worshiped gods that other Greeks took little or no notice of, but all Greeks were

The Temple of the Wingless Victory stands on the Acropolis in Athens. It has been restored, using the stones and columns of the original. The columns are of Ionic style: slender, graceful, and with scroll capitals. (Alinari)

united in paying homage to the twelve gods who dwelt on Mount Olympus in northern Thessaly. The greatest of the Olympian gods was Zeus (or Jupiter, as the Romans called him). He took an active interest in earthly affairs but was not so powerful that he could control the course of earthly events. Nor did he have absolute control over the other gods. He was specially regarded by the Greeks as the god who sent rain and lightning upon the earth. The other Olympian gods had special areas of activity too. Sailors prayed to Poseidon (Neptune) for a safe journey upon the sea. Warriors prayed to Ares (Mars) for victory in battle.

The power of the gods, however, was not necessarily limited to specific activities. For instance, Aphrodite (Venus), who was primarily regarded as the goddess of love and beauty, was called upon to give victory in battle or a safe journey upon the sea to those who were specially devoted to her. Sometimes it was impossible to please one god without offending another, for the gods were very jealous of one another. If they wished, they could as easily bring harm to a mortal as help him. The dramatist Aeschylus told how the god Apollo commanded the mortal Orestes to kill his mother for a terrible crime she had committed. Orestes obeyed Apollo, but in so doing angered the goddesses called the Furies, who sought to destroy him for his terrible deed. The Greeks sympathized with Orestes for his sad predicament but blamed it on Fate—a divine force which no man or god, not even Zeus, could change.

How the Greeks honored their gods. The Greeks honored their gods through processions, sacrifices, choruses, hymns, and even athletic contests. Periodically they held great Pan-Hellenic ("all-

Greek") religious festivals, in which Greeks from every corner of the Greek world participated. The most famous of the Pan-Hellenic festivals was the Olympic Games. These were great athletic contests held every four years at Olympia in honor of Zeus. The real core of Greek religion, however, lay not in the Pan-Hellenic festivals but rather in the worship of the patron god of the city-state. Every city-state had a certain god to whom it paid special homage. This god was considered the protector of the city-state, and every citizen was bound to worship him. Thus, civic religion could not be separated from patriotism. The Greek who openly doubted the truth of the civic religion was in danger of being tried for treason. The penalty for such treason was, at best, exile; at worst, death.

Though the gods encouraged virtues such as hospitality and generally condemned murder and pride, they did not bind their followers by a strict moral code. Greek religion was formalistic; that is, it consisted mostly of ceremony and ritual. It did not demand righteous living. In return for faithful service the gods promised their followers to help them in this life. They did not promise a happy afterlife. The Greek religion taught that the souls of the dead descended to Hades, where they were doomed to moan and groan for all eternity. Achilles, the hero of the Trojan War, declared that he would rather be the slave of a poor man on earth than king in Hades.

The mystery religions. While every Greek was expected to take part in the civic religion, he could, if he wished, join one of the non-civic religions, called mystery religions. Unlike the civic religions, the mystery religions taught a moral code and promised eternal happiness to their faithful members. Their ceremonies and teachings were secret; so secret, indeed, that scholars today know very little about them. There was no question of rivalry between the civic religions and the mystery religions, for membership in the mystery religions in no way interfered with the citizen's participation in the civic rites, or vice versa.

Few activities of Greek life escaped the influence of religion. The Greeks believed that faithful service to the gods brought good fortune and that failure to perform this service was liable to bring disaster. In such an enterprise as colonization, for example, no step was taken without due regard for the gods. Before the Greeks set out to found a new city, they made certain that the gods, speaking through their priests or priestesses, approved their venture. They asked the god Apollo, through his priestess at Delphi, to name a suitable site for founding a city. They called on the gods to give them a safe journey. En route to their new home they performed the usual services in honor of the gods. When they disembarked, they solemnly thanked the gods for their safe arrival, prayed for the success of their colony, and immediately laid out a plot of ground for divine worship.

Early Greek philosophy. The Greeks were an inquiring people. They loved to ask questions and, better still, to find answers. They wondered about the origin of things—of the world, the human race, vegetation, thunder and lightning, etc. Their earliest solutions to such problems belong to that great body of literature which we call Greek mythology. The Egyptians, Babylonians, and other ancient peoples created great mythologies too, but the difference between the Greeks and them was that the Greeks did not remain satisfied with mythological answers. The Greeks observed that there were numerous and often contradictory stories about the origin of things. Which stories were true? Obviously all of them could not be true, since some contradicted others. With their genius for logical thinking, the Greeks sought to find answers which would stand the test of reason. Some Greeks wondered, for instance, if thunder and lightning were really caused by Zeus hurling thunderbolts down to the earth. They wondered if thunder and lightning might not really be explained by certain weather patterns which no one, up to that time, had bothered to investigate. The fact that some Greeks doubted that Zeus hurled thunderbolts did not mean that they doubted Zeus's existence. After all, there were many stories about Zeus that were quite contradictory, and many indeed that were really quite scandalous. Was it not possible for the universe to be governed by certain basic laws which Zeus or some other divine power had originally set in motion?

From such questions as these Greek philosophy and science were born. Philosophy means "the love of wisdom." It has also been called the search for truth. What we call *philosophy* and *science* were, for the Greeks, the same body of knowledge. One of the earliest philosopher-scientists was

The Iliad *and* Odyssey, *epics attributed to Homer, were always considered as moral poems by the Greeks and were the source of inspiration for later Greek artists. (Library of Congress)*

Thales of Miletus (*c.* 585 B.C.), who believed that the origin of all things was water. He arrived at this conclusion because water was the most universal of substances. It fell from the sky; it lay on and under the earth. It could be a liquid, a solid (ice), and a gas (steam or vapor). Thales even conceived of the earth itself as a flat disk floating on water. Another Greek from Miletus, Anaximenes, believed that the origin of all things was air, which condensed to form the material things of this world.

Early Greek literature. From their commercial contacts with the Phoenicians, the Greeks acquired the Phoenician alphabet and adapted it to their own use. The Greek alphabet was already fully developed before the writing of the two great epic poems, the *Iliad* and the *Odyssey,* around 800 B.C. The Greeks, and later the Romans, regarded these two poems as the finest pieces of Greek literature. They looked back with envy to the period of the Trojan War as a golden age, when men were mighty warriors. A more somber picture of Greece is drawn by the poet Hesiod, who lived many years after Homer. He lived in unhappy times, when the city-states were torn by political and economic troubles. In his long poem entitled *Works and Days,* he deplores the widespread belief that might makes right. He complains that the poor are oppressed by the nobles and that the judges give favorable verdicts only to those who bribe them. In another long poem, the *Theogony,* Hesiod gives an account of the origin and generation of the gods and the universe.

In the sixth century B.C. Greek poets originated *lyric poetry,* so called because it was sung to the accompaniment of the lyre. The lyric poets were a restless lot and wrote about everything they experienced: love, war, politics, athletic games, travels, shipwreck, the seasons, and even drinking parties. Their poetry fully reflects the turbulent times they lived in. Many of the city-states were experiencing political and economic troubles similar to Athens' and were progressing painfully toward democracy. War among them was common. But early in the fifth century B.C. they were suddenly faced with a danger that required them to unite—at least temporarily—or else lose their freedom. That danger was Persia's ambition to conquer Greece.

REVIEW

10. The Early History of Greece

A. Which of the two Greek epic poems is more important historically? What is its subject?

B. What were the results of the Dorian invasions of the Mycenaean kingdoms?

C. Mention some of the principal colonies established by the Greek city-states.

D. What was the meaning of *tyranny* in the time of the Greek city-state?

11. Sparta and Athens

A. What was the necessity of the military discipline that characterized Spartan life?

B. Identify the following elements of the Spartan state: helots, Assembly of Citizens, Council of Elders, five ephors.

C. How did the Athenians differ from the Spartans in solving their economic problems?

D. What were the principal reforms introduced by Draco and Solon?

E. Mention the significance of the following Athenian institutions: Assembly, Council of the Four Hundred, Supreme Court.

F. What were the principal democratic safeguards introduced by Cleisthenes?

12. Early Greek Religion, Philosophy, and Literature

A. Identify five of the gods of the Greek religion.

B. How did Greek "civic religion" differ from "mystery religions"?

C. What were the contributions to Greek culture of Thales, Anaximenes, and Homer?

THE CHAPTER IN REVIEW

A. On a relief map study the physical features of the southern Balkan peninsula, the area we know as Greece. How could this geographic environment lead to the development of many city-states?

B. Are there any similarities in the culture and life of Sparta and that of Assyria? Explain.

c. What characteristic of Western government, thought to be essential today, originated in the Greek city-state?

D. The Greeks with their inquiring natures went beyond their mythology in seeking answers to certain basic questions. What were some of the results of this intellectual curiosity?

FOR YOUR NOTEBOOK

Most historians believe that the Greeks were the first distinctively Western people. They also believe that Homer's epic poems are folk tales which contain a great deal of historical information. From your reading of either the *Iliad* or the *Odyssey* show what we can learn of Greek ideals, civilization, and differences from other ancient peoples.

A second entry in your notebook for this chapter should be a tracing of the textbook map of the eastern Mediterranean and of Greece proper. Add to this map the physical relief of the area shown. In a paragraph show how the geography of this area encouraged the Greeks to settle in city-states and to engage in seafaring ventures.

A third section of your notebook for this chapter should contrast the Spartan and Athenian ideals of manhood, government, and social life.

Fourth, pick out those features of Athenian life which distinguish Athenian Greeks not only from the Spartans but also from the other ancient peoples.

SELECTED READINGS

Homer's *Iliad* and *Odyssey* are epic poems handed down from one generation to another and put in written form by Homer. They are found to contain much historical truth, and they are a record of what Greeks believed about their early history. Each student would do well to read through either epic poem to see what the Greeks believed about their predecessors.

Marjorie and Charles H. Quennell, *Everyday Things in Ancient Greece* (New York: G. P. Putnam's Sons, 1954) is an excellent, well-illustrated account of how people lived in early Greece. More detailed and more specialized in that it concentrates on Athens is the work of the historian William Stearns Davis, *A Day in Old Athens* (Boston: Allyn & Bacon, 1952), in which the author takes you to the temple, the market place, the academy, and into the homes of the Athenians. An interesting piece of historical fiction is Caroline D. Snedecker's *The Spartan*—also published as *The Coward of Thermopylae* (New York: Doubleday & Co., 1914), in which the author faithfully follows the history of these critical years of struggle between Athens and Persia. Many students will find absorbingly interesting the *Story of the Olympic Games*, by John Kieran (New York: Frederick A. Stokes Co., 1936).

Socrates Plato Aristotle

Chapter 5. The Classic Age of Greece

13. THE PERSIAN WARS AND THE RISE OF ATHENS

The threat of Persia. In the seventh century B.C. the Greeks of Asia Minor came under the rule of Lydia, a kingdom in western Asia Minor. Lydian rule was far from oppressive, for the Lydian kings were great admirers of Greek culture and allowed the Asian Greek cities to conduct their own affairs pretty much as they pleased. When King Cyrus of Persia defeated King Croesus of Lydia in 546 B.C., both Lydia and the Asian Greeks passed under the rule of Persia. Like the Lydians, the Persians interfered very little in the affairs of their Greek subjects. The Asian Greeks, however, yearned to be completely free and in 499 B.C. staged a great rebellion. They begged the European Greeks across

the Aegean Sea to help them, but only Athens and the little city-state of Eretria, on the island of Euboea, sent aid. By 494 B.C., King Darius of Persia had completely crushed the rebellion. He gave the defeated rebels easy terms and even allowed them to have democratic governments, so long as they paid tribute to him and supplied soldiers and ships for his army and fleet. Darius now began to give serious thought to conquering the Greeks across the Aegean, for he knew that as long as some Greeks were free the Asian Greeks would never be content under Persian rule. Furthermore, he was determined to punish Athens and Eretria for helping the rebels.

The first Persian attack. In 490 B.C. Darius sent a great expedition of ships and infantry across the Aegean Sea. The Persians landed on the island of

Euboea and destroyed the city of Eretria. Next they crossed over to Attica and landed at Marathon, about fifteen miles east of Athens. None of the Greeks, not even the Athenians, had made any plans to repel them. When the Athenians learned that the Persians had landed in Attica, they dispatched the runner Pheidippides to Sparta to implore aid. Pheidippides ran the 150 miles between Athens and Sparta in two days. The Spartans were celebrating a religious festival at the time and told Pheidippides that they could not send an army until after the next full moon. Only the little city of Plataea, in Boeotia, sent an army to help the Athenians.

Battle of Marathon. The Athenian general Miltiades hastily led a joint army of Athenians and Plataeans over the mountains to Marathon. Having encamped a few miles from the Persians, he learned that they planned to move their army and navy along the coast of Attica until they reached Athens. When the Persians began to move south, Miltiades suddenly attacked them in the flank. They were caught completely off guard and were driven into the sea (490 B.C.). Miltiades immediately marched his army back to Athens. On the next morning the Persian fleet, with the remnants of the army aboard, arrived off the coast of Attica only five miles from Athens. When the Persians saw the victorious Athenian army waiting for them at the shore, they dared not risk an engagement and sailed home.

Xerxes and Themistocles. While planning a second expedition against the Greeks, King Darius died in 486 B.C. His successor Xerxes soon made known that he was no less determined than Darius to conquer the Greeks. In Athens, meanwhile, a new statesman, Themistocles, had come to the fore. He believed that in a second land engagement with the Persians the Athenians might not be so fortunate as they were at Marathon. Convinced that no foreign power could hold Greece without command of the seas, Themistocles urged the Athenians to build a mighty fleet. Athens had never been a great sea power before this time, and many Athenians balked at the expense of undertaking such a project. Themistocles won out, however, and in 493 B.C. the Athenians— for the first time in their history—began building a great fleet.

Battle of Thermopylae. The Athenians were not the only Greeks preparing for the renewed Persian onslaught. The leading Greek states, including Athens, met at Corinth in 481 B.C. and formed a land and sea alliance under the supreme command of Sparta. They made these arrangements just in time, for King Xerxes, in 480 B.C., crossed the Hellespont into Europe and began advancing with a great fleet and army along the north shore of the Aegean Sea. The allied Greek army, under the command of King Leonidas of Sparta, moved north to meet the Persians. In advance of the main Greek army, King Leonidas led a guard of three-hundred Spartans to hold the pass at Thermopylae. His position became hopeless when a pro-Persian Greek showed the enemy a path through the mountains that led round to the Spartans' rear. Leonidas and his men had time to retreat but refused to do so. They fought until the

Themistocles encouraged foreign business-men to settle in Athens, thus making it the busiest trade center in Greece. This bust was made about 460 B.C. (Fototeca Unione, Roma)

last of them had been killed. The Greeks never forgot the heroism of the men who died at Thermopylae and later erected an inscription on the spot which reads:

> Tell them in distant Sparta,
>   passer-by,
> That here, obedient to their word,
>   we lie.

Battles of Salamis and Plataea. With the loss of Thermopylae, the allied Greek army and fleet retreated southward. The Spartans, who were still in command, refused to defend Athens. They preferred to meet the Persians on the narrow isthmus of Corinth, a spot far more defensible than the open plains of Attica. While the Athenians debated whether or not to defend their city, Themistocles recalled a prophecy of Zeus, addressed to Athena, patron goddess of Athens:

> Far-seeing Zeus grants this to the
>   prayers of Athena:
> Safe the wooden wall shall be for
>   thee and thy children.

Themistocles convinced the Athenians that the wooden wall was none other than the wall of their ships. He evacuated the population of Athens to a safe spot and persuaded the Greek commanders to station the Greek fleet in the narrow Bay of Salamis, situated between the coast of Attica and the island of Salamis. Unopposed, the Persian army entered Attica and seized and burned the city of Athens, while the Persian fleet moved to within a short distance of the Greek fleet. Then the Persian fleet fell into the trap which Themistocles had laid for it. Entering the narrow ends of the Bay of Salamis, the heavy Persian ships were set upon by the lighter Greek ships. One after another the Persian ships were rammed and sunk, boarded, or driven aground by the Greeks. By day's end the naval victory of the Greeks was complete. The bulk of the Persian fleet lay in ruins (480 B.C.). The discouraged Xerxes returned to Persia but left a great part of his army in Greece. He still hoped that his generals would defeat the Greeks. In the following year (479 B.C.) a powerful Greek army, comprised chiefly of Spartans, utterly defeated the Persians at Plataea. The remnants of the Persian army straggled back to Asia. The Persians had been driven from Europe forever.

The League of Delos. Swept along by the thrill of their victories, the Greeks spent the next few years clearing the Persians out of the Aegean islands and the Greek cities of Asia Minor. When the Spartans gave up their supreme command of the allied Greeks shortly after their victory at Plataea, the Athenians stepped in to take their place. In 478 B.C., Athens formed a new Greek alliance, called the League of Delos, whose purpose was to drive the Persians from whatever Greek states they still ruled. The League drew its membership mostly from the Greek states of the Aegean Sea and Asia Minor; that is, from those states that lay most exposed to a renewed Persian offensive. The member states contributed to the support of the League by supplying either money or ships. Every year they sent deputies to the island of Delos, where they met under the presidency of Athens to decide on a common course of action. The League acted so energetically that by 468 B.C. it had driven the Persians from all the Greek cities of the Aegean Sea and Asia Minor.

The Athenian empire. Since Greeks everywhere were now freed from the Persians, the island state of Naxos decided that the Persians were no longer a menace and therefore announced its withdrawal from the League. The Athenians, however, felt that a weakening of the League would encourage the Persians to resume the offensive. With a show of force they compelled Naxos to remain in the League. Next they stripped the island of its fleet and compelled it thereafter to contribute money instead of ships to the League. When another member state attempted to withdraw a few years later, it was given the same treatment as Naxos. Slowly the League was being transformed into an Athenian empire.

Pericles. In 461 B.C. the Athenian nobleman, Pericles, was elected to the office of general. No other position in

Note the three tiers of oars, which were manned by slaves, on this model of an Athenian trireme of the fourth century B.C. *Ships similar to this were used to defend Athens against the Persians. (Commercial Museum, Phila.)*

Athens gave its holder greater influence, and Pericles was re-elected to this post almost every year until his death in 429 B.C. Under Pericles' influence the Athenians moved the headquarters of the League from Delos to Athens, forced still other states to join, and compelled most of the member states to make their contributions in money instead of ships. By the middle of the fifth century B.C., the League had become, in reality, an Athenian empire. The so-called member states were actually subject states of Athens, and the Athenians made little effort to conceal the fact. They kept a close watch over the governments of the subject states and sometimes placed garrisons in their cities. Athenian juries heard all important law cases that arose in the subject states. The subject states were made to adopt the coinage and weights and measures in use at Athens and to pay whatever tribute Athens demanded.

In the middle of the fifth century B.C., Athens was at her peak. She ruled scores of states in the Aegean Sea, in Asia Minor, and along the Black Sea straits. Her prosperity was assured by the tribute from her subject states and by the revenues from her greatly expanded commerce and industry. Militarily she was rivaled only by Sparta. Culturally and in every other respect her position as the leading city of Greece was questioned by no one.

14. ATHENIAN SOCIETY IN THE FIFTH CENTURY, B.C.

Pericles and the Athenian empire. The position of general which Pericles held for over thirty years enabled him to

Under Pericles, Athens flourished politically and artistically. The political structure of the polis was defined, and the sculpture and architecture in the city reflected the "Golden Age of Athens." (British Museum)

exert great influence. There were ten such generals in Athens, annually elected, whose duties consisted chiefly of commanding the army and navy and handling foreign affairs. Theoretically Pericles had no greater authority than any of the other nine generals. But he was held in such high esteem that the Athenian people were content to let him guide their affairs for over thirty years. In an age of Athenian imperialism, Pericles was the very symbol of Athenian ambitions. His policies led to the transformation of the League of Delos into an Athenian empire.

Pericles sought to enlarge this empire, which consisted chiefly of maritime states, by bringing a number of land states into alliance with Athens. His attempts to build up a land empire, however, brought Athens into conflict with Sparta and Corinth and other Greek states, who feared that the Athenian thirst for empire would not be quenched until all of Greece was brought under subjection. In 445 B.C., after suffering several defeats at the hands of Sparta and her allies, Athens was forced to dissolve her land alliances. Her maritime empire, however, remained as strong as ever.

Pericles' success in building up a maritime empire assured the Athenians of numerous markets where their goods could be sold, numerous sources of cheap raw materials, and considerable revenue from the tribute-paying subject states. Under Pericles' leadership Athens easily became the most prosperous city in Greece. But Pericles stood for much more than imperialistic and commercial ambitions. He wished to make Athens the leading cultural center of Greece. He encouraged poets, dramatists, sculptors, and craftsmen from all over the Greek world to come and settle in Athens. He adorned the city with beautiful public buildings, including the Parthenon, the loveliest of Greek temples.

Athenian democracy: the Assembly. In the fifth century B.C., the long progress of Athens toward democracy was completed. Every male citizen over eighteen was eligible to vote in the Assembly, the supreme law-making body of Athens. There were over fifty thousand such citizens, but no more than a few thousand regularly attended the sessions of the Assembly. Any citizen could introduce a bill in the Assembly or propose changes in one under consideration.

The Council of Five Hundred. Most of the measures which the Assembly passed into law were drawn up and submitted to it by the Council of Five Hundred. Male citizens over eighteen could serve in this Council, whose members were annually chosen by lot from the entire citizen body—fifty from each of the ten tribes. The Council handled routine matters of state. The measures which it presented to the Assembly were often suggested by the ten generals. Thanks to his dominant position among the

Model of the Parthenon, temple dedicated to Athena. It is an excellent example of Doric architecture, in which strength and beauty are combined in the orderly Hellenic tradition.

ten generals, Pericles was able to draw up measures which the Council passed on to the Assembly, which then passed these measures into law. When Pericles introduced the practice of paying the Council members a salary, it even became possible for poor citizens to devote time to this office.

The magistrates and other public officials of Athens were chosen by lot from the entire citizen body. The Athenian theory of democracy was that every citizen could be trusted with responsibility in office. There were, however, two notable exceptions. The ten generals and the financial officials were elected rather than chosen by lot, and eligibility for these offices was restricted to property holders. Thus, even at the height of Athenian democracy, the most responsible positions in the state were entrusted only to men of means and of proven ability.

The juries. The duty which practically every Athenian citizen could expect to perform, perhaps many times in his life, was that of serving on the juries. Every year six thousand jurors were chosen by lot from a list of the citizens over thirty years old. The six thousand were assigned to juries which ranged in size from 201 to 1,001. All civil and criminal cases were heard by these juries, the importance of a case determining how large a jury should hear it. The operation of the Athenian juries is best illustrated by an example. If a citizen thought that he had been unjustly deprived of a piece of property by another citizen, he laid a formal charge before a city magistrate. The magistrate then notified the plaintiff (the accuser) and the defendant (the accused) to appear before him. If the

The English word "ostracism" is derived from the Greek ostraka, *meaning ballots. Note the names of famous Greeks —Pericles, Aristides, Themistocles—on the stone ballots. (American School of Classical Studies, Athens)*

defendant thought that the accusation was unjust, he solemnly swore before the magistrate that his cause was just and presented whatever evidence he had to sustain his case. The plaintiff did the same. If the magistrate decided that one of the parties had no real evidence, he awarded the case to the opposite party. But if he considered that each party had good evidence, he assigned the case to a jury. The jury reviewed the same evidence which the litigants—that is, the plaintiff and defendant—had presented to the magistrate. The litigants were required to present their cases in person. They could bring in witnesses and, if they wished, noted orators to plead on their behalf before the jury. A majority vote of the jury decided the case. After returning its verdict, the jury asked both the plaintiff and the defendant to name a penalty for the guilty party. In a second vote the jury decided which penalty to impose. The guilty party did not necessarily suggest a light penalty, for if he suggested too light a

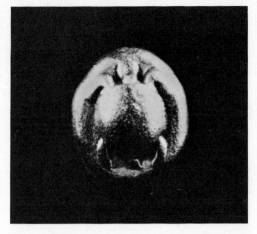

The earliest silver coin, the stater, dates back to about 700 B.C. On the right is a fifth-century tetradrachm, a silver coin based on the drachm unit, a measure of silver. (Chase-Manhattan Museum of Moneys of the World)

penalty the jury was inclined to impose the penalty suggested by the winner of the case.

Military service. Every able-bodied Athenian male between the ages of eighteen and twenty received military training. Thereafter, each one was liable to be called up for active service until he was fifty. Since the soldiers had to provide their own military equipment, the nature of the citizen's military duties depended on his wealth. The wealthiest citizens served as commanders of ships; they bore the cost of the ships' upkeep and paid the crews. Less wealthy citizens served in the cavalry. Athenians of moderate means served as heavy-armed infantry, while the poor served as light-armed infantry, bowmen, and rowers.

The Athenian economy. The Athenian concept of wealth, by modern standards, was very modest. Few Athenians could afford to build themselves great mansions, while the largest "estate" in Attica covered a mere sixty-four acres. The Athenians, even the wealthy ones,

lived very sparingly. They spent most of the day outdoors, rarely ate meat, and even considered fish a luxury. Like most other Mediterranean peoples of antiquity and even of the present day, they lived mostly on bread, wine, and cheese. The wealthiest men in Athens were the landowners and merchants. From the farms came clay, olives, and grapes, which were converted into pottery, oil, and wine and were sold abroad by the merchants. Industry was concentrated in small shops, where the manufacturing was done by the owner, his family, and several apprentices and slaves. There were no factories or large-scale business establishments.

Population. The total population of the city-state of Athens in the fifth century B.C. has been estimated at 315,500. Of these, some 172,000 were citizens (including women and children), 115,000 were slaves, and 28,500 were *metics*, a name given to the foreign residents of Athens. In the city of Athens and its nearby port of Piraeus lived 155,000 persons.

The metics. Like citizens of other ancient city-states, the Athenians prized their citizenship very highly and were slow to confer it on others. Of the 28,500 metics, or foreign residents living in Athens, many were Greeks whose families had lived in Athens for generations. They were not eligible for citizenship for the simple reason that one or more of their ancestors had not been Athenians. Their only chance of attaining citizenship was through adoption by some influential Athenian family. Though the metics had to perform many of the citizens' duties, such as serving in the armed forces, they were not, strictly speaking, entitled to the protection of Athenian law. The custom developed, however, whereby influential Athenians took metics under their protection and represented them in the courts.

The slaves. Athenian slaves were mostly of non-Greek extraction. They were bought from slave merchants, who in turn had bought them from the slave pirates who flourished throughout ancient times. The slaves were mostly employed in household and industrial work. Some held re-

On this gravestone, now in the National Museum in Athens, a slave girl is shown fastening the sandal of her mistress. (Fototeca Unione, Roma)

The agora, *or market place, of Athens was the center of municipal activity. The* agora *was surrounded by public offices and food shops. People congregated here to discuss politics and philosophy. (American School of Classical Studies, Athens)*

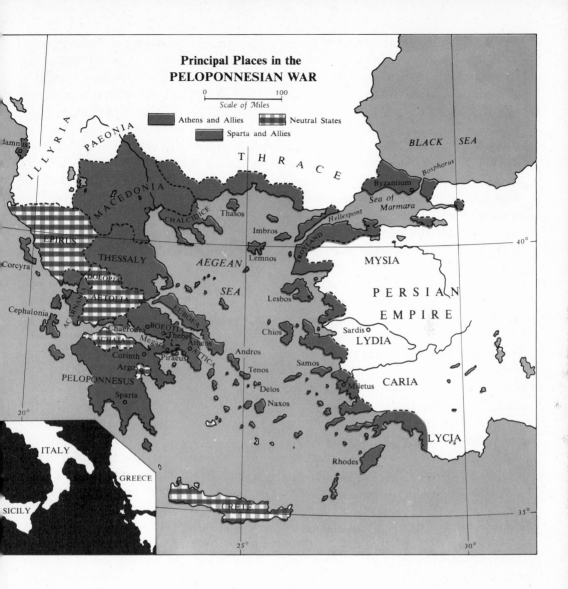

Principal Places in the PELOPONNESIAN WAR

Scale of Miles
0 — 100

Athens and Allies Neutral States
Sparta and Allies

ILLYRIA
PAEONIA
Epidamnus
BLACK SEA
THRACE
MACEDONIA
Bosphorus
Byzantium
CHALCIDICE
Thasos
Sea of Marmara
Imbros
Hellespont
EPIRUS
Corcyra
THESSALY
AEGEAN
Lemnos
40°
MYSIA
DOLOPIA
PERSIAN
ACARNANIA
AETOLIA
SEA
Cephalonia
Lesbos
EMPIRE
EUBOEA
Chios
Sardis
LYDIA
Chaeronea
BOEOTIA
ACHAIA
Thebes
Athens
Megara
ATTICA
Andros
Samos
Corinth
Piraeus
CARIA
Argos
Tenos
Miletus
PELOPONNESUS
Delos
20°
Sparta
Naxos
LYCIA

ITALY
GREECE
Rhodes
SICILY
CRETE
35°
25°
30°

sponsible positions, such as managing
the estates or businesses of their owners. On the whole, the city slaves were
well treated, but the farm slaves were
worked very hard, while those who
worked in the state-owned silver mines
of southern Attica were in a pitiable
condition. Some businessmen, and
even the state, owned gangs of slaves
who were rented out for various
employments.

15. THE PELOPONNESIAN WAR AND THE MACEDONIAN CONQUEST OF GREECE

Athens vs. Sparta. The rise of Athens
as the leading commercial and naval
power of Greece and as virtual ruler
of the Aegean Sea alarmed many
Greek states, particularly Sparta and
Corinth. They feared that Athens' imperialistic ambitions would not be satisfied until all of Greece was subject

to her. Though the enemies of Athens forced her to give up her land empire, they saw her maritime empire steadily growing as she brought one Aegean island after another under her control and established her power in the city-states that ringed the coasts of the Aegean Sea and the Black Sea straits. In 435 B.C. a series of incidents began that led to the outbreak of a deadly war between Athens and Sparta—a war that was to involve practically every Greek state. In that year Athens made an alliance with Corcyra, an island city-state which dominated the sea lanes between Greece and Italy. This alliance, which combined the Athenian and Corcyrean naval forces, caused great alarm in the anti-Athenian camp. In 432 B.C. the Athenians caused further alarm by forbidding Megara, a rival commercial power, to use the facilities of any port in the Athenian empire. This prohibition meant the economic ruin of Megara, and other Greek states trembled lest the same measure be applied to them. As a result of these and other incidents, Sparta and her allies declared war on Athens in 431 B.C. Their announced intention in declaring war was to free Greece from the danger of Athenian domination.

Athenian strategy. Even before Sparta declared war, Pericles had carefully mapped out the strategy which he hoped would lead to an Athenian victory. He had no intention of engaging Sparta's army, for he recognized Sparta's superiority on land. The Athenian hopes lay in their naval superiority. Pericles planned for the Athenian fleets to make constant attacks on the enemy coast and destroy

the enemy commerce. Thus would Sparta and her allies be forced to sue for peace. Pericles foresaw, of course, that the Athenian refusal to engage Sparta's army meant that Attica lay open to the enemy. Consequently he collected almost the entire population of Attica behind the high thick walls of Athens and Piraeus and in the walled area that connected these two cities. Pericles assured the Athenians that as long as Athens remained supreme on the sea and kept her empire intact, the city would be well provisioned from abroad. Meanwhile the Athenians would simply have to put up with the Spartan devastation of their land. The Athenians grumbled, but Pericles steadfastly refused to let their army engage the enemy.

Sparta was just as confident of victory as Athens. She hoped that the destruction of Attica would demoralize the Athenians, or at least force them to send out their army. She tried to stir up rebellions in the Athenian subject states and placed great faith in the ability of her naval allies to match Athens on the sea.

The Sicilian expedition. Athens and Sparta were so evenly matched that the war dragged on inconclusively for many years. After Pericles' death in 429 B.C., the Athenians remained faithful to his strategy for several years. But no statesman of equal ability arose to take his place. Impatient for victory, the Athenians came more and more under the domination of rabble-rousers. In 415 B.C., Alcibiades, a brilliant young nobleman, urged the Athenians to undertake the conquest of Sicily. Though the Greek cities of Sicily had hitherto taken no part in

the war, Alcibiades warned that several of them, particularly Syracuse, were preparing to enter the war on the side of Sparta. Furthermore, he argued, the conquest of Sicily would greatly enlarge the Athenian empire. Swayed by his arguments, the Athenian Assembly voted to equip a great fleet and army for this purpose and appointed three generals, with equal power, to head the expedition. One of the three, Nicias, was appointed against his will, for he believed that the expedition was a great act of folly. Alcibiades, too, was one of the generals, but his political enemies succeeded in having him recalled to Athens shortly after the arrival of the expedition in Sicily. He was summoned to stand trial on a charge of sacrilege. Fearing for his life, he fled to Sparta and revealed the Athenian plans to the enemy. When the third general, Lamachus, died in Sicily, Nicias was left in sole charge of the expedition. His bungling leadership and Alcibiades' treason sealed the fate of the Athenians. Sparta sent an army

to aid Syracuse. Nicias foolishly allowed the Athenian fleet to be blockaded in the harbor of Syracuse, and in 413 B.C. the entire Athenian fleet and army were captured. Forty thousand Athenians and allies were either slain or held as prisoners.

Collapse of Athens. Despite their great defeat at Syracuse and the subsequent rebellion of many of their subject states, the Athenians rallied and managed to hold out until 404 B.C. Their final defeat was due to an act of almost unbelievable carelessness. Unaware that a Spartan fleet lay nearby, the officers and crew of the main Athenian fleet anchored their ships in the Hellespont and went ashore in search of food. They made the fatal mistake of leaving their ships unguarded. The Spartans moved in and easily captured the Athenian ships. Deprived of their fleet, the Athenians could no longer be provisioned from abroad or hold together what little empire remained to them. In 404 B.C. Athens surrendered. Sparta was urged by her allies to wipe Athens off the face of the earth, but the Spartans refused. They were content to dissolve the Athenian empire, tear down the walls of the city, and install a pro-Spartan government.

The Athenians were soon able to expel their pro-Spartan government and restore democracy, but they never succeeded in rebuilding their empire. They still counted as a leading Greek state, however, and soon joined the other states in their ancient pastime of warring on one another. These constant wars alarmed a number of Greeks, who warned that the city-states would destroy each other or be conquered by an outside power unless they formed some kind of union. But the independence of the city-state was so basic to their way of thinking that the Greeks never even considered forming an effective confederacy. For centuries their freedom had been assured by what amounted to a balance of power among the leading states. When Athens upset that balance in the fifth century B.C. she was laid low by Sparta.

The rise of Macedon. The balance of power was upset once and for all by the rise of Macedon, a half-Greek, half-barbarian kingdom north of Thessaly. Macedon was a land of powerful landowning nobles, farmers, shepherds, and hunters. Many of these spoke a Greek dialect but were generally considered barbarians by the more civilized Greeks to the south. For centuries Macedon had been ruled by kings who had tried in vain to control their half-wild subjects. Even as late as the first half of the fourth century B.C. the kings had been unable to prevent the expansion of Greek city-states into southern Macedon.

Philip of Macedon (359 to 336 B.C.). Macedon was at length transformed into a first-rate power under her extraordinary king, Philip II. Philip dreamed not only of making Macedon a strong, united kingdom under his command but of conquering Greece and Persia as well. He began his reign by subduing the numerous tribes of Macedon and bringing them firmly under his control. He organized his warlike countrymen into a splendid army. When he ran short of money, he boldly seized the gold mines of Thrace. Part of the revenues from these mines trickled into the city-states, where high-placed officials were bribed to influence public opinion in Philip's favor.

The Macedonian conquest. The Athenian orator and statesman, Demosthenes, clearly saw the threat of Macedon to the freedom of the city-states. He appealed to the Greeks to unite and crush Macedon, but his appeals went unheeded. Indeed the Greeks themselves unwittingly contributed to Philip's growing influence over Greek affairs. With so powerful a state nearby, they turned to Philip to help them solve their own differences. In 346 B.C., Thebes invited Philip to punish an enemy state. When Philip responded, the Thebans hailed him as a friend of Greece. But the Thebans shortly learned that their friend was likely to become their master. In 338 B.C., Philip was again requested—this time by several other Greek states—to punish an offending state. This request was made over the protest of Thebes and Athens, who were now convinced that Philip's ambition was to dominate Greece. They joined forces to stop his advance into Greece. On the battlefield of Chaeronea in Boeotia, their armies were thoroughly beaten by the Macedonians, led in person by King Philip and his eighteen-year-old son Alexander.

Though the Greeks were now at Philip's mercy, he announced that he had no intention of taking away their freedom. His aim, he said, was to bring peace and unity to Greece. For this purpose he organized a number of city-states, including Athens and Thebes, into a military alliance under his presidency. Nominally the Greeks entered this alliance of their own free will, but actually they had little choice. With the Macedonians henceforth keeping a close watch over Greek affairs, the city-states were reduced, in effect, to the position of Macedonian satellites. The classic age of the city-state had come to an end.

16. THE PHILOSOPHERS: SOCRATES, PLATO, AND ARISTOTLE

In no other area have the Greeks so influenced mankind as in their philosophy. Fifth-century Greek philosophers were concerned with very much the same problems as were the philosophers of the sixth century B.C. The philosopher Empedocles, whose home was in Sicily, maintained that all things were composed of four basic elements: earth, air, fire, and water. This theory was later accepted by the great philosopher Aristotle (384–322 B.C.) and by many noted philosophers and scientists for hundreds of years thereafter. Democritus (*c.* 460–*c.* 370 B.C.), however, believed that all things

Legend tells us that Demosthenes practiced oratory on the seashore and that he placed pebbles in his mouth to overcome a speech defect. In his orations against Philip of Macedon (the Philippics), he warned Greece of the growing influence of Philip. (Library of Congress)

were composed of innumerable particles called atoms—so small that the naked eye could not see them—which moved through space and were joined together and separated by chance.

The Sophists. Every philosopher had his school, or group of followers. One of the most famous schools in the fifth century B.C. was that of the Sophists ("wise men"), who taught mostly in Athens. The Sophists prided themselves on being "practical" men. They laid great stress on earthly success and taught that men ought to discard those beliefs or practices that stand in the way of success. Since they doubted the truth or usefulness of many Greek customs and religious beliefs, they were

Although Socrates never sought office, he willingly performed public duties and twice served in the military.

often accused of teaching views that were irreligious and immoral—for example, *might makes right*.

Socrates (469 to 399 B.C.). One of the greatest of the Greek philosophers was the Athenian Socrates, a stonecutter by trade. He never taught in any school but spent his free moments in the market place and shops of Athens, talking with men of every class. The question he constantly asked himself and others was: What is truth? Like the Sophists, Socrates doubted the truth or value of many of the beliefs which his fellow Athenians simply took for granted. But, unlike the Sophists, he did not believe that earthly success should be the rule that determines whether a belief is accepted or rejected. He taught that men should have concern only for the truth, no matter what the consequences. Socrates sought to arrive at the truth through the question-and-answer technique. An illustration of what is commonly called the *Socratic method* follows:

In conversation with a friend, Socrates asks if Zeus is a good god. Naturally the friend answers yes. Next Socrates asks if his friend believes that Zeus has ever caused the death of innocent persons. Again the friend answers yes, for the Greeks told any number of stories of how Zeus had caused the death of some innocent person as a favor to one of his fellow gods or to one of his devoted mortals. Socrates next asks whether Zeus, in causing the death of innocent persons, is guilty of what the Greeks call murder. His friend becomes somewhat uneasy at this question but has no choice except to answer yes. Finally Socrates asks if murder is evil. The friend answers yes. Socrates has now forced his friend into the position where he must reject one of the following statements: If Zeus commits murder, which is evil, he is not a good god; or, if Zeus is a good god, he does not commit murder.

The death of Socrates. Many Athenians looked with suspicion upon Socrates. They accused him of being a Sophist and of twisting words to arrive at any conclusion he wished. In 399 B.C., Socrates was brought into court on the charge of teaching disbelief in the gods and of corrupting the young men of Athens by his teaching. He was tried by a jury of his fellow citizens, who found him guilty and sentenced him to death. Although Socrates had the opportunity to escape from Athens, he preferred to remain a good Athenian to the end by obeying the laws of Athens, even though obedience in this case meant his death. He was condemned to drink a cup of poison—a common form of execution in Athens at that time. Surrounded by his friends in his last hours, he sought to calm them by his certainty of a good life in the next world. With the utmost peace of mind he drank his cup of poison and died. He lived and died in the belief (as he said) that no harm could come to a good man in this life or in the next.

Plato (428 to 347 B.C.). Socrates' most famous disciple was Plato, an Athenian aristocrat. Like Socrates, Plato thought that men must seek the truth above all else. In Plato's thinking, truth, or reality, was another name for what is good. He maintained that once a man knows what is good he cannot help *doing* good, since his mind (where knowledge of the good is stored) and his will (which directs his actions) are always in harmony. But truth, or reality, is not an easy thing to grasp, since it exists in all its perfection only in another world. All earthly things are but a dim reflection of reality. For instance, although there are millions of trees on earth, none of these tree is a really perfect tree. Each of them is merely a reflection of the perfect tree—the universal tree.

He asserted that since reality does not exist on this earth it cannot be learned from perishable things known through the senses. It can be grasped only by man's *spiritual mind,* which existed in the other or real world before it was joined to the body on earth. Even when the spiritual mind is joined to the body, it still retains a hazy notion of the reality which it knew in its preincarnate existence. But only a few individuals are fortunate enough to grasp reality. Plato compares mankind to prisoners chained inside a cave with their faces to the wall. Outside is the

Plato's works are part of the world's best literature, because of the excellence and charm of his language and his vivid portrayal of contemporary life. (Library of Congress)

real world, and its light helps the prisoners in the cave see distant reflections of reality on the wall, which they are facing. Chained mankind sees only this world of shadows and thinks that *it* is the real world. But if one of the prisoners could break away from his chains and go outside into the real world, he could return to the cave and explain to the prisoners what the real world is like. What they think is reality is nothing but a reflection of the real world!

Plato's Republic. Plato describes the real (or what we would call the "ideal") state in *The Republic.* In this republic, which would be a city-state of no more than five thousand citizens, every citizen would be assigned to one of three classes—workers, warriors, and guardians—according to his natural abilities. The highest class would be the guardians, who would watch over the republic. They would be trained from childhood for their position and would be carefully shielded from any experience that would harm them. They would remain unmarried so that they could give all their attention to governing the state. At their head would be a philosopher-king. It is obvious that Plato's republic would be no democracy, since the great mass of the citizens, the workers and warriors, would have no hand in ruling the state. The republic would be, rather, an aristocracy—not an aristocracy of blood, but an aristocracy of talent. Though the ruling guardians would be few in number, they would be chosen solely on the basis of their natural ability.

Aristotle (384 to 322 B.C.). Plato's most noted disciple was Aristotle, a native of southern Macedon. At the age of seventeen he went to Athens and studied under Plato until the latter's death in 347 B.C. Returning to Macedon he tutored Alexander, the young son of King Philip of Macedon, for several years. He went back to Athens in 335 B.C. and spent practically all the remaining years of his life there, teaching in his school, which he called the Lyceum.

Aristotle's universal knowledge. Aristotle wrote on a greater number of subjects than any other Greek thinker. He was the first Greek who carefully separated one branch of knowledge from another. He wrote books on such varied subjects as physics, astronomy, biology, physiology, ethics, metaphysics, politics, the drama, rhetoric, and poetry. Not all of his contributions to these fields were by any means original. He took full advantage of the knowledge which the Greeks had already accumulated, and he had numerous assistants to whom he as-

A student of Plato and the tutor of Alexander the Great, Aristotle influenced Moslem, Jewish, and Christian philosophy. (Fototeca Unione, Roma)

signed topics for further investigation. Nevertheless, the contributions which he personally made to these fields were probably greater than those of any other thinker in ancient times.

Inductive and deductive reasoning. Aristotle popularized the methods of inductive and deductive reasoning. Through inductive reasoning, one arrives at general notions through observing and understanding a number of particular things. For instance, if one observes that every tree which one has seen has leaves, and if this observation is confirmed by reliable reports, one may arrive at the general notion that *all* trees have leaves. Deductive reasoning operates in the opposite manner. One begins with a general notion and applies it to a particular. For instance, if one accepts the general notion that all trees have leaves, then one may safely conclude that the particular trees in China have leaves.

The method by which deductive reasoning operates is known as the syllogism. An example of deductive, or syllogistic, reasoning is found in Socrates' discussion of whether Zeus was a good god (p. 100). What Socrates did, in effect, was to force his friend to two contrary conclusions, which can be expressed in syllogisms as follows:

A good god does no evil.
Zeus is a good god.
Therefore, Zeus does no evil.

But since the friend admitted that Zeus committed murder, and that murder is evil, he found himself following the line of reasoning in this second syllogism:

Whoever commits murder does evil.
Zeus commits murder.
Therefore, Zeus does evil.

Though neither Socrates nor his friend talked in syllogisms, the reasoning found in the above syllogisms was *implied* in their conversation. Since the conclusions of the two syllogisms are contradictory, the friend must reject one or the other. The only way he can still maintain that Zeus is a good god is by rejecting the old notion that Zeus committed murder.

17. GREEK DRAMA, HISTORIOGRAPHY, AND ART

The drama. The Greek drama developed from processions in honor of Dionysus, the god of reproduction and vegetation. The chief participants in these processions were the chorus, which sang the praises of Dionysus. With the passing of time the chorus began to sing songs about other sub-jects out of the Greek past as well. In the sixth century B.C. the processions were changed somewhat when the chorus was made to do most of its singing on a stage, and a performer was added who did not sing at all. The new performer carried on a dialogue with the leader of the chorus, while the chorus itself fell more and more into the background. Still later the performer began to play the role of several characters, changing his dress for each character. Finally, in the fifth century B.C., Greek drama reached maturity with the addition of several more performers who played the different characters.

A Greek drama, or play, was generally characterized by the "three unities": unity of action, time, and place. Unity of action meant that the drama had a single plot, around which the dialogue of the actors and the songs of the chorus centered. Unity of time meant that the action, or plot, took place within a very short time, generally less than a day. Unity of place meant that the action occurred within a rather restricted area, such as a palace. Most Greek dramas were tragedies, but the dramatist never intended to depress his audience with a story of woe and sorrow. His intention was to impress the onlookers with the grandeur of the tragedy and to have them leave the theater with the feeling that they were better persons for having seen it. This feeling was (and still is) called *catharsis*.

The greatest of the Greek dramatists were Athenians. Of the hundreds of plays which they wrote, only a small fraction have survived. Aeschylus (525–456 B.C.), for instance, wrote

about ninety plays, but only seven are extant. His most famous work is a trilogy, or series of three plays, which deals with the family of Agamemnon, the King of Mycenae, who led the Greek expedition against Troy in the twelfth century B.C. Sophocles (496–406 B.C.) produced many of his great plays during the trying days of the Peloponnesian War. His most famous play, *Oedipus Rex*, the story of a king who unknowingly marries his own mother, is still a favorite with playgoers all over the world. The tragedies of Euripides (480–406 B.C.) were so admired all over the Greek world that the Syracusans, after defeating the Athenians in 413 B.C., freed any prisoner who could recite from memory verses from the plays of Euripides.

Not all Greek dramas were tragic in tone. Aristophanes (*c.* 444–380 B.C.) wrote comedies which ridiculed Athenian politicians (e.g., Pericles), intellectuals (e.g., Socrates), silly stories about the gods, and even Athenian democracy. He lived throughout the Peloponnesian War and hated every minute of it.

More of a realist than Aeschylus or Sophocles, Euripides wrote penetrating tragedies. This statue of him, holding the tragic mask, is in the Vatican Museum. The theater of Dionysius was the center of drama for Athens. (Alinari)

Herodotus. (The Metropolitan Museum of Art)

Sophocles.
Thucydides.   *(Library of Congress)*

The historians. The early Greeks were fond of writing descriptions of the places they visited and of drawing up genealogies, or family trees, of their ancestors and of the gods. These writings naturally touched on the history of the places and individuals concerned. Gradually writers began to concentrate more on history and less on geographical and genealogical information. By the fifth century B.C., the Greeks were writing history in the modern sense of the word.

Herodotus. The first Greek historian was Herodotus (484–425 B.C.). He came from Asia Minor but spent much of his literary life in Athens. He traveled to distant places such as Babylon and Egypt and gathered information wherever he went. In his great history, *The Persian Wars,* he gives a detailed account of the events leading up to the war and of the war itself. He tells many interesting stories about the persons and places involved. Many of these stories, strictly speaking, are not related to the war, but they are always interesting and have provided later historians with considerable knowledge of the ancient world. Though Herodotus wrote his history to keep the memory of the Persian wars forever alive, he shows no bitterness whatsoever toward the Persians. As a matter of fact, he presents the Persian emperors as likable, civilized men.

Thucydides. The Athenian Thucydides (*c.* 460–*c.* 395 B.C.) is generally regarded as the greatest of the Greek historians. When the Peloponnesian War broke out, Thucydides began collecting material for his history, *The Peloponnesian War.* Though he was a general in the Athenian army, he succeeded in being fair in presenting the causes and the course of the war. His history is neither pro-Athenian nor pro-Spartan. Thucydides' scientific approach to history is revealed by his own words on how and why he wrote his history:

. . . with regard to my factual reporting of the events of the war I have made it a principle not to write down the first story that came my way, and not even to be guided by my own general impressions; either I was present myself at the events which I have described or else I heard of them from eyewitnesses whose reports I have checked with as much thoroughness as possible. Not that even so the truth was easy to discover: different eyewitnesses give different accounts of the same events, speaking out of partiality for one side or the other, or else from imperfect memories. And it may well be that my history will seem less easy to read because of the absence in it of a romantic element. It will be enough for me, however, if these words of mine are judged useful by those who want to understand clearly the events which happened in the past and which (human nature being what it is) will, at some time or other and in much the same ways, be repeated in the future. My work is not a piece of writing designed to meet the taste of an immediate public, but was done to last forever.

Xenophon (c. 434 to 355 B.C.). Xenophon was the last of the great historians of the Greek classical age. His *Anabasis* is regarded as one of the greatest military histories of all time. It is the story of a military expedition in which a number of mercenary Greek soldiers, including Xenophon, took part against Artaxerxes, King of Persia. Xenophon's reputation for impartiality is not as high as that of Herodotus or Thucydides. He purposely omitted de-

Xenophon. (Library of Congress)

tails that might have given offense to his friends, particularly to the Spartans, with whom he was on excellent terms.

Architecture and sculpture. The eagerness of the Greeks to honor their gods resulted in their building some of the most beautiful temples the world has ever seen. Early Greek architecture shows considerable Egyptian influence. But the Greeks did more than merely copy. After centuries of building they produced an architecture that was unlike any other found in Egypt or the Near East. Its influence on the Western world, and even to some extent on oriental countries, has been so great that even today numerous buildings are erected which, especially on the outside, are hardly more than copies of Greek models. The ruins of hundreds of Greek buildings are still to be seen in Asia Minor, Greece, Sicily, and southern Italy. The most famous of Greek ruins is the Parthenon, which was built in Athens in the fifth century B.C. Though built as a temple of the goddess Athena, the

Parthenon continued to receive excellent care long after Athena had become only a memory. In the sixth century A.D., when most Greeks had become Catholics, it was dedicated as a church to the Blessed Virgin Mary. In the fifteenth century the Turks conquered Greece and turned the Parthenon into a mosque. Thus for a thousand years the beauty of the Parthenon was recognized by pagan, Catholic, and Moslem alike, who employed it for what they considered man's noblest activity—divine worship. In the seventeenth century, during a war between Turkey and Venice, the Turks used the Parthenon as a powder magazine. An explosion was touched off which laid most of the Parthenon in a heap of ruins. Ruined though it is, it still rises above the city of Athens and stands as a constant reminder of the ancient glory of Greece.

As in architecture, so in sculpture the Greeks learned much from the Egyptians. At first they carved in a stiff, formal style which clearly shows an Egyptian influence. As they gained more experience, they gradu-

The Winged Victory of Samothrace, sculptured about 306 B.C. to commemorate a naval victory, is one of the finest examples of Hellenic art. It is in the Louvre, Paris. (Caisse Nationale des Monuments Historiques)

ally developed a style all their own. By the fifth century B.C. they had learned to make statues of beautiful proportion and grace. Most Greek statues were of the gods and were placed in temples, public buildings, squares, and homes. The stone of these buildings, and also of tombstones, was often carved with statues in relief.

Medicine. It was the custom of ailing Greeks to visit the shrines of Asklepios, god of healing. The priests who were in charge of these shrines not only interceded with the god to cure the patients, but often played the role of physician too. From observing their patients and studying the medical knowledge of Egypt and Babylon, they learned much about the nature and cure of disease. The most famous of the priests of Asklepios was Hippocrates (c. 460–377 B.C.), who is generally regarded as the founder of scientific medicine. Though Hippocrates did not doubt that disease might result from the curse of the gods or of

The southern portico of the Erectheum, a temple on the Acropolis, has the only faultless example of caryatid architecture, wherein sculptured forms are used for support. (Kidder-Smith)

Hippocrates. (Photo Mate, Toronto)

evil spirits, he was equally convinced that, in some cases at least, disease could be traced to organic causes alone. Thus he laid great stress on the scientific observation of disease. He and his disciples tirelessly searched for the causes and symptoms of disease and were ever on the lookout for better treatments. Hippocrates is also called the founder of medical ethics, for he insisted that physicians should always act according to the highest principles. His medical ethics are summed up in the Hippocratic Oath, which, after more than two thousand years, is still taken by medical students the world over:

You do solemnly swear, each man by whatever he holds most sacred, that you will be loyal to the profession of medicine and just and generous to its members; that you will lead your lives and practice your art in uprightness and honor; that into whatsoever house you shall enter, it shall be for the good of the sick to the utmost of your power . . . that

you will exercise your art solely for the cure of your patients and will give no drug, perform no operation, for a criminal purpose . . . that whatsoever you shall see or hear of the lives of men which is not fitting to be spoken, you will keep inviolaby secret. These things do you swear. . . .

REVIEW

STUDY SECTIONS IN REVIEW
13. The Persian Wars and the Rise of Athens
A. Why did King Darius of Persia embark upon an invasion of Greece?
B. Identify the following battles: Marathon, Thermopylae, Bay of Salamis.
C. Explain the purpose and membership obligations of the League of Delos.
D. How did the members of the League of Delos react to the leadership of Athens?

14. Athenian Society in the Fifth Century, B.C.
A. Mention three contributions by Pericles to the rise of Athens over other city-states.
B. How were public officials chosen under the Athenian version of democracy?
C. Identify the following classes within a city-state: metics, slaves, citizens.
D. Who were eligible for citizenship in the Greek city-state?

15. The Peloponnesian War and the Macedonian Conquest of Greece
A. What events led to the outbreak of war between Athens and Sparta in 431 B.C.?
B. Discuss the results of the defeat of Athens by Sparta and her allies.
C. How did King Philip unite Macedon into a powerful kingdom?
D. How did the Greeks unknowingly help Philip gain control of the city-states?

16. The Philosophers: Socrates, Plato, and Aristotle
A. What were the principal contributions of the Sophists, Democritus, and Empedocles?
B. Explain the basic purpose and approach of the "Socratic method."

c. What ideal form of government was set forth by Plato in his book, *The Republic?*

D. Distinguish between *inductive* and *deductive* reasoning as defined by Aristotle.

17. Greek Drama, Historiography, and Art

A. What were the "three unities" of Greek drama?

B. Indicate the dramatic contributions of Sophocles, Euripides, and Aristophanes.

c. Cite the principal historical works of Herodotus, Thucydides, and Xenophon.

D. Why is Hippocrates considered the father of modern medical ethics?

THE CHAPTER IN REVIEW

A. The Greek city-state of Athens is considered one of the birthplaces of democracy. Cite some examples of Athenian "government by the people" which illustrate this fact.

B. Although Aristotle was the pupil of Plato, their respective philosophies were not completely in agreement. Discuss briefly their differing views on the possibility of acquiring knowledge through the senses.

c. Mention an achievement in each of the following fields which would demonstrate that Greek culture was not only pre-eminent in its time but also the originator of modern practice: science, medicine, historical writing, politics.

D. Despite their highly developed culture and civilization, the Greek states fell easily to the Macedonian conquerors. Can an explanation for this fact be found in the very nature of the Greek city-state system? Explain.

FOR YOUR NOTEBOOK

In this chapter we enter into the first period of history that still has direct and distinct influence on our own world, for the plays of Sophocles and Euripides are still presented in our theatres, and Plato and Aristotle are still studied in our universities. The Greeks asked the great questions in philosophy and they formulated the various possible answers. It is therefore important for the student to have a more detailed knowledge of Greek history and civilization than that of preceding periods. To help you obtain this, you should make the following entries in your notebook:

1. What is the significance for later history of:
   a) The battle of Marathon
   b) The battle of Salamis

2. Make a list of and evaluate the factors contributing to Athenian greatness in the age of Pericles.

3. What contribution was made to Greek and to our own civilization by:
   a) Pericles   b) Themistocles
   c) Socrates   d) Plato
                 e) Aristotle

In your answer be careful to explain why an educated American should understand what each of these Greeks did.

4. Look up Herodotus and Thucydides in one of the standard encyclopedias, and from your understanding of history as described in Chapter 1 explain why these two great Greek historians are frequently contrasted.

5. Summarize the Greek contribution to the civilization of which we are heirs.

SELECTED READINGS

Everyday Things in Ancient Greece, by Marjorie and Charles H. Quennell, follows the authors' pattern of showing you how people lived in this age (New York: G. P. Putnam's Sons, 1954).

The story of Greek history is told in simple fashion by Eva M. Tappan, *The Story of the Greek People* (Boston: Houghton Mifflin Co., 1947). A more complete picture of Greek history in its critical years is to be found in William Stearns Davis, *A Victor of Salamis* (New York: The Macmillan Co., 1953). The former work is strictly historical; the latter is a fictionalized account in which the author respects the facts of history but tries to write a more interesting account by imagining what men thought and what individuals did in the excitement of the conflict.

Alexander the Great

ΣΤΟΙΧΕ

Euclid

Chapter 6. Alexander the Great and Hellenistic Civilization

18. ALEXANDER'S CONQUESTS AND EMPIRE 336 to 323 B.C.

Shortly after King Philip of Macedon united the Greeks in a military alliance under his command he was assassinated by a fellow Macedonian. His successor was his twenty-year-old son, Alexander. Alexander was fully the equal of his father in military genius and ambition. From his childhood he had dreamed of doing great things. His heroes were the valiant warriors of the *Iliad* and *Odyssey,* especially Achilles, whose mighty deeds he hoped to equal. Like his father, Alexander planned a war of revenge against the Persians, to punish them for their expeditions against the Greeks a hundred and fifty years earlier. Considering

his genius and the superb army he inherited from his father, Alexander was well equipped to make his dreams come true.

Destruction of Thebes. By sternly suppressing any signs of rebellion among his subjects, Alexander quickly showed the Macedonians that he would rule just as firmly as his father. When Thebes attempted to shake off his rule, he swooped down from the north and utterly destroyed the city. Out of reverence for Greek culture, he allowed only the house of the poet Pindar to be saved. The destruction of Thebes taught the Greeks to be submissive for the remainder of Alexander's reign.

Persian empire attacked. In 334 B.C. he was ready at last to begin his war against Persia and led an army of

Macedonians and Greeks across the Hellespont into Asia. His total army consisted of probably no more than forty thousand men. Potentially, the Persian emperor could throw hundreds of thousands of men in his path. But mere numbers were not the decisive factor in this contest between Europe and Asia. Alexander's army was far superior to the Persian armies in organization, enthusiasm, and brilliant leadership. Though the Persian empire contained millions of men subject to military service, these men belonged to many different nationalities and had little or no love for their Persian masters. The Great King, Darius III, was dependent on his loyal native Persians and on his army of mercenaries. His mercenaries were far more reliable than conscripted men and fought very well so long as they were well paid. But their enthusiasm was not equal to that of Alexander's men, who had a devotion to their king which only a few generals in history have been able to arouse.

Alexander conquers "the world." After crossing the Hellespont, Alexander met the Persians at the Granicus River in northwestern Asia Minor. He won a resounding victory and began a triumphant march across Asia Minor. Meanwhile the Persians assembled another army, led in person by Darius III. Alexander smashed this army at the River Issus in southeastern Cilicia, on the border of Syria. Darius fled from the battlefield, leaving his family and treasure to be captured by the victor. Alexander proceeded down the coast of Syria, captured the great port city of Tyre after an eight-month siege, and marched on to Egypt. To the Egyptians a change of masters was a welcome relief, and they enthusiastically con-

In this detail of a mosaic, now displayed in the Naples Museum, Alexander the Great is shown in the battle of Issus. What has been preserved of the art is enough to show us its delicate craftsmanship. (Alinari)

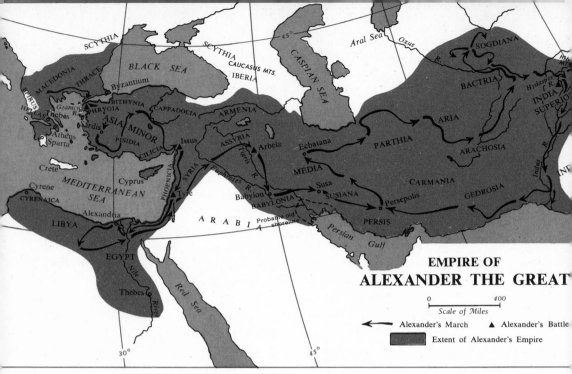

**EMPIRE OF
ALEXANDER THE GREAT**

0   400
Scale of Miles

←———— Alexander's March   ▲ Alexander's Battle

Extent of Alexander's Empire

ferred on Alexander the titles of Pharaoh and god. After founding the city of Alexandria at the mouth of the Nile River, Alexander struck across Syria and into the Tigris-Euphrates Valley. At Arbela he met and defeated the Persians for the last time. Darius fled and was pursued through Media, where he was assassinated by his own men. Alexander then proclaimed himself King of Persia. Babylon and other Persian cities threw open their gates to receive him.

Knowing only success, Alexander would not stop. He led his army east into an unknown world until he reached the borders of India. There he crushed a great Indian prince in the battle of the Hydaspes River. He planned to conquer all of India, but his troops mutinied. They refused to enter the great sub-continent in order to satisfy Alexander's ambition. Devoted though they were to their king, they complained of their many hard-

ships and of not having seen their homes for many years. Alexander had no choice but to return to the West. In 323 B.C. he was once again in Babylon. From the time of his departure from Greece until his return to Babylon, Alexander and his army had marched fifteen thousand miles.

Alexander's plan of empire. Unlike the Persian and Assyrian kings of old, Alexander did not intend to rule over a conglomeration of peoples who had nothing in common except that they were ruled by the same king. Alexander's aim was to rule a truly united empire in which all his peoples would be welded into one. He aimed to bring about this unity by giving his peoples a common religion and, most of all, a common culture. Alexander himself, ruling as a god-king, would be the focus of this common religion. He would make the worship of himself an act of patriotism binding on all his peoples. From the Adriatic Sea to the

Himalaya Mountains, all his subjects would join as one in paying divine honors to their mighty king. King worship was a very old institution in the East and was therefore an easy thing to accomplish among the Orientals. Among the Greeks, however, king worship was unknown. They balked at the idea of paying divine honors to a mortal man.

Alexander's best hope of uniting his peoples lay in his determination to spread among them a common culture —Greek culture. As a means of spreading this single culture he founded seventy new cities throughout his empire and settled them with Greek colonists. Though he was firmly convinced of the superiority of Greek culture and planned for the Greek colonists to spread it among the "barbarians," he did not treat the Asians as inferiors. He treated all his peoples as equals. He placed Asians in high government and military posts, enrolled great numbers of them in his army, encouraged his Greek officers and troops to marry Asian women, and himself married Roxana, the daughter of the last Persian king.

The death of Alexander. Alexander is said to have wept because "there were no more worlds to conquer." But the fact was he keenly regretted that the mutiny of his army had prevented his conquest of India. In the West, too, there were still new worlds to conquer. After his return to Babylon in 323 B.C., Alexander began to lay plans for the conquest of Arabia, Carthage, and the Greek city-states west of the Adriatic Sea. But death cut him short. Before his plan of a still larger and truly united empire could be realized, he died in Babylon at the age of thirty-three.

The breakup of the empire. Alexander had only an infant son to succeed him. At the news of Alexander's death, rebellions broke out in various parts of the empire. The regents who ruled in the name of the infant king were unable to restore order. Even Alexander's generals began fighting among themselves for the control of the empire. After a generation of civil wars the empire split up into several independent states, known as the *successor states*. The greatest of the successor states were the three kingdoms of Macedon, Syria, and Egypt. Each of these kingdoms was ruled by a Macedonian general who had served under Alexander, and they continued to be ruled by the Greek-speaking descendants of these generals until the Roman conquests of the second and first centuries B.C. Off the southwestern coast of Asia Minor, the island of Rhodes became a powerful free state. Athens and other Greek city-states regained their independence.

The Seleucid kingdom of Syria. The largest of the successor states was the kingdom of Syria, founded by Seleucus, one of Alexander's generals. At first the Seleucid kingdom stretched from western Asia Minor to the Indus River. The Seleucids proved unable, however, to hold their vast "empire" together. In the middle of the third century B.C., both Asia Minor and the eastern provinces successfully revolted. In Asia Minor were formed the kingdoms of Pergamum, Bithynia, Pontus, and Cappadocia. In the east several kingdoms were established; the most important was the Parthian kingdom, which had its center in northern Iran, east of Mesopotamia.

The Ptolemaic kingdom of Egypt. Though smaller than the Seleucid kingdom of Syria, the Ptolemaic kingdom of Egypt was undoubtedly the greatest of the successor states. Its first king was Ptolemy, a Macedonian general who had served under Alexander. Ptolemy founded a Greek-speaking dynasty which ruled Egypt for almost three hundred years. The last member of this dynasty to rule Egypt was also its most famous—Cleopatra. Like the Pharaohs of old, Ptolemy and his decendants were worshiped as gods, claimed ownership of every acre of Egyptian land, and acquired tremendous wealth from their monopolies in banking and in various Egyptian industries. Their capital, Alexandria, became the largest city in the world, with half a million inhabitants. The shops of Alexandria produced paper, perfume, leather goods, and olive oil. Ships from the port of Alexandria traded as far west as Spain; and, reaching the Red Sea through the canal built in the sixth century B.C., traded with Arabia and east to India. They returned with the luxury goods of the East: ebony, ivory, precious stones, spices, and incense. Besides being the largest city and the greatest commercial and industrial center in the world, Alexandria also became the intellectual capital of the world. At the invitation of the Greek-speaking kings of Egypt, Greeks poured into Alexandria by the thousands. They built

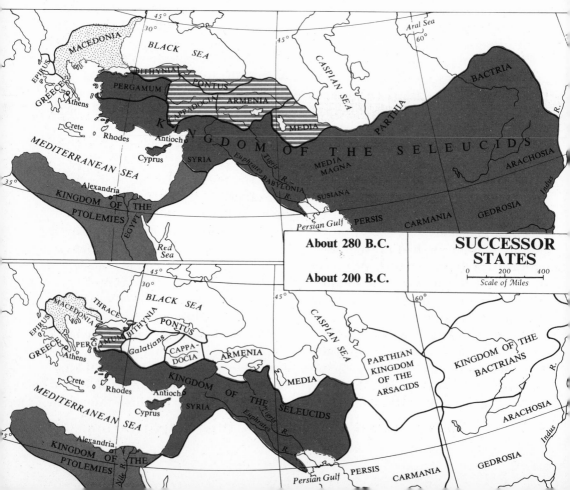

About 280 B.C.

About 200 B.C.

SUCCESSOR STATES

0   200   400
Scale of Miles

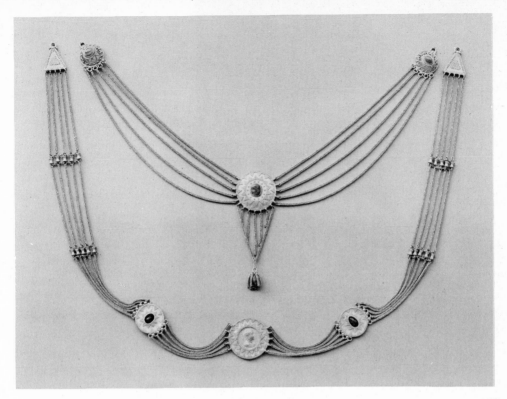

This beautifully wrought jewelry of the Ptolemaic period is of gold and precious stones. The necklace is set with amythests, and the girdle has the coin of Ptolemy III in the central medallion. (The Metropolitan Museum of Art)

schools, libraries, temples, theaters, and stadia. Alexandria became a Greek-speaking city and a home to teachers, authors, and scientists from every part of the Greek world.

The decline of Athens. Though Athens and other Greek city-states regained their freedom after Alexander's death, they never recovered their former importance. They lost many of their most talented citizens when, at the invitation of the Macedonian kings of the East, thousands of Greeks migrated to the newly founded kingdoms. Even Athenians began to look to the great cities of the East, such as Alexandria and Antioch, as places where opportunity was knocking at the door and where their talents would be properly

appreciated. So successful were the immigrant Greeks in setting up a new Greece, so to speak, in the East, that much of the cultural activity which had formerly been centered in Athens now shifted to the East. The loss of her position as the center of Greek culture was a fatal blow to Athens.

19. THE HELLENISTIC AGE 323 to 31 B.C.

The Hellenization of the East. Even before the death of Alexander the Great, Greek (or Hellenic) civilization was spreading in the Eastern lands he had conquered. In the seventy cities Alexander himself had founded he settled Greek colonists. After the breakup of

his empire, the Greek-speaking rulers of the successor kingdoms continued his policy of encouraging Greeks to migrate to the East. These kings, all of whom were Macedonians, aimed at nothing less than founding a new Greece in the East. They showed the immigrant Greeks every favor and did everything in their power to make them feel at home. They built temples where the Greek gods were worshiped, schools where the Greek language and literature were taught, theaters where Greek plays were given, libraries where Greek scholars studied, and stadia where Greek games were presented. They granted the Greeks large estates, appointed them to the highest government and army posts, and helped them get a start in business. Lastly, they made Greek the official language of the government, army, and business.

The king's native subjects—Egyptians, Syrians, Jews, Babylonians, and the various peoples of Asia Minor— were quick to see that there was little chance of getting ahead in the world unless they learned the language and customs of their rulers. It is not surprising, therefore, that many of the native inhabitants became *Hellenized;* that is, adopted the Greek language and many of the Greek customs. Hellenization was especially prominent in Asia Minor, in the coastal areas of the eastern Mediterranean, and in the great cities of the successor kingdoms. Outside the great cities, however, and especially in the countryside, the native inhabitants continued to speak their own language and practice their ancient customs. These non-Hellenized natives actually formed the majority of the population. Often they were hostile to their Greek rulers and bitterly resented the favor shown to the Greeks and their Hellenized fellow countrymen. They were waiting for the day when they could reassert themselves and drive the Greeks from their shores.

The meaning of Hellenistic civilization. Even in those places where Greek culture was transplanted with great success, the influence of the native oriental cultures remained very strong. Consequently, the meeting of the two cultures —Greek and oriental—was followed by a mixing of Greek and oriental elements. From this mixing came a culture which, though it was predominantly Greek, was rather different from the classical Greek culture of the fifth and fourth centuries B.C. This new Greek culture, therefore, is called *Hellenistic* culture, to distinguish it from classical Greek culture. Hellenistic means *Greek-like.*

The age of Hellenistic civilization is generally considered to have begun with the death of Alexander (323 B.C.) and to have ended with the conquest of the Hellenistic kingdoms by the Romans. The Roman conquest got under way in the second century B.C. and ended in 31 B.C., when Egypt was annexed to the Roman Empire. The life span of Hellenistic civilization, covers, therefore, a period of approximately three hundred years.

Culturally, the Hellenistic world was one, though politically it was divided into a number of independent states. From Sicily in the West to Babylon in the East, every government official, every military commander, every merchant, every educated man spoke Greek. Ideas spread rapidly from one country to another, even to non-Hellenistic states like Rome. This easy spread of ideas was due, of course, to a common language and also to the ease of communication and travel provided by the great merchant fleets that plied the Mediterranean. A glance at the diverse places of origin of the leading Hellenistic figures—writers, philosophers, scientists, etc.—is evidence enough that much of the Mediterranean world had become, indeed, one world.

Hellenistic science. Many of the greatest achievements of the Hellenistic world were made in the field of science. Some of the scientists were far ahead of their time, and their theories have been accepted only in recent centuries. *Aristarchus of Samos* (c. 310–230 B.C.), for instance, proposed the heliocentric ("sun-centered") theory of the universe,

The water clock was used to time speakers in Athenian courts. This clock ran for about six minutes. Antiochidos is the name of an Athenian tribe. (American School of Classified Studies, Athens)

which is that the center of the universe is the sun, around which the earth and the other planets revolve. His theory found few supporters at the time and was not accepted by scientists until recent centuries. The geographer *Eratosthenes of Cyrene* (*c.* 275–195 B.C.) computed the earth's circumference to be 24,662 miles, falling 168 miles short of its true circumference. He was the first to use latitudinal and longitudinal lines in map making. He contended that if a ship sailed due west from Europe it would eventually reach India. He added to this the possibility of there being undiscovered lands in between. He also believed that it was possible to reach India by sailing around the southern tip of Africa. The physician *Herophilus of Chalcedon* (*c.* 300 B.C.) discovered the circulation of blood through the arteries to and from the heart. Nineteen-hundred years later this fact was rediscovered by the English physician William Harvey.

In the field of mathematics, *Euclid of Alexandria* (*c.* 300 B.C.) wrote a textbook on geometry, entitled *Elements,* which is so thorough that very little has been added since. *Apollonius of Perga* (*c.* 250 B.C.) began the study of trigonometry. The physicist *Archimedes of Syracuse* (287–212 B.C.) discovered the law of specific gravity, invented the compound pulley and the water screw, and calculated the value of π. When Syracuse was besieged by the Romans in 214 B.C., Archimedes constructed a gigantic catapult which hurled giant rocks into the harbor, crushing the Roman ships. He is said to have set Roman ships on fire when he focused the sun's rays on them by means of a giant mirror he had built.

Little is known about the life of Euclid, his works having so completely overshadowed his personal history. (Library of Congress)

Other scientists of the Hellenistic age studied the principles of hydraulics and the uses to which compressed air and the expansive power of steam could be put. Among their inventions were clocks, washing machines, water mills, music organs, and such curiosities as mechanical toys and automatic door openers. Most of the great advances in science, however, were never put to any practical use. Science was valued as theory, as intellectual exercise, and not for its practical use in improving machinery. Very few people, indeed, were even interested in more efficient machinery. Labor was cheap and plentiful, and some people feared that improved methods of production would upset the economic structure of their country. Indeed, the attitude of many ancient people toward improved machinery was quite

"Give me place to stand and I will move the world," Archimedes is said to have stated when he illustrated the principle of the lever. (Library of Congress)

similar to that of many people today toward automation.

Religion in the Hellenistic age. One feature of their civilization which the Greeks failed to transplant in the East with any notable success was their religion. Since the Greek religion was primarily a religion of the free city-state, it was never really at home in the Hellenistic monarchies, where there were no free city-states. Another reason why the Greek religion failed to take root in the East was that, even in the old city-states themselves, the Greeks were losing faith in their gods. The gods had allowed the Macedonians to conquer the Greeks and had therefore failed in their primary duty of preserving the freedom of Greece. Though many Greek states regained their independence after the breakup of Alexander's empire, their faith in the gods was not revived. In the great new world of Hellenistic civilization the old city-states of Greece counted for very little.

Philosophy, too, contributed to the decline of the Greek religion. The philosophers had pointed out spiritual values and hopes for which the Greek religion, earth-centered as it was, had no room. The philosophers had stressed that man's highest goal on earth was the pursuit of truth and a virtuous life. They had made the hope of a life after death far more attractive than a dreary underworld. The impact of the philosophers' teachings made many Greeks dissatisfied with their old religion, which began to seem very hollow. In ever-increasing numbers they turned to the mystery religions for guidance. We have already seen that the mystery religions were found in Greece even at the heyday of the city-states. They were secret religions that taught a moral code and promised eternal happiness to the righteous. The original homeland of the mystery religions was in the East, where they had flourished for centuries. In the Hellenistic age the Greeks came in contact with these religions at their source and spread a firsthand knowledge of them back to Greece.

Hellenistic philosophy. Not all Greeks turned to the mystery religions for guidance. Some looked to philosophy to provide them with an aim in life and rules of right living. Philosophy itself became almost a religion, though it could not guarantee a happy afterlife. Three philosophies in particular had many followers in the Hellenistic world. These were *Cynicism, Epicureanism,* and *Stoicism.* Originally taught at

Athens in the late fourth and early third centuries B.C., they spread from Athens over the Hellenistic East, especially among the educated classes.

Cynicism. This was the least popular of the three. There was nothing new in the Cynical teaching that man's greatest good is the attainment of truth and virtuous living. What was new in the Cynics' teaching were the things they named as obstacles to truth and virtue. Among the outstanding obstacles, they taught, were religion, law, government, even the family. These were foolish things, they said, which the wise man would brush aside. He would concentrate solely on the pursuit of truth and virtue. Therefore, he could not let his mind be cluttered with the things of this world.

The Cynics carried their anti-social thinking so far that many of them withdrew altogether from the life of their times. They wandered in bands over the countryside, begging for their food, sleeping in the open, abstaining from marriage, dressing in rags, and occasionally preaching their doctrine of the good life. The Greeks called them Cynics ("dogs") because they had the reputation of snarling at everything. The Cynics, however, did not care what people thought of them. They expected no good from a world which they despised. Their indifference to the things of this world is illustrated by the well-known story of Diogenes, a Cynic philosopher. While sunning himself one day, Diogenes received a visit from none other than Alexander the Great. The mighty king asked the philosopher if there was any favor he might do him. "Yes," Diogenes replied. "There is a favor you can

For Epicurus, pleasure was not heedless indulgence but the avoidance of pain. He taught that social conduct should be governed by honesty, prudence, and justice. (The Metropolitan Museum of Art)

do me. Step a little to the other side—you're blocking out the sun."

Epicureanism. Epicurus, a native of Samos, taught in Athens around 306 B.C. He taught that if the gods existed at all (which was doubtful) they took no interest in this world or in men's affairs. He believed that the world came into being solely by chance, simply because a number of atoms happened to come together in a certain way. Man himself was no more than a bundle of atoms, which were joined together to form a body during life and fell apart again after death.

This pessimistic attitude toward religion led the Epicureans to stress happiness as man's highest goal. They recognized that virtue was one means of attaining happiness, but they did not insist that virtue was the *only* road to happiness. It was for each man to find out for himself what best led to his personal happiness. Many Epicureans thought happiness could best be achieved through study, friendship, and detachment from the world. Other Epicureans taught an "eat-drink-and-be-merry" formula for happiness.

Stoicism. The Hellenistic philosophy that made the deepest impression on the world was Stoicism. Its founder was Zeno, a Semite from Cyprus, who taught in Athens around 302 B.C. He taught that truth and virtue were the highest goals that a man could seek. Happiness came only from being virtuous; unhappiness came only from not being virtuous. Hence the virtuous man, the happy man, could not be made unhappy by any of the troubles of this world, since these troubles in no way took away his virtue. Imprisonment, torture, slavery, the loss of one's family—none of these could make the virtuous man unhappy. Indeed, by bearing patiently such misfortunes the virtuous man grew still more virtuous and his happiness increased.

The Stoics did not shy away from society but took an active part in the life of their times. They were noted for their public spirit, fortitude, and devotion to duty. They believed in a supreme god, the Artisan Fire that orders and rules the world. It was the duty of every virtuous man to try to learn what the order and nature of the world was and to bring the conduct of his life into harmony with it. Thus the Stoics recognized law higher than the laws of any individual country. They called this law *natural law*. They believed that natural law should become the law of all nations, thereby joining all the peoples of the world into one. This doctrine of the natural law found its staunchest supporters in a nation whose citizens were acting like Stoics

long before they had ever heard of Stoicism. This nation was Rome.

REVIEW

STUDY SECTIONS IN REVIEW
18. Alexander's Conquests and Empire, 336 to 323 B.C.
A. What factors led to the defeat of the Persians despite numerical superiority over Alexander's forces?

B. What was Alexander's opinion of Greek culture and civilization?

C. What was the destiny of Egypt after the dissolution of Alexander's empire?

D. Was Athens able to regain her former glory as a "successor state"?

19. The Hellenistic Age, 323 to 31 B.C.
A. Describe the content of Hellenistic culture and the reasons for its spread.

B. Mention the principal scientific contribution of Aristarchus, Euclid, and Archimedes.

C. Why did Greek religion make little impact on the Eastern world?

D. Mention the principal philosophical characteristic of the schools of Cynicism, Epicureanism, and Stoicism.

THE CHAPTER IN REVIEW
A. What areas came under the domination of Alexander of Macedon? Note the extent of Alexander's empire on your classroom or textbook map.

B. Discuss the two methods by which Alexander hoped to unite his widespread empire.

C. Why were the rulers of "successor kingdoms" eager to attract Greek emigrants to their lands? Was this an indication of the quality of the Greek culture of the period?

D. What factors in communications helped to spread Hellenistic culture throughout the Mediterranean world?

FOR YOUR NOTEBOOK

Alexander the Great, who died at the age of thirty-three, is one of the world's greatest conquerors. In outline form trace his achievements and compile a list of factors which explain how he could make such extensive conquests in so short a time.

Explain the attitude toward life and fundamental issues taken by Cynics, Stoics, and Epicureans.

Enumerate the accomplishments made by scientists in the Hellenistic period. After each listing, explain briefly why this accomplishment is important in the development of scientific knowledge.

Study the illustrations of Hellenic and Hellenistic architecture and sculpture that appear in the textbook and in standard encyclopedias. Compare the features of each period and list them in your notebook with typical examples from each period.

SELECTED READINGS

The complete story of the building and disintegration of Alexander's empire is told in the biography by Harold Lamb, *Alexander of Macedon* (Garden City, N. Y.: Doubleday & Co., 1946). Lamb is scrupulously faithful to historical truth, but he fills in the story imaginatively to give you an account of how things probably happened.

Dorothy Mills, *Book of the Ancient Greeks* (New York: G. P. Putnam's Sons, 1925), is a well-written and easy-to-read account of Greek history from its beginnings through the Hellenistic period. The student will find the later history of the Hellenistic period covered in treatments of the Roman Empire, which will be listed in readings for the next unit.

CHRONOLOGICAL REVIEW

2000 Greek-speaking barbarians enter southern Balkans
1184 End of the Trojan War
1100 *Dorian invasion of southern Greece*
800 *Homer's* ILIAD *and* ODYSSEY
735 Founding of Syracuse by Corinth
716 Spartan conquest of Messenia
683 Hereditary monarchy abolished in Athens
650 Height of Greek colonizing
621 *Draco's law code*
600 Founding of Marseilles (Massilia)
Age of the tyrants in Greece
Philosophy begins to flourish
594 Constitutional reforms of Solon
539 The Asian Greeks come under Persian domination
510 End of tyranny in Athens
508 Democratic reforms of Cleisthenes
494 Darius crushes the Ionian Revolt
490 The Persian War; battle of Marathon
482 Athenians build a strong navy
481 The Greeks unite against Persia
480 Battles of Thermopylae and Salamis
479 Battle of Plataea
478 League of Delos
468 Revolt of Naxos
461 *The Age of Pericles begins*

456 *Death of Aeschylus*
454 Defeat of the Athenians in Egypt
450 Athenian empire at its height
446 Athens loses its land empire
445 The Thirty Years' Peace
432 *Completion of the Parthenon*
431 Outbreak of the Peloponnesian War
430 *The great plague in Athens*
429 *Death of Pericles*
425 *Death of Herodotus*
413 The Sicilian expedition
404 End of Peloponnesian War
399 *Death of Socrates*
371 Theban victory over Sparta
356 King Philip of Macedon (to 336)
347 *Death of Plato*
338 Battle of Chaeronea
333 Battle of Issus
331 Founding of Alexandria
326 Battle of the Hydaspes
323 Death of Alexander
322 *Death of Demosthenes and Aristotle*
301 Battle of Ipsus
300 *Cynicism, Epicureanism, and Stoicism*
260 Height of Hellenistic civilization
250 Seleucid kingdom of Syria loses its eastern provinces
235 Founding of the Parthian kingdom

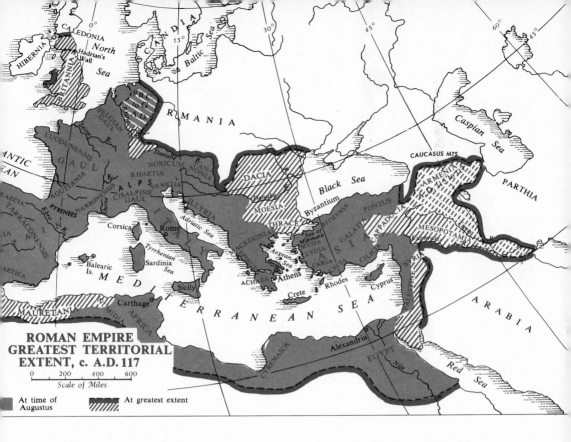

ROMAN EMPIRE
GREATEST TERRITORIAL
EXTENT, c. A.D. 117

0   200   400   600
Scale of Miles

At time of
Augustus

At greatest extent

UNIT THREE
Rome and the Rise of
the Catholic Church

The Kingdom of Rome and the Founding of the Republic · Rome Unites All Italy · Roman Imperialism and the Decline of the Farming Class · The Last Century of the Roman Republic, 133 to 27 B.C. · Roman Society and Culture during the Republic · The Pax Romana, 27 B.C. to A.D. 180 · The Advent of Christ and the Rise of the Church · Diocletian and Constantine · The Church in the Roman Empire after A.D. 313 · Barbarian Penetration into the Western Empire, 378 to A.D. 511 · East vs. West: The Age of Justinian

Chapter 7. The Roman Monarchy and the Early Republic 753 B. C. to 264 B. C.

20. THE KINGDOM OF ROME AND THE FOUNDING OF THE REPUBLIC

We have seen that when Greek colonists went to Italy in the eighth century B.C. they had very little trouble establishing footholds. The peoples of Italy were much too disunited to oppose them, for they were divided into hundreds of independent tribes. They spoke many different languages and followed different customs. They were constantly at war with one another. Culturally, they were barbarians.

The Etruscans. Among the peoples whom the Greeks found living in Italy was one group which was civilized. These were the Etruscans, who lived mostly in the northern half of the peninsula facing the Tyrrhenian Sea. No one knows where they came from

or how they developed their high civilization. Some scholars believe they lived originally in western Asia Minor; that they were driven from their homes around 1100 B.C. by the Mycenaean Greeks; that eventually the dispossessed Etruscans settled in Italy, where they transplanted their Eastern civilization with great success. Like the Greeks, they never formed a single state but lived in independent city-states ruled by nobles. They traded with the Carthaginians and the Greeks, and their cities became very wealthy. They were a pleasure-loving people and took special delight in gladiatorial games. They built fine homes and temples, produced beautiful art work in terra cotta and bronze, and buried their nobles in magnificent tombs. Unfortunately the written

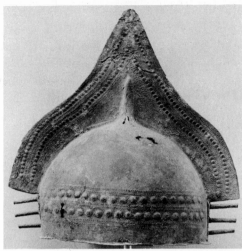

Bronze was widely used by the Etruscans. The cuirass, eighth century B.C., *provided adequate protection against sword thrusts. The helmet is from the seventh century* B.C. *(The Metropolitan Museum of Art)*

records which they left have never been deciphered.

The legendary founding of Rome. Immediately south of the Etruscans lived the Latins. In the eighth century B.C. the Latins were still a barbarous people who lived in numerous independent tribes and small towns that stretched from the Tiber River almost to the Greek city of Naples. The Latins, therefore, were wedged between the two most civilized peoples in the western Mediterranean: the Etruscans and the Greeks. The northernmost of the Latin tribes was that of the Romans, whose hill town of Rome lay on the Tiber River about ten miles from the sea.

The earliest history of Rome is very

This two-horse chariot, or biga, dates from the sixth century B.C. *It is made of bronze and is believed to be of Etruscan design. (The Metropolitan Museum of Art)*

obscure, for there are no written records from that period. Like most other ancient peoples, the Romans invented legends to account for their origin. They especially tried to link the founding of their city with Troy. They told how Aeneas, the son of King Priam of Troy, fled Troy when the Greeks destroyed the city. Eventually Aeneas settled in Italy and married the daughter of a Latin king, and his descendants became powerful kings. One of his descendants, the princess Rhea Silvia, gave birth to twins by the god Mars. She named them Romulus and Remus. The uncle of the twins, who had unlawfully seized the kingship from the twins' grandfather, feared that when the twins grew up they would deprive him of his power. Therefore, he had them put on a mountainside to die. They were nursed by a wolf, however, and were later found by a shepherd who raised them as his own sons. When they reached manhood they drove their uncle from his throne and restored their grandfather as king. Then they went off to found a new city in 753 B.C. They called this city Rome, and Romulus became its first king.

The Roman monarchy (753-509 B.C.). Though the story of the founding of Rome is legendary, it had a powerful hold on the minds of the Roman people. Perhaps it has some elements of truth in it. Whether Romulus was Rome's first king is doubtful, but there is no doubt whatsoever that early Rome was a monarchy. Some of the kings of Rome were Etruscans and introduced many features of Etruscan civilization among the Romans. The Etruscan influence on the Romans is most noteworthy in the fields of religion and architecture. From the Etruscans the Romans learned the art of divination and the worship of their three principal gods, Jupiter, Juno, and Minerva. They followed Etruscan models in building their houses, temples, city walls, sewers and arches.

Altogether, Rome had seven kings, who ruled successively for 145 years. These kings ruled in a fashion very similar to that of the early Greek kings. A council of nobles, called the Senate, advised the king; and an assembly of all the citizens elected the king, declared war, and made peace. The nobles, who were the great landowners, were called patricians. The common people, who were small farmers and shopkeepers, were called plebeians. Rome was prosperous under her kings and became the leading Latin city. But the Romans considered their last king, Tarquin the Proud, a tyrant and drove him from Rome in 509 B.C. They resolved never to let a king rule Rome again.

The Roman Republic. The Romans established a new form of government which they called a republic, *res publica,* which means "the public thing"; that is, "the people's thing." To the Romans, "republic" expressed not only the idea that the state should exist for the welfare of the people but also that it should be governed by the people. The second part of this idea—namely, that the state should be governed by the people—was to cause considerable trouble in Roman history. For the question was: What people should govern the state? Should the patricians hold the chief offices and have the leading voice in the government?

Should they share their power with the wealthy plebeians? Or should all the people of Rome have an equal voice in the government and equal opportunity to rise to the highest positions?

Republican government. In the early history of the republic, the patricians clearly held the greatest power. It was they who had taken the leading part in expelling the last king, and they considered themselves the rightful successors to his powers. Therefore, they set up a republic in which they enjoyed a privileged position.

Under the republic, the Romans annually elected two chief magistrates, called consuls, to head the state. The consuls were chief executives, chief judges, and supreme commanders of the Roman army. Each of them held exactly the same authority as the other, and each had the right to veto the actions of the other. Consequently, in order to get things done, the two consuls had to agree on the same

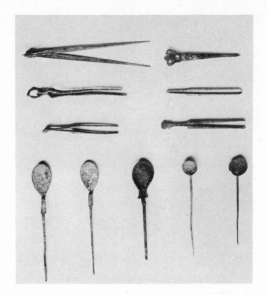

Surgical instruments from ancient Rome are an indication of the early Romans' knowledge of medicine. Some of the instruments are similar to those used in modern medicine. (The Metropolitan Museum of Art)

course of action. In times of great crisis the two consuls were authorized to appoint a dictator, to be in supreme charge of Rome and the army for a period of no more than six months.

One institution that carried over from the monarchy to the republic was the Roman Senate. In the early republic it consisted of three hundred patricians, who acted as an advisory council to the consuls. The senators were appointed by the consuls and were generally among the most intelligent men in Rome. All of them were wealthy landowners and could therefore devote a great deal of time to their duties. According to the law, the Senate had no authority other than that of an advisory council. The custom developed, however, whereby the Senate handled foreign affairs. In the early years of the republic this author-

ITALY AT TIME OF
ROMAN MONARCHY
(753-509 B.C.)

0   100
Scale of Miles

Greek Colonies
Phoenician Colonies

Rubicon R.

Illyrians

ADRIATIC SEA

CORSICA

Rome
Latins

Etruscans
Parthenope
(Naples)

Tarentum

SARDINIA

TYRRHENIAN
SEA

Thurii

MAGNA
GRAECIA

Croton

Panormus   Messina

Rhegium

SICILY   Naxos
Catana
Megara Hyblaea
Gela   Syracuse

Cicero denounces Catiline in the Roman Senate. During the monarchy the Senate was merely an advisory body. Although in theory this was true later, actually the Senate was the ruling oligarchy until the collapse of the republic. (Alinari)

ity meant very little, for Rome was still only a small city-state. But as Rome gradually expanded and foreign affairs became the primary concern of the Romans, the Senate became the most powerful body in Rome.

The other great political body in the early republic was the Centuriate Assembly. It was so called from the fact that its members voted in groups of hundreds (centuries). The Centuriate Assembly elected the consuls and other officials, passed laws, declared war, and made peace. Although all Roman citizens, including the poorest, could vote in the Assembly, it was so organized that the vote of a patrician counted much more than the vote of a plebeian.

Character of the Roman people. Despite the unusual constitution of the Roman Republic, particularly the double consulship, the republic functioned smoothly for hundreds of years. One reason for its success was that the Roman people were solidly behind it. From earliest childhood they were taught to love their city and honor the gods of Rome above all else. They were taught the virtue of *pietas,* which meant a strong sense of respect and

responsibility toward the gods, the city, one's family, friends, kinsmen, and even slaves. They were taught *sanctitas,* which meant letting actions be guided by right principles at all times. Another virtue was *constantia:* perseverance. *Constantia* was strengthened by *tenacitas:* holding on, not letting go, no matter what the consequences. Other virtues which Romans stressed were *industria,* hard work; *frugalitas,* thriftiness; *probitas,* uprightness; *fides,* keeping faith; *modestia,* moderation or temperance; *fortitudo,* courage.

The Roman family. The family was a sacred institution among the Romans. Every Roman family had a special guardian spirit all its own, called the *genius.* The earthly ruler of the family was called the *pater familias,* "father of the family." His family included his wife, his sons and their wives and children, his unmarried daughters, and the servants and slaves of the household. So great was the Romans' respect for the authority of the *pater familias* that they gave him absolute authority over his family, even allowing him to put to death any members of it who were guilty of a great wrong. Every

Roman family honored the gods in family ceremonies, and every Roman father, whether he was a *pater familias* or not, was a priest in his own home. At every meal he offered up a simple sacrifice of food to the gods. He taught his sons the correct prayers and ceremonies with which to honor the gods so that they too would worship the gods in a fitting manner when they, in turn, had their own homes.

21. ROME UNITES ALL ITALY.

When the Roman Republic was founded in 509 B.C., Rome covered no more than a few square miles, and her citizens numbered no more than a few thousand. Rome was but one of hundreds of little independent communities in Italy. Wars between the many Italian tribes and city-states were frequent, and Rome herself was in constant danger of attack. North of Rome were the Etruscans, ever seeking to ex-

The face above this painting of a patrician's home (100 B.C.) is that of the "genius." (The Metropolitan Museum of Art)

pand south of the Tiber River. East and southeast of Rome were barbarous mountaineers who periodically made raids into Roman and Latin territory. With common dangers, Rome and the Latin cities drew closer together.

The Roman Confederation. For a long time many of the Latin cities had been joined in a defensive alliance called the Latin League. In 493 B.C., Rome and the Latin League joined hands. Rome did not become a member of this League but rather created a new alliance which consisted of herself on the one hand and the Latin League on the other. Though Rome was a Latin city, the Romans considered themselves a people apart from the other Latins. They were determined not to lose one iota of their prized freedom. Therefore, instead of joining the Latin League, the Romans had the Latin League join them. This larger alliance, consisting of Rome and the Latin League, was called the Roman Confederation.

Rome begins to expand. In the fifth and fourth centuries B.C., Rome and her Latin allies fought many wars against their non-Latin neighbors. Though they occasionally suffered setbacks, the allied armies under the command of Roman consuls and dictators were always victorious in the end. Rome early developed a unique way of dealing with defeated enemies. First, whenever Rome concluded a war, she annexed large portions of the defeated enemy's territory and settled these annexed lands with Roman and Latin veterans. Second, she forced the defeated enemy to join the Roman Confederation. By adopting these policies toward defeated

Officers and men of a Roman legion. The legion was made up of 4,000 to 6,000 heavy infantry, who were citizens of Rome, in contrast to auxilia, *allies who had no political status. Crack troops, the legionaries were the most trustworthy and truly Roman. (Fototeca Unione, Roma)*

enemies, Rome increased the size of the Roman state and the size of the Roman Confederation every time she concluded a war.

By the middle of the fourth century B.C., Rome was clearly the leading power in central Italy. Since the founding of the republic one hundred and fifty years earlier, the size of the Roman state and of the Roman Confederation had grown enormously. The number of Roman citizens was growing too, for Rome frequently granted the rights of citizenship to allied cities, especially to the Latins. Though the allies in the Roman Confederation considered themselves independent, they were quite aware that in military matters and in foreign affairs they were dominated by Rome. Occasionally a discontented ally rebelled, but Rome always succeeded in bringing the rebellious ally back into the Confederation. Since there was no chance of breaking away from Rome, the allies sought to become full partners of Rome by gaining the rights of Roman citizenship.

Advance to the Rubicon. In 327 B.C., Rome received an appeal from the Greek city of Naples to drive out the Samnites, a powerful mountain tribe that had recently occupied the city. The Romans were quick to answer Naples' appeal, for they considered the Samnites as great a danger to their own security as to the Neapolitans'. The war with the Samnites was long and bitter. The Samnites were aided by armies of Etruscans and Gauls from northern Italy, who were fearful of Rome's growing power. Rome suffered several terrible defeats at the hands of her enemies, but in the end her iron determination and the loyalty of her allies won out. By 290 B.C. the Samnites were utterly defeated. The Romans then marched north and defeated the Etruscans and Gauls. As usual, Rome annexed great portions of her defeated enemies' territories, founded colonies in the annexed lands, and forced the Samnites, Etruscans, and Gauls to join the Roman Confederation. By 283 B.C., Rome's northern frontier reached to the Rubicon

River, which was then considered the boundary between Italy proper and Cisalpine Gaul (modern northern Italy). Rome controlled the entire Italian peninsula except for a few Greek cities and barbarous hill tribes in southern Italy.

Rome advances southward. Rome's last war for the control of Italy was launched in 282 B.C. Again Rome responded to the appeal of a Greek city, Thurii, for help against barbarian neighbors. Rome's appearance in southern Italy, however, alarmed another Greek city, Tarentum. The Greeks of Tarentum felt that if Rome was not stopped all of Italy would be forced into the Roman Confederation. To the Tarentines, alliance with Rome meant subjection to Rome. They invited Pyrrhus, the King of Epirus in Greece, to cross the Adriatic and crush Rome. Pyrrhus was an ambitious man and dreamed of becoming King of Italy. He crossed the Adriatic with a powerful army and defeated the Romans in two engagements. But he lost so many of his own men in these two battles that ever since his time a victory gained at too great a cost has been called a "Pyrrhic victory." Eventually the Romans defeated Pyrrhus and he returned to Epirus in 275 B.C. In 272 B.C., Tarentum and her Greek allies in southern Italy surrendered and were granted peace on the usual terms. Rome was now the mistress of the entire Italian peninsula.

The plebeians improve their status. While Roman armies were conquering Italy, great changes were taking place in the Roman constitution. These changes were brought about chiefly through the pressure of the plebeians; that is, the non-noble class of Roman citizens. The early republic, as we have seen, was dominated by the patricians. Only patricians were eligible to the magistracies, priesthoods, and the Senate; only patricians commanded the army and administered the law. The plebeians took no part in the government; they tilled the soil, worked in industry and commerce, and, above all, served in the army. They knew that their strength lay in their numbers and that the republic could not possibly function without them.

One of the earliest complaints of the plebeians was that there was no official in the government who was concerned with their welfare, since all of the magistrates were patricians. They asked the patricians to allow them to elect their own officials, but the patricians refused. When the plebeians threatened to secede from Rome and found a new city of their own, the patricians, in 494 B.C., gave in. They allowed the plebeians to elect four annual officers, called tribunes, who were henceforth recognized as the special protectors of the plebeians. The tribunes could veto any act of a magistrate, the Senate, or the Centuriate Assembly, which the tribunes considered unjust to the plebeians. The establishment of the tribuneship was a great gain for the plebeians, but the effectiveness of this office was somewhat limited by the fact that the four tribunes had to agree among themselves before they could exercise the veto. For they, like the consuls and other Roman magistrates, had the right to veto one another's actions. Another right which the plebeians gained in 494 B.C. was that of organizing themselves into an assembly of their own. This plebeian assembly, called the Tribal Assembly, could henceforth pass laws binding on the entire plebeian population.

In the following generations the patrician privileges were abolished one by one. In 451–449 B.C. the Roman laws were inscribed on twelve tablets and set up in a public place for all to see. These were the famous *Twelve Tables of the Roman Law,* the starting point for that great development of law which was to be one of Rome's chief contributions to mankind. The publication of the laws was followed by other improvements in the lot of the plebeians. Slavery for debt was outlawed, pay was introduced for soldiers, and land was distributed to the poor of Rome. But the plebeians no sooner got one right than they clamored for another. One of their chief complaints was that most of the land which Rome annexed as a result of her wars went to the patricians. This annexed land was part of the public land of Rome and belonged therefore to all the citizens. But most of it—and the best of it—was leased to patrician families, who treated it as their own property. The plebeians made such an issue over this point that in 367 B.C. the Licinian-Sextian laws were passed which strictly limited the amount of public land any citizen could lease. The patricians, however, managed to evade these laws and continued to get the lion's share and treat the public land as their own.

The plebeians are taken into the government. In the fourth century B.C. the plebeians became eligible by degrees to all the chief magistracies of Rome. In 367 B.C. they were made eligible to the highest of all the magistracies: the consulship. After that the barriers to the other magistracies were removed one by one. By 300 B.C. they were eligible to all the magistracies and priesthoods of Rome. They were eligible to the Senate, too, since the Senate was made up generally of ex-magistrates. In 287 B.C. the plebeians achieved their greatest triumph when the Hortensian Law was passed which provided that laws passed by the plebeian Tribal Assembly were binding on the entire Roman population, patricians and plebeians alike. The older Centuriate Assembly henceforth restricted its activities primarily to electing the higher magistrates.

It would not be true to say that the passage of the Hortensian Law made Rome a democracy, for the direction of affairs remained in the hands of the wealthy class. As the patricians lost their political privileges, they tended to form an alliance with the wealthier plebeians. The patricians and wealthy plebeians closed ranks and were henceforth regarded as a single class: the aristocrats. The aristocrats used their great wealth and social prestige to maintain their hold on the government. On the whole, the aristocrats served Rome well, and the plebeians were willing enough to follow them. In the years immediately ahead, the leadership of the aristocrats and the character of the Romans would be sorely tested, for Rome was about to embark on a series of wars which would end only when the entire Mediterranean world had been brought under her rule.

REVIEW

STUDY SECTIONS IN REVIEW

20. The Kingdom of Rome and the Founding of the Republic

A. What elements of Etruscan civilization influenced the early Romans?

B. How did the Senate become the most powerful governmental institution in Rome?

C. Discuss the origin and meaning of the term "republic."

D. Identify the following: patricians, plebeians, consuls, *pietas.*

E. What was the role of the *pater familias* in Roman family life?

21. Rome Unites All Italy

A. Mention three factors that led to the founding of the Roman Confederation.

B. What methods were used by Rome in dealing with a defeated enemy people?

C. What peoples or nations were defeated by Rome in her progress to control the Italian peninsula?

D. How was the office of tribune introduced into Roman government?

E. Mention at least five reforms that benefited the plebeians between 451 and 287 B.C.

THE CHAPTER IN REVIEW

A. Discuss the present meaning and the origin of the term "Pyrrhic victory."

B. What peoples lived on the Italian peninsula before the area was unified under Roman rule? Locate on your textbook or classroom map the area in which each group lived.

C. What caused Rome to turn from a monarchy to a republic? What is the difference between these two forms of government?

D. Compare the "government by the people" in Rome with that in Athens. Did one class of people come to dominate either system?

FOR YOUR NOTEBOOK

By this time you have found that certain devices help you to remember and understand history. Three of these devices are charts or diagrams, outlines, and lists or enumerations. Let us employ them in this chapter.

1. Make a chart to illustrate the organization of government in republican Rome. Be sure your chart shows where legislative, military, and other powers reside, what the relations are between various offices, and what checks there are on each office and institution.

2. Outline the principal steps taken by Rome to unite all of Italy. In a parallel column put down contemporary events in Greece, which you will find in your notes for Unit Two.

3. The authors list Roman virtues that help account for Rome's greatness. In two or three sentences for each, show the connection between the four most important of these virtues and the stability and strength of the Roman state.

4. Make a list of the ways in which the plebeians improved their lot after 500 B.C.

SELECTED READINGS

Dorothy Mills, *Book of the Ancient Romans* (New York: G. P. Putnam's Sons, 1927), is a reliable, readable account of Roman history that covers the matter of this and the next two chapters. A similar, simply told tale of Roman history from the beginning down to the Augustan age is Gordon King, *The Rise of Rome* (New York: Doubleday, Doran & Co., 1932). Less concerned with political events than with the changing life of the Roman people is Eva M. Tappan, *The Story of the Roman People* (Boston: Houghton Mifflin Co., 1938). A good description of how the average plebeian lived in the days of the republic is to be found in Frank F. Abbot, *The Common People of Ancient Rome* (New York: Charles Scribner's Sons, 1911).

Tiberius

Chapter 8. The Rise of Rome to World Domination, 264 to 27 B.C.

22. ROMAN IMPERIALISM AND THE DECLINE OF THE FARMING CLASS

Rome and Carthage. We have seen that Rome's response to the appeal of Greek cities in Italy involved her in wars that led to the Roman conquest of Italy. Now, several years after Rome's defeat of King Pyrrhus and Tarentum, Rome received an appeal from the Greek city of Messina, in Sicily. The Carthaginians, who ruled over half of Sicily, had recently occupied Messina, and in 264 B.C. Messina appealed to Rome to expel the Carthaginians from that city.

The Romans hesitated, for Carthage was a greater power than Rome had ever opposed before. Situated in North Africa (modern Tunisia), less than a hundred miles from Sicily, Carthage was the greatest land and sea power in the western Mediterranean. The Carthaginians were of Phoenician stock, descended from Phoenicians of Tyre who founded Carthage as a commercial colony in the ninth century B.C. Though the Carthaginians were few in numbers, they controlled a great commercial empire which consisted of the entire coast of North Africa west of Egypt, the southern coast of Spain, and the islands in the western Mediterranean, including half of Sicily. They ruled over a large population of native peoples who produced the raw materials and finished products which Carthage sold abroad and who served as mercenaries in the Carthaginian army and navy.

The Carthaginians were steadily expanding their empire. Messina was but the latest addition to it. The

Romans feared that if Carthage remained in possession of Messina the Carthaginians would seize the entire island of Sicily. They feared, too, that the Carthaginians would use Messina, which lay directly across from Italy, as a base from which to interfere with shipping in the waters off southern Italy. Such action would seriously inconvenience Rome's Greek allies in southern Italy who depended on sea trade for their livelihood. Rome's concern for her own safety, and Roman pride too, demanded that Messina's appeal be answered.

First Punic[1] War (264 to 241 B.C.). The Romans realized that they could not defeat Carthage without control of the sea. Therefore, for the first time in their history, they built a great fleet. Their land and sea forces were commanded by the two annually elected consuls. The Carthaginians were led by generals of great ability, the most distinguished of whom was Hamilcar Barca. For twenty-three years the war raged on land and sea. On both sides the cost in lives and money was staggering. Finally, in 241 B.C., the Romans destroyed a great Carthaginian fleet off the coast of Sicily, and Carthage sued for peace. Carthage was made to pay a large war indemnity and to surrender her possessions in Sicily to Rome. Several years later the Romans, taking advantage of Carthage's exhaustion, seized the Carthaginian islands of Sardinia and Corsica. The seizure of these islands gave Rome an overseas empire consisting of Sicily, Sardinia, and Corsica. Toward these islands Rome adopted a new policy, for she did not take them into the Roman Confederation but sent out governors to rule them as provinces. The Romans added still another province to their rapidly growing empire when in 222 B.C. they defeated the Gauls of Cisalpine Gaul (modern northern Italy) and pushed the Roman frontier to the Alps.

Second Punic War (218 to 201 B.C.). After their defeat by Rome the Carthaginians worked hard to regain their former strength. They sent Hamilcar Barca to Spain, where he labored to develop the economic resources of Spain and to rebuild the Carthaginian army. After his death his son Hannibal continued his policies. Hannibal was a most gifted leader of men and a brilliant soldier. He built up a mercenary army completely devoted to him. Thanks to the leadership of the Barcas, Carthage rapidly recovered from her defeat in the First Punic War. Rome followed Carthage's recovery closely and realized that it was only a matter of time before the two great powers would clash again. In 218 B.C., when Hannibal refused to evacuate a Spanish city which Rome claimed was her ally, Rome declared war.

The Romans expected the war to be

CARTHAGE AND ROME on Eve of Second Punic War

0   200   400
Scale of Miles

Roman Dominions and Allies
Carthaginian Dominions and Allies

---

1. From *Punicus,* the Latin word for Phoenician.

fought in Spain, but Hannibal caught them completely off guard. He quickly led his army across the Pyrenees into Gaul and then over the Alps into Italy. Hostile natives, bad weather, and disease cost him thousands of men, and he arrived in Italy with only twenty thousand infantry and six thousand cavalry. The Romans and their allies had a total reserve of nearly eight hundred thousand men, though hardly more than a hundred thousand were ever in the field at a single time. Hannibal realized that his forces were greatly outnumbered, but he hoped to attract to his side Rome's Italian allies. Here he made a serious miscalculation, for Rome's allies in the Roman Confederation were not as unhappy under Rome's domination as Hannibal thought. Most of them stood by Rome throughout the war.

Though his forces were greatly outnumbered, Hannibal was eager to engage the Romans in battle. In the first two years of the war he met the Romans in three great battles. Using brilliant strategy, he made every battlefield a trap for the Romans and annihilated every army the Romans threw against him. The worst of the Roman defeats was at Cannae, in southern Italy, in 216 B.C. In a single day Hannibal's army slaughtered seventy thousand Romans and allies. For the moment Rome had no army at all, and Hannibal marched quickly on Rome. But the great walls of the city and the determination of its people saved Rome from capture. As quickly as they could the Romans called out their reserves to form another army. But they dared not engage Hannibal in battle again. For the next thirteen years Hannibal roamed about Italy at will, burning cities, setting fire to grain fields, slaughtering sheep and cattle, and cutting down orchards. The devastation was staggering, and several of Rome's allies deserted. The Roman army, which followed Hannibal at a respectful distance, tried to keep the allies in line and harassed the Carthaginians from the rear. During all these years in Italy, Hannibal did not receive a single reinforcement from Carthage because Carthage did not control the sea. In 208 B.C. his brother Hasdrubal led a relief army from Spain to Italy, but it was destroyed by the Romans in northern Italy before Hannibal could arrive on the scene.

The proconsulship. The war with Hannibal proved to the Romans that their system of military command was outmoded. When Hannibal invaded Italy, it was still the custom for Roman armies to be commanded by the two annually elected consuls. Sometimes these consuls were men of little military experience. Often they did not agree on military policy. At the time of the disastrous battle of Cannae, for instance, both consuls were in command of the same army. Every day they took turns at commanding the army. One of the consuls decided on his day of command to fight Hannibal. The other was opposed to the idea but gave in. The result was the total annihilation of a great Roman army. After Cannae, the Romans realized that it was better for a single general of proven military ability to hold command continuously. They named a young aristocrat, Publius Cornelius Scipio, as commander of a large army and sent him to Spain to drive out the Carthaginians. Since

Hannibal (After engraving by Geo. Cooke)

command of an army was regularly entrusted to the consuls, Scipio was given the title of proconsul; that is, one who acts in the place of a consul.

Hannibal's defeat at Zama (202 B.C.). Scipio conducted a vigorous campaign against the Carthaginians in Spain and drove them over into Africa. He

Scipio Africanus (After engraving by Geo. Cooke)

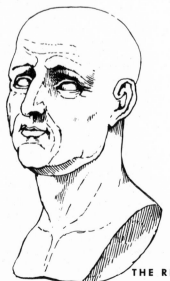

followed them with his army and prepared to attack Carthage. Hannibal, who was still in Italy at the time, then crossed over to Africa to defend his native city. In 202 B.C., Hannibal's and Scipio's armies met at Zama, a few miles from Carthage. Scipio employed tactics which he had himself learned from Hannibal and defeated him. In 201 B.C. the Carthaginians sued for peace. As the price of peace, the Romans made the Carthaginians pay a huge war indemnity, surrender Spain to Rome, reduce their army and navy to mere token size, and promise to wage no future war without Rome's consent. These terms meant the utter ruin of Carthage as a great power.

Rome's eastward expansion. Now that Rome was the dominant power in the western Mediterranean, she turned her eyes eastward. First she annexed Illyria, on the eastern coast of the Adriatic Sea. She fought several wars with Macedonia and reduced that kingdom to a province in 146 B.C. In the same year she completely destroyed Carthage and Corinth. In 133 B.C. the King of Pergamum, in western Asia Minor, died without heirs, and his will disclosed that he had left his kingdom to the Roman people. He had preferred to have the Romans take over his kingdom rather than let it become a bone of contention among the other Asian kingdoms.

The effects of empire on Rome. Rome's acquisition of an overseas empire naturally had great effects on Roman society at home. The most obvious effects were those produced by the great wealth that flowed into Rome: costly temples and homes, the growth of great estates, the construction of splendid

Drawn by Giuseppe Lugli and Itale Gismondi. (Fototeca di Architettura e Topografia Dell'Italia Antica) roads, bridges, and aqueducts—and a decay of the old Roman virtues. Most citizens profited little by Rome's wealth, however, for it was concentrated in the hands of a few, the aristocrats. Since the aristocrats held the chief offices in the government and army, they were in a position to pocket most of the wealth that came Rome's way. The office that best enabled its holder to acquire great wealth was that of proconsul, or governor, in a province. The governor headed both the civil government and the military forces in a province. When there was a war on the frontier, he and his lieutenants (always aristocrats) got the lion's share of the booty from plundered cities and the proceeds from the sale of captured prisoners of war. When there was peace, he and his lieutenants lined their pockets by overtaxing the provincials and pocketing the surplus, by accepting bribes for favors, and by extorting money for "protection." The magistrates and senators in Rome winked at these practices, since they, likely as not, had themselves profited (or hoped to profit) by the same practices.

The growth of great estates. Since the aristocrats considered it beneath their dignity to go into business, they used their great wealth to build up their estates, which were tended by great gangs of slaves. They leased from the government (which they controlled) great blocks of public land, which they treated as their own property and passed on to their heirs. In order to get still more land, they undersold the small farmer on the open market; when the small farmer went into debt as a result, they purchased his land at a cheap price. Rome's farming class suffered not only from this practice but also from Rome's constant wars and the demands of military service. When veterans returned to their farms after years in service, they often found them in a run-down condition. The expense of restoring them was so great that many veterans found it easier to sell their farms to great landowners and move to Rome to find what work, if any, they could. During the Second Punic War thousands of farms in Italy were ruined by Hannibal, and only the aristocrats could afford to build them up again.

The changing citizen body. As the empire grew, the character of Rome's citizens changed greatly, often for the worse. This change was particularly noticeable in the citizens who lived in the city of Rome itself. Citizenship was frequently granted to provincials and emancipated slaves, who cared little for Rome's history or traditions. Many citizens were constantly idle, as there was little industry or commerce in Rome to provide jobs. The poorer citizens, who were in the majority, looked to the government and to the wealthy aristocrats to provide them with food and entertainment. By the middle of the second century B.C., the citizen body in Rome was becoming a great mob.

23. THE LAST CENTURY OF THE ROMAN REPUBLIC, 133 to 27 B.C.

Tiberius Gracchus' land reform. In 133 B.C. a young Roman aristocrat, Tiberius Gracchus, was elected tribune. Gracchus was disturbed by the fact that Italy was becoming a land of great estates cultivated by slaves and that more and more landless citizens were crowding into Rome. He was convinced that these conditions were undermining the moral and military qualities of the Roman people. The only way to restore the old Roman character, he believed, was to take the landless citizens out of the city and resettle them on the land. To achieve this, he introduced a bill in the Tribal Assembly which provided for the distribution of the public lands of Rome among the citizens. The Senate, most of whose members were land-owning aristocrats, strongly opposed this bill. The aristocrats had been in possession of the public land for many years, sometimes for centuries; they had built splendid homes and made many improvements upon it and had come to regard it as their private property.

When one of the tribunes obliged the Senate by vetoing Gracchus' land bill, Gracchus persuaded the Assembly to depose him. While the senate protested that the deposing of a tribune was unconstitutional, the Assembly proceeded to pass the land bill. The Senate then sought to prevent the land law from going into effect by refusing to grant the funds necessary for its operation. Gracchus, however, quickly came up with a solution. He persuaded the Assembly to take the funds from the revenues of the kingdom of Pergamum, which, as we have seen, had recently been willed to the Roman people. Since the Senate had heretofore handled the revenues of Rome's foreign possessions, the Senate again objected that Gracchus and the Assembly were acting unconstitutionally. When Gracchus broke with ancient custom a third

time by running for re-election to the tribuneship, a number of senators slew him and three hundred of his followers in the streets of Rome. A few years later Gracchus' younger brother, Gaius, attempted to introduce reforms even bolder than his brother's. In so doing he antagonized the Roman aristocracy, and in 121 B.C. he and three thousand of his followers were attacked by a veritable army of senators and senatorial sympathizers and were slain.

The schism in Roman society. The attempted reforms of the Gracchus brothers accomplished little. Though the land bill went into effect and thousands of landless citizens were settled on the land, the transplanted citizens had little enthusiasm for country life. As soon as they could, they sold their land to the aristocrats and returned to the city. The real significance of the Gracchi is that they showed that a deep schism, or division, existed in Roman society. The two chief organs of government, the Senate and the Tribal As-

Marius (After engraving by Geo. Cooke)

sembly, were at deadly odds. The one was made up of wealthy aristocrats, the other of the Roman mob. On one side were the "haves," on the other side the "have-nots." The Senate was determined to keep the Roman constitution as it was and insisted that time-honored customs could not be lightly brushed aside. The Tribal Assembly, on the other hand, insisted that it *was* the Roman people, that the will of the people was supreme, and that the will of the people, as expressed in the acts of the Tribal Assembly, overrode every other consideration. There seemed to be no way out of the deadlock. The issue was aristocracy against democracy.

Marius and the volunteer army. The inability of the Senate and the Tribal Assembly to work together was a certain sign that Rome's republican form of government was decaying. In 107 B.C. still another force was organized that helped to bring about the ruin of the republic. This was the volunteer army, founded by Marius, consul for the year 107 B.C. Marius was dissatisfied with Rome's old custom of allowing only property-owning citizens to serve in the army. He saw in Italy thousands of landless men who could be molded into good soldiers. He decided, therefore, to enlist these men as volunteers for a period of sixteen years, promised them booty while in service, and pensions and land upon discharge. Volunteers by the thousands answered his call. With this new army Marius waged a successful war in Africa and completely destroyed two great armies of Germanic barbarians seeking to invade Italy from the north. The new volunteer army was a stunning success, but

Marius had forged a dangerous weapon. Hereafter the soldiers looked to their general, not to the Roman state, to provide for their welfare. They expected their general to reward their loyalty with plunder and pensions and lands. The general, in turn, expected his army of devoted followers to help him advance his career in the state.

Violence in Rome (88 to 82 B.C.). The rift between the Senate and the Assembly, and the threat of the volunteer army, combined to form an explosion in 88 B.C. In that year the Senate, exercising an old prerogative, appointed the consul Sulla to command the Roman forces in a war in Asia Minor. The Tribal Assembly promptly transferred the command to Marius. Sulla, however, was not the man to be deprived of a command. He marched into Rome at the head of his own volunteer army and slaughtered all who opposed him. This action marks the first time in Roman history that a Roman general led his army into Rome. After dealing with the opposition, Sulla placed the Senate in control of Rome and left for his Eastern war. During his absence, however, Marius' supporters seized Rome and, following the example set by Sulla, butchered the opposition. Sulla, meanwhile, remained in the East, concluded the war, and returned to Italy in 84 B.C. His return to Rome two years later at the head of his victorious army marked the greatest bloodbath Rome had yet seen. Over five thousand Romans suspected of being unfavorable to the Senate and to Sulla were massacred. Sulla next drew up a new constitution which placed the government squarely in

Julius Caesar (Library of Congress)

the hands of the Senate. He then laid down his dictatorial powers and died in retirement in 78 B.C.

Pompey and Caesar. Sulla sought to strengthen Rome's government by putting supreme power in the hands of the Senate, but his work did not endure. The half century after Sulla's death was one of the greatest confusion and witnessed the final collapse of the Roman Republic. Sometimes the Senate was in control, sometimes the Assembly, and sometimes a "strong man." The strong man usually had the support of either the Senate or the Assembly, but always of an army. One of these strong men was Pompey (106–48 B.C.), whose power, like that of most of the great Romans of the first century B.C., rested on his military victories. From 78 B.C. to 63 B.C. he put down a serious revolt in the province of Spain, ended a slave rebellion in Italy, cleared the Mediterranean Sea

of pirates, and fought several victorious wars in the East. He brought to an end the Hellenistic kingdom of Syria and added several new provinces, including Syria, to Rome's empire. Pompey, however, never became the outright ruler of the Roman state, for he had several powerful rivals. Among these were Crassus, an enormously wealthy businessman who had achieved some distinction in politics and war, and Julius Caesar (100–44 B.C.), who had achieved little distinction in either politics or war but who was extremely popular with the Roman masses. In 60 B.C., Pompey, Caesar, and Crassus formed a political alliance called the First Triumvirate and distributed the chief offices in the Roman state among themselves and their supporters. It has been said that Caesar supplied the brains, Pompey the military prestige, and Crassus the money to make this alliance effective.

Julius Caesar and the conquest of Gaul. When Caesar joined the First Triumvirate he was already a man well into middle life. His career up to that point had been relatively undistinguished. He had had a few military successes as governor of Spain and had made himself popular with the Roman masses by providing them with free entertainment. Caesar was determined, however, to use his alliance with Pompey and Crassus to advance his career both militarily and politically. In 59 B.C. Caesar was consul, and from 58 to 49 B.C. he was proconsul, or governor, in the Roman provinces of Cisalpine and Transalpine Gaul (northern Italy and southern France). North of his provinces lay barbarian Gaul, a vast area inhabited by numerous tribes of Gauls who spoke a common language but had no political unity. Caesar knew that he could win the favor of the Roman masses and the support of a loyal army only by waging victorious war and adding new provinces to Rome's empire. To achieve this end, he deliberately provoked war with the barbarian Gauls. The struggle with the Gauls was long and bitter, but by 51 B.C. Caesar's conquest of Gaul was complete. He had even crossed the English Channel and invaded Britain in 54 B.C., although he did not establish a Roman province there. Rome's northern frontiers now reached to the English Channel and the North·Sea and east to the Rhine River. Whatever were Caesar's motives in conquering Gaul, the results of that conquest were momentous in the history of civilization. For the first time in their history the Romans had pushed into northern Europe. Caesar's conquest not only brought Gaul within the pale of Roman civilization but paved the way for future conquests in Britain and Germany.

Caesar becomes the ruler of the Roman world. Caesar's success in Gaul made him the man of the hour. The Roman masses hailed him as a great con-

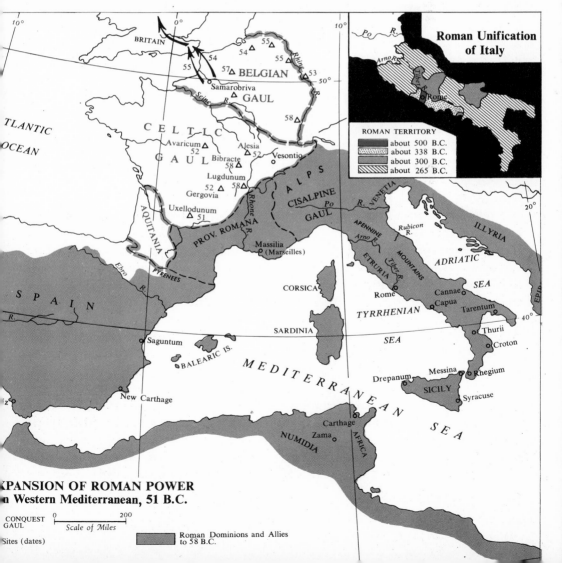

Roman Unification of Italy

ROMAN TERRITORY
- about 500 B.C.
- about 338 B.C.
- about 300 B.C.
- about 265 B.C.

XPANSION OF ROMAN POWER
n Western Mediterranean, 51 B.C.

CONQUEST
GAUL

0   200
Scale of Miles

Sites (dates)

Roman Dominions and Allies
to 58 B.C.

queror, and his troops were willing to follow him to the ends of the earth. In Rome, Pompey and the Senate feared that Caesar's aim was to make himself ruler of Rome; and in January, 49 B.C., the Senate declared Caesar a public enemy and authorized Pompey to take whatever steps were necessary to protect the republic. When Caesar heard the news he crossed the Rubicon River (which divided his province of Cisalpine Gaul from Italy proper) and marched on Rome. Pompey fled to Greece, where he gathered together a great army. After defeating Pompey's commanders in Spain, Caesar crossed over into Greece and hurled his army against Pompey's at Pharsalus in 48 B.C. Pompey was defeated and fled to Egypt. There he was murdered by agents of the Egyptian king, who mistakenly thought that in murdering Pompey he would win favor with Caesar. After his victory over Pompey, Caesar spent the next three years waging brilliant campaigns against all who challenged his power —in Asia, in Africa, and in Spain. After defeating one of his enemies with comparative ease, Caesar made his famous pronouncement: *"Veni, vidi, vici* [I came, I saw, I conquered]." In 45 B.C. he returned to Rome and received from the Senate and the Assembly every important office in the Roman Republic. He was dictator, consul, tribune, commander-in-chief of the Roman armies, head of the Roman religion, and was empowered to appoint all provincial governors, military officers, and senators. He was king in everything but name.

In 45 and 44 B.C., Caesar started many reforms which he hoped would cure the ills of the Roman state. He settled landless Romans throughout the empire. He provided employment by compelling landowners to employ free laborers on their great estates. He appointed governors who would rule the provinces justly. He granted citizenship to many provincials and even named provincials to the Senate. He reformed the 365-day calendar of the Romans by adding a day every fourth year to keep the calendar in line with the solar year.

Death of Caesar, 44 B.C. Though Caesar was popular with the Roman masses, he was hated by many aristocrats. They wanted to restore fully Rome's old republican government, in which the Senate had the leading voice. In their eyes Caesar was destroying the republic; the only way to restore it was to destroy Caesar. Sixty senators formed a conspiracy to assassinate Caesar, and on March 15, 44 B.C., he was stabbed to death in the Senate building at Rome. The leader of this aristocratic effort to save the republic was Brutus.

The end of the Roman Republic. The slayers of Caesar were sadly mistaken in thinking that his death would enable the Senate to regain power. Caesar had been enormously popular, and the mass of the Roman people rallied to those leaders who claimed to be Caesar's successors. Caesar's popularity was inherited by two men. One was Mark Antony, a Roman politician who had been a close friend of Caesar and his comrade-in-arms. The other was Octavian, Caesar's eighteen-year-old great-nephew, adopted son, and heir to his wealth. Antony and Octavian regarded one another with sus-

Jupiter, the chief Roman god, is etymologically identified with the chief Greek god, Zeus, through the root-word diu, *"bright." (Fototeca Unione, Roma)*

picion but for the moment joined forces and destroyed a senatorial army led by Brutus (42 B.C.). For the next ten years they divided the rule of the Roman world between them. Antony was supreme in the East, while Octavian ruled the West. In 36 B.C. Antony married Cleopatra, the Queen of Egypt, a beautiful woman who had once briefly captivated Caesar. When Antony and Cleopatra began carving up Rome's Eastern provinces into kingdoms for their children, Octavian declared war. The struggle for the control of the Roman world was concluded at Actium, in northwestern Greece, in 31 B.C. In a great naval battle Octavian's fleet overwhelmed the naval forces of Antony and Cleopatra. Octavian's victory at sea was followed by the surrender of Antony's land forces, and both Antony and Cleopatra committed suicide. Octavian was now the sole ruler of the

Roman world. After establishing peace throughout the empire, he announced in 27 B.C. that he was restoring the Roman Republic. Ironically, at the very moment that Octavian announced the "restoration of the republic," the Senate and the Assembly granted him so much authority that he became, in effect, the Emperor of Rome. Rome's ancient republican government, under which she had risen from an obscure city-state to become the ruler of the Mediterranean world, had vanished forever, although the outward forms of it were preserved in what was now the Roman Empire.

24. ROMAN SOCIETY AND CULTURE DURING THE REPUBLIC

Roman religion. In their very early history the Romans practiced a rather simple religion. They did not have the widespread notion that the gods were immortal supermen, but conceived of them rather as spiritual forces that had no shape whatsoever. But as early as the days of the monarchy (753–509 B.C.) Roman religion began to be affected by foreign influences. From the Etruscans the Romans borrowed the notion of anthropomorphism; that is, the belief that the gods had human forms. They also borrowed the three Etruscan gods, Jupiter, Juno, and Minerva. Later, when the Romans came in contact with the Greeks of southern Italy and Sicily, they identified Jupiter, Juno, and Minerva with the Greek gods Zeus, Hera, and Athena. In the second century B.C., when the Romans expanded into Greece and Asia, they borrowed wholesale from the Greek religion and mythology. They also introduced the Asiatic mystery religions into Rome.

Despite foreign influences on their religion, the Romans kept many of their ancient religious customs and beliefs virtually unchanged throughout the entire period of the republic. They honored many hundreds of gods, each of whom, like the Greek gods, had a sphere of activity. The *lares,* for example, watched over the grain fields, the *penates* protectd the family's storeroom, the *genius* was the family's guardian spirit. While every Roman father was a priest in his own home, the religious festivals and ceremonies of the city as a whole were entrusted to associations of priests. Three of these associations, or "colleges" as they were called, were especially prominent. The college of pontiffs was in charge of the city's religious festivals and ceremonies. The college of augurs learned the will of the gods by looking for omens in the flight of birds and in the entrails of animals. The college of the Vestal Virgins served Vesta, the goddess of fire, and kept the sacred fire of Rome burning at all times in her temple.

The impact of the Hellenistic East. In the third and second centuries B.C., Hellenistic civilization began to exert a strong influence on the Romans. Old-time Romans deplored this influence, for they feared that it would undermine Rome's ancient way of life. This viewpoint, however, was never more than a minority opinion, and the floodgates of Hellenistic civilization were opened toward Rome. The tide was irresistible. Soldiers and travelers returned to Rome from the East with unbounded enthusiasm for what they

had seen and learned. Rome became filled with thousands of Eastern slaves, physicians, teachers, and merchants. The basis of Hellenistic civilization was that of classical Greece, and it can be said that the Greeks captured Rome with their culture just as they had earlier captured the East. Greek-speaking Easterners set up schools in Rome, and after a while the ability to read, write, and speak Greek became the sign of an educated Roman. Everywhere the Greek influence could be seen. The great literary works of Greece were translated into Latin and were used as models in the composition of Latin poetry, drama, and histories. Roman architecture, sculpture, and painting were little more than copies of Greek models. Greek philosophy made a deep impression on the Roman mind, especially Stoicism, which had so much in common with the ancient Roman concept of virtue.

Decline of Roman morals. If some Romans strengthened their character through a study of Stoicism, other Romans used another Greek philosophy, Epicureanism, to justify immoral conduct. Indeed, the old-time Romans blamed the influence of Greece and the East for a general lowering of moral conduct in Rome. "Easy living" became the fashion. More and more marriages were arranged solely for financial or political reasons. Divorce, which was almost unheard of in the early republic, became common. The practice of birth prevention became widespread. Women became "emancipated" and mingled loosely in the society of men. Rich and poor alike craved entertainment and flocked to the circuses, where they wildly applauded the great chariot races, animal hunts, and gladiatorial games.

Roman literature. The influence of Greece on Rome is seen most clearly in the field of literature. As early as the third century B.C. the Romans, under Greek influence, began to produce a notable literature of their own, most of which has been lost. The best of this early literature survives in the plays of Plautus (*c.* 254–184 B.C.) and Terence (*c.* 195–159 B.C.). It was not until the first century B.C.—a century filled with violence—that Roman literature reached its peak. Catullus (*c.* 84–54 B.C.) wrote love poems in the Greek lyric style. Lucretius (*c.* 99–55 B.C.) wrote poetry in which he expounded the philosophy of the Epicureans. In his long poem, *On the Nature of Things*, he expresses the belief that the world is just one great mechanism made up of innumerable atoms which join together, only to fall apart again. He scorned the mystery religions which were sweeping Rome at this time, and held out no hope for the immortality of the soul. The historian Sallust (86–34 B.C.) wrote of Roman wars in Africa and of a conspiracy led by a corrupt aristocrat Catiline in 64–63 B.C., to overthrow the republic. Caesar himself found time in the midst of all his activities to write a history of his wars. In his *Commentaries* he wrote of his conquest of Gaul and of the civil wars that followed after he crossed the Rubicon. He wrote in the third person and appears to have described himself in a very impartial manner. Yet he emerges from his pages as a man of great judgment, generosity, and military genius.

Terence, Roman comic poet and playwright, was born in Carthage and came to Rome as a slave. He took the name of his master, who freed him. (After engraving by Geo. Cooke)

Cicero (106 to 43 B.C.). Caesar's contemporary, Cicero, is generally considered the greatest of Roman authors. His orations, letters, legal and philosophical writings are important not only as literary works but also for the wealth of information they contain of the history of the late republic. His Latin style is of such a high order that

Bust of Cicero in the Vatican. (Fototeca Unione, Roma)

it was imitated by numerous later Roman and medieval writers. Cicero had a profound knowledge of Greek philosophy and literature, yet no Roman was ever more devoted to Rome's ancient customs and republican form of government. Cicero, indeed, was no scholar living in an ivory tower. He was a patriot of the old school and devoted the greater part of his life to government. As consul in 63 B.C., he delivered a series of famous orations in which he exposed Catiline's plot to seize the government. Cicero was gravely suspicious of Caesar and sided with Pompey and the Senate when Caesar crossed the Rubicon. Later he reconciled himself with Caesar and was not associated with the senators who brought about Caesar's death. After Caesar's death Cicero delivered a series of brilliant orations, called the *Philippics,* in which he warned the Roman people against Mark Antony's ambition to rule the Roman state. His orations recalled those of Demosthenes, who three hundred years earlier had warned the Athenian people against Philip of Macedon's ambition to rule Greece. Cicero urged the Roman people to put aside their differences and unite to save the republic. Like Demosthenes, however, Cicero was a voice crying in the wilderness; for, like Demosthenes, he was striving to preserve a way of life that had almost passed away. Cicero's reward for his efforts to save the republic was death by Antony's order in 43 B.C.

Roman law. One of the greatest achievements of the Roman Republic was in the field of law. In the early republic, the Roman concept of law

Ruins of the Temple of Saturn. First built in 498 B.C. and rebuilt in 42 B.C., the temple was dedicated to the god of the harvest. (Fototeca Unione, Roma)

was very severe and narrow. The types of cases that could be heard in the courts were very few. Death was the penalty for stealing, arson, libel, and false witness. The debtor was commonly sold into slavery or could even be put to death.

The earliest republican officers in charge of hearing cases were the consuls. In 367 B.C. the office of praetor was created to relieve the consuls of their judicial duties. With the establishment of the praetorship, Roman law began to undergo a great change. The praetors knew that Roman law, including procedure, was too strict and narrow for a state that was constantly growing and meeting new kinds of legal problems. The Romans, however, were so attached to their old law that the praetors did not dare change it outright. In order to bring about needed changes, the praetors fell back on their power to *interpret* the law. They interpreted it so broadly that, for all practical purposes, they made new law. They allowed new types of cases to be brought to court, placed greater emphasis on evidence and less on oaths, and generally improved the procedure by which cases were decided. The praetors brought about these changes so gradually that very few Romans were aware of them.

Another factor that helped to hasten the development of Roman law was Rome's contact with foreigners. Since foreigners could not claim the protection of Roman law, the Romans appointed another praetor, called the foreign praetor, to handle cases involving foreigners. The foreign praetors had great freedom in making law for foreigners, for there were very few precedents to go by. Their knowledge of law in other countries helped them to develop a law for foreigners that was often far more reasonable and just than Rome's law for citizens. After a while the law for foreigners began to be used as a guide for improving the citizen law.

Still another factor that aided the development of Roman law was the rise of the jurists. In the third century B.C. the praetors began consulting learned men for advice in legal questions. These men were called *juris prudentes;* that is, "men wise in the law." Such men today are known as jurists. The answers which the jurists gave to legal questions were called *responsa,* and many *responsa* were so admired that they took on the force of law. Many of the *responsa* touched on the principles and theory of law, and in this way the systematic study of law, called jurisprudence, was begun.

Court procedure. The method by which the Romans decided cases was essentially simple. The litigants appeared before the praetor, and each stated his case. The praetor decided exactly what the issue was, drew up a brief, and handed the case over to a judge for a verdict. The judge was not a city official but was simply a private citizen who was noted for his honesty and fair dealing. The judge considered the evidence which the litigants presented to him, and rendered a verdict accordingly. In these two distinct stages of a legal action, both the praetor and the judge often consulted jurists for advice. Jury trials were known to the Romans but were reserved chiefly for cases involving high government officials accused of misconduct in office.

REVIEW

STUDY SECTIONS IN REVIEW

22. Roman Imperialism and the Decline of the Farming Class

A. Why did the Romans launch a war against Carthage?

B. What were the results of the First Punic War?

c. Discuss the peace terms forced on Carthage after Hannibal's defeat in the Second Punic War.

D. Did the old Roman virtues still prevail among government officials as the Roman Empire grew? Explain.

E. What was the fate of the small farmer during the period of imperial expansion?

23. The Last Century of the Roman Republic, 133 to 27 B.C.

A. What defects in Roman society were revealed by the struggles over the land reforms of the Gracchi?

B. Why was the "volunteer" army of the consul Marius a possible threat to the Roman state?

c. Who composed the First Triumvirate that came to power in Rome in 60 B.C.?

D. How did Julius Caesar set about winning the favor of the Roman masses?

E. After his rise to supreme power, what reforms did Caesar introduce?

F. Why was Caesar assassinated by the Roman senators?

G. Was republican government restored after the death of Caesar and the triumphs of Octavian? Explain.

24. Roman Society and Culture during the Republic

A. Mention the principal characteristics of Roman religion during the period of the republic.

B. Cite some of the Hellenistic influences on the culture of Rome.

C. What changes were evident in Roman morals in the imperial period?

D. Discuss the contributions of Cicero to Roman culture and politics.

E. How did the praetors "make" new law in Roman legal procedure?

THE CHAPTER IN REVIEW

A. What areas had come under the domination of the Roman Empire by the end of the reign of Julius Caesar? Locate these on your textbook or classroom map.

B. What were the results of Sulla's attempts to make the Senate the most powerful institution in Roman government?

C. Discuss the rise of Caesar from the First Triumvirate to supreme power in Rome.

D. List various evidences which demonstrate that the Roman empire was being weakened from within during the period of the republic.

FOR YOUR NOTEBOOK

Most Romans and Carthaginians seemed to believe that war between their two expanding states was inevitable. Although we know that nothing is "inevitable" in history, explain why Romans and Carthaginians believed as they did. You will have to study a map of the western Mediterranean carefully and find out about the Carthaginian and Roman economies to gather material on this topic.

From biographical sketches of Hannibal in standard encyclopedias and from articles on the Punic Wars, follow Hannibal's exploits in Italy from the time he crossed the Alps until he left for Africa. Try to account for his amazing survival in Italy.

Re-read the paragraphs in the text dealing with the reforms of the Gracchus brothers. After careful thought write out a paragraph on what we can learn from these attempted reforms that might be of value to us as American citizens.

Political history in the Roman Republic from 107 B.C. to 31 B.C. is extremely confusing. On a single page in your notebook outline the events of this period by using words or phrases instead of sentences. Your object is to get the full story on a single page in outline form.

Summarize the individual contributions to history of Marius, Caesar, and Cicero. Which, in your opinion, was the most important? the longest lasting? Explain the reason for your choice.

SELECTED READINGS

The greater part of the Punic Wars is covered by Mary Dolan, *Hannibal of Carthage* (New York: The Macmillan Co., 1955). This biography is built on solid scholarship, but it is filled in to read like historical fiction. Equally interesting to the good student is one of the English translations of Livy's *Punic Wars*. A good description of Rome and of everyday things in the last days of the republic is Alfred J. Church, *Roman Life in the Days of Cicero* (New York: The Macmillan Co., 1916).

A more thorough knowledge of the important period of Roman history toward the end of the republic can be obtained from one of the following biographies: H. J. Haskell, *This Was Cicero* (New York: Alfred A. Knopf, 1949), which discusses Cicero as a politician and enters into considerable detail in studying the political maneuvers and intrigues of the time; Victor Thaddeus, *Julius Caesar and the Grandeur That Was Rome* (New York: Brentano's, 1927); F. R. Crowell, *Cicero and the Roman Republic* (Baltimore: Penguin Books, Inc., 1956).

Chapter 9. The Empire and the Church

25. THE PAX ROMANA, 27 B.C. TO A.D. 180

With the restoration of the Roman Republic by Octavian in 27 B.C., all the old republican forms of government were apparently back in operation. There was, however, a silent understanding between Octavian and the people of Rome that he would continue to watch over the safety of Rome. Therefore, no sooner had he surrendered his dictatorial powers than the Senate and the Roman Assemblies granted him such a great number of offices and titles that he became, in effect, the Emperor of Rome. He was given the authority of consul and tribune. He was authorized to name the members of the Senate, to preside over the Senate and the Assemblies, and to nominate candidates for office. He was made governor over all provinces where Roman armies were stationed; this power made him, in effect, the commander-in-chief of all the Roman armies. He was granted a private bodyguard of nine thousand men and the titles of *Imperator* ("victorious general"), a word which gradually took on the meaning of "emperor"; *Princeps* ("first citizen"), which came to mean "prince"; and *Augustus* ("the sacred one").

Octavian becomes Augustus. Octavian's favorite title was *Augustus*. After 27 B.C. this title became the equivalent of his personal name, and he has been known as Augustus ever since. Augustus' position in the Roman Empire was indeed sacred, for in the Eastern half of the empire he was worshiped as a god. Ruler worship was an ancient institution in the East, but in the West the people were not accustomed to worship living men and balked at the idea of worshiping

Augustus. A compromise was reached by having them worship the *genius,* or guardian spirit, of Augustus.

Augustus and the Senate. In view of his own great power, Augustus saw little point in retaining the Roman Assemblies and gradually deprived them of their functions. He had more faith in the Senate, however, and made the Senate his associate in ruling Rome. He allowed the Senate to pass laws, elect magistrates, act as a Supreme Court, and appoint governors to provinces where no armies were stationed. But the Senate was very much under Augustus' control, since it was he who appointed its members, prepared the measures it passed into law, and nominated the candidates it elected to office.

While keeping a firm hold on the reins of government, Augustus encouraged men of ability to enter government service. He built up an efficient civil service which any able Roman, no matter what his background, could hope to enter. Outside Rome, Augustus earned the loyalty and gratitude of millions of provincials by seeing to it that the provinces were ruled by honest governors. To protect the frontiers he kept a standing army of about three hundred thousand men, who were stationed mainly in the outlying provinces where the frontiers were least secure. He also assigned troops to provinces where there was danger of rebellion. Near Rome he kept his personal bodyguard, the Praetorian Guard, whose nine thousand members were drawn exclusively from Romans of Italian birth.

Religion and culture. Augustus was not content merely with giving Rome or-

The Augustan Age of Rome was truly named, for Augustus was a generous patron of the arts. He was the personal friend of Vergil, Ovid, Livy, and Horace, and encouraged their work during his reign.

derly government. He was disturbed by the declining morality of the Roman people and sought to revive the high moral standards and patriotism of the Romans of old. He banished immoral persons from Rome, rededicated Rome to the gods, built numerous temples, and revived many of the old religious practices of the Romans. Good government, he felt, could not survive unless it was supported by a people who were religious, moral, and patriotic. To Augustus' mind, these three ingredients of a good citizen body—religion, morality, and patriotism—went hand in hand and could not be separated. One could not be had without the others.

The poets and historians supported Augustus' attempt to revive the ancient character of the Roman people. The poet Vergil (70–19 B.C.), in his great epic poem, the *Aeneid,* retold to the Roman people the story of their ancestor, Aeneas, who went to such great labors to found the Roman people. The historian Livy (59 B.C.–A.D. 17) wrote a long history of Rome that aimed to show the Roman people how they had progressed from being an insignificant but virtuous city-state to the point where they were the rulers of the world. The poet Horace (65–8 B.C.) praised the simple life, the old Roman virtues, and the greatness of Augustus. The poet Ovid (43 B.C.–A.D. 18) wrote about Rome's ancient religious festivals and in his *Metamorphoses* retold the story of the great Greek myths.

The succession problem. In his reorganization of Roman government and society, Augustus left one problem unsolved. This was the problem of a successor to his powers. Augustus purposely had no laws passed on this matter, for the Roman people, and perhaps Augustus himself, still considered Rome a republic. Augustus was, in fact, an emperor, but the Romans would not recognize that fact. Had Augustus passed a law naming a successor, he would have destroyed the illusion that Rome was still a republic. Worse still, he would have destroyed perhaps the good will which he had so painfully built up. Before he died, however, there was a silent understanding be-

This mosaic of Vergil was unearthed in Tunisia. Vergil intended to burn his manuscript of the Aeneid, *but Augustus persuaded him to save the great epic. (Fototeca Unione, Roma)*

tween him and the Roman people that his adopted son Tiberius would succeed to his powers. During Augustus' last years, Tiberius was the emperor's right-hand man and the heir to his wealth. He distinguished himself in several military campaigns and was very popular with the army. When Augustus died in A.D. 14, the Senate, as expected, conferred on Tiberius the same authority Augustus had held.

The fact that there was no law of succession proved very inconvenient several times in the first century A.D. On one occasion the Praetorian Guard named the emperor; on another, four generals fought one another until one of them emerged victorious. In A.D. 96, the Senate seized the initiative and named one of its own members, Nerva, as emperor. Nerva (A.D. 96–98) realized that the succession problem was a

Marcus Aurelius, the last of the "Five Good Emperors." (After engraving by Geo. Cooke)

serious one and sought to solve it by starting the practice whereby the emperor adopted as his legal son and successor the man whom he considered best qualified to succeed him. This procedure was followed until A.D. 180. The five emperors who ruled during this period are known as the Five Good Emperors (A.D. 96–180), and the period of their rule is often called the Golden Age of Rome.

The Pax Romana (27 B.C. to A.D. 180). Thanks in great part to Augustus' reorganization of the Roman government, there was almost constant peace within the Roman Empire for more than two hundred years. This great era of peace is known as the *Pax Romana,* "the Roman Peace." Owing to the efficient civil service started by Augustus, the government functioned quite smoothly even when there were incompetent emperors. Rome continued to fight wars, of course, but these wars were fought on or beyond the frontiers. Within the empire there was peace.

The Roman provinces. When Augustus took over Egypt in 30 B.C., after Antony's and Cleopatra's defeat at Actium, Rome's conquest of the Mediterranean world was complete. Earlier, Caesar had pushed Rome's northern frontier to the North Sea. Augustus undertook further conquests in northern Europe and conquered Germany as far east as the Elbe River. But in A.D. 9 the Germans staged a great revolt and drove the Roman legions back to the Rhine River. The successful revolt of the Germans cost the Roman army thousands of men, and neither Augustus nor any of his successors ever attempted again to conquer Germany. In A.D. 42 the Romans invaded Britain and thereafter conquered the island as far north as present-day Scotland. The last great conquests of the Romans were made by the emperor Trajan (A.D. 98–117). In 106 he conquered Dacia (modern Rumania), north of the Danube River; and in 114–115 he conquered Armenia (east of Asia Minor), Mesopotamia, and Assyria. For a brief moment the Roman Empire included the Tigris-Euphrates Valley, the very birthplace of civilization. But Trajan's successor, Hadrian (117–138), voluntarily abandoned Armenia, Mesopotamia, and Assyria. He felt that Rome, in conquering so far to the East, was at last overreaching herself. He therefore withdrew westward to the older, more defensible boundaries provided by the mountains of Asia Minor, the Euphrates River, and the Syrian Desert. Trajan was the last Roman ever to add any considerable areas to Rome's empire. The centuries of the Roman conquest had come to an end.

Greek East and Latin West. The Roman Empire was almost evenly divided between the Greek East and the Latin West. East of Illyria (modern Yugoslavia) and southern Italy the dominant language was Greek. In the rest of the empire the dominant language was Latin. The great Hellenistic kingdoms of the East had fallen to Rome one by one: Macedonia in 168 B.C., Syria in 64 B.C., and Egypt in 31 B.C. Rome had turned the once proud kingdoms into provinces, but a change of masters meant little to the majority of the inhabitants. So long as the Easterners paid their taxes and occasionally supplied auxiliary troops for Rome's armies, they were allowed to pursue their ancient ways. The Latin language and Roman customs made no headway in the East, for the Easterners were quite convinced of the superiority of their own language and civilization (which were primarily Greek). The Romans apparently were convinced of the same thing, for, as we have seen, Hellenistic civilization made a deep impression on Roman life. One thing the Romans offered which the Easterners were eager to acquire—Roman citizenship.

In the West the picture was quite different. There the Romans had conquered barbarians. The Greeks of southern Italy and Sicily long held onto their Greek ways, but elsewhere the Latin language and culture spread north through Italy, westward to Spain, eastward to Illyria, southward to Africa, and northward to Gaul and Britain. The Romans did not force their barbarian subjects to adopt the Latin language and culture. The barbarians accepted these voluntarily,

Trajan's Column, Rome, commemorates his conquest of Dacia, now modern Rumania. Encircling the columns are sculptures that wind their way to the top, telling the story of Trajan's two vigorous campaigns. In the background is the Church of Santa Maria Loretto. (Alinari)

Hadrian's Mole, now known as Castel Sant'Angelo, was originally built by the emperor as a mausoleum for himself and his successors. Connected to the Vatican by a secret passage, it was often used as a place of refuge by the popes. (Italian State Tourist Office)

This view of the aqueduct at Segovia, Spain, shows the Romans' wide use of arches. A trough at the top carried the water many miles in an efficient system that was not excelled until the nineteenth century. (Spanish Tourist Office)

for they had little to offer in their place. The process of Romanization was hastened by the presence of thousands of Roman soldiers and colonists in the Western lands. The Romans taught the barbarians to build cities and to establish municipal governments, modeled after Rome's, for running local affairs. By the second century A.D., the Western provinces had become so Romanized, especially Gaul, Spain and Africa, that they produced many of Rome's leading writers, artists, soldiers, politicians—and even emperors.

A United Mediterranean world. Despite the cultural differences between the Eastern and Western halves of the empire, the Mediterranean world was united as never before. All men recognized one supreme ruler—Rome; and one supreme law—Rome's. These were centuries not only of peace but also of prosperity. Commerce and industry flourished in the Mediterranean as never before. Merchant ships sailed all the way from Britain to the Black Sea without fear of pirates or the expense of customs barriers. Travel and

communications by land were made easy by a great network of Roman roads. In Gaul alone, for example, there were thirteen thousand miles of excellent roads. One could travel on good roads all the way from the Atlantic Ocean to the Black Sea without having to stop at a single border or pay a single toll. Neither Europe nor Asia nor Africa had ever seen anything like it before, nor has ever seen it since.

26. THE ADVENT OF CHRIST AND THE RISE OF THE CHURCH

During the reigns of the first two Roman emperors, Augustus and Tiberius, there lived in the little Roman province of Judea a man whose influence on world history has been greater than that of any other man who ever lived. This man was Jesus Christ, Who claimed, and Whose followers fervently believed, that He was the long-awaited Messiah of the Jews, the Son of God, God incarnate, Who assumed the mortal body of man in order to save men from their sins.

Judea before the coming of Christ. The prophets of ancient Israel had foretold that a Messiah, or Saviour, would be sent by God. After the Persian king Cyrus allowed the Jews to return from Babylonia and establish the independent Jewish state of Judea, there continued a steady stream of prophecies that the Messiah's coming was growing near. Most Jews imagined that the Messiah would be a great earthly ruler who would unite Jews everywhere under his throne, conquer their enemies, and bring an everlasting reign of justice on earth. They longed for his coming.

In 332 B.C., Judea had been conquered by Alexander the Great. After Alexander's death, Judea was ruled by the Hellenistic kings of Egypt, the Ptolemies. Finally in 198 B.C. Judea was conquered by the Hellenistic kings of Syria. The Syrians were less tolerant of the Jews than had been the Persians and Egyptians, for they were determined to unite all their subject peoples by means of a common Greek culture and religion. In 168 B.C. the King of Syria placed a statue of the Greek god Zeus in the temple at Jerusalem and commanded the Jews to observe the religious rites of the Greeks. Led by the Maccabee family, the Jews revolted. After a struggle of twenty-five years they succeeded in setting up an independent kingdom of Judea. The new kingdom, however, was torn by religious differences and by civil wars among the Maccabees. Obviously the kingdom of the Maccabees was not the kingdom of the Messiah that the Jews were longing for. Many Jews began to suspect that the Messiah, when He came, would

The Appian Way, built in 312 B.C., extended 350 miles and was the principle highway to Greece and the East. Some of the cement and stone block construction has endured to this day. (Alinari)

not be a temporal ruler at all, but a spiritual ruler only.

In matters of religion, there were serious disagreements among the Jews. There were several Jewish sects, all at odds with one another. The most notable of the sects were the Pharisees and the Sadducees. Closely allied with the Pharisees were the Scribes, men who were learned in the law. The Pharisees paid great respect to tradition, believed in the resurrection of the body and the immortality of the soul, and held that the Jews should have as little dealings with Gentiles as possible. The Sadducees had no sympathy at all for these views. Pharisees and Sadducees were very much alike, however, in that both insisted that the written law must be observed to the letter. They emphasized most of all the outward forms and ceremonies of religion. To the Pharisees and Sadducees, as to the pagans, religion had little to do with the inward disposition.

The kingdom of Judea remained independent until its conquest by Roman armies under Pompey in 63 B.C. For a while the Romans created a king over the Jews, Herod, who ruled from 43 B.C to 4 B.C. After Herod's death, however, Judea became a Roman province under a Roman governor called the procurator. The Romans were tolerant and allowed the Jewish religion, law, and courts to function as before. The most that the Romans hoped for in Judea was to keep peace.

Jesus of Nazareth. Sometime between 7 B.C. and 4 B.C.[1] Jesus of Nazareth was born. Even before His birth certain prophecies began to be fulfilled that indicated that Jesus was the long-awaited Messiah of the Jews. The circumstances of His birth and events in His early life bore out still more prophecies. He had no earthly father but was born of the Virgin Mary.

At the age of thirty or so Jesus began to preach publicly and gathered about Him specially chosen followers called the Apostles. He declared Himself to be the Messiah, the son of God, Whose mission it was to show all men, Jew and Gentile alike, the way of salvation and to redeem them from their sins by His own death. As evidence of His mission and divinity, Jesus performed many miracles. To all who obeyed His commands He promised eternal life; to all who disobeyed Him, eternal damnation.

The teachings of Jesus. Many of the evils which Jesus condemned were those that good-living men in every

age had condemned: lying, cheating, pride, impurity, hypocrisy, etc. He condemned other practices that were not so obviously evil, even to good-living men: the love of material possessions, judging one's fellow men, observing the letter of the law while ignoring its spirit. The greatest—and the hardest—commandment which Jesus imposed on His followers was that they should love God and their fellow men. When one of the Pharisees asked Jesus what was the greatest commandment, Jesus replied: "Thou shalt love the Lord thy God with thy whole heart, and with thy whole soul, and with thy whole mind. This is the greatest and the first commandment. And the second is like it, Thou shalt love thy neighbor as thyself." (Matthew 22: 37–39.)

It was this element of love, directed toward God and one's fellow men rather than toward oneself, that became the distinguishing mark of Jesus' followers. This love, combined with a deep humility and renunciation of self, demanded of men a religious *heroism* quite unlike anything the world had seen till then. "I say to you, love your enemies, do good to those who hate you, and pray for those who persecute and calumniate you, so that you may be children of your Father in heaven." (Matthew 5: 44–45.) To the young man who led a good life but still felt that something was missing, Jesus said: "If thou wilt be perfect, go, sell what thou hast, and give to the poor, and thou shalt have treasure in heaven; and come, follow me." (Matthew 19: 21.)

The sacraments. Jesus recognized that it would not be easy for men to follow

---

[1] The year of Christ's birth is uncertain; confusion of calendars explains these dates.

The mystery of the Eucharist, in which the body and blood of Jesus are offered in sacrifice, was first performed by Jesus Himself at the Last Supper. By His words to His Apostles on that occasion, "Do this in remembrance of me" (Luke 22: 19), Jesus founded a priesthood to carry on His work (the essential mark of a priest being that he offers sacrifice). Jesus founded the sacrament of Penance for the forgiveness of sins when He said to His Apostles, the first priests: "Receive the Holy Spirit; whose sins you shall forgive, they are forgiven them; and whose sins you shall retain, they are retained." (John 20: 22–23.)

Jesus founds the Church. To provide an organization for carrying on His work, Jesus founded the Church. The Apostles, besides being the first priests, were also the first heads, or bishops, of this Church. Jesus summed up the essential duties of bishops and promised that He would preserve their authority and continued existence when He said to His Apostles: "Go . . . and make disciples of all nations, baptizing them in the name of the Father, and of the Son, and of the Holy Spirit, teaching them to observe all that I have commanded you; and behold, I am with you all days, even unto the consummation of the world." (Matthew 28: 19–20.)

To one of the Apostles, or first bishops, Jesus gave pre-eminent authority. This was Simon, whom Jesus renamed Peter, meaning "rock." The impact of Jesus' naming Peter the head of His Church can be appreciated only in the full gospel passage:

Now Jesus, having come into the district of Caesarea Philippi, began to ask

"The Crucifixion," by Velásquez, is in the Prado, Madrid. (Anderson, Roma)

His commands without His special assistance. Therefore, He provided special means or outward signs, called sacraments, which men would find not only helpful but *necessary* for salvation. One of these sacraments was Baptism. "Unless a man be born again of water and the Spirit, he cannot enter into the kingdom of God." (John 3: 5.) Another sacrament was the Eucharist. "Unless you eat the flesh of the Son of Man, and drink his blood, you shall not have life in you." (John 6: 54.)

his disciples, saying, "Who do men say the Son of Man is?" But they said, "Some say, John the Baptist; and others, Elias; and others, Jeremias, or one of the prophets." He said to them, "But who do *you* say that I am?" Simon Peter answered and said, "Thou art the Christ, the Son of the living God." Then Jesus answered and said, "Blessed art thou, Simon [son of] Jona, for flesh and blood has not revealed this to thee, but my Father in heaven. And I say to thee, thou art Peter, and upon this rock I will build my Church, and the gates of hell shall not prevail against it. And I will give thee the keys of the kingdom of heaven; and whatever thou shalt bind on earth shall be bound in heaven, and whatever thou shalt loose on earth shall be loosed in heaven." (Matthew 16: 13–19.)

The death, resurrection, and ascension of Jesus. The teachings of Jesus were not welcome to the religious leaders of the Jews: Pharisees, Scribes, and Sadducees. Though these men had little use for one another, they saw in Jesus a common enemy and joined forces to destroy Him. They summoned Him to the highest religious court of the Jews and judged Him guilty of blasphemy for calling Himself the Son of God. According to Jewish law, the crime of blasphemy deserved the death penalty; but only the Roman governor, Pontius Pilate, could order the execution of Jesus. This he did, not because he personally saw any wrong in Jesus, but because he feared that there would be disorders in Judea if Jesus, whom the Jewish leaders unanimously condemned, were not removed from the scene. Jesus was therefore made to undergo a most cruel passion and was publicly crucified as a common criminal. But as He had prophesied to His Apostles, He rose from the dead three

Nero started the first Roman persecution. His victims included St. Peter and St. Paul. (Library of Congress)

days after His death, thereby giving final proof that He was indeed the Son of God. Forty days after His resurrection He ascended bodily into heaven.

The spread of the infant Church. Shortly after Jesus' ascension, the founding of the Church was completed when the Holy Spirit, on the day of Pentecost, descended in the form of tongues of fire upon the Apostles. From that moment on the Apostles began to preach the gospel and organize the Catholic Church. The Jewish religious leaders in Judea persecuted the early Church, but one of them, Saul of Tarsus, had a vision of Jesus and was converted to Christianity. Renamed Paul, he went on to become a bishop and the greatest missionary the world has ever seen. Paul and the other Apostles, aided by Christ's disciples and the new converts to the Faith, preached the gospel throughout the Near East and westward to Rome. Around A.D. 44, St. Peter founded the bishopric of Rome. Other bishoprics were established in many of the key cities of the Roman Empire.

Subterranean vaults and galleries were used for both services and burial by the early Christians. The catacombs were frequently decorated with frescoes of religious motif. Pictured are those outside the city walls of Naples. (Fototeca Unione, Roma)

Nero's persecution of the Christians (65 to 67 A.D.). At first the Roman authorities outside Judea paid little attention to the Christians, for they regarded them as a Jewish sect. They soon discovered their error, however. They observed that the Christians, unlike the Jews, were busy making converts and that their numbers were growing very fast. Other customs of the Christians gave offense not only to the Roman authorities but to many simple pagans as well. The Christians, looked upon many of the customs of the Romans, such as divorce and birth prevention and gladiatorial games and indecent plays, as sinful. Consequently the pagans accused the Christians of being "anti-social." The Christians held their religious services in secret and were therefore accused of holding obscene and horrible rites which they would be ashamed for others to know about. Worst of all, the Christians refused to worship the gods of Rome or to regard the emperor as divine. Therefore, they were accused of being unpatriotic.

In A.D. 64 the city of Rome was swept by a great fire. When the emperor Nero (A.D. 54–68) was accused of having started it, he shifted the blame to the Christians. In the persecution that followed, hundreds of Christians, including St. Peter and St. Paul, were put to death. Nero's persecution is described below by the Roman historian Tacitus (*c.* A.D. 55–120), whose attitude shows how even the educated Romans misunderstood the early Christians: [2]

To suppress this rumor [that he had set Rome on fire], Nero fabricated scapegoats—and punished with every refinement the notoriously depraved Christians (as they were popularly called). Their originator, Christ, had been executed in Tiberius' reign by the governor of Judea, Pontius Pilatus. But in spite of this temporary setback the deadly superstition had broken out afresh, not only in Judea (where the mischief had started) but even in Rome. All degraded and shame-

---

[2] Tacitus, *On Imperial Rome,* translated by Michael Grant (Baltimore: Penguin Classics, 1956), p. 354.

Roman coinage dates from the fourth century B.C. Pictured are a denarius (silver coin) with the head of Augustus Caesar, an aureus (gold coin) of the time of Nero, and a bronze follis from the age of Constantine. The three emperors are depicted on the coins, which are shown twice their actual size. (Chase-Manhattan Museum of Moneys of the World)

ful practices collect and flourish in the capital.

First, Nero had self-acknowledged Christians arrested. Then, on their information, large numbers of others were condemned—not so much for incendiarism as for their anti-social tendencies. Their deaths were made farcical. Dressed in wild animals' skins, they were torn to pieces by dogs, or crucified, or made into torches to be ignited after dark as substitutes for daylight. Nero provided his Gardens for the Spectacle, and exhibited displays in the Circus . . . Despite their guilt as Christians, and the ruthless punishment it deserved, the victims were pitied. For it was felt that they were being sacrificed to one man's brutality rather than to the national interest.

Nero's persecution was followed by many more in the next two hundred and fifty years. But despite persecution (or rather, aided by it), Christianity continued to spread. Soldiers, merchants, neighbors, travelers, and, above all, missionaries spread the Faith from one end of the Mediterranean to the other, southward to Abyssinia and northward to Britain. By the end of the second century A.D., the Church was entrenched in even the remotest provinces of the empire. The empire itself was about to enter a period of grave troubles that would finally end only with the empire's collapse. Ironically, only the Church, which the pagan empire sought to destroy, would in the end save Rome's achievements for future generations.

27. DIOCLETIAN AND CONSTANTINE

The Pax Romana is broken. For almost a hundred years the method of choosing an emperor, devised by the emperor Nerva, worked very well. It broke down when Marcus Aurelius (161–180) chose his own son, Commodus, rather than the man best qualified, to be his successor. Commodus was a very poor ruler and in 192 was assassinated. Peace within the empire rapidly gave way to civil war as one general after another began fighting for the imperial title. Finally the general Septimius Severus (193–211) emerged triumphant. Knowing that he owed his success solely to the support of the army, Septimius increased the pay and pensions and other benefits of the soldiers.

The all-powerful army. The army, upon which Severus heaped favors and upon which his successors would heap still more favors, was quite different from the citizen army of former times. During the long period of peace which Rome enjoyed under the early empire, the citizens developed a distaste for military life. They grew "soft" and preferred to take advantage of the *Pax Romana* by following a comfortable career in civilian life rather than the hard career of the army. The citizens were still subject to conscription, but they no longer made good soldiers. Consequently, more and more soldiers were recruited from the distant frontier provinces, where life was rough, and even from among barbarians beyond the frontiers.

The civil wars of the third century. Septimius Severus hoped to solve the succession problem by founding a dynasty. His family, the Severi, ruled Rome until 235. The most noteworthy act of this dynasty was the proclamation by Caracalla (211–217) granting citizenship to all free men in the Roman Empire. In 235 the last of the Severi to rule Rome lost favor with the army and was assassinated. Almost immediately the empire was thrown into chaos as the Roman world witnessed the maddest scramble for power it had ever seen. From 235 to 285, hundreds of generals were proclaimed emperor by their troops. Twenty-six of these gained sufficient power to be seriously considered emperor. Yet of these twenty-six, only one died a natural death: the rest were either murdered or killed in battle. The emperors of this chaotic period are known as "the barracks emperors."

The empire totters. The civil wars of the third century gave the barbarians beyond the frontiers an opportunity to invade the empire. The greatest threat in the West came from the Germanic barbarians east of the Rhine River. The Saxons spread terror along the coast of Britain; the Franks and Alemanni left a path of destruction across Gaul and even invaded Spain; the Goths occupied the province of Dacia (Rumania). East of the empire, the Persians, who were rebuilding their own empire after centuries of inactivity, began to pound at the Roman frontiers all the way from the Black Sea to Syria. On one occasion they pushed as far west as the Black Sea straits and several times occupied the great Syrian city of Antioch.

Within the empire, law and order were almost nonexistent. Civil war was being waged at every level: the greater generals fought to rule the empire, while lesser generals fought to rule provinces or cities. The highways became infested with robbers, and pirates attacked ships at sea. Commerce and industry rapidly declined, prices rose, and the cities and countryside were ravaged by rival Roman armies or by the barbarians. The great Roman Empire seemed to be on the verge of complete collapse.

Diocletian (285 to 305) reorganizes the empire. In the midst of all this confusion a general of outstanding ability gained recognition as emperor. He was Diocletian, who united the armies behind him and drove the barbarians and Persians back across the frontiers. Having restored law and order throughout the empire, Diocletian took several drastic measures which he hoped would prevent the empire from ever again falling into anarchy.

Diocletian (Library of Congress)

First he divided the empire in half and appointed the general Maximian to rule as emperor over the Western half. This division of the Roman world into an Eastern and a Western empire was prompted in great part by the threat of the barbarians and Persians on Rome's borders. Diocletian was convinced that the constant presence of an emperor on both of Rome's frontiers, East and West, would better enable Rome to keep the foreign enemy in check. Both emperors established their headquarters at cities convenient to the frontiers: Diocletian at Nicomedia, on the eastern side of the Black Sea straits; Maximian at Milan, in northern Italy. The boundary between the two halves of the empire was roughly the boundary that separated the Greek East from the Latin West. Thus the ancient cultural division of the empire now became a political division too.

Like many of his predecessors, Diocletian tried to solve the vexing problem of succession. His plan was that henceforth the two emperors should each choose an able general to assist in ruling the empire. The two emperors, after twenty years of rule, should resign and be succeeded by their two assistants, who in turn should name two new assistants. Diocletian hoped that this succession rule would be observed ever thereafter. He and Maximian faithfully observed it, but after their retirement in 305 it broke down.

In order to restore economic stability to the empire, Diocletian decreed that the price of food and other commodities, and also wages, be frozen; that every man stay on his job and not leave it for another; and that every father train his son in his own occupation. To finance the cost of the new double government, Diocletian increased taxation and rigidly enforced its collection. He decreed that the local aristocrats in every municipality should collect the taxes. If they failed to collect the taxes that were due, they had to make up the remainder out of their own pockets. This practice ruined many aristocrats, especially in the West, where the economy had been so damaged by the civil wars and barbarian invasions of the third century that many communities never recovered.

It was inevitable that such policies and measures, destructive as they were of all freedom and natural rights, should bring on the greatest persecution the Catholic Church had as yet suffered. Diocletian aimed at transforming the empire into a sacred and mysterious absolutism. He became an oriental despot, demanding divine honors from his subjects. Evidently he thought he could strengthen the empire by reviving that religious spirit of Romans in earlier times which showed in their attributing divinity to both empire and emperor. The Church was now established throughout the empire and was the strongest cohesive force within it. Diocletian saw clearly that he could not succeed in his despotic policies without destroying the Church.

Persecution of the Christians. The minimum which Diocletian demanded was that all Romans pay divine honors to the emperor. Naturally the Christians refused to comply. During the third century the Christians had been persecuted on a greater scale than ever before, for many Romans claimed that Rome's misfortunes were due to the anger of the gods over the refusal of so many Romans (namely, the Christians) to worship them. Diocletian endorsed this view. Therefore, in the name of religious unity, he launched in 303 the greatest persecution of the Christians which the Roman world had yet seen. But every means which Diocletian employed to destroy the Catholic Church failed. Neither the loss of their jobs, confiscation of their property, destruction of their churches, imprisonment, torture, nor a painful martyrdom could sway the majority of Christians from their Faith.

Two years after he got his great persecution of the Christians under way, Diocletian and his colleague Maximian resigned their imperial titles. Within the year Diocletian's elaborate plan for peaceful succession to the emperorship broke down, as Roman armies resumed their old habit of proclaiming their favorite general emperor.

The Colosseum. Built between A.D. *72 and 80, this vast amphitheater accommodated about 50,000 spectators. Here, gladitorial contests were staged and persecuted Christians were thrown to wild beasts. (Italian State Tourist Office)*

Constantine. This marble head, sculptured in the fourth century A.D., is now in the Metropolitan Museum of Art.

Constantine and the Edict of Milan. By 312 the struggle for the Western half of the empire had narrowed to two leading contenders. One of these contenders, Constantine, dreamed on the eve of a great battle with his rival that he saw a cross in the sky, under which were the words: "In this sign, conquer." He knew the cross to be the sign of the Christian God and had it inscribed on his standard. Under the sign of the cross, he defeated his rival at the Milvian Bridge outside Rome in 312 and became the ruler of the Western Empire. Convinced that the Christian God had led him to victory, Constantine put an end to the great persecution and announced his own intention of becoming a Christian. In 313 he and his co-emperor in the East, Licinius, issued the Edict of Milan, which granted freedom of conscience to all Roman citizens. They recognized Christianity as a lawful religion and restored to the Christians their rights and property.

Needless to say, the Edict of Milan was of momentous importance for the Church. For the first time since her founding, the Church could operate in complete legality, knowing that the law was henceforth her protector. The Edict of Milan was also of momentous importance for the state. In every society we have studied up to this point, the state had an official religion in which all the citizens were expected to take part. Now the state officially recognized that the religion of its citizens was purely their own private affair.

Perhaps the most momentous development of all was that the emperor soon was a Christian. This fact posed a problem which the Church had not had to face before; namely, the role that the Christian ruler should play in the Church. The emperors were long accustomed to being the absolute rulers of the Roman state; their word was law; they were the chief priests of the Roman religion and were worshiped as gods. Were the Christian emperors now to take their place among the laymen of the Church and leave the direction of Church affairs entirely to the bishops, or were they to play a more active role?

During his reign, which continued until A.D. 337, Constantine became a Christian and took deep interest in the Church. Also, he unified the empire under his sole authority and removed his seat of government from Rome to Byzantium, which was renamed Constantinople.

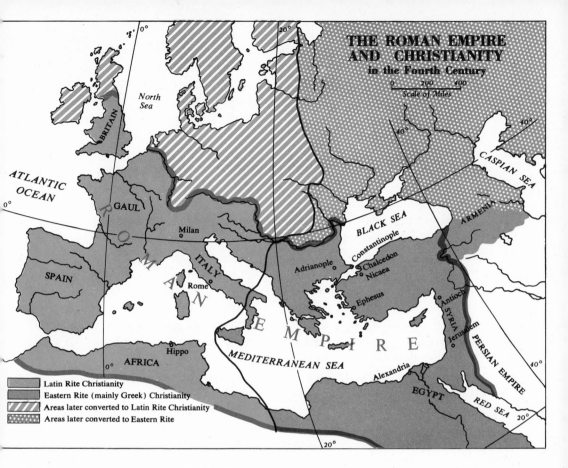

THE ROMAN EMPIRE AND CHRISTIANITY in the Fourth Century

Scale of Miles

Latin Rite Christianity

Eastern Rite (mainly Greek) Christianity

Areas later converted to Latin Rite Christianity

Areas later converted to Eastern Rite

28. THE CHURCH IN THE ROMAN EMPIRE AFTER A.D. 313

The Arian heresy. Shortly after the Edict of Milan, a controversy over Catholic teaching broke out that gravely disturbed the peace of the Church. The role played by Constantine and his successors in this controversy plainly showed that the emperors did not intend to leave the direction of Church affairs solely to the Church's lawful rulers, the bishops. The controversy was provoked by the teachings of Arius, a priest of Alexandria. Arius was an educated man, thoroughly trained in Greek philosophy. Like so many Greeks before him,

he tried to explain things in such a way that they would be understandable to human reason. After pondering for a long time on the nature of Christ, Arius concluded that Christ was not truly God. He reasoned that since Christ is the son of God the Father, He must have come into existence after the Father, just as every son comes after his father. Arius maintained, therefore, that Christ could not be truly God, since He could not have existed from all eternity. Against the doctrine of Arius, the greatest voice was that of St. Athanasius (296–373).

The Council of Nicaea. Despite its condemnation by many Catholic bishops, Arianism spread quickly through the

Greek-speaking parts of the empire. The heresy was debated so heatedly in some cities that the two opposing parties, Athanasians and Arians, came to blows. Constantine was greatly upset by these disturbances and played his first great role in Church affairs by inviting all the bishops in the world to meet in a council at Nicaea (325) and settle the Arian question once and for all.

The Council of Nicaea was attended by 318 bishops, most of whom were Greek-speaking. It is known as the first ecumenical, or general, council in the history of the Church. It is called ecumenical ("world-wide") because the participating bishops spoke for the entire Church, and their decrees, approved by the Pope, were binding on all Catholics. The Council of Nicaea overwhelmingly condemned Arianism and wrote a creed, called the Nicene Creed, which states emphatically that Christ is truly God. When the Council was over, Constantine again stepped into the picture by exiling all those who continued to hold Arian views.

Arianism spreads with the emperors' support. Arianism was not stopped by the Council of Nicaea. There were many priests and bishops who were secretly Arians, and Constantine himself came under the influence of an Arian bishop. Now the emperor entered the picture as a friend of heretics. In 335 the Arians persuaded Constantine to exile St. Athanasius, who was Archbishop of Alexandria.

Before Constantine died in 337, he divided the empire among his three sons. One of these sons, Constantius (337–361), outlived the others and became the sole ruler of the empire.

Constantius was an out-and-out Arian and used all the resources of the empire to force Arianism on the Catholic people. Catholic bishops who refused to sign Arian documents were exiled. In their place Constantius put bishops of his own choosing. Years later the great Church writer, St. Jerome, wrote concerning this period: "The whole world groaned to find itself Arian."

Council of Constantinople (381). The history of the Church after the Edict of Milan shows clearly that the Christian emperor, depending on his attitude, could just as easily do harm to the Church as good. By 380 the empire was once again in the hands of Orthodox emperors, Gratian and Theodosius, who issued a decree outlawing Arianism:[3]

We will that all the peoples who are ruled by the authority of our clemency shall hold to the religion which the Divine Apostle Peter delivered to the Romans, and which is recognized by his having preserved it there until the present day, and which it is known that the Pontiff Damasus follows, and Peter, Bishop of Alexandria, a man of apostolic holiness, that is to say, that according to the teaching of the apostles and the doctrine of the Gospel, we should believe in one Godhead of the Father, Son, and Holy Ghost, in co-equal majesty and Holy Trinity. We order those who follow this law to take the name of Catholic Christians; all others, mad and insane, we condemn to the infamy of heresy, and they will be punished in the first place by Divine vengeance, and also by our penalties, wherein we follow the will of Heaven.

---

[3] Quoted in Father John Laux, *Church History* (New York: Benziger Brothers, 1930), pp. 122–123.

The interior of St. Paul's Outside the Walls. Originally built by Constantine, St. Paul's is one of Rome's five patriarchal basilicas.

To restore complete unity in the Church, Theodosius summoned a council of bishops to meet at Constantinople in 381. The bishops at the Council of Constantinople not only condemned Arianism again and reissued the Nicene Creed (as we have it in the Mass today), but decreed that the Bishop of Constantinople should hold second place in the Church after the Pope.

The Fathers of the Church. In the fourth and early fifth centuries, when the Church was so gravely threatened by heretics and, to some extent, by the still-powerful pagans, a number of brilliant men arose who defended the Church both by their actions and by their writings. These men, who for the most part were bishops, are called the Fathers of the Church. They were well equipped to defend the Church against both pagans and heretics, for they had unswerving loyalty to the Catholic Faith, keenness of mind, and great learning. They knew the history and literature of Greece and Rome as well as any pagan, and the Bible and tradition of the Church better than any heretic. Various problems in the Church, especially the Arian danger, set the Fathers to thinking about the whole body of Catholic teaching. Consequently they wrote numerous works in which they explained with great clarity and detail the Church's doctrine. They added much to the body of Catholic theology; that is, to our knowledge of God and the Faith.

The Latin Fathers. There were great theologians in both the Eastern and the Western Church; that is, in those parts of the Church where Greek and Latin were used respectively. In the Greek

East, St. Athanasius, St. Basil, and St. John Chrysostom were among the staunchest defenders of the Faith. In the West the greatest were St. Ambrose, St. Jerome, and St. Augustine. St. Ambrose (*c.* 340–397), the Bishop of Milan, is noted not only for his theological writings but also for his clear vision of the Church's authority. On one occasion Ambrose forbade the emperor Theodosius to enter the cathedral of Milan and receive Communion until he had done public penance for putting to death a number of innocent people. For weeks Theodosius resisted Ambrose's order. When Ambrose stood his ground, Theodosius repented, put on the rags of a penitent, and publicly confessed his sin. Many of Ambrose's fellow bishops thought that Ambrose went too far in demanding that the emperor publicly confess his sin. But Ambrose, and Theodosius too, clearly saw that even the mightiest of men could claim no special privilege from God.

The great Church Father, St. Jerome (*c.* 340–420), is noted for many theological writings and particularly for his great translation of the Bible into Latin. This translation, known as the Vulgate, was commissioned by Pope Damasus I (366–384) and is still the official Latin text of the Bible. The greatest of the Latin Fathers was St. Augustine (354–430). Augustine was raised as a pagan in his native Africa and later went to Italy to be a teacher. In Milan he came under the influence of St. Ambrose and was converted to Christianity. Subsequently he became a priest and Bishop of Hippo, in Africa, where he spent the remainder of his life. In his autobiography, the *Confessions,* he tells of the follies of his youth and of his painful search for truth which ended in his conversion to Catholicism. He wrote numerous works against the heretics, especially the Pelagians, who maintained that men could save their souls without God's grace. Augustine, on the other

St. Athanasius　　　　　　　*St. Jerome*　　　　　　　*St. Ambrose*

St. Benedict (Library of Congress)

hand, emphasized man's utter dependence on God's grace for salvation. His most important work is *The City of God,* which he wrote to refute the pagan charge that Rome's misfortunes were due to the abandonment of the pagan religion.

Monasticism. Before the fourth century, when the Church was still outside the law, it was physically impossible for Catholics dedicated to God to form the organized community life which we know as monasticism. After the Edict of Milan such communities began to spring up. The first monasteries were founded in Egypt around 318, and from Egypt spread to all parts of the Catholic world. Eventually most of the monasteries in the East were organized under the monastic Rule of St. Basil, while those in the West followed the Rule of St. Benedict. These two great saints, Basil (c. 329–379) and Benedict (480–543), realized that monasticism, in order to be strong, must have strict discipline. They organized monasteries, therefore, where the religious (either monks or nuns) lived under a single roof,

worked together, ate together, and prayed together. St. Basil and St. Benedict wrote their Rules, of course, with the sole purpose of providing Catholics with a means of saving their souls. As we shall see, the monasticism they helped to found was the strongest missionary and civilizing force in the world for the next five hundred years.

REVIEW

STUDY SECTIONS IN REVIEW

25. The Pax Romana, 27 B.C. to A.D. 180

A. What was the significance of the title *Augustus* which was granted to Octavian?

B. List five measures by which Augustus sought to solidify the Roman state.

C. What were the contributions of Vergil, Livy, and Ovid to the reviving of the spirit of the Roman people?

D. Explain the meaning of the *Pax Romana.*

E. Did the Roman Empire expand after the reign of the emperor Trajan? Explain.

26. The Advent of Christ and the Rise of the Church

A. What was the significance of the "Messiah" in the Jewish religion?

B. Explain the place of the Pharisees and Sadducees in the religion of the Jews.

C. Why, and in what manner, did Jesus of Nazareth establish the Church?

D. What became of the followers of Jesus after his death and resurrection?

E. What was the attitude of the Roman authorities toward Christianity?

27. Diocletian and Constantine

A. What were the principal internal and external threats to the Roman Empire in the third century?

B. How did Emperor Diocletian attempt to deal with these problems?

C. What was the fate of Christianity under Emperor Diocletian?

D. Identify the emperor Constantine and the Edict of Milan.

28. The Church in the Roman Empire after A.D. 313

A. Explain the Arian heresy and its condemnation by the Council of Nicaea.

B. Was the Arian heresy stopped after the Council of Nicaea? Explain.

C. Give the significance of the following Fathers of the Church: St. Ambrose, St. Jerome, St. Augustine.

D. What were the contributions of St. Basil and St. Benedict to Christianity?

THE CHAPTER IN REVIEW

A. Why did Greek culture prevail in some parts of the Roman Empire and Roman culture in other areas? On your textbook or classroom map indicate the areas in which each was predominant.

B. What were the causes and results of the Roman civil wars of the third century?

C. What essentials of the teachings of Jesus of Nazareth distinguished His doctrines from those of previous religions?

D. How were the conversion of Constantine and the Edict of Milan significant for both the Christian Church and the Roman state.

FOR YOUR NOTEBOOK

Historians distinguish between "primary" and "secondary" sources of historical information. A primary source is the testimony of an eyewitness or at least a contemporary of the event described, whereas a secondary source is one that deals with the information *secondhand* by using another person's evidence. Secondary sources will differ according to the use the author makes of his primary sources. Thus some authors will quote the Gospels to show that Christ was merely a good man and a moral reformer, and others will use the full Gospel story to show that He claimed to be God and made good His claims.

Now look in the Acts of the Apostles and make a list of things you find in Chapter 2 about the early Church.

Tacitus and Livy are "primary sources" for Roman history. Look in one of the many translations of either Tacitus'

Germania to see what he says in *one chapter* about the Germans, or look at one chapter of Livy's *Punic Wars* to see what he says about Hannibal's march through the Alps.

Diocletian effected drastic reforms in the Roman Empire. Explain how these **reforms temporarily** halted the empire's decline but were permanently unsuccessful. Do this in no more than two paragraphs.

In the *Catholic Encyclopedia* read the biographical sketches of St. Ambrose and St. Benedict. Now state simply what St. Ambrose did about the relationship of secular and spiritual authority and what contribution St. Benedict made to monasticism.

SELECTED READINGS

This chapter deals with two entities: the Roman Empire, which has reached its peak; and the new Christian Church, which is the dynamic and even revolutionary institution within the empire.

In addition to the general readings suggested in the previous two chapters, see Genevieve Foster, *Augustus Caesar's World* (New York: Scribner's Sons, 1947), for an adequate treatment of the empire.

The four Gospels are eyewitness accounts of Christ's life, and they tell the story in simple, straightforward language. The Acts of the Apostles are the best and most immediate account of apostolic times. The Gospel story is popularly told by Fulton Oursler, *The Greatest Story Ever Told* (Garden City, N. Y.: Doubleday & Co., 1949), and the same author gives an interesting account of the Apostles in *The Greatest Faith Ever Known* (Garden City, N. Y.: Doubleday & Co., 1953).

The early years of Christianity, especially the persecutions, have been the setting of many famous stories. Four of the best known, all of which have appeared in many editions, are Henryk Sienkiewicz, *Quo Vadis;* John Henry Cardinal Newman, *Callista;* Nicholas Patrick Stephen Cardinal Wiseman, *Fabiola;* and Lew Wallace, *Ben Hur.*

Chapter 10. The Passing of the Ancient World

29. BARBARIAN PENETRATION INTO THE WESTERN EMPIRE, 378 TO A.D. 511

The Germanic barbarians. We have seen how Rome's civil wars of the third century enabled Germanic barbarians and the Persians to weaken seriously the frontiers of the empire. The emperor Diocletian (285–305) ended the civil wars, drove back the foreign enemy, and re-established strong frontiers. During most of the fourth century his Christian successors were able to keep these frontiers intact. But the situation remained a precarious one.

In northern Europe, beyond Rome's frontiers, were numerous Germanic tribes. These tribes were not necessarily regarded as enemies, for the Romans and the Germans were often in friendly contact. The Germans were great admirers of Roman civilization and were anxious to share in its benefits. To a large extent the Roman armies were made up of German recruits. Frequently, individual Germans received permission to settle in the empire in order to farm or trade. Sometimes whole tribes were allowed to settle in the empire on condition that they guard the frontiers against less friendly tribes. After the middle of the fourth century many of the Germanic tribes were Christian. Their Christianity, however, was Arian, for they were converted when Arianism was at its peak.

The Huns and the Visigoths. Around the middle of the fourth century a savage band of Mongolian warriors, called Huns, swept across the steppes of Asia into eastern Europe. They quickly conquered the Germanic tribe of the

Ostrogoths, who were living north of the Black Sea. The western neighbors of the Ostrogoths, the Visigoths, fearing that they were next in the line of Hunnish conquests, applied to the Eastern emperor for permission to settle in the empire. Since the Visigoths were already on the move and were determined to enter the empire at any cost, the Eastern emperor, Valens, considered it more prudent to admit them as allies than to try to hold them back. In 376, therefore, the Visigoths were made Roman allies and were allowed to settle south of the Danube River on condition that they protect the frontier. After crossing the Danube, however, the Visigoths complained that they were being mistreated by Roman officials. Armed violence broke out between the Visigoths and the Romans, and the emperor Valens rushed at the head of an army to suppress the Visigothic "rebellion."

At Adrianople, in eastern Thrace, the Romans and Visigoths met in battle in 378. The Romans were thoroughly defeated, and Valens was killed. The battle of Adrianople marks the beginning of the Germanic penetration into the empire that was not to end until almost the entire Western Empire was in the hands of the barbarians.

The Visigoths sack Rome (410). After the battle of Adrianople, the Visigoths, who were still officially Roman allies, roamed through Thrace and other Balkan provinces of the Eastern Empire. Sometimes they plundered cities and sometimes they settled down for a while to live peaceably. They were far too warlike and too well organized under their king for the Eastern Romans to attempt seriously to subject them or expel them from the empire. Finally, in order to clear them from the Eastern Empire, the Eastern em-

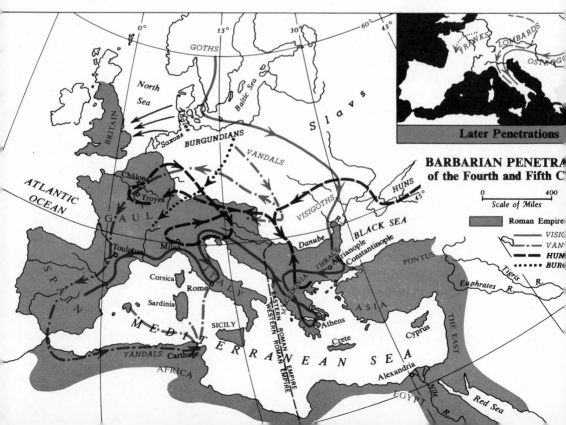

BARBARIAN PENETRA
of the Fourth and Fifth C

Later Penetrations

peror, Arcadius, encouraged them to seek their fortune in the West. Led by their king, Alaric, the Visigoths entered Italy. When the Western emperor, Honorius, refused to have anything to do with them, they marched down the Italian peninsula and sacked Rome. The capture and looting of this city by Alaric caused a sensation throughout the Roman world.

Barbarian kingdoms in the Western Empire. The Visigothic penetration into Italy was the signal for other barbarian Germans to break into the empire. One Germanic tribe, the Vandals, crossed the Rhine and swept across Gaul into Spain. Another tribe, the Burgundians, crossed the Rhine and set up a kingdom in southeastern Gaul. The Western emperor, Honorius, hoping at least to clear the Visigoths out of Italy, commissioned them to drive the Vandals from Spain. The Visigoths accepted the commission and by 429 had driven the Vandals completely from Spain. The Visigoths set up a kingdom in Spain which the Western emperor had no choice but to recognize. Technically the Visigothic king ruled Spain as a Roman ally and representative of the Western emperor. Thus Spain remained officially a part of the Roman Empire. In reality, however, Spain was firmly in the hands of the Visigoths and had passed forever from Roman rule. The Vandals, defeated by the Visigoths, crossed into Africa and carved themselves a kingdom out of the African provinces. The Western emperor shut his eyes to the fact that another huge piece of the Western Empire had been lost, and recognized the Vandal king as his ally and representative.

The Invasion of the Huns. While Rome was losing her Western provinces to Germanic barbarians, the Huns were pushing ever farther into Europe. By 450 they had conquered a vast area that stretched from the Ural Mountains to the very heart of Europe. Led by their fierce king, Attila, they crossed the Rhine River in 451 and prepared to conquer Gaul. The Huns were regarded as brutal savages bent on the destruction of civilization and posed as great a threat to the security of the Germans as to the Romans. Germans and Romans joined hands, therefore, and were molded into a great army by the Roman general, Aetius. This combined army of Germans and Romans fought the Huns at Châlons in 451 and stopped their westward advance. Attila was, for the moment, stopped but by no means conquered. Suddenly he turned south and invaded Italy. As he prepared to march on Rome, he was met by Pope Leo I (440–461), who persuaded him to spare the city. Attila withdrew his army from Italy and died shortly thereafter. The unity of his empire was broken when it was divided among his sons, none of whom was as capable as Attila. Very soon the subject peoples overthrew their Hunnish lords and the great Hunnish empire fell to pieces.

Germanic Tribes occupy Britain (449). Though the Huns were no longer a menace, the Western Empire was still in the process of disintegrating. Already the Vandals were ruling Africa, the Visigoths Spain, and the Burgundians southeastern Gaul. Meanwhile another Roman province, Britain, was being lost. After making raids on the island for many years, the Germanic

The historic event of Pope Leo I turning back Attila was painted by Raphael. The mural is in the Vatican. (Fototeca Unione, Roma)

Angles and Saxons began to settle in Britain around 449. Whereas the Vandals, Visigoths and Burgundians were Arians and had settled in the midst of the native Africans, Spaniards, and Gauls, the Angles and Saxons were pagan and drove the native Britons to the western fringes of the island. In Wales the descendants of the displaced Britons, the Welsh, still live.

The end of the Western Empire (476). During most of the fifth century the Western emperors were pitifully weak. Gradually they became little more than the puppets of various German officers in the Roman army. Though Italy was not occupied by a Germanic tribe, it was, to all intents and purposes, German-controlled. In 476 a German officer, Odoacer, decided at last to abolish the sham office of Western emperor. He deposed the puppet emperor, Romulus Augustulus, and sent the insignia of the imperial office to Zeno, the Eastern emperor. Following in the footsteps of former emperors, Zeno appointed Odoacer to rule Italy in the Eastern emperor's name. Thus ended Diocletian's system of two emperors. There was no further need of it, for the barbarians ruled practically all of the Western Empire.

The Eastern Empire escaped Germanic occupation. Its survival as an independent state was due to the competence of its emperors, to the accident of geography (for the West was more accessible to the Germans than the East), and to its greater wealth (which enabled the emperors to build up a strong professional army). After the collapse of the Hunnish empire, however, the Eastern Empire was momentarily threatened by the Germanic

Ostrogoths, who were now free to roam again. Following an established precedent, the emperor Zeno commissioned Theodoric, the king of the Ostrogoths, to remove Odoacer from authority in Italy. Theodoric led his Ostrogoths to Italy and killed Odoacer. Following another established precedent, Zeno allowed Theodoric to set up a great kingdom which included not only Italy, but Sicily and Illyria. Northward the Ostrogothic kingdom extended to the Danube River.

The reign of Theodoric (493 to 526). Theodoric was no barbarian king in the usual sense of the word, for he was a man of excellent education. He had lived for several years in Constantinople and had acquired a deep appreciation of Eastern Roman culture. His reign in Italy was a happy one for both Romans and Ostrogoths. Though Theodoric and his Ostrogothic followers were Arian Christians, he allowed his Catholic subjects to practice freely their religion. Theodoric patronized scholarship and the arts and sponsored the building of many splendid churches, several of which are still standing. Centuries later, when Italy was split up into many warring sections, the Italians would look back to Theodoric's reign as a golden age.

Clovis as the king of the Franks. One of the last Germanic tribes to set up a great kingdom in the Western Empire were the Franks. As early as the fourth century, various tribes of Franks had occupied the northeastern corner of Gaul and had acquired the status of Roman allies. Until the reign of the Frankish king Clovis (481–511), the Franks were a pagan people and were politically disunited. Clovis united all the Franks, on both sides of the Rhine River, under his rule. In 496 Clovis was converted to Catholicism, and the rest of the Franks soon followed suit. Though other Germanic tribes had earlier adopted Arian Christianity, the Franks were the first of the Germanic tribes to become Catholic.

Clovis' conquest of Gaul was very systematic. After asserting his rule over all the Frankish tribes, he attacked and defeated Syagrius, a Roman gen-

The Basilica of San Vitale in Ravenna is an excellent example of Byzantine architecture. Its interior is rich in mosaics. The tombs of Theodoric and Dante are enshrined there. (Fototeca Unione, Roma)

Engaged in battle with the Alemanni, Clovis vowed to become a Christian if he was victorious. He was baptized by St. Remi, who instructed him: "Adore what thou has burned, and burn what thou has adored." (Library of Congress)

eral who was ruling northwestern Gaul as king. In 496 he conquered the Alemanni, an Arian Germanic tribe that lived on both sides of the Rhine River in the area of modern Strasbourg. In 507 he conquered the Arian Visigoths who ruled southwestern Gaul. Last, he began the conquest of the Arian Burgundians but died before the conquest of Burgundy was complete. In his conquest of the Arian Germanic tribes, Clovis was aided by the fact that he and his followers were Catholic. Most of the native Gauls were Catholic, and they welcomed the replacement of their Arian masters by a Catholic king. When Clovis died in 511, his kingdom included practically all of Gaul and a considerable area of

German territory east of the Rhine River. The kingdom he founded was to play a remarkable role in the history of the world.

30. EAST VS. WEST: THE AGE OF JUSTINIAN

While the Western Empire was gradually being occupied by Germanic barbarians, the Eastern Empire managed generally to keep itself intact. Several factors helped to keep the Eastern Empire strong. Industry and commerce still flourished in the East, and the emperors collected great sums of money in taxes. The Eastern Empire's wealth enabled the emperors to keep well-equipped professional armies in the field—armies that could be counted on to remain loyal and fight well as long as they were well paid. When the Germanic barbarians occasionally threatened the Eastern Empire, the emperors bribed them to move westward. When the Persians threatened the eastern frontier, they too were bribed to cease their attacks.

Another source of strength to the Eastern Empire was that its capital was almost impregnable. On three sides Constantinople was bordered by water, and the Roman fleet was at all times in control of the sea. On its land side, facing Thrace, Constantinople was protected by a series of high, strong walls. (Indeed, so well situated is Constantinople, now called Istanbul, for defense, that from the time of its founding in 325 to the present day it has been taken by a foreign enemy only twice.)

Decline of the Western cities. While the Eastern economy remained strong, that of the West steadily declined. Indeed, the West had never known the type of economic prosperity so common in the East. As we have seen, the Western peoples—Italians, Gauls, Spaniards, Africans, and Britons—became civilized much later that the Easterners, and they were never able to build up industries and commerce that could compete with those in the East. As long as Rome was expanding and prosperous, however, this economic unbalance made little difference. The Western cities were assured of a certain prosperity by the presence of Rome's great military and administrative establishments, just as many cities today owe their prosperity to the presence of great government offices and nearby military camps. From the late second century onward, however, the Western cities began to decline. Rome was no longer extending her frontiers, and consquently she was deprived of the wealth that had formerly come from the booty of conquered cities and the sale of captured prisoners. The civil wars of the third century, which were fought mainly in the West, caused great damage to what little industry and commerce the Western cities possessed. Once Rome's great military and administrative structure began to crack, the Western cities rapidly declined. They owed their very existence to this structure, and when it collapsed, they collapsed. Under the Germanic barbarians, the cities practically disappeared, and the West returned to an almost purely agricultural economy.

Religious dissension between East and West. Even when the Roman Empire had been at its height, it could always be neatly divided into two halves: the Greek East and the Latin West. Dio-cletian recognized this division when he founded the double emperorship. The division became final when the barbarians occupied the Latin West. Though the barbarian occupation separated the peoples of East and West, they still had one thing in common— the Catholic Faith. Here too, however, we find the cultural division between East and West reflected in the two great liturgies of the Church, Greek and Latin. This cultural division was also reflected in what might be called the "temperament" of the two churches. Like the Romans of old, the Latin churchmen were inclined to be conservative and to preserve at all costs Christianity as it had been delivered to them. The Greek churchmen, on the other hand, were like the Greeks of old in that they endlessly searched to explain Christianity, to make it fit into the scheme of human logic, and to bring to light, if possible, more truth. In their attempts to explain Christianity, many Greek churchmen shed much light on the great mysteries of the Catholic Faith. Other Greek churchmen, however, explained Christianity in such a way that they distorted it and thus produced heresy. We have already seen how the Greek-trained Arius explained Christ's nature in such a way that he explained away Christ's divinity. After Arianism died down, other heresies arose in the Greek East and gravely disturbed the peace of the Church. These heresies were always promptly condemned by the popes and eventually by ecumenical councils. But the period from the rise of a heresy until its eventual condemnation by an ecumenical council always produced great tension between the Greek East, where the heresy flourished, and the Latin West, which was less troubled by heresy. During such periods of tension there was often a schism, or breaking off of relations, between the Western Church (which remained loyal to the Pope) and the Eastern Church (which followed the lead either of the emperor or of the Archbishop of Constantinople).

Nestorianism. In the fifth century a great heresy called Nestorianism arose in the East. Its name is derived from Nestorius, the Archbishop of Constantinople, who was its leading supporter. Nestorius taught that the Blessed Virgin Mary was not rightly called the Mother of God. She was, he said, merely the mother of Christ as man, not the mother of Christ as God. So sharp was the distinction he drew between the divinity and manhood of Christ that he taught, in effect, that there were two persons in Christ. Pope Celestine I (423–432) promptly condemned the Nestorian heresy and appointed St. Cyril, the Archbishop of Alexandria, to preside over a council where judgment should be passed on Nestorius. The council which met at Ephesus (in western Asia Minor) in 431 was the third ecumenical council of the Church. It excommunicated and deposed Nestorius and condemned his heresy, thereby upholding the Church's traditional teaching that Mary is truly the Mother of God.

Monophysitism. No Catholics were more prominent in the fight against Nestorianism than the Egyptians. The Egyptian Church had always laid great stress on the oneness of Christ and therefore could not tolerate the insinuation that there were two persons in Christ.

So much did the Egyptians insist on the oneness of Christ, however, that they too fell into heresy only a few years after the condemnation of Nestorianism. Led by Dioscurus, the Archbishop of Alexandria, the Egyptians taught that Christ had but one nature, the divine—contrary to the Church's traditional teaching that Christ has two natures, a human and a divine. The new heresy, called Monophysitism ("one nature"), found numerous supporters not only in Egypt but also in Syria. Pope Leo the Great (440–461) condemned it and urged the Eastern emperor to call a council of bishops. The council (the fourth ecumenical) met at Chalcedon, across the straits from Constantinople, in 451. It confirmed the excommunication and deposition already pronounced against Dioscurus by Pope Leo, condemned Monophysitism, and endorsed a letter written by Leo in which the Pope set out the traditional teaching of the two natures in Christ.

Egypt and Syria in Schism. Despite the condemnation of Monophysitism by the Pope and the council of Chalcedon, the Egyptians and Syrians continued to cling to it. In so doing they produced a schism (or breach) between their churches and the Catholic Church. They made an independent Monophysite Church. This action marks the first great breaking away from the Catholic Church in her history. The split in religious unity was equally serious for the stability of the Eastern Empire. The Egyptians and Syrians had long been restless under the rule of the Greek emperors at Constantinople, and now they rallied to Monophysitism as to a great national cause.

BARBARIAN KINGDOMS
ROMAN EMPIRE
A.D. 565

| 00 | 400 | | 800 |
Scale of Miles

The emperor Justinian (527 to 565). By the early sixth century the unity that had long characterized the Mediterranean world was rapidly disintegrating. Already the entire Western half of the Roman Empire had been occupied by various barbarian tribes. Religious unity had been broken by the separation of the Egyptians and Syrians from the Catholic Church. This religious separation was interwoven with a growing Egyptian and Syrian nationalism which, in turn, threatened the complete separation of Egypt and Syria from the Eastern Empire.

Attempts to halt the forces of dis-

integration were made by the emperor Justinian. He was determined not only to hold together the Eastern Empire but to conquer back the Western Empire from the barbarians as well. From 533 to 554 he staged several gigantic wars of reconquest and succeeded to the point of reconquering Africa from the Vandals, Italy from the Ostrogoths, and southeastern Spain from the Visigoths. He also turned his attention to the problem of religious unity and succeeded by various compromises in momentarily appeasing the Monophysites.

The greatest achievements of Jus-

Santa Sophia is considered the supreme masterpiece of Byzantine architecture. The massive dome is about 180 feet high and has forty arched windows that let in a flood of light to illuminate the brilliant colors of its interior columns. (Turkish Information Service)

tinian's reign were not his military conquests or appeasement of the Monophysites—for ultimately they failed—but lay rather in the field of culture and law. Justinian was a great patron of culture, especially of architecture and the decorative arts. He tried to give Constantinople all the splendor of old Rome by adorning it with beautiful churches, monasteries, government buildings, and theatres. Of the numerous churches which he built, the greatest was the cathedral of Santa Sophia in Constantinople. This great cathedral, which is still standing, has a great dome that reaches 180 feet above the floor. Mosaics and various

colored stones made its interior a riot of colors—colors that remained undimmed until many years later in 1453, the Turks captured Constantinople and whitewashed the brilliant mosaics.

The Corpus Iuris Civilis. Justinian's most lasting achievement was in the field of law. By Justinian's time Roman law filled hundreds of volumes. Much of it was outmoded and contradictory and had fallen into disuse. Justinian appointed a group of lawyers to go through all the Roman laws and legal writings and to combine in a single work whatever was still of use. The result was the *Corpus Iuris Civilis*, "the

Body of Civil Law." This great work is divided into three parts: the *Code*, which contains the laws still in force in Justinian's time; the *Digest*, which contains the legal writings of the great jurists; and the *Institutes*, a textbook of law for students. At first the *Corpus* was used only in the Eastern Empire. Many years later it was adopted in western Europe and became the foundation of much of European law. Today it forms the basis not only of the law of many Western countries, but has influenced the development of law in non-Western countries as well.

Conclusion. The projects to which Justinian gave his greatest efforts—the appeasement of the Monophysites and the reconquest of the West—ultimately were failures. After his death in 565 the split between the Monophysites and the Catholics became greater than ever, and the empire's hold on Egypt and Syria became precarious in the extreme. In the West, the Visigoths reoccupied southeastern Spain, and the Germanic tribe of the Lombards conquered much of Italy. Only Africa and certain sections of Italy remained under Justinian's immediate successors. But even there the imperial officials ruled like little kings and paid scant attention to the emperors in far-off Constantinople. Justinian's wars of reconquest, which were achieved at a tremendous cost in lives, money, and property, proved in the end but one thing: that the great Roman Empire was a thing of the past. Henceforth the West—half barbarian and half Roman but entirely Catholic—would pursue an independent course and would build on the wreckage of the ancient world a new

civilization which would spread someday to the farthest corners of the earth.

REVIEW

STUDY SECTIONS IN REVIEW

29. Barbarian Penetration into the Western Empire, 378 to A.D. 511

A. Identify the following: Huns, Ostrogoths, Visigoths, the Battle of Adrianople.

B. How did the Visigoths and the Vandals gain at the expense of the weakened Western Empire?

C. Discuss the invasion of the Italian peninsula by the Huns under Attila.

D. What events marked the end of the Western Empire?

E. Indicate the significance of Theodoric and Clovis.

30. East vs. West: The Age of Justinian

A. What factors enabled the Eastern Empire to survive despite the collapse of the West?

B. What was the fate of the Western cities after the fall of the Western Empire?

C. Define the principal teachings in the Nestorian and Monophysite heresies.

D. What attempts were made by Justinian to save the empire? Were they successful?

THE CHAPTER IN REVIEW

A. In what area did the Huns originate? Where were they finally halted? Trace the extent of their invasions on your textbook or classroom map.

B. To what extent had the Germanic peoples infiltrated the Western Empire by the mid-fourth century? How did these encroachments weaken the Western Empire?

C. Discuss the great cultural and legal contributions of Emperor Justinian.

D. Characterize the "temperaments" of the Latin and Greek divisions of Christianity.

FOR YOUR NOTEBOOK

The barbarians differed considerably from one federation of tribes to another. From material in your textbook and from encyclopedia articles, prepare a brief summary of the physical appearance, the clothing, weapons and tools, the habits and general culture of: (1) the Huns, (2) the Goths, (3) the Celts, (4) the Vandals, and (5) the Franks. How many of these are Germanic?

Use one of the standard encyclopedias to prepare a biographical sketch of Theodoric and one of Clovis. Be sure your sketches show how each built up his state. Now see if your sketches explain adequately why Clovis' state lasted permanently, whereas Theodoric's soon disintegrated.

Justinian is one of the great figures of this period. Make a list of his accomplishments, and after each one of them write "fleeting," "temporary," or "permanent," according to how long it lasted.

For a start you should use reference books in your library and add to your notes as you study later chapters in this text.

SELECTED READINGS

Interesting stories on the period of the barbarian invasions are to be found in Eva M. Tappan, *Old World Hero Stories* (Boston: Houghton Mifflin Co., 1911). Contrasting types of "barbarian invaders" can be seen in the following two biographical studies: Marcel Brion, *Attila: The Scourge of God* (New York: Robert M. McBride & Co., 1929); and Thomas Hodgkin, *Theodoric the Goth: The Barbarian Champion of Civilization* (New York: G. P. Putnam's Sons, 1894).

A very interesting and historically authentic account of the Eastern Empire under Justinian is given by Harold Lamb, *Theodora and the Emperor* (Garden City, N. Y.: Doubleday & Co., 1952).

CHRONOLOGICAL REVIEW

753 Founding of Rome
509 Founding of the Roman Republic
494 Establishment of the tribuneship
493 Rome's alliance with the Latin League
449 *Twelve Tables of the Roman Law*
390 Gauls sack Rome
300 Plebeians eligible to all offices
241 End of the First Punic War
227 First Roman provinces
146 Destruction of Carthage
133 Tribuneship of Tiberius Gracchus
 82 Sulla's dictatorship in Rome
 64 Pompey's conquests in Asia Minor
 60 The First Triumvirate
 58 Julius Caesar, proconsul in Gaul
 51 Caesar completes conquest of Gaul
 48 Battle of Pharsalus; death of Pompey
 43 The Second Triumvirate
 31 Battle of Actium
 27 Octavian receives supreme power
 19 *Death of Vergil*
  8 *Death of Horace*
  4 *Birth of Jesus Christ in Bethlehem*

A.D.
  9 Defeat of the Romans in Germany
 14 Death of Augustus
 33 Death and Ressurection of Jesus Christ and the founding of the Catholic Church
 43 Roman invasion of Britain
 64 *Great fire at Rome*
180 *End of the Pax Romana*
212 *Edict of Caracalla*
235 Anarchy in the Roman Empire
313 *Edict of Milan*
407 Romans abandon Britain
410 Sack of Rome by the Visigoths
449 Anglo-Saxons invade Britain
476 Deposition of last Western emperor
496 *Conversion of Clovis to Catholicism*
511 Division of the Frankish kingdom
533 *The* CORPUS IURIS CIVILIS
534 Vandal kingdom falls to Justinian
554 Ostrogothic kingdom falls to Justinian
568 Lombard invasion of Italy
604 *Death of Pope Gregory the Great*

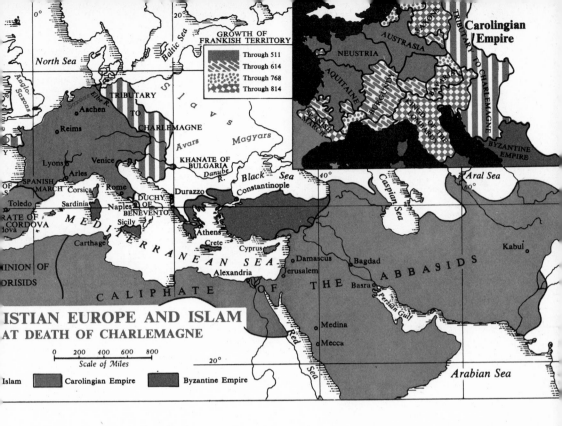

UNIT FOUR
The Early Middle Ages:
The Catholic Church and Islam

The Barbarian West and the Church · Mohammed and the Spread of Islam in the Seventh and Eighth Centuries · The Carolingian Empire · The Formation of France, Germany, and England · The Feudal Constitution of Europe · The Papacy and the Church in the Feudal Age · Byzantium · The Moslem Civilization · Gregory VII and the Reform of the Church · The Launching of the Crusades

Charlemagne

Chapter 11. The Frankish & Moslem Empires

31. THE BARBARIAN WEST AND THE CHURCH

Western Europe under the barbarians. By the end of the sixth century, most of Western Europe was in the hands of Germanic barbarian kings. Only North Africa and parts of Italy (including Rome) still acknowledged the authority of the emperor. Though he called himself Roman emperor, the emperor was henceforth always a Greek; his capital was the great Greek city of Constantinople; his empire was restricted mostly to the eastern Mediterranean; the people whom he ruled were mostly Greeks and Orientals. The so-called Roman Empire had become, in reality, a Graeco-Oriental empire. This Graeco-Oriental empire was such a different thing from the older Roman Empire that historians give it an entirely new name.

They call it Byzantium, or the Byzantine Empire (from "Byzantium," the site on which Constantinople was built).

. In the West, Gaul was ruled by Frankish kings; Spain by Visigothic kings; most of Britain by Anglo-Saxon kings; and, after 568, most of Italy by Lombard kings and dukes. The native Romans complained very little of being ruled by barbarian kings. Life went on as it had under the late empire. Though at first the barbarian rulers in Spain and Italy were Arians, they did not interfere with the freedom of the Catholic Church. Very few Romans were deprived of their land, since the barbarians were never more than a small minority in the midst of a large Roman population. The barbarians themselves admired Roman civilization and tried to run their governments in the manner of the Romans. They appointed officials with Roman titles, collected some of the old Roman taxes, and enforced Roman law among their Roman subjects. They used native Romans, both laymen and bishops, to help them in administration.

Decline of civilized life. Life under the barbarians went on as before—or so it seemed. But civilized life, as it had been known for centuries, was declining more and more all the time. This decline cannot be blamed exclusively on the barbarians, for it had started long before their coming. But after their arrival it declined all the more rapidly. While the barbarians, it is true, became partially civilized under the influence of the Romans, the Romans, in turn, became partially barbarized under the influence of the barbarians. After a while the two peoples — Romans and barbarians — tended to blend. The barbarians, always a minority, intermarried with the Romans and adopted the Latin language. Those barbarians who were Arians were converted by degrees to the Catholic religion. Eventually the distinction between Romans and barbarians ceased to exist.

Britain: an exception. There was one notable exception to this process of blending. This was in Britain. The Anglo-Saxons who settled in Britain after 449 were pagans and had little knowledge of Roman civilization. The native Britons, who were Catholics and at least partially Romanized, were slaughtered in great numbers by the invading tribes. Many who survived fled to the western parts of the island, where their descendants, the Welsh,

still live. Others fled across the English Channel to a peninsula in northwestern Gaul. They called this peninsula Britain (or Brittany), and their descendants, the Bretons, live there to this day.

By the sixth century the Anglo-Saxons had occupied the greater part of Britain and had made it into a thoroughly Germanic country. They kept their Germanic language, their pagan religion, and their Germanic customs. Of all the Germanic tribes, they alone succeeded in transplanting an entire culture to a distant Roman province. Not until the seventh century, after the arrival of Catholic missionaries, did most Anglo-Saxons abandon their pagan religion and begin to become civilized.

Germanic customs. Though the Germans on the Continent were greatly influenced by what remained of Roman civilization, they kept certain customs of their own. One such custom was their intense loyalty to their tribal kings or chieftains. To the state they had no loyalty at all, for they did not know what a state was. A Frank, for instance, had no feeling of loyalty or patriotism toward the "kingdom of the Franks." This was no more than a phrase to him. His loyalty was to the King of the Franks. When he served in the government, he served the King of the Franks; when he fought, he fought for the King of the Franks. The idea of serving or fighting for the kingdom of the Franks was completely strange to him.

Germanic law. The Germans also preserved their law and legal system. These were very different from the Roman. Unlike the Romans, the Germans had no notion of what was meant by legislation, or "making law." To the Germans, law was simply the customs of their ancestors. So sacred were these customs that, theoretically, they could not be changed by the king, nor even by the king in consultation with the nobles. The Germanic notion of crime, also, was very different from the Roman. Under Roman law a person guilty of a serious crime was prosecuted by the state, on the theory that he had committed a crime against the state; that is, against society. The Germans, however, thought of crime only as a personal thing. Only the injured party, or the injured party's family, could bring a criminal to justice.

Germanic court system. Though crime was considered a personal thing, the kings provided public courts where justice could be done. An official of the king presided over such a court, but the method of determining the innocence or guilt of an accused person was decided by a group of private citizens, called Law Men, who were learned in the local customs and had a reputation for good character. There were several such methods or proofs. The proof known as *compurgation* allowed the accused party to clear himself by producing in court a certain number of men, called compurgators, who swore that the accused was a man of good character. Another proof was the *ordeal,* of which there were several kinds. The ordeal of hot iron required the accused to carry a red-hot iron a certain distance in his bare hand. The ordeal of boiling water required the accused to pull a pebble from a pail of boiling water. After the ordeal, the accused's hand was band-aged. If after three days the wounded hand was healing, the accused was judged to be innocent; if it was still festering, he was judged guilty. In the ordeal of water, the accused was bound and thrown into a deep stream. If he sank to the bottom, he was judged innocent; if he floated immediately to the top, he was judged guilty. The principle underlying this ordeal was that water, being pure, rejects what is evil and keeps what is good. Still another proof was trial by combat, which was reserved for noblemen. The aim of this proof, in which accuser and accused fought one another, was not to kill one's opponent but to prove one's case by disarming him or making him cry for mercy.

These proofs, though primitive, were not as senseless as they might sound. Before any proof was allowed, the accuser and the accused swore mighty oaths to God that their cause was just and asked that they be struck dead if they were guilty of perjury. Many a guilty man, if he had any faith in God at all, would think twice before swearing such an oath. The Law Men set the exact conditions for the proof and could make it very hard for a man of bad reputation to clear himself.

From the sixth to the thirteenth centuries Germanic law held sway in most of western Europe. Roman law, however, was never completely eclipsed, for it continued to be administered in southern Gaul and in much of Italy, where Roman civilization was least affected by the barbarians. The Church, too, kept up the spirit of Roman law, for she frequently used Roman law as a model in drawing up

Church (canon) law and in organizing her court procedure.

The Church saves civilization. The Church was, indeed, the single institution that saved civilization in the West from extinction. While secular schools were closing their doors, monks and bishops did what they could to provide a basic education for the boys in their locality, especially for boys who desired to be monks or to enter the ranks of the clergy. But fewer and fewer parents chose to have their sons educated. In a barbarian society it was the warrior who mattered most; and since warfare was mainly a matter of brute force, the warrior saw little need for an education. By the end of the sixth century there were few educated men in the West other than churchmen. Even among the churchmen the level of education continually sank. The Greek language, which had been a standard item in Roman education for centuries, was almost completely forgotten. Even many of the great Roman writings were no longer read and were lost through neglect. Anthologies, condensations, and review books took the place of the great classics. In northern Europe there were bishops and priests who could hardly write their own names.

The Irish monks. The men who did the most to save civilization from utter ruin were the monks. Most of the monks in the Western Church followed the Rule of Saint Benedict. In the quiet of their monasteries they copied ancient manuscripts, built libraries, and taught school. In the sixth century another group of monks made their appearance on the European scene. These were the monks of Ire-

St. Patrick, Ireland's patron saint, converted the island in the fourth century. It became a bulwark of Christian civilization, with fine schools and monasteries from which missionaries were sent to the Continent to spread the faith along the valley of the Rhine. (Year, Inc.)

land. A century and a half earlier, Ireland had been converted to Catholicism by St. Patrick (*c.* 389–461), and monasticism had quickly taken root there. The Irish monks were eager for knowledge and imported to Ireland as many Roman and Greek manuscripts as they could get their hands on. Within one hundred years of their conversion the Irish had the finest schools in western Europe. In the sixth century, bands of Irish monks began to appear on the Continent. From the sixth to the eighth centuries

This page from the Book of Kells illustrates why it is regarded as one of the finest examples of Gothic illumination. (Trinity College, Dublin)

Pope Gregory the Great, a Doctor of the Church, was an exponent of the doctrine of divided powers—the emperor was God's vicar in things temporal, the Pope in things spiritual. Pope Gregory upheld the prerogatives of the Holy See.

(Alinari)

the Irish converted thousands of pagans in the Rhine Valley and in southern Germany, did mission work among the Catholic people, and founded scores of monasteries and schools in western Europe. At the same time they brought over from Ireland and put back into circulation many ancient writings which the Europeans had already forgotten.

Pope Gregory the Great (590 to 604). When the Western Empire was split up into barbarian kingdoms, there remained but one authority whom all the West acknowledged: the Roman Pontiff. No Pope was more conscious

of his authority or of the duties which that authority involved than was Gregory the Great. He corresponded with bishops and rulers all over western Europe, giving them both spiritual and temporal advice, settling their disputes, encouraging them when their actions were good and sternly warning them when their actions were bad. In the many books he wrote he explained the teachings of the Catholic Church, advised bishops how to govern their dioceses, encouraged the spread of monasticism and the conversion of the heathen, and held up the lives of the saints for all Catholics to imitate.

Gregory's temporal duties were many. He was, in effect, the ruler of Rome; for, though Rome was still officially in the Byzantine Empire, the emperors were too far away to exercise effective control. To finance the expense of the papal activities, Gregory personally managed the great estates of the Roman See and assured it of a steady annual income.

In 596, Gregory sent a band of Italian Benedictine monks to convert the Anglo-Saxons. While the Benedictines converted England from the south, Irish monks converted it from the north. With the conversion of the people of England, all of Europe west of the Rhine River was at last Catholic. Within a generation of Gregory's death, however, there arose in the East a new non-Christian force that threatened for a while to engulf all of western Europe. This force did, indeed, virtually destroy the Christian Church and Graeco-Roman civilization in Syria, Egypt, and North Africa and shook the Byzantine Empire to its very foundations. This new force was Islam.

32. MOHAMMED AND THE SPREAD OF ISLAM IN IN THE SEVENTH AND EIGHTH CENTURIES

As we have seen, the occupation of the Western Empire by the Germanic barbarians was accomplished gradually over a period of about a hundred and fifty years. The transition from Roman to Germanic rule came as a

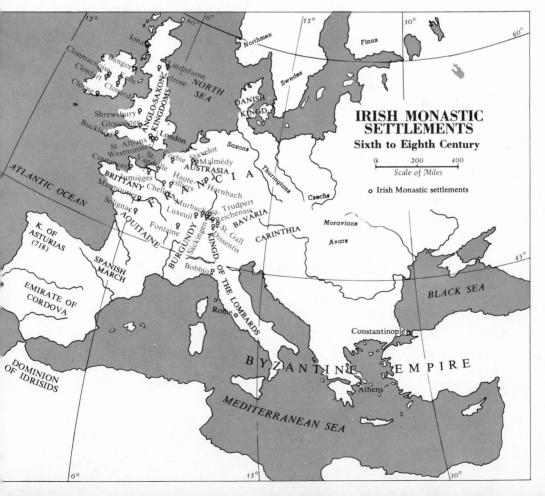

IRISH MONASTIC SETTLEMENTS
Sixth to Eighth Century

0   200   400
Scale of Miles

o Irish Monastic settlements

shock to very few. In the seventh century, however, both Europe and Asia were shocked by the expansion of a people who forced their way, with lightning speed, deep into the Byzantine and Persian empires, thence eastward to the borders of India and westward to the Atlantic Ocean and Spain. These new invaders, inspired by a new religion called Islam, were the Arabs.

The Arabs before Mohammed. The Arabs were no strangers to the peoples of the Mediterranean world. Egyptians, Mesopotamians, Assyrians, Persians, and Romans had traded with them since time immemorial. But the great homeland of the Arabs, Arabia, was virtually unknown to outsiders. Arabia was mostly desert; no roads crossed it; no single ruler before the seventh century ever controlled it. The inhabitants were mostly nomads called Bedouins, who were ruled by chieftains called shieks. They were a warlike folk, constantly raiding enemy tribes and attacking the caravans that traveled up and down the Arabian coast.

There were also Arabs who lived in towns, which were situated chiefly on the western coast of Arabia. The towns had a little industry but depended for their prosperity on the caravan trade up and down the coast. The principal town, Mecca, was an important trading station and religious center. Though the Arabs did not have a single religion, most of them considered Mecca a holy city. It housed a sacred building called the Kaaba, which contained numerous idols and a sacred black stone. Frequently the Arabs made pilgrimages to Mecca in order to worship the idols and the sacred stone. In addition to the heathen Arabs, there was a small minority of Christian Arabs and Jews who lived in the towns and made their living from trade. Thus the Arabs were touched by the great religious traditions of the Jews and Christians.

The prophet Mohammed (570 to 632). The man who changed the history of Arabia and of the world was Mohammed. He was born in Mecca in 570. Though his family belonged to the great tribe that ruled Mecca, they were very poor. At the age of six Mohammed became an orphan and was taken in by relatives. He received hardly any education at all and at an early age had to make his own living. As a young man he became a camel

Moslem pilgrims are shown in the courtyard of the great mosque in Mecca as they face the Kaaba, symbolic building covered with hand-woven hangings. (Arab Information Center)

driver and traveled in the great caravans to Syria. At the age of twenty-five he married a wealthy widow named Khadija and thereafter had time for leisure and began to devote himself to religious meditation. He prayed often in the desert, where he believed he had visions of the archangel Gabriel. When he was about forty years old Mohammed announced to the people of Mecca that he had been commanded by God to preach the true religion. At first he was laughed at, but later, as he made more and more converts, he was threatened with death. In 622 he and his followers fled for their lives to Medina. The flight to Medina is called the Hegira ("emigration") and, in the Moslem calendar, marks the beginning of the Moslem era.

The teachings of Islam. In Medina, Mohammed made many converts, and gradually his new religion took shape. Its fundamental creed was: There is only one God, and Mohammed is His prophet. This creed, though very simple, carried with it heavy obligations. The Arab who accepted it had to give up entirely his worship of the old gods of Arabia and to believe and observe everything that Mohammed, as God's prophet, taught. Mohammed put so much emphasis on submission to the one God that the Arabic word *Islam,* meaning "submission to God," was adopted as the name for the new religion. A follower of Islam was called a Moslem, which means "one who submits himself to God."

The Five Pillars of Islam. Altogether, Mohammed taught that there were five things essential for salvation.

This page is from a tenth-century parchment copy of the Koran, the teachings of Mohammed, written in Persian.

These are called the Five Pillars of Islam. First, the Moslem must believe in the one God and accept Mohammed as His prophet. Second, he must pray frequently, at least five times a day. Third, he must be generous in almsgiving. Fourth, he must fast for one month of every year, abstaining completely from food and drink from sunrise to sunset. Fifth, he must make a pilgrimage to Mecca at least once during his lifetime. Mohammed assured faithful Moslems that they would enjoy eternal bliss in heaven, and threatened those who ignored his teachings with eternal damnation. After Mohammed's death his teachings were gathered into a single volume called the Koran, which has remained ever since the bible of Islam.

Mohammed's political triumph. Mohammed won so many converts at Medina that he was eventually chosen as the town's ruler. Thereafter he often used his political power to win converts by force, and on one occasion he put to death six hundred Jews because they refused to accept Islam. He dreamed of returning in triumph to Mecca, his native city, and he deliberately provoked war with the Meccans by attacking their caravans. Mohammed was victorious and returned triumphantly to Mecca in 630. He promptly reconciled the Meccans to his political and religious authority by making Mecca the holy city of Islam. From Mecca, Mohammed extended his authority over a great part of Arabia. The new religion always followed in the wake of his armies.

The establishment of the caliphate. Mohammed died in 632 without naming a successor to his all-embracing authority. Thereupon his followers met and elected an old friend of Mohammed's, Abu Bakr, to succeed him and gave him the title of caliph ("successor"). During his short caliphate (632–634), Abu Bakr united all of Arabia, both politically and religiously. The Arabs became, so to speak, one great family. They were filled with enthusiasm for their new religion and were anxious for its spread among other peoples. Abu Bakr's successor, the caliph Omar (634–644), decided to put the fighting spirit and religious zeal of the Arabs to use by sending his armies on raids into the Byzantine and Persian empires.

The Arab conquest of Syria, Egypt, and western Persia (634 to 644). Omar quickly discovered how pitifully weak were Arabia's two great northern neighbors, the Byzantine and Persian empires. They had recently concluded a great war between themselves, and each was on the point of military exhaustion. Omar also discovered that the Byzantine hold on Egypt and Syria was very precarious. The Egyptians and Syrians detested the Byzantine Empire, which taxed them heavily for its wars and persecuted them for clinging to the Monophysite heresy. When Omar sent his armies into Egypt and Syria, the native populations offered little resistance. Many Egyptians and Syrians actually welcomed the Arabs with open arms. The armies which the Byzantine emperor threw into the field could not stand up to the vigorous, warlike Arabs, who were convinced that their cause was God's cause and that death in battle assured them of eternal salvation. In the mere space of eight years (634–642) all of Egypt and Syria fell into Arab hands. The conquest of Persia was even more spectacular than that of Egypt and Syria. As in the time of Alexander the Great, the capture of a few cities and the defeat of a few armies spelled the downfall of the Persian Empire. Before Omar's death in 644, the Arabs had pushed to the borders of India.

The Arab conquest of North Africa and Spain (644 to 715). A mere dozen years after Mohammed's death, the successor of the prophet ruled a considerable empire, which included several of the most ancient, civilized, and prosperous lands of the ancient world. Still the Arabs did not stop. They spent the remainder of the seventh century in consolidating their conquests east of the Tigris-Euphrates Valley and in conquering the Byzantine provinces in North Africa westward to the Atlantic Ocean. Several times they pushed through Asia Minor and besieged Constantinople by land and by sea. But they could neither penetrate the mighty defenses of the city nor

The Eastern Gate to the old city of Damascus was built by the Romans. (Arab Information Center)

break the will of its people to survive. Elsewhere the Arabs were more successful. By the end of the seventh century they had wiped the Persian Empire from the map forever, had conquered at least half of the Byzantine Empire, and were the masters of Asia and Africa all the way from the Indus River to the Atlantic Ocean. In 711 they crossed the Strait of Gibraltar into Spain and destroyed the Visigothic army in a single battle. By 718 they were making raids into the kingdom of the Franks. As always, raids were followed by conquest, and by 732 the Arabs were advancing deep into the heart of Gaul. North of Poitiers they were stopped by a great Frankish army under Charles Martel, and they withdrew to southern Gaul. The great era of Arab expansion had come to an end.

The caliphate moves to Bagdad. The capital from which Mohammed's successors, the caliphs, first ruled the growing Arab empire was Medina, in Arabia. But in 661, the great Arab family of the Ommiads gained control of the caliphate and moved the capital to the more centrally located city of Damascus, in Syria. In 750 the Ommiads were overthrown, and a new dynasty, the Abbasids (750–1258), moved the capital eastward to Bagdad on the Tigris River.

Religious divisions within Islam. Religious unity within Islam lasted only fifty years after the death of Mohammed. Rivalry between Arab families and conflict over the interpretation of Mohammed's teachings tended to split the Arabs into religious factions. The first great religious split occurred around 681. This split resulted from the belief of many Arabs that the caliphate could rightfully be held only by the descendants of Mohammed, through his one surviving child, Fatima, and her husband Ali. They refused to regard the Ommiads as lawful caliphs and further accused them of adding false teachings to the Moslem religion. In 681 they formed a sect within Islam called the Shi'ites, who sought to overthrow the Ommiads and restore Islam to its original purity. Disagreement among the Shi'ites themselves produced still further divisions within Islam which have lasted down to the present day.

Spread of Islam and the Arabic language. The military and political expansion of the Arabs, remarkable as it was, was not nearly so remarkable as the spread of the Moslem religion and the Arabic language. From the Indus River to the Atlantic Ocean, the great majority of the conquered population gradually became Moslem. And in many areas, especially from the Tigris-

Euphrates Valley westward, most of the natives adopted the Arabic language. The successful spread of the Arabs' religion and language cannot be attributed to persecution alone. Contrary to the popular notion, the Arabs only occasionally spread their religion by the sword. Generally they were very tolerant, especially toward Christians and Jews, whom they carefully distinguished from the heathen. Aside from the appeal that Islam had for the minds of the conquered natives, there were social pressures that induced the natives, Christian and heathen alike, to become Moslem. Non-Moslems were heavily taxed by the Arabs and were not eligible to many high government and military posts. Only by becoming a Moslem could a native become a first-class citizen.

Islam's blow to Christianity. In Egypt, Syria, and North Africa, Christianity suffered a staggering blow as millions of Christians gradually accepted Islam. These ancient lands had a distinguished Catholic history. The Church had first taken root there; monasticism had been born there; many great saints and theologians had lived and died there. But in the fifth century, as we have seen, the Monophysite heresy triumphed in Syria and Egypt. North Africa, too, was racked by a heresy called Donatism. The triumph of Islam meant not only the near disappearance of Christianity in these areas but the blotting out of much of Graeco-Roman civilization as well. Of all the great Christian countries conquered by the Arabs, only Catholic Spain clung tenaciously to Christianity. But south of Spain in Africa, east-ward to northern Syria, Islam was triumphant. The unity which the Mediterranean world had derived from Graeco-Roman civilization and the Catholic Church was destroyed forever.

33. THE CAROLINGIAN EMPIRE

Of all the barbarian tribes that settled in the Western Roman Empire, only two founded permanent kingdoms. These were the Anglo-Saxons and the Franks. The others were destroyed one by one. In the sixth century the Burgundian kingdom of southeastern Gaul was conquered by the sons of the Frankish king Clovis. In that same century Justinian destroyed the kingdoms of the Ostrogoths in Italy and of the Vandals in Africa. In the early eighth century the Visigothic kingdom of Spain was destroyed by the Arabs; and in the late eighth century, as we shall see, the Lombard kingdom in Italy was conquered by the great Frankish king Charlemagne.

The Merovingian kingdom of the Franks (481 to 751). The greatest of the western kingdoms was Frankland, which was ruled for nearly three hundred years by kings of the Merovingian dynasty. Beginning with Clovis (481–511), the Merovingian kings conquered not only Gaul but also a considerable portion of Germany east of the Rhine River. Since, however, the Merovingian kings considered their kingdom a piece of property to be divided among their sons, Frankland was constantly being divided into smaller kingdoms. The only thing that saved the Frankish kingdom from being per-

Charles Martel, who defeated the Arabs at Poitiers in 732, probably saved Europe from Islamic rule. (Library of Congress)

manently partitioned was the fact that one of the sons was usually able to conquer his brothers' kingdoms and thus re-establish the unity of Frankland. But after almost one hundred and fifty years of constant civil war, the Merovingian dynasty was so weakened that the kings lost all effective control over Frankland. The real power in Frankland passed to high government officials called mayors of the palace. Like the Merovingian kings, the mayors fought among themselves until one of them, Pepin of Heristal, gained control of the entire kingdom in 687. The Merovingian kings continued to reign, but they did not rule. The mayors of the palace may be thought of as "prime ministers."

The Carolingian mayors of the palace (687 to 751). Though Pepin was the sole mayor of the palace for all Frankland (687–714), it was no easy matter for him to enforce his authority. This was due in part to the administrative form of the Frankish kingdom. Ever since the time of Clovis, Frankland had been divided into counties, which were governed by counts appointed by the kings (and later by the mayors). The counts, who were generally great noblemen, dispensed justice, collected taxes, and commanded the army in the counties which they governed. Often they paid little attention to the king or mayor and tried to make the office of count hereditary in their own families. When Pepin became sole mayor, many of them refused to recognize his authority. Pepin, consquently, spent most of his rule putting down the rebellions of the counts.

Charles Martel (714 to 741) and the Frankish army. Pepin's family, the Carolingians, continued to hold the office of mayor after his death. During the mayorship of his son, Charles Martel (714–741), the Franks faced a great crisis as the Arabs completed their conquest of Spain and prepared to conquer Frankland. To meet the threat of the Arabs, who fought on horseback, Martel reorganized the Frankish army. Customarily the Franks fought on foot, and every Frank was obliged to serve in the army. Martel, however, revolutionized the army by converting it primarily into a cavalry force composed of wealthy landowners. Since most Franks were too poor to maintain a stable and did not have the time to train themselves to fight on horseback, Martel confiscated many estates belonging to the Church and granted these to certain Franks on condition that they serve him as cavalrymen. Thus began the feudal practice whereby a relatively small corps of landowners served as cavalry fighters in return for grants of land. With his new cavalry force, Martel met the Arabs at Poitiers in 732 and drove them back to the Mediterranean. Had the Franks not had a stout ruler who could stand up to the Arabs, all of Europe might have been engulfed by Islam.

Pepin the Short (741 to 768) founds a new dynasty. When Martel's son, Pepin the Short, became mayor of the palace in 741, the Carolingian mayors had already been ruling Frankland for over fifty years. All this while there had been Merovingian kings who ruled in name only. Pepin decided at last to bring this sham monarchy to an end and become king himself. But before he could take the momentous step of deposing a lawful monarch, he felt that he needed the highest authority in Christendom to back him up. In 751 he sent an embassy to Pope Zachary (741–752) asking the question: Who should be King of the Franks— the one who has the title or the one who actually rules? Zachary's answer was that he who ruled should also have the title of king. When the Pope's answer was taken back to the Frankish nobles, they deposed the last Merovingian king and hailed Pepin as king of the Franks (751).

The founding of the Papal States (756). If Pepin had needed the Pope's support, the Pope also badly needed Pepin. The Lombard kings, who had ruled northern Italy since the sixth century, began to make a determined effort in the eighth century to bring all of Italy under their sway. By 751 the Byzantine territories north of Rome had fallen to the Lombards, and the Lombard king was preparing to march on Rome. Pope Zachary feared that if the Lombard king got control of Rome

This painting of Charlemagne by Albrecht Dürer shows the emperor in the costume of the Germanic court of the ninth century. The arms of Germany and France are at the top.

he would try to control the Papacy just as he tried to control the Catholic bishoprics in northern Italy. To whom, other than to the Franks, could the Pope look for protection? In 754 Zachary's successor, Stephen II (752–757), went in person to Frankland and asked King Pepin for aid against the Lombards. The Pope also took the occasion to anoint Pepin as King of the Franks and to confer on him the Roman title of patrician. In gratitude for the assistance he had received from the Papacy, Pepin led an army into Italy and defeated the Lombard king. He seized a great strip of Lombard territory, including the recently conquered Byzantine territories, and handed it over to the Pope. This action, known as the Donation of Pepin (756), marks the founding of the Papal States. Henceforth the popes were the tem-

St. Peter in this mosaic from St. John Lateran Church is flanked by Charlemagne and Pope Leo III, who crowned the emperor. (Library of Congress)

poral rulers of a large part of Italy. In addition, they felt that they could count on the protection of the Frankish king. The continued independence of the Papacy seemed assured.

Charlemagne (768 to 814) enlarges the Frankish kingdom. Pepin was succeeded as King of the Franks by his son Charles, the greatest of the Carolingian rulers and known to history as Charlemagne (Charles the Great). Charlemagne spent much of his reign in warfare and greatly increased the size of the Frankish kingdom. From 772 to 804 he waged almost constant war against the heathen Saxons, finally subduing them and converting them forcibly to Christianity. In 774, when the Lombards were again threatening the Papacy, he led an army into Italy, defeated the Lombards, and himself became King of the Lombards. In 778

he led an expedition to Spain to fight the Moslems but succeeded in taking only a small part of northeastern Spain. Failure though it was, Charlemagne's expedition to Spain inspired one of the greatest medieval epic poems, *The Song of Roland.* From 788 to 805 he fought and finally destroyed the pagan Avars, a Hun-like people who had settled in the Danube Valley. He also fought numerous wars against the Slavs, barbarian peoples who lived on his eastern frontier. By the end of his reign the Frankish kingdom stretched all the way from Barcelona in northeastern Spain to the Elbe River in eastern Germany. Southward it reached to Rome, for even the Pope, who had so recently been given possession of the Papal States, was hardly more than Charlemagne's subject.

The revival of the empire (800). By the year 800 it was clear that Charlemagne was the greatest ruler in the West since the days of the Roman Empire. Men began to say, indeed, that the Roman Empire had been born again and that Charlemagne was its emperor. The Pope, Leo III (795–816), shared this view. On Christmas Day, 800, as Charlemagne prayed during Mass at St. Peter's in Rome, the Pope crowned him emperor of the Romans. Three times the congregation in the great church shouted out: "Hail to Charles Augustus, the great and peace-bringing emperor of the Romans—crowned by God!"

The revival of culture. Though Charlemagne now called himself Roman emperor and his kingdom the Roman Empire, he continued to rule very much as before. He considered Rome his capital, but he lived mostly at Aachen in northern Frankland. From Aachen he supervised the affairs of his great empire. He appointed good administrators to rule the counties of the empire and kept a close watch on all their actions. He issued decrees for all his subjects to obey. Though he had so little education that he could hardly write his own name, he was keenly interested in restoring the West to a high level of culture. To this end he ordered bishops and monks throughout his empire to set up schools for the instruction of future clerics and the sons of noblemen. He encouraged the collection, copying, and redistribution of manuscripts. He commanded that the calligraphy (method of writing) which the Irish monks had earlier introduced to Europe be universally used. From this calligraphy developed our modern handwriting and print. He assembled at Aachen scholars from all over western Europe—from Ireland, England, Spain, Italy, and Gaul. These scholars taught and wrote books and paved the way for a later day when creative writing and original thought would once again reach the high level they had reached in antiquity.

Charlemagne's control of the Church. Charlemagne ruled the Church as firmly as he ruled his empire. Indeed, he considered that the Church and the empire were inseparably bound together and therefore could not conceive of ruling the one without ruling the other. Very few churchmen complained on this score, for the idea that the Church is an independent society answerable only to God and that she should run her own affairs independently of lay rulers was not yet clearly re-established. Far from opposing Charlemagne, most churchmen gave him their enthusiastic support, for he saw to it that good bishops and abbots were appointed and that people obeyed the Church's laws and contributed to the Church's support. His control over the Church was so great that he called together councils of bishops and told them what decrees to pass and instructed the priests of the empire how they should say Mass. The Pope and some churchmen saw that Charles was overstepping the limits of his authority, but the prestige of the emperor was so great that they had little choice but to bide their time.

When Charlemagne died in 814, it seemed that the empire would go on forever and that Europe would quickly recover from the barbarism of recent centuries. Charlemagne was survived by only one son, and thus the empire remained united under a single emperor. The Carolingian Roman Empire, however, was doomed to perish. It was the creation of one of the most extraordinary men in history. For lack of another such extraordinary man, it would fall to pieces.

REVIEW

STUDY SECTIONS IN REVIEW
31. The Barbarian West and the Church
A. Did the Roman and barbarian peoples remain distinct from each other? Explain.

B. What culture was introduced to Britain by the Anglo-Saxon invaders?

C. Explain the nature of Germanic law.

D. What was the role of the monasteries in the early Middle Ages?

32. Mohammed and the Spread of Islam in the Seventh and Eighth Centuries
A. Identify: Mohammed, Islam, the Koran, Mecca.

B. What areas came under the control of Mohammed's successors in the seventh and eighth centuries?

C. What explanation can be offered for the rapid and widespread acceptance of the Moslem religion?

D. What was the impact of Islam on Christianity?

33. The Carolingian Empire

A. Identify the following: Frankland, Clovis, Pepin of Heristal.

B. What feudal practice was begun in connection with Martel's changes in the Frankish army?

C. Explain the relationship between Pepin's coronation as king of the Franks and the Donation of Pepin.

D. What was the extent of the Frankish kingdom after the wars of Charlemagne?

E. What was Charlemagne's view of the relationship between the Church and empire?

THE CHAPTER IN REVIEW

A. What remained of the Roman Empire at the beginning of the sixth century?

B. Discuss the major characteristics of Germanic civilization of this period. In what areas did it predominate?

C. Discuss the basic principles of Islam, the religion founded by Mohammed.

D. What were the principal achievements of the reign of Charlemagne? Why did his empire begin to decline after his death?

FOR YOUR NOTEBOOK

By now it should be apparent that the course of world history is something like a great river and that various individuals and peoples, like rivulets and tributaries, make their contribution to the stream of history. Make a list of the distinctive German elements, such as personal loyalty, which become part of Western civilization.

By means of a diagram show how much of Greek and Roman civilization was passed on to medieval times by the Church and her institutions.

Using encyclopedias and other reference works in your library, trace Mohammed's personal development. Show how he changed the history of Arabia and of the world.

List reasons why the Moslem religion spread so rapidly.

Historians sometimes speak of the "Carolingian Renaissance." Look up the word *renaissance* and then list all the reasons you can find for saying that there was a renaissance in Carolingian times.

SELECTED READINGS

Dorothy Mills, *The Middle Ages* (New York: G. P. Putnam's Sons, 1935), is a popular history of the entire medieval period. The first sections cover this chapter's material adequately. The Carolingian Empire is well described in the fictional but historically sound biography by Harold Lamb, *Charlemagne: The Legend and the Man* (Garden City, N. Y.: Doubleday & Co., 1954). The spirit and feeling of the age can be obtained by reading the *Chanson de Roland,* edited by Merrian Sherwood (New York: Longmans, Green & Co., 1957). This epic poem is about one of Charlemagne's great warrior knights.

The best single-volume coverage of the Moslem world is the short survey in the Home University Library by H. A. R. Gibb, *Mohammedanism, a Historical Survey* (London: Oxford University Press, 1949); reprinted in Mentor Books (New York: New American Library, 1955).

A very interesting description of the Middle Ages, which is applicable to the Carolingian period, is Eva M. Tappan, *When Knights Were Bold* (Boston: Houghton Mifflin Co., 1956). This is a description of life in a castle, on a manor, in the military orders, the way that tournaments were conducted, and such other aspects of everyday life.

Chapter 12. The Beginning of the Feudal Age

34. THE FORMATION OF FRANCE, GERMANY, AND ENGLAND

After the death of Charlemagne's son, Emperor Louis the Pious, in 840, the luck of the Carolingians ran out. Louis was survived by three grown sons, each of whom was intent on getting as large a share of the empire as possible. The oldest of the three sons, Lothair, hoped to rule the entire empire, but his two younger brothers, Louis the German and Charles the Bald, joined forces against him. They defeated him and forced him to divide the empire. This division was made at Verdun in 843. Lothair was recognized as king over the middle part of the empire, stretching from the North Sea to Rome. He was also awarded the title of emperor as a consolation prize. Louis the German be-

came king over the lands east of Lothair's Middle Kingdom, while Charles the Bald became king over the lands west of it. Theoretically the empire remained united under three kings, one of whom was emperor. But in reality its unity was broken. What had been formerly one great empire under Charlemagne and his son Louis the Pious was now three kingdoms each going its separate way.

When the three brothers divided the empire at Verdun, they made no attempt to set up the new kingdoms along linguistic or geographical lines. Lothair's Middle Kingdom was long and narrow and was cut up by great mountain ranges. It contained a hodgepodge of peoples speaking various Germanic and Latin dialects. Quite by chance, however, the other two kingdoms had a certain linguistic and geographical unity. Louis the German's eastern kingdom contained mostly German-speaking peoples, while Charles the Bald's western kingdom contained mostly Latin-speaking peoples. Eventually Louis' kingdom came to be known as Germany, and Charles's kingdom as France.

The disappearance of the Middle Kingdom. The life of the Middle Kingdom was very short. When Lothair died in 855, his kingdom was divided among his three sons. After their deaths the kingdom was further divided, until by the end of the ninth century it had been broken up into several small kingdoms and states. The kings of the eastern and western kingdoms, Germany and France, seized what they could of the northern part of the old Middle Kingdom. Certain sections, like the province of Lorraine, were continually fought over by the German and French kings and long remained a bone of contention between Germany and France.

Unlike the Middle Kingdom, Germany and France managed to survive. The notion that a kingdom was a state, that ought to remain one and indivisible, was gradually gaining ground. For a while it became the custom for the sons of a king to rule as co-kings over the same area. But even this arrangement was unsatisfactory. More and more the notion gained ground that a kingdom should not only remain undivided but should be ruled by one king only.

The Viking invasions of Europe. Though Germany and France kept their identity, they—and all the rest of Europe —were subjected in the eighth, ninth, and tenth centuries to barbarian invasions that threatened for a while to destroy all semblance of law and order. The most ferocious of the invaders were the Northmen, or Vikings, an uncivilized, pagan people who came from Norway, Sweden, and Denmark. Toward the end of the eighth century they began to make great raids on the coasts of Britain and Ireland. At that time Ireland and Scotland were ruled by numerous tribal chieftains, while England was composed of several independent kingdoms. Consequently, in neither Britain nor Ireland was there a single ruler powerful enough to hurl the Vikings back. As long as the Carolingian Empire remained

The Oseberg ship is typical of those which the Vikings used in their raids on Europe and the British Isles. These ships were as much as 80 feet long and were propelled by sixteen oarsmen. (Norwegian Information Service)

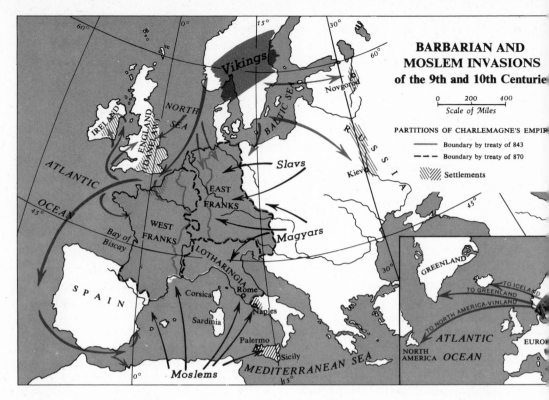

Scale of Miles

PARTITIONS OF CHARLEMAGNE'S EMPIR

——— Boundary by treaty of 843

– – – Boundary by treaty of 870

///// Settlements

united under Charlemagne and his son Louis the Pious, the Continent suffered little from the Viking attacks. But once the unity of the empire was broken by the Treaty of Verdun in 843 and war broke out between the various Carolingian kingdoms, the way was opened for Viking invasions. No European country in the ninth century had any fleet to speak of, and the coasts were unfortified. Armies of Vikings, great and small, sailed up the rivers of the British Isles and the Continent and landed wherever they chose. They attacked all along the coasts of Europe from the Baltic Sea to the Strait of Gibraltar. They even sailed into the Mediterranean and attacked eastern Spain, southern France, Italy, and North Africa. Christians and Moslems alike suffered.

The Vikings were a savage people

and often killed the entire populations of towns and villages. The object of their attacks was not only to plunder but to kill and burn as well. Having done their damage, they sailed away as quickly as they had come. The great monasteries and churches of Europe suffered most from the Viking attacks. After being looted of their precious objects they were often burned to the ground. The clergy and monks who avoided being massacred fled in all directions. The Church in England and Ireland was especially hard hit by the Viking invasions. Hardly a cathedral or monastery escaped destruction, and the great monastic schools and libraries went up in flames. England came close to being thrown back into barbarism. Ireland was so wrecked that her great civilization, which had made her the

Isle of Saints and Scholars, never recovered.

The Slavic, Moslem, and Hungarian invasions. As if the invasions of the Vikings were not enough, Christian Europe suffered still more attacks in the course of the ninth and tenth centuries. On the eastern borders of Germany, the Slavs began making raids into Germany. From North Africa came Moslems who raided Italy and southern France. The Moslems even attacked Rome, and on two different occasions the Pope himself had to muster an army and drive them away. But the greatest of the barbarian threats, after the Vikings, came from the Magyars. The Magyars, or Hungarians as they later came to be called, were an Asiatic people who, after settling in the Danube Valley in the ninth century, almost immediately began sending great plundering armies into Germany, France, and Italy.

The growing strength of the Western nobles. The West reeled from these barbarian attacks and was thrown into chaos. Since the barbarians struck unexpectedly in many different places at the same time, the kings were hardly ever on hand to oppose them. Most localities, therefore, were left to defend themselves under great noblemen who called out the army and did what they could to repel the attacks. On the whole, the nobles succeeded very well. By the middle of the tenth century the invasions had come to an end. But now that the West was relatively secure again, the nobles refused to surrender the great powers they had assumed for the defense of the land.

Italy. So powerful had the nobles in Italy grown that there was no central authority at all. Though the Byzantine Empire still claimed southern Italy and the popes the Papal States, their control of those areas was very shaky. Northern Italy was split into hundreds of little states ruled by nobles and bishops who acknowledged no higher authority at all.

France. In France the nobles had grown so powerful that the Carolingian kings were left with very little authority. When the throne became vacant in 987, the nobles by-passed the Carolingians and chose a king from among their own numbers. The new king was the powerful nobleman Hugh Capet (987–996), the founder of the Capetian dynasty whose various branches were to rule France until 1848. Surrounded on all sides by powerful nobles, the early Capetian kings were content to rule as figureheads and pass on the crown to their sons.

England. The invasions of the Vikings, or the Danes as the English called them, had been extremely destructive to the number of small kingdoms in Anglo-Saxon England. In the long run the Danish invasions helped to unify the English people. There was a time, however, when it seemed that the independence of the English would be completely wiped out, for by the middle of the ninth century the Danes had destroyed all of the English kingdoms but one. That one remaining kingdom was Wessex, and the Danes were preparing to wipe it out too. But Wessex was saved by a very able king, Alfred the Great (871–899), who defeated the Danes at Edington in 878. Alfred lacked the strength, however, to drive them com-

Alfred the Great, King of Wessex, defeated the Danish invaders at Edington in 878, thus paving the way for a united England. (Library of Congress)

ENGLAND
on the
Eve of the Norman Conquest

0   50   100
Scale of Miles

pletely from the island and made a treaty with them whereby England was divided in half. In the tenth century Alfred's descendants, supported by all the English people, conquered the Danish half of England and united the entire country under their rule. By this time we may speak of a king of England and an English nation formed of Angles, Saxons, Danes, and native Britons.

Germany. During the barbarian invasions, events in Germany followed very much the same pattern as in France. The nobles took over the defense of the country and consequently grew very powerful. In 911 the Carolingians ceased to rule, and in 919 the nobles elected Henry the Fowler, Duke of Saxony, as king (919–936). Henry made a great reputation for himself and his family by repelling the Slavs and Hungarians and by adding new territories to the German kingdom. He was succeeded by his son Otto I, called the Great (936–972). When the Hungarians began to invade Germany again during Otto's reign, Otto inflicted such a crushing defeat upon them that they never again threatened western Europe.

The founding of the Holy Roman Empire (962). Otto restored to the German monarchy a great deal of the power and prestige it had lost during the barbarian invasions. Taking advantage of the confusion in Italy, he led an army into Italy in 951 and assumed the title of King of Italy. This step made him the greatest ruler in all of Europe, for he now ruled over a great area that stretched from the North and Baltic seas southward to Rome. So great was his power that in 962 the Pope crowned him Roman emperor. Historians call Otto's empire the Holy Roman Empire. It was destined to play a leading role in Western history, not only in the Middle Ages, but even into modern times.

35. THE FEUDAL CONSTITUTION OF EUROPE

The West in the year 1000. By the year 1000 the political map of western Europe was very different from what it had been in the early ninth century under Charlemagne. The great Carolingian empire had vanished forever. In its place were several new states, great and small. Of these, the greatest were the kingdoms of France and Germany. In the borderland between these two kingdoms were several states that were theoretically subject to either the King of France or the King of Germany. But by playing off one king against the other, these

Otto III (980-1002), Holy Roman Emperor, was also recognized as king of the Lombards. He settled in Rome, seeking to make the city the center of a universal empire. (Detail from painting in Brussels Royal Museum)

small border states managed to maintain an almost complete independence. Italy, after 951, was claimed by the King of Germany and after 962 was part of the Holy Roman Empire. But the authority of the Holy Roman Emperor (who was always the King of Germany) over Italy was very uncertain. When the emperor (always with an army) visited Italy, the Italian cities acknowledged him as their emperor and king; but as soon as he returned to Germany, they began running their own affairs as if he did not exist.

Outside the lands of the old Carolingian empire, England was at last united under a single king. Spain was still ruled by the Moslems, but in northwestern Spain the Catholic

HOLY ROMAN EMPIRE
OUT THE YEAR 1000

0   100   200
Scale of Miles

Spaniards were organizing a resistance that would someday drive the Moslems into the sea. In Scandinavia and in eastern Europe the pagan barbarians were being converted to the Catholic Faith, and new Catholic kingdoms were being formed.

The rise of feudalism. The political system that was at last taking recognizable shape was one in which kings had relatively little power and nobles had great power. This situation, which is known as feudalism, came about through the breakup of the Carolingian empire and through the great barbarian invasions of the ninth and tenth centuries. The nobles took advantage of these circumstances by

This contemporary illustration of serfs at work outside their lord's manor shows the costumes, occupations, tools, and architecture of feudal England. (Pierpont Morgan Library)

exercising powers which the kings were no longer able to exercise. All over the West the nobles assumed control of districts which they defended and governed with the authority ordinarily reserved to kings. When the West returned to a state of relative calm, the nobles held onto the powers they had assumed. The kings were very much in their power, for it was the nobles who elected them.

The fief. Powerful as they were, few nobles ever went so far as to claim complete independence of the king. They acknowledged (for the sake of legality, at least) that the land they held and the political and military powers they exercised were granted them by the king. The land and all the powers a noble held over it were together known as a fief (from the Latin *feudum,* hence feudalism). In the fief which he ruled, the noble maintained law and order, protected the Church, collected taxes, held law courts, and raised armies for the defense of the fief or to aid the king. In return for the king's grant of a fief, the lord of the fief obligated himself to fight in defense of the kingdom, serve on the king's advisory council, and help the king decide great lawsuits. The king's duty to the great lords was to look after their interests and to see especially that justice was done.

Vassalage, homage, and fealty. The great lords who held their fiefs from the king were known as the king's "men," or vassals. When a vassal died, his fief was inherited generally by his oldest son, but before the son could officially take possession of the fief he was expected to take an oath of

Characteristic of feudalism was war. Here a castle is being besieged. Note the variety of weapons and protective armor being used. (Pierpont Morgan Library)

homage and fealty to the king. Homage was the act by which the heir to a fief swore to be the king's man; i.e., vassal. Fealty was the new vassal's promise that he would be faithful and carry out all his duties to the king.

Many of the vassals in western Europe, especially in France and Germany, were extremely powerful. Their fiefs consisted sometimes of thousands of square miles of land. These great fiefs were generally called duchies or counties, and their rulers dukes or counts. Like the king, the dukes and counts had vassals, too, whom they needed to help administer their fiefs and to serve in their armies. Since there was very little money in circulation, they could pay their officials and soldiers only in land. Consequently a duchy or county was always divided into smaller fiefs which the dukes and counts granted to their own vassals on very much the same

terms and in very much the same way as dukes and counts received fiefs from the king. Their vassals served only them, however, not the king, for the rule in the feudal society was that a vassal served only the lord from whom he received his fief and to whom he swore homage and fealty. Thus we see how the notion of loyalty had changed from the days of Rome. In the days of the Roman Empire, the Roman served the state; in the days of the Frankish monarchy, the Frank served the king; in the feudal age, the vassal served his lord.

War and tournaments. The chief occupation of the feudal lords, both vassals of the king and vassals of the king's vassals, was war. If a duke or count did not think that he was getting his due from the king, he did not hesitate to go to war against the king himself. Then the king had to call on his other vassals to put down the rebellious vassal. Frequently the great lords fought among themselves, and there was little that the king could do to stop them. When a foreign enemy threatened the kingdom, however, the great lords were usually loyal to the king. They called up their own vassals and fought by the side of the king.

When a feudal lord was not engaged in war he often engaged in mock battles, called tournaments, between individuals and even between small armies. They provided the countryside with entertainment and at the same time kept the lords in fighting shape. Though it was not the intention of the men engaged in tournaments to maim or kill their opponents, casualties were a common occurrence. The Church regarded the tournaments as brutal and barbarous, but not even the threat of excommunication could stop the men of the feudal age from engaging in this favorite pastime.

Castles. The feudal lords built themselves great castles, for they never knew when they might be attacked or subjected to a long siege. They surrounded their castles with high, thick walls of stone and encircled them with deep ditches called moats. Castles that were well stocked with food could stand a siege of many months. Many of them were so powerfully constructed that only treachery within the castle itself could enable the enemy to break in.

The origins of serfdom. During the feudal age, which reached its peak between the ninth and the twelfth centuries, society was dominated by two classes: feudal lords and clergy. There was but one other class of men besides

Detail of an illustration from a medieval Bible depicts the building of the Tower of Babel. Workmen are using building methods known to craftsmen of the Middle Ages. (Pierpont Morgan Library)

these: the peasants. Many of the peasants were unfree, and had been ever since the days of the late Roman Empire. During the Roman civil wars of the third century and the barbarian penetration of the fourth, fifth, and sixth centuries, the agricultural life of the West was seriously damaged. As a result, the small farmers of those times often found themselves deeply in debt and unable to pay off either their mortgages or taxes. Furthermore, they were in need of someone to protect them from the violence of the age. Many of them, consequently, surrendered their farms to powerful, wealthy landowners in return for protection and permission to remain on the land as tenants. They made a contract with their new landlords whereby they and their descendants were obligated to remain on the land and farm it, to turn over a certain portion of the harvest to the landlord, to cultivate that portion of the estate which

All members of the serf's family worked to maintain the manor of their lord, supply him with food, and take his crops to market—in return for his protection. (Pierpont Morgan Library)

the landlord reserved for the needs of his own family and servants, and to help keep the estate in good repair. Farmers who agreed to these conditions were obviously no longer free men. They were called serfs, and their state of dependence was known as serfdom.

The final blow to those farmers who still owned their land came in the ninth and tenth centuries. As the barbarians spread destruction far and wide and bandits roamed the countryside, law and order came close to vanishing. Since the kings offered little protection, the landowning peasants turned to the nobles to protect them. In return for the protection of a noble, the peasant surrendered the title to his land and became the noble's serf. By the opening of the eleventh century very few free farmers remained in Europe.

Mutual dependence of lord and serf. Though the serf did not have an outright title to the land which he worked, there was little danger that he or his descendants would be dispossessed. After all, the land had to be worked by somebody, and it was as much to the lord's advantage as to the serf's that the serf and his descendants continue to work it. In reality, lord and serf were bound together by a mutual dependence. The lord depended on the serf to supply him with food, to take his produce to market, and to keep his estate (called a manor) in good repair. The serf depended on his lord to protect him against outside enemies, to provide officials to run the village, and to settle village disputes. In other words, the serf depended on his lord for those services which the citizen today looks to his government to provide.

36. THE PAPACY AND THE CHURCH IN THE FEUDAL AGE

During the brief years of the Carolingian empire it had seemed that the West would quickly recover from the barbarism of the previous centuries. But the collapse of the Carolingian empire and the new waves of barbarian attacks threatened to wipe out civilized life altogether. In the chaotic ninth and tenth centuries no institution suffered greater harm than the Church. The Papacy, in particular, was dragged down to very low depths.

Pope Nicholas I and papal supremacy. At first the wars of the Carolingians and the barbarian invasions affected the Papacy very little. Until near the end of the ninth century the Papacy continued to be held by popes of high caliber who exercised in a very striking manner the spiritual leadership entrusted to them. An outstanding example is Pope Nicholas I (858–867), who demonstrated that kings and churchmen alike must submit themselves to papal authority. When Nicholas was informed that a council of bishops had granted an annulment of marriage to Lothair II, a descendant of Charlemagne and King of Lorraine, the Pope personally reviewed the case and found that grounds for an annulment were lacking. He ordered Lothair under pain of excommunication to take back his lawful wife. Lothair replied by threatening to take the Pope prisoner, and marched on Rome. But when he met the Pope face to face, his boldness failed him. He took back his wife and, in atonement for his sins, did public penance.

Nicholas I also had to contend with bishops who sought to ignore his authority. When Hincmar, the powerful Archbishop of Reims, in France, refused to reinstate a bishop whom he had deposed, the Pope threatened to lay the Archbishopric of Reims under an interdict. Rather than see all Church services in his archbishopric suspended, which is what an interdict would have meant, Hincmar submitted and did as the Pope commanded him. Nicholas gave close attention to affairs in the Greek Church and excommunicated an Archbishop of Constantinople who had taken unlawful possession of that see.

The Papacy in the tenth and early eleventh centuries. Within a generation of Nicholas' death the Papacy was engulfed by the disorders of the age. The complete collapse of the Carolingian empire left Italy without any central authority, and the barbarians were striking at the West from all sides. Italian noblemen scrambled madly for power. The Roman nobility seized control of Rome and put the Papacy, so to speak, in their pocket. There was no one now, as in the days of Pepin the Short, on whom the popes could call for aid. The Carolingian rulers north of the Alps were too busy fighting among themselves and trying to ward off the barbarians to hearken to a papal call. For a period of one hundred and fifty years—from the late ninth to almost the middle of the eleventh century—the Papacy was treated by various noble Roman families as a family possession. The nobles threatened and bribed the Roman clergy to elect to the Papacy whomever they designated. They took over the great estates and income which belonged to the Papacy and sought to rule the Papal States. The Papacy was repeatedly disgraced by a number of popes who had hardly any qualifications for that very great office. The lowest point was reached in the eleventh century when a twelve-year-old boy was chosen Pope. In a matter of days he was ordained priest and consecrated Bishop of Rome. Under the name of Benedict IX (1032–1045) he utterly disgraced the Papacy until, in 1045, he resigned in order to get married. When such things could happen, we may well call those times "the Dark Ages."

Nothing illustrates better the barbarism into which the West fell than the history of the Papacy during this period. The moral life of the West declined as rapidly as its civilized life. Though there were many good men who were shocked by the condition of the Papacy, there was little they could do about it. Many Catholics had only a vague inkling of what was going on at Rome, for their own affairs were in such confusion and communications were so poor that very little news from Italy reached north of the Alps. After the coronation of Otto the Great in 962, the Holy Roman Emperors began to show a concern for the welfare of the Papacy. On their periodic visits to Rome they tried to put papal affairs in order. But the Italians respected the emperor only when he was present in person with an army. As soon as the emperor withdrew from Rome, the Roman nobility again seized control of the city, and the condition of the Papacy became as bad as ever.

Destruction of the monasteries. In the terrible chaos of the ninth and tenth centuries, monasticism, too, suffered a terrible decline. Hardly a monastery in western Europe escaped destruction by either the Vikings, Saracens, or Hungarians. The great monastic li-

The noted Abbey of Monte Cassino, situated on a mountaintop, was founded by St. Benedict during the sixth century. It became the vanguard of Western monasticism.

braries and schools were destroyed, and the monks were often either killed or fled in all directions.

The Church in the feudal system. Another evil that began to afflict the Church at this time was that it became deeply involved in the feudal system. Bishops and abbots became the vassals of kings and nobles, and the great estates of the Church became fiefs. Churchmen who were vassals had to render the same services to their lords as did lay vassals. Some churchmen even fought in the feudal armies, though generally most of them sent knights to fight in their place. Besides being vassals themselves, bishops and abbots were the lords of other vassals, for they divided the Church estates into fiefs and apportioned these out among knights.

Lay investiture. When the Church became involved in the feudal system, kings and feudal lords began to exercise considerable control over the election of bishops and abbots. For if a bishop or abbot was to be a lord's vassal, the lord naturally hoped to see a man elected who would serve his interests. After a while the free election of bishops and abbots almost disappeared. It became so common for feudal lords, in effect, to appoint bishops and abbots that most Catholics simply took such action for granted. Some lords took great care to see that good men were elected to Church offices, but others appointed men who were noted only for their devotion to their lord. Consequently, there were bad bishops and abbots.

Laymen did more, however, than merely appoint churchmen to office. They even took part in the ceremonies of consecration and presented the bishop or abbot with the crozier and ring that were the symbols of his office. The practice of appointing and investing churchmen is known as lay investiture.

Simony and clerical marriage. Other evils that plagued the Church were simony and clerical marriage. Simony was the practice whereby a cleric paid money for a Church office or was appointed only because of his faithful service to a lay lord. Clerical marriage was regarded as an evil not only because the Church forbade clerics to get married but also because married clerics tried to pass on their Church offices to their sons.

The monastic revival of Cluny (tenth century). The ninth and tenth centuries were by no means a completely dark period for the Church. The Church was never so downtrodden that she did not show signs of great vitality at the same time. Monasticism, in particular, rose quickly again from the ashes of wrecked monasteries. In 910 a group of Benedictine monks who wanted to get a fresh start founded a monastery at Cluny, in France. They were given the land on which to build their monastery by the Duke of Aquitaine, one of the most powerful feudal lords in France. To enable the monks to lead holy lives undisturbed by worldly affairs, the duke gave them their land in outright ownership. Consequently, the monks of Cluny were not dependent on any feudal lord and did not have to render services to anybody.

Cluniac monks lived very holy lives and after a while began to found new monasteries. Though they followed the Rule of St. Benedict, their organization and way of life differed so much from that of other Benedictine monks that they came to be regarded as a separate order. Whereas every Benedictine abbey was independent of other abbeys and there was no superior general of the Benedictines, all the Cluniac abbeys were joined together under the supreme authority of the Abbot of Cluny. Other religious orders similar to Cluny sprang up, and by the end of the tenth century monasticism was flourishing again throughout most of the West.

The call for reform of the Church. The monks not only led holy lives them-

The Benedictine Abbey of Cluny sparked a reform movement throughout the Western world. It enjoyed a unique exemption from local jurisdiction guaranteed by the Pope. (Giraudon)

The Abbey of Mont-Saint-Michel was founded in 708 by Aubert, Bishop of Avranches, according to directions given to him by the Archangel Michael in a vision. (French Govt. Tourist Office)

selves but called on Catholics everywhere to imitate Christ. They urged that the Church be reformed and singled out simony and clerical marriage as two of the greatest evils. Their cries were taken up by many churchmen and laymen as well. As yet there were few complaints about lay investiture, for this practice was so tied up with feudalism that most Catholics simply took the appointment of churchmen by lay lords for granted.

The monks and the heathen nations. During those very years when the Papacy and the Church as a whole were suffering such great ills, the monks of the Church were converting the pagan peoples of northern, central, and eastern Europe to the Catholic Faith. The conversion of a people was always followed by their admission to the ranks

of the civilized nations, for the Church was the greatest civilizing force in Europe. The monks taught the newly converted how to read and write, set up governments, build homes and churches, and cultivate the land.

In the ninth century the Czechs, in central Europe, were converted to Catholicism. Shortly thereafter they organized a state called the Duchy of Bohemia. Their duke was a vassal of the Holy Roman Emperor and in the eleventh century was awarded the title of king. The newly converted Czechs assisted German monks in the conversion of Poland in the tenth century. Like Bohemia, Poland was at first a duchy, but in the eleventh century was recognized as a kingdom. At the very end of the tenth century the Hungarians were converted, and in 1001 their ruler,

Duke Stephen, was awarded the title of king by Pope Sylvester II. By the eleventh century the three Scandinavian countries, Norway, Sweden, and Denmark, were converted. Under the influence of Christianity the Scandinavians lost the savage habits that had made them the terror of Europe. They organized the three kingdoms of Norway, Sweden, and Denmark, which were destined to take their places among the civilized nations of the West.

REVIEW

STUDY SECTIONS IN REVIEW

34. The Formation of France, Germany, and England

A. How was the Carolingian empire divided after the death of Louis, son of Charlemagne?

B. What were the fates of the various kingdoms that resulted from the division?

C. Identify the various barbarian tribes that invaded Europe in the ninth and tenth centuries.

D. How did the nobles build their power at the expense of the kings during this period?

35. The Feudal Constitution of Europe

A. Explain the meaning of the term "feudalism."

B. Identify each of the following feudal terms: fief, vassal, oath of fealty.

C. What is the feudal meaning of the word "serf"?

D. Discuss the mutual dependence between lord and serf in the feudal system.

36. The Papacy and the Church in the Feudal Age

A. Give an example that illustrates the upholding of papal supremacy by Pope Nicholas I.

B. How did the results of the barbarian invasions affect the Papacy?

C. What was "lay investiture"?

D. What was the origin of the monastic revival of the tenth century?

THE CHAPTER IN REVIEW

A. Discuss the breakdown of the Carolingian empire and the origins of Germany and France.

B. How did the barbarian invasions affect both Church and State during the ninth and tenth centuries?

C. Outline the principal relationships and obligations that constituted the feudal system.

D. In what way did the Church display her vitality in the tenth century despite the fact that some churchmen had fallen into evil ways?

FOR YOUR NOTEBOOK

Explain how the "second barbarian invasion," or the Viking raids, enhanced the power of the nobles.

In four parallel columns place the dates and events of importance in the (1) Viking, (2) Moslem, (3) Slavic, and (4) Hungarian invasions of western Europe.

Feudalism is a most important concept to understand in studying the Middle Ages. You will help yourself to understand this concept if you draw up a list of rights and duties which the lord and his vassal owed each other.

Illustrate the position of churchmen in feudal society by means of a chart showing a typical bishop's position relative to the Pope, the emperor, his lay vassals, and the priests in his diocese.

SELECTED READINGS

An excellent picture of medieval life is found in William Stearns Davis, *Life on a Medieval Barony* (New York: Harper & Bros., 1928). Feudalism is well presented by Rafael Sabatini's *Chivalry* (Boston: Houghton Mifflin Co., 1938), and by Marion Florence Lansing's *Page, Esquire, and Knight* (Boston: Ginn & Co., 1953). More recent than Davis' study is Gertrude Hartman, *Medieval Days and Ways* (New York: The Macmillan Co., 1937).

Chapter 13. The Byzantine and Moslem Civilizations

37. Byzantium

From the seventh to the tenth centuries, the peoples of the West had relatively little contact with the two great civilizations of the eastern Mediterranean—the Byzantine and the Moslem. This lack of contact was not due to any great distance separating the West from the Byzantine and Moslem empires. On the contrary, both Byzantium and Islam had outposts situated directly on the western European continent. The Moslems were in control of most of Spain and had a brilliant civilization there at the very time when civilization in the West was at its lowest ebb. The Byzantines held territories in northern Italy until the eighth century and held a great part of southern Italy until the eleventh century. Unlike Moslem Spain, however, Byzantine Italy was never more than a dim reflection of its mother civilization, which was centered in Constantinople.

The shrinking of the Byzantine Empire. The Byzantine Empire maintained a high level of civilization for centuries. Yet all the while, it scarcely ever had a moment's rest from enemy attacks. From the sixth century on, the Balkan provinces and Thrace were continually ravaged by barbarians of Slavic or Hunnish origin. Often these barbarians reached the very gates of Constantinople, but they were never able to take the great city. In the seventh century the empire was stripped of half its territories when Egypt, Syria, and North Africa fell to the Arabs. In the same century the Slavs and the Bulgarians, a Hunnish people, permanently settled in the Balkan provinces north of Greece. In the eighth century the Byzantine territories in northern and central Italy were conquered by the Lombards. These were the same territories which, after Pepin's defeat of the Lombards (756), were handed over to the Pope and became the Papal States. In the ninth century the Moslems took Crete and Sicily from the Byzantines.

The Byzantines preserve Greek and Hellenistic culture. Despite a state of constant war and the steady shrinking of their empire, the Byzantines clung fiercely to their independence. Their spirit could not be broken. They gloried in the fact that they were Greeks and were the heirs to the great Greek and Hellenistic civilizations of antiquity. They gloried in the fact that theirs was the Roman Empire and that their emperor was successor to Augustus, Constantine, and Justinian. They gloried in the fact that they were Catholics, and believed that the Faith was kept with no greater devotion than in their empire. They gloried in their great capital of Constantinople, the greatest city in Christendom, with its million inhabitants and hundreds of splendid churches, parks, and public buildings.

The Byzantines worked tirelessly to keep alive the great civilization they had inherited from antiquity. Though they all but forgot the classic achievements of the Roman West, they carefully preserved many of the great Greek and Hellenistic works of literature, philosophy, and science, and the writings of the Greek Fathers of the Church. Except in the field of art, they made few original contributions of their own. They copied and studied, wrote textbooks, digests, anthologies, and encyclopedias. Their greatest importance in civilization is that they helped to preserve it and pass it on to others. Moslem civilization was in great part based on that Byzantine civilization which the Arabs found in Egypt and Syria. In the ninth, tenth, and eleventh centuries the Byzantines spread their civilization among the Slavic peoples of eastern Europe. Later, the Catholic West absorbed much of Byzantine civilization both directly from Constantinople and indirectly through the Moslems of Spain. When we consider that the term "Byzantine civilization" includes the preservation of Greek and Hellenistic civilization, we can appreciate the debt which we owe to the Byzantines.

Conversion of the Slavs of eastern Europe. Like their fellow monks in the West, Byzantine monks spread Christianity and civilization among barbarian peoples, especially among the Slavs of eastern Europe. One of the greatest missionaries to the Slavs, St. Cyril (827–869), invented the Slavic, or Cyrillic, alphabet and translated the words of the Byzantine liturgy into the Slavic language. The Cyrillic alphabet and Slavonic (Slavic) liturgy were later adopted by all but a few of the Slavic peoples and are found to this day in Russia, Bulgaria, and Yugoslavia.

The founding of Russia (ninth century). Of all the Slavic peoples Christianized and civilized by the Byzantines, none has played a greater role in the history of the world than the Russians. Before their conversion, the great Slavic tribes living north of the Black Sea were conquered and first organized into states by the Vikings, who penetrated as far south as the Black and Caspian seas. The conquering

Vikings were called *Rus,* or Russians, and their name was given to the Slavic people whom they dominated. The Vikings, who came in bands at different times, founded several Russian states. The greatest were the princedoms of Novgorod and Kiev, which were founded in the ninth century and became great trading posts. From Novgorod and Kiev the Vikings sailed down the great rivers of Russia to Constantinople and to other trading centers on the Black and Caspian seas. They exchanged slaves, furs, honey, and wax for the finished wares of Byzantium and the East. On their return trip they sold these wares as far north as the Baltic Sea.

The conversion of Russia. The Russians under their Viking princes were but another people who made life uneasy for the Byzantines. In the ninth and tenth centuries they constantly made raids into Byzantine territories and several times attacked Constantinople itself. Despite their hostile acts, the Russians had great admiration for Byzantine Christianity and civilization. In 989 the Grand Prince of Kiev, Vladimir, was baptized into the Catholic Church by Byzantine missionaries. After that the conversion and civilizing of Russia began in earnest. Byzantine monks introduced into Russia the Cyrillic alphabet and Slavonic liturgy and spread Byzantine civilization. The most exposed of the Russian cities to the Byzantine influence was Kiev, the greatest commercial center north of Constantinople. Within a hundred years of Vladimir's conversion, Kiev boasted hundreds of churches, schools, and monasteries and was the most splendid Christian city in Europe after Constantinople.

Catholic Europe. By the eleventh century almost all of Europe was Catholic. Many peoples who had been heathen barbarians only a few generations earlier were now becoming civilized. All the Christians of Europe were one in Faith and accepted the basic Catholic doctrines taught by the Roman pontiffs. They worshiped God in three great liturgies. The Catholics of the West followed the Latin liturgy, the Byzantines the Greek liturgy, and most of the Slavs the Slavonic liturgy.

Tension between the Western and Eastern churches. We have seen earlier that relations between the Western and Eastern churches were not always good. Through the centuries several factors operated to cause tension. One was the frequency of heresy in the Eastern

VIKING ORIGINS OF RUSSIA

0   100   300
Scale of Miles

■ Byzantine Empire

Vikings

Novgorod 840

DANISH KINGDOM

BALTIC SEA

ESTHONIA

Elbe R.

Slavs

Kiev 864

Dnieper R.

Magyars

KINGD. OF BULGARIA

Danube R.

BLACK SEA

Venice

Adriatic Sea

Rome

Naples

Durazzo

Constantinople

Chalcedon

Aegean Sea

Sicily

Athens

Ephesus

Church. From the fourth to the eighth century there originated in the Eastern Church no fewer than five great heresies. Though the Eastern Church always accepted papal teaching in the end, there were frequently long periods of schism before the heresy was finally stamped out. The factor of heresy was complicated by the powerful position of the emperor in the Eastern Church. Frequently the emperor himself was the chief supporter of heresy, and he tried to force the Eastern heresies on the Pope as well. If Eastern bishops refused to endorse the emperor's heresy, he simply deposed them and replaced them with more compliant bishops.

A second factor causing tension was the attitude of the Greeks toward the Western Church. They felt that they were culturally superior to the West (as for centuries they undoubtedly were), and believed that their cultural superiority somehow made their church superior to the Western Church. They were fond of describing the Pope, and the West in general, as barbarous. Any customs of the Western Church that they did not find in their own they did not hesitate to stamp as barbarous and wrong.

The Patriarch of Constantinople. A third factor causing tension was the role played by the Archbishop of Constantinople himself. As early as the fourth century he had tried to make himself the head of the Eastern Church. He assumed the title of "patriarch," a title that had hitherto been reserved only to bishops who occupied sees founded by the Apostles: Rome, Jerusalem, Antioch, and Alexandria. With the emperor's backing, the new patriarch rapidly assumed control of much of the Eastern Church. When Egypt and Syria were lost to the Church in the fifth and sixth centuries, the Patriarch of Constantinople was left without a rival in the Eastern Church.

From the sixth to the tenth century, East and West drifted farther apart, and communication between the churches became very difficult. The patriarchs tightened their control of the Eastern Church and developed more and more an independent attitude toward Rome. They denounced certain practices of the Western Church, such as clerical celibacy, the use of unleavened bread for consecration, and the eating of cheese and milk on fast days. Occasionally they even accused the Western Church of heresy for having inserted the phrase *filioque* into the Nicene Creed. Needless to say, the terrible decline of the Papacy from the late ninth to the middle of the eleventh century greatly damaged its prestige in the eyes of the patriarchs. Their own authority, meanwhile, was greatly extended by the control they exercised over the church of the newly converted Slavs.

The final schism (1054). In the eleventh century the patriarch Michael Cerularius became so contemptuous of the Western Church that he closed all the Latin churches in Constantinople and ordered that the Blessed Sacrament be taken from these churches and trampled underfoot. When he refused to cancel these orders he was excommunicated by papal ambassadors on July 16, 1054. Cerularius' control of the Eastern Church was so great that the Catholics of both the Greek and Slavonic rites went into schism with him.

Despite two great attempts by Rome to heal the schism, the great majority of Eastern Christians (called the Orthodox) remain in schism with Rome to this day.

The Turks threaten Byzantium. Shortly after Cerularius' break with Rome, the Byzantine Empire came upon very hard times. New waves of Asiatic barbarians, called Patzinaks, pushed through the Balkans to the gates of Constantinople. Normans from France seized southern Italy from the Byzantines. From the East came the greatest threat of all: the Turks. In the first half of the eleventh century the Asiatic Turks conquered the Moslem Near East and in the second half of the eleventh century conquered Asia Minor from the Byzantines. By 1072 the Turks were encamped at Nicaea, across the Bosphorus from Constantinople. The Byzantine Empire seemed on the verge of extinction.

38. THE MOSLEM CIVILIZATION

Political disunity. The greatest civilization that flourished in the early Middle Ages was that of the Moslems. From Spain and Morocco in the West to the borders of India and China in the East, one religion, one language, and one culture were supreme. Until the middle of the eighth century this vast area was ruled by one man, the caliph—the successor of the prophet Mohammed. But after the Abbasid dynasty moved the caliphate to Bagdad in 762, family rivalries and disagreements over religious matters broke the political unity of the Islamic world. The first province to break

away from the caliph was Spain, which set up an independent dynasty of its own in 756. In the ninth and tenth centuries, other dynasties were established all the way from Morocco to eastern Persia. Sometimes these dynasties paid lip service to the Abbasid caliph at Bagdad, but in reality they ran their affairs as they pleased.

Cultural unity. Though Islam kept its political unity only a little over a hundred years after Mohammed's death, its cultural unity remained. The history of Islam reminds us in many respects of the history of the Hellenistic world after the death of Alexander the Great (323 B.C.). Like Alexander's great empire, the Moslem empire broke up into a number of independent states. But the Moslems still had a unity—cultural unity—that had far more meaning than mere political unity. A common religion, Islam; a common language, Arabic; and a common book of basic laws, the Koran, gave them a solidarity far greater than that of mere political unity. Like the Hellenistic states, the Moslem states exchanged ideas and commercial goods with equal ease. From the Atlantic Ocean to the Indus River, a distance of over four thousand miles, the Moslem could travel with ease and always feel at home. For wherever he went, the God of Mohammed was worshiped, the Arabic language was spoken, and the Koran provided the basic laws of society.

The meaning of "Arab." After the seventh century, the Arabs of Arabia proper had small part in directing the affairs of the Islamic world. When the capital was moved to Bagdad in the

The interior of the Sultan Ahmet Mosque, or the Blue Mosque, is an outstanding example of Ottoman architecture and design. (Turkish Information Office)

eighth century, the leadership of Islam passed to Arabs whose families had long since left Arabia, and to native Syrians, Mesopotamians, and Persians who placed their talents at the disposal of the Abbasid caliphs. Thereafter Arabia had little importance save for the city of Mecca, which was always revered as Mohammed's birthplace and as the holy city of Islam. In the eighth and following centuries the "Arabs" who held the caliphate, ruled the Moslem states, and produced the brilliant civilization of Islam must not be thought of as natives of Arabia. They were, for the most part, the descendants of Arabs who, after migrating from Arabia in the seventh century, intermarried with the natives of the conquered lands. Wherever the migrating Arabs settled in great numbers, Arabic became the language of the people, especially from Mesopotamia (Iraq) westward to the Atlantic Ocean. Viewing the natives of that area as one great linguistic and religious group, we may properly call them Arabs; but viewing them as national groups, we must distinguish between Iraqi, Syrians, Egyptians, etc.

Islamic cities. Islamic civilization reached its height from the eighth to the twelfth century. Like all great civilizations, it was an *urban* civilization and was dotted with many great cities. The greatest of the cities was Bagdad, which contained a population of around two million inhabitants. Other great Moslem cities were Damascus, Aleppo, and Antioch in Syria; Jerusalem in Palestine; Alexandria and Cairo in Egypt; Tunis in North Africa; and Cordova, Seville, and Toledo in Spain. All these cities were adorned with beautiful houses of worship called mosques, great public buildings, including schools and baths, and splendid residences. Parks, gardens, and fountains adorned the newer sections of these cities.

Industry and commerce. While Islamic civilization was at its height the Moslems enjoyed industrial and commercial supremacy in the Mediterranean and far to the east. They excelled in the production of textiles, metalware, leather goods, jewelry, and perfumes. In the ninth century the Moslems conquered the islands of Crete, Malta, Sicily, Sardinia, and the Balearic Isles. The Mediterranean became almost a Moslem lake. Merchant ships from the great ports of Islam freely plied the waters from Spain to Syria. They sailed down the west coast of Africa and eastward—through the old canal linking the Nile with the Red Sea—to India.

Islamic civilization. In literature, philosophy, and science the Moslems made notable advances. Here again they present an interesting parallel with the great Hellenistic civilization of antiquity. As we have seen, Hellenistic civilization had strong Greek overtones, but in actuality it was built on the cultural achievements not only of classic Greece but of Egypt, Syria, Asia Minor, Mesopotamia, and Persia as well. So, too, Islamic civilization had strong Arabic overtones, thanks to its foundation in the religion and language of Arabia, but its great cultural achievements were built on those of the Hellenistic East, Rome, Persia, India, and even distant China (whose western borders Islam touched). If Arabia had little other than her religion and language to give to the formation of Islamic culture, she could boast that her religion and language spread over a far greater area and took much deeper root than the Greek religion and language ever did. Hellenistic civilization is long since dead, and Greek is hardly spoken outside of European Greece and the Aegean Islands. But from Morocco to Pakistan, Islam is as strong as ever, and Arabic is the language of the educated and peasants alike from Morocco to Iraq. Since the Middle Ages, Islam has penetrated to the very heart of Africa and eastward to China and Indonesia. The only explanation for Islam's remarkable expansion and for its survival against the attacks of secularism and modern rationalism is that it is a religion that for centuries has satisfied the hearts and stimulated the minds of millions. It is still expanding.

This intricate illustration of a water wheel was taken from a thirteenth century Egypto-Arabic manuscript, Treatise of Al Jazari on Automata *and displays the Arabian interest in scientific invention. The Arabs had a tremendous curiosity in the fields of chemistry, physics, astronomy, geography and mathematics. (Museum of Fine Arts, Boston)*

In physics, mathematics, chemistry, astronomy, medicine, and geography the Moslems made notable advances. Eventually Moslem scientific knowledge found its way into the Catholic West, where the foundations were laid for the great scientific progress of recent centuries. From the Hindus of India the Moslems borrowed the cipher, or zero, a concept that revolutionized the study of mathematics. They founded the mathematical sciences of algebra and plane and spherical trigonometry. In medicine they correctly analyzed the symptoms and progress of many diseases and developed the sciences of surgery, dissection, and anatomy. In the liberal arts the Moslems were serious students of the Greek philosophers, especially of Aristotle. Their translations of Aristotle and their commentaries on his works were introduced to the Christian West in the twelfth century and made possible the work of the greatest of all Catholic philosophers, St. Thomas Aquinas (1225–1274). The Moslems wrote excellent histories, beautiful poetry such as the well-known *Rubáiyát of Omar Khayyam*, and prose works such as the *Arabian Nights*. Their literary works, as well as their scientific and philosophical works, have had wide influence far beyond the borders of Islam.

Moorish Spain and the Catholic Reconquista. One of the most flourishing centers of Moslem culture was in Spain. Spain, however, was never thoroughly Islamized, for the Moslems, who were mostly of Moorish (North African) extraction, were never more than a ruling minority in the midst of a people who clung fiercely to their Cath-

The Alcazar at Seville, a masterpiece of Moorish architecture, is famous for its glazed tiles. The mosque-cathedral in Cordova was begun in the eighth century by the Moors. (Spanish Tourist Office)

olic religion and Roman language. Extreme northwestern Spain, indeed, was never conquered by the Moslem Moors at all, and in this region originated the Spanish offensive to drive the Moslems from Spain. This Catholic offensive against the Moors is known as the *Reconquista*. By the tenth century several Catholic kingdoms had formed in northern Spain, and the *Reconquista* was well under way. Two kingdoms, Castile and Aragon, eventually emerged as the strongest. They rallied not only the Spaniards but Catholics from all over Europe to help them drive the Moors into the sea.

The Turks take over western Asia. In the eleventh century a new barbarian people, the Turks, made their appearance on the Islamic scene. Moving down from the interior of Asia, they were converted to Islam and steadily extended their conquests southward and westward. In 1055 the Abbasid caliphate at Bagdad fell into their hands. Thereafter, members of the Abbasid dynasty continued to rule as caliphs, but the actual control of much of southwestern Asia remained in the hands of the Turks. The Turks were zealous Moslems and were noted for a religious fanaticism, especially against Christians, which other Moslems rarely displayed. Although it had been a Moslem custom, ever since the Holy Land fell to the Arabs in 640, to allow Christians to make pilgrimages to the holy places, the Turks had little use for this kind of toleration. The difficulties of the Christian pilgrims were increased by the fact that Syria, in the late eleventh century, was ruled by several Turkish governors, called emirs, who were frequently at war

with one another. Farther south, in southern Syria and in Palestine, there was constant war between the Turks and the Egyptians. Control of the holy places shifted from Turk to Egyptian and then back again. These Moslem wars made it so dangerous for Christian pilgrims that pilgrimages became armed expeditions, prepared if necessary to fight their way to the holy places.

The Turks presented a grave problem to Christians other than the pilgrims. In the second half of the eleventh century they advanced steadily into Byzantine Asia Minor. During the reign of the emperor Alexius Comnenus (1081–1118) they entrenched themselves all along the Black Sea straits. Opposite them they saw the great city of Constantinople and Europe. The Catholic West would shortly hear that Islam was once again on the march, profaning the holy places and threatening to cross the Black Sea straits into Europe.

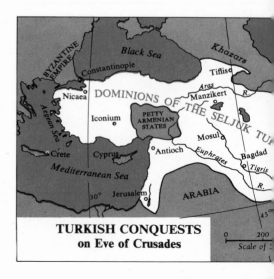

TURKISH CONQUESTS on Eve of Crusades

REVIEW

37. Byzantium

A. What was the fate of the Byzantine Empire through the seventh, eighth, and ninth centuries?

B. What great contributions to world culture were preserved by Byzantium?

C. How were the early Russian peoples influenced by Byzantine culture?

D. What three major liturgies characterized Catholicism in the eleventh century?

E. Give the immediate cause and result of the final schism of 1054.

38. Islam

A. What factors enabled Islamic cultural unity to survive after its political unity ended?

B. Mention a Moslem contribution to mathematics, philosophy, and literature.

C. Explain the meaning of the *Reconquista* in Spanish history.

D. What areas were conquered by the Turks in the eleventh century?

THE CHAPTER IN REVIEW

A. What areas were influenced by Byzantine culture and civilization?

B. Explain the three major causes of tension between the Eastern and Western churches that led to the schism in 1054.

C. Why are peoples of many Middle Eastern nations called "Arabs"? What have they in common throughout history?

D. Compare the survival of Islamic cultural unity with the survival of Hellenistic cultural unity of earlier history. What explanation can be offered for the vitality of Islamic culture even in today's world?

FOR YOUR NOTEBOOK

List and evaluate the factors that led to a final schism between the East and the West by 1054.

Make a list of cultural accomplishments achieved by Islam and passed on to western Europe.

Prepare a list of twenty-five words that have come into the English language from Arabia. Examples of such words are "coffee," "gauze," and "zero." After you have compiled the list, check to see in what categories they tend to fall —such as commercial, scientific, etc.

Prepare three parallel columns for Islam, Byzantium, and Western civilization. In these columns enter the principal events and important persons in the history of each civilization that you have studied thus far in this unit.

SELECTED READINGS

The best coverage of the Byzantine civilization as a whole is N. H. Baynes, *The Byzantine Empire* (London: Oxford University Press, 1926). This volume, which has been reprinted many times, is one of the Home University Library series. Another excellent treatment of Byzantium, though rather long, is S. Runciman, *Byzantine Civilization* (London: Edward Arnold & Co., 1933).

Rafael Sabatini presents an interesting fictional tale of adventure of Italian privateers fighting against the Moslems in *Sword of Islam* (Boston: Houghton Mifflin, 1939); and William Stearns Davis writes an equally interesting story of the Saracens in his *Beauty of the Purple* (New York: The Macmillan Co., 1924).

Chapter 14. The Popes Assume the Leadership of the West

By the opening of the eleventh century the West was at last taking recognizable form. A number of states had come into being which, in one form or another, have lasted down to the present day: Germany, France, England, Bohemia, Poland, Hungary, Norway, Sweden, and Denmark. Spain was divided between the Moors and the Catholic kingdoms of the north. But the great *Reconquista* was in full swing, and the foundations of the future Catholic kingdoms, Spain and Portugal, were being laid. Italy had no political unity whatsoever. The King of Germany laid claim to Italy as part of the Holy Roman Empire, but he hardly ever exercised ef-

fective control there except when he was personally present with an army. In reality, Italy was composed of many states. In the north were a number of duchies, counties, and city-states that had come into being after the breakup of the Carolingian empire. Often these states were at war with one another, and some of them, for safety's sake, were closely allied with the King of Germany. In central Italy were the Papal States. Southern Italy was feebly held by the Byzantines. Sicily, since the ninth century, had been held by the Moslems.

Scandinavian vitality. In the eleventh century we no longer speak of Vikings but of Norwegians, Swedes, and Danes. Catholicism and civilization were spreading fast in the Scandinavian kingdoms, but the descendants of the Vikings were slow to lose that roving instinct that had carried their ancestors so far afield. The Viking Danes, who had wrought so much destruction in England in the ninth century, returned as conquerors under a Catholic king in the eleventh. The Danish king Canute (1014–1035) ruled over a great northern empire made up of England, Denmark, and Norway. But Canute, like so many kings before him, divided his empire among his sons. In 1042 the Danish rule in England was overthrown, and England was ruled again by an English king, Saint Edward the Confessor (1042–1066). But after Edward's death, other descendants of the Vikings, the Normans of France, descended upon England and conquered it. The conquest of England by William, Duke of Normandy, and the effects of that conquest on English life, will be discussed in a later chapter.

The Normans and their conquests. Of all the descendants of the Vikings, those who were most venturesome no longer lived in Scandinavia at all but settled in France. When the great Viking invasions were drawing to a close, a number of Vikings established themselves in northwestern France in 910. They called themselves Normans (North-men), and the land they settled, Normandy. Under powerful dukes, Normandy became the strongest feudal state in France. Though the Normans were converted to Catholicism and became thoroughly French in language and culture, they lost none of their old Viking energy. Like their Viking ancestors, they wandered far afield, and in 1016 a band of Norman noblemen began the conquest of

The tomb of Edward the Confessor is in Westminster Abbey, London. Through the childless Edward, William the Conqueror claimed the throne of England. (British Information Services)

Byzantine southern Italy. By the middle of the century the Normans had driven the Byzantines from most of southern Italy and were preparing next to conquer Moslem Sicily.

The council of Sutri and the reformed Papacy. As it turned out, the institution that showed the greatest vigor in the eleventh century was not any particular kingdom or state, but the Papacy. In 1046 the Holy Roman Emperor, Henry III (1039–1056), visited Rome and found that no fewer than three men were claiming to be Pope. To settle the dispute, Henry called together a council of bishops at Sutri, a suburb of Rome, where they deposed two of the claimants and accepted the resignation of the one who had the best claim to be Pope. For the next ten years Henry III, in effect, appointed the popes by indicating to the Roman clergy whom they should elect. All of the popes whom Henry named were excellent men, for Henry was genuinely anxious that the Papacy recover its spiritual leadership of the Church. Overnight the prestige of the Papacy soared, and Catholics everywhere became aware that it was once more in the hands of popes of high caliber. This news was not welcome to everybody, for the popes were determined to reform the Church, and reform always means that the unreformed are going to be discomfited.

The Lateran Decree and the Treaty of Melfi: 1059. Henry III died in 1056 and was succeeded as King of Germany by his six-year-old son, Henry IV (1056–1106). The German nobles took advantage of the king's youth to assert their own power, and for the moment German authority in Italy vanished. Many Catholics expected that the Papacy, without strong German support, would fall again under the domination of the Roman nobility. This did not happen, however, for the tradition of a reformed Papacy was already so strong and had so much popular support that the popes carried on very well without German backing. For the first time in almost two hundred years the Roman clergy were free at last to elect a pope of their own choice. And the popes were free at last to govern the Church as they saw fit.

In order to guarantee the freedom of papal elections and to prepare against the day when lay powers might try again to dominate the Papacy, Pope Nicholas II (1058–1061) took two significant steps. First, in or-

der to guarantee the freedom of papal elections, he issued the Lateran Decree of 1059. By this decree Nicholas organized the leading (cardinal) clergy of Rome into a body called the College[1] of Cardinals and assigned to them—and to them alone—the right and the duty to elect future popes. The Lateran Decree is a historic landmark in the history of the Church and remains in effect to this day. Second, in order to provide the Papacy with a protector who (it was hoped) would not meddle in papal affairs, Nicholas signed the Treaty of Melfi with the Normans of southern Italy. By this treaty, Nicholas recognized the Norman duke, Robert Guiscard, as the ruler of southern Italy and Sicily on condition that he and his successors hold these lands as papal fiefs. Thus Nicholas established a feudal relationship with the Normans which obligated them, as vassals, to come to the defense of their lord, the Pope. At the time of the treaty, parts of southern Italy were still in Byzantine hands and all of Sicily was held by the Moslems. For the next thirty years the Normans fought to wrench these territories from the Byzantines and Moslems, and by 1091 were in full possession of southern Italy and the island of Sicily.

Gregory VII forbids lay investiture. In 1073 the monk Hildebrand, a leading reformer and one of the cardinals in the Roman Church, was elected Pope. He is known as Gregory VII (1073–1085). In surveying the state of the Church in his day, Gregory became convinced that many of the ills of the

[1] *Collegium,* meaning "society," "corporation," "group of colleagues."

Church could be traced to lay investiture, that is, the practice whereby lay rulers appointed bishops and abbots and took part in their consecration. He believed that the Church would fully achieve the mission given her by God only if she were free to run her own affairs independent of lay interference. If we take this notion for granted today, it is because Gregory VII was our teacher.

In 1075, Gregory issued a decree which absolutely forbade, under pain of excommunication, the laity to appoint Church officers or the clergy to accept such appointments. This decree was nothing less than revolutionary and dealt a serious blow to the feudal constitution of Europe. For many years now emperors, kings, and feudal lords had practically regarded it as a law of nature that they should appoint bishops and abbots. Nor did they lack a good feudal argument for making such appointments. Since bishops and abbots were their vassals and were therefore obliged to render the same services that lay vassals rendered, the rulers considered the choice of such churchmen of vital interest to themselves.

The excommunication and deposition of Henry IV. When Gregory issued his decree, Henry IV had come of age to rule Germany and was in fair control of much of Italy too. He was the most powerful ruler in Europe and was looking forward to the day of his coronation as Holy Roman Emperor by the Pope. He expected to exercise the same control over the Papacy as his father Henry III had done, and he reacted to Gregory's decree by promptly appointing bishops to five German and

Italian sees. When Gregory warned Henry to cancel these appointments, Henry replied by summoning a council of German bishops which "deposed" the Pope from office (1076). Gregory's reply, in turn, was such as captured the attention of all of Europe. Not only did he carry out his decree by excommunicating Henry but, declaring that Henry was a sinful man and not fit to rule a Christian people, he deposed him. Thus did Henry's disobedience cost him not only his membership in the Catholic Church but his throne too.

Canossa (1077). The nobles and bishops of Germany supported the Pope and began to make plans for the election of a new king. Henry was determined to save his throne but realized that he could do so only by being readmitted into the Church. In the dead of winter he crossed the Alps and pre-

Pope Gregory VII (Library of Congress)

sented himself before the Pope at Canossa. For three days he stood outside the Pope's window in the cold and snow, begging forgiveness. Gregory doubted the sincerity of Henry's repentance, but as a priest he knew that he had no choice but to grant absolution to a man professing repentance and begging forgiveness. He granted Henry absolution, but only on condition that Henry henceforth follow the Pope's counsels.

Gregory's death in exile. When Henry failed to keep his promise, Gregory excommunicated him again in 1080. The second excommunication, however, meant little to Henry, for he had greatly strengthened his position in Germany by waging skillful warfare and by convincing many Germans that he was unjustly persecuted by the Pope. In 1084 he led an army into Italy and seized Rome. But he quickly retreated when Gregory's Norman vassals came to the Pope's rescue. In taking Rome, the Normans caused considerable damage, and the Romans blamed Gregory for all their troubles. For safety's sake, Gregory took refuge with his Norman vassals in southern Italy. He died shortly thereafter, saying before his end: "Because I have loved justice and hated iniquity, I die in exile."

With the Pope's death in exile, Henry's triumph seemed complete, and the Papacy appeared to have suffered a terrible defeat. Whether the Papacy would maintain the leadership it had so recently regained was questionable. All would depend on the caliber of future popes and on the support of the Catholic people. Neither of these was found wanting.

40. THE LAUNCHING OF THE CRUSADES

Pope Urban II (1088 to 1099). The spirit of a vigorous and independent papacy had made so deep an impression on Catholics that, with few exceptions, they rallied to its support. After the brief pontificate of Pope Victor III, the College of Cardinals in 1088 elected as Pope a man who had been a close friend and advisor of Gregory. This was Urban II, a former monk of Cluny who had long been identified with the reform movement in the Church. Henry IV of Germany and some of his German bishops and nobles refused to recognize Urban as Pope and tried to replace him with false popes (called anti-popes) of their own choosing. But Henry's opposition was weakened by the loyalty of most Catholics to Urban and by frequent rebellions on the part of German nobles against Henry's rule.

Urban II and the reform movement. Like his predecessors of the previous fifty years, Urban fought the great evils that plagued the Church, especially simony, clerical marriage, and lay investiture. He traveled extensively throughout Italy and France, holding councils of bishops where he dealt with local abuses and publicized the papal prohibition of the great evils. Thanks to the efforts of Urban and his predecessors, simony, clerical marriage, and lay investiture were gradually becoming less common. If they did not disappear completely, at least Catholics were aware that such practices were wrong, whereas a hundred years earlier these practices had bothered the consciences of very few.

Urban calls for a crusade. In 1095, Urban received an appeal of an unusual nature. From the Byzantine East, already in schism with Rome for forty years, came a cry for Western military forces to help turn back the tide of the advancing Turks. Urban weighed this appeal carefully and decided on a course of action that went far beyond the expectations of the Byzantine emperor, Alexius Comnenus. In November 1095, Urban traveled to Clermont, in central France, and called together a great council of churchmen and nobles. On November 27, when a great throng had assembled, Urban delivered what was perhaps the most momentous speech in history. He called on the Catholics of Europe to unite and launch a great attack on the Turks in Asia and drive them forever from the holy places of the East. He noted, furthermore, that Europe was becoming too crowded and that the East contained much land that could be carved into fiefs by those who fought in Christ's name. But, above all else, Catholics must unite their efforts to rescue the Holy Sepulcher of our Lord in Jerusalem from the Turks. Urban promised an abundance of graces to all Catholics who, with a pure heart, fought in Christ's name, and eternal salvation to those who died in His cause.

Those who heard Urban deliver his speech were swept with a great enthusiasm. They cried out excitedly: "God wills it! God wills it!" Thousands immediately patched a cross upon their shoulders as a symbol of their vow to rescue the Holy Sepulcher. Clergymen were dispatched throughout Europe to preach the crusade, so called from the Latin word *crux,* meaning "cross." Wherever the crusade was preached, men by the thousands vowed themselves to fight in Christ's holy name.

This was one of the Papacy's greatest moments. The Catholic West was filled with religious enthusiasm and the spirit of reform. The Papacy was the one power in the Catholic world that commanded the allegiance of all men. The feudal nobility, which showed scant respect to the authority of kings, placed itself in the service of the Pope.

The Peasants' Crusades. Pope Urban planned the crusade as a great organized military expedition under his own direction. He did not intend to lead it in person but placed in supreme command of the crusade a French bishop, acting under the Pope's orders. But so eager were thousands of Catholics to rescue the Holy Sepulcher and find a new home in the East that they would not wait for the Pope's crusade to be organized. They packed all their belongings into carts and began the long trek to the Holy Land. Expeditions such as these, of which there were several, are called the Peasants' Crusades. Having little money at their disposal with which to buy provisions, they fought and pillaged their way through the Balkans to Constantinople. When they arrived at Constantinople, the emperor Alexius hardly knew what to do with them. They were, in reality, a great undisciplined army, and the emperor feared that they were as likely to seize Constantinople as Jerusalem. At their own insistence and for the safety of his empire, he shipped them across the Bosphorus to Asia, where they hoped to

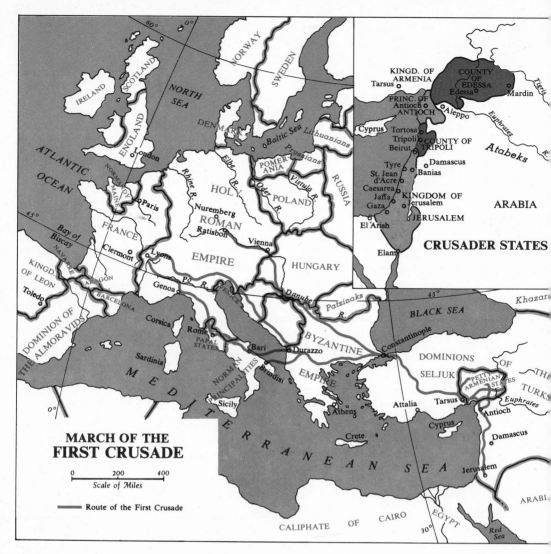

MARCH OF THE FIRST CRUSADE

0   200   400
Scale of Miles

━━━ Route of the First Crusade

CRUSADER STATES

begin the final march to Jerusalem. But they were quickly cut to pieces by the Turks.

The First Crusade. In 1096 Urban's official crusade, called the First Crusade, got under way. Four great armies, marching in good order, made their way across the Balkans to Constantinople. The French supplied the greatest number of crusaders, but the combined armies, which consisted of about one hundred thousand men, were made up of Germans, Italians, Englishmen, Irishmen, Bohemians, Hungarians, and Scandinavians as well. In 1097 the crusading armies assembled at Constantinople and crossed the Bosphorus into Asia. They were not opposed by a united Islam but rather by several armies of fierce, well-disciplined Turks fighting under the command of Turkish emirs (governors). The crusaders defeated the Turks in two important battles in Asia Minor and allowed the emperor Alexius to take possession again of that great area. In 1098, after a siege of eight months, the crusaders captured the great fortified city of Antioch on the Syrian coast. In June of 1099 they undertook the siege of Jerusalem. On July 13, 1099, they stormed Jerusalem, killed many of the inhabitants, and raised the Cross over a city which had been held by the infidel for four and a half centuries. Shortly before the news reached the West that the Holy Sepulcher was once more in Christian hands, Pope Urban died in Rome.

The Kingdom of Jerusalem. When the crusaders conquered Syria and the Holy Land, they set up four Christian states. The southernmost was the Kingdom of Jerusalem. North of it were the County of Tripoli, the Principality of Antioch, and the County of Edessa. These states were organized in the only manner the crusaders knew —that is, on a feudal basis—and consequently the four states became a patchwork of fiefs. Theoretically the four states together formed one great Kingdom of Jerusalem. But owing to the feudal constitution of the so-called kingdom, the King of Jerusalem exercised as little control over his great vassals, the Counts of Tripoli and Edessa and the Prince of Antioch, as they in turn exercised over their own vassals.

The failure of the crusaders to set up one strong state in the East obviously made it difficult for them to present a united front to the ever-threatening Turks. For a while the Turks were not too great a threat to the independence of the newly founded states, for they themselves had little unity. Their lack of unity, however,

was not deliberately planned, as was that of the Christian rulers. The Turks had a tradition of powerful monarchy and awaited only the rise of a strong ruler to drive the crusaders from the East.

Italian cities and the revival of commerce. One great result of the First Crusade and the establishment of the crusader states in Syria and the Holy Land was the opening up of new trading opportunities for the West. Even before the First Crusade, however, the beginnings of commercial activity were in evidence all the way from Scandinavia to Italy. The foremost leader in this new commercial activity was Venice, a north Italian city situated on the Adriatic Sea. Originally founded in the fifth century by Italians fleeing the advancing Huns, the city was built on a number of islands a short distance from the Italian shore.

The doges (dukes) of Venice fought opposition to the rise of Venice as mistress of the Mediterranean. This painting of the Doge Loredan is by Bellini. (Alinari)

The construction of St. Mark's Basilica in Venice, one of the most influential examples of Byzantine architecture, was begun in 1043. (Italian Tourist Service)

Thanks to the marshy lagoons that separated the islands from the shore, the Venetians were able to escape domination by the foreign invaders who periodically descended into Italy. For several centuries after her founding, Venice was a Western outpost of the Byzantine Empire. Throughout the period of the Western barbarian kingdoms, the expansion of the Arabs, and the Viking, Magyar, and Saracen invasions, Venice remained untouched and maintained almost uninterrupted commercial and cultural contact with Byzantium. After the Byzantines lost their north Italian territories in the eighth cen-

tury, Venice gradually asserted her independence. Her commercial contact with Constantinople remained as strong as ever, however, for Venice was an important source of Western raw materials for Constantinople, and she purchased from the Byzantines Eastern products which she sold in the West.

The Venetians were not the only ones who contributed to the growth of commerce in the West before the First Crusade. In the tenth century merchants from Flanders and Germany began to travel eastward to trade with the Russian Vikings, who brought the products of the East up the great rivers of Russia and thence to Baltic ports. In the eleventh century, Pisa and Genoa, following the lead of Venice, began to look around for trading opportunities. But first, in order to make the Mediterranean safe for their ships, they drove the Moslems from Sardinia and helped the Normans capture Moslem Sicily.

The commercial cities of Italy profited greatly by the First Crusade. During the crusade they shipped foodstuffs and munitions to the Christian armies. After the founding of the crusader states, Italian ships were regularly hired to carry pilgrims, military reinforcements, and munitions to the East. They returned laden with Eastern products. Other Mediterranean cities, such as Marseilles in France and Barcelona in Spain, imitated the Italian cities and joined in the East-West traffic.

The bourgeoisie. New towns sprang up and old towns grew larger as merchants set up markets, and workers their shops, outside the walls of feudal fortresses and episcopal cities. The rise of the towns and the growth of the new commercial and industrial class introduced an element into feudal society which it had not known before. For the first time in centuries the West had an appreciable class of people who were not bound to any lord, lived in towns, and (most important of all, perhaps!) sought to make money. The merchants and workers who formed this new class came to be called the *bourgeoisie*, from the fact that they settled so often next to the great feudal fortresses called *bourgs*. Eventually the word "bourgeoisie" came to denote only those townsmen who had

considerable incomes; in other words, the upper middle class. In the eleventh century the bourgeoisie was still quite insignificant. Who could have suspected that it would someday grow so powerful that it would determine, in large measure, the course of world history and even topple kings from their thrones?

REVIEW

STUDY SECTIONS IN REVIEW

39. Gregory VII and the Reform of the Church

A. What areas fell to the Normans in the tenth and eleventh centuries?

B. What were the results of the Council of Sutri?

C. Explain the effects of the Lateran Decree issued by Pope Nicholas II.

D. What steps were taken by Pope Gregory VII to eliminate lay interference in Church affairs?

40. The Launching of the Crusades

A. What motives prompted Pope Urban II to call for a crusade?

B. Were the "Peasants' Crusades" successful? Explain.

C. What new states were established after the success of the First Crusade?

D. Which European areas prospered as a result of the commerce stimulated by the crusades?

E. Explain the meaning of the term "bourgeoisie."

THE CHAPTER IN REVIEW

A. What steps were taken by Pope Nicholas II to guarantee papal independence from temporal authorities?

B. Explain the principal causes of the struggle between Pope Gregory VII and King Henry IV.

C. How did the crusades demonstrate the renewed vigor of the Papacy?

D. Discuss the great European commercial growth that indirectly resulted from the crusades.

FOR YOUR NOTEBOOK

The monk Hildebrand, later Pope Gregory VII, is one of the important popes in medieval times. From reading his biographical sketch in the *Catholic Encyclopedia* or another standard reference work, make a list of his important historical accomplishments.

Pope Urban II's speech at Clermont, in which he called for a crusade, has been called the "most momentous speech in history." In a paragraph enter into your notebook reasons for this statement.

Many motives sent men on the crusades. Make a list of these motives in descending order of importance so that you explain why (1) the average crusader, (2) the bored second son, (3) a common peasant, and (4) an Italian merchant went to the Holy Land. Remember that many persons had more than one motive.

Enter into your notebook (1) the immediate result of the Crusades, and (2) their ultimate and indirect effects.

SELECTED READINGS

A popular and easy-to-read book on the Papacy is John Farrow, *Pageant of the Popes* (New York: Sheed and Ward, 1950). The book is arranged by centuries, and it is easy for the student to pick out the appropriate chapters for each period covered in our world history.

The spirit of the crusades is well captured by William Stearns Davis in *God Wills It* (New York: The Macmillan Co., 1924). Harold Lamb uses his ability to put an interesting story into an authentic historical setting in two books dealing with the crusades. *The Crusades* (Garden City, N. Y.: Doubleday & Co., 1945), is a general treatment of the subject; and *Durandal, a Crusader in the Horde* (Garden City, N. Y.: Doubleday & Co., 1931) is a biographical account of one of the crusaders. A brief but excellent account of the crusades is R. A. Newhall, *The Crusades* (New York: Henry Holt and Company).

CHRONOLOGICAL REVIEW

597 *Conversion of England begins*
604 *Death of Pope Gregory I, the Great*
622 *Mohammed's flight to Medina*
632 *Death of Mohammed*
644 Arabs reach India and Libya
687 Pepin of Heristal becomes mayor of the palace for all Frankland
711 Arabs defeat the Spanish Visigoths
732 Battle of Poitiers
751 Pepin becomes king of the Franks
756 Bagdad becomes the capital of the Arab empire; the Donation of Pepin
774 Charlemagne conquers the Lombards
787 First Viking raids on Britain
800 Coronation of Charlemagne
814 Death of Charlemagne
843 Treaty of Verdun; Vikings sail into the Mediterranean
863 *Pope Nicholas I condemns King Lothair*
864 *Conversion of Boris, King of Bulgaria*

868 *SS. Cyril and Methodius made bishops*
878 Alfred the Great defeats the Danes
910 *Founding of Cluny*
911 End of Carolingian rule in Germany; settlement of the Normans in France
955 Otto the Great defeats the Magyars
962 Coronation of Otto the Great
966 Conversion of Mieszko, Duke of Poland
987 Founding of the Capetian dynasty
989 Conversion of Vladimir, Prince of Kiev
1046 *The Synod of Sutri*
1054 *The Greek schism*
1059 *The Lateran Decree and Treaty of Melfi*
1055 Turks capture Bagdad
1066 Battle of Hastings
1072 Turkish conquest of Asia Minor
1075 *Decree against lay investiture*
1077 *Henry IV's penance at Canossa*
1085 *Death of Pope Gregory VII*
1095 *Council of Clermont*
1099 *Capture of Jerusalem*

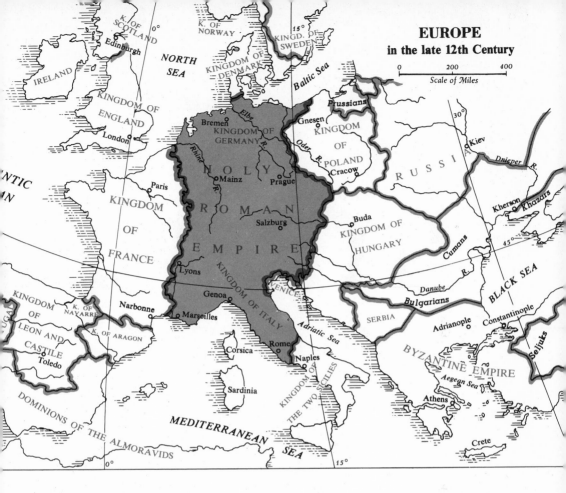

EUROPE
in the late 12th Century

0   200   400
Scale of Miles

UNIT FIVE
Western Christian Civilization
in the Twelfth and
Thirteenth Centuries

The Church and Civilization · Literature and Learning · Towns in Western Society ·
The Papacy and the Empire; Norman England · Innocent III and the Western
Monarchies · Innocent III and the Religious Life of the West · Last Great Struggle
between Empire and Papacy; England in the Thirteenth Century · The Rise of the
French Monarchy; Spain and Medieval Parliaments · The Mongol Conquests: West
Meets East · Theology and Science in the Thirteenth Century

Chapter 15. The Twelfth-Century Recovery and Creative Advance

41. THE CHURCH AND CIVILIZATION

With the collapse of the Western Roman Empire in the fifth and sixth centuries, the Western provinces had sunk into a low state of civilization. Grave political and social disorders served to keep them in that condition for many centuries. When we say that the state of civilization in the West was low, we mean that very few great books were written, very little great art or architecture was produced, very few scientific advances were made. We mean, too, that the economy, government, and law of the West were very crude. Nevertheless, the centuries (sixth to eleventh) of low civilization in the West were very important in world history. All that while the Church was toiling to pre-serve what civilization she could and to convert the many heathen tribes of northern and central Europe. Slowly the Church was laying the foundations on which a new civilization—Western Christian civilization—was to be built.

As society became more stable in the eleventh century, the West began to recover the arts and techniques of civilization. It did far more, however, than merely recover civilization. Building on the contributions of the ancient world, of the Byzantine Empire, and of Islam, the Catholic peoples of the West brought into being a new civilization—Western Christian civilization. From the twelfth century to the present day no civilization in the world has shown greater vitality and strength or made greater advances than has Western Christian civilization, which is *our* civilization.

The foremost institution in this new civilization was, of course, the Church. Since all the Western peoples were Catholic, the Church touched practically every great activity in which they were engaged. Before we consider the progress of the Catholic West in the twelfth century, we shall look briefly at the Church's organization and at certain twelfth-century events closely connected with that organization.

The papal curia. In governing the Church, the Pope was assisted by a great staff of ecclesiastical officers and clerks. This staff made up the papal court, which was called the *curia.* The highest officers in the papal curia were the cardinals, most of whom in those days resided in Rome. Besides electing the Pope, the cardinals had other very important duties. They formed the Pope's advisory council (called the consistory), headed various departments of the curia, and performed whatever missions the Pope assigned them. The Pope made known his will to the prelates and rulers of Europe by issuing decrees that were known as bulls (so called from the papal seal, or *bulla,* which was attached to them). Papal ambassadors, called legates, carried these bulls to their places of destination. Since the legates were the Pope's representatives, they enjoyed to a limited extent the Pope's own authority and outranked all the archbishops and bishops of the countries they visited.

Excommunication and interdict. The chief means by which the Pope sought to bring disobedient Catholics into line was fatherly persuasion. If this failed, he used more severe methods, such as taking away certain privileges of the offenders or suspending them from their offices. If these means failed, the Pope resorted to excommunication. Excommunication was, of course, very serious, for it not only deprived the excommunicate of the sacraments (thereby threatening his soul with damnation) but it made him an outcast of society. In the most extreme cases of disobedience (usually involving mighty persons) the Pope used the interdict, which was a papal command that all Church services and the dispensing of the sacraments be suspended in a certain area until further notice. Usually an area was placed under interdict because its ruler was guilty of some grave offense against the Church. In the twelfth and thirteenth centuries the interdict was a powerful means of forcing rulers to return to the Church's obedience.

Ecumenical councils. When the Pope had matters of very special importance which he wished to make known to the Catholic world, he called together an ecumenical council. An ecumenical council was attended by bishops from all over the Catholic world, and its decrees, when approved by the Pope, were binding on all Catholics. Before the Greek schism of the eleventh century, ecumenical councils always met in the East, but after the schism they met exclusively in the West.

The first great ecumenical council of the West was the First Council of the Lateran, which met in 1123 in the church of St. John Lateran, the great cathedral church of Rome. There the bishops solemnly voiced their approval of the Concordat of Worms, which was an agreement reached the previous year by Pope Calixtus II and Henry V, the Holy Roman Emperor, wherein the emperor finally abandoned his claim to appoint bishops and invest them with their authority. The next ecumenical council met in 1139; and the third, the Third Council of the Lateran, in 1179. The latter council amended the famous Lateran Decree of 1059 to read that a two-thirds majority vote of the cardinals was needed to elect a pope. This rule is still in effect. The council also decreed that no man might be ordained a priest before the age of twenty-five, and no priest be consecrated a bishop before the age of thirty. These rules, too, are still in effect. Ecumenical councils dealt mostly with matters of doctrine and discipline in the Church, but they also issued decrees for the general betterment of society as a whole. For instance, the Third Lateran Council, after considering how tournaments frequently ended in bloodshed and even death, condemned tournaments as immoral and forbade them under pain of mortal sin.

Archbishops and bishops. In the various Catholic countries the chief officers of the Church were the archbishops and bishops. An archbishop headed a large district called a province, which consisted of his own archdiocese and the dioceses of the bishops under him. Generally there were several ecclesiastical provinces in a single country. In most cases the only ecclesiastical superior of an archbishop was the Pope. In some countries, however, a single archbishop was the superior of all the other archbishops in the country. Such an archbishop was called a primate. In England, for example, the Archbishop of Canterbury was the primate; in Spain, the Archbishop of Toledo.

Archbishops and bishops had courts that were modeled on the papal curia, though on a much smaller scale. Their chief assistants were the priests who were attached to the cathedral. These priests, called canons, were organized in a body called the cathedral chapter. The canons elected the bishop (or archbishop), acted as his advisory council, headed various departments in the bishop's court, conducted the cathedral services, and ran the cathedral school.

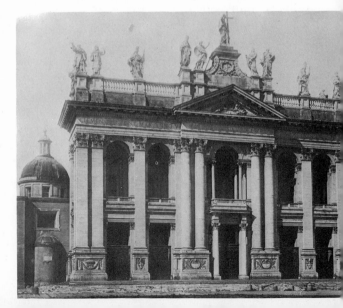

The Basilica of St. John Lateran is the cathedral of Rome, the Pope's church. The basilica was presented to the Church by Constantine, with most of its decoration dating from the Middle Ages. (Alinari)

New religious orders. Beginning in the late eleventh century, a common feature in the Church was the rise of new religious orders. While the older Benedictines and Cluniacs remained strong, several new orders came into great prominence. The Carthusians, founded by St. Bruno in 1084, built their monasteries in very remote places. They were dedicated to a life of solitude, great austerity, and almost perpetual silence. The Cistercians, founded by St. Robert of Molesme in 1098, lived a busy community life in their monasteries and followed to the letter the Rule of St. Benedict. Why they were distinguished from the older Benedictines we shall see in the next paragraph. The Premonstratensian canons, founded in 1120 by St. Norbert, staffed cathedral chapters, taught school, and worked as missionaries and teachers of agriculture among the backward peoples of central and eastern Europe. The most unusual religious orders were the Knights of the Temple and the Knights of the Hospital, popularly called the Templars and the Hospitalers. These were "soldier monks." Their orders were founded after the First Crusade to guard the frontiers of the crusader states in Syria against the Moslems.

The Cistercian constitution. When St. Robert of Molesme established a community of monks at Cîteaux (Cistercium) in Burgundy in 1098, he had no intention of founding a new order. His aim was to found a monastery where the Rule of St. Benedict would be followed in all its strictness. When the Cistercians branched out and founded new abbeys, however, they organized themselves in a way very different from the Benedictines. Every Benedictine abbey was independent of the others, whereas the Cistercians adopted a constitution that bound all the Cistercian abbeys very closely together. Every September all the abbots of the Cistercian Order met at Cîteaux and formed a body called the general chapter. The general chapter was the supreme legislative, executive, and judicial body of the order, and the statutes it passed were binding on every abbot and monk in the entire order. Thus, by means of the general chapter, the Cistercians became the first truly unified religious order in the history of the Church.

St. Bernard of Clairvaux (1091 to 1153). Early in their history the Cistercians produced an outstanding saint, Bernard, Abbot of Clairvaux. For over a quarter of a century he was the most listened-to man in the West, and his advice was sought by popes and kings alike. When the Moslems began encroaching on the crusader states in Syria, Bernard preached a second crusade in France, Germany, and the Low Countries. Men who did not even understand his French tongue were so moved by his eloquence that they hastened to take the Cross. In 1130, when the College of Cardinals split into two factions and each faction elected its own Pope, Bernard's opinion concerning who was the lawful Pope carried such weight that all Catholics accepted it. In Bernard's day heresy was again becoming a problem for the Church, and Bernard fought it tirelessly. He was the author of many devotional works and poems which have become classics of Catholic literature. Bernard's love for the Mother of God was very great, and he instilled into Catholics a devotion to Mary that has never been dimmed. With such an outstanding saint in the Cistercian Order, it is no wonder that by the time of Bernard's death the Cistercian Order numbered over three hundred and fifty abbeys and several thousand monks.

42. LITERATURE AND LEARNING

The use of Latin. In our earlier discussion of the Roman Empire we saw that Latin became the vernacular (spoken language of the natives) of most of the inhabitants of the Western Roman Empire. After the barbarian occupation of the Western Empire, however, Latin as a vernacular language lost ground. In Britain, the Britons reverted to their original Celtic speech. In eastern Britain (England) the Anglo-Saxon invaders clung to the Germanic speech they had brought from overseas. A heavy migration of Slavs into Illyria made that region Slavic-speaking. In North Africa, Latin was replaced by Arabic. In Italy, Gaul, Spain, and Dacia, however, Latin remained the spoken language.

While Latin lost ground as a spoken language, it actually gained ground as a written, or literary, language. Throughout the entire West— that is, in all those countries Christianized by missionaries of the Latin Rite —Latin became the chief literary language. From Sweden in the north and Poland in the east, westward to the Atlantic Ocean, Latin was the written

St. Bernard of Clairvaux has been regarded as "the conscience of medieval Christianity." He had a profound contempt for the materialism of the world and attacked the spreading secularism within the Church. (Library of Congress)

language of the Church, of governments, of literature, and of scholarship. Even in countries where Latin was not the vernacular, as in England, Germany, and Poland, it was a spoken language to the extent that all educated men spoke it among themselves.

Early vernacular literature. Though Latin was the chief literary language of the West, it was never so used exclusively. As early as the fourth century the Bible was translated into an old form of German called Gothic. From the seventh century on, the Anglo-Saxons frequently wrote their laws and kept official records in Anglo-Saxon (Old English), and as early as the eighth century they were writing poetry in the vernacular. The greatest poem surviving from Anglo-Saxon England is the epic poem *Beowulf.* Before the year 1000 the Norse and the Germans, too, were writing great epic poems called *sagas.*

The Romance languages. After the sixth century, vernacular Latin changed rapidly. By the eighth century it had changed so much that it was actually developing into several new languages, notably Italian, French, and Spanish. These are the Roman, or Romance, languages. Other important Romance languages developed, too, and are spoken to this day. These are Provençal, spoken in southern France; Catalan, spoken in northeastern Spain; Romansh, spoken in southeastern Switzerland; Portuguese and Rumanian.

Of the Romance languages, the first that achieved a fine literary form was French. The earliest literary works in French were epic poems, of which the greatest is the *Song of Roland.*

Love lyrics and romances. Epic poems had their greatest popularity in the days when bloodshed, violence, and barbarian attacks were a common occurrence. But as Western society became more stable, the epic poems lost much of their popularity. In the twelfth century, love lyrics and romances became the most popular forms of poetry. Love lyrics were composed by men called troubadours and were sung by wandering minstrels who went from castle to castle. The romances were very long poems that told of never-never lands that knights and ladies loved to dream of. They told of beautiful maidens in distress who were rescued by gallant knights; of separated lovers who pined away

A page from the oldest English epic, Beowulf. *The poem, derived mainly from Scandinavian history, folk tale, and mythology, presents a vivid picture of old Germanic life. (British Museum)*

for love of one another but who, in the end, were whisked off to enchanted castles where they lived happily ever after. Some romances told of King Arthur and his Round Table and of Sir Galahad's search for the Holy Grail, the chalice which our Lord used at the Last Supper. In some romances the characters were animals who behaved very much like human beings. The most popular of the animal romances were those that told the story of Reynard, a clever fox who was the vassal of King Noble, a lion.

Mystery plays. Another popular literary form of the twelfth century was the drama. Like the earlier Greek drama, Western drama grew directly out of religious ritual. In the early Middle Ages the church choir sometimes acted out the story that was celebrated in the liturgy on a particular feast day, such as the story of the Resurrection at Easter or the story of the Nativity at Christmas. At first the acted-out story was sung, but after a while it came to have spoken parts too. Later the subject matter of these early dramas was enlarged to include stories from the Bible and the saints' lives. Costumes and sound effects were added, and the language of the plays was changed from Latin to the vernacular so that as many people as possible could understand them. Finally, the performance of the plays was moved from inside the church to the church porch or to an outside stage. Medieval plays are called mystery plays, from the fact that they dealt with the great mysteries of the Bible and of the life of Christ, the Blessed Virgin Mary, and the saints.

Faith and reason. As early as the eleventh century there was a widespread revival of interest in Greek philosophy. This interest centered primarily in philosophy's chief tool, logic, which is the science of correct reasoning. Around the middle of the eleventh century the Italian theologian Lanfranc used his knowledge of Greek philosophy to uphold the Church's doctrine of transubstantiation. He did so in reply to Bérenger of Tours, a French canon, who was teaching that it was contrary to reason to believe that the bread and wine consecrated at Mass are truly the Body and Blood

of our Lord. Lanfranc replied that such a belief is not at all contrary to reason, and he used the classic Aristotelian distinction between substance and accident to uphold the Church's traditional teaching. The senses, Lanfranc pointed out, perceive only the accidental (the apparent); they do not perceive the substantial (the essential). The Eucharist is *accidentally* bread and wine; but *substantially,* it is the Body and Blood of Christ. The true nature of the Eucharist, he argued, is no more apparent to the senses than is the true nature of man, for who can tell by sense perception alone that man has a soul?

St. Anselm. One of the foremost theologians and philosophers of this period was St. Anselm (1033–1109). Like other scholars, Anselm believed that reason can be a great aid to understanding the Faith, but he always cautioned against relying on reason too greatly, for human reason is imperfect. In matters of Faith, he taught, one must believe before attempting to understand. "I believe *in order that* I may understand," he said. Once reason is enlightened by Faith, however, it is capable of arriving at great truths. Anselm himself was a noted logician, and he drew up a purely logical proof of God's existence—a proof which he believed that every rational man, even the atheist, was bound to accept. He even proved that logically the rational man is incapable even of thinking that there is no God.

Abelard. The most famous thinker after Anselm was the Frenchman Abelard (1079–1142). Abelard shocked his contemporaries by insisting that much of Catholic teaching was unclear, even

St. Anselm, archbishop, theologian, and philosopher, after leading the life of a carefree nobleman, became a monk in Normandy. (Alinari)

contradictory. He said that the authorities on which Catholic teaching was based—the Bible, the Fathers of the Church, and Church councils—were not always in agreement. To illustrate his point, he wrote a book called *Sic et Non* ("Yes and No"), in which he listed one hundred and fifty-eight propositions concerning Catholic belief. After each proposition he quoted authorities that seemed to support it and others that seemed to contradict it. When *Sic et Non* caused a storm in Church circles, Abelard insisted that it was not his aim to deny Catholic teaching or to shake anyone's faith, but rather to stimulate men to use their reason to solve difficulties. Several times in his life, however, Abelard admitted that certain of his teachings were erroneous.

Peter Lombard. Abelard's technique of pointing out what seemed to be con-

tradictions in the Catholic sources was adopted by the theologian Peter Lombard (1100–1164). Lombard, however, went a step farther: by delving into the meaning of the sources, he showed that there were no real contradictions. He used this method in his great theological work, the *Four Books of the Sentences*. In the *Sentences* ("opinions"), as this work was popularly called, Lombard arranged the main teachings of the Church in an orderly, systematic fashion. In support of each teaching he quoted authoritative sources. Where the sources seemed to conflict, he explained them to show that the conflict was only apparent, not real. Lombard issued the *Sentences* as a purely unofficial collection, but this great work presented Catholic teaching so thoroughly and so accurately that it was approved by the Pope as an official presentation of Catholic doctrine.

One of the doctrines stated in Peter Lombard's Sentences, *adopted by the Church, was that a sacrament is both a symbol and a means of grace. (Library of Congress)*

Gratian and the canon law. Another great scholar who presented his material in a very systematic manner was the monk Gratian. His field was canon law. Around 1140, Gratian issued a great work on canon law in which he arranged the laws of the Church in logical order according to subject matter. Where the laws were unclear, Gratian interpreted them; where they seemed to conflict, he reconciled the differences. Lastly, through inductive and deductive reasoning he arrived at general principles that could be applied to situations not explicitly covered by the then existing laws. Gratian's work, which was popularly called the *Decretum,* was at first a purely unofficial collection. But its excellence was recognized by the Pope, and it was made the Church's official Code of Canon Law.

Recovery of science. In the twelfth century, Western scholars turned once again to a serious study of science. The obstacles they faced were enormous, for the scientific tradition had been all but lost in the West for hundreds of years. The primary task of twelfth-century scholars was, therefore, to recover the scientific knowledge of antiquity and to acquaint themselves with the more recent scientific discoveries of the Moslems. In Spain they found the scientific knowledge they were seeking; for the Moors, as they retreated south before the victorious advance of the kings of Castile and Aragon, left their great scientific libraries behind them.

With the assistance of learned Moslems, Spaniards, and Jews, Western scholars translated into Latin hundreds of Arabic works. Among these were the famous works of Avicenna on medicine and of al-Khwarizmi on algebra and trigonometry. For the first time Western scholars learned to use Arabic numerals and the zero— discoveries that were to revolutionize the study of mathematics. Many of the works which the Western scholars translated from Arabic into Latin had been written originally in Greek. Among these were the works of Aristotle on the various sciences; of Hippocrates and Galen on medicine; of Euclid on mathematics; of Archimedes on mathematics and physics; and of Ptolemy on geography and astronomy.

The first universities. A direct outcome of the great scholarly activity of the twelfth century was the founding of the first universities in the history of the world. They began in the following manner. As scholars, most of whom were teachers, became more specialized in their various fields, they formed professional teacher guilds. Four such guilds were founded whose specialties were theology, law, medicine, and arts. The members of the guilds were called master or doctor. A teacher guild was known in Latin as a *universitas;* and the first universities, as we understand the word today, were the schools organized and controlled by the teacher guilds (*universitates*). The goal of the students at the universities was to gain admission to one of the guilds. The requirements for admission to a guild were long years of study under masters or doctors, participation in scholarly debates, and the passing of strenuous oral examinations. Admission to a teacher guild was the equivalent of our modern-day university degree.

Four great universities were founded in the twelfth century: Paris, Bologna,

Salerno, and Oxford. Paris specialized in theology, Bologna in civil (Roman) and canon law, Salerno in medicine, and Oxford in the arts (literature, grammar, logic, rhetoric, and mathematics). The basic course in all universities was the arts. At the end of four or five years of study in the arts, the qualified student received his degree; that is, he was admitted to the guild of arts masters. If the master of arts aspired to become a doctor of law, theology, or medicine, he then entered upon a new course of studies for his higher degree. Four years of study beyond the arts degree were required for the degree of doctor of medicine, and as much as ten or twelve years for the doctorate in either civil and canon law, or in theology.

While studying for the master's degree in arts or for the doctorate, the student took a bachelor's degree. But the bachelor's degree had no great importance: it merely entitled the bachelor to do a limited amount of student teaching until he received his higher degree. At the commencement ceremony, which was held directly before the qualified student was admitted to the guild, the candidate "commenced" his teaching career by giving a prepared lecture before the assembled masters or doctors of the guild. After his commencement he received his degree; that is, he was formally admitted to the guild.

43. TOWNS IN WESTERN SOCIETY

The eleventh century, as we have seen, saw a great revival of industry and commerce in the West and of renewed trade between West and East. The tempo of this movement was quickened by the First Crusade. In the twelfth century, as industry and commerce continually expanded, there was a veritable revolution in the structure of Western society. Peasants left their manors to add to the ever-growing number of working people in the cities; new cities were founded and old cities grew larger; and the bourgeoisie—the new middle class in Western society—grew larger, wealthier, and more powerful.

Town revolts. The feudal lords, on whose lands the new cities of the West sprang up, tried at first to rule the townsmen in much the same way that they ruled their peasants. The townsmen resented this, for they found it very difficult to manufacture good products or carry on trade when their working hours were likely to be interrupted by a lord's demand for services of one kind or another. They disliked the fact that their cases were heard in the lord's court according to manorial law, that they had to pay a toll every time they entered a town gate or crossed a bridge, or that they were obliged to use the lord's mill and oven for grinding their wheat and baking their bread. The townsmen began to demand that their lords relieve them of peasant obligations and rule them in a manner that favored, rather than hindered, industrial and commercial activity. Many a lord gave in to this demand when the townsmen promised him large annual sums of money in the place of peasant services. Lords who did not give in soon found that their townsmen were in full revolt against them.

Town revolts were a very common occurrence in the twelfth century, with the result that the townsmen generally gained most of the rights they were seeking. Sometimes, aided perhaps by their lord's enemies, the townsmen actually beat their lord and his knights in the field. The victorious townsmen then forced their lord to grant them a charter that guaranteed the rights they were seeking. Other lords simply grew tired of the struggle with their townsmen and granted them charters in return for large sums of money and promises of still more.

Towns of limited liberties. In granting charters, feudal lords rarely signed away their authority over their towns. What they did was allow the townsmen certain privileges in return for annual sums of money. The privileges, or liberties, which most chartered towns enjoyed were these: The townsmen were recognized as free men; no townsman could be claimed as a runaway serf if he had lived in the town for a year and a day; the townsmen had full title to their property and could sell or will it to whomever they pleased; the townsmen could be tried only in the town court and by the special law of the town; the professional associations, or guilds, of the townsmen were protected by law, and no outside merchant or craftsman could sell his goods or set up shop in the town without the express permission of the guilds.

Communes and city-states. Some towns shook off the authority of their lords almost completely. Such towns were called communes. They elected their own officials, made their own laws, dispensed justice, and in some cases even coined their own money and had their own armies. In Italy the communes were so independent that they were really city-states. The Italian city-states formed alliances, went to war against one another, made treaties of peace, and in every way acted like sovereign states.

Flanders and Italy. The greatest concentration of towns was in Flanders and in northern Italy. There the towns were freest too. While the Italian towns were generally city-states, the Flemish towns were communes that recognized the higher authority of the Count of Flanders. The Italian and Flemish cities owed their prosperity to their old established industries and to geographical locations that were ideal for commerce. Fearing to sail through the Strait of Gibraltar up the Atlantic coast, merchant ships of the Mediterranean naturally chose the ports of northern Italy to unload their goods.

From northern Italy the merchant goods were carried by pack horse over the Alps and were then loaded onto barges that sailed down the great rivers into France, Germany, and the Low Countries. Flanders was the most industrialized region in the entire West. Its woolen industry employed thousands of workers, and Flemish cloth was in demand from Lisbon to Bagdad. Flanders was ideally situated for commerce too. Its central location in northwestern Europe and its ports on the North Sea made it easily accessible to ships from western France, England, Scandinavia, and Germany. Also, the rivers that flowed through or near Flanders made its cities accessible to river-borne traffic from all parts of western Europe.

City leagues. For commercial advantage and for their own protection, many cities formed leagues (called *hanses* in northern Europe). The cities of Flanders formed a great league called the London Hanse, so called from the great trade which these cities had with London. Many of the north Italian cities were organized as the Lombard League. In the thirteenth century the north German cities formed the great Hanseatic League. The member cities of a league regulated commercial dealings with one another, agreed on a common policy concerning trade with outsiders, and in some cases even had armies and navies which they threw at foreign powers that threatened the league's security.

The guilds. On the local level, the craftsmen of a town formed associations called guilds. Every craft had its own guild. There were guilds of shoemakers, metalworkers, furniture makers, hatmakers, dressmakers, candlemakers, etc. The members of the guilds were called master craftsmen. They were both manufacturers and retailers, for they sold the products they made directly to the public. Unlike modern manufacturers and retailers, the craftsmen were not in competition with one another. On the contrary, the chief aim of guild organization was to ensure that each guild member had equal opportunity to make a living. To achieve this aim, the guild regulated the number of hours the masters should work, the number of apprentices (trainees) and journeymen (hired craftsmen) they should employ, the quality of raw material they should use, the quality of work-

A goldsmith's workshop of the eighteenth century is depicted on this elaborate invitation to a meeting. The guilds set up standards of workmanship and price and established status for members in society.

manship they should turn out, and the price they should charge for their products.

The guilds were very exclusive and had a strong *esprit de corps*. Before a craftsman could become a member, he had to serve many years as an apprentice worker in the shop of a master craftsman. After that he worked several years as a journeyman or hired craftsman. When the journeyman could prove to the masters that he was proficient in his chosen craft and could afford to set up shop for himself, he was admitted to the guild as a master craftsman.

The activities of the guilds were more than strictly professional. The guilds had many religious and social functions which all members were required to attend. Every guild had its own chaplain, and the masters often attended Mass in a body. When one of the masters died, the guild saw to his proper burial, had Masses said for the repose of his soul, and provided for his widow and children.

The middlemen. The guild system worked best in towns where the craftsmen obtained their raw materials locally and sold their finished products to the local population. But in towns whose economy was geared for the international trade, the formation of guilds was very difficult. In Flanders, for example, the clothworkers had very little control over the cloth industry. The prosperity of this industry depended on the importation of raw wool from England and on the exportation of finished cloth to foreign countries. The business of getting wool into Flanders and shipping cloth abroad was very complicated. It was handled by big businessmen called middlemen or entrepreneurs. The clothworkers were merely the hired workers of these middlemen. It was not uncommon for such hired workers to demand higher wages and shorter working hours. Sometimes when their demands were not met they went on sitdown strikes and even resorted to physical violence.

Commercial institutions. By the end of the twelfth century the commercial institutions of the West were developing fast. Joint-stock companies, banking, and insurance had already come into existence. In joint-stock companies merchants pooled their resources for commercial enterprises involving great expense or risk. The percentage of the profits received by each mem-

This French or Flemish tapestry of the late fifteenth century is titled "The Hunt of the Unicorn." It is woven of wool and silk with silver and silver-gilt threads. (The Metropolitan Museum of Art)

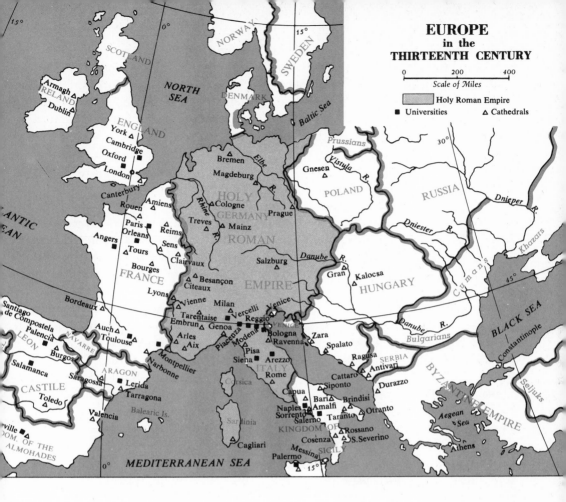

EUROPE
in the
THIRTEENTH CENTURY

Scale of Miles
0   200   400

☐ Holy Roman Empire
■ Universities   △ Cathedrals

ber depended on the number of shares he held in the company. Banks paid annual rates of interest to their depositors, lent money at interest, and insured merchants against the destruction of their goods by fire, theft, or shipwreck. Checks and letters of credit spared merchants the bother of shipping money when they did business with far-off places.

Decline of manorialism. The rise of the towns had a profound effect on rural life. The feudal nobles, who ruled great estates, were jealous of the wealthy townsmen, but nevertheless they craved the goods which the towns produced. At first, few nobles

had the money with which to buy goods. Their wealth was mostly in land, and most of the payments they received from their tenants and serfs were in the form of labor services. One way of getting money was to charge their peasants money rents in the place of labor services. The peasants were happy to make this change. With burdensome labor services out of the way, the peasants could find the time to grow more food and produce more raw materials. These, in turn, could be exchanged at the town markets for money. When labor services were replaced by money payments, manorialism and serfdom began to decline in western Europe. Serfs became, in effect, tenant farmers. It was many centuries, however, before every form of labor service was abolished. Lords still depended on their tenants to do such tasks as repairing the local roads and bridges.

From the twelfth century on, manorialism and serfdom declined at a rapid rate in western Europe. But in central and eastern Europe, where industry and commerce developed very slowly, manorialism and serfdom remained unchanged for centuries to come.

44. THE PAPACY AND THE EMPIRE; NORMAN ENGLAND

The Concordat of Worms (1122). The great struggle between Empire and Papacy which had begun under Pope Gregory VII and Emperor Henry IV continued into the twelfth century. The basic cause of dispute remained the same: whether the prelates of the Church were to be freely chosen by lawful electors or appointed by the emperor. In 1122 the emperor Henry V (1106–1125) finally agreed to make peace with the Papacy on terms that were drawn up by a council of bishops in the German city of Worms. Henry swore that he would allow cathedral chapters the freedom to elect bishops, and monks the freedom to elect abbots, provided that such elections were held in his presence. He swore never again to invest bishops and abbots with the ring and the staff, the symbols of their spiritual office.

Frederick Barbarossa (1152 to 1190). For over thirty years after the Concordat of Worms there was peace between the popes and the emperors. Then, in 1152, the German nobles elected as their king a man who was to threaten the freedom of the Church even more than had his predecessors. He was Frederick Barbarossa, a member of the great German family of the Hohenstaufen. Relations between Frederick and the Papacy were at first very cordial, and the Pope crowned Frederick Holy Roman Emperor. Frederick's concept of the imperial office, however, was bound to make trouble between himself and the Papacy. As "Emperor of the Romans," Frederick considered himself the heir to all the authority that had ever been exercised by Augustus, Constantine, Justinian, and Charlemagne. Whatever authority the Christian emperors had ever exercised over the Church and Italy, Frederick considered to be rightfully his. He claimed, in effect, universal authority, and he justified this claim by an appeal to the Roman law. In Frederick's day the Roman law, as preserved in Justinian's great *Corpus Iuris Civilis,* was being studied by many scholars, some of whom interpreted it in a manner most agreeable to Frederick. They said that the emperor was the supreme lawmaker in the world, that the imperial office was created by God, that the emperor was responsible to God alone, and that the emperor was commissioned by God to rule all Christians and to supervise the affairs of all institutions, including the Church.

The popes did not accept these interpretations, of course. They claimed, on the contrary, that the empire, as it then existed, was actually a creation of the Papacy; that no man could become emperor unless approved by the Pope; that all institutions, including the empire, were subject to the moral supervision of the Papacy; and that unjust emperors and kings could be deposed by the Pope.

The break between Frederick and the Papacy. Obviously Frederick's and the popes' positions were irreconcilable. A break between Frederick and the Papacy was almost inevitable and was finally brought on by a disputed papal election in 1159. Following the death of Pope Adrian IV in 1159, the cardinals split into two factions, and each faction elected its own Pope. The larger faction elected Alexander III (1159–1181); the smaller faction, Victor IV (antipope, 1159–1164). Frederick looked upon the double papal election as a golden opportunity to put into practice his claim to supervise the affairs of the Church. He therefore took it upon himself to decide who was the true Pope, and he awarded the title to Victor IV. Outside Germany, however, Alexander III was recognized as true Pope.

Frederick's defeat at Legnano. Frederick was determined not only to place his antipope in control of Rome but also to bring all of Italy under his control. Politically the Italians had no unity whatsoever. In northern Italy were the great city-states such as Milan, Genoa, Pisa, Florence, and Venice. In central Italy were the Papal States, ruled by the popes. In the south was the Norman state, which since 1130 had been called the Kingdom of Sicily. Under the leadership of Pope Alexander III, the north Italian cities formed a great alliance called the Lombard League. To this alliance Alexander added contingents from his own Papal States, and he succeeded in getting the Norman King of Sicily to send aid too. In 1176 the army of the Lombard League met Frederick's German army at the north Italian city of Legnano. The Germans were overwhelmingly defeated.

The union of the empire and Sicily. After Legnano, Frederick recognized Alexander III as the true Pope and acknowledged the almost complete independence of the Italian cities. For the moment, at least, the Papacy and Italy were free of imperial control. Several years later, however, a new danger loomed when Frederick succeeded in marrying his son and heir, Henry VI, to Constance, heiress to the Kingdom of Sicily. In 1189 the childless King of Sicily died and was succeeded by Henry and Constance as King and Queen of Sicily. On the death of his father Frederick in 1190, Henry was elected King of Germany, and in the following year he was crowned Holy Roman Emperor by Pope Celestine III.

The Papacy now found itself in an extremely dangerous position. Formerly the popes had counted on the Sicilians for aid against the empire. Now Sicily and the empire had a single ruler. The Pope was caught in between. Henry VI turned out to be just as ambitious as his father to control the Papacy, but before he could do any great damage he died suddenly in 1197. His heir was his three-year-old son, Frederick II. Frederick became King of Sicily by hereditary right, but he had no such claim to the imperial throne, which was elective. Since the

German nobles had no intention of electing a three-year-old child as their king, the danger which the Papacy had faced from a united empire and Sicily seemed to be past.

Weakness of the French kings. During the chaotic ninth and tenth centuries the kingdom of France became the most feudal of all countries. The Capetian kings, who reigned in France from 987 on, had little authority except in the Ile de France, the region around Paris. This region was the king's special domain, the Royal Domain. It was, in a sense, the king's own province, for it was the only part of France that was not ruled by some great duke or count. Only if the Royal Domain grew and absorbed the other French provinces could the King of France become a powerful king. Eventually the kings of France did succeed in adding all the French provinces to the Royal Domain, but this was a process that took several centuries.

William the Conqueror and the conquest of England (1066). In the eleventh century the most powerful noblemen in France were the dukes of Normandy. One of these dukes, William, wanted very much to be a king—King of England, to be exact. He claimed that England's king, Edward the Confessor (1042–1066), had made him the heir to the English throne. He also claimed that England's most powerful nobleman, Harold Godwin, the Earl of Wessex, had sworn to accept him as Edward's successor. But after Edward's death the English nobles chose Harold Godwin as king.

William of Normandy was not the only man who thought he had been cheated out of a kingdom. Harold Hardrada, the King of Norway, also claimed the English throne and invaded England with a powerful army in September, 1066. The armies of the two Harolds met at Stamford Bridge in northern England. Hardrada's army was crushed and Hardrada himself killed. William of Normandy, meanwhile, had landed on England's southern coast. No sooner, therefore, did Harold Godwin win his great victory at Stamford Bridge than he had to rush with his exhausted army to meet William. On October 14, 1066, Harold Godwin and William of Normandy met in deadly battle at Hast-

The coronation of William I in Westminster Abbey. William the Conqueror granted English lands to the Normans who aided him in his invasion and conquest of England. (British Information Services)

ings. Harold was struck and killed by an arrow, and his army of English foot soldiers, armed with primitive battle-axes, was dispersed by William's Norman cavalry. From that day until his death, William "the Conqueror" was England's king (1066–1087).

Shortly after his conquest of England, William began to give that country a decided Norman character. He divided England into a great number of fiefs, which he distributed to his Norman followers. The English landholders whom he dispossessed fled either to Scotland or overseas, or were absorbed into the common people of England. As the English bishops and abbots died off by degrees, William replaced them with churchmen from France. Thus England came under the rule, both political and ecclesiastical, of Frenchmen (called Anglo-Normans to distinguish them from the Frenchmen of France). England's culture, too, began to be affected in a marked degree by French culture. The Anglo-Norman nobles and churchmen introduced French styles of architecture in building castles, cathedrals, churches, and monasteries. The literature and learning that were flourishing in France were also brought over to England.

The "English lands" in France. Even before his conquest of England, William had been a powerful rival of his own feudal lord, the King of France. Not only did William hold the Duchy of Normandy, but he also was the overlord of two French provinces, Maine and Brittany.[1] After his conquest of

The reign of Henry II in England was one of reorganization, order, and progress. Through his efforts, royal justice was strengthened and expanded. (Library of Congress)

England, William, as Duke of Normandy, was still the vassal of the King of France. As King of England, however, William was no one's vassal. He was the royal equal of the King of France. In actual power, indeed, he was more than the equal of the French king. Not only did he rule England and Normandy with a firm hand, but as King of England he was the overlord of Scotland and Wales. How could the King of France ever hope to become a strong ruler when one of his own vassals was a king far more powerful than himself?

Instead of brightening, the picture steadily grew darker for the Capetians. In 1154 Henry of Anjou, a great-grandson of William the Conqueror, became King of England (Henry II, 1154–1189). From his Norman mother

---

[1] This meant, in feudal terminology, that the counts of Maine and Brittany were the vassals of William.

Henry inherited England, Normandy, and the overlordship of Brittany and Maine. From his father, the Count of Anjou, Henry inherited the French counties of Anjou and Touraine. Through his wife, Eleanor of Aquitaine, Henry became the duke of the largest of all the French provinces, Aquitaine. As if he did not have titles enough, Henry assumed the title of Lord of Ireland after several of his vassals acquired a foothold in that land in 1170. Henry was the most powerful king of his time, and the King of France had every reason to fear him; for Henry ruled no less than two-thirds of France at a time when the Capetian king still had little authority outside the Royal Domain.

Henry II and Ireland. From the beginning of his reign Henry gave thought to making Ireland a part of his dominion. He doubted that the Irish would offer unified resistance, for they were far from being a united people. The island was divided into several kingdoms, and the kings were often at war with one another. In 1166 one of these kings, Dermot MacMurrough, was driven from his kingdom of Leinster. Determined to regain his throne, Dermot sought assistance from England. He struck a bargain with Richard de Clare, Earl of Pembroke, whereby de Clare promised to help Dermot regain his throne; and Dermot, in return, recognized de Clare as his heir.

In 1170, Richard de Clare (called "Strongbow" by the Irish) landed in Ireland. With the help of his own and Dermot's followers, he conquered Leinster. On Dermot's death in 1171, Strongbow assumed the title of King of Leinster. The Irish, however, were not content to let an Anglo-Norman rule as an Irish king. Led by Rory O'Connor, King of Connaught, they hemmed in Strongbow in the fortress of Dublin.

Late in 1171, Henry II came to Strongbow's assistance. He landed with a strong army, and most of the Irish kings submitted. Henry granted fiefs in eastern Ireland to a number of his Anglo-Norman vassals, and he recognized Strongbow as King of Leinster. Dublin and its surrounding countryside he annexed outright to the English crown. This area became known as the Irish Pale (i.e., enclosure), and for centuries it was the only part of Ireland which the English effectively governed. As time went on, the Norman lords in Ireland tended to blend with their Irish subjects, and in the west of Ireland native kings continued to rule until the sixteenth century.

Henry II and the common law of England. In the long run Henry II had a far greater influence on England than on France. Though he spent most of his reign in France and never even learned to speak English, he greatly influenced the development of English law. When Henry became King of England, English law was still very Germanic. Cases were still settled by the old methods of trial by battle, compurgation, and the ordeal, and legal customs varied greatly from county to county.

The changes that Henry made in English law had far-reaching effects. He improved legal procedure by introducing trial by jury. He introduced the system of writs, which entitled a man to have a case settled according

Thomas à Becket, Archbishop of Canterbury, was martyred by knights who broke into the cathedral. Henry II was indirectly responsible for the death of his former chancellor. (Pierpont Morgan Library)

to the king's law and by a jury. He promoted the use of circuit judges, who traveled to all parts of England enforcing the king's law. All these innovations—trial by jury, writs, and circuit judges—helped to establish one law, the king's law, throughout all of England. Thus was founded the common law of England.

The grand jury. Henry laid down several of his legal reforms in a famous document called the Assize of Clarendon (1166). Following the instructions contained in the assize, royal judges periodically visited the county courts of England. In every county court the judges assembled a number of free men whom they organized as a jury. This jury, called the presentment jury, was required to "present" the names of all persons in the county who were suspected of crime. When this was done, the accused were summoned to the court and were made to undergo the ordeal of water to determine their innocence or guilt. The presentment jury was, of course, the ancestor of the modern grand jury. Its naming of persons suspected of crime is known as indictment.

The petit jury and writs. Henry also founded the petit jury, which is the jury that gives verdicts in court cases. In Henry's day the petit jury heard only property cases, which it settled according to the king's law. Any Englishman who wanted a property dispute settled in this manner first applied to the chancellor of England for a writ. A writ was an order instructing the sheriff of a particular county to assemble a jury of twelve men for the purpose of settling a dispute according to the king's law. Unlike modern juries, the juries in Henry's day were made up of men who were already familiar with the case in question. Thus the jurors were, in effect, witnesses too.

REVIEW

STUDY SECTIONS IN REVIEW
41. The Church and Civilization
   A. Why do we say that civilization was in a low state from the sixth to the eleventh century?
   B. Identify the following: papal curia, papal bull, excommunication, ecumenical council.

c. Explain the position of an archbishop in the hierarchy of the Church.

D. How did the Cistercian Order differ from the older Benedictine Order?

42. Literature and Learning

A. What languages developed from vernacular Latin from the sixth century forward?

B. Identify the following: *Beowulf, Song of Roland,* mystery play.

c. Cite a contribution to knowledge by St. Anselm, Peter Lombard, and Gratian.

D. What universities came into being during the twelfth century?

43. Towns in Western Society

A. What caused the "town revolts" of the twelfth century?

B. Describe at least four privileges usually granted by a lord in a town charter.

c. What was the purpose of the guild system?

D. What was the effect of the rise of towns on rural life?

44. The Papacy and the Empire; Norman England

A. How did Frederick Barbarossa differ with the Pope over the authority of the emperor?

B. Why was France "the most feudal of all countries" in the tenth century?

c. How did French influences come to be introduced into England in the eleventh century?

D. Was the domain of the English king, Henry II, confined to the British Isles? Explain.

E. Identify the following: common law, grand jury, petit jury.

THE CHAPTER IN REVIEW

A. Review the decrees of the great ecumenical councils of the twelfth century. Are any of these decrees still in effect?

B. Discuss the purpose and work of the guilds in the twelfth century.

c. How did the guild system influence the founding of early universities? What major divisions of knowledge were taught in twelfth-century universities?

D. What were the principal legal reforms introduced in England by William the Conqueror and his successors?

In two or three paragraphs describe the work of St. Bernard of Clairvaux. Quote a few lines of his poetry written in honor of our Blessed Mother.

Analyze the *Song of Roland* or one of the mystery plays, which you can obtain in your library, to show what it reveals of the ideals, the attitudes, and the standards of the age.

Analyze the ways in which the development of the towns tended to weaken the structure of feudal society.

Enter an essay in your notebook showing how Henry II's legal and judicial reforms might affect you as an American citizen claiming certain political and civil rights.

SELECTED READINGS

The best general description of the twelfth century is Urban Tigner Holmes, Jr., *Daily Life in the Twelfth Century* (Madison, Wis.: University of Wisconsin Press, 1952). This book is written for adults, but high school students should have no difficulty reading it and enjoying it.

Louise Lamprey, *Masters of the Guild* (Philadelphia: Lippincott, 1920), is a good study on the high school level of guilds and of medieval industry. Equally useful is the same author's *In the Days of the Guild* (New York: Frederick A. Stokes Co., 1918).

The relationship between Church and civilization is well covered in two biographies. Written for general consumption, these books should not be difficult for high school students: Robert Speaight, *St. Thomas of Canterbury* (New York: G. P. Putnam's Sons, 1938); and Helen Waddell, *Peter Abelard* (New York: Henry Holt & Co., 1933). Miss Waddell is a medieval scholar who has reconstructed Abelard's life in the form of a novel; Mr. Speaight's study is a simple, interestingly written biography.

Pope Innocent III

Chapter 16. Papal Supremacy in Feudal Europe

In 1198 the cardinals elected to the Papacy Innocent III, who in the opinion of all historians was one of the greatest popes in history. In his effort to make men follow Christ's law, Innocent was involved in practically every major event of his time. His decisions affected the history of nations. Yet Innocent's reign was by no means an unqualified success. He had his failures and disappointments too. Perhaps the important lesson to be learned from Innocent's reign is that no Pope, however great his concern for justice, can ensure the triumph of justice when the men on whom he relies betray him.

Innocent and Philip Augustus of France. Early in his reign Innocent showed in his handling of a dispute with the King of France that his concern for justice far outweighed his fear of offending the great. The issue between Pope and king concerned the sanctity of the marriage vow—a matter on which earlier popes had taken a firm stand and on which later popes would take an equally firm stand. Before Innocent became Pope, the King of France, Philip Augustus (1180–1223), persuaded a council of French bishops to annul his marriage with Ingeborg, a Danish princess. Ingeborg, however, stubbornly refused to recognize the annulment, even after Philip had taken another wife. When her appeal reached Innocent, the Pope reviewed the case and ruled that there were no valid grounds for annulment. He ordered Philip to put away his unlawful wife and reinstate Ingeborg as his wife and queen. When Philip refused,

Pope Innocent III (Library of Congress)

Innocent placed France under interdict in 1199. The severity of the interdict forced Philip to have second thoughts on the matter, and in 1200 he bowed to the Pope's wishes.

Philip Augustus and John of England. On the field of battle Philip Augustus was somewhat more successful than in his quarrel with the Pope. We have already seen that the Capetian kings wielded little authority in France outside the Royal Domain. The kings of England, who held about two-thirds of France in fief, actually had greater power in France than the Capetians. From the beginning of his reign Philip waited for the opportunity to weaken his great English vassal. King John of England (1199–1216) finally presented him with such an opportunity.

John, a very unpopular king, oppressed his subjects, both English and French, by extorting money from them and by abusing them in numerous other ways. Philip sensed, therefore, that John's subjects would not support him in any great action. In 1202, when John failed to fulfill his feudal obligation of appearing at Philip's court, Philip declared that all of John's fiefs in France were forfeit. Many of John's French vassals promptly recognized Philip as their lord and offered him their services. Beginning in Normandy, Philip began to occupy the English lands. Brittany, Normandy, Maine, Anjou, Touraine, Poitou, La Marche, and Auvergne fell to Philip's armies. By 1208, Philip was in control of all the English king's lands except those in southwestern France. As we shall see, the rivalry between Philip and John made both kings seek European allies and involved them in a yet greater conflict over the Holy Roman Empire.

Innocent and the Holy Roman Empire. Germany during Innocent's reign was a land of troubles. After the death of King Henry VI in 1197, the German nobles could not agree on a successor. One faction of nobles chose Otto of Brunswick as king. Another faction chose Philip of Swabia, a brother of the late King Henry. Both Otto and Philip petitioned Innocent for recognition.

Innocent believed that there were two good reasons why he should decide who was King of Germany. First, because both Otto and Philip had presented their claims to him; second, because he who was King of Germany would someday be crowned Holy Roman Emperor, and the Pope considered that it was his duty to pass on

Richard I, King of England (1189–1199), also known as Richard the Lionhearted, was a central figure in English romance and a symbol of chivalry because of his participation in the Third Crusade. (British Information Services)

the fitness of the candidate for such high office. After reviewing the claims and fitness of each candidate, Innocent recognized Otto as king (1201). Philip refused to accept the Pope's decision and prepared to win the throne by force. Otto of Brunswick found an ally in his uncle, King John of England. Philip Augustus of France allied with Philip of Swabia. Never before had the Pope and so many monarchs of Europe been involved in a single struggle.

Innocent and John of England. In the years that followed, Philip of Swabia steadily gained the upper hand in Germany, while at the same time his ally, Philip Augustus of France, busily seized John's lands in France. John himself, though he supported the Pope's candidate for the German throne, shortly entered into a dispute with the Pope over the archbishopric of Canterbury. In 1206 the cathedral chapter of Canterbury elected Cardinal Stephen Langton as archbishop. John had wished one of his own favorites to be chosen archbishop and refused to recognize the election of Langton. He confiscated the property of the archbishopric of Canterbury and persecuted and robbed whoever took Langton's side. These acts moved Innocent to place England under interdict in 1208.

In that same year Philip of Swabia, who had all but won the German throne by force, was assassinated. Otto of Brunswick, the Pope's original candidate, was then accepted by the German nobles as King of Germany. But no sooner had Innocent crowned Otto Holy Roman Emperor than Otto was seized with the imperial ambitions of his predecessors. He laid claim to Italy as part of his empire, occupied the Papal States, and invaded the kingdom of Sicily, a vassal state of the Holy See.

Innocent and Frederick II. In 1210, Innocent came forward with a new candidate for the German throne: Frederick II, the King of Sicily. In return for the Pope's support, Frederick swore that he would never unite the kingdoms of Germany and Sicily. He promised to turn over Sicily to his son as soon as the latter came of age. Many of the German nobles rallied to the youthful Frederick, who was a member of the old royal family of the Hohenstaufen.

Meanwhile King John of England came back into the Pope's favor in 1213. After five years of terrible interdict, England was on the verge of rebellion, and King Philip Augustus of France was preparing to cross over to

The lifetime of Frederick II (1194–1250) was spent in almost constant conflict with the Papacy, which he had grown to despise. With the death of Frederick II in 1250, the House of Hohenstaufen fell and the great days of the empire ended. (Library of Congress)

Augustus won a stunning victory over the forces of Otto of Brunswick and John of England. The results of this battle were momentous. Otto of Brunswick's cause was ruined, and Frederick II was assured of the German throne. Philip Augustus' hold on the provinces he had taken from John was assured, and thus the Capetian monarchy was set firmly on its feet. John's prestige suffered its final blow, and the English nobles were spurred to unite and force John to accept the Magna Carta, an event we shall consider in the next chapter.

The battle of Bouvines was, of course, a great victory for Innocent III, since it meant the ruin of Otto of Brunswick and the triumph of the Pope's candidate, Frederick II. What the Pope did not know was that the man whom he had made King of Germany would someday prove to be one of the greatest enemies the Papacy ever had.

The Fourth Crusade (1202 to 1204). One of the projects closest to Innocent's heart was the crusade. In the half century prior to Innocent's reign, the crusader states of Syria suffered a terrible decline. The Turks steadily gained strength and captured one crusader city after another. Under their great leader Saladin, they shocked the Christian world in 1187 by capturing Jerusalem. Though the West organized two major crusades during the twelfth century, neither crusade was able to do much for the rapidly disintegrating crusader states. By the end of the twelfth century nothing remained of these states except a few fortified cities on the Syrian coast.

In 1202, Innocent finally got

England and take the crown for himself. To save his throne, John surrendered to the Pope. Not only did he recognize Langton as archbishop and promise to make amends for all the damage he had done the Church, but he also put himself in vassalage to the Pope.

The battle of Bouvines (1214). Still John was not entirely in the Pope's good graces, for he continued to support Otto of Brunswick in Germany. Philip Augustus of France threw his support to the Pope's candidate, Frederick II. Finally, the great contest involving the Pope and the four kings was decided on the battlefield of Bouvines, in Flanders. On July 27, 1214, Philip another crusade under way. Instead of going to the Holy Land as the Pope ordered, the crusaders sailed to Constantinople. They did so in response to the plea of a deposed Byzantine emperor, Isaac Angelus. Isaac promised to supply the crusaders with soldiers and money for the crusade if they first restored him to his throne. The crusaders accepted the offer, and in 1203 they forced the Byzantines to take back Isaac as their emperor.

The Latin Empire of Constantinople (1204 to 1261). In 1204 the Byzantines revolted against Isaac and drove him from his throne. Shortly afterward, Isaac died. The crusaders, who had never received the soldiers and money that Isaac had promised them, attacked the Byzantines and captured Constantinople for themselves. They installed one of their leaders, Baldwin of Flanders, as emperor. Next they conquered Thrace and the Greek peninsula, which they carved into great fiefs. Thus the old Byzantine Empire passed out of existence—for the time being. The Latin Empire which took its place was nothing more than a great conglomeration of fiefs. It had no more unity than the old crusader kingdom of Jerusalem had had. East and west of the Latin Empire, the Byzantines still clung to large areas of their own fallen empire. Like the Turks after the First Crusade, the Byzantines needed only a strong leader to deliver a mortal blow to the unwanted feudal state in their midst. They found such a leader in the Byzantine nobleman Michael Palaeologus. In 1261, Michael drove the Western feudal lords from Constantinople and refounded the Byzantine Empire.

The crusade in Spain. The failure of the Fourth Crusade to reach the Holy Land was, of course, a bitter disappointment to Innocent III. But in Spain, where there was a "perpetual crusade" against the Moors, Innocent's efforts to check the Moslem advance met with great success. At the beginning of Innocent's reign, the outlook had been none too bright for the Spanish Christians. A warlike Moorish dynasty, called the Almohades, ruled the southern half of the Spanish peninsula and was slowly pushing to the north. Christian resistance was feeble, since the five Christian kingdoms of northern and western Spain—Portugal, Leon, Castile, Navarre, and Aragon—were more often at war with one another than with the Moors. In 1211, Pope Innocent made a fervent plea to the Spanish kings to put aside their differences and turn again to the task of reconquering Spain from the Moors. The Pope also sent pleas to Christians north of the Pyrenees to join the Spaniards. The response to the Pope's appeals was gratifying. All of the Spanish kings, save the King of Leon, joined forces to drive back the Moors. Volunteers poured into Spain from beyond the Pyrenees, twenty thousand knights coming from France alone. The Almohades, seeing that the Christians intended a showdown battle, assembled a great army, but on July 16, 1212, they were overwhelmingly defeated at Las Navas de Tolosa. So decisive was this battle that the power of the Moors in Spain was broken forever, and the way was open for the rapid advance of the Christian kingdoms into the south.

The Gate of Glory in the cathedral in Santiago, Spain, a masterpiece of Romanesque art, was built in the twelfth century by the architect Mateo. (Spanish Tourist Office)

46. INNOCENT III AND THE RELIGIOUS LIFE OF THE WEST

The Waldensians. A matter which engaged much of Innocent's attention was the problem of heresy. Two great heresies, Waldensianism and Albigensianism, were disturbing the Church in several parts of Europe. The Waldensians were a sect that foreshadowed in many ways the later Protestants. They taught that every good man was a priest; that the Bible contained all the truth that could be known about God; that the Eucharist was only a symbol of the Body and Blood of our Lord; that only persons who had reached the age of reason could be lawfully baptized; that private confession to a priest was of no more value than public confession to the whole congregation; that all religious services should be held in the vernacular; and that indulgences, veneration of relics, and Masses for the dead were superstitions. The Waldensians accused the Catholic clergy of greed and luxury, and they taught that all true Christians should choose voluntarily to live in poverty.

The Waldensians had many followers, especially in France, Italy, and Germany, but also in as widely separated places as Spain and Poland.

Pope Innocent sent out preachers to counteract their influence and worked tirelessly to win back the Waldensians to the Church. His success was notable, and many of them returned to the Church. Some, however, have persisted to the present day, especially in the Alps.

The Albigensians. A far different heresy was Albigensianism. In fact, Albigensianism strayed so far from Christian doctrine that it became a religion entirely different from Christianity. The Albigensians were strong in southern France, a cosmopolitan region where ideas from the pagan and Moslem East were constantly filtering in. Many of the Albigensian teachings can be traced to the ancient mystery religions of the East and to the Zoroastrianism of the Persians.

The Albigensians taught that there were two gods, a god of good and a god of evil. All spiritual things were created by the god of good, while all material things were created by the god of evil. Our souls, for example, were created by the god of good; our bodies by the god of evil. Since the body was an evil thing, it was wrong to reproduce it. Consequently, marriage and the begetting of children were evil. Death was good, since it destroyed the body; death by suicide was especially good.

The Albigensian Crusade (1209 to 1229). Innocent III saw that Albigensianism, if it continued to spread, would do far more than damage the Church. If its inhuman, or rather anti-human, teachings prevailed, civilization itself might be destroyed. He dispatched preachers to southern France to counteract the Albigensians, but the preachers met with little success. He pleaded with the powerful Count of Toulouse and other nobles of southern France to stop tolerating the heresy, but in vain. The Albigensians had grown so strong that the Catholics themselves were in danger of their lives. Finally, when the Albigensians murdered a papal legate, Innocent declared a crusade against them. He deposed the Count of Toulouse and other lords of southern France from their positions of authority, and authorized the crusaders to assume the vacant posts. Many nobles from northern France responded to the Pope's appeal for a crusade.

The war that broke out lasted twenty years. Scores of cities were destroyed, and thousands of persons,

St. Francis of Assisi preached the virtues of poverty, simplicity, and manual labor. (Library of Congress)

Albigensian and Catholic alike, died in the fighting. Peace came only in 1229. By the terms of the Treaty of Meaux, which ended the struggle, the Count of Toulouse was obliged to recognize Alphonse, the brother of the King of France, as his heir to the County of Toulouse. Many years later, when Alphonse died without heirs, the County of Toulouse was annexed to the Royal Domain of France. Thus the Albigensian Crusade had both religious and political significance. It led to the destruction of a great heresy and to the ultimate annexation of a large French province to the Royal Domain, thus adding to the ever-growing power of the King of France.

The Franciscans and Dominicans. The spread of heresy and the need of combating it help explain why Pope Innocent encouraged the founding of two new religious orders during his reign. These new orders were the Franciscans and Dominicans. Their founders, St. Francis of Assisi (1182–1226) and St. Dominic (1170–1221), were greatly disturbed by the spread of heresy. They saw that if people were first taught the truth they would be far less likely to fall into error later. Before the time of Francis and Dominic, the common people rarely had a thorough knowledge of Christian doctrine. They did not learn it in school, since most of them did not go to school. Nor did they learn it in church, since it was not the custom in those days for priests to deliver sermons at Mass. The danger that the common people would fall into religious error was particularly great in the cities. City people had far more contact with one another than people in the country, and ideas

To counteract the Albigensian heresy, St. Dominic devoted his life to the conversion of heretics and the defense of the Faith. (Alinari)

spread quickly. Moreover, many city people were completely out of contact with priests, for the cities of Europe had grown so quickly that there were not nearly enough parishes.

The friars' vocation. Encouraged by Pope Innocent III, St. Francis and St. Dominic founded groups of religious who went into both city and country to preach to the Catholic people and to heretics, and to minister to the religious needs of the people in general. The members of the new orders were called friars (from the Latin *fratres*, "brothers"). As proof of their detachment from the things of this world, the friars gave away all their worldly possessions and lived in strictest poverty. They craved but one thing that this world could offer them—souls for Christ. They preached in city market places and in village squares; they heard confessions, baptized children, sought out fallen-away Catholics, visited the sick and the dying, and assisted the poor in their needs. From the friars the common people learned to know Christ better than before, and the tide of heresy was in great part stemmed.

St. Francis and St. Dominic, it must be noted, were the first to found great religious orders that were specially dedicated to preaching the Word of God and ministering to the spiritual needs of the Catholic people. Other religious orders had often done such work in response to the crying needs of the time. But no religious order, before the Franciscans and Dominicans, had ever been expressly founded for that purpose. Thus, with St. Francis and St. Dominic, a whole new concept of the religious vocation entered the Church. Of the many religious orders founded since their time, the great majority have been dedicated to ministering to the needs of the Christian people, as in mission work, hospital work, social work, and teaching.

The Fourth Lateran Council (1215). In 1215, Innocent held the greatest ecumenical council the West had yet seen. Some of the dogmas that it infallibly defined and some of the laws it decreed are familiar to every Catholic. Owing to attacks on the Eucharist by such persons as Bérenger of Tours and the Waldensians, the council defined in very precise terms the doctrine of transubstantiation. The council established two new laws of the Church when it decreed that Catholics must confess their sins to a priest at least once a year and receive Communion during the Easter season. It also took steps to correct abuses that were especially prominent at that time. It condemned the writings and teachings of certain heretics and ordered bishops to try heretics in the episcopal courts. It forbade lay rulers to tax the clergy without papal permission. It condemned a number of abuses within the Church, such as the system of pluralities (the holding of two or more bishoprics by a single bishop). It condemned trial by battle and trial by ordeal as barbarous customs, and it strictly forbade the clergy to be present at such trials. As a result of this prohibition, trial by battle and trial by ordeal quickly disappeared as official proofs in the courts of the old Germanic law.

As Innocent lay dying in 1216, he could look back on a pontificate that was filled with many accomplishments and with many disappointments. He had played an energetic role in most of the great events of his day, and to a great extent he had directed their course. Few of Innocent's successors were to play directly so decisive a role in world affairs. Already great changes were taking place that would weaken the Pope's influence in such affairs.

45. Innocent III and the Western Monarchies

A. What was the cause and result of the original dispute between King Philip Augustus and Pope Innocent III?

B. What action was taken by Philip against English possessions in France?

C. Why did Innocent III believe that he should settle the dispute over the German kingship?

D. Identify the following: Otto of Brunswick, Frederick II, Cardinal Langton.

E. What was the result of the Fourth Crusade?

46. Innocent III and the Religious Life of the West

A. What were the principal points of the Waldensian heresy?

B. How did the Albigensian heresy depart from Christian doctrine?

C. How did the Dominican and Franciscan orders help to combat these heresies?

D. What significant dogmas were defined by the Fourth Lateran Council?

THE CHAPTER IN REVIEW

A. List those who supported Otto of Brunswick for the German throne. What events split this alliance?

B. Review the important results of the climactic battle of Bouvines (1214).

C. Why did Innocent III believe strong action was necessary to end Albigensianism? What were the results of the Albigensian Crusade?

D. How did the Dominican and Franciscan orders differ from earlier monastic orders such as the Benedictines?

FOR YOUR NOTEBOOK

Draw a diagram in which you make the battle of Bouvines the waistline of an hour-glass figure. In the upper section put down all the events, circumstances, and alliances that lead up to this decisive battle; in the lower section list the results that followed the decision rendered at Bouvines.

Put yourself in the position of a typical medieval Catholic and explain why you consider heresy more serious a crime than we consider treason today.

One of the truisms in Church history is that "new needs produce new orders." Analyze the "new needs" that produced (1) the Franciscans, and (2) the Dominicans.

SELECTED READINGS

Good coverage of this chapter's material is given in a little book by Sidney Packard, *Europe and the Church under Innocent III* (New York: Henry Holt & Co., 1927). This is one of the "Berkshire Studies in European History," short books on restricted periods of European history written by scholars for students and put into simple form.

A popular biography covering most of this material is that by Joseph Clayton, *Pope Innocent III and His Times* (Milwaukee, Wis.: Bruce Publishing Co., 1941). Also helpful for filling in your knowledge of this period are biographies of two great saints and founders of religious orders: Bede Jarrett, *Life of St. Dominic* (Westminster, Md.: The Newman Press, 1947); and Johannes Jorgensen, *St. Francis of Assisi* (Garden City, N. Y.: Doubleday & Co., Image Books, 1955). An interesting view of social, religious, and cultural life can be found in the unusual study of Robert Gordon Anderson, *The Biography of a Cathedral* (New York: Longmans, Green & Co., 1945). This book is written for general popular consumption, and it should not prove difficult for high school students.

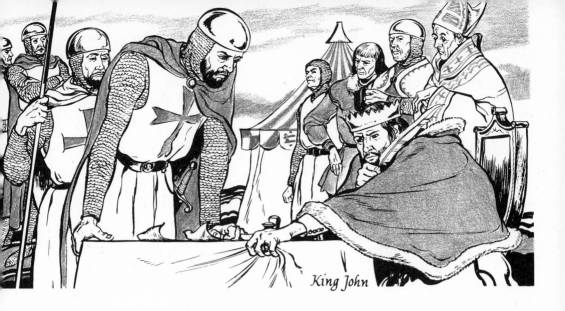

King John

Chapter 17. The Weakening of Papal Leadership

47. LAST GREAT STRUGGLE BETWEEN EMPIRE AND PAPACY; ENGLAND IN THE THIRTEENTH CENTURY

Emperor Frederick II. Frederick II, King of Sicily, King of Germany, and Holy Roman Emperor, owed all three of his crowns to the Papacy. When in 1197, at the age of three, he inherited the Kingdom of Sicily, a vassal state of the Holy See, the Sicilian nobles would never have accepted Frederick as their king had not Pope Innocent III zealously protected Frederick's interests. In 1211, Innocent persuaded the German nobles to elect Frederick King of Germany. In 1220, Innocent's successor, Honorius III, crowned Frederick Holy Roman Emperor. If the popes thought that their support of Frederick would make him a friend to the Papacy, they were sadly mis-

taken. Frederick and his sons became involved in the greatest struggle with the Papacy the West had yet seen. The basic cause of this struggle was, as usual, the emperor's desire to dominate Italy and the Church. The final result was nothing less than the complete destruction of the Hohenstaufen dynasty.

Before Frederick was elected King of Germany, he made three solemn promises to Pope Innocent III: first, to keep his kingdoms of Germany and Sicily separate; second, to respect the liberties of Italy and the Church; third, to make a crusade to the Holy Land. By 1227, Frederick had broken all three promises, and he was excommunicated by Pope Gregory IX. Frederick's excommunication was the signal for the outbreak of the last great struggle between Empire and Papacy.

Aided by the Italian cities and by rebellions in Germany and Sicily, Pope Gregory and his successor, Innocent IV, barely managed to hold their own with Frederick. At one point Innocent IV had to flee for safety to France, and in 1245 he held a great ecumenical council at Lyons which deposed Frederick from all his thrones. Deposition disturbed Frederick not in the least. It merely made him more determined than ever to subject Italy and the Papacy to his rule.

The destruction of the Hohenstaufen. Before he could realize his aims, Frederick died in 1250. His son Conrad followed him to the grave four years later, leaving only an infant son, Conradin, to succeed him. The German nobles would not accept Conradin as their king, nor could they agree on any other candidate. Germany, consequently, fell into great confusion.

Since the Hohenstaufen no longer ruled Germany, the popes concentrated on defeating Frederick's son Manfred, who had unlawfully made himself King of Sicily. Needing powerful support, Pope Urban IV offered the Kingdom of Sicily to Charles of Anjou, the brother of the King of France. In 1266, Charles led an army of Frenchmen into southern Italy and defeated and killed Manfred at the battle of Benevento. Two years later he defeated and captured the fifteen-year-old Conradin, the last of the Hohenstaufen. Charles executed Conradin in Naples, and thus the house of Hohenstaufen came to an end.

The Sicilian Vespers. In making Charles of Anjou King of Sicily, Pope Clement IV had failed to consider one thing: the sentiments of the Sicilians. It was the popes, not the Sicilians, who wanted to get rid of the Hohenstaufen. On the island of Sicily itself (which was the southern half of the Kingdom of Sicily) the Hohenstaufen had been popular rulers. The Sicilians, therefore, hated Charles of Anjou as an intruder and hated him all the more because he ruled them severely. On Easter Monday, 1282, at the hour of vespers, the Sicilians rose in a great

Monte S. Giuliano, a Sicilian castle. Because of the conditions of medieval life, in which wars were frequent, castles had the twofold function of residence and fortress. (Alinari)

rebellion. They offered the crown of Sicily to Manfred's son-in-law, King Peter III of Aragon, and with Peter's help they drove the French from the island. When Peter refused to evacuate the island of Sicily, Pope Martin IV excommunicated him. Next the Pope deposed him. Finally, in 1284, the Pope proclaimed a crusade against him. But all to no avail: Peter stayed in Sicily.

The result of the War of the Sicilian Vespers was the splitting of the Kingdom of Sicily into two separate kingdoms. The southern kingdom (comprising the island of Sicily) was ruled by Peter III and his descendants. The northern kingdom (comprising mainland Italy south of Rome) was ruled by the descendants of Charles of Anjou. Both kingdoms kept the official name of Kingdom of Sicily, but historians call the mainland kingdom the Kingdom of Naples to distinguish it from the island Kingdom of Sicily. In the fifteenth century the two kingdoms of Sicily were reunited under a single ruler. From that time until the eighteenth century the reunited kingdom was called the Kingdom of the Two Sicilies.

Decline of papal prestige. Though the Papacy had rid itself of the Hohenstaufen and of the threat of a united Germany and Sicily, its victory obviously was not undimmed. The War of the Sicilian Vespers taught the popes that neither excommunications nor crusades could force Catholic peoples to accept rulers they did not want. Though most Catholics were sympathetic to the Papacy's determination to maintain its rights, they did not necessarily approve what the main-

tenance of those rights led to. The proclamation of a holy crusade against the Catholic King of Aragon over a matter that many Catholics regarded as purely political came as a profound shock. To many Catholics it seemed that the popes were acting more as great temporal princes than as the supreme spiritual leaders of the world. The bitter struggle with the Hohenstaufen and the War of the Sicilian Vespers undoubtedly lowered papal prestige.

To meet the great expense of the papal administration and, above all, of the papal wars, the popes had to make increasing demands on the clergy for money. The clergy grumbled, as did the laity too, for in the long run the papal revenues came from all their pockets. Despite their increased revenues, the popes still did not have enough money to pay the many clerical officials who staffed the curia. Consequently the popes began the practice of paying their assistants and clerical staff in benefices. (A benefice was an ecclesiastical position that provided its holder with a good income; e.g., the post of canon in a cathedral or the pastorate of a wealthy church.) The practice of "providing" clergy with benefices was known as *provisions*. Most of the "provided" clergy were Italians, and they were sometimes provided with benefices far from Rome; e.g., in Poland and Ireland. Only rarely did the provided clergy perform the duties of their benefices in person. Usually they hired local clergy to perform such duties and had the bulk of the revenues of their benefices forwarded to themselves.

Rudolf of Hapsburg (1273 to 1291). The struggle between Empire and Papacy had one very important result for Germany: it virtually assured the autonomy of the great German nobles and cities. While occupying themselves with Italian, papal, and Sicilian affairs, the German emperors had neglected to build up a strong monarchy in Germany. Indeed, they had deliberately surrendered some of their royal rights to the German nobles and cities in order to gain support for their ventures south of the Alps. How the imperial ambitions in Italy came to ruin, we have already seen.

For many years after the death of Frederick II, the German nobles could not agree on whom to elect as king. Finally, in 1273, they chose Rudolf of Hapsburg, a rather obscure German nobleman. Rudolf was the first of the German kings to whom the Pope granted the title, but did not crown, Holy Roman Emperor. After Rudolf, it became the custom for the German king to be called automatically Holy Roman Emperor.

Rudolf had no ambitions in Italy and stayed away from that land altogether. In Germany his authority over the nobles and cities was very slight. The one great achievement of his reign was that he added a number of German territories, including the Duchy of Austria, to his family possessions. The ability to acquire new lands proved to be a Hapsburg trait. This ability would one day make the Hapsburgs the greatest territorial family in the world.

England and the Great Charter. The reign of King John of England (1199–1216) was an unbroken series of fail-

The signing of the Magna Carta by King John at Runnymede. The charter was forced upon the king by the nobles, who demanded a guarantee of respect for their rights.

ures and misdeeds. He lost most of the English lands in France to the Capetians; he brought a terrible interdict on England by refusing to recognize Stephen Langton as Archbishop of Canterbury; he made an alliance with his nephew, Otto of Brunswick, that ended in the terrible defeat at Bouvines; and throughout his reign he repeatedly violated the rights of his English subjects, nobles and commoners alike—especially by extorting large sums of money from them. In 1215 the English nobles rebelled against John. He had few supporters, and in order to save his throne he had to accept the terms of peace which the nobles dictated. These terms were drawn up in a great document called the Magna Carta ("the Great Charter").

The Magna Carta is in the form of a long list of promises on John's part to respect certain rights of the English people and to bring about certain reforms in the government. Few of the articles in the charter contained anything new. For the most part they merely restated or clarified the time-honored rights of the English people, especially of the nobles. Even the most famous of the articles, such as Articles Twelve and Thirty-nine, merely confirmed the ancient customs of England. In Article Twelve, John swore that he would levy aids (i.e., taxes) "only with the common assent of our kingdom." In Article Thirty-nine he swore that "no free man shall be arrested, or imprisoned, or dispossessed from his land, or outlawed, or exiled, or in any way destroyed, nor will we go against him, nor will we send against him, except by the legal judgment of his peers and by the law of the land."

The importance of Magna Carta lay in the fact that a number of very important rights of the English people, and John's promise to respect those rights, were set down *in writing*. Also, Magna Carta served to remind the English people how they could force a king to do their bidding, since by it *everyone* was under the law. For centuries after John's death the English were frequently to appeal to Magna Carta when they thought their rights were being violated. With the passing of time they even forgot the literal meaning of the charter and mis- interpreted some of its articles to justify liberties which the authors of the charter never even dreamed of.

Henry III and the Provisions of Oxford. As might have been expected, John failed to respect the promises he made in the charter. Again the nobles rebelled, but before they could drive him from his throne John died. His son, Henry III (1216–1272), promptly reissued the charter in order to pacify the nobles, thus holding onto the throne which his father almost lost. Over the years, however, Henry proved to be almost as bad a ruler as his father. He was dominated by unscrupulous persons and allowed his favorites to mismanage the government. He went to war with France in the hope of winning back the lost English lands but was promptly defeated. He tried to conquer Wales but failed. He tried to get his brother elected King of Germany and his son appointed King of Sicily, but in the end he had nothing to show for his efforts but a pile of debts.

In 1258 the English nobles resolved to call a halt to Henry's misadventures by forcing the king to accept a number of reforms, called the Provisions of Oxford, which greatly curtailed his power. The chief reform was the setting up of several committees (appointed mostly by the nobles) whose advice Henry was bound to follow in all important matters of government. Henry, of course, detested this arrangement, and in 1264 he announced that he would no longer abide by it. Thereupon the nobles, led by Simon de Montfort, the Earl of Leicester, banded together and captured the king.

The first English Parliament. After Henry's capture, Simon de Montfort was virtually the ruler of England for an entire year. To enlist support for changes he intended to make in the government, de Montfort summoned (in the king's name) a great assembly of nobles, bishops, knights, and burgesses (townsmen). This assembly was the first Parliament in English history. Though it had long been the custom for the king to meet separately with groups of nobles, bishops, knights, and burgesses (especially when he was seeking money from them), these groups had never before met as a single body. De Montfort's Parliament, however, was far from being representative of the English nation, since it was attended only by men who sympathized with his rule. Indeed, de Montfort had many more enemies than friends, and in August 1265 he was defeated and killed in battle by the king's son, Edward.

Edward I (1272 to 1307) and Parliament. Edward I was the first King of England since the Norman Conquest whose everyday language was English rather than French. He was also the first king since the Conquest who was really popular with the English people. His great intelligence, high sense of honor, and strong devotion to duty steered him away from the pitfalls into which his father and grandfather had fallen.

The most notable event in Edward's reign was the growth of Parliament. Edward called Parliament frequently, not because he felt obliged to do so, but because he chose to do so. Parliament granted the king money, approved his decrees, acted as

Edward I, popular King of England, was outstanding for his efforts to extend the English rule to all of Britain. In his first campaign against Scotland, he humiliated Scotland by removing the Coronation Stone from Scone to Westminster. (Library of Congress)

a high court of justice, and attended to various matters of government. Edward accomplished through Parliament, therefore, what would otherwise have had to be done in a much more bothersome way. Moreover, by sounding out the opinions of his people before he took any important step, Edward found that he was far more likely to get co-operation from them. Thus Parliament was a source of strength to Edward. Also, he learned by contact with Parliament how far he might go in the exercise of his authority, and so he avoided the difficulties that had plagued his father and grandfather.

Edward's wars in Wales and Scotland. Parliament made generous grants of money to Edward to enable him to wage two great wars of conquest, in Wales and in Scotland. Like the English kings before him, Edward claimed that Wales and Scotland were vassal states of England. Neither the Welsh nor the Scots, however, took this claim very seriously. Consequently, when they failed to give Edward the respect which he considered his due, he set out to conquer them. In 1284 he defeated Llewelyn, the Prince of Wales, and annexed Wales to England. To make the Welsh think that they still had a prince, he conferred the title of Prince of Wales upon his son. Ever afterward it has been the custom for the heir of the English throne to be called Prince of Wales.

In Scotland, Edward's wars of conquest (1295–1307) failed completely. First under William Wallace, and later under Robert Bruce, the Scots stoutly resisted all of Edward's attempts to conquer their country. The Scots were assisted by the French, and thus began an historic alliance between Scotland and France that would last for more than three hundred years. Seven years after Edward's death (1314) the English gave up their attempt to conquer Scotland when Robert Bruce annihilated the English forces at the great battle of Bannockburn.

48. THE RISE OF THE FRENCH MONARCHY; SPAIN AND MEDIEVAL PARLIAMENTS

Growth of the Royal Domain. During the thirteenth century France grew into a powerful monarchy, as the Capetian kings added more and more provinces to the Royal Domain. We have already seen that the rapid rise of the French monarchy began in the reign of Philip Augustus (1180–1223). From

John of England, Philip seized the provinces of Normandy, Maine, Anjou, Touraine, Poitou, La Marche, and Auvergne. Through marriage and inheritance he acquired several feudal districts in northeastern France. Before the end of the century two other great provinces were annexed to the Domain: the counties of Toulouse and Champagne. The County of Toulouse was annexed when its count died without heirs in 1271. Champagne was annexed when King Philip the Fair (1285–1314) married its heiress.

St. Louis (1226 to 1270). If Philip Augustus strengthened the monarchy by giving it a firm territorial basis, his grandson, Louis IX, gave it even greater strength by winning for it the devotion of the French people. Louis, who was canonized in 1296, was a rarity among kings. From his earliest childhood he strove to live as closely

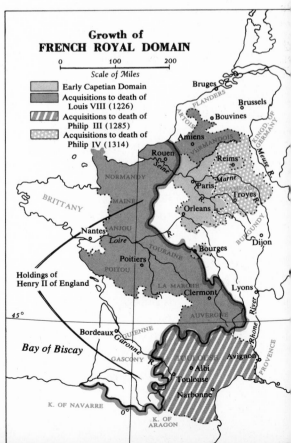

Growth of
FRENCH ROYAL DOMAIN

0   100   200
Scale of Miles

Early Capetian Domain
Acquisitions to death of
Louis VIII (1226)
Acquisitions to death of
Philip III (1285)
Acquisitions to death of
Philip IV (1314)

Holdings of
Henry II of England

Louis IX, saintly King of France, encouraged the religious orders, rebuilt monasteries, and assisted his mother, Queen Blanche, in founding the convent of Maubuisson. (Alinari)

handful of Christian cities along the Syrian coast still held out against the Turks. The Christians in the East looked to the West for help, but in the West there was little enthusiasm for a crusade. Louis managed, nevertheless, to organize a crusade in 1248, but it was only devotion to the king or the offer of money that induced men to follow him. Five years Louis fought in Egypt and Syria; few of his men stayed with him, and the crusade was a failure. On a second crusade in 1270, Louis died. Twenty-one years later the Moslems captured the last of the crusader cities in Syria, and the history of the crusades in the Holy Land came to an end.

The bourgeoisie strengthens the monarchy. As the Royal Domain grew larger, the power of the French nobility was naturally weakened. The expansion of the Domain meant, of course, the elimination of great dukes and counts. Though many nobles remained, none was so powerful as to rival the king himself. The power of the nobility was weakened, too, by the rise of the bourgeoisie. Formerly the king had depended almost exclusively on the nobles to provide him with an army and to serve in his government, but the rise of the bourgeoisie relieved the king of this dependence. The bourgeoisie voted the king taxes, which enabled him to hire professional soldiers. From the bourgeois class came well-educated men who served as the king's councilors and officials. Though the nobles continued to play an important role in the army and the government, their monopoly was broken.

Some of the educated bourgeois who served in the king's council were

to Christ as possible. Though he sought praise from no man, all men knew of the spotless purity of his personal life, of the devout spirit in which he daily heard Mass, of the trustworthiness of his word, and of his wholehearted devotion to the happiness and spiritual welfare of the French people. So great was St. Louis' reputation for justice that rulers of foreign countries called on him to arbitrate their disputes with one another and even to settle their internal problems.

St. Louis' crusades. One of St. Louis' greatest ambitions was to bolster the declining strength of the Christians in the Holy Land. By his day only a students of the Roman law, and they helped to give the king a new concept of monarchy. The king, they said, was entitled to exercise just as much authority over his kingdom of France as the emperors of Rome had exercised over the old Roman Empire. Since the king was responsible for the well-being of his subjects, he should take whatever steps he considered necessary to ensure that well-being. The bourgeois advisers of the king were fond of quoting the old Roman dictum, "What pleases the prince has the force of law." How seriously a French king could take this dictum was seen in the reign of Philip the Fair.

Philip the Fair and Pope Boniface VIII.
St. Louis' grandson, Philip IV, the Fair, was heir to the powerful monarchy built by his ancestors, Philip Augustus and St. Louis. The way in which he used his great authority was no credit to him, however. For several years of his reign he engaged in a great quarrel with the Pope, Boniface VIII (1294–1303). This quarrel broke out in 1296 when Philip levied a tax on the French clergy to help finance a war he was waging with England. Taxation of the clergy without papal consent violated the rights of the Church, and Boniface promptly reminded Philip of this fact in a bull entitled *Clericis laicos*. Philip replied to *Clericis laicos* by forbidding all shipments of money from France. His aim was to cut off the Pope from all papal revenues that ordinarily came from, or through, France. Boniface retreated to the point where he declared that kings could tax the clergy without papal permission, provided such taxes were used for the defense of the realm.

Through his lack of statesmanship, Boniface VIII failed to stop Philip IV from his illegal levies on the clergy. He was the first Pope to declare a holy year. (Alinari)

Philip and the Estates-General (1302).
Having successfully defied the Pope on one score, Philip proceeded to violate other rights of the Church. In 1301 he arrested a French bishop, whom he accused of treason and intended to put on trial in a secular court. When Boniface condemned this action, Philip began a campaign to make the Pope hated by the French people. He and his councilors drew up false bulls in which they pretended that Boniface claimed that the King of France was no more than the Pope's underling and that the Pope could squash the king at a moment's notice. These false bulls were publicized as genuine among the French people. To gain further backing for his campaign against the Pope, Philip called together a great assembly of the French people

in 1302. This assembly was composed of representatives of the three social classes of France—clergy, nobles, and commoners. Such classes were known in France as "estates," and thus this general meeting of all three estates was called the Estates-General. The Estates-General which Philip summoned was the first to meet in French history. Taken in by Philip's propaganda against the Pope, the Estates-General sent letters to Boniface, protesting his "mistreatment" of their king.

The Pope's patience was now at an end. In November 1302 he issued a great bull entitled *Unam sanctam,* in which he affirmed that the spiritual authority of the Papacy is the highest authority on earth and that kings who misuse their temporal authority are subject to the correction of the Pope. Shortly afterward the Pope warned Philip to respect the rights of the Church—or face excommunication.

The Crime of Anagni (1303). Philip, meanwhile, had shrewdly sized up the Pope's position in Italy. It was unstable, to say the least. There was no great power in Italy that could come to the Pope's defense in case he was attacked. Since the collapse of imperial rule in Italy, the north Italian city-states had broken off their alliance with the Papacy and were constantly engaged in struggles with one another. Southern Italy and Sicily were just coming out of the War of the Sicilian Vespers. Moreover, Boniface's position in his own city of Rome was very insecure. The noble Italian family to which Boniface belonged had many enemies, several of whom, including two cardinals, sought to undermine the Pope's authority by falsely accusing him of horrible misdeeds, such as murdering his predecessor and buying his way into the Papacy.

Seeing the weakness of the Pope's position, Philip planned one of the boldest—and most shameful—acts of the century. He sent several of his officials with a small army to Italy with instructions to seize the Pope and bring him to France for trial! In September 1303, Philip's agents made their way to Anagni, where Boniface was staying. They broke into the Pope's quarters, struck him in the face, and held him prisoner for three days. They were preparing to drag him to France when the townspeople, aided by a small army of the Pope's relatives, drove the French from the city. So dazed and famished was Boniface after his three-day imprisonment that he wandered into the market place of Anagni and begged: "If there be any good woman who would give me an alms of wine and bread, I would bestow upon her God's blessing and mine." Boniface was escorted back to Rome, where he died a month later.

The Avignon Papacy. Men everywhere pointed an accusing finger at Philip, but none was prepared to punish him for his crime. The cardinals were so frightened of what Philip would do next that after the brief pontificate of Benedict XI (1303–1304) they elected a Frenchman as Pope. This was Clement V (1305–1314). Since Rome and the Papal States had fallen into great disorders after Boniface's death, Clement established a "temporary" residence at Avignon, in southern France. For the next seventy years the popes, all of whom were Frenchmen, resided in this city.

The Destruction of the Templars. Clement V chose to tread softly with Philip, and so emboldened the king all the more. After Boniface VIII, Philip chose as his next victim the great military order of the Templars. To gain the Templars' wealth and to cancel the debts which he personally owed them, Philip resolved to destroy them. To do so "legally," he put them on trial for such various crimes as heresy, sorcery, and immorality. The verdict of Philip's courts was a foregone conclusion. The Templars were tortured into making confessions, and later when they retracted their confessions they were sent to the stake as relapsed heretics. Clement V highly disapproved of these proceedings but, remembering the fate of Boniface VIII, dared not stop them. Without sustaining Philip's charges against the Templars, Clement issued a bull in 1311 that simply dissolved the order. The Pope ordered the property of the Templars to be turned over to other religious orders, but Philip managed by various devices to seize most of it for himself.

Obviously the world of the fourteenth century was a rather different place from that of the twelfth and thirteenth. In the centuries just ahead, it would change even more.

The Spanish reconquista nears its end. After the power of the Moors was broken at Las Navas de Tolosa in 1212, the three kingdoms of Castile, Portugal, and Aragon expanded quickly into the south. By 1270 they had conquered all of Moorish Spain except the kingdom of Granada at the tip of the Spanish peninsula. Granada became a vassal state of Castile, and so the *reconquista,* or Christian reconquest of Spain, was almost completed. Castile was the largest of these expanding kingdoms. In 1230 its king had inherited the kingdom of Leon, and the Castilians had gone on to conquer the lion's share of the Moorish lands in the south. In the north the little kingdom of Navarre came under the rule of French princes and consequently ceased to play an important role in Spanish affairs.

The Spanish Cortes. Culturally and linguistically, the differences among the three Spanish kingdoms were very great. In one very important respect, however, the kingdoms were very much alike. Each of them developed a parliament, or *cortes,* at an early date. As early as the twelfth century the kingdom of Leon had a powerful *cortes,* made up of clergy, nobles, and townsmen. By the thirteenth century, the Cortes was an established institution in all the Spanish kingdoms. In Castile the king could levy taxes only with the consent of the Cortes, and the Cortes introduced legislation in the form of petitions, as the English Parliament was to do in the following century.

In Aragon the Cortes was even stronger than in Castile. In 1283 the Aragonese Cortes forced King Peter III (of Sicilian Vespers fame) to accept the *Privilegio General.* The "General Privilege" was an Aragonese Magna Carta. In accepting it, King Peter guaranteed that the laws, customs, and privileges of the Aragonese would be respected, that no man would be condemned without due process of law, and that representatives of the three estates would sit on the king's council. Several years later Alfonso III of Aragon recognized the right of the Cortes to appoint members to his council, and he formally admitted that the Cortes could depose a king for mismanagement of the royal office. The oath which the Aragonese nobles swore to the king at his coronation illustrates their independent attitude toward the monarchy:

We who are as good as you swear to you who are no better than we, to accept you as our king and sovereign lord, provided you accept all our liberties and laws; but if not, not.

Medieval parliaments. Parliamentary government was a unique contribution of the High Middle Ages (twelfth and thirteenth centuries) to the development of political institutions. To what degree the founding of parliaments was influenced by the example of such religious parliaments as the Cistercian general chapter and the later general chapters of the Franciscans and Dominicans is not known. But it is very likely that the influence of the religious parliaments was very great. The Dominicans, as a matter of fact, established in the thirteenth century the most representative government the world had ever known. Their general chapter, which was the supreme executive, legislative, and judicial body in the order, was made up not only of the elected heads, or priors, of the various Dominican houses but also of friars who were specially elected by each Dominican house and by the friars at large to sit in the general chapter. It would be many centuries before secular governments established parliaments that represented their nations as well as the Dominican general chapter represented all the Dominican friars.

By the end of the thirteenth century there were parliaments in most of the Western monarchies. According to the feudal concept of monarchy, when a king planned an important step (such as issuing a law or levying taxes), he was bound to get the consent of those whom his action would most affect. Until the twelfth century, kings ordinarily consulted only their nobles and bishops. When the townsmen grew wealthy, well educated, and trained in practical affairs, kings began to consult them too. Parliaments developed for the simple reason that they were the most convenient way of consulting those whom the king was obliged to consult—clergy, nobles, and townsmen.

The function of the medieval parliament was, in brief, to aid and advise the king in running the government and to authorize him to do such things (e.g., issue laws and levy taxes) as the king, by virtue of his office alone, had no right to do. Occasionally, of course, parliaments acted as a check on kings who tried to overstep the limits of their authority. With the passing of time, parliaments often tended to invade the legitimate authority of kings. When this happened, kings began looking for ways to weaken their parliaments, and eventually most kings succeeded in rendering their parliaments ineffectual.

49. THE MONGOL CONQUESTS: WEST MEETS EAST

The West, as we know, had suffered many barbarian attacks. After the Germanic barbarians and the Huns of the fifth and sixth centuries, there came in rapid succession the Moors, the Avars, the Vikings, and the Magyars. Finally, with the defeat of the Magyars in the tenth century, the barbarian invasions came to an end. After that, the West itself went on the offensive. Though the West failed in its design to set up permanent Christian states in the Holy Land and in the Byzantine Empire, it succeeded in making the Mediterranean virtually a Christian lake, and in the thirteenth century it broke the power of the Moors in Spain. Then, all of a sudden, the barbarians returned.

The Mongols and Genghis Khan. The new barbarians were the Mongols, or Tartars, as the West called them. Their homeland was north of China in east-

central Asia, where their descendants, the Mongolians, live to this day. Before the twelfth century the Mongols, who were nomads, were divided into many independent tribes. East and west of them lived kindred tribes. Toward the end of the twelfth century a young Mongol chieftain, Temujin (born 1162), began the conquest of all the Mongols and of the many kindred tribes. By 1206 he was in firm control of a vast area stretching from the Aral Sea in the west to the Sea of Japan in the east. In that year he assumed the name Genghis Khan ("Perfect Warrior") and set out to conquer the world.

Rarely had civilized men seen the like of the Mongols. Whatever Genghis Khan commanded, they did. Their

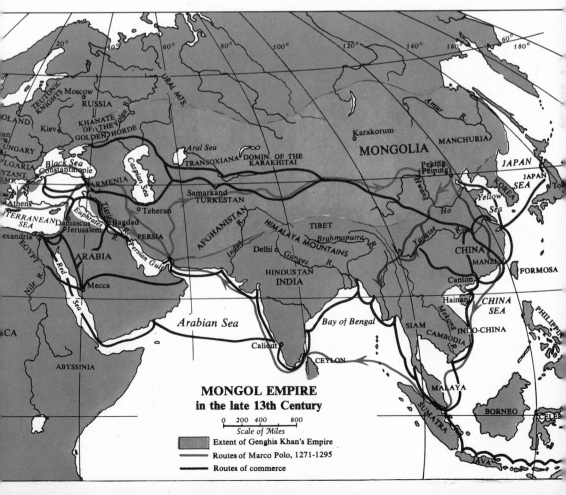

MONGOL EMPIRE
in the late 13th Century

0   200 400   800
Scale of Miles

Extent of Genghis Khan's Empire
Routes of Marco Polo, 1271-1295
Routes of commerce

horsemanship was superb, and they could aim an arrow as well from a fast-moving horse as when they were standing still. They needed very little food to sustain themselves, and they frequently ate their meals while riding at full speed. In war they were very savage, caring nothing whatsoever for human life. They often put to death every inhabitant of the towns they captured, and their tortures were as fiendish as any ever thought up by man. Yet the Mongols, once they conquered a land, were no harder on their subjects than other conquerors have been. Provided their subjects were submissive and paid tribute, the Mongols allowed them to practice their ancient ways.

The Mongol conquests. During the reign of Genghis Khan (1206–1227) the Mongols conquered northern China, Korea, and all southwestern Asia between the Indus River and the Caspian Sea. Under Genghis' son Ogodai, who succeeded his father as Great Khan (1229–1241), one group of Mongol armies attacked southern China, while another pushed into Russia. Russian resistance was very disorganized, since Russia was divided into several independent principalities and had no acknowledged leader. From 1237 to 1240 the Mongols, led by Batu, a grandson of Genghis Khan, captured one princely Russian city after another. With the destruction of Kiev in 1240, almost all of Russia became subject to the Mongols and remained under Mongol domination for the next two centuries. Only one Russian city, Novgorod, in the northwestern part of Russia, remained free of the Mongol yoke.

The Mongols invade the Catholic West. Batu led the Mongols on into Poland and Hungary. Cracow and Budapest, the leading cities in Poland and Hungary respectively, were captured and destroyed. The Mongols advanced to the Adriatic Sea, sacking the cities along its shores. Batu called his westward march to a halt when he heard that Ogodai, the Great Khan, had died. It was the custom for all the Mongol leaders to participate in the election of a new Great Khan, and so Batu returned with his armies to the East. What would have been the fate of western Europe had Batu not withdrawn, we shall never know.

Destruction of the Abbasid caliphate. The Mongols never returned to the West. Henceforth they concentrated on southeastern and southwestern Asia. During the khanate of Kublai Khan (1257–1294), a grandson of Genghis Khan, the Mongols destroyed Bagdad and brought to an end the five-hundred-year-old Abbasid caliphate. From Bagdad the Mongols moved to Syria, capturing Damascus and Antioch. Preparing to move into Egypt, the Mongols suffered one of their rare setbacks when the Egyptian sultan defeated their army a few miles north of Jerusalem. The Mongols continued to hold northern Syria for a while, but after a second defeat by the Egyptians, in 1281, they withdrew to Mesopotamia.

Kublai Khan (1257 to 1294). In the East, Kublai Khan ruled more as a Chinese emperor than as a Mongol war lord. He adopted the Buddhist religion, spoke Chinese, and built the city of Peiping. He conquered southern China and Burma but failed in

Kublai Khan, Emperor of China and the last great ruler of the Mongols, encouraged foreign commerce and allowed several Europeans to visit his magnificent city of Peiping. (Hulton Picture Library)

his attempt to bring Japan under his rule. Kublai gave little attention to Mongol affairs outside China, and during his reign the great Mongol empire began to split into independent khanates.

Western travelers in the East. In 1245, when the West was still expecting a renewed Mongol attack, Pope Innocent IV dispatched a Franciscan friar, John Carpini, to the court of the Great Khan in far-off Mongolia. Carpini's mission was to convert the Mongols to the Catholic Faith and to arrange an alliance between them and the West against the Moslems. Several years later St. Louis of France entrusted another Franciscan friar, William of Rubruck, with a similar mission. Both Carpini and Rubruck safely made the overland journey to and from the court of the Great Khan, but neither man succeeded in converting the Mongols or in making an

alliance. Their journeys, however, were not in vain. When they returned home they wrote official accounts of their travels, in which they gave detailed descriptions of the countries and peoples they had encountered. Thus, for the first time in Western history, men began to acquire accurate knowledge of the vast lands that lay to the east of Europe.

Marco Polo (1254 to 1324). The man who did more than anyone else to acquaint the West with the fabulous East was Marco Polo, a Venetian merchant. From 1275 to 1292, Polo lived in China (which the West called Cathay) as the guest of Kublai Khan. He learned the Mongol and Chinese languages and rose to high office in the khan's court. He even served as the governor of a Chinese province and performed many missions for the khan which took him to distant parts of the Mongol empire.

After his return to the West, Marco Polo wrote an account of his travels.

Marco Polo, Venetian traveler to the court of the Emperor of China, found favor with Kublai Khan and remained for seventeen years. (Hulton Picture Library)

This work, *The Travels of Marco Polo,* was the most accurate description of Asia and its peoples that had ever been written. He described not only the lands he had visited—Persia, central Asia, Mongolia, China, Indo-China, Malaya, Sumatra, Burma, India, and Mesopotamia—but also many lands of which he had gained knowledge from oriental travelers—Asia north of the Arctic Circle, Japan, Java, Ceylon, Arabia, Abyssinia, and the eastern coast of Africa as far south as Madagascar.

The Catholic Church in the Far East. As long as Mongol khans ruled the greater part of Asia, communications between East and West were fairly easy. The khans allowed Catholic missionaries, travelers, and merchants to visit the East, and the missionaries made little groups of converts all the way from the Caspian Sea to the Sea of Japan. The greatest of the missionaries was the Franciscan John of Montecorvino, who labored in China from 1291 to 1338. He set up an archbishopric in Peiping, nine bishoprics in other parts of China, and fifty Franciscan monasteries. Though several Mongol khans expressed great interest in Christianity, none of them was ever converted. Most of the Mongols became either Moslem or Buddhist. The khans of Persia, for instance, became Moslem, while the Mongol emperors of China became Buddhist.

Toward the end of the fourteenth century the Mongol power rapidly declined, and Asia fell into a great deal of confusion. In 1368 the Chinese drove out their Mongol emperors. Since the Church had been introduced into China under the patronage of the Mongol emperors, the Chinese denounced it as a Mongol institution. In other Mongol khanates the subject peoples imitated the Chinese and sought to throw off the Mongol yoke. During these years the Church suffered a great setback, and communications between East and West became very difficult. The West, however, was not content to let China and the East pass from its mind. Since Westerners could no longer go overland to the East, men began to dream of finding a water route to the land of Cathay and the other lands of the fabulous East.

50. THEOLOGY AND SCIENCE IN THE THIRTEENTH CENTURY

The recovery of Aristotle's philosophy. Great thinkers of the eleventh and twelfth centuries—St. Anselm, Abelard, and Peter Lombard—leaned heavily on Aristotle to teach them how to think logically, but they had been acquainted with only a small number of his works. During and after the lifetime of these men, scholars were working hard at the task of translating Aristotle's works (covering almost every branch of human knowledge) into Latin. By the early thirteenth century all of Aristotle's works were at last available in Latin.

We saw in Chapter 15 that many of Aristotle's works were translated, not from the Greek in which they had been written, but from Arabic. The Moslems had long regarded Aristotle as the greatest of philosophers. They had translated all his works into Arabic and had written lengthy commentaries interpreting these works. When Western scholars translated Aristotle from Arabic into Latin, they translated the Arabic commentaries as well. Indeed they were nearly as interested in reading what the Moslem commentators had to say about Aristotle as they were in reading Aristotle himself.

The greatest of the Moslem commentators was Averroës, who lived in Moorish Spain in the twelfth century. Averroës was greatly respected by Western scholars, but his interpretations of Aristotle were opposed by Catholic teachers on many points.

St. Thomas Aquinas, the "Angelic Doctor," quoted St. Hilary in setting forth the reason for writing the Summa Contra Gentiles: *"I am aware that I owe this to God as the chief duty of my life, that my every word and sense may speak of Him." (Alinari)*

St. Thomas Aquinas (1225 to 1274).

St. Thomas Aquinas was an Italian nobleman who at the age of twenty entered the Dominican Order. He was educated at the universities of Naples and Paris and studied at Cologne under a great Dominican teacher, Albert the Great (c. 1193–1280). St. Thomas was himself a great teacher and for several years was professor of theology at the University of Paris. He taught that "it is impossible that the truth of faith should be opposed to those principles that the human reason knows naturally." The ability to reason is given to man by God. If man uses his reasoning power *correctly*, he cannot possibly arrive at conclusions that conflict with the revealed word of God. Truth is one. The truths of reason and revelation come from the same divine wisdom and are by nature in harmony with one another.

St. Thomas wrote many works on philosophy and theology. To show that Aristotle had been misinterpreted in places by the Moslem commentators, St. Thomas wrote detailed commentaries on the works of Aristotle in which he set forth the meaning of Aristotle.

The Summa Contra Gentiles. In one of his greatest works, the *Summa Contra Gentiles,* St. Thomas aimed to show how the truths of philosophy led man toward the Christian religion. Among the truths Thomas proves from reason are: that God exists, that God is one, that God is everywhere, that God knows all things, that God is eternal, and that God created the world out of nothing.

The Summa Theologiae. The crowning work of St. Thomas' career was his unfinished *Summa Theologiae*—a truly great synthesis of Christian teaching. The subject of the *Summa Theologiae* is God, in Whose love all reality is born and also completed. St. Thomas' single-minded aim in this long work is to understand, as far as man can, the life of God and how it was that God created man in order to give him a share in that life. To St. Thomas, God is a perfect being, and this means not only that He is powerful and wise, and true and good, beyond all measure, but also that He is generous. The whole story of the creation of man, of his life on earth, of the means that God has given him to lead that life, is the story of God's generous desire to share His life with the angels and with man. St. Thomas follows this story from God the generous Creator to God the compassionate Redeemer, giving to man the help to journey to the eternal happiness that God has offered him.

Experimental science. Thanks to the labors of the twelfth-century translators, the scholars of the thirteenth century had at their disposal a vast body of science, mostly Greek and Moslem in origin. The task of mastering this material, and of making it available to as many readers as possible, was enormous. Some scholars wrote digests and encyclopedias of science; others wrote learned commentaries on the Greek and Moslem scientific works. One of the greatest of the commentators was Albert the Great, the teacher of St. Thomas Aquinas. Albert carried on many experiments of his own and occasionally corrected errors he found in Aristotle. He instilled into his students the "scientific attitude"—the attitude of the man who seeks to determine

Albertus Magnus, or "Albert the Great," the teacher of St. Thomas Aquinas, was a great scientist and scholastic philosopher and was called Doctor Universalis *because of his vast knowledge in all fields. (Alinari)*

through experiment the natural causes of things, who does not accept explanations simply because they are time-honored or because somebody else said so. When people insisted to Albert that it was common knowledge that ostriches ate iron, Albert, like a good scientist, put this "common knowledge" to the test. He tried in vain to get ostriches to eat iron, offering them all their hearts could desire.

Roger Bacon (1214 to 1294). The most zealous of the thirteenth-century students of science was the English Franciscan, Roger Bacon. Bacon was keenly aware of what science could achieve. He conceived of flying machines, underwater craft, and horseless carriages. He was acquainted with gunpowder and knew of the terrible uses to which it could be put. Though thoroughly absorbed in science, Bacon never lost sight of the fact that science must not be sought merely to make life more comfortable or to make the weapons of war more deadly. He continually stressed that science must serve the moral and spiritual betterment of mankind. If it fails to do this, he taught, it had best be left alone.

Though the great age of scientific inventions and discoveries still lay in the future, scientific advancements of a very practical nature were constantly being introduced. In the thirteenth century we hear for the first time of eyeglasses, mechanical clocks, and the mariner's compass. Eyeglasses and mechanical clocks are believed to have originated in China. Whether the mariner's compass was invented in the West or in one of the Moslem countries remains uncertain.

REVIEW

STUDY SECTIONS IN REVIEW

47. Last Great Struggle between Empire and Papacy; England in the Thirteenth Century
A. What was the goal of King Frederick II of Germany in his struggle with the Papacy?

B. How did the factors surrounding the War of the Sicilian Vespers weaken papal prestige?

C. How did the struggles between German emperors and the Papacy benefit German nobles?

D. Why did the English nobility rebel against King John?

E. Identify the following: Provisions of Oxford, Simon de Montfort, Edward I.

F. What resulted from Edward I's two wars of conquest?

48. The Rise of the French Monarchy; Spain and Mediaeval Parliaments
A. Why could St. Louis, King of France, be said to be "a rarity among kings"?

B. How did the rise of the bourgeoisie strengthen the French monarchy?

C. Explain the importance of the papal bull, *Unam sanctam.*

D. Why did a Frenchman succeed Boniface VIII, and why was the papal residence moved to Avignon?

E. Describe the function of medieval parliaments.

49. The Mongol Conquests: West Meets East
A. Describe the Mongols. Where did they originate?

B. Describe the achievements of Genghis Khan.

C. What was the significance of the journeys of Carpini and Rubruck? Of Marco Polo?

D. Describe Catholic missionary work in the Far East during this period.

50. Theology and Science in the Thirteenth Century
A. Who was Averroës?

B. What was the aim of St. Thomas Aquinas in the *Summa contra Gentiles?*

C. What was the greatest work of St. Thomas?

D. Indicate the contributions of Albert the Great and Roger Bacon to scientific knowledge.

THE CHAPTER IN REVIEW

A. How did the first English Parliament come to be called? What classes were represented?

B. Why was the Magna Carta granted by King John? What is the importance of this document in British history?

C. Explain how the convening of the first French parliament was related to the dispute between Philip the Fair and Boniface VIII.

D. Describe the development of mediaeval parliaments during the twelfth and thirteenth centuries.

E. How did St. Thomas Aquinas explain that truth arrived at correctly by reason could never be in conflict with revealed truth?

FOR YOUR NOTEBOOK

Read a short biographical sketch of Frederick II in one of the standard encyclopedias. Then enter a list of reasons in your notebook for his being called "an un-medieval man," or a "modern man who lived in medieval times."

List all the reasons you can find for considering the Magna Carta an important document to you personally.

Between 1066 and 1300 many important constitutional and legal developments took place in England. Make a chronological list of these developments and indicate the importance of each with a phrase, such as 'beginning of trial by jury," or "origins of representative government."

What principles were at stake in the quarrel between Boniface VIII and Philip IV?

What were St. Thomas Aquinas' contributions to the history of the world and especially Christianity?

SELECTED READINGS

One of the most widely discussed and read books about the Middle Ages is

James J. Walsh, *Thirteenth, the Greatest of Centuries* (New York: Fordham University Press, 1952). Mr. Walsh wrote his book in answer to those who disparaged the Middle Ages; it is popularly and interestingly written, and it should attract the student who has become interested in history by this time.

Three biographies give good, balanced coverage to the material of this chapter. The most interesting biography of the unusual saint-king of France is that by his companion on the last crusades, Jean Sire de Joinville, *The History of St. Louis* (London: Oxford University Press, 1938). This is the best of many editions of Joinville's biography. An excellent biography of St. Thomas is G. K. Chesterton, *St. Thomas Aquinas* (New York: Doubleday & Company, Inc., Image Books, 1956). An interesting biography that covers much of the French and English stories is *Eleanor of Aquitaine and the Four Kings,* by Amy Kelly (Cambridge, Mass.: Harvard University Press, 1950).

CHRONOLOGICAL REVIEW

1122 *Concordat of Worms*
1153 *Death of St. Bernard*
1166 Assize of Clarendon
1170 Anglo-Norman invasion of Ireland
1176 Battle of Legnano
1179 *Third Council of the Lateran*
1187 Saladin captures Jerusalem
1190 Death of Barbarossa; Henry VI, King of Germany and Sicily (to 1197)
1201 *Innocent III supports Otto of Brunswick*
1202 *The Fourth Crusade (to 1204)*
1203 Forfeiture of English lands in France
1208 *England placed under interdict; death of Philip of Swabia*
1209 *Beginning of Albigensian Crusade*
1212 Battle of Las Navas de Tolosa
1213 Genghis Khan overruns China
    King John surrenders to Innocent III
1214 Battle of Bouvines
1215 *Fourth Lateran Council; Magna Carta*
1227 Death of Genghis Khan
1240 Mongols overrun Russia

1245 *First Council of Lyons; Carpini's mission to the Khan*
1248 *St. Louis' crusade (to 1254)*
1258 Mongols capture Bagdad; Provisions of Oxford
1265 First English Parliament
1268 Execution of Conradin of Hohenstaufen
1270 *Death of St. Louis on the last crusade*
1273 Election of Rudolf of Hapsburg
1274 *Death of SS. Thomas Aquinas & Bonaventure*
1275 Marco Polo arrives in China
1282 Sicilian Vespers
1291 Fall of Acre
    John of Monte Corvino in China
1294 Death of Kublai Khan
1296 *The bull* Clericis laicos
1302 First meeting of Estates-General
1303 *The crime of Anagni*
1309 *Clement V moves to Avignon*
1311 *Suppression of the Templars*
1314 Battle of Bannockburn

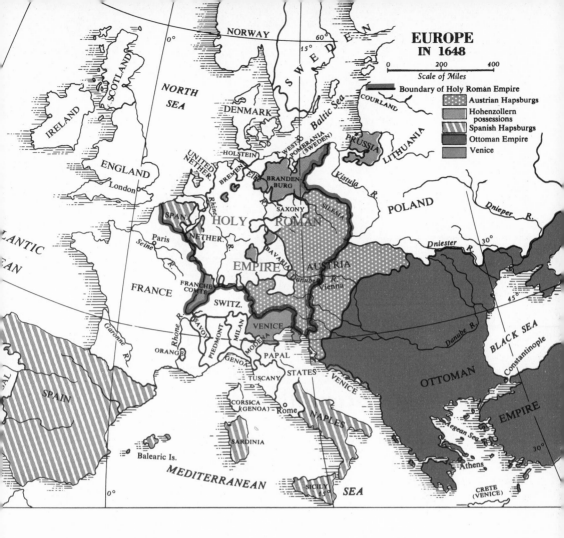

EUROPE
IN 1648

Scale of Miles

0   200   400

Boundary of Holy Roman Empire
Austrian Hapsburgs
Hohenzollern possessions
Spanish Hapsburgs
Ottoman Empire
Venice

UNIT SIX

The Breakup of Medieval Christendom

The Beginnings of the Hundred Years' War · Joan of Arc Rallies the French Nation ·
England, France, and Spain in the Second Half of the Fifteenth Century · The Holy
Roman Empire and Its Slavic Neighbors · The Rise of the Ottoman Turks and Russia ·
The Papacy and Church under Severe Attack · The Crisis and Triumph of the Papacy ·
Italy and the Renaissance · Luther and Protestantism in Germany · The Spread of the
Protestant Revolt · The Era of Catholic Reform

Joan of Arc

Chapter 18. The Monarchies of Western Europe and the Hundred Years' War

51. THE BEGINNINGS OF THE HUNDRED YEARS' WAR, 1337 to 1453

From the time of the first Capetian King of France, Hugh Capet (987–996), to the early fourteenth century, every King of France had a son to succeed him. After King Philip the Fair, however, the luck of the Capetians ran out. Philip was succeeded by his three sons successively, none of whom had a son. When the last of Philip's sons died in 1328, the French faced the problem of finding a king. One of the candidates for the throne, Edward III of England (1327–1377), traced his claim through his mother Isabella, the daughter of Philip the Fair and sister of the last king. But the French nobles and lawyers decided

that the throne could be claimed only by one who traced his descent *through the male line* from a previous king. The French nobleman Philip of Valois was so descended, and he was accordingly named King of France (Philip VI, 1328–1350).

Causes of the Hundred Years' War. From the very outset, relations between Philip and Edward were bad. Philip wanted to annex Guienne, the great fief Edward held in southwestern France. Edward, on the other hand, was determined not only to keep Guienne but to recover some of the fiefs which his ancestor, King John, had lost more than a hundred years earlier. Edward dreamed, too, of conquering Scotland, but Philip urged the Scots to resist and sent them mili-

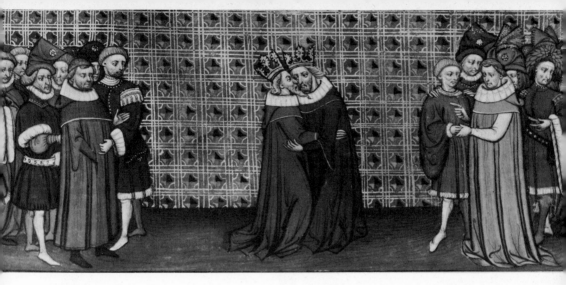

This illustration taken from a fourteenth-century French manuscript depicts Edward III paying homage to King Philip.

tary aid. The biggest source of tension between Philip and Edward was over Flanders. Politically Flanders was tied to France, since the Count of Flanders was the vassal of the King of France. But economically Flanders was tied very closely to England, since the great cloth industry of Flanders was dependent on wool from England. The Count of Flanders and the wealthy Flemish towns were often at odds. The count looked for support to the King of France, while the towns looked to England. In 1337 the Flemish towns rebelled against the count and, in the hope of receiving aid from England, recognized Edward III as King of France (thus making him their overlord). Edward chose this moment to proclaim himself King of France and made ready to win the French throne by force. So began the great Hundred Years' War between France and England.

Misery and defeat in France. For France the first phase of the Hundred Years' War was a series of disasters. On land

and sea the French were worsted by the English. In 1346, at Crécy, a great army of French knights was mercilessly mowed down by English bowmen, who used a new instrument of war, the longbow. After Crécy, Edward continued his advance into France, but the war was soon interrupted by a terrible plague called the Black Death. In 1348–1349 the plague ravaged France, the British Isles, and much of the Continent, and carried away as much as a third of the population of western Europe.

After the plague had died down, Philip's successor, John the Good (1350–1364), resumed the war with England. John was so short of funds that he could hardly raise an army. In 1355 he called a meeting of the Estates-General and begged the deputies of the three great estates of France for money. They granted it, but only on condition that it be used to build up the army under the direct supervision of the Estates. In the following year, at Poitiers, John engaged an

In the battle of Crécy, August 26, 1346, the flower of French nobility was destroyed by Englishmen using the English longbow for the first time in continental warfare. (Giraudon)

English army commanded by Edward the Black Prince, heir to the English throne. The French were overwhelmingly defeated, and their king was captured.

The failure of the Estates-General. With the king in enemy hands, France was thrown into the greatest confusion. Bandits roamed the highways, and unemployed soldiers devastated France. The Estates-General, meeting in Paris, placed the blame for France's misfortunes on the monarchy and decided therefore to limit the king's authority once and for all. In 1357 it issued a great charter called the Grande Ordonnance, which gave the Estates-General virtual control of the government and army. King John was still a prisoner of the English, but his son Charles, the dauphin (that is, heir to the throne), accepted the Ordonnance. The Es-

tates-General, however, could not restore order in France. Conditions became worse than ever. In 1358 the peasants of northern France rose in a great rebellion. After causing much destruction of castles and towns, the peasants were put down by the dauphin. Charles now assumed the leadership of France and drove from power the leaders in the Estates-General who had issued the Grande Ordonnance.

The Treaty of Bretigny (1360). In order to bring the war with England to a close, but primarily to ransom the captive King John, Charles made a very disadvantageous treaty with the English. Eleven French provinces, comprising over a third of France, were turned over to Edward III. In addition, the French promised to pay an enormous sum of money for the release of King John. Edward III promised to renounce his claim to the French throne if the terms of the treaty were carried out.

France's recovery under Charles V (1364 to 1380). The terms of the Treaty of Bretigny were only partially carried out. Each side accused the other of breaking them, and made ready to resume the war. On the death of King John in 1364 (still a captive in England), the French welcomed to the throne the dauphin Charles. Charles had more intelligence than his immediate predecessor and came to be called Charles the Wise. He had learned much from the turbulent events of the 1350's and he took care to provide the monarchy with two things it had then lacked: sufficient funds and good generalship. Charles could have obtained money by grants from the Estates-General, but he preferred not to assemble it for fear of the demands it might make on him. He chose, rather, to collect the taxes which the Estates-General had granted on a purely temporary basis in 1355 and 1356. Though some Frenchmen contested Charles's right to collect these taxes, most Frenchmen were willing to put up with them so long as the king preserved order in France and drove back the English.

Charles reorganized the French army and entrusted its command to a great general, Bertrand du Guesclin. Du Guesclin never fought a pitched battle with the English. Instead, he wore them down by attacking their scouting parties, cutting off their food supplies, and encouraging the French inhabitants of the English-occupied towns and countryside to resist. The English fought back. very poorly. Edward III had become very senile and no longer took any interest in the war. His son Edward, the Black Prince, who had been his best general, was suffering from an incurable disease and died in 1376. Edward III died in 1377 and was succeeded by his ten-year-old grandson, Richard II (1377–1399). While Richard's uncles argued over who should rule England in the name of the child king, the French steadily drove the English from France. When Charles V died in 1380, the English held no more than five towns on the western coast of France.

Growth of the English Parliament. While English armies were fighting on the soil of France in the fourteenth century, the English Parliament at home was becoming a powerful force in the government. Parliament was made up of the nobles and bishops of England and representatives of the knights and burgesses. The nobles and bishops attended Parliament by virtue of their rank alone. The knights and burgesses were elected by the county courts and boroughs, respectively. By the fourteenth century the "knights" of England had become little more than country gentlemen, and they had more in common with the burgesses than with the nobles and bishops. The knights and the burgesses in Parliament tended, therefore, to act as one group. By the middle of the fourteenth century they had definitely organized themselves into a distinct house of Parliament, the House of Commons. The nobles and bishops made up the House of Lords.

Parliament's power of taxation. The king called Parliament primarily to ask for money. Naturally this put Parliament in an excellent position to bargain with the king. If Parliament had some grievance against the king, it simply withheld funds until the king corrected the grievance. To use the language of the day, Parliament demanded redress of grievances before it voted supply. Edward III called Parliament frequently, since he was continually in need of money to finance his war in France. Thanks to its control of the purse strings, Parliament gained two important rights during Edward's reign. One right was that only Parliament could authorize the king to collect taxes. The other was that Parliament could pass laws.

Parliament's legislative power. Most of the parliamentary laws originated in the House of Commons; in other words, the Commons "initiated legislation." In the fourteenth century the custom developed whereby the Commons, when it wanted a law passed, drew up the proposed law in the form of a petition, which it presented to the king. If the king and the House of Lords approved the petition, it then became a law, or statute. (Laws passed by legislative bodies are called statutes.)

Though Parliament's gains were great, it had by no means stripped the king of his authority. Theoretically the king was as powerful as ever. He was the chief executive and highest judge in England. He appointed all the government officials—his own councilors, the heads of departments of government, the royal judges, and the sheriffs. He commanded the army, declared war, made alliances and treaties of peace.[1] Indeed, if the king

The coronation Chair and Stone in Westminster Abbey. Tradition has it that the stone was the "pillow" used by Jacob at Bethel, where he had a vision of angels ascending and descending the ladder to heaven. (Hulton Picture Library)

could have managed to live on his regular income (from his private estates, court fines and fees, feudal dues, customs on imports and exports, etc.), he need not have called Parliament into session at all.

In reality, the king had to watch his step. His dependence on Parliament for taxes was actually a grave limitation on his power. The nobles of England were still very powerful and very independent in their thinking.

52. JOAN OF ARC RALLIES THE FRENCH NATION

Parliament deposes Richard II (1399). For many years after France's remarkable recovery under Charles the Wise, France and England gave little attention to war and concentrated on internal affairs. For a while both countries had child kings, and in both countries the nobles struggled for power. In England the boy king, Richard II (1377–1399), stood by helpless while control of the government was shifted from one party of nobles to another. In 1388 one group of nobles went so far as to seize the government by force and, with the consent of Parliament, execute two of the king's leading ministers. Many years later, after Richard had become a strong ruler, he resolved to revenge himself on the men who had killed his ministers. Murder, execution, confiscation, or exile was the fate of those whom the king singled out for punishment. One of those who suffered by confiscation and exile was the king's

[1] It is interesting to note that theoretically (very theoretically indeed) all the above-mentioned authority still resides in the English monarch.

Richard II lacked the strength of character and devotion to the royal business which characterized his predecessors and which may have helped him to surmount the domestic crises of his reign. (Hulton Picture Library)

own cousin, Henry of Lancaster. In 1399 Henry led a rebellion against Richard and forced him to abdicate. Parliament proclaimed Henry King of England (Henry IV, 1399–1413). Shortly afterward Richard died under very suspicious circumstances.

The houses of Lancaster and York. The fact that Richard II was childless made it easier for Henry of Lancaster to become king. But Henry had a cousin, Edmund Mortimer, who was descended from an older branch of the royal family and had therefore a better hereditary claim to the throne. Several attempts to put Mortimer on the throne failed, and eventually

Mortimer died childless. But his sister Anne married into the house of York, which thereby inherited the claims of the Mortimers to the throne of England.

Charles the Mad of France. With the accession of the boy king, Charles VI (1380–1422), France entered upon one of the most troubled periods of her history. Charles's childhood was a time of great confusion, for his uncles, who ruled in his name, governed France very badly, and there were several uprisings. Then in 1392, at the age of twenty-four, Charles went hopelessly insane. A bitter struggle for power arose among his relatives, and gradually two great factions developed. One was led by Louis of Orleans, the king's brother; the other by Duke Philip of Burgundy, the king's uncle.

The rise of Burgundy. Philip, Duke of Burgundy, was by far the most powerful nobleman in France. He owed the beginnings of his power to his father, King John. In 1361 John took over the great Duchy of Burgundy, whose last duke had just died without heirs. Instead of adding Burgundy to the Royal Domain, however, John gave it to his son Philip. Through marriage, Philip later acquired the provinces of Flanders and Franche Comté. All these lands he passed on to his successor, John the Fearless.

Henry V of England invades France. John the Fearless also inherited the old rivalry with Orleans, and in 1407 he had the Duke of Orleans assassinated. This action touched off the most terrible civil war France had ever seen. Taking advantage of the confusion in France, King Henry V of England

Henry V, from a drawing by Prince Alfred, Duke of Edinburgh in 1855. Through Henry V the English came closest to reaching the throne of France. (Hulton Picture Library)

renewed the old claim of the English kings to the French throne. In 1415 he invaded France. While the Duke of Burgundy remained neutral, the Orleanists hastily assembled a great army of French knights, which they hurled against Henry at Agincourt. This battle was the story of Crécy and Poitiers over again; the French were annihilated. When Henry followed up his victory at Agincourt by capturing one French town after another, John the Fearless grew alarmed and made overtures of peace to the Orleanists. The Orleanists, however, had not forgotten John's murder of the Duke of Orleans. Craving revenge more than Henry's defeat, they murdered John at the very moment that he was nego-

tiating with them for an alliance. When John's successor, Philip the Good, heard the news of his father's death, he went over immediately to the side of Henry V.

The Treaty of Troyes. In 1420, Henry V and Duke Philip the Good forced France's mad king, Charles VI, to sign a treaty of peace with the English. By the terms of this treaty, Henry V was to marry Charles's daughter Catherine, and Henry was recognized as the regent of France and heir to the French throne. Charles's own son, the dauphin Charles, was thus excluded from the succession to the throne. In 1422 both Henry V and Charles the Mad died, and Henry's infant son, Henry VI, was proclaimed King of England and of France. Many Frenchmen, however, recognized the dauphin Charles as true King of France, and they urged him to take the field against the English.

France's darkest hour. Paris, with all its machinery of government, was in English hands, and the influential University of Paris declared that Henry VI was true King of France. The dauphin Charles, who claimed to be France's true king, took refuge south of the Loire River. He constantly talked of taking the field against the English, but in reality he and his followers were thoroughly demoralized and had little hope of ever beating the English-Burgundian alliance. As Charles whiled away his time, the English began the siege of Orleans. This city was the last barrier to the English advance into southern France. In February of 1429, when the fall of Orleans seemed only a matter of time, a seventeen-year-old peasant girl, Joan of Arc, made her way to the court of the dauphin to tell him that God had chosen her to lead France to victory.

Joan of Arc. At the age of thirteen, Joan of Arc first began to hear heavenly voices, which she said were those of St. Margaret, St. Catherine, and St. Michael the Archangel. The saints told Joan many things: to be a good girl, to obey her parents, and to go often to Mass. But they also told her what a terrible condition France was in and that God had chosen her to save France from its enemies.

Joan persuaded a French officer to provide her with an escort to the court of the dauphin. Charles, mostly out of curiosity, agreed to see her, but before she came into his presence he decided to play a trick on her to test whether she really came from God. He dressed up one of his courtiers in royal clothes and made him sit upon the throne, while the dauphin, dressed in ordinary clothes, mingled among the other courtiers. When Joan entered the dauphin's court she made her way straight to the dauphin and announced: "Most noble dauphin, I have come from God to help you and your kingdom." Her voices had never told Joan in full detail exactly what she must do to save France. But two things she did know: that she would save Orleans from the English and lead the dauphin to Reims for his coronation as King of France.

Joan saves Orleans. Charles and his court were impressed by Joan's obvious sincerity and saintliness, but still they were very skeptical. They thought it absurd that France, which had many good generals, should have its destiny placed in the hands of a seventeen-year-old country girl who could not even write her own name. Nevertheless, Charles placed her at the head of an army and sent her to relieve the besieged city of Orleans. Joan's soldiers followed her enthusiastically to battle, and word quickly spread throughout the country that a maiden girl had come from God to save France. In two days' fighting, May 6–7, Joan's army captured all the fortifications the English had thrown up around the city of Orleans. Joan herself was in the thick of the fighting, spurring on her men, but she carried in her hand only a banner, never a sword. On May 8 the English were in full retreat, and Orleans was saved.

The Dauphin's coronation. Next Joan proceeded to lead the dauphin to Reims for his coronation. Militarily, such an action was very inadvisable,

FRANCE, 1429

0   100   200
Scale of Miles

English rule
Charles VII
Burgundian lands of 1479

NETHERLANDS
Sluys
Strait of Dover
FLANDERS
BRABANT
Calais
Brussels
ARTOIS
Agincourt
Crécy
LUXEMBOURG
Luxembourg
English Channel
Rouen
VALOIS
Reims
Seine
NORMANDY
Paris
Marne
LORRAINE
Brétigny
CHAMPAGNE
MAINE
Troyes
Orleans
BRITTANY
NEVERS
DUCHY OF BURGUNDY
FRANCHE COMTÉ
Loire
R.
Poitiers
Lyons
Bay
of
Biscay
Bordeaux
GUIENNE
45°
DAUPHINÉ
Rhone
GASCONY
Garonne
Toulouse
Narbonne
Mediterranean Sea

299

since Reims lay deep in the heart of the English-occupied country. Nevertheless, Joan insisted that the trip be made, and she had her way. As she led the dauphin and the French army across the enemy country, the English watched her from the safety of their walls. They would not engage her in battle. Towns that had no English garrison threw open their gates, and in the great cathedral of Reims, Charles, with Joan at his side, was solemnly crowned and anointed King of France. Kneeling before Charles after his coronation, Joan addressed him as king for the first time: "Gentle King, now is fulfilled the will of God that I should raise the siege of Orleans and lead you to the city of Reims to receive the holy coronation, to show that you are indeed the king and the rightful lord of the realm of France."

The death of Joan. At Charles's request, Joan remained in the service of the king, but he gave her very little support. In 1430 she was captured by the Burgundians, who sold her to the English for ten thousand pieces of gold. The English tried to destroy her reputation in the eyes of the French people. If they could make the French believe that Orleans owed its deliverance and the king his crown to a girl who was a witch and a heretic (for thus did they label Joan), they might destroy the newly awakened spirit of the French people. To achieve this end, the English turned Joan over for trial to an ecclesiastical court headed by a French bishop, Pierre Cauchon, who was sympathetic to the English cause. For three months Joan heroically stood trial while the court tried in vain to make her confess to a num-

The Burning of Joan of Arc at the Stake, *a painting by J. E. Lenepveu. The tragedy following her triumph was not in vain. She had aroused a new spirit of patriotism among the French which brought them to final victory over the English. (Giraudon)*

ber of crimes. The court's verdict was a foregone conclusion. On the morning of May 30, 1431, Joan was informed that she had been found guilty of heresy and sorcery. She was turned over to the English, who burned her at the stake. As the smoke rose about her she kissed the crucifix which a French soldier had brought her, and before she died she was heard to utter the name "Jesus." She was a true saint. Almost five hundred years later she was canonized at Rome.

End of the Hundred Years' War. The English were very much mistaken in thinking that the death of Joan of Arc would strengthen their hold on France. Instead of believing that Joan was a witch and a heretic, the French mourned their dead heroine as a martyr for God and for France. Even King Charles, who was very lazy by nature, was inspired by Joan's example, and he began at last to make a determined effort to drive the English from his kingdom. In 1435 he succeeded in breaking up the English-Burgundian alliance, and he captured Paris in the following year. Year by year the English were beaten back, until by 1453 they had been driven from all of France except Calais, a town on the English Channel. The Hundred Years' War was over, and England's threat to the unity of France was ended forever.

France is stronger. The French monarchy, which had come so close to being destroyed, came out of the Hundred Years' War more powerful than ever. During the war the French kings had often levied taxes by royal decree. Such taxation was contrary to the notion of feudal monarchy, but in the terrible crisis of war the French people had accepted it. By the end of the Hundred Years' War, the principle of taxation by royal decree was well established.

After the defeat of the English, the French kings still had one more great task to perform before they could truly become the masters of France. That task was to break the power of Bur-

gundy. Here they were aided by a rare piece of good fortune. In 1477 the Duke of Burgundy, Charles the Bold, was killed fighting the Swiss. He left only a daughter, Mary of Burgundy, as his successor. King Louis XI of France refused to recognize Mary as Charles's successor, and he annexed the Burgundian provinces of Burgundy, Artois, and Picardy to the Royal Domain. The remainder of the Burgundian possessions, consisting chiefly of the Netherlands (Belgium and Holland) and Franche Comté, were taken over by the German Hapsburgs when Mary of Burgundy married Maximilian of Hapsburg, the son of the Holy Roman Emperor.

Louis XI, the Spider King. Louis XI (1461–1483) annexed other provinces, notably Provence, when their rulers died without heirs. On several occasions the French nobles, who were alarmed at the growth of the king's power, rebelled against him, but Louis put them down. The tactics he used against his enemies were often very unscrupulous. He freely made promises and freely broke them whenever it suited him. Like the spider that painstakingly weaves its web to trap the unsuspecting insect, Louis was constantly scheming the downfall of his enemies and for that reason has been called the Spider King.

With the bourgeoisie of France, Louis was very popular. He encouraged the growth of industry and commerce, and he chose his advisers and ministers of state from the bourgeois class. In fact, Louis acted very much like a bourgeois himself. When he traveled about France he seldom stayed at his royal residences or at the

Louis XI, haunted by a guilty conscience and the fear of assassination by his enemies, spent his last years in self-imprisonment in a château. (Giraudon)

châteaux of the nobles. Generally he stayed at the homes of wealthy merchants, and sometimes he spent the night at the local innkeeper's. In return for the king's protection and favor, the bourgeoisie paid Louis heavy taxes. With these taxes he built up a strong standing army, which he used against any who challenged his authority.

The rounding out of France. When Louis XI died, all the great French provinces except the Duchy of Brittany had been added to the Royal Domain. In 1491 this province, too, was annexed when Charles VIII (1483–1498) married its duchess. With the annexation of Brittany, the shaping of France was more or less completed, and the king was supreme. So certain was Charles VIII that he was master in France that he left his kingdom for a considerable period of time, confident that his ministers could safely rule in his absence.

England: the Wars of the Roses. After the English were driven from France, England became the scene of a series of devastating civil wars. These wars were caused by the rivalry between the houses of Lancaster and York for the throne of England. On hereditary grounds the Yorkists undoubtedly had a better claim to the throne than had the Lancastrians. The third of the Lancastrian kings, Henry VI (1422–1461), was discredited by England's defeat in France, and in 1453 he became insane. The king's inability to rule gave the Yorkists the chance they were looking for, and in 1455 the Duke of York raised the standard of revolt. Almost the entire nobility of England allied itself with one side or the other, and thus began the terrible Wars of the Roses, so called from the symbols of the two contending houses —the white rose of York and the red rose of Lancaster.

Bosworth Field. After six years of bitter fighting the Yorkists succeeded in deposing Henry VI and proclaimed the Duke of York as King of England. The new king, Edward IV (1461–1483), sat on a very shaky throne, and several times during his reign he had to put down Lancastrian rebellions. The whole age was a violent one, and Englishmen seem to have forgotten the meaning of law. After Edward's death, his brother, Richard III (1483–1485), became king, and it was said that he murdered Edward's young sons in the Tower of London. Shortly thereafter a conspiracy was formed to put Henry Tudor, a relative of the Lancastrians, on the throne. On August 22, 1485, Henry Tudor defeated and killed Richard III in the battle of Bosworth Field. England was Henry's by right of conquest, and he ascended the throne as Henry VII (1485–1509).

Henry VII founds the strong Tudor dynasty. Henry Tudor had no hereditary claim to be King of England, but a number of circumstances and his own shrewd-

Coats of arms for the House of Lancaster (left) and the House of York (right), contenders in the Wars of the Roses. (Hulton Picture Library)

ness placed him and his family securely on the throne. In the first place, England was weary of war and welcomed a ruler who could maintain law and order. Second, so many nobles had been killed in the Wars of the Roses that very few were left who could challenge the king's authority. Favored by such circumstances, Henry proceeded by carefully planned steps to build a powerful monarchy.

Henry satisfied many Englishmen by having Parliament proclaim him King of England. He brought over many of the Yorkists to his side by marrying Elizabeth of York, the daughter of King Edward IV. He won the favor of the middle class by sponsoring commerce and the growth of such industries as clothmaking, shipbuilding, and fishing. He improved his relations with foreign powers by marrying his daughter Margaret to King James IV of Scotland, and his son Arthur to Catherine of Aragon, the daughter of King Ferdinand and Queen Isabella of Spain. When Arthur died prematurely, Henry conveniently had Catherine marry the new heir, Henry, the future Henry VIII.

Henry sought to make himself fi-

nancially independent of Parliament. He achieved this aim by avoiding foreign wars (the greatest of all expenses) and by scrupulously collecting every penny that was due him from his regular revenues (court fines and fees, feudal dues, customs on imports and exports, income from the royal estates). Sometimes, when he was short of money he forced Englishmen to make him loans, which he had no intention of repaying. These loans were known by the deceptive name of "benevolences."

In order to deal quickly with his enemies, Henry relied on a special court, the Court of the Star Chamber. This court, whose judges were hand-picked by Henry, ignored the English common law and trial by jury—the two great safeguards of English liberty. Another measure Henry used to get rid of men whom he considered dangerous was the bill of attainder, which was simply an act of Parliament declaring someone guilty of treason. Any man suspected of treason but whose guilt could not be proved could be "attainted" by act of Parliament and quickly sent to the block. The strong Tudor monarchy was founded, obviously, at the expense of liberties long enjoyed by the people of England.

The unification of Spain. In the fifteenth century Spain progressed toward unification and strong monarchy with surprising speed. Even as late as the middle of that century Spain was still divided into five kingdoms: Portugal, Castile, Aragon, Navarre, and Moorish Granada. In 1469, the union of the two largest kingdoms was forged by the marriage of Ferdinand, the heir of Aragon, to Isabella, the heiress of Castile.

Ferdinand (1439–1516) and Isabella (1474–1504) believed that two conditions were necessary for a united Spain: a single monarchy and a single church. In 1492 they conquered the Moorish kingdom of Granada, thus bringing the entire peninsula under Catholic rule for the first time in nearly seven hundred years. In 1512, Ferdinand conquered Spanish Navarre. After that, only Portugal remained outside the united kingdom of Spain.

Expulsion of Moors and Jews. As a team, Ferdinand and Isabella naturally had far greater power than would have been the case had they ruled separately. They succeeded in depriving the nobility of many of its ancient privileges and they drastically reduced the representation of the towns in the Cortes. At the same time they turned to another element in the population which they considered an obstacle to strong monarchy and Spanish unity. This was the presence in Spain of numerous Moors and Jews. In 1492 the two monarchs gave the Jews the choice of either being baptized or leaving the country. Ten years later the Moors were given the same choice. Most of the Moors became Catholic (at least nominally), but the great majority of the Jews (possibly 165,000) left the country. Most of the Spanish Jews had been engaged in industry and commerce, and it has often been noted that their departure inflicted a grave blow on the Spanish economy.

The premature death of Ferdinand's and Isabella's only son left their daughter Joanna the heiress of Spain. Joanna was the wife of Philip of Hapsburg, the son of the Holy Roman Emperor. In 1500 Joanna gave birth to a son, Charles. Heir to both Spain and all the Hapsburg lands, and future Holy Roman Emperor, Charles would one day play a mighty role in world history.

REVIEW

STUDY SECTIONS IN REVIEW

51. The Outbreak of the Hundred Years' War

A. Mention three causes of the Hundred Years' War.

B. Identify: battle of Crécy, Black Death, John the Good, Treaty of Bretigny.

C. How did Charles V avoid the troubles his predecessors had with the Estates-General?

D. Cite two rights gained by the English Parliament during this period.

52. Joan of Arc Rallies the French Nation

A. Identify: Henry of Lancaster, House of York, Louis of Orleans, Philip of Burgundy.

B. What were the results of the Treaty of Troyes (1420)?

C. What areas of France were under English control in 1429?

D. Why did the English try Joan of Arc for heresy and sorcery?

53. England, France, and Spain in the Second Half of the Fifteenth Century

A. What two factors immensely strengthened the French monarchy after the Hundred Years' War?

B. What is the significance of the French annexation of Brittany in 1491?

C. Identify: Wars of the Roses, Edward IV, Richard III, Henry VII.

D. Cite three steps taken by Henry VII to ensure Tudor control of the English throne.

E. Note three measures taken by Ferdinand and Isabella to unite Spain.

THE CHAPTER IN REVIEW

A. How did Joan of Arc affect the course of the Hundred Years' War?

B. Review the developments, from the Wars of the Roses onward, which brought the Tudor dynasty to the throne of England.

C. Compare the condition of France and the French monarchy at the beginning and at the conclusion of the Hundred Years' War.

D. Compare the development of the English Parliament and the French Estates-General during the fourteenth century. Note also how the monarchy in each country was affected by such development.

FOR YOUR NOTEBOOK

A good knowledge of history requires an understanding of *causes* and *effects*. Both can be listed under the following convenient headings: political (including dynastic and international), economic, social, cultural, religious. Read through Section 51 again and enter into your notebook, under the above headings, the causes of the Hundred Years' War.

A student of history should understand the relationship of international and domestic events. You can highlight this in your notebook by drawing a graph of the Hundred Years' War, showing periods of English success and of French success. Now run a time-line for England and another for France parallel to the graph line for the Hundred Years' War. Study your three lines carefully to see what re-lationship the events of the war had on domestic developments in each country.

List the results of the Hundred Years' War under the headings used for your first entry for this chapter.

In the Appendix to this book you will find a genealogical table of the Valois kings of France. Enter this table into your notebook. Now do the same for the Plantagenet, Lancastrian, and Yorkist kings of England. From these tables you should understand how the hereditary principle is usually, but not always, followed in England, and how it was invariably followed in France.

Section 53 shows how England, France, and Spain became strong monarchies. Draw three parallel time-lines for these countries and enter the principal developments toward a strong monarchy in each country.

SELECTED READINGS

The best full account of the Hundred Years' War is E. Perroy, *The Hundred Years' War,* translated by W. B. Wells (New York: Oxford University Press, 1951), but the decisive period of the struggle can more easily be followed in the biography of Joan of Arc by Stanislas Fumet, *Joan the Saint* (New York: Sheed and Ward, 1937).

The formation of the national state in Spain can be followed in William Walsh, *Isabella of Spain* (New York: The Tudor Publishing Co., 1938), and in France in *King Spider,* by D. B. Wyndham Lewis (New York: Coward-McCann, Inc., 1929). English development in this period is well handled—both for spirit and for major historical events—by the series of historical plays by Shakespeare. These are *Henry IV, Henry V, Henry VI, Richard II,* and *Richard III.* Reading one of these, especially *King Richard III,* is a good exercise in seeing the close relationship between literature and history, the former serving as "the mirror" of the latter.

Chapter 19. Central and Eastern Europe in the Late Middle Ages

54. THE HOLY ROMAN EMPIRE AND ITS SLAVIC NEIGHBORS

The Holy Roman Empire. Unlike France and England, Germany was not destined to have a strong national monarchy until modern times. The struggle between the Hohenstaufen dynasty and the Papacy had left the monarchy in a very weakened state. The German nobles continued to elect kings, and the kings continued to assume the title of Holy Roman Emperor, but the power of the emperor-king was very little. However weak the emperor, the Holy Roman Empire was still very impressive in size. Within its borders were several hundred states, ranging in size from a few square miles to several thousand. Most of these states were German-speaking, but on the fringes of the empire were several non-German states. The most important of the non-German states was Bohemia, whose king was the vassal of the emperor. Most Bohemians were Czechs, but in the thirteenth and fourteenth centuries thousands of skilled Germans (craftsmen, merchants, and farmers) settled in Bohemia at the invitation of the Bohemian kings. The Germans concentrated heavily in the Sudeten Mountains of northern Bohemia and in the cities. They never blended with the native Czechs but kept their own language and customs, thus forming a large minority in the midst of the Czech population.

The Hapsburg emperors. In one respect the office of Holy Roman Emperor was of great advantage to its holder.

Since the feudal customs of forfeiture and escheat were still practiced in the empire, the emperors were able by these means to increase their family holdings. Often a German prince, on account of lawlessness, had to forfeit his land to the emperor, or a ruling family died out and its land escheated to the emperor. Most of the emperors of the fourteenth and fifteenth centuries belonged to either the Hapsburg or Luxembourg family.

The Hapsburgs were unusually skillful in acquiring lands, not only through forfeiture and escheat, but also through carefully planned marriages. The chief possession of the Hapsburgs was the Archduchy of Austria, but they held many other lands scattered throughout the empire. Late in the fifteenth century the Hapsburgs arranged two marriages that increased their holdings enormously and made them the most powerful family in Europe. In 1477, Maximilian of Hapsburg married Mary of Burgundy, daughter of Duke Charles the Bold. We have already seen how Louis XI of France seized some of Mary's lands, but she and Maximilian managed to hold the bulk of them, which included the Netherlands (Belgium and Holland) and Franche Comté. Then, in 1496, Maximilian's son Philip married Joanna, the daughter of Ferdinand and Isabella of Spain. On the death of Joanna's older brother, she and Philip became the heirs not only of Castile and Aragon but also of the Aragonese possessions of Sicily and Naples.

The Diet and the seven electors. Like other Western monarchies, the Holy Roman Empire had a parliament, called the Diet. Clergy, nobles, and townsmen sat in the Diet, but as a governing body the Diet did very little. The men who made up the Diet were practically independent in their own states, and so they had no desire to pass laws or levy taxes that would be binding on themselves. Before the fourteenth century it was the custom for the clergy and nobles, assembled in the Diet, to elect the emperor. Often they could not agree on a candidate, with the result that frequently there were double elections. To provide for orderly elections, the emperor

The magnificent doors of the Gothic cathedral of Cologne. Cologne is the center of north German Catholicism and has long been famous for its impressive religious processions and Mardi Gras celebrations. (German Tourist Information Office)

Charles IV (1347–1378) issued, with the Diet's approval, a constitution entitled the Golden Bull (1356). The Golden Bull limited the number of electors to seven—the archbishops of Mainz, Cologne, and Trier, the Duke of Saxony, the Margrave of Brandenburg, the Count Palatine of the Rhine, and the King of Bohemia. Election was to be by majority vote. The Golden Bull remained in effect, with some modifications, until the end of the Holy Roman Empire in 1806.

The Swiss Confederation. Owing to the absence of a strong central government in the empire, many German towns and states formed leagues for their own protection and advantage. Two of these leagues, the Swiss Confederation and the Hanseatic League, deserve mention. The original holdings of the Hapsburg family included several lands (called cantons) that are today a part of Switzerland. Between the Hapsburgs and three of the Swiss cantons there was a running dispute as to whether the cantons were directly subject to the Hapsburg family or to the emperor (regardless of the family he belonged to). Naturally the cantons preferred to be directly subject to the emperor, since the emperor had hardly any power over the lands of the empire. In 1291 the three cantons formed an alliance by which they sought to assert their independence of the Hapsburgs. From that time on there was an almost constant state of war between the cantons and the Hapsburgs. The Hapsburgs had great military resources, but they were very inexperienced in mountain fighting. In every major battle between the two sides, the Swiss won.

The success of the three cantons attracted the attention of other southern German lands and cities, which hastened to join the Swiss Confederation. By 1350 there were eight cantons in the Confederation, and the feudal lords of southern Germany were very alarmed. Already they had lost control over the lands that had joined the Confederation, and they feared that still more of their lands would be lost. Determined to destroy the Swiss Confederation, the Hapsburgs and southern German nobles formed a grand alliance. But three times, in 1315, 1386, and 1388, they were decisively beaten by the Swiss. Thereafter the independence of the Swiss was not seriously challenged.

By the end of the fifteenth century the Swiss Confederation contained fifteen cantons, including such cities as Zurich, Berne, and Lucerne. The Confederation was not a state, but merely an alliance. Technically, each of the cantons was independent of the others, but in military and foreign affairs they acted as a unit. Once their freedom was assured, the Swiss began to hire themselves out as mercenary soldiers. In the fifteenth and sixteenth centuries they served in practically every army of western Europe. Frequently they fought in the papal armies, and they formed the Pope's special guard. Though the modern Swiss have long ceased to hire themselves out as soldiers, the Swiss Guard of the Vatican still reminds the world of the time when the Swiss were Europe's finest soldiers.

The Hanseatic League. The other great German league was the Hanseatic League. All its members were north

German commercial cities that had joined together to keep the North and Baltic seas free of pirates and to obtain favorable trading treaties with the countries of northern Europe. In England, Flanders, the Scandinavian kingdoms, and Russia, the Hanseatic cities had greater trading privileges than any other commercial group. In the Baltic, the League had virtually a monopoly on trade, and it even maintained its own army and navy. When Waldemar IV, King of Denmark (1340–1375), tried to break the League's hold on his country's commerce, the League went to war against him. Waldemar was beaten and was forced to accept the Treaty of Stralsund (1370), which gave the Hanseatic League a near monopoly of Danish commerce and even allowed the League to be consulted in the election of Danish kings.

German colonization. Many of the member cities of the Hanseatic League were situated on the south shore of the Baltic Sea. Before the twelfth century there were very few Germans on the Baltic coast or even east of the Elbe River. Beginning in that century, however, German nobles began to conquer eastward as far as the Oder River. The inhabitants of the lands they conquered were Slavs, who were either subjected, displaced, or killed, and German colonists were settled in their land. In the thirteenth century the Germans began to expand eastward up the Baltic coast. The Teutonic Knights, a religious military order, paved the way. Originally the Knights had been founded to help garrison the Holy Land, but with the decline of Christian power in that area

they transferred their activities to Europe. First they conquered the pagan Prussians, who lived north of Poland. Then they proceeded up the Baltic coast, conquering the pagan lands of Samogitia, Courland, Livonia, and Esthonia. The fate of the pagan Baltic peoples was very much the same as had been that of the Slavs between the Elbe and the Oder. Those who remained as subjects of the Knights were converted to Christianity, often by force. In the wake of the Knights came thousands of German colonists. So thickly did the Germans settle in Prussia that Prussia became a thoroughly German land.

After reaching Esthonia, on the Gulf of Finland, the Knights found

The gates to the north German city of Lubeck, "Queen of the Hanse." The sturdy buildings date back to the time of the Hanseatic League. (Fremdenverkehrsverband Nordmark)

further progress blocked. North of them lay Finland, which in the thirteenth and fourteenth centuries was being taken over and converted to Christianity by the Swedes. East of them lay that part of Russia which was dominated by Novgorod, the city that had remained free of the Mongol yoke. Southeast of them lay Lithuania, still a pagan land in the fourteenth century. And south of them lay the Catholic kingdom of Poland.

Poland and Lithuania united (1386). The pagan princes of Lithuania were very warlike, and in the fourteenth century they extended their power as far south as the Black Sea. Poland and Lithuania were often at war with one another, but they had one complaint in common: the Teutonic Knights blocked them from access to the Baltic Sea. In 1386, Poland and Lithuania were joined by the marriage of Jagiello, Grand Duke of Lithuania, and Jadwiga, Queen of Poland. On the occasion of his marriage, Jagiello became a Catholic, and the Lithuanians followed their prince into the Church. The conversion of the Lithuanians was a historic moment in the history of the Church, for the Lithuanians had been the last of the European peoples to remain pagan. The conversion of the European peoples to Christianity was at last completed.

In 1410, King Jagiello (called Vladislav V by the Poles) defeated the Teutonic Knights in a great battle at Tannenberg. The Knights were forced to accept the Treaty of Thorn (1411), by which they ceded Samogitia to Lithuania, thus giving Lithuania access to the sea. Later King Casimir IV defeated the Knights a second time

and, by the second Treaty of Thorn (1466), forced them to cede West Prussia to Poland. The Knights retained East Prussia, holding it as a fief of the Polish crown. For centuries to come, West Prussia would form a Polish corridor separating the great mass of Germans to the west from the Germans of East Prussia.

55. THE RISE OF THE OTTOMAN TURKS AND RUSSIA

The conquests of the Mongols in the thirteenth century displaced many Asian tribes from their homelands. One such tribe was the Ottoman Turks. For many years the Ottomans wandered about western Asia, serving as mercenaries in the armies of various Moslem rulers. The Ottomans themselves became converts to Islam. Asia Minor escaped permanent occupation by the Mongols, and in this area the Ottomans were allowed to settle, around 1240, by the Turkish Sultan of Roum. Toward the end of the century the power of the Sultan of Roum declined, and the various Turkish tribes in Asia Minor, including the Ottomans, set up independent states. The Ottoman state proved to be the most vigorous, and early in the fourteenth century it began to expand at the expense of its Turkish neighbors.

The Ottomans cross into Europe (1354). The growth of Ottoman power was very rapid. The Ottoman leaders assumed the title of sultan (commander of the faithful), and by 1340 they had conquered all of northern Asia Minor. Across the Black Sea straits they could see Constantinople, which it was their fondest dream to capture. Constantinople was still the most splendid city in Christendom, but it was no longer the capital of a great empire. The Byzantine Empire was but a shadow of its former self. Various Balkan peoples, such as the Serbs and the Bulgars, encroached on its territory, and within the empire there was an almost constant state of civil war.

As the power of the Ottomans grew, rival Byzantine leaders looked to the Turks for assistance. At the invitation of one of these leaders, the sultan Orkhan (1326–1359) crossed the Hellespont into Europe. Orkhan's crossing, incidentally, marked the first time that an Eastern power had crossed the straits into Europe since the Persian king Xerxes crossed the Hellespont into Greece in 480 B.C.

The Janissaries. Once they were settled on the European side of the straits, the Ottomans would not leave. The Byzantine Empire was much too weak and divided to expel them. The Ottoman army was numerous and well disciplined, and it is one of the ironies of history that the most loyal and warlike of the Ottoman troops—who eventually subjugated the Christians of southeastern Europe—were themselves former Christians. These were the Janissaries. Under the sultan Orkhan, the Turks began the practice of demanding as tribute from their Christian subjects a certain number of very young Christian boys. These boys were made to adopt the Moslem religion and were brought up to serve as soldiers. The only life they knew was that of serving their Ottoman masters, and they became noted for their intense loyalty.

The crusade of Nicopolis (1396). In 1365 the Turks occupied Adrianople, in Thrace, and established that city as their capital. Steadily they encroached on the remnants of the Byzantine Empire in Greece, and by the end of the century they had subjected Greece's northern neighbors, Serbia and Bulgaria. The advance of the Moslem Turks into Christian Europe alarmed the West, and the Pope called for a crusade. Sigismund, the King of Hungary, led a short-lived crusade against the Turks in 1396, but his army of Western knights was disastrously defeated at Nicopolis, on the lower Danube River. The victorious sultan, Bayazid (1389–1402), then turned his attention to Constantinople. By this time Constantinople had become a Christian enclave in Turkish territory, and Bayazid knew that he could not safely advance into central Europe while Constantinople, far to his rear, remained free. His efforts to take Constantinople were cut short, however, by an unexpected invasion of Ottoman territory from the east.

Tamerlane and the new Mongol empire. Ever since the time of Kublai Khan, the great Mongol khanates from the Black Sea to the South China Sea had been independent. As we have already seen, the Mongol khanates began to weaken in the latter part of the fourteenth century as the khans warred on one another and the subject peoples rose in revolt. In the midst of the Mongol disintegration, there arose a new Mongol leader, Tamerlane, who briefly restored the Mongols to some of their former power. In 1369, Tamerlane gained control of Transoxiana, north of India, and from there he sent his conquering armies in all directions but east. India, which had escaped the earlier Mongol conquests, was invaded, and the leading city of Delhi was sacked. Westward the Mongols conquered to Asia Minor and Syria. The Ottoman sultan Bayazid sought to stop Tamerlane's advance into Asia Minor, but at Angora (Ankara), in 1402, the Mongols inflicted a severe defeat on the Ottomans, and Bayazid himself was captured. Tamerlane then turned south and ravaged Syria. Planning to conquer China, he returned to the East but died en route to China in 1405.

The crusade of Varna (1444). The Mongol empire of Tamerlane was the creation of a single man, and at Tamerlane's death it fell to pieces. For several years thereafter the Ottoman state was in confusion as rival sultans sought for control of the growing Ottoman empire. The sultan Murad II (1421–1451) restored order and resumed the Turkish penetration of Europe. Again the West became alarmed, and the Pope called for a crusade. Led by King Vladislav VI of Poland, a crusading army of Western knights was routed by Murad at Varna, on the Black Sea coast. Sporadic fighting continued between the West (especially Hungary) and the Ottomans, who were stopped at Belgrade from advancing into central Europe.

The fall of Constantinople (1453). On April 7, 1453, Sultan Mohammed II (1451–1481) began the final siege of Constantinople. The Byzantines were reinforced by troops sent by Genoa and Venice, but still they were hopelessly outnumbered. One hundred and fifty thousand Turkish troops assaulted the city, while the defenders numbered no more than ten thousand. Besieged by land and by sea, cut off from outside help and reduced to starvation, the Byzantines and their Western allies held out, nevertheless, as long as was humanly possible. On May 29 the walls of the city were breached, and the ancient capital of

The Fall of Constantinople, *by Tintoretto. Although its greatest asset was a system of massive walls, Constantinople fell before overwhelming numbers. During the siege, Emperor Constantine XI was killed. (Alinari)*

Byzantium fell amidst terrible scenes of massacre and destruction. The last of the Byzantine emperors, Constantine XI, did not witness the sack of his city, for he had died fighting on the walls. After the fall of Constantinople, the sultan Mohammed captured the isolated Byzantine fortresses in Greece, and so the Byzantine Empire passed forever from the scene of history.

The Ottoman Empire. Mohammed II, the captor of Constantinople, was called "the Conqueror." He completed the Turkish conquest of all the Balkan peninsula south of Belgrade, except a section of Dalmatia held by Venice and the little mountain principality of Montenegro. For many years he was at war with Venice, and he seized the Venetian commercial colonies in the Aegean Sea and in southern Greece. Twice Mohammed landed armies in Italy, but the Turks did little more than give the Italians a fright. In the eastern Balkans, Mohammed subjected Wallachia and Moldavia to his rule, and he conquered the Mongol khanate of Crimea in southern Russia.

Mohammed's immediate successors expanded east and south of Asia Minor, and in 1517 added Syria and Egypt to the Ottoman Empire. By the early sixteenth century the entire eastern Mediterranean area was under Turkish control. Only the islands of Cyprus, Rhodes, and Crete remained in Christian hands. When the sultanate passed to Suleiman the Magnificent in 1520, the Turks made ready to resume their march toward the heart of Europe.

Russia: the Khanate of the Golden Horde. After the Mongol conquest of Russia in 1237–1240, the Mongols set up a khanate, called the Golden Horde, in southern Russia. From that time the Mongols were not so much the rulers as the masters of Russia. So long as the Russians remained submissive and paid yearly tribute to the Mongols, the Mongols allowed them to be ruled by Russian princes and to follow their ancient ways. The Mongols never interfered with the Russians' practice of the Orthodox religion.

The Grand Dukes of Moscow. The Mongols did not personally make the rounds of Russia collecting tribute. Instead they deputized one of the Russian princes to do the job for them. The prince who received this job was designated grand duke by the Mongols. At first the Mongols bestowed the office of grand duke on whichever prince they wished, but from 1328 on they allowed the title to become hereditary among the princes of Moscow.

Before the Mongol conquest the Duchy of Moscow had been of little importance. But once the office of grand duke became vested in its princes, Moscow rapidly became a leading principality. Besides collecting tribute from the other Russian princes, the grand dukes assumed the duty of keeping peace among the various principalities and settling their differences. Officially the grand dukes performed these services on behalf of the Golden Horde, but they also used their superior position to expand the Duchy of Moscow at the expense of other Russian principalities.

Toward the end of the fourteenth century there was a general weakening of the Mongol khanates, and the Khanate of the Golden Horde was no exception. For many decades the grand dukes of Moscow had faithfully discharged their duties for the khan, but they were quick to take advantage of the khan's weakness to claim greater freedom for themselves. This move was challenged by the khan, but in 1380 the Grand Duke Dmitri defeated the khan at the battle of Kulikovo. Dmitri's victory was regarded by the Russians as a heartening sign, for it proved that the Mongols were far from invincible. Since it was the Grand Duke of Moscow who had beaten the khan, the prestige of Moscow soared.

Tamerlane attacks the Golden Horde. In 1395 the Golden Horde received a blow from which it never recovered. Tamerlane suddenly appeared in eastern Russia at the head of a great Mongol army. The khan of the Golden Horde looked upon Tamerlane not as a fellow Mongol but as a rival who had come to seize his land. Tamerlane inflicted a shattering defeat on the Horde, and for the moment both the Horde and the Russians became for a time the subjects of Tamerlane. The Golden Horde was never able to regain its former strength. Rival khanates were formed in southern Russia, and the Horde's hold on Moscow steadily grew weaker.

Ivan III ends the Mongol domination. Now the grand dukes of Moscow acted more and more as if they were sovereign rulers. They continued to expand their duchy at the expense of other Russian principalities, and they grew very careless about paying tribute to the khan. Under Ivan III (1462–1505), Moscow absorbed so many other Russian principalities that

from that time the Duchy of Moscow and Russia became practically synonymous terms. Ivan's greatest feat was his conquest of Novgorod, the one Russian city that had never been subjected to the Mongols. Ivan also reconquered much of western Russian that had been seized by the Lithuanians in the fourteenth and fifteenth centuries. In 1480, Ivan felt strong enough to announce that he would no longer pay tribute to the Golden Horde. So weak had the Horde become that it did not even challenge Ivan in the field, and very shortly it fell to pieces.

Moscow, the "Third Rome." Unlike other European rulers, Ivan did not regard the fall of the Byzantine Empire merely as a calamity. He married Zoë, the niece and heiress of the last emperor, and claimed, therefore, to be the heir to the Byzantine Empire. This meant that he considered himself the successor of the Caesars. Whatever power they had had, he should have. He considered also that—with the fall of Constantinople and the subjection of the Greek church to the Turks—the religious leadership of the Orthodox Church had passed to Moscow. Just as Constantinople had been the Second Rome, so was Moscow now the Third Rome. Ivan's successors would never forget this. During the reign of Ivan's son, a Russian monk summed up the sentiments of Russia's political and religious rulers when he wrote: "Moscow is the successor of the great capitals of the world—of old Rome and of the Second Rome. Moscow is the Third Rome, and a fourth there will never be."

54. The Holy Roman Empire and Its Slavic Neighbors

A. By what three means did the Holy Roman Emperor add to his lands?

B. Identify: the Diet, the Golden Bull, Hanseatic League.

C. Describe the Swiss Confederation.

D. How did the German state of Prussia come into being?

55. The Rise of the Ottoman Turks and Russia

A. What was the purpose of the crusade of Nicopolis (1396)?

B. Cite the conquests of Tamerlane and his Mongol armies.

C. What events marked the end of the Byzantine Empire?

D. How did the Mongols govern southern Russia in 1237–1240?

E. Why was Ivan III able to free Russia from Mongol domination in 1480?

THE CHAPTER IN REVIEW

A. How did the Germans of East Prussia come to be separated from the Germans of the West?

B. What areas of the world had come under the domination of the Ottoman Empire by 1520? How was Russia freed from this Mongol rule?

C. Discuss the position of the Holy Roman Emperor in the fourteenth and fifteenth centuries.

D. What was the composition of the Diet of the Holy Roman Empire? Were its powers comparable to those of the English Parliament? Explain.

FOR YOUR NOTEBOOK

You will notice that the pattern of development toward a strong national monarchy did not prevail in central Europe as it did in western Europe. Look through your text carefully to prepare a list of reasons why a strong German monarchy did not develop.

Certain common conditions, such as a need for mutual defense, prevailed among the Swiss cantons and the Hanseatic cities. There were also certain marked differences, such as the Hanseatic cities being port towns and the Swiss cantons being landlocked. Make a list of these common conditions and differences. Examine your list carefully to see if it helps explain the differing developments in each area.

Developments in eastern Europe and the Near East during this age are complex and can be confusing. You will get a clearer picture of these developments if you make four parallel columns for (1) the Ottoman Empire, (2) the Mongol Empire, (3) the Khanate of the Golden Horde, and (4) the Duchy of Moscovy, and then enter the principal events in each column.

SELECTED READINGS

Harold Lamb has written two popular biographies that are historically sound even though they are classified as "historical fiction." These are *Genghis Khan, Emperor of All Men* (New York: Doubleday & Co., Inc., 1952), *The Earth Shakers* (Garden City, N. Y.: Garden City Publishing Co., 1949).

Less imaginative histories for adult readers are the two works of an authority on Russian history, George Vernadsky: *Kievan Russia* (New Haven, Conn.: Yale University Press, 1953), and *The Mongols and Russia* (New Haven, Conn.: Yale University Press, 1953). These books are not difficult to read, and the student will find that two or three chapters from each book will increase his understanding of early Russian history considerably.

Affairs in Germanic Europe, including Switzerland, are well handled in Volume I of *The Hapsburg Monarchy*, by Arthur J. May (Cambridge, Mass.: Harvard University Press, 1953). The interesting story of the Hanseatic League is well told by Elizabeth Gee Nash, *The Hansa, Its History and Romance* (New York: Dodd, Mead & Co., 1929).

Cellini

Michelangelo

Council of Constance

Chapter 20. The Papacy in the Late Middle Ages and the Italian Renaissance

56. THE PAPACY AND CHURCH UNDER SEVERE ATTACK

The Avignon Papacy. Two years after the death of Boniface VIII (the Pope whom Philip the Fair of France had treated so badly), the cardinals elected a Frenchman as Pope. This Pope, Clement V (1305–1314), never left France. He established his residence at Avignon, on the Rhone River, where the popes were to live until 1377. The Avignon popes were under no pressure to remain in Avignon, but stayed there as a matter of choice. Italy in the fourteenth century was a land of violence, where war between rival families and states and insurrections of the Roman populace were very common. The popes felt that they could carry out their duties much better at Avignon than in Rome.

The Avignon popes knew, of course, that the Catholic people expected the Pope to reside in the city whose bishop he was—Rome. The popes themselves admitted that their proper place was in Rome, but most of them continually put off returning. One of them, Urban V (1362–1370), did return to Rome in 1367, but conditions there were so unsettled that he returned to Avignon in 1370.

Effects of the Avignon residence. The popes' residence at Avignon aroused much unfavorable comment in Europe. The charge was often made that the popes were the tools of the French kings. There was much grumbling, too, about certain policies of the

Avignon popes. These popes granted a greater number of "provisions" than had any of their predecessors. Whereas it had been the custom for cathedral chapters to elect bishops, the popes deprived the chapters of this privilege and began making more and more appointments to bishoprics. The papal appointment of bishops is a practice that has continued to the present day. The Avignon popes also made many appointments to the posts of abbot, canon, and pastor in widely separated parts of the Catholic world. Few men denied the papal right to make such appointments, but many complained that the popes did not always appoint suitable men.

Papal expenses were very heavy. Papal States, which had once provided the popes with a good income, had now become the Papacy's greatest expense.

In their effort to restore order to Rome and the Papal States, the Avignon popes had to maintain in Italy, at great expense, an army and a large body of officials.

The growing resentment against the Papacy revealed itself in various ways. Sometimes this resentment expressed itself in the acts of governments, as when the English Parliament passed the statutes of Provisors (1351) and Praemunire (1353). The aim of Provisors was to stop the Pope from making appointments to church offices in England. The aim of Praemunire was to stop Englishmen from having cases heard in the papal court. Similar legislation was passed by other European parliaments.

The heretical ideas of Marsiglio of Padua. On more philosophical grounds, Marsiglio of Padua attacked the

The Return of Pope Gregory XI to Rome from Avignon, *by Bartolo. This event in 1377 ended the Babylonian captivity of the popes. (Alinari)*

Papacy in a revolutionary manner. He set forth his ideas in a work entitled *The Defender of the Peace* (1324). The Church, as Marsiglio saw it, should have the same relationship to the community (whether city-state, monarchy, or empire) as the pagan Greek religion had to the ancient city-state. The Church could not be thought of as something distinct from the community, since the Church and the community were made up of the same body of Catholics. Marsiglio wrote that the sole function of the clergy— Pope, bishops, priests—was to preach, and no more. They had no right to hold Church property, or to try Catholics in special Church courts, or to impose excommunications or interdicts. Church property, he said, belonged to the community, and the community should receive the income from it.

Marsiglio's views were a radical departure from anything the Church had ever known. His views on supreme authority in the Church were equally as radical, for he maintained that the Pope was merely the highest-ranking Church officer (something like a chairman of the board). The supreme teaching and governing authority in the Church, Marsiglio maintained, belonged, not to the Pope, but to the general council. A general council, being representative of the whole Church, spoke for the whole Church. It alone could make decisions binding on all Catholics. The general council had the duty of electing the Pope and, if it saw fit, of deposing him. Its members should be chosen by the various Catholic communities from among men of good life and learning. Marsig-

John Wycliffe (Hulton Picture Library)

lio's views on the role of the general council became known as conciliarism, or the conciliar theory of government.

Marsiglio placed control of the Church in the hands of the Catholic community. But how, precisely, was the community to exercise its power? Marsiglio answered that the community might exercise its power through elected representatives, or by delegating it to a council or even to a single ruler. Obviously the ruler who thought of himself as the community's delegate —and who thought that his will was the community's will—could not fail to be impressed by Marsiglio's theories.

The heresies of John Wycliffe. After Marsiglio, came heretics who attacked many of the Church's fundamental doctrines. The Englishman John Wycliffe (1320–1384), an Oxford professor, rejected the Church's teachings on papal supremacy, penance, clerical celibacy, masses for the dead, purgatory, confirmation, extreme unction, transubstantiation, pilgrimages, indulgences, and veneration of the saints and relics. None of these, he claimed, could be found in the Bible. He taught that everyone was predestined by God either to be saved or damned, and that the only true members of the Church were the "elect." Wycliffe had many of the ideas of the earlier Waldensians and, like them, he claimed that the Bible was the sole source of truth. Like them, too, he set himself up as the interpreter of the Bible.

Wycliffe constantly lashed out against the clergy, from the Pope on down, accusing them of luxury, greed, and pride. The clergy, he said, should be stripped of all their property and be forced to live a life of strict poverty. Temporal lords should seize Church property and divide it among themselves.

The Peasants' Revolt. Wycliffe reached a very large audience, for he wrote in both Latin and English. He claimed that the common people were hungering for religious knowledge, and he had much of the Bible translated into English. He formed an association of priests and laymen, called the Lollards, who preached his doctrines throughout England. The peasants at that time were suffering from many injustices, and a spirit of revolt was brewing. Many of the peasants found that the accusations of greed and luxury which Wycliffe hurled against the clergy could be leveled against the temporal lords as well. In 1381 the English peasants rose in a great revolt that was very anti-aristocratic in tone. A common saying among the peasants was:

When Adam delved and Eve span
Who was then the gentle-man?

The peasants demanded that they be given full benefit of the law and that the lands of the Church and the nobles be equally distributed among the people of England. Wycliffe disavowed any connection with the Peasants' Revolt, and the revolt was put down by the nobles with merciless cruelty. The Lollards, however, continued to preach. They were frequently persecuted by the English government, but the Lollard movement continued into the six-

The Peasant's Revolt (1831) involved the destruction of church lands and property. (Alinari)

teenth century, when it eventually merged with sects that sprang up as a result of the Protestant Revolt.

John Hus, heretic and nationalist. It was a significant sign of the times that neither Marsiglio of Padua nor John Wycliffe suffered any harm on account of his heretical teachings. Marsiglio was protected by the Holy Roman Emperor and Wycliffe by the English nobility. John Hus (1369–1415), a Czech heretic, was not so fortunate. Hus, the head of the University of Prague, absorbed many of Wycliffe's ideas. He began preaching and writing these ideas in the Czech tongue and quickly became a celebrity in Bohemia, a kingdom within the Holy Roman Empire which had long had a large minority of Germans. Hus made himself popular with many Czechs by calling on the Czech people to free themselves from the German influence. Consequently Hus, besides being a heretic, became the champion of Czech nationalism. Even Czechs who had no sympathy for Hus's religious views sided with him on the question of Czech nationalism. As we shall see, Hus's popularity was no guarantee that he would continue to preach and write in safety, and eventually his ideas embroiled the Czech people in a terrible civil war.

57. THE CRISIS AND TRIUMPH OF THE PAPACY

The Great Western Schism (1378–1415). In 1377, Pope Gregory XI, the last of the Avignon popes, returned to Rome. He was begrudgingly accompanied by the cardinals, most of whom were Frenchmen who wanted nothing bet-

John Hus
(Hulton Picture Library)

ter than to return to Avignon. In 1378, Gregory died, and the cardinals met in St. Peter's to elect a successor. The people of Rome, fearing that the cardinals would elect a Frenchman who would return to Avignon, clamored outside St. Peter's for an Italian or a Roman pope. The cardinals were threatened with death if they did not comply with the mob's wishes. On April 8, 1378, the cardinals elected an Italian archbishop who took the name Urban VI (1378–1389).

The Roman people were satisfied with the choice, and so, apparently, were the cardinals. The cardinals insisted that Urban was their free choice and they paid him all the honor that is due a pope. About a month or so after the election, however, Urban began to displease the cardinals, more so when he announced that he was going to reform the Church, beginning with the Sacred College of Cardinals. The cardinals then began to pine for the good old days at Avignon, and one by one they left Rome. In September they met in southern Italy. Claiming that Urban's election was invalid (owing to mob pressure), they proceeded to elect a new pope, Clement VII (1378–1394). Later Clement and the cardinals returned to Avignon. Urban, who had been abandoned by all his cardinals, created an entirely new College of Cardinals.

Confusion in the Catholic world. The double papal election threw the Catholic world into confusion. Who was the true Pope? The alignment of the various Catholic governments with one or the other pope was dictated mainly by political considerations. France recognized Clement VII, the Pope who resided at Avignon. England, which was then fighting the Hundred Years' War with France, recognized Urban, the Roman Pope. France's political friends, Aragon, Castile, and Scotland, recognized the Avignon Pope. England's political friends, Portugal and Burgundy, recognized the Roman Pope. Germany and Italy, being divided politically, were also divided in their allegiance to the Papacy. Many German and Italian states recognized Urban; others recognized Clement. The Catholic countries of eastern Europe, on the whole, recognized Urban. Even the saints were confused by the situation. St. Catherine of Siena adhered to Urban; St. Vincent Ferrer, a famous Spanish Dominican, recognized Clement. Each of the popes excommunicated all the followers of the other; and so, in a sense, every Catholic in the world was excommunicated.

St. Catherine of Siena, who because of her great wisdom and saintliness was a counselor to the popes, believed that Urban VI was the legitimate successor to the throne of Peter. (Alinari)

The way out of this unprecedented situation would have been for each of the popes to resign and for their cardinals to meet and agree on a new pope. But each Pope was convinced that he was the true Pope, and neither trusted the other to resign, and so all efforts toward this end failed. When Urban and Clement died, their cardinals elected successors, and so the schism continued. The conciliar theory of Church government, which had been proposed by Marsiglio of Padua, now began to loom very large in the minds of the Catholic people. How could the schism be solved except by a general council?

The Council of Pisa. In 1409 the cardinals of both the Roman and Avignon popes called a council, which met at Pisa. The Council deposed the two popes and elected Alexander V as pope. When Alexander died shortly afterward, the cardinals elected John XXIII (1410–1415). But both the Roman and the Avignon popes continued to have large followings, and so there were now three popes.

The Council of Constance. In 1414 another council was called, which met at Constance, in southern Germany. This was the most splendidly attended council the Church had ever seen. Cardinals, primates, archbishops, bishops, abbots, doctors of theology, doctors of canon law, and temporal princes flocked to it by the hundreds. The Council was called not only to heal the schism but also to end the Hussite heresy in Bohemia and to reform the Church in general.

In 1415 the Council summoned Hus to appear before it and tried him on charges of heresy. He was condemned, turned over to secular authority, and burned at the stake. The Council issued several decrees calling for various reforms in the Church. It also issued the decree *Sacrosancta,* which stated that a general council was superior to the Pope, and the decree *Frequens,* which stated that a general council should henceforth be held at stated intervals, at least once every ten years.

The end of the schism. In 1415 the Council succeeded in ending the Great Western Schism. The Pisan Pope, John XXIII, and the Roman Pope, Gregory XII, voluntarily resigned. The Avignon Pope, Benedict XIII, refused to resign and was deposed by the Council. In 1417 the cardinals and the other delegates to the Council unanimously elected Martin V (1417–1431). Martin was recognized by the entire Catholic world, and so ended the Great Western Schism. Benedict XIII never gave up his claim to the Papacy, but after his death in 1422 the handful of cardinals who had remained faithful to him made their submission to Martin V.

The election of Martin V ended one of the gravest crises the Church had ever gone through. Were the Church purely a human institution, she might well have been wrecked by the schism. Though the unity of the Church was restored, Martin V and his successor, Eugene IV (1431–1447), were in a very difficult position. Conciliarism was still very much in the air, and the popes had to proceed very diplomatically to restore the Papacy to its supremacy. That the Catholic world did not really believe in conciliarism was proved very shortly. In accordance with the Council of Constance's decree *Frequens,* Martin V called a council to meet at Pavia in 1423. But so little interest was shown in the Council that it shortly broke up on account of poor attendance. Martin's successor, Eugene IV, also called a council, which met at Basel in 1431. It, too, was poorly attended at first. But when it was on the verge of breaking up, the Hussite troubles in Bohemia became so serious that many Catholics felt that the troubles could be solved only by a general council. Consequently the attendance improved.

The Council of Basel and the Hussites. The death of John Hus had not ended

The dome of St. Peter's in Vatican City, Rome. The Vatican City is an independent sovereign state with the Pope as its absolute ruler. (Italian Tourist Office)

the Latin *calix,* chalice). The other group, the Taborites (from Mount Tabor in the Old Testament), were far more radical and accepted all of Hus's heresies. The Taborites could not keep their unity and split into several sects, but reunited in the face of renewed German invasions. In 1431 the Hussites sent the Germans fleeing in panic across the border.

The Calixtines were anxious to remain within the Church, and in 1432 they opened a series of conferences with the Council of Basel. The Council finally agreed to allow the Calixtines to receive Communion under both species. Subsequently, the Calixtines drove the Taborites from power, and so the more serious of the Hussite troubles came to an end. But like the Lollards in England, the Taborite movement continued into the sixteenth century.

The Greek union with Rome (1439). The Council of Basel acted rather independently of Pope Eugene, but there was not an open break between the Council and Eugene until 1436. In that year the Council demanded that Eugene accept the decree *Sacrosancta,* which stated that a general council was superior to the Pope. Eugene refused, and announced that he was transferring the council to Ferrara, in Italy, in order to begin negotiations with the Byzantines for their reunion with Rome. Many of the delegates obeyed the Pope and went to Ferrara, but others stayed on at Basel, claiming that their council was the true council. In Italy, Eugene moved the council from Ferrara to Florence and scored a major triumph when the Greek Church recognized papal

the Hussite heresy. Hus's followers armed themselves and resisted all attempts of the Holy Roman Emperor to put them down. For a while the Hussites were so successful that they invaded Germany. In the flush of victory, however, they split into two camps and began fighting among themselves. The more moderate group of Hussites was really not heretical at all. Its chief demand was that the Czechs be allowed to receive Communion under both species.[1] This group was called the Calixtines (from

---

[1] The consecrated wine as well as the consecrated bread.

supremacy. The Greeks at that time were being hard pressed by the Ottoman Turks, and they hoped that their union with Rome would be followed by military help from the West. Unfortunately the submission of the Greek Church was very short-lived, for the Byzantine Empire soon fell to the Turks, and the union gradually dissolved.

The end of conciliarism. The delegates who remained at Basel refused to recognize the Council of Ferrara-Florence. They accused Eugene of heresy and schism, deposed him, and elected another to fill his place. The new "pope," Felix V (1439–1449), was the last antipope in history. Few Catholics took either Felix or the so-called Council of Basel very seriously. In 1449 the Council, having become the laughingstock of Europe, dissolved itself and made its submission to the Pope. Felix resigned and made his submission too.

Conciliarism gradually disappeared, and there was never again any serious question concerning papal supremacy over the Church. The Papacy had survived a terrible ordeal, and its triumph was complete. There were many troubles in store for the Papacy and the Church, but future troubles were not to be of such a nature as were the Great Western Schism and the conciliar movement. The schism and conciliarism were problems *within* the Church and caused genuine confusion in the minds of many honest Catholics. The Protestant Revolt of the sixteenth century, terrible though it would be, would not cause confusion of this sort. It would be both a breaking away from the Church and an *outside* attack upon it. There would never be any doubt as to who was the true Pope or where the unity of Christ's Church was to be found.

58. ITALY AND THE RENAISSANCE

During the fourteenth and fifteenth centuries Italy assumed the cultural leadership of all Europe. In the two previous centuries that position had been occupied by France. Paris, with its great university, had been the intellectual capital of Europe. The most splendid Gothic churches and the finest Gothic sculpture had been done in France. France, too, had produced the finest vernacular literature in Europe.

The poet Dante (1265 to 1321). The shifting of the cultural leadership of Europe to Italy began with the poet Dante. Dante Alighieri, a native of Florence, is universally acclaimed as one of the greatest poets in world literature, ranking with Greece's Homer and England's Shakespeare. His fame rests chiefly on his poem *The Divine Comedy,* which tells of Dante's imaginary journey through hell, purgatory, and heaven. Dante wrote in the Tuscan dialect of his native Florence. So well did he mold this dialect to express beautiful poetic images and profound thought that the Tuscan dialect became the foremost literary and vernacular language of Italy.

The Renaissance. Before Dante's death a movement was already underway in Italy that eventually was given the name *Renaissance,* which means "rebirth." The rebirth which men of the Renaissance considered was taking place was that of antiquity. Classical writings, buildings, and art were studied with renewed interest. Writers tried to reproduce the style and content of the ancient authors, and artists tried to produce works of art and architecture inspired by ancient models. This movement meant, of course, a breaking away from the cultural trends of the High Middle Ages. Gothic art and architecture came to be looked upon as barbarous. In fact it was during the Renaissance that the art and architecture of the High Middle Ages were first labeled Gothic, a term the Italians equated with "barbarous." The men of the Renaissance went to great pains to cultivate a Latin style based on the classical authors, such as Cicero. Unfortunately the movement to revive a classical Latin style resulted generally in a style that was extremely artificial and clumsy. Unfortunately, too, this same movement effectively killed Latin as a living literary language of great naturalness and beauty and simultaneously set back the development of literature in the vernacular languages.

Petrarch (1304 to 1374). The greatest name associated with the early Renaissance is that of Petrarch, a Florentine. Petrarch collected all the classical manuscripts he could get his hands on and studied them intently in order to recapture the atmosphere of the ancient world.

The "fountains" of Italian literature: Dante, Petrarch, and Boccaccio. Boccaccio's admiration for Dante inspired him to write a biography of the poet, one of his earliest works. In later years, the city of Florence engaged him as expositor of Dante's Divine Comedy. *(Alinari)*

ANTE ALLIGHIERI   FRANCESCO PETRARCA   GIOVANNI BOCCACCIO

He laboriously composed letters and other works in what he thought was a pure Latin. Petrarch was widely acclaimed for his Latin works and was hailed on both sides of the Alps as a rival of the ancient authors. Petrarch also wrote in Italian, but was somewhat embarrassed at writing in the language of the people and apologized profusely for doing so. His chief Italian works are his sonnets addressed to Laura, the lady of his dreams. Apologetic though Petrarch was for writing in Italian, he wrote beautifully in his native language, and his sonnets to Laura still retain a high place in Italian literature.

The art of the Renaissance. In the arts the Renaissance was remarkably productive. Though in architecture and in sculpture its imitation of classical models marks the Renaissance as a period of far less originality than the High Middle Ages, in painting the Renaissance is unrivaled. The earliest of the great Italian painters belongs more properly to the High Middle Ages. This was Giotto (*c.* 1276–*c.* 1337), a Florentine, who typified the medieval spirit in his exclusive concern with religious themes. After Giotto the techniques of painting steadily improved, as the treatment of subject matter, under the influence of the Renaissance, steadily changed. As in literature, so in painting the artists looked to antiquity for inspiration. Since few paintings from antiquity had survived, the artists looked to classical sculpture to provide them with models for the canvas. Greek and Roman sculpture had a strong naturalistic, at times an almost photographic, quality, and we find this

Leonardo da Vinci, Italian painter, sculptor, architect, musician, engineer, and scientist—a man born before his time. His most notable painting is The Last Supper. *(Alinari)*

quality reproduced in the paintings of the Renaissance. Though the painters of the Renaissance still used religious themes, there is often lacking a genuine spiritual quality in their work. Remove the halos from the "Holy Family" of many a Renaissance painter and you have a painting that might as well be labeled "Italian Family." The same observation may be made of Renaissance sculpture. Here we see the influence of the ancient models at its greatest. One need only turn from the statuary on the cathedrals of Chartres, Amiens, or Reims to that of the Renaissance to see how far the world had moved from a highly spiritual conception of art to an art that reflects a highly secular outlook.

In painting, three names stand out particularly: Leonardo da Vinci

Moses, *by Michelangelo. This colossal figure rests on the tomb of Pope Julius II, who commissioned him to work on the ceiling of the Sistine Chapel. (Fototeca Unione, Roma)*

(1452–1519), Raphael (1483–1520), and Michelangelo (1475–1564). Of the three, Michelangelo was undoubtedly the greatest. He is remembered not only as the painter of the splendid *Last Judgment,* which adorns the ceiling of the Sistine Chapel in the Vatican, but also as a brilliant sculptor, architect, and even poet. Leonardo, too, was a man of broad interests. Like Roger Bacon in the thirteenth century, Leonardo had an extremely inventive mind and drew sketches of such things as airplanes and submarines.

The secular spirit of the Renaissance. The atmosphere of the Renaissance was rather worldly. It has often been said that the several centuries previous to the Renaissance were theocentric (i.e., God-centered), while the Renaissance was anthropocentric (i.e., man-

centered). Certainly during the Renaissance there was much talk about "man" and of man's realizing to the fullest his earthly potential. The models for this "full living" were, of course, the ancient Greeks and Romans. As the men of the Renaissance became more and more man-centered, they became less and less concerned with God-given laws. In business and politics an unscrupulousness arose that in the previous centuries had been very exceptional. Immorality became almost the fashion. Life became very luxurious (for those who could afford it). Even the Papacy became rather worldly-minded. In the latter half of the fifteenth century the popes tended to live more and more luxuriously. They became known as great patrons of art and had the Vatican and St. Peter's rebuilt in the latest Renaissance styles. They entered actively into the game of Italian politics, seeking temporal power for themselves and their relatives.

The Northern Renaissance. Italy, during N, 13. the fourteenth and fifteenth centuries, was the school of Europe. From north of the Alps students flocked to Italy to study ancient manuscripts and to sit at the feet of the Italian masters of painting, architecture, and sculpture. Returning to their homelands, German, French, English, and Flemish students ushered in what is called the Northern Renaissance. Naturally the Northern Renaissance bears a strong resemblance to its parent Renaissance of the south. It differs, however, in having a somewhat more religious tinge. Northern scholars studied closely the Latin and Greek manuscripts of the Bible. They talked a great deal about the "primitive Christianity" found in the New Testament and of the need to reform the Church so that a "purer" Christianity might prevail. There were strong religious movements, too, in the north. Though perfectly orthodox, these movements laid less emphasis on the organization and externals of Christianity than had earlier religious movements. Much less was heard about the role of the hierarchy or the seven sacraments than was heard about the individual's mystical union with God. Many of the northern scholars found great fault with the Church as it then existed, and ridiculed the abuse of such practices as the veneration of the saints and relics, indulgences, and pilgrimages.

The firearm and the printing press. During the fourteenth and fifteenth centuries, two inventions, the firearm and the printing press, came into widespread use. The first of these was to revolutionize the science of warfare; the second was to influence to an incalculable degree the spread of ideas. Gunpowder, which had been known to Roger Bacon in the thirteenth century, was first put to destructive use in the fourteenth. It was not until the following century, however, that the cannon and hand gun were developed to the point that they became indispensable instruments of war. The Hussites used gunpowder with great effect against the Germans in the 1420's and 1430's, and the Turks employed sixty-two pieces of artillery to break down the walls of Constantinople in 1453.

The first printed book, a Bible, came from the printing press of John

Page of the Gutenberg Bible, the first printed book. (American Bible Society)

Gutenberg of Mainz, Germany, possibly as early as 1454. Prior to Gutenberg's time, books were always laboriously copied by hand. Hand-copying made books very expensive, of course, the more so since they were copied on parchment, a very expensive material. Paper was known in the West as early as the thirteenth century. It was much cheaper but also much less durable than parchment, and it was used mostly by businessmen in keeping accounts. Though printing from letters carved on wooden blocks was an old art, it was not until the invention of movable metallic type that it became feasible to print books. Gutenberg's printing of the Bible was quickly followed by the setting up of printing presses all over Europe. By 1500 there were seventy-three printing presses in Italy alone.

The states of Italy. As we have noted so often, Italy was a land of many states. During the period of the Renaissance there were at least a dozen important states in Italy, of which six were large enough to maintain a kind of balance of power. These six were Milan, Venice, Florence, the Papal States, Naples, and Sicily. Before the fourteenth century the north Italian states generally had republican governments, with the suffrage vested in at least the middle-class citizens. In the fourteenth century, however, political strife became the rule of the day as the lower-class citizens made increasing demands for participation in government. Usually the only way out of the confused political situation that followed was to vest supreme political authority in the hands of a single man. Thus in Florence the Medici became the rulers, in Milan the Visconti and later the Sforzas. The Venetian government became the monopoly of a small circle of aristocratic families.

In southern Italy the two kingdoms of Sicily and Naples had been separated ever since the time of the Sicilian Vespers (1282). Sicily was ruled by a branch of the royal house of Aragon, while Naples was ruled by the Angevins, the descendants of Charles of Anjou. In 1435, Alfonso the Magnanimous, King of Aragon, succeeded in reuniting the two kingdoms under his own scepter. But on his death in 1458 the union was again broken. Alfonso's older son, John, the King of Aragon, received Sicily, while Naples went to a younger son, Ferrante.

Charles VIII of France invades Italy. In the late fifteenth century King Charles VIII of France, a descendant of the Angevins of Naples, claimed the throne of Naples for himself. In 1494 he led an expedition through Italy to Naples to seize the kingdom by force. Up to this point, foreign expeditions of this kind had been very rare in Western history. Now they were to become part and parcel of Western politics.

With the invasion of Italy by Charles VIII, the Italians began to pay bitterly for their political disunity. They offered Charles no united opposition; in fact, some Italians encouraged his coming. Charles marched triumphantly through Italy and drove Ferrante from Naples. But the French were no more popular in Naples than they had been in Sicily two centuries earlier, and in 1496 the Neapolitans drove them out.

Conflict between France and Aragon over Naples. Charles VIII's successor, Louis XII, did not give up the claim of the French kings to Naples. Louis did more than merely claim Naples, however. From his grandmother he inherited a claim to the Duchy of Milan. In 1499 Louis invaded Italy and drove the ruling family of the Sforzas from Milan. Next he reduced Naples to subjection. King Ferdinand of Aragon, however, had no intention of letting Louis keep Naples, a kingdom which Ferdinand regarded as rightly belonging to himself. In 1503, Ferdinand drove Louis from Naples and made himself King of Naples. Louis remained in possession of Milan, while

Louis XII, King of France, was called "the father of the people." In vain, he pursued the claim of the French kings to Naples. (Alinari)

Naples and Sicily (the Kingdom of the Two Sicilies) were reunited once again under the royal house of Aragon. Thereafter the Kingdom of the Two Sicilies (also called the Kingdom of Naples) remained under Spanish rule until the eighteenth century.

Italy at the mercy of foreign powers. Italy's troubles had only just begun. Venice's turn was next. Louis XII of France claimed that Venice had usurped part of the territory of his Duchy of Milan; Maximilian I, the Holy Roman Emperor, claimed that Venice had encroached on imperial territory; Pope Julius II claimed that Venice had seized papal territory. In 1508 these three rulers and Ferdinand of Aragon formed an alliance called the League of Cambrai and invaded Venice. By 1511, Maximilian and the Pope had got what they had set out for and thereupon deserted the League of Cambrai. The Pope and Maximilian had grown very suspicious of France's power in Italy, and in 1511 they formed a new alliance called the Holy League, which was aimed at France. The members of the Holy League were the Pope, Maximilian, the Venetians, the Swiss, Ferdinand of Aragon, and even England; in short, every power that had any grievance against France. In 1512 the Holy League drove the French from Italy, but in three years' time the French were back again, this time under their new king, Francis I.

If the student is bewildered by what he has just read, he has every right to be, for a bewildering age of international relations had begun. The age of power politics in Europe was well under way, and Italy had provided the setting for the first act. Across the Alps from Italy still another age was dawning—an age of religious revolt that would deal a mortal blow to the centuries-old religious unity of the West.

REVIEW

STUDY SECTIONS IN REVIEW

56. The Papacy and Church under Severe Attack

A. Why did the popes reside at Avignon rather than at Rome during the fourteenth century?

B. Mention two policies of the Avignon popes that were received unfavorably.

C. What was the "conciliar" theory of Marsiglio of Padua?

D. How did the heresies of John Wycliffe differ from those of Marsiglio?

E. Identify the following: Peasants' Revolt, the Lollards, John Hus.

57. The Crisis and Triumph of the Papacy

A. Why did the cardinals declare the election of Pope Urban VI to be invalid?

B. Which nations supported the Avignon Pope and which recognized the Roman Pope?

c. How was a third pope introduced into the midst of the schism?

D. How did the Council of Constance end the Great Western Schism?

E. Identify: Calixtines, Council of Basel, Felix V.

58. Italy and the Renaissance

A. What was the "rebirth" that characterized the Renaissance period?

B. Mention a contribution to the Renaissance of each of the following: Dante, Petrarch, Michelangelo.

c. Why was the Renaissance said to be "anthropocentric"?

D. How did the lack of unity among the Italian states work to their disadvantage during this period?

THE CHAPTER IN REVIEW

A. Why was the Avignon Pope unpopular during the fourteenth century?

B. Summarize the heresies of Marsiglio of Padua, John Wycliffe, and John Hus.

c. Discuss the causes and solution of the Great Western Schism. How did this schism differ in nature from the Hussite and later Protestant heresies?

D. What was the cultural emphasis of the Renaissance? What was the effect of the Renaissance on the spirituality of the age?

FOR YOUR NOTEBOOK

A real appreciation of what happened in the past is possible only through use of what is called "controlled imagination." Imagine yourself a young Englishman who hears in 1305 that the popes have moved to Avignon. (Remember you are a loyal Englishman and a good Catholic). List the reasons why you might be put out by this turn of events in Church history. Now imagine yourself an elderly English gentleman in 1345 (in the course of the Hundred Years' War). Write down what your attitude would likely be to the popes' staying at Avignon at this time.

Religious developments, such as the decline of the Church and the Papacy in this period, often have political, social,

and economic as well as religious causes. Look in one of the standard one-volume Church histories, such as Neill and Schmandt, *History of the Catholic Church* (Chapters 16–18), and make a list of these non-religious causes. Put them under the headings of political, economic, and social.

The ideal of the Renaissance was the "universal man." Read a biographical sketch of Leonardo da Vinci in one of the encyclopedias and list reasons why he was such an ideal.

"Humanism" is a term often used in connection with the Renaissance. Read the article on humanism in one of the standard encyclopedias and then enter in your notebook a list of reasons for considering this a key cultural development of the Renaissance.

SELECTED READINGS

You will find the Avignon Papacy, the Western Schism, and the conciliar movement best covered in Church histories. Good brief treatments are Dom Charles Poulet, *Church History*, translated by S. A. Raemers (St. Louis: B. Herder Book Co., 1940), Volume I, Part iii; and Thomas P. Neill and Raymond Schmandt, *History of the Catholic Church* (Milwaukee, Wis.: Bruce Publishing Co., 1957), Chapters 16–19.

A good general treatment of this period and that of the next chapter, designed especially for young people, is Dorothy Mills, *Renaissance and Reformation Times* (New York: G. P. Putnam's Sons, 1939). An excellent survey of the Renaissance, written by a scholar in simple language, is George Clarke Sellery, *The Renaissance* (Madison, Wis.: University of Wisconsin Press, 1950). Good biographies that are interesting reading and give a good view of the age are Leo Lerman, *Michelangelo, A Renaissance Profile* (New York: Alfred A. Knopf, 1942); and E. C. Lansing, *Leonardo, Master of the Renaissance* (New York: Thomas Y. Crowell, 1942).

Luther   Calvin   Henry VIII

Chapter 21. Protestant Revolt and Catholic Reform

59. LUTHER AND PROTESTANTISM IN GERMANY

Martin Luther (1483 to 1546). Martin Luther started out to be a lawyer, and his parents scrimped and saved to send their son to the University of Erfurt, in Germany. Luther later told how he gave up his law studies when, at the age of twenty-two, he was caught in a frightening thunderstorm and promised to become a monk if God would spare him from death. This was in 1505, and Luther entered the order of Augustinian Hermits. As an Augustinian, he turned to the study of theology, was ordained a priest in 1507, and later received the degree of Doctor of Theology. He was then sent to be a professor of theology in the newly founded University of Wittenberg, in Saxony.

The doctrine of justification by faith alone. For many years after becoming an Augustinian, Luther was tormented by the problem of salvation. He doubted that he could effectively do anything to save his own soul, and he feared the everlasting pain of hell. He found some comfort, however, in reading Scripture, especially the epistles of St. Paul, where he was struck by the sentence: "He who is just lives by faith" (Romans 1:17). Luther came to put more and more emphasis on faith as the means of salvation, at the same time putting the necessity of doing good works into the background. Eventually he arrived at the doctrine of justification (salvation) by faith *alone.* Luther believed that man was so utterly depraved that he could do absolutely nothing toward his own salvation—except throw himself completely on God's mercy. The act of throwing oneself completely on God's mercy was a sure sign that one had faith, and from that moment on the believer could rest assured that he was saved. The doctrine of justification by faith alone was, of course, contrary to Catholic teaching. In fact, Luther's doctrine undermined the whole structure of the Catholic Church. For if man were saved by faith alone, he would have no need of the sacraments.

The ninety-five theses. It was not Luther's teaching on faith (which he kept pretty much to himself) that brought him into the limelight. It was, rather, his teaching on indulgences. In 1517 a German Dominican, John Tetzel, was commissioned by the Pope to issue indulgences in Germany. Indulgences could be gained not only by good works and prayers but also by donations of money, and, of course, not without the proper interior disposition. A donation of money was equated with a good work, since the giving of money represented a sacrifice on the part of the donor. Tetzel, unfortunately, did not so much issue indulgences as sell them, and he gave the distinct impression that cash on the counter meant the automatic release of one's deceased relatives or friends from purgatory. Luther was shocked by Tetzel's indulgence-hawking and in 1517 drew up a list of ninety-five theses, or propositions, in which he challenged the whole notion of indulgences and of good works in general. On October 31, 1517, he posted his ninety-five theses on the church door at Wittenberg.

Luther an active heretic. Luther's ninety-five theses created a sensation in Ger-

Martin Luther and His Friends, *a wood panel by Lucas Cranach, who did numerous paintings of the Reformation leaders. In the above, Henry VIII is in the foreground. On the left is Luther; on the right are Zwingli and Melancthon, other reformers. (The Toledo Museum of Art)*

many. Pope Leo X ordered an investigation of Luther's teachings, and the papal legate in Germany tried in vain to get Luther to retract. In 1519 a renowned German theologian, Dr. John Eck, debated publicly with Luther in Leipzig. Eck repeatedly forced Luther into a corner, making him reveal that he held many of the heresies of Wycliffe and Hus. When in the following year the Pope issued a bull excommunicating Luther, the heretic publicly burned the bull in Wittenberg to show his contempt of papal authority.

Pope Leo X issued the bull Exsurge Domine *(1520), which condemned the heresies of Martin Luther and excommunicated the reformers. (Alinari)*

Many Germans rally to Luther. Luther's defiance of the Papacy was enthusiastically hailed by many Germans. Some Germans thought that Luther would bring about a genuine reform of the Church; others hailed him as the liberator of the German Church from the "Italians"; still others were casting a covetous eye on the Church's property in Germany. Luther promptly set about making a very conscious play for the support of as many Germans as possible, especially of the nobility. In a pamphlet entitled *An Address to the German Nobility,* he appealed to the nobles' sense of German nationality and asked them how long they would allow their land to be "milked dry" by the Italian Pope at Rome. He called on the nobles to seize the Church's property and to take the reform of the German Church into their own hands. In other public writings Luther outlined his own teachings, which were mostly of a negative sort. He rejected papal supremacy, the apostolic succession of bishops, the sacred character of the priesthood, several of the sacraments as defined by the Church, pilgrimages, fasting, indulgences, and the veneration of relics, images, and saints.

The emperor Charles V (1519 to 1556). In the very year in which Luther debated with Eck and disclosed himself an active heretic, a new Holy Roman Emperor was elected in Germany. This was the Hapsburg prince, Charles V. The new emperor was indeed an imposing figure. Thanks to the skillful marital policies of his Hapsburg ancestors, Charles was the hereditary ruler of Austria and of the many Hapsburg lands in Germany, of the Netherlands, Luxembourg, and Franche Comté, of Castile and Aragon, of Sardinia, the Two Sicilies, and the recent Spanish acquisitions in the New World.

Charles was a devoted son of the Catholic Church, and in the normal course of events it was to be expected that he would do something to suppress Luther and his heretical teachings. But we have already seen what little control the emperor had over the various German lands in the empire. Had Luther lived in one of the hereditary Hapsburg lands, Charles would have had no trouble in dealing with him. But as it was, Luther resided in the Electorate of Saxony and was not under Charles's immediate jurisdiction. The Elector of Saxony, Frederick the

Wise, was theoretically subject to Charles but, like the other German princes, he did as he pleased. Frederick was a warm partisan of Luther and zealously protected the heretic from harm.

Even if Charles had ruled a more united Germany, he could never for long have given his undivided attention to Luther and the German situation. He had far too many other things to do and was constantly looking after his scattered dominions. Then, too, his reign was an almost endless series of wars with the French and the Turks. Often when he was on the verge of taking vigorous steps against Luther, he was called away from Germany by pressing events elsewhere. During the 1520's—a crucial period in the Protestant Revolt—Charles was at war with Francis I of France, successfully driving the French from Italy once and for all. The French were practically surrounded by the Hapsburg lands, and they would stop at nothing to injure the emperor. Catholic though they were, the French gladly allied with the Turks and the Lutherans in order to weaken the Catholic Charles. After the French, the Ottoman Turks were Charles's worst enemies. In 1520 the Turkish sultan, Suleiman the Magnificent, resumed his march toward central Europe, overrunning Hungary and advancing to the very gates of Vienna in 1529. The Turks were driven back, but eventually Charles had to recognize the Turkish possession of the greater part of Hungary.

Luther organizes his church. In 1521, Luther was summoned to appear before the German imperial Diet, or parliament, at Worms. He refused to retract

Erasmus of Rotterdam, Dutch humanist and classical writer. Luther first looked upon him as an ally because of Erasmus' attacks on clerical abuses. However, Erasmus made his position clear and remained a believing Catholic. (Fototeca Unione, Roma)

any of his teachings, and after his departure the Diet proclaimed him an outlaw. The Elector Frederick of Saxony hid Luther in a castle for safekeeping, and Luther spent the next year translating the New Testament into German. Luther was a master of the German language (in the Saxon dialect), and his translations of the New Testament and later of the Old Testament established him as one of the molders of the modern German language.

In 1522 he returned to Wittenberg and began to organize a new church based on his own teachings. Already a number of German princes had seized the Church property in their states and were setting up new churches. In the new Lutheran (or Evangelical) church there were no bishops or priests at all. The Mass was abolished and replaced by a communion service, which consisted mainly of prayers, hymns, and a sermon. The communion service was conducted by a "minister" who claimed no priestly character. The monasteries were abolished, and Luther encouraged the monks and nuns to enter civil life. Luther himself married a former nun in 1525. He did not obtain any governing authority over the new church. In each German state the head of the church was the prince of that state, who on adopting the new religion seized all the property of the Catholic Church and thereby greatly increased his own wealth. Often the seizure of Church property was accompanied by great destruction of statues, stained-glass windows, paintings, and illuminated manuscripts. The monastery churches, which were generally of great beauty, were often totally destroyed. The wanton destruction of religious art by the Protestants is one of the most saddening features of the entire Protestant Revolt. Though the Northern Renaissance produced many beautiful objects of art in the sixteenth century, it is safe to say that the Protestants destroyed far more things of beauty than the artists produced.

The Peasants' Revolt. Luther's heresies had a more unsettling effect on the Germans than Luther himself had bargained for. New religious sects began to crop up completely outside the Lutheran movement. Some of these sects, the Anabaptists in particular, took Lu-

ther's teaching of the private interpretation of Scripture in an extremely literal fashion. They ignored the newly founded Lutheran Church and oftentimes announced their independence of the state too. Luther had no use for the new sectarians and called on the princes to put them down by force. Another result of Luther's teachings was great unrest among the German peasants. They misinterpreted his words as calling for a new social equality among men, and in 1524–1525 they rose in a great revolt. The whole episode was very similar to the rising of the English peasants in 1381, inflamed in part by Wycliffe's teachings. As long as the peasants directed their attacks against the holdings of the Catholic Church, Luther was very sympathetic to them. But when they began to attack the persons and property of the German princes, many of whom were Lutheran, Luther disclaimed any connection with the revolt. In a brochure called *Against the Murderous and Thieving Rabble of the Peasants,* Luther called on the German princes to slaughter the rebellious peasants one and all. His advice was very succinct: "Whoever can, should smite, strangle, or stab, secretly or publicly." The princes gladly obliged, and the revolt was mercilessly suppressed. When the revolt was over, the butchered bodies of fifty thousand German peasants lay strewn across the fields of Germany.

The Peace of Augsburg. Several times Charles V and the imperial Diet issued decrees outlawing Lutheranism and other sects, but Charles, as noted above, was always prevented from taking effective action owing to the need of his presence elsewhere. When the Diet of Speyer, in 1529, renewed the outlawing of Lutheranism, the Lutheran princes banded together and drew up a formal *protestation* of the Diet's action. From that time on, the Lutherans and all others who broke with the ancient Church were known as *protestants*. Toward the end of his reign Charles fought an inconclusive war with the Lutheran princes of Germany, who received great assistance from the French. In 1555, on the eve of his abdication, Charles and the Lutherans agreed to compromise. At Augsburg an imperial Diet was held which issued the Peace of Augsburg, designed to end the fighting in Germany. According to the Peace, the princes and governments of the free cities of Germany should determine what religion their subjects should follow. Each state was to be either Catholic or Lutheran. No other religion was to be tolerated. In case a bishop-prince turned Protestant, he was to surrender his authority in his ecclesiastical state, leaving it in the hands of the Catholic Church. Lutherans were to keep whatever Church property they had seized before 1552. In many of its provisions the Peace of Augsburg was very vague. It far from settled the religious problems of Germany. In the following century these problems would rise again to the fore and lead to the most murderous civil war Europe had ever seen.

60. THE SPREAD OF THE PROTESTANT REVOLT

Scandinavia. Outside Germany, Scandinavia provided the most congenial atmosphere for Lutheranism. The kings of Denmark (who also ruled Norway) and the kings of Sweden (who also ruled Finland) imitated the German princes by seizing Church property and setting up national churches. The seizure of Church property enriched the kings enormously and gave them the strength wherewith to put down Catholic opposition. The Scandinavian kingdoms adopted the Lutheran faith as approved by Luther, and by the end of the sixteenth century Catholicism had been nearly wiped out in Scandinavia.

Switzerland. The Protestant Revolt in Switzerland was almost simultaneous with that in Germany. Its leader was Huldreich Zwingli, a preacher at the cathedral of Zurich. From 1518 on, Zwingli actively denounced many of the basic doctrines of the Catholic Church. His teachings, which were even more revolutionary than Luther's, found considerable support among the Swiss people, especially the townsmen. The Swiss break from the Church was followed by the usual seizure of Church property and the destruction of monasteries and religious art. Luther and Zwingli recognized that they had a lot in common, but they could never agree on certain fundamentals. Their biggest disagreement was in their belief about the Eucharist. Luther believed that God was present *in* and *with* the consecrated bread and wine; Zwingli maintained that the Eucharist was no more than a mere symbol of the Body and Blood of our Lord. Zwingli had no use for sects other than his own, and he sought to convert the non-Zwinglian Protestant sects and the Catholics of Switzerland to his own brand of Christianity by force of arms.

He was killed in battle by the Catholic Swiss in 1531, and shortly afterward the Protestant leadership of Switzerland passed to John Calvin.

John Calvin (1509 to 1564). After Luther, the most important of the Protestants was John Calvin, a Frenchman. Calvin broke away from the Church at the age of twenty. Later, fearing persecution at the hands of King Francis I of France, he fled to Basel, in Protestant Switzerland. Calvin was a man of great learning and intellect, and in 1536 he published the *Institutes of the Christian Religion.* In this work he aimed to show how the Christian religion was practiced in the early days of the Church. In the same year in which he published the *Institutes,* Calvin took up residence in Geneva, an independent city which had just expelled its count and bishop. Geneva was fast becoming Protestant, and Calvin was invited to become its head. Except for one period of exile, Calvin spent the remainder of his life in Geneva.

Geneva: a Calvinist theocracy. Though Geneva had a republican form of government, Calvin was really its absolute ruler. The aim of his government was to have the Genevans live the "perfect" Christian life which he had described in the *Institutes.* Under Calvin, Geneva was a theocracy. Theoretically God was Geneva's ruler; no distinction was made between religious law and civil law; and the law —God's law—was backed up by the police. Disobedient children were whipped in the public square; anyone who used blasphemous language was placed in the public pillory; dancing, card-playing, and non-attendance at

John Calvin. Calvinism which spread from Switzerland to Hungary in the East and Scotland in the West was finally curbed by the great Catholic Reform.
(Hulton Picture Library)

church were punished by fines and imprisonment. Heresy (i.e., disagreement with any of Calvin's notions of Christianity) was punished by death. On one occasion an eminent Spanish physician, Servetus, was passing through Geneva on his way to Italy. Servetus was himself a heretic, holding views very similar to those of the ancient Arians. Such views were later known as Unitarianism. Calvin did not share these views. Before Servetus could get out of Geneva, he was arrested by Calvin's police. He was tried, found guilty of heresy, and burned at the stake.

Calvin's doctrine of predestination. Calvin's distinctive contribution to Protestant theology was his doctrine of predestination. He taught that man could do absolutely nothing toward his eternal salvation; neither good works nor faith were of any use. Calvin taught that all men deserved to be damned but that God in His infinite mercy had arbitrarily chosen a few to be saved. Long before a man was born God had predestined him either to eternal joy or eternal woe. At this point one might ask, Why try to be good or attend church at all, since these could do nothing to help save a person? The answer Calvin gave was very simple. Man, whether he is to be saved or damned, nevertheless owes respect to God, and this respect takes the form of good conduct and churchgoing. Also, the man who lives a good life and goes to church is certainly more likely to be one of the saved than the man who lives a bad life. Thus, living a good life was a great source of comfort to those who thought themselves among the saved. Calvin expected, too, that the saved would naturally associate with one another and set themselves apart from the damned by their good conduct and attendance at church.

The spread of Calvinism. Geneva became the headquarters of a Calvinist world. Calvin founded the University of Geneva, and students from all over Europe flocked to Geneva to sit at the feet of the master. Calvinism so captured the minds of Protestants that it practically brought the spread of Lutheranism to a halt, and Calvinism was transplanted with considerable success in Switzerland, southwestern Germany, eastern Germany, Bohemia, France, Poland, Hungary, and Scotland. We shall see in the next section how the great Catholic Reform of the sixteenth century halted the spread of both Calvinism and Lutheranism and swept Calvinism out of many of the areas where it seemed to have entrenched itself.

Henry VIII of England breaks with Rome. In England the Protestant Revolt took a rather different course. King Henry VIII (1509–1547), the initiator of the revolt, was at first a devout Catholic. When the Lutheran heresy first appeared Henry wrote a book in defense of the seven sacraments and of papal supremacy, and he was rewarded by the Pope with the title of Defender of the Faith—a title which English monarchs use to this day. Henry's enthusiasm for papal leadership began to wane, however, when the Pope failed to grant him an annulment of his marriage with Catherine of Aragon. Henry wanted very much to have a son, but all of his children by Catherine had died in infancy, save their daughter Mary. When Catherine passed the childbearing age, Henry began to agitate for an annulment. He claimed that his marriage with Catherine was never valid in the first place, since she had earlier been married to his older brother. Marriage with a brother's widow was indeed contrary to canon law, but the Pope had granted a dispensation to Henry and Catherine at the time of their marriage.

The Pope to whom Henry appealed for an annulment was Clement VII (1523–1534), who constantly put off making a decision. In the first place, Clement was loath to declare that a dispensation granted by his predecessor was invalid. Second, even if Clement had wanted to give Henry an annulment he would hardly have dared to. Catherine of Aragon herself fought the annulment tooth and nail, and she was backed by her nephew,

Charles V, the Holy Roman Emperor. Charles let it be known that Clement would rue the day he ever granted an annulment to Henry VIII.

Finally Henry grew tired of waiting and began to take steps that weakened the power of the Papacy in England. In 1531 he assembled the English clergy and induced them to recognize him as head of the English Church "as far as the law of Christ allows." In the next two years the English Parliament stripped the Pope of several of his revenues from England and of certain rights over the English clergy. In 1533 Henry went through a marriage ceremony with Anne Boleyn, even before he had got an annulment of any kind whatsoever. Following his "marriage" with Anne, the Archbishop of Canterbury, who was very subservient to Henry and who had many Protestant leanings, pronounced the invalidity of Henry's marriage with Catherine of Aragon. Three months later Anne Boleyn gave birth to a daughter, Elizabeth.

The Act of Supremacy (1534). Henry's marriage with Anne Boleyn and his divorce were followed by his excommunication by the Pope. In 1534, Parliament declared Henry "the only supreme head on earth of the Church of England." Anyone who denied the king's supremacy over the church was declared guilty of treason. Sir Thomas More, the chancellor of England, and Bishop John Fisher of Rochester were sent to the block for refusing to recognize Henry's supremacy.[1]

Henry's schismatic church. The church which Henry VIII founded was not strictly Protestant. It separated itself from Rome, thereby becoming a

Sir Thomas More, the chancellor of England, attracted the friendship of King Henry VIII but was later beheaded because of his staunch opposition to the king's divorce. (The Frick Collection)

schismatic church, but it retained the basic teachings of the Catholic Church. In fact, Henry was just as severe on Calvinists and Lutherans in England as he was on Catholics. By the time of his death in 1547, Henry had executed hundreds of Catholics and Protestants for refusing to accept him as the head of the Church. Those who were executed were not charged with heresy but with treason (for refusing to accept the King's religious supremacy).

The English Church becomes Protestant. Altogether, Henry VIII had six wives. Two of these he divorced, two he be-

---

[1] Four hundred years later (1935) they were canonized as saints by Pope Pius XI.

headed, one died a natural death, and the sixth wife outlived him. Henry's third wife, Jane Seymour, gave birth to a son, Edward, who succeeded Henry as king. Edward VI (1547–1553) was only a child when he became king, and he was easily dominated by the Protestants, who came out of their hiding places as soon as Henry died. The Protestant nobles who dominated the young king soon made the English Church Protestant. English was substituted for Latin in the church services, and priests were encouraged to marry. A uniform book of services, called the Book of Common Prayer, was issued for use in all churches. The Book of Common Prayer contains an implicit denial of the nature of the Eucharist, substituting the words "Holy Communion" and "Lord's Supper" for "Mass," and "table" for "altar."

Catholicism restored. When Edward died England had not yet become so Protestant that it could not take the road back to Catholicism. Edward's successor was Mary I (1553–1558), the daughter of Henry and Catherine of Aragon. Mary was a devout Catholic and promptly set about restoring England to the Catholic fold. Parliament was as co-operative in making Catholic legislation as it had been in making schismatic and Protestant laws under Henry VIII and Edward VI. There was some Protestant resistance to Mary's actions, and she had about three hundred Protestants burned for heresy. Protestant historians in England have criticized Mary severely for this, but the three hundred who died during her reign is a paltry figure compared with the thousands of Catholics who were executed for "treason" during the reigns of Henry VIII, Edward VI, and Elizabeth I.

When Mary died it seemed that England was firmly within the Catholic fold again. Her younger sister Elizabeth, however, would soon undo all of Mary's work and permanently impress the Protestant stamp upon the English Church.

61. THE ERA OF CATHOLIC REFORM

Demand for Church reform. Long before the Protestant Revolt ever broke out there were insistent demands for reform within the Catholic Church. The Renaissance popes were none too eager for reform, but in several of the Western countries the Catholic rulers took the lead. This was particularly true in Spain, where Ferdinand and Isabella saw to it that good bishops were appointed, that the clergy set a good example, and that heretics were put down. Several new religious orders were founded early in the sixteenth century. The Theatines worked to reform the Church and combat heresy in Italy; and the Capuchins, an offshoot of the Franciscans, sought to revive the spirit of St. Francis among the clergy and people.

Paul III (1534 to 1549) reforms the Papacy. The Protestant Revolt speeded the process of Catholic Reform. The first two popes of the early days of the Protestant Revolt, Leo X and Clement VII, were still very much popes of the Renaissance and hardly knew what to do about the Protestants except repress them by force. Beginning with Pope Paul III, however, the reform movement within the Church took on great momentum. Paul lived a very austere life, expelled all corrupt elements from the papal court, appointed only worthy men to the posts of cardinal and bishop, and sought to instill a spirit of reform throughout the entire Church.

The Council of Trent. Many Catholics felt that the Church could best take stock of the religious situation by meeting in general council. In 1545, Pope Paul III assembled a general council at Trent, on the border of Italy and Germany. Thereafter the Council met at various intervals until 1563, when its work was done. The Council did not compromise any Catholic doctrine. It reasserted in clear and forceful language the ancient teachings of the Church. It proclaimed anew that the source of truth is not only the Bible but tradition too; that the Church, under the guidance of the Holy Spirit, is the sole interpreter of the Bible and of tradition and cannot err; that the seven sacraments are essential for salvation; that such ancient practices as the veneration of relics, and invoking of saints are praiseworthy. The Council also reasserted the Church's ancient belief in purgatory and indulgences and in the Pope's supremacy over the Church.

Disciplinary decrees of Trent. These doctrines were issued in clear and ringing tones so that Catholics, clergy, and laity alike could never again be in doubt concerning Catholic teaching. To prevent future abuses, the Council decreed that no charge could be made for indulgences or for the sacraments or for Church offices; that bishops must reside in their dioceses and all clerics in their proper posts. It decreed that every diocese must maintain a seminary for the training of priests and that priests should instruct the faithful frequently in sermons.

St. Ignatius Loyola and the Jesuits. The Church's right arm during the age of Catholic Reform was the Society of Jesus. The founder of this order was St. Ignatius Loyola (1491–1556), a Spanish nobleman who had spent his early life as a soldier. In his fighting days he was very little interested in the things of the spirit, but in 1521, while convalescing from a wound received in

The Council of Trent, which stated and clarified Catholic doctrines and undertook needed reforms, spanned the reigns of five popes. (Caisse Nationale des Monuments Historiques)

St. Ignatius Loyola as painted by Rubens. The Society of Jesus, which he founded, served as a chief instrument of the Pope in the Catholic Reform. Its members gained renown as teachers and writers. (Alinari)

battle, he determined to spend the rest of his life in the service of God. Loyola knew that he would be a far greater force for good if he were a man of education; but, like other members of Europe's military aristocracy, he had received very little schooling. Consequently, in 1524, at the age of thirty-three, he swallowed his pride and enrolled in grammar school with little boys to begin the study of Latin. He made rapid progress in his studies and several years later enrolled at the University of Paris.

At Paris, Loyola gathered around him a group of men as zealous to serve God as he. Some of his followers, attracted to the things of this world, wavered in their loyalty. But Loyola gave them food for thought when he asked, as he did frequently: "What does it profit a man if he gain the whole world and suffer the loss of his soul?" Originally Loyola planned that his group should become missionaries among the Moslems, but later he became convinced that he could better serve the Church in Europe, which was then in the throes of the Protestant Revolt. In 1540, Pope Paul III approved the infant Society of Jesus. Old soldier that he was, Loyola thought of his men primarily as a military company whose duty it was to win battles for Christ. Indeed, "society" is actually a poor translation of the Latin *societas,* which properly means "company" (in the military sense of the word).

The Jesuit achievement. The Jesuits sought to keep Catholics in the fold and to reconvert Protestant Europe to the Faith through preaching and teaching. They set up schools in all the Catholic countries and soon acquired the reputation of being the best educators in Europe. They attached themselves to the courts of kings and princes, where they became court preachers and the confessors of the ruling families. Wherever they could they preached to heretics and they brought back into the Church thousands of Catholics tottering on the verge of heresy. The Jesuits worked especially hard in Poland, Hungary, Austria, Bohemia, the southern Netherlands (Belgium), Bavaria, and the Rhineland. When the Jesuits began preaching in these lands Protestantism had already taken a firm grip, and it seemed for a while that all the inhabitants would become Protestant. With the preaching of the

Jesuits, however, these lands were brought back into the Catholic fold, with only Protestant minorities remaining. In countries where the Jesuits were outlawed, as in England and Protestant Germany, they risked their lives to minister to the needs of the remaining Catholics. Many of the Jesuits died for the Faith, and their names, such as that of Edmund Campion in England, add luster to the long list of Catholic martyrs.

The Wars of Religion in France. In some Catholic countries, such as Spain and Italy, the Protestant Revolt never made much impression. The rulers of those countries remained faithful to the Church, encouraged Church reform, and were ever on the lookout for heresy. In France, on the other hand, Calvinism made great inroads, especially among the nobility and bourgeoisie. The French Calvinists, who were called Huguenots, became so powerful that they formed a political party that sought to get control of the state. This attempt led to a series of terrible civil wars in France, called the Wars of Religion, which lasted intermittently from 1562 to 1598. The Huguenots were fanatical in their hatred of the Catholic Church, and to this day the ruined façade of many a French church attests to Huguenot vandalism. The leader of the Huguenot party was Henry of Navarre, a member of the Bourbon branch of the royal family. The Catholic party was, on the whole, victorious, but on the death of the king in 1589 the throne passed to none other than the Huguenot Henry of Navarre, a cousin of the late king. For several years Henry received hardly any recognition at all from the French people, for they were determined that a Protestant should not rule them. Then in 1593 Henry became a convert to the Catholic Church, and so the new Bourbon dynasty was set securely on the throne. Henry still remained friendly to the Huguenots, however, and in 1598 he issued the Edict of Nantes, which granted religious toleration to the Huguenots. In certain towns of France, Henry gave the Huguenots such power that they became practically a state within the state. Privileged though they were, the Huguenots made very few converts thereafter, and France remained a predominantly Catholic country.

Philip II of Spain. Spain during the sixteenth century was ruled by two kings noted for their devotion to the Catholic Faith. The first of these, Charles V, we have already encountered. When Charles abdicated his thrones in 1555, he left his German possessions to his brother Ferdinand, who was also elected Holy Roman Emperor to succeed Charles. To his son Philip II, Charles left all the other Hapsburg possessions, which were Spain and its New World empire, Sardinia, the Two Sicilies, the Netherlands, Luxembourg, and Franche Comté. Philip was a great champion of the Catholic Church. He was ever watchful for heretics, and during his reign what little Protestantism there was in Spain disappeared. He was no less opposed to the Moslems than he was to the Protestants. In the early part of his reign the Turks were making great inroads into the western Mediterranean. They constantly destroyed Christian shipping, ravaged Sicily and other Christian islands, and even attacked

The tomb of Philip II, designed by P. Leoni. The gilt bronze figures of Philip and his royal family are thirteen feet high. The scene is to one side of the main altar in the Escorial, which was the palace, the monastery, and the mausoleum of the royal family. (Spanish Tourist Office)

the mainland of Italy. In 1571, Philip, co-operating with the Pope, Genoa, and Venice, assembled a great fleet, whose command he entrusted to his half brother, Don John of Austria. On October 7, 1571, the Christian fleet met a numerically superior Turkish fleet in the Gulf of Lepanto, off the western coast of Greece. The Christian fleet utterly destroyed the Turks, and Turkish naval power suffered a blow from which it never recovered. In 1580, Philip enjoyed a victory of another sort when he succeeded to the kingdom of Portugal, thus realizing his ancestors' dream of a truly united Spain. The Portuguese, however, never liked the union with Spain and after sixty years shook off Spanish rule.

The revolt of the Netherlands. In the Netherlands, Philip II suffered another great disappointment. From his father

Charles V, Philip inherited the title of Prince of the Netherlands. Charles had been raised in the Netherlands and had been loved by his subjects, but Philip was a Spaniard by birth and rearing and was looked upon as a foreigner by the Netherlanders. The Netherlanders frequently accused Philip of being a tyrant and of ruling the Netherlands in the interests of Spain. They complained that they were overloaded with taxes, that their commerce was hampered in favor of Spanish shipping, and that their ancient political rights were being suppressed. But the worst cause of tension between Philip and the Netherlanders was that many of the Netherlanders, especially in the seven northern provinces, were Calvinist. Philip introduced the Inquisition into the Netherlands and sought to restore the Calvinists to the Church.

During the greater part of Philip's reign the Netherlands were in rebellion against their Spanish lord. No sooner did Spanish armies suppress one revolt than another cropped up. A Calvinist nobleman, William of Orange, arose as the champion of the Netherlands and enlisted considerable support from the Calvinists. Most of the southern Netherlands were Catholic, and Philip made use of this fact to separate the Catholic part of the Netherlands from the Protestant.

The founding of the Dutch Republic. In 1581 the seven northern provinces, united under the leadership of William of Orange, declared their independence of Philip. The northern Netherlanders (hereafter called the Dutch) stubbornly resisted Philip on both land and sea, and eventually the Spaniards had to accept the independence of the United Provinces. Thus the Netherlands were divided into two parts: the Spanish Netherlands (Belgium), which remained predominantly Catholic; and the United Provinces (also called the Dutch Republic or Holland) which remained predominantly Calvinist.

Before the Protestant Revolt, the Dutch had played little part in European or world history. Once the Dutch gained their independence, however, they quickly rose to be one of the foremost nations in Europe. They achieved this eminence through commerce and colonization. Already these two activities—commerce and colonization—were ushering in a new age of world history.

Elizabeth I of England. Philip paid a great deal of attention to affairs in other Western countries, trying in particular to uphold the Catholic Faith wherever he could. He was the husband of Mary I of England and thus king of that country too, but his brief influence over England came to an end with Mary's death. He hoped to marry Mary's successor, Elizabeth I, but Elizabeth refused to accept him. Elizabeth, indeed, took a course in religious matters that caused Philip great distress. Shortly after she became queen, Elizabeth had Parliament pass a new Act of Supremacy, which declared her the supreme governor of the English Church. The heretical Book of Common Prayer was reissued for use in all English churches. Parliament passed an act called the Thirty-nine Articles, which declared that Scripture was the sole source of truth and that man was saved by faith alone. Thus the English Church became Protestant again, and

Elizabeth I, Queen of England. Her reign opened a new era of economic and cultural development for England. This painting depicts the fashions of her day. (The Metropolitan Museum of Art)

the Thirty-nine Articles became its basic creed. Unlike the Protestant churches on the Continent, the Protestant Church of England (the Anglican Church) retained many of the externals of the Catholic Church. The change in religion was not very apparent to most Englishmen, and the majority of them quietly accepted the new church. There was, nevertheless, considerable Catholic resistance, which was put down by force of arms. Elizabeth tried to impose the new church on the Irish, but they stoutly clung to their ancient Faith.

Mary Queen of Scots. During Elizabeth's reign, seagoing Englishmen knew no law, and they frequently preyed upon Spanish shipping in the New World and off the coasts of Spain. Philip II, hoping to stop English lawlessness on the sea and to restore the Catholic Church in England, intrigued to remove Elizabeth from the throne and replace her with her Catholic cousin, Mary Queen of Scots. Mary was a great-granddaughter of the first of the Tudors, Henry VII, and was next in line to the English throne. In Mary's kingdom of Scotland, Calvinism had made great inroads under the fiery preacher John Knox, and the Catholic Mary had fled her native land in 1568. From that time on, Elizabeth kept Mary in confinement in England. Fearing Mary as a rival to the throne, Elizabeth had her beheaded in 1587. For Philip, Mary's execution was the last straw, and he prepared to conquer England, remove Elizabeth from the throne, and restore the Catholic Church. In 1588 he dispatched a great fleet, called the Invincible Armada, against England. The seagoing prowess of the English and a timely storm in the Channel, however, dashed the Armada to pieces.

REVIEW

STUDY SECTIONS IN REVIEW

59. Luther and Protestantism in Germany

A. Explain Luther's doctrine of "justification by faith alone."

B. Identify: the "ninety-five theses," Leo X, John Eck.

C. Cite three reasons why many Germans rallied to Luther.

D. What were the causes and results of the peasant revolts of 1524–1525?

E. What was the significance of the Peace of Augsburg (1555)?

60. The Spread of the Protestant Revolt

A. How did Zwingli differ with Luther in doctrine?

B. Why do we say that Geneva, under Calvin, had a theocratic government?

C. Explain Calvin's doctrine of predestination.

D. What caused the break between Henry VIII and Rome?

E. Identify: Act of supremacy, Sir Thomas More, Edward VI, Mary I.

61. The Era of Catholic Reform

A. Mention at least four pronouncements of the Council of Trent.

B. Cite three achievements of the Society of Jesus during the Catholic Reform.

C. Identify: the battle of Lepanto, Elizabeth I, Mary Queen of Scots.

D. What was the fate of the English Church during the reign of Elizabeth I?

THE CHAPTER IN REVIEW

A. Discuss the causes and results of the dispute between Henry VIII of England and the Papacy.

B. Discuss the doctrines of Martin Luther and the form of worship of the church he established.

C. How can Luther's doctrines be said to have brought about political and economic as well as religious upheavals?

D. How did the Catholic Church set about reversing the Protestant Revolt? Mention particularly the works of Pope Paul III, St. Ignatius Loyola, and the Council of Trent.

FOR YOUR NOTEBOOK

The personal element is often very important in historical developments. Look up short biographical sketches of Luther, Calvin, and Henry VIII in one of your standard reference works. Now make a list of each man's religious doctrines (with Luther, for example, jusification by faith alone, and with Henry VIII denial of papal supremacy), and show how these doctrines met their personal desires.

Go through your text carefully to make a list of the (1) religious, (2) political, (3) economic, and (4) social causes of the Protestant revolt from the Catholic Church. Make a similar list to account for the lasting success of this movement.

Make four parallel columns to state briefly (1) Catholic, (2) Lutheran,

(3) Calvinist, and (4) Anglican teaching on each of these subjects: (a) salvation or justification, (b) the sacraments, (c) the Mass, (d) Church organization. This can be done quickly by looking under the appropriate headings in the Catholic Encyclopedia—Lutheranism, Calvinism, Anglicanism.

The various Protestant movements treated in this chapter were not exactly simultaneous, but they did overlap each other. You will see their time relationship more clearly if you prepare four parallel columns for the principal events in (1) the Lutheran movement, (2) the Calvinist movement, (3) the Anglican movement, and (4) Catholic Reform.

SELECTED READINGS

A good biography of each of the major figures in the Protestant movement and the Catholic Reform will increase your understanding of what happened in this eventful period and how personal considerations influenced events. A good introduction is Hilaire Belloc, *Characters of the Reformation* (New York: Sheed and Ward, 1940. This provides the reader with character sketches of some twenty major figures of the Reformation.

The three major Protestant figures are well handled by Joseph Clayton, *Luther and His Work* (Milwaukee, Wis.: Bruce Publishing Co., 1937); Georgia Harkness, *John Calvin: The Man and His Ethics* (New York: Henry Holt & Co., 1931); and Theodore Maynard, *Henry the Eighth* (Milwaukee, Wis.: Bruce Publishing Co., 1949).

Major aspects of the Catholic Reform movement can be followed in the biography of St. Ignatius Loyola by Ludwig Marcuse, *Soldier of the Church* (New York: Simon & Schuster, 1939); and in the gripping story of Don Juan of Austria by Louis de Wohl, *The Last Crusader* (Philadelphia: J. B. Lippincott, 1956).

CHRONOLOGICAL REVIEW

1291 Swiss independence
1324 *Marsiglio of Padua's* DEFENSOR PACIS
1328 Beginning of Valois-Capetian dynasty
　　　Rise of the duchy of Moscow
1337 Beginning of Hundred Years' War
1354 Ottoman Turks cross into Europe
1356 Battle of Poitiers; the Golden Bull
1360 Treaty of Bretigny
1378 *Beginning of Great Western Schism*
1384 *Death of John Wycliffe*
1386 Union of Poland and Lithuania;
　　　Conversion of the Lithuanians
1399 Deposition of Richard II of England
1409 *Council of Pisa; triple schism*
1414 *Council of Constance (to 1418)*
1415 Battle of Agincourt
　　　End of Great Western Schism; burning of John Hus
1420 Treaty of Troyes
1429 *St. Joan of Arc saves Orleans*
1431 *Trial and execution of St. Joan of Arc*
1453 End of Hundred Years' War; fall of Constantinople
1469 Union of Castile and Aragon

1477 Death of Charles the Bold of Burgundy
1480 Independence of Russia from Mongols
1485 Battle of Bosworth Field
1494 Charles VIII's expedition to Italy
1517 *Luther's ninety-five theses*
1520 *Excommunication of Luther*
1524 Outbreak of Peasants' Revolt
1529 Turks besiege Vienna; Diet of Speyer
1533 Henry VIII marries Anne Boleyn
1536 *Calvin arrives in Geneva*
1540 *Founding of the Society of Jesus*
1545 *Council of Trent (to 1563)*
1553 *Restoration of Catholicism in England*
1555 Abdication of Charles V
　　　Peace of Augsburg
1558 Elizabeth I, Queen of England (to 1603)
1562 *Wars of Religion in France (to 1598)*
1571 *Battle of Lepanto*
1581 Founding of Dutch Republic
1588 Destruction of Invincible Armada
1598 *Edict of Nantes*

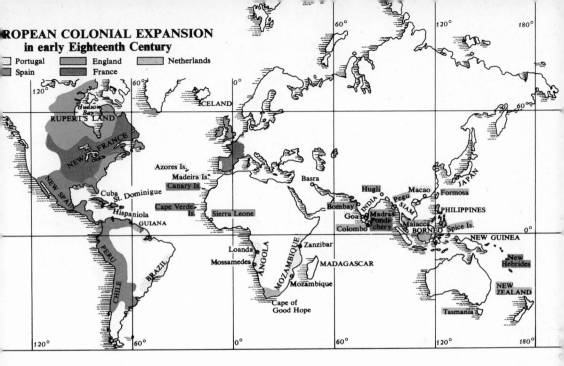

ROPEAN COLONIAL EXPANSION
in early Eighteenth Century

Portugal ▢   England ▢   Netherlands ▢
Spain ▢   France ▢

UNIT SEVEN
Transition to the Modern World

Commercial Empires in the East · European Colonies in North and South America · Consequences of the Discoveries and Colonization · The Progress of Science · Political Disunion of Europe and the Increased Power of Kings · Thirty Years' War and Puritan Revolution · France under Louis XIV · Repulse of the Turks and Rise of Russia · Glorious Revolution in England and War of the League of Augsburg · War of the Spanish Succession and Great Northern War

Chapter 22. Geographical Revolution and Beginnings of Modern Science

62. COMMERCIAL EMPIRES IN THE EAST

From 1500 to 1700, far-reaching changes so altered Europe that little of the medieval world remained. Two of the major changes, the Renaissance and the Protestant Revolt, have already been discussed. In this unit the spotlight turns on great geographical discoveries and the commercial and scientific "revolutions"; the downfall of the medieval political system (which had been marked by divided authority and weak central government) and its replacement by strong kings and bitter rivalry that pitted country against country; and the rise of new states.

Europeans and other lands. A main feature of the history of the world is the expansion of Europeans into Africa, Asia, and North and South America. Although Europe in the Middle Ages resembled a beleaguered fortress of Christians pressed by alien peoples, it steadily gained strength. Confident of their power, Europeans reached out to learn about other peoples, then to trade with and, eventually, to dominate them. Between the crusades and the discovery of America, Europeans increased their wealth by expanding their simple industries, exploiting their natural resources, and promoting a brisk overland trade among various regions and especially with overseas lands.

Italian merchants from Genoa, Pisa, and Venice carried woolen cloth and metals from European ports and returned with cargoes of spices and luxuries from the Near East, where many of them had been brought from India and the East Indian islands. This long-distance sea-borne trade enabled the merchants to reap handsome profits, which were reinvested. This trade prospered because of the breakdown of feudalism and manorialism. Medieval economy based upon barter and personal services was replaced by an economy based upon money. The local authorities who were powerful in the Middle Ages could not easily throw obstacles in the path of merchants who had the support of kings.

Throughout most of the Middle Ages people had lived in rather isolated communities. Toward the close of that period, however, men became more curious about the outside world and especially the trade routes to the Orient. The journeys of Marco Polo and other medieval travelers caught their imaginations. They wondered if there were other ways—perhaps by sea—to avoid the tiring overland routes to the fabled lands and riches of the East. Some suggested sailing around Africa; others advised sailors to sail west in order to reach the East. But he was a brave sailor who ignored popular legends that the earth was flat (though wise men knew that the earth was round) and that horrible sea monsters waited in the deep to devour mariners. Even if they could forget sea dragons, sailors still feared a long journey of thousands of miles in frail vessels that could not sail into the wind. However, the advances in geographical knowledge and in the science of sailing emboldened sailors. Better maps, the compass, and the conviction that the earth *was* round encouraged explorers and merchants to seek new routes to the Indies, as they called the Orient.

The Atlantic countries lead. The heroic journeys of exploration and discovery and the planting of colonies throughout the non-European world constitute amazing exploits in history. For a variety of motives which may be summarized as the three "G's"—for God, glory, and gain—Europeans left the safety of their homes to sail uncharted seas, conquer strange lands and peoples, and often to die of wounds or disease. The principal leaders of this epic served the kings of the countries that faced the Atlantic, such as Portugal and Spain. The old Italian city-states were thus left behind when the Mediterranean was replaced as the main highway for the exchange of goods by the Atlantic, which now carried the commerce of the world.

The Portuguese. The Portuguese led the way by first exploring and controlling nearby waters and islands. They rediscovered Madeira and the

The astrolabe, developed from a land-measuring instrument invented by the Arabs, was much used on voyages of discovery in the fifteenth century to determine latitude, longitude, and time of day. (Museum of the City of New York)

Prince Henry the Navigator and Vasco da Gama opened the way for the Portuguese to expand commerce outward across the Atlantic, thus establishing the first overseas European colonial empire. (The Metropolitan Museum of Art)

Azores. Under the leadership of the royal Prince Henry the Navigator (1394–1460), they prepared for greater deeds. Bartholomew Diaz reached the Cape of Good Hope in 1488 by hugging the coast of Africa. Vasco da Gama braved the open sea by rounding the tip of Africa and making his way to the east coast of Africa. There he picked up an Arab pilot who led him across the Indian Ocean to Calicut, India, in 1498. The valuable cargo he brought back to Lisbon excited other mariners to follow his example.

The Portuguese Empire. The Portuguese set out to build up an empire in West Africa and Asia. In the East they first had to get rid of Arab interference. The Arabs had been in the East Indies since 1300 and had introduced Moslemism among the native peoples, a majority of whom became Moslems during the fourteenth and fifteenth centuries. Once rid of the Arabs, the Portuguese established a

monopoly over trade in Indian waters, especially around the city of Goa. At their bases they established "factories,"[1] which were trading centers. Control over the island of Ceylon gave them a valuable supply of cinnamon. Their hold over Malacca in the Malay archipelago led in turn to the Moluccas, or the Spice Islands, which were rich in costly spices such as nutmeg and cloves. The Spice Islands brought the Portuguese closer to China.

Contact with China. The first Portuguese ships arrived at Canton, China, in 1516. By 1557 a Portuguese settlement near Canton became the principal European outpost in China. The Portuguese were soon followed by the Spanish, Dutch, and English. While western Europeans came by sea, Russians entered China from Siberia. Russia threatened northern China,

---

[1] The term *factory* comes from *factor*, the permanent representative of a foreign firm in a country such as India or China. His residence was over the warehouse or office, called factory.

but her ambitions were halted by the victory of the Chinese over Russian armies in 1689.

Missionaries. One of the features of European contact with the East was the reintroduction of Christianity. St. Francis Xavier (1506–1552), a Jesuit missionary, did remarkable work in evangelizing Goa, Malacca, and Japan but died before he could begin work in China. However, other Jesuit and Franciscan and Dominican missionaries followed his example there. They won friends by their inspiring lives and by their study of the Chinese language and literature. Besides, their knowledge of science and such mechanical things as clocks made them sought-after advisers. One of the most important missionaries in China was Father Matthew Ricci, an Italian Jesuit, who reached Macao in 1582 and remained in China until his death in 1610. Ricci permitted Chinese Christians to take part in the ceremonies honoring Confucius and their ancestors—a vital part of family and village life—because he did not consider the ceremonies to be religious rites. However, in 1694 the Pope ordered the missionaries to stop tolerating these Chinese ceremonies on the ground that they were forbidden religious rites.[2]

Chinese Reaction against Europeans. The attitude of the missionaries toward the ancestral ceremonies angered the Chinese, who were already disturbed by the bad conduct of some white men. The murders, pillaging, and

St. Francis Xavier in Agony, *by Carlo Maratta. St. Francis soothed the antagonism of the Indians exploited by unethical Portuguese traders. (Fototeca Unione, Roma)*

rivalry among various European nationalities led to stern action against them. When Christianity was outlawed, the missionaries went underground. Severe restrictions were placed on European merchants, and by the mid-eighteenth century European trade was confined to the port of Canton. The Chinese were convinced of their superiority and the excellence of their civilization in contrast to that of the "barbarians." Under the Ming Dynasty (1368–1644) Chinese people could boast of a brilliant culture and civilization. It was symbolized in the

[2] This action handicapped the work of missionaries in China until 1939, when the Pope permitted these ceremonies as long as they were civic and not religious.

Interior of the Exchange at Amsterdam, *by Job Berckheyde. Amsterdam was a major port and became the financial center of the sixteenth century. Merchants met in the Exchange, where they offered for sale the goods in their warehouses. (Rijksmuseum, Amsterdam)*

marvelous "Forbidden City" of Peking with its beautiful buildings and great treasures. The fall of the Ming Dynasty and the coming of the Manchus in 1644 brought with it hostile feeling toward the white men.

The Dutch in the East. Until 1600 the Portuguese controlled the trade between Europe and India. But they were unable to hold off their ambitious rivals. In addition, governmental corruption and heavy losses of life in establishing their trade weakened the Portuguese Empire.

The Dutch, who had successfully revolted against Spanish rule (1568–1609) now transferred some of their hatred of Spaniards to the Portuguese because from 1580 to 1640 Portugal was united with Spain. In the 1590's the Dutch moved into the Malay islands. In 1602 they chartered the United East India Company, which directed efforts to build a Dutch East

Indies empire. Control of Java, Sumatra, and the Spice Islands supplied them with tea, spices, indigo, sugar, and camphor. They introduced the coffee bush into Java and reaped great profits later. In 1658 the Dutch drove the Portuguese out of Ceylon and soon afterward dominated the East Indies. By controlling the spice trade between the Far East and Europe and the commerce between the East Indies and India, they grew rich. They bought cheap cotton goods in India, which they exchanged in the East Indies for spices, and then exported spices to India and to Europe.

Europeans in Japan. Like the Chinese, the Japanese were able to resist European pressure. Their military disposition was proved in their sixteenth-century attempt to invade Korea, a province of China. Warlike clans seized political power and gave the Japanese islands a strong and stable government. Now Portuguese seamen entered Japanese waters and were soon followed by their European rivals. The Dutch and English prejudiced the Japanese against the Portuguese and Spanish. These quarrels worked against the men from the West, and the introduction of Christianity worried some Japanese leaders.

The work of St. Francis Xavier in preaching the gospel in Japan (1549–1551) was fruitful. It is estimated that before 1600 there were 150,000 Christians, and by 1625 the figure jumped to three hundred thousand in a population of about twenty-five million. Persecution soon faced Japanese Christians. They were either killed or driven underground when all foreigners were expelled in 1639. After

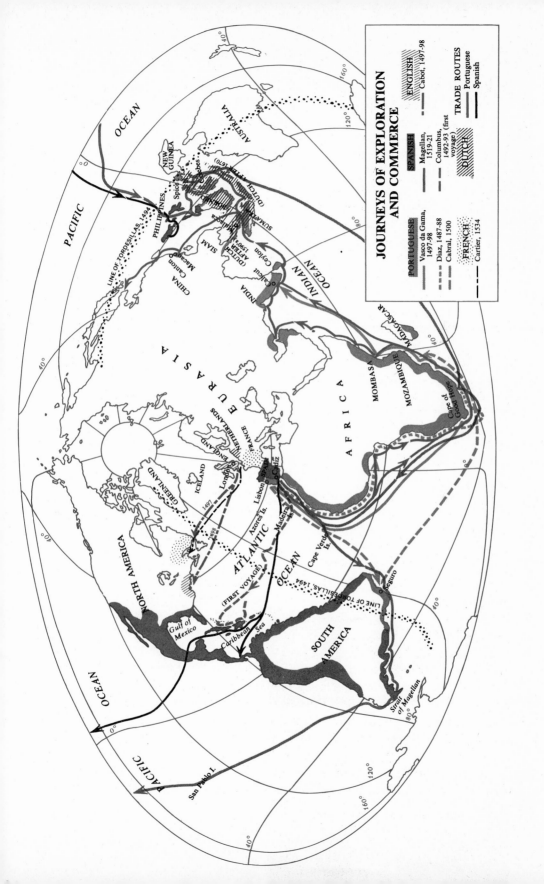

JOURNEYS OF EXPLORATION
AND COMMERCE

PORTUGUESE
Vasco da Gama, 1497-98
Diaz, 1487-88
Cabral, 1500

FRENCH
Cartier, 1534

SPANISH
Magellan, 1519-21
Columbus, 1492-93 (first voyage)

DUTCH

ENGLISH
Cabot, 1497-98

TRADE ROUTES
Portuguese
Spanish

that, Europeans were not permitted to enter until Commodore Perry of the United States reopened Japan in 1854.

Spain and the Philippines. Another country in the East which was brought into the main stream of world history by the discoveries was the Philippines. Spain laid claim to the islands as a result of the discovery of Ferdinand Magellan (1480–1521), who reached the Philippines and died there in 1521 after sailing around South America and across the Pacific. Magellan's exploit in many ways is typical of the sacrifices and heroism of the early explorers. His journey across the Pacific was described by Antonio Pigafetta, who noted in his diary:[3]

We were three months and twenty days without getting any kind of fresh food. We ate biscuit, which was no longer biscuit, but powder of biscuit swarming with worms, for they had eaten the food. . . . We drank yellow water that had been putrid for many days. We also ate some ox hides that covered the top of the mainyard to prevent the yard from chafing the shrouds, and which had become exceedingly hard because of the sun, rain, and wind. We left them in the sea for four or five days and then placed them for a few moments on top of the embers, and so ate them; and often we ate sawdust from boards. . . . But above all the other misfortunes the following was worst: the gums of both the lower and upper teeth of some of our men swelled, so that they could not eat under any circumstances and therefore died. . . . We sailed about four thousand leagues during those three months and twenty days through an open stretch in that Pacific Sea. In truth it was pacific, for during that time we did not suffer any storm. . . . Had not God and His Blessed Mother given us so good weather, we would all have died of hunger.

Spain followed up Magellan's discovery by sending expeditions to hold the islands. In 1571 the main settlement was made at Manila, on the island of Luzon.

The Mogul Empire in India. European merchants now reached for the fabulous riches of India. This vast subcontinent of Asia had fallen under the domination of the Mongols (or Moguls), who, under Babar (1526–1530), a descendant of Tamerlane and Genghis Khan, founded the Mogul Empire, with the capital at Delhi. By the end of the sixteenth century, as a result of the conquests of Akbar (1556–1605), the Moguls controlled all of northern India, and by 1630 they subjugated the Deccan. The Mogul Capital at Delhi contained the Pearl Mosque, and the city of Agra boasted the celebrated Taj Mahal, the marble tomb of the emperor Shah

Ferdinand Magellan (1480–1521). The explorer was killed in the Philippines, but his crew continued and completed the first voyage around the world. (The Metropolitan Museum of Art)

---

[3] Quoted from J. E. Gillespie, *A History of Geographical Discovery, 1400–1800* (New York: Henry Holt & Co., 1933), pp. 36–37.

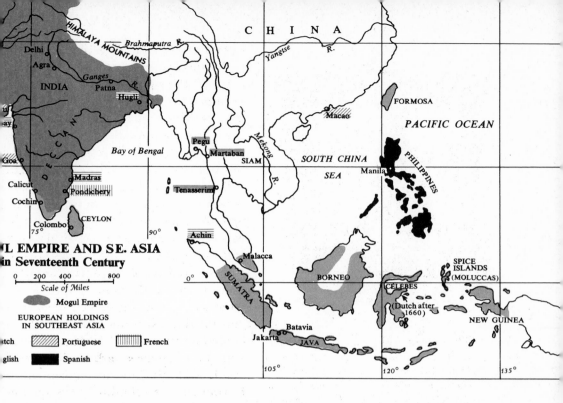

MOGUL EMPIRE AND S.E. ASIA
in Seventeenth Century

0   200   400   800
Scale of Miles

Mogul Empire

EUROPEAN HOLDINGS
IN SOUTHEAST ASIA

Dutch · Portuguese · French

English · Spanish

Jahan and his wife. No sooner had the Moguls established their power than many of the Hindu lords began to throw off the yoke of the invaders, who overtaxed and misgoverned India. Hence, in the last half of the seventeenth century the Mogul Empire declined. Into this troubled scene Europeans entered. They came as traders but soon exploited the lack of political unity and began to seize power themselves. Missionaries continued their labors; Jesuit fathers had been admitted during the reign of Akbar.

European merchants in India. As in the East Indies, China, and Japan, sharp rivalry occurred among the European merchants. The English and the French became bitter enemies and carried over to India the wars of Europe and to the homeland their commercial rivalry over India. The English came to India as employees of the East India Company, which had received a monopoly of all trade from the Cape of Good Hope eastward to the Strait of Magellan. Having set up strategic outposts and having defeated the Portuguese for control of the Persian Gulf, the English East India Company established itself at Madras, Bombay, and Calcutta, during the seventeenth century.

The French similarly came to India under the auspices of their own East India Company. This venture was encouraged by Colbert, minister of King Louis XIV (1660–1715). The center of French activities in India was at Pondicherry and the chief leader was Joseph Dupleix (1697–1763). It was his idea to prevent the draining of gold and silver from France to India to pay for French imports by taxing the natives under his

HET HUIS VAN DEN
OOST INDISCHE COMPAGNIE IN
LON DEN

THE OLD EAST INDIA HOUSE IN LEADENHALL STREET 1648 TO 1726

The Home of the English East India Company, *engraving from a Dutch painting. The company traded exclusively with India, concentrating on the exports of textiles. (The Metropolitan Museum of Art)*

rule and using these sums to buy goods for export to Europe. Unfortunately (for the French) the lack of foresight of the government at Paris undermined Dupleix and caused his dismissal. Eventually the English East India Company won political control over India and defeated its French rival as a result of the victories of Robert Clive (1757–1759).

63. EUROPEAN COLONIES IN NORTH AND SOUTH AMERICA

Columbus. The opening of the New World in the fifteenth and sixteenth centuries had important consequences. The greatest of the Atlantic discoveries resulted from the journeys of Christopher Columbus, an Italian born at

Genoa in 1446. An experienced sailor, Columbus appealed to the crusading spirit of the Spanish monarchs, Ferdinand and Isabella, who were driving the Moors out of Spain and were eager to continue their crusade by preaching the gospel far and wide. Columbus was convinced that God had called him to explore the unknown Atlantic on his way to the Indies. The first of his journeys resulted in the discovery of America in 1492, though Columbus believed until his death that he had reached the Indies. It is possible that Irish monks had reached America in the ninth century; it is certain that Norsemen from Iceland landed on the coast of North America. But these journeys had no historical result and left America unknown to Europeans. Columbus' discoveries caused Portugal to fear for her colonies on the coast of Africa. To prevent controversy, Spain and Portugal appealed to Pope Alexander VI, who in 1493 authorized Spain to possess all lands west of a north-south line about three hundred miles west of the Azores. By

Christopher Columbus (1451–1506). His discoveries disproved many theories in navigation and established Spain's claim to the New World. (The Metropolitan Museum of Art)

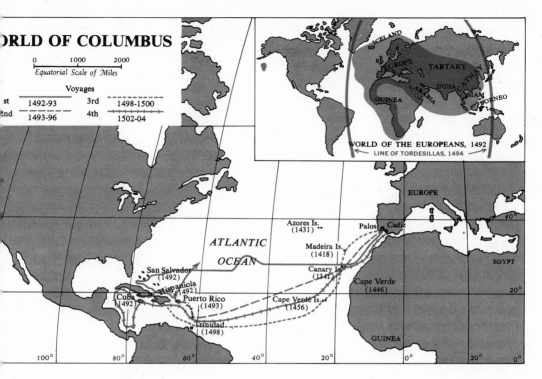

0   1000   2000
Equatorial Scale of Miles

Voyages

st	1492-93	3rd	1498-1500
nd	1493-96	4th	1502-04

WORLD OF THE EUROPEANS, 1492
◄── LINE OF TORDESILLAS, 1494 ──►

ATLANTIC OCEAN

EUROPE

EGYPT

GUINEA

Azores Is. (1431)
Palos Cadiz
Madeira Is. (1418)
Canary Is. (1341)
Cape Verde (1446)
San Salvador (1492)
Hispaniola (1492)
Cuba (1492)
Puerto Rico (1493)
Cape Verde Is. (1456)
Trinidad (1498)

100°   80°   60°   40°   20°   0°   20°   0°

40°   20°

the Spanish-Portuguese Treaty of Tordesillas the next year the line was somewhat changed. As a result, Spain got North and South America, exclusive of Brazil.

The Spanish Empire. Within comparatively few years after Columbus' discoveries, Spain undertook the exploration and colonization of the New World. The gold, silver, and labor of the skilled Indians in Mexico, Central America, and Peru attracted adventurers and explorers to organize expeditions for the conquest of certain areas in the name of the King of Spain. Conquests of the New World proceeded outward from the first colony on Santo Domingo to other islands in the West Indies. The highlights of the settlement of the mainland were the discovery of the Pacific by Balboa in Panama in 1513, the conquest of Mexico by Cortez in 1519

and of Peru by Pizarro in 1531–1532. Spaniards founded a colony in Buenos Aires in 1536 and established control over the Rio de la Plata area. Footholds were established in what is now the United States Southwest. From 1539 to 1542 Hernando de Soto journeyed across a wide stretch of land from Florida to Arkansas and saw the Mississippi; while in 1540–1542 Coronado explored the Southwest and reached Kansas. The northern borderlands of the Spanish Empire ultimately extended from Florida to California.

The Spanish king exercised direct authority over his colonies. He granted the Catholic Church extensive powers in Christianizing and civilizing the Indians. The missions of the Carmelites, Dominicans, Franciscans, and later the Jesuits spread the Catholic religion and Spanish culture among the natives. The king also granted to the upper classes extensive privileges and power over the natives. However, the policy of the king protected the Indians. They were not killed but were compelled to work under the rule of their conquerors. Despite many shortcomings, the Spanish Empire produced beneficial results. Its missionaries preached the gospel, and their work was crowned by the canonization of saints such as St. Rose of Lima (1586–1617). They also established schools to educate the clergy, mining engineers, lawyers, and doctors. The universities of Mexico and of San Marcos (Lima, Peru) were founded as early as 1551. Printing presses existed in Spanish America as early as 1539. Spain held her empire in peace for hundreds of years, and the Spanish Empire had a long life. Despite weakness at home and the pressure of eager rivals such as the Dutch, English, and French, Spaniards held a wide area extending from California in the north to Cape Horn at the tip of South America until the early nineteenth century.

The Portuguese in America. The Portuguese, too, established an empire in South America as a result of the journey of Cabral to Brazil in 1500. No serious effort to colonize Brazil was made until the 1530's, when Martin Alfonso de Souza and Thomé de Souza established colonies. The central coastal region of Brazil provided the Portuguese with sugar, tobacco, and cotton. The introduction of Negro slavery brought a third element into the European and Indian populations.

International rivalry in the New World. As early as 1522, when Cortez sent a treasure ship filled with gold, silver, mosaics, and other fineries to the King of Spain and it was captured by a French corsair, other countries tried to win a share of the wealth and colonies of the New World. Spain admitted no other country, for she claimed that the New World had been divided between herself and Portugal. But other countries refused to recognize this division. In the latter half of the sixteenth century, English pirates, with the support of Queen Elizabeth, descended upon Spanish ships in European and Caribbean waters. During the seventeenth century, while Spain weakened, the English, French, and Dutch did get footholds in the Caribbean and on the coast of South America. The bitter rivalry of the three new aggressive countries who sought the lion's share of trade and empire prevented any single country from winning all.

North America had for long blocked the path of English, French, and Dutch in their search for a water passage to the Indies. Early explorations of the coast are clothed in mystery. Portuguese, Basque, Breton, and English fishermen probably were familiar with the coastal areas off the great fishing banks of Newfoundland but would not reveal the information for fear of revealing their secret sources of fish. Early journeys of explorers charted the rivers and the waterways of North America. As the Spanish Empire was rising, two Italians, John and Sebastian Cabot, in the service of King Henry VII of England, explored the northeast coast, and John Verrazzano, an Italian in the service of the King of France, did much the same in 1524. Jacques Cartier, a

Frenchman, explored the Gulf of St. Lawrence, 1534–1541. These men labored against great odds—fog, icebergs, reefs and shallows, mists, and ocean currents.

England and France knew about North America about a century before they decided to colonize it. Cut off from the more profitable tropical and subtropical areas such as the Caribbean, they fought for the fish and furs of North America. Because of the large number of fast days in Catholic Europe and the high price of meat, fish was an important item in diet. Furs were widely demanded for clothing and especially for hats, because Europeans considered it a mark of distinction to wear a fur hat.

English colonization. The defeat of the Great Spanish Armada that sailed against England in 1588 enabled English ships to challenge Spanish supremacy in the New World and to

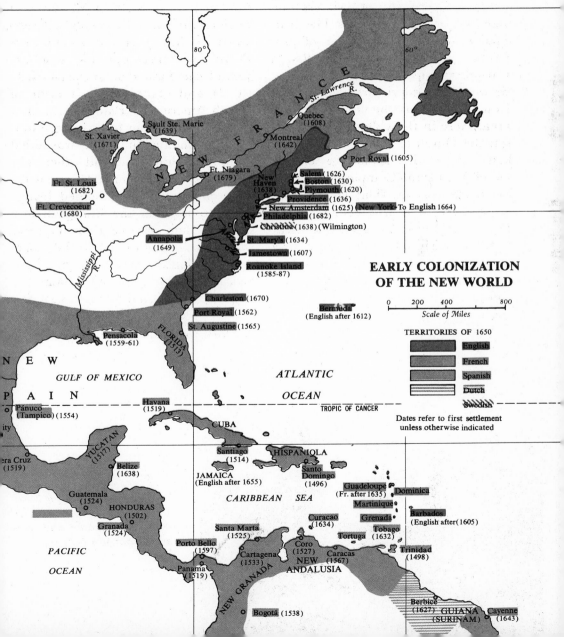

EARLY COLONIZATION OF THE NEW WORLD

Scale of Miles
0   200   400   800

TERRITORIES OF 1650
English
French
Spanish
Dutch
Swedish

Dates refer to first settlement unless otherwise indicated

St. Xavier (1671)
Sault Ste. Marie (1639)
Ft. St. Louis (1682)
Ft. Crevecoeur (1680)
NEW FRANCE
St. Lawrence R.
Quebec (1608)
Montreal (1642)
Port Royal (1605)
Ft. Niagara (1679)
New Haven (1638)
Salem (1626)
Boston (1630)
Plymouth (1620)
Providence (1636)
New Amsterdam (1625) (New York—To English 1664)
Philadelphia (1682)
Christina (1638) (Wilmington)
Annapolis (1649)
St. Mary's (1634)
Jamestown (1607)
Roanoke Island (1585-87)
Charleston (1670)
Port Royal (1562)
St. Augustine (1565)
Pensacola (1559-61)
FLORIDA (1513)
Bermuda (English after 1612)
Mississippi R.

GULF OF MEXICO
ATLANTIC OCEAN
TROPIC OF CANCER
NEW SPAIN
Pánuco (Tampico) (1554)
Havana (1519)
CUBA
Vera Cruz (1519)
YUCATAN (1517)
Belize (1638)
Santiago (1514)
HISPANIOLA
Santo Domingo (1496)
Guadeloupe (Fr. after 1635)
Dominica
Martinique
JAMAICA (English after 1655)
Guatemala (1524)
HONDURAS (1502)
Granada (1524)
CARIBBEAN SEA
Curacao (1634)
Grenada
Barbados (English after 1605)
Santa Marta (1525)
Tobago (1632)
Porto Bello (1597)
Coro (1527)
Caracas (1567)
Tortuga
Trinidad (1498)
PACIFIC OCEAN
Cartagena (1533)
Panama (1519)
NEW ANDALUSIA
NEW GRANADA
Bogotá (1538)
Berbice (1627)
GUIANA (SURINAM)
Cayenne (1643)

bring settlers to North America. Efforts to colonize failed in the sixteenth century. Not until the settlement of Jamestown in Virginia in 1607 did English colonists gain a solid foothold. For religious motives the Pilgrims settled at Plymouth (1620) and the Puritans at Massachusetts Bay (1629). These two settlements merged and led the colonization of the rest of New England. Meanwhile the English kings made grants of large territories in America to proprietors who undertook to found colonies. The principal results of the initiative of proprietors were Maryland (at first a Catholic colony) and the Carolinas. Between the proprietary colonies and New England lay the vital New York area. Here in the valley of the Hudson the Dutch erected New Netherland under the leadership of the Dutch West India Company primarily for trade reasons. The Dutch then absorbed a Swedish settlement in the Delaware Valley. They posed a threat to the English not only because New Netherland cut the English colonies in two but also because they controlled the rich fur trade with the Indians.

While the English valued the American mainland colonies, their principal ambition was a Caribbean empire. Toward this purpose they occupied the Bermudas, the islands of St. Kitts and Barbados, and Jamaica (captured in 1655 from Spain), and gained a foothold on the coast of South America (British Guiana).

Founding of New France. The French built a New France in Canada and in the Mississippi Valley. Samuel Champlain settled Quebec, the nucleus of the French colony, in 1608. Intrepid explorers and missionaries pushed westward to the Great Lakes and then down the Mississippi. La Salle explored the Father of Waters (1679–1683) and claimed the interior of North America for France, naming it Louisiana in honor of his king, Louis XIV. French colonization was aided by Jesuit, Sulpician, and other missionaries and by a mixed French-Indian population that helped bridge the gap between the European and the red man. Heroic French priests were determined to preach the gospel to the Indians even at the risk of their own lives. King Louis XIV poured in settlers, soldiers and munitions, money and equipment in an effort to put new life into New France and to end the

The landing of the Pilgrims at Plymouth in December 1620. The Pilgrims separated from the Church of England and came to the New World to practice their religion without discrimination and criticism. (Library of Congress)

menace of the Iroquois Indians. Great hopes were entertained in the eighteenth century for the development of Louisiana. The French settlements led to friction with the English, who were also developing North America. The rival ambitions clashed over the Hudson Bay area, Acadia (Nova Scotia), and the area south of the Great Lakes.

Defeat of the Dutch. The English and Dutch fought repeated wars over the carrying trade of Europe, trade in the East Indies, and over colonies in the New World, especially New Amsterdam and those in the Hudson Valley. For a time the Dutch swept everything before them. However, Holland was unequal to the task of holding her empire against the pressure of stronger powers. The Dutch population was small and weakened by the effort to hold the trade empire and by the casualties suffered in Europe in wars against Louis XIV. England won New Amsterdam in 1664 and renamed it New York. Thus she won control of the vital Hudson River Valley, which linked New England with the rest of her colonies in North America.

The Indians. There were hundreds of tribes speaking different languages and ranging from savages to civilized people. Spanish settlers encountered the Pueblo, Maya, Aztec, Chibcha, and Inca Indians. The Pueblos of the highlands of southwestern United States were either cliff dwellers or residents of the floors of canyons. The Mayas lived in Central America from Guatemala to Yucatan and had passed the peak of their achievements long before the Spaniards arrived. Their league of city-states had fallen to the powerful Toltec and Aztec invaders.

This calendar, used by the Aztec Indians of Central America, was developed before A.D. *400. It was more accurate than the Julian calendar used by the Europeans when America was discovered. (Chicago Natural History Museum)*

The fiercest tribe north of Panama was the hunting tribe of the Aztecs who lived on the Mexican plateau. They built a strong empire and a civilization on the achievements of other Indian tribes. Their picture-writing, pottery, textiles, astronomy, and art reached high levels. They worshiped the sun, to which they offered human sacrifices. The Chibchas and Incas were in South America, the first living in Colombia and the Incas on the Peruvian highlands. The Incas had established a kingdom in Peru and along the west coast of South America. They had an intricate machinery of government, extensive irrigation works, and perhaps the best cultural achievement of the Indians at the time of the Spanish conquest. Before Pizarro arrived with his soldiers, the Incas were weakened by civil wars.

English and French explorers and settlers in North America also met a variety of tribes, such as the Algonquian family, which included the Blackfoot and the Shawnee tribes; and the Iroquois, consisting of the "five nations" (Mohawk, Cayuga, Seneca, Oneida, and Onondaga tribes who were organized in a federal league). The Iroquois occupied an area that straddled the only water-level route across the Appalachians, the Hudson River–Lake Champlain route. A Jesuit missionary wrote of them that "they approach like foxes, fight like lions, and fly away like birds."

The white men succeeded in taking Indian lands in North America not only through superior numbers and power but because the Indians never banded together effectively. Instead of joining forces to resist the Europeans, the Indians fought each other as fiercely as they attacked the white invaders. The white men had only to pick off one tribe at a time.

The significance of the Indians. The Indian has had great importance in the history of the New World. In some lands, such as Bolivia, Peru, and Mexico, he still forms the greater part of the population. Further, the Indian taught the white man much about agriculture, introducing him to maize, kidney and lima beans, tobacco, cocoa, quinine, rubber, sisal, the white potato, sweet potato, pineapple, pumpkin, peanut, and tomato. The European learned the importance of fertilizing crops, of evaporating water for salt, dressing skins, making rubber, and the use of herbs as medicines. Using the Indian's tracks through the wilderness, the white man picked his way westward in search of furs and then in quest of farms and homes. The

existence of Indians on the frontier, raiding European settlements at intervals, slowed down the march of white men. Indian outbreaks occurred from the days of the English settlement on Roanoke Island in North Carolina to the closing days of the settling of the American West in the late nineteenth century. During the interim, Indian life was profoundly affected by the white man. The European introduced the horse, which revolutionized the life of the plains Indians who hunted buffalo. Some of the horses that got away from the early Spanish explorers and settlers ran wild on the plains and were later tamed by Indians. The weapons of the European were soon mastered by the red man, who used them to advantage in slowing down the settlement of the wilderness.

64. CONSEQUENCES OF THE DISCOVERIES AND COLONIZATION

The discoveries and the colonies resulted from stupendous human adventures that widened the horizon of Europe to include the East and the Americas. Europeans bridged the gap between East and West and pushed North and South America—previously unknown continents—into the main stream of world history. There was produced an exchange of people, ideas, and things. Europeans brought their civilization and religion to the East Indies, India, China, Japan, and especially to the New World. Millions became Catholic converts at a time when the Church suffered heavy losses in Europe as a result of the Protestant Revolt. Further, millions of Europeans emigrated to Argentina, Brazil, Canada, the British colonies, and other "new Europes" overseas. In these new lands Europeans realized ambitions they were unable to satisfy in the Old World. European languages are still spoken everywhere, even in former colonies where European influence is resisted.

East and West. Asia and the New World left their imprints on Europe. Oriental languages, art, literature, and philosophy were studied by Europeans. At first the white men wanted to study oriental civilization in order to carry on business with the East. and to preach the gospel. Later Europeans pondered the ideas of the Chinese and Indian wise men, such as Buddha and Confucius, and studied Chinese and Japanese art. Similarly the art and the designs of the American Indians were examined and copied.

Effects on the state. The discoveries and colonization tended to increase the power of kings and central governments. Mercantile interests supported royal power because kings could unify the country by enforcing the same laws, weights, and measures and similar aids to trade, and eliminate the barriers to the movement of goods within the country. The king could use his power to keep out foreign goods and thus enable his own merchants to prosper. Monarchs found in merchants and capitalists the sources of loans necessary for political purposes, for hiring troops, and for building ships. The wealth coming from trade and the colonies enabled some of the rulers of Europe to establish absolute control over their subjects.

Mercantilism. The merging of the economic interests of the crown and merchants led to *mercantilism*. In this form of economy the national state built up its power by means of an empire and overseas trade conducted to promote industry and trade for essentially political reasons.

Its main aim was to increase the country's revenue and power for the purpose of preparing the nation for getting the better of its enemies. The slogan was "national wealth through the regulation and protection of commerce." Mercantilists prevailed upon kings and parliaments to enact laws discriminating against foreign merchants in domestic and colonial trade. Laws were passed to encourage shipbuilding and other industries associated with national defense, and to encourage a favorable balance of trade.

The English Navigation Acts of the seventeenth century illustrate the efforts of the new states to squeeze out their commercial competitors and make their country self-sufficient. The Navigation Acts were aimed first at the Dutch, who brought into English ports spices from the East and sugar from the West Indies and threatened the profits of English shippers. These laws prohibited all foreign merchants, shippers, and manufacturers from benefiting from the English colonies. All goods entering or leaving the English colonies had to be carried on ships built by Englishmen and manned by British subjects.

Colonies were branches of national commerce, and their function at first was to supply tropical products and markets for the goods of the mother country. Naturally they could not compete with the mother country. If colonies were not profitable, they were not useful. Hence the great powers fought to get footholds in tropical and subtropical areas because products such as sugar, rice, indigo, and spices were sought throughout the world. Northern colonies were not considered so valuable. Among the English colonies of the seventeenth century, for example, the tiny island of Barbados with its sugar plantations was considered more valuable than all the mainland colonies from Massachusetts to South Carolina. Some northern colonies did not pay their way but were a burden on the ruling power.

Slavery. The development of the tropical and subtropical colonies producing sugar and other articles needed by Europeans led to Negro slavery. A steady labor supply was needed to man the sugar plantations of Brazil and the West Indies. The American Indians failed to supply the demand for labor because of heavy losses suffered in war and as a result of disease. White men were not practical as laborers on the sugar plantations; they were too difficult to handle, for they could escape and mingle with the free population. The Negroes, on the other hand, were considered suitable because of their strength, their ability to work long hours in the sun, and their color, which singled them out in the event of escape. The first Negroes were shipped to the West Indies in 1501. They were brought in large numbers as the sugar colonies developed. Later, when tobacco became a principal crop in the southern colonies of British North America,

scores of thousands entered the New World. Slave raiders captured Negroes in Africa and transported them to the New World in "slavers." The "middle passage," as the trip from Africa to the Caribbean, Brazil, or other colonies was called, was a nightmare of filth, disease, seasickness, and imprisonment.

In Spanish and Portuguese America, in contrast to the English colonies in North America, the law accepted the doctrine of the moral personality of the slave. He was recognized as a moral person and therefore capable of freedom. The Church insisted in these countries that slave and master were equal in the sight of God and both must recognize relationship to each other as moral human beings and as brothers in Christ.

Rise in prices. The economic results of the discoveries and colonization were similarly important. They hastened the development of a money economy. In addition, gold and silver from the New World and later from the Orient led to inflation and a "price revolution." Prices increased fourfold while wages lagged behind. The result was much suffering and discontent in the seventeenth century. The New World proved a safety valve for European society.

Chartered companies. The increase in commerce led to the *chartered company*. Individual persons were unable to supply money and supervision of large-scale ventures, so two company forms developed. In the *regulated company* each member traded for himself but agreed to follow the rules of the company and contributed in proportion to his share for the protection and operation.

Brazilian sugar works of the sixteenth century, employing Negro slaves in the sugar fields and the processing plant. (From Pierre vander Aa, La Galeries Agréable du Monde, *Vol. III, Leyden, 1733, Bibliothèque Nationale)*

In the *joint-stock company* (illustrated by the British East India Company) persons invested in the company but did not participate directly in trade, leaving these problems to hired clerks and sailors, and a board of directors who distributed profits according to the proportionate investment of each. No distinction existed between companies chartered for commerce and those for colonization.

Banking. Trade and colonies led to new developments in banking. Private individuals or family banking houses no longer possessed the supply of money that trading companies or kings wished to borrow. Big banks,

such as the Bank of Amsterdam (1609) and the Bank of England (1694), were in effect agents of their governments and filled the need. Transactions involving buying and selling of shares of companies led to the establishment of stock exchanges in Europe.

65. THE PROGRESS OF SCIENCE

The scientific advances of the seventeenth and eighteenth centuries mark brilliant achievements of the human mind in seeking to discover the secrets that God locked into the universe. By giving man greater control over nature than ever before in history and by helping to solve problems in manufacturing, mining, transportation, and warfare, these advances increased the might of Europe. With their scientific knowledge, self-assurance, and optimism, Europeans knew they could create more wealth and arm themselves so that they could dominate the rest of the world. A distinguished historian maintains that the scientific advances outshine everything since the rise of Christianity, reducing the Renaissance and the Protestant Revolt to the rank of mere episodes or "internal displacements within the system of medieval Christendom." In his judgment, the scientific advances are the real origin of the modern world and the modern mentality, for through them science was able to become the main directive force of civilization.[4]

Modern science—associated with observation and experiment—did not prosper in the early Middle Ages. In the later Middle Ages (after about 1200) science made remarkable advances. Men became trained in the habit of exact and clear thinking. Medieval thinkers bequeathed to modern scientists the conviction that the human mind *can* learn the secrets of nature, and they taught them the lesson of patient study, love of learning, and the habit of collecting and respecting facts. Scientific study was then filled with reverence for and curiosity about the world God had made. Medieval scientists were religious men, reasoning that God had put order into the universe and had given them light of the mind to learn of His creation.

Early modern science. The growth of commerce and colonies, together with the increase in the wealth of the middle classes that followed, allowed some persons the necessary leisure for study and money to purchase equipment for research. Merchants and bankers encouraged scientists and endowed research.

Francis Bacon (1561–1626), an English nobleman and Lord Chancellor, is popularly considered the prophet of natural science and the scientific method. He was not a scientist, but a writer advocating science. Bacon denounced reliance on deductive reasoning and on old books and urged scientists to observe nature and collect facts in order to explain and master the world about them. Bacon's writings helped the development of the scientific method. He was, however, more interested in science as a means of power than in truth.

Francis Bacon (Library of Congress)

---

[4] Herbert Butterfield, *The Origins of Modern Science, 1300–1800* (London: The Macmillan Co., 1950), viii.

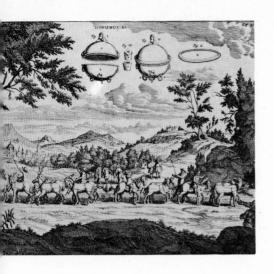

Demonstration of atmospheric pressure by Otto von Guericke, German physicist. Two metal hemispheres (the Magdeburg hemispheres) were fitted together and air was pumped out. Because of the atmospheric pressure, the horses could not pull them apart. (Ullstein)

The scientific advances were not the work of a few, but of hundreds and even thousands of investigators, many of whom are forgotten. In proportion to the population of Europe, they were a handful of men. Their influence on the ruling classes and on the small elite that dominated European thought was out of proportion to their numbers. Few of them were full-time or professional scientists. The age of specialization was still to come, so that only a small number devoted themselves exclusively to the study of science, and still fewer to a single branch of science, such as anatomy or astronomy. For the most part, early scientists were brilliant amateurs who pursued their studies and conducted their experiments along with their other activities. Gottfried Leibnitz (1646–1716), the universal genius who invented calculus and discovered that light is transmitted from the sun to the earth by means of ether, pursued a varied career. He mastered mechanics, optics, physics, economics, history, philosophy, and theology while a busy diplomat. His contemporary, Isaac Newton (1642–1727), who discovered the law of gravity, was engrossed in biblical studies as well as in astronomy, mathematics, and physics.

"Century of Genius." While scientific progress was notable in the whole modern period, it was especially brilliant in

Isaac Newton (British Information Services)

Blaise Pascal (Library of Congress)

the seventeenth century, or the "Century of Genius." Among the exceptional scientists in addition to Leibnitz and Newton were Robert Boyle (1627–1691), a chemist; René Descartes (1596–1650), a mathematician; Galileo Galilei (1564–1642), an astronomer; William Harvey (1578–1657), a physiologist; Christian Huygens (1629–1695), a physicist; Johannes Kepler (1571–1630), an astronomer; John Napier (1550–1617), a mathematician, and Blaise Pascal (1623–1662), a mathematician.

The results of scientific investigation were diffused by means of books and magazines which were made possible by the improvements in printing. Scientists corresponded with each other and exchanged information and criticism. Thus the learned men of Europe developed a sense of solidarity and mutual interest and, in a way,

promoted unity in Europe at a time when conflicting national ambitions and religious rivalry were dividing nations. The various scientific societies played an important role in encouraging and aiding scientific research. Most of the members of the Academy of the Lynxes in Rome, the Academy of Sciences in Paris, the Royal Society of London, and others were not teachers of science but scholars, scientists, and influential men in the political and social world who wished to stimulate research and offered prizes for improvements and inventions. By the late seventeenth century, science had captivated the minds and hearts of the upper classes and professional people, many of whom built private laboratories in their homes and studied science as a hobby.

Mathematics. Scientists needed two tools before they could progress fur-

A new interest in science and general advances in all knowledge led to the founding of scientific societies, such as the Academy of Sciences and Fine Arts in France, chartered by King Louis XIV. (Giraudon)

ther: a mathematical language that could express accurately quantities and relations among things, and instruments that could weigh, measure, and count. A series of instruments such as the barometer, delicate balances and scales, the microscope, the pendulum clock, the telescope, and the thermometer made possible more precise observations and experiments.

One of the greatest names in the history of mathematics is René Descartes (1596–1650), who applied algebra to geometry and thus invented analytical geometry. Descartes believed mathematics was the queen of the sciences and hoped to apply the mathematical method to all sciences. Above all, his readers were impressed with the idea that the world about them could be translated into mathematical form.

Astronomy. The progress of science in astronomy triggered off a series of advances in other studies. From ancient times scholars believed that the earth was the center of the universe. The Ptolemaic theory, as it was called, suited the idea that just as man was the center of creation, so too was his home, the earth, the center of the planets. It did not seem to need proof. If a person looked up at the starlit sky at night, he felt as if he were looking out of a dome, with the stars and planets arranged over and around the earth. Nevertheless, some thinkers rejected this idea and proposed instead that the sun, not the earth, was the center of the universe and that the earth and other planets revolved around it.

The person who propounded the heliocentric (sun-centered) theory was

René Descartes (1596–1650). Descartes' works included essays and books on analytical geometry, meteors, philosophy, physiology, and psychology. (Library of Congress)

Nicholas Copernicus (1473–1543), a Polish monk. Without telescope or other instrument, Copernicus scrutinized the notion that the earth was the center. With his naked eye he studied the heavens and concluded that the sun was stationary. He explained the fact that the sun and planets appeared to move from east to west by noting that the earth moved on its axis from west to east. Many remained unconvinced and ridiculed Copernicus. Others, however, added proofs. Tycho Brahe (1546–1601) established an observatory in Denmark and collected data about the stars which proved to him that the earth and planets traveled around the sun. Johannes Kepler (1571–1630) added to the heliocentric theory the observation that the earth and planets travel around the sun in ellipses, not in circles.

Galileo. These ideas received strong support from the Italian scientist, Galileo Galilei (1564–1642). Filled with curiosity, Galileo asked himself

Galileo Galilei, great Italian astronomer, mathematician, and physicist. Using his improved telescope, Galileo noticed that the moon had an uneven mountainous surface and that numerous stars made up the Milky Way. (Library of Congress)

and spots on the surface of the sun. His studies and observations led him to the conclusion that Copernicus was right and that the earth was not the center of the universe. He published his findings in *Dialogue on the Two Principal Systems of the Universe,* which started a heated controversy.

As a result of this work, Galileo was summoned before the Congregation of the Index in Rome and forced to cease teaching as a fact what seemed still only a theory. Churchmen feared that people would not be able to reconcile the Copernican theory with certain concepts drawn from the Bible. Many learned scholars and scientists also denounced him. "Look how the sun moves across the heavens, rising in the east in the morning and setting in the west at night!" And they asked, "Does the sun not travel across the skies, as we can all see?" Time proved Galileo's critics wrong.

The studies of Sir Isaac Newton (1642–1727) ended the argument. Newton showed that the earth and other planets were held in their course around the sun by the power of gravity. According to the old story, Newton saw an apple fall from a tree in his garden and wondered why the fruit fell down instead of up. The answer to his question was the force of gravity that brought everything down to earth. Newton reasoned that the same force that pulled the apple to the earth kept the earth and her sister planets from wandering in space and set them revolving around the sun. Newton's impact on his time was so strong that popular versions of his difficult book *Principia* were widely read. The poet Alexander Pope said:

how things happened in nature. Without relying on the answers supplied by books or persons, he determined to find out for himself by studying and checking. For example, after contemplating the old idea of Aristotle that heavier bodies fall faster to the earth than lighter ones, he experimented. Before a large audience he climbed to the top of the Tower of Pisa and dropped two shots, a one-pound and a ten-pound weight. Both weights reached the ground at the same time. Galileo thus exploded a myth.

Galileo perfected a telescope—originally invented by a Dutchman—so that he could magnify objects four hundred times. With this instrument he scanned the skies at night and saw stars not detected before. He observed the satellites around the planet Jupiter

Nature and Nature's laws lay hid
in night:
God said, let Newton be, and all
was light.

Newton's achievements in astronomy, mathematics, color, and biblical studies so impressed his countrymen that he was buried with royal honors in Westminster Abbey.

Biology and medicine. Progress in other branches of science were of equal importance. The human body was studied systematically. The invention of the microscope by the Dutch Zacharias Janssen (*c.* 1590) and its improvement by Anton van Leeuwenhoeck (1632–1723) enabled scientists to study human tissues and bacteria. A notable achievement was the study of the circulation of the blood. Michael Servetus (1511–1553) traced the course of the blood in the lungs, but it was not until the time of William Harvey (1578–1657) that the circulation through the body was mapped. In his studies of the structure of tissues, kidney, spleen, and other organs, Marcello Malpighi (1628–1694) discovered the capillaries and thus solved the medical mystery of how blood got from the arteries to the veins. Andreas Vesalius (1514–1564), a Fleming, studied animals and the human body by dissecting cadavers. These dissections proved that many statements about the human body in the old medical books based on the ideas of the ancient Roman, Galen, were erroneous. However, ridicule was heaped on Vesalius for daring to question the old masters of medicine and anatomy. Another old myth was disproved when Francesco Redi (1626–1697) demonstrated that maggots do not come from putrid meat but

only use it as nests. Redi showed that "spontaneous generation" does not occur.

The advances in the healing arts were a boon to mankind. The Swiss Philippus Paracelsus (1493–1541) prepared the way for modern pharmacists and physicians who rely on medicines and drugs to restore good health to the body. Ambroise Paré, a French surgeon (1517–1590), reviewed existing notions about surgery, discarded many, and improved on others. For example, he adopted the technique of tying up arteries instead of cauterizing them with a hot iron; and he rejected the widespread practice of treating gunshot wounds as poisonous burns and pouring scalding oil into them.

Applications of science. The scientific advances found many applications. Of course science was studied not only for its practical use but for its own sake. No immediate application was made of the new knowledge. But more often than not, uses followed quickly upon the heels of discovery. The principle of the pendulum was applied to the construction of accurate clocks. Studies in atmospheric pressure led to a practical model of a steam engine. Improvements in surveying land and in mapmaking enabled individuals and states to draw precise boundaries and aided trading companies and mariners. Italian engineers employed principles of hydrostatics (the science of the pressure and equilibrium of liquids) in building canals, locks, and harbors. Furthermore, scientific advances aided kings to wage war. Military engineers improved fortifications and artillery. Even in music and art the impact of science was strong. Painters and architects, for ex-

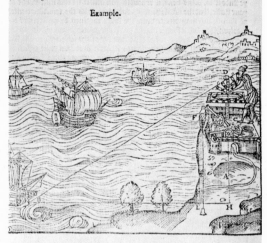

The first Booke

f the perpendiculare intercepted with the scale in the cliffes altitude
before measured, and divide by the partes of the scale cutte, the quotient
will shew the lyne hypothenuial, or distance of that parte of the shippe
which your lyne visuall touched from your eye, or adioyning the square.
if the longitude firste founde to the square of the altitude, the roote qua-
rat of the product is also the true length of the line visuall.

Example.

Admit I stande on the cliffe A, and see the shippe B lying at rode in the
sea, I desire to know how farre of she is from me, mine instrument conu-
iently placed at C (as is tofore declared) I turne my dimetient of my semicir-
le towarde the shippe, mouing it vp and downe till I espye through the sightes

Reproduction of a page from Leonard Diggess's Geometrical Practise Named Pantometria *in 1571, with illustration and instruction of an early method of measuring. (Hulton Picture Library)*

ample, used the principles of light, color, proportion, and perspective that they learned from physicists and mathematicians. The Church also found use for the new knowledge. The accurate observations of astronomers helped churchmen fix correct dates for the annual fixed and movable feasts. Pope Gregory XIII sponsored astronomical studies that led to the reform (1582) of the old Julian calendar (which was then eleven days behind the astronomical year). The new calendar was called the Gregorian calendar and is still in use.

REVIEW

62. Commercial Empires in the East

A. What were the motives behind the European explorations in the period under study?

B. Identify the following: Bartholomew Diaz, Vasco da Gama, Goa.

c. What trade monopolies enabled the Dutch Empire to surpass the Portuguese Empire?

D. Explain the significance of the Mogul Empire, Joseph Dupleix, and the English East India Company.

63. European Colonies in North and South America

A. Mention the contribution of five Spanish explorers to Spain's empire in the New World.

B. What beneficial results came from the American settlements of the Spanish Empire?

c. Identify the following: the Cabots, Verrazzano, Cartier, Pilgrims, New Netherland, Jamestown.

D. What is the importance of the Indians in the history of the New World?

64. Consequences of the Discoveries and Colonization

A. Mention at least five beneficial consequences of the European explorations in this period.

B. How did colonization aid in strengthening monarchies?

c. What was meant by "mercantilism"? Cite an example.

D. Why was Negro slavery so prevalent in the New World?

65. The Progress of Science

A. How did the writings of Francis Bacon aid the development of modern science?

B. Mention the contributions to mathematics made by Leibnitz and Descartes.

c. How did the theories of Copernicus revolutionize astronomy?

D. Mention a contribution to science by each of the following: Galileo, Newton, Harvey.

THE CHAPTER IN REVIEW

A. On your textbook world map that

shows European expansion, note the areas of the world which European exploration, trade, or colonization had reached by 1700. List these areas and indicate which European country was principally concerned with each area.

B. How did the rise of science in the sixteenth and seventeenth centuries add to European dominance of the world?

C. What motives brought the English to the New World around 1600? Why had they not attempted colonial expansion in the Americas before this time?

D. Unlike the Mogul Empire in India, China and Japan were successful in resisting European pressures. What were the reasons for and the results of this resistance?

E. Review the major consequences of European expansion to new areas of the world in the period between 1500 and 1700.

FOR YOUR NOTEBOOK

You are halfway through your course in world history, and by now you should see that your notebook is designed (1) to supplement material in the text; (2) to organize material so that you understand it thoroughly; (3) to enable you to see simultaneous events in various parts of the world; (4) to show how the big developments in history have many "causes" and many "results," and (5) to let you see that the contributions of individual *persons* are the important material out of which history is made. It is well to keep these purposes in mind as you enter the second half of this course. Also, look back through your notebook to see if you can "touch it up" with the above purposes in mind.

In any of your standard reference works or in a history of science, look up the scientific and technological discoveries of the later Middle Ages and early modern times, such as the compass, and show how they enabled sailors to leave sight of land.

Read a biographical sketch of Prince Henry the Navigator to see how he set about systematic exploration. In your notebook list the steps he took to prepare his captains for their tasks.

Enter the name of each of the following in your notebook, and after each name describe the contributions the man made to the development of science:

Bacon	Harvey
Kepler	Boyle
Copernicus	Leibnitz
Galileo	Newton

Make up parallel columns for Portugal, Spain, the Netherlands, England, and France. In these columns enter events connected with overseas discoveries and explorations from 1400 to 1700.

Make a list of effects that exploration and overseas discoveries had on the European countries.

SELECTED READINGS

The best general accounts of explorations are Harold Lamb, *New Found World: How North America Was Discovered and Explored* (Garden City, N. Y.: Doubleday & Co., 1955), and Ralph Edgar Bailey, *Argosies of Empire* (New York: E. P. Dutton & Co., 1947). Both are absorbing, fast-moving stories.

Biographies have been written about many persons you encountered in this chapter. Perhaps the most helpful and interesting are Samuel Eliot Morison, *Christopher Columbus, Mariner* (Boston: Little, Brown & Co., 1955), a condensation of Morison's larger and authoritative *Admiral of the Ocean Seas;* and *The Fire of Francis Xavier,* by Arthur R. McGratty, S.J. (Milwaukee, Wis.: Bruce Publishing Co., 1952).

Sarah Bolton, *Famous Men of Science* (New York: Thomas Y. Crowell Co., 1946), gives short accounts of the major figures of this chapter in the first part of her study of famous scientists down to the time of Einstein. Francis Bacon gives an excellent picture of what a scientist hoped might come about in his *New Atlantis,* of which there are many editions in English.

Chapter 23. Post-Reformation States and Wars in Europe

66. POLITICAL DISUNION OF EUROPE AND THE INCREASED POWER OF KINGS

Medieval Europe had been composed of many and various political bodies; kingdoms, principalities, small republics, and free cities. Yet a sense of unity, of belonging to a grand society called Christendom, had held these bodies together in a loose system. In this grand society of states the Pope was not only the head of the Church but in a rather undefined sense the supreme diplomatic arbiter of disputes between states. In a similar sense the Holy Roman Emperor (in reality the German emperor) was the political chief of Christendom. Few governments controlled large areas effectively. Nobles, bishops, abbots, knights, and cities shared public

authority with the various kings and the emperor. Within each kingdom individual persons, classes of people, religious or municipal corporations enjoyed rights and privileges that few rulers dared to violate. The king might legally stand over all, but in practice he had little real power. Moreover, he was bound to fulfill certain duties and respect the rights of others because, like everybody else, he was considered to be bound by law. No medieval king was sole master in his kingdom.

Immense changes took place in the general political and governmental system of Europe in the sixteenth and seventeenth centuries. The Protestant Revolt reduced the sense of unity in Christendom. Religious divisions stood out more prominently than religious unity. Protestant churches denied the authority of the Pope, and Protestant rulers tended generally to elevate the state above the Church. Even some Catholic rulers showed a similar disposition, although of course they could not completely subordinate the Church to the state without ceasing to be Catholic. Another great change that took place was the development of certain very large and well-centralized territorial states ruled by dynasties that directed almost all their energies to acquiring and exercising power. A comparison of the maps of medieval and of seventeenth-century Europe shows that the number of political bodies decreased, because smaller principalities were absorbed by the larger dynastic powers. No longer did kings merely *claim* to be the lords of their kingdoms: they acted as if no doubt existed. Old limitations on royal power fell away, and the seventeenth century became an age of monarchical absolutism.

Public affairs were now directed from a single center, a fixed capital. Officials appointed to carry out the royal will and enforce royal laws were civil servants who were paid by the king and hence were completely dependent on him. These servants did not possess the independence of the nobles and clergy who had served the monarch in the Middle Ages. They were usually recruited from middle-class persons who were trained in law, finance, or administration—"men of the pen," as they were scornfully called by the nobles, who were "men of the sword." Civil servants had wide powers to act in the name of the king. They collected money to clothe, feed,

and train the king's paid soldiers; they administered justice, enforced laws, and promoted the country's domestic and foreign trade. Kings tended to employ nobles only as officers in the army or diplomats in foreign affairs.

Reasons for the emergence of the modern state. Several developments explain the transition from the feudal political system to the modern state. An important reason was the replacement of the agricultural economy of the Middle Ages by a money economy, which was a result of the expansion of trade and manufacturing and the influx of gold and silver. In a self-sufficient agricultural economy, people living in a neighborhood produce what they need, barter among themselves, and buy from the outside world only luxuries or a few articles such as iron and salt. In a money economy, however, money takes the place of barter, and goods and services from faraway lands are bought and sold.

The expansion of trade and colonies, as we have seen, helped to increase royal power. The fact that money was available permitted kings to tax their subjects and to use these sums to clothe, feed, and train a standing army; that is, paid soldiers who were always ready to march at their king's command. Kings were thus freed from reliance on their vassals for knights to do battle.

Armies increased in size, so that it was no longer practical for a local strong man to raise an adequate army and supply it with new and costly weapons. New infantry weapons, improved artillery, advances in the sciences of building fortifications and warships changed the character of warfare and rendered it unlikely that the local man could make good his claim against the central government. With armies far larger than those of rivals within his kingdom, the king could move quickly against the rebel.

Divine right of kings. The modern state, with absolute power vested either in the king or in the central government, was aided also by political writers who praised royal power. Some maintained that, as God's ministers on earth, kings were supreme in spiritual and temporal matters; that they could not be held responsible to anyone on earth, either people or parliament, for what they did. They were responsible to God alone. This is the idea of the *divine right of kings.* James I of England (1603–1625) supported this position by writing that people sinned if they did not obey the king; he argued that the laws of God and reason decreed that subjects had duties but no rights. Similar views

James I of England (Library of Congress)

were voiced later in France by Bishop Jacques Bossuet, who said that the royal throne was not the throne of men but the throne of God Himself and that the king need give no account of his acts save to God. The vast majority of people obeyed their kings. The king seemed more than human because at his coronation he was anointed by holy oils that made his person sacred.

Kings and central governments did not increase their power and prestige without a fight against nobles, religious minorities, and writers who advocated limited monarchy and local liberties. Revolts against central power erupted in many lands, but prior to 1689 they succeeded in limiting it only in the Holy Roman Empire and in the Republic of Poland. From 1640 to 1660, six revolutions occurred against royal government. The authority of the King of Spain was challenged by rebellions in Catalonia (the northeast corner of Spain), in Portugal (which made good her claim of independence under the Braganza dynasty), and in Naples (where a fruit peddler named Masaniello led a mob). Other outbreaks were in France, Netherlands, and England. In most of these outbreaks the immediate cause of violence was arbitrary taxation or religious persecution.

Religious minorities. A big obstacle to national unity and the power of the central government was the existence of religious minorities in all countries. Religion, which had been a bond of union in the Middle Ages, now divided countries. A religious minority in one country often felt it had more in common with its co-religionists in another land than with fellow countrymen who belonged to a different church. French Protestants (called Huguenots), for example, looked for sympathy to the Protestants of the British Isles, Holland, and Germany. Such minorities weakened national unity and popularized the idea that royal authority was limited, or they even encouraged disloyalty and rebellion. Because of the force of the written word in winning men's minds, kings were disturbed by political writers who ridiculed divine right or justified the murder of tyrants (tyrannicide). Thorns in the side of divine-right monarchs were persons who placed the source of authority in the state not in kings but in the people, who received it from God. These "popular" ideas, the work of Jesuit thinkers Francisco Suárez (1548–1617) and St. Robert Bellarmine (1542–1621), laid the philosophical foundations for Christian democracy.

Certain countries took advantage of religious troubles within other lands by encouraging minorities to weaken the king. England, for example, sympathized with and at times aided French Protestants, while the Catholic kings of France, fearing a strong Germany, encouraged German Lutherans and Calvinists to defy the Catholic emperor who was trying to unify Germany. Today it is difficult to appreciate the intense hatred generated by religious differences. But in the sixteenth and seventeenth centuries it was hard for men to see how a state could flourish if people were not united in religion. How could one be saved— through faith, or faith and good works,

or was one predestined by God to be saved or damned for all eternity? Such questions aroused great controversy and produced civil strife.

Each side in a controversy depicted the other in the darkest colors and charged base motives. Books, sermons, and newspapers were weapons in a cold war waged by Catholics and Protestants, and by Protestant against Protestant.

In the sixteenth century the Tudor dynasty in England had vastly augmented its power by seizing the wealth of the Catholic Church and strongly supporting Protestantism in Europe. The Spanish monarchy under a Hapsburg dynasty had grown powerful in part through its championing of Catholicism. In the seventeenth century the most striking example of increased royal power was in France under the Bourbon dynasty.

Religious wars in France. The fight for a strong monarchy in France was a hard one. The kings first had to overcome the divisions between Catholics and Huguenots that had resulted in the Wars of Religion (1562–1598). Catholics tried to stem the tide of Protestantism, while Huguenots wished not only to retain what they had already gained but to better their political and religious position. But without firm government, France fell apart as bands of soldiers wandered about the countryside, looting and killing.

Henry IV and Louis XIII. In the reign of the first king of the Bourbon dynasty, Henry IV (1589–1610), the king and central government in Paris triumphed over all rivals. Henry IV, at one time a Protestant, tried to end the Catholic-Protestant feud by adopting the

Catholic religion and tolerating the Protestants. His Edict of Nantes of 1598 granted Huguenots religious toleration and equal rights with Catholics, who formed a vast majority of the nation. In effect, the Edict recognized the Huguenots as an armed political party with the right to garrison certain fortresses. However, the Huguenots proved to be a state within a state, and the royal authority continued to fear them.

Louis XIII (1610–1643) continued the effort to make the royal will supreme. His minister, Cardinal Richelieu, reduced the power of the Estates-General or representative assembly, organized a strong army, reduced the military strength of the Huguenots and some of the privileges of the nobility. He made noblemen subject to the death penalty and to exile, and compelled them to dismantle their fortifications. To centralize control of the provinces in the capital, he dispatched

Cardinal Richelieu, Louis XIII's chief minister and one of the world's great statesmen.

Political cartoon showing Cardinal Richelieu controlling a card game with Louis XIII and Ferdinand II, first German Emperor. (Bibliothèque Nationale)

agents (intendants) to supervise the administration of the country and see to it that the will of the king was obeyed.

67. THIRTY YEARS' WAR AND PURITAN REVOLUTION

The ambition of rulers and religious antagonisms led to the outbreak of the Thirty Years' War (1618–1648). Three main developments led to war. First, following the Peace of Augsburg of 1555, the growth of Calvinism upset the Lutheran-Catholic equilibrium which that peace had created in the Holy Roman Empire. Second, the emperor (a Hapsburg) tried to tighten his grip over the states of the empire. These states, including Catholic areas, resented a loss of local liberties and looked for outside help against their

---

[1] The Holy Roman Emperor was the hereditary ruler of Austria and was also King of Hungary and Bohemia. It was his hereditary possessions rather than the emperorship that made him strong. The word Austria, as used here, signifies the Hapsburg hereditary lands —Austria, Bohemia, Hungary.

emperor. And last, the rivalry between Hapsburg and Bourbon and between the Netherlands and Spain spilled over into Germany.

Revolt in Bohemia. Fighting began in Bohemia (now Czechoslovakia) when the Czechs, who were zealous to maintain their local liberties, rebelled against the emperor and elected a Calvinist prince as their king. Emperor Ferdinand II sent an army to crush the rebels, who were defeated at the Battle of the White Mountain (1620). The emperor not only reconquered Bohemia but now attempted to restore the Catholic religion there.

Denmark intervenes. Protestants feared the worst, but their spirits were lifted by the intervention on their side of the Lutheran King of Denmark. Christian IV had already made Denmark the leading power in the Baltic. He encouraged commerce and immigration of merchants and skilled workers and organized a strong army. His motives for going to war against the emperor were not primarily to save the Protestant cause but to seize control of German North Sea ports and the Elbe and Weser rivers. However, his armies were defeated by Generals Tilly and Wallenstein in the service of Ferdinand II. Christian IV thus was forced to pledge not to interfere in the affairs of the Holy Roman Empire (1629).

German affairs were now complicated by Spanish, French, and Swedish ambitions. Spain, under a Hapsburg king allied with Emperor Ferdinand, strengthened her position in Belgium and the Franche Comté and thus threatened the frontiers of France and Holland. Faced by a double Hapsburg threat from Spain and the em-

The beginning of the Thirty Years' War. Revolt began with violence against the royal officers in Prague. (Ullstein)

peror, France sought aid from their enemies. The French thereupon detached from the emperor some German Catholic states and also paid the King of Sweden to intervene in Germany.

Sweden. Sweden aspired to dominate the Baltic. While the Danish king intervened in the Thirty Years' War, the King of Sweden, Gustavus Adolphus, consolidated Swedish power in northern Germany. Using his competent armies, Gustavus Adolphus made the Baltic a Swedish lake. He undertook to remove two rivals before moving against the emperor: the Russians and the Poles. He cut off Russia from the Baltic and took the province of Livonia at the mouth of the Vistula River from Poland. Christian IV of Denmark sought unsuccessfully to block his rival, the King of Sweden, from intervening in Germany.

Gustavus Adolphus entered the German war in 1630 because he feared that the victories of Wallenstein's imperial armies menaced Protestantism and the Swedish position in northern Germany. Swedish armies, toughened by campaigns against Russians and Poles, defeated the imperial forces. But at the battle of Lützen (1632), Gustavus Adolphus fell, although his troops carried the day. Swedish victories continued and established Sweden as the principal military power of northern Europe.

Despite these victories, the Protestant coalition seemed to fall apart. Peace was in sight. But neither France nor Spain wanted peace, and therefore the struggle continued. Spanish troops raided France, while French armies invaded Catalonia. The King of France recognized the independence of Portugal which had been under Spanish control from 1580 to 1640.

French intervention. The last phase of the Thirty Years' War was a combined Swedish-French effort to defeat the Holy Roman Emperor. France no longer confined her efforts to intrigue and subsidies. French troops took the field on German soil. Many Protestants, however, supported the Catholic emperor because they resented foreign intervention in German affairs. The emperor's Spanish ally fought to subdue the Dutch and to hold a band of territory stretching from Milan, in northern Italy, to the Netherlands, and thus to encircle France.

Peace of Westphalia. After heavy fighting, peace was made in 1648. Because the negotiations were carried on at two cities in Westphalia (in Germany), the settlement is called the Peace of Westphalia. The conferences there were the first in a series of meetings of European diplomats that have taken place from

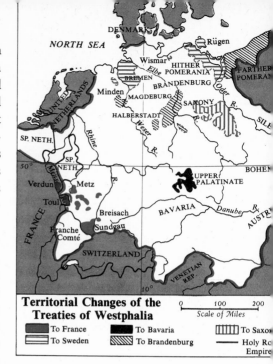

Territorial Changes of the Treaties of Westphalia

Scale of Miles — 0, 100, 200

- To France
- To Sweden
- To Bavaria
- To Brandenburg
- To Saxony
- Holy Roman Empire

time to time to the present day. The results of the war and the treaties are important in world history.

Germany weakened and divided. Already divided by Protestantism, Germany was further weakened. Whereas Germany in 1500 had been prosperous, a century and a half later German life, property, and moral standards were destroyed as a result of the movements of hungry and destructive armies of foreign soldiers. Large provinces, though technically still in the Holy Roman Empire, were now under the control of princes and kings whose main interests were non-German. Thus France received Metz, Verdun, and Alsace, while Sweden held part of the German coast on the Baltic and three votes in the Diet of the Holy Roman Empire. The Dutch and the Swiss won European recognition of their independence. The two chief German states, Austria and Brandenburg, had interests outside the empire. Austria controlled much of Hungary, and Brandenburg had succeeded (1618) to the Duchy of Prussia in the east. Austria lost her hope of establishing a Hapsburg power over all Germany. Yet the emperor managed to root out Protestantism and rebellion in Austria, to recover Bohemia, and thus to unify his domains. He was still titular head of Germany.

The Thirty Years' War broke Germany politically. The emperor could not raise taxes or declare war without the permission of the imperial Diet, consisting of representatives of 343 princes, bishops, free cities, and others in the Holy Roman Empire. This situation allowed the neighbors of the empire to interfere in German affairs. France and Sweden saw to it that "German liberties" were written into the peace treaties of Westphalia so that they could intervene in Germany to "protect" any one of the 343 states from the emperor.

The treaties of Westphalia in effect greatly retarded Catholic recovery in Germany, for they confirmed the principle that German princes could dictate the religion of their subjects. Besides, much property belonging to Catholic bishops was annexed by princes without permission of the Pope. By drafting these treaties as if the Church did not exist, the great powers decided that the Pope was no longer the supreme diplomatic arbiter of Europe.

In short, the Thirty Years' War confirmed the political disruption of Christendom. Westphalia ended the great war in the disaster-torn empire, but conflict between France and Spain continued until 1659. By the Peace of the Pyrenees in 1659 the French acquired new territory along the Pyrenees boundary and in Flanders at the expense of the Spanish. This treaty of peace marks the beginning of the decline of Spain as the leading power in western Europe and the establishment of France in that position.

The Stuart kings in England. England took no part in the Thirty Years' War but instead plunged into a great civil war of her own. King James I of England was, as we have seen, a believer in the divine rights of kings. He and his son, Charles I, claimed that Parliament should advise the crown only on matters in which such advice was solicited and should not interfere with the royal government. These rulers of the Stuart dynasty thus ran counter to what the members of the House believed to be their lawful and traditional rights. What the House of Commons had been willing to put up with under the Tudor rulers, who had been popular, the Parliament resented and resisted under the Stuart kings. They were a Scottish dynasty which had succeeded Queen Elizabeth in 1603.

The Peace of Münster (1642), a preliminary treaty before the final settlement and the Peace of Westphalia in 1648. (Hulton Picture Library)

Taxes and religion. King and Parliament came to blows over two related problems, money and religion. Since the Stuarts did not possess the wealth of the Tudors and since they lived at a time of rising prices and depression, they depended on Parliament to supply them with necessary funds to run the government. But when they called Parliament into session, they supplied their opponents with the opportunity to be heard and to demand that public grievances be redressed before money was voted. A religious quarrel was related to the financial. Puritans—a substantial segment of the English middle classes represented in the House of Commons— did not think that the Protestant Revolution had been carried far enough in England. They wanted

The trial of Charles I of England (British Information Services)

to purify the Church of England of "popish" or Roman Catholic tendencies, hence their name "Puritans." Inspired by the ideas of John Calvin, their complete reliance was on the Bible as the rule of faith, and on preaching instead of ritual. Puritans favored the congregational form of church government, in which every parish should be a self-governing unit without the rule of bishops. To accept these views would have meant radical changes in the Anglican Church. Therefore, the kings as heads of the Church of England, denounced the Puritans and sought to force them to conform to the national church.

Reign of Charles I. James I (1603–1625), son of Mary, Queen of Scots, came early into conflict with Parliament and the Puritans. His insistence on governing England with responsibility to God alone produced a series of crises. His son and successor, Charles I (1625–1649) came to blows with his enemies over the program of Archbishop Laud to coerce the Puritans and over new taxes imposed without parliamentary approval. Laud forced conformity to the Church of England, with the result that large numbers of Puritans left England for a haven in the New World.

For eleven years (1629–1640) Charles I ruled his kingdom without Parliament. Finally in 1640 he convened Parliament, which forced him to renounce unparliamentary taxes and arbitrary practices and to summon Parliament every three years. However, the opposition to the King disintegrated when Parliament tried to remove control of the army from him and so restrict his authority that

Cromwell dissolving the Parliament. Cromwell purged Parliament of all Presbyterian members, leaving about sixty members of a "Rump" (or sitting) Parliament. (British Information Services)

he would not really be an effective king. His supporters rallied to his colors and Charles I declared the leaders of the House of Commons to be rebels. A civil war between the king's allies, or Cavaliers as they were called, and his enemies in the Parliament, principally Puritans or "Roundheads," occurred between 1642 and 1649.

Oliver Cromwell. The parliamentary party was victorious because of the military genius of Oliver Cromwell and his so-called New Model Army. Charles I was defeated, captured, tried as a "tyrant, traitor, murderer, and public enemy," and executed in 1649. Between 1649 and 1660, England was a commonwealth and protectorate under Oliver Cromwell (1599–1658) and his son Richard, who soon failed as a ruler. Backed up by a strong army, Cromwell maintained a Puritan dictatorship. The-

aters and bowling alleys were closed and games and sports prohibited on Sunday. Cromwell conquered Ireland, too, and confiscated the lands of his enemies. He received eloquent support for his regime from the pen of John Milton, the talented author of *Paradise Lost.* Cromwell, after subduing all the British Isles, carried on a vigorous foreign policy. A successful naval war, arising over trade questions, was fought against the Dutch in 1652–1654. The capture of Jamaica by the British in 1655 led to war with Spain (1656–1659).

The Restoration. The death of Cromwell marked the practical end of Puritan rule. The effort to have his son take his place was short-lived. The English tired of Puritans, civil war, and military government, so that in 1660 their leaders invited Charles II, the son of Charles I, to return to England. The return of the Stuarts is called the Restoration.

The Restoration was a compromise between the royal and parliamentary power. Monarchy, but without an absolute king, was restored, as was the position of the Anglican Church. Dissenters from the Church of England were denied equal civil and political rights with persons who conformed to the state church.

68. FRANCE UNDER LOUIS XIV

King Louis XIV of France reigned for seventy-two years: from 1643 to 1715. Prior to 1661, however, the French state had been directed by the king's minister, Cardinal Mazarin, who had carried on the vigorous system of Richelieu. Louis had succeeded to the throne at the age of five and was only twenty-three in 1661, the year Mazarin died. On the morning after the death of the minister the young king made the announcement that henceforth he would personally direct the government. In the years that followed he not only made the French monarchy dominant in western Europe —so that the period has been called by historians "the age of Louis XIV" —but made himself the very heart of France. A man of great energy, he supervised every detail of government. His spirit so infused the country that he could say, *L'état, c'est moi* [I am the state]!"

The period of this great king was marked by numerous wars and an immense revolution in the state system of Europe. England rid itself of the Stuart dynasty and became the chief maritime power in the world. Sweden rose to immense power in the north and then declined. The Spanish empire in Europe was dissolved. The Ottoman Empire made new attacks on Christian Europe and then went into a state of permanent decline. Russia under Czar Peter the Great became a great power for the first time. These important changes in the international system of Europe had an impact on the world beyond Europe, especially in North and South America.

The energies of France. Louis XIV reinforced France by ordering his war minister, Louvois, to reorganize French armies, and Controller-General Colbert to develop policies for increasing French wealth. Colbert encouraged industry and established minute regulations for French manufacturing, assisted shipbuilders, improved roads, built canals and harbors, enlarged the navy, founded trading companies for overseas and European trade, and put new life into the Canadian colony of New France. His main object was to get more money for France because he believed that abundant money was the difference between a mighty country and a weak one. Hence he recommended laws to encourage French industry and commerce to earn money and to discourage foreign merchants. Much of the wealth that came to France as a result of his labors was spent on the costly wars and the magnificent court life in the palace at Versailles.

The court of Louis XIV. To have a fitting home for himself and his government, Louis XIV ordered the construction of a series of beautiful buildings at Versailles, located about twelve miles from Paris. Here the king—who likened himself to the sun that shone brilliantly in the heavens and was the source of light and energy—held court in regal splendor. Soon all Europe marveled at his beautiful palace and other rulers tried to imitate him. At Versailles, Louis XIV entertained large numbers of nobles and foreign visitors and patronized the arts, letters, and sciences.

Europeans marveled, too, at the excellence of French literature of the "Splendid Century." The great masters of literature included La Fontaine, who wrote *Fables;* Corneille, whose plays (especially *Le Cid*) reflected his staunch Catholic faith; and Molière, whose plays poked fun at human

Night illumination of the magnificent Palace of Versailles, the "showcase" of King Louis XIV, whose tastes were luxurious and expensive. (French Embassy Press & Information Division)

weaknesses, the meanness of customs, and the social-climbing of the middle classes. For example, Molière's *Would-Be Gentleman* lampoons the efforts of a merchant to become a nobleman. Drama was encouraged by the king, who established a theater, the Comédie Française, which still survives.

The Turks advance. If there was peace in western Europe when Louis XIV began personally to direct French policy, the same could not be said of eastern Europe. There the Ottoman Turks were undergoing one of their periodic revivals and onslaughts upon Christian Europe. They were fighting to take the great island of Crete from Venice, and their advances in Hungary led to war with the Holy Roman Emperor, who held the crown of that kingdom. In 1664, after being defeated by the emperor, they made a twenty-year truce with him in Hungary. But the war for Crete continued until a peace was made in 1670 which in effect delivered that island to the Ottoman Empire. These wars against the Turks had something of the aspect of a crusade from the viewpoint of Christians, and some states, including

France, sent military aid to the Venetians. But such acts were little more than gestures.

Natural frontiers. Louis XIV and his ministers were more interested in taking advantage of the Turkish menace in eastern Europe by developing aggressive power policies in the West. Thus, in 1667–1668 the French king laid claim to certain territories in the Spanish Netherlands (Belgium) and fought to secure them. This aroused the fears and hostility of the Dutch Republic. When England and Sweden allied with the Dutch, a peace was made in 1668 that left France in control of some twelve fortified towns in the Spanish Netherlands. This was the first of Louis XIV's wars to gain for France what was thought of as her "natural frontiers"—that is, the boundaries of ancient Gaul—the Rhine, the Alps, and the Pyrenees. To achieve his purpose Louis developed a policy of neutralizing the English by subsidies, allying himself with certain German princes who feared the emperor, and encouraging the Turks to create new diversions in eastern Europe.

The Dutch War. In 1670, Louis XIV and Charles II of England signed the Treaty of Dover. In return for siding with France against the Dutch, Charles was to receive a large annual subsidy. Next, similar treaties of alliance were made by France with Sweden and certain German princes. Then Louis was ready to attack the Dutch and make good his claim in the Spanish Netherlands, which of course would involve him in conflict also with Spain. The great target of the French king's anger was the Dutch Republic, not only because it had blocked him in 1668, but because it had given political refuge to certain writers who had attacked him. In 1672, French forces moved against the Dutch and easily conquered southern Holland. The Dutch, however, overthrew the oligarchical rulers of their republic and placed at the head of the state as *stadholder* Prince William III of Orange, a descendant of the great William the Silent who had led the Dutch revolt against Spain a century earlier. The Dutch halted the French by opening the dykes and flooding the land. Soon the English, who had helped the French navally, made peace with the Dutch; and about the same time the emperor Leopold I entered the war against France (1674). Thus most of western Europe was at war and the struggle continued until 1678. France and Sweden were allied against a combination of the Dutch, the emperor, Spain, and Denmark. By the treaties of Nimwegen, 1678–1679, the Dutch emerged from the war without territorial loss but were obligated to form no more alliances against France. Spain ceded to France what France claimed in Belgium and also Franche Comté. The emperor ceded to France the strong military position of Freiburg, east of the upper Rhine. Louis XIV can hardly be said to have won a resounding victory, but in this so-called Dutch War he had succeeded in advancing a long step toward gaining the "natural frontiers" of France. His generals also had won for France an undisputed military superiority in Europe. From this time French power was greatly feared.

The reunions. Louis XIV soon declared that all lands and cities that had ever been part of the territories he had annexed since he became king must be "reunited" with France. These annexations alarmed German princes, who feared that their possessions also would be swallowed up by the French. But the emperor was too deeply involved in combating the Turks to defend the interests of German princes. Louis also marched his armies into the Spanish Netherlands and into Catalonia. Unable to help the King of Spain against the French, Leopold accepted a French truce. Spain surrendered Luxembourg, while the emperor recognized the French "reunions" of Spanish territory. In 1684 it seemed that Louis XIV could not be stopped. He had successfully terrorized his neighbors, humbled the Holy Roman Emperor, and still had a first-class army to use against a rival.

Louis XIV and Catholicism. The king was an ardent Catholic but fell victim to the intolerant spirit of his age. Because he believed his office was not less sacred than that of the Pope, he determined to dominate the Church in France. This led to a famous clash between the French monarchy and Pope Innocent XI. It began with Louis' claim to the revenues of all vacant bishoprics in France; this the Pope could not allow. Then there surged up the spirit of Gallicanism with the ideal of a sort of French national Catholic Church: a spirit that had emerged from time to time in France since the fifteenth century. In 1682 the king's supporters among the clergy drew up certain articles of belief which in effect allowed the king a veto over the acts of the Pope and the Church in France. The Pope annulled these articles, and

Pope Innocent XI (Fototeca Unione, Roma)

the king retaliated by refusing to nominate bishops for confirmation by the Pope. A bitter quarrel and prolonged deadlock followed, but in the end Louis conceded all to the Pope. The Gallican articles were cast aside by the king, but they were never wholly abandoned by many of the French clergy.

One reason why Louis XIV had been able to sway the clergy in France was that the Church there had been seriously weakened by a great dissension. The heretical ideas of a Dutch bishop, Cornelius Jansen (1585–1638), had come to influence many French Catholics. These doctrines, known as Jansenism, exaggerated the Catholic teaching concerning the fall of man and brought into Catholic minds an essentially Calvinistic conception of grace along with the doctrine of predestination. Great disputes arose, especially between Jesuits and Jansenists. The latter showed strong tendencies of Gallicanism. Ultimately (in 1713) the main doctrines of Jansenism were condemned by the Pope. By that time Louis XIV, in his old age, had seen a dangerous enemy in Jansenism.

The attack on Protestantism. The French king was at the height of his quarrel with the Pope when he struck a deadly blow at the religious liberty of the Huguenots. Bent on enforcing a strict religious uniformity in France, he revoked the Edict of Nantes and commanded the Huguenots to give up their religion in favor of Catholicism. Many Huguenots fled the country, although the king sought to prevent their going. Thus Louis XIV committed a serious violation of freedom of conscience. His act was deeply disapproved by Innocent XI. The Huguenots who managed to escape to England, Denmark, Holland, and other parts of the Protestant world took with them wealth and various business and technical skills, which were lost to France. Thus the king unintentionally strengthened his enemies. The exiled Huguenots were bitterly hostile to France and to the Catholic Church.

69. REPULSE OF THE TURKS AND RISE OF RUSSIA

The siege of Vienna. As Louis XIV was trampling upon the liberties and rights of the Church, new aggressions of the Turks drew the attention of all Europe. The Ottoman Empire then held most of eastern Europe and encircled the Black Sea. From 1672 to 1676 the Turks had carried on a successful war against Poland, then a large, sprawling, and ill-organized state that included much territory that later would be Russian. From 1677 to 1681 the Turks fought, but with less success, against Russia; and in 1682 a new war broke out between Emperor

Leopold, as King of Hungary, and the Turks. Advancing north and westward, the Turks under Kara Mustafa laid siege to the city of Vienna. The greatest alarms spread through Europe. Pope Innocent XI supplied funds for defense and ordered prayers for the victory of Christian arms. Protestants and Catholics alike feared the consequences of a Turkish victory and hence responded to the call for volunteers. The nobility of Europe gallantly served in what was really the last crusade of Christian Europe.

While Austrian defenders held the invaders, relief armies from Germany and Poland arrived before Vienna. On September 12, 1683, John Sobieski, King of Poland, led his cavalry in a charge against the Turkish lines and saved Vienna.

Afterward hopes were high for the liberation of Christian areas held by the Turks. A Holy League was formed by the emperor, Poland, Venice, and the Pope (1684). The battle against the Turks continued for sixteen years. Almost all of Hungary was liberated. The city of Budapest fell to the Christians in 1686 after having been held by the Turks for a hundred and forty-five years; and soon Belgrade capitulated (1688). Christians now held the keys to the outer defenses of Constantinople. Meanwhile Russia attacked the Turks in the Crimea, so that they were pressed on many fronts.

Treaty of Karlowitz. Renewed aggressions of France in the west (which we shall presently notice) doomed prospects for the liberation of the Balkans. To make matters worse, France gave aid to the Turks to save them from defeat. France had even hoped for a Turkish victory at Vienna in 1683, reasoning that an Austrian loss would make Louis XIV instead of the emperor the first Prince of Christendom. The defeat and disgrace of Austria, the French argued, would leave France the director of Europe. The attacks of French armies in the west meant that the emperor had to wage a two-front war. Fortunately his general, Prince Eugene of Savoy, drove the Turks out of Hungary.

The Treaty of Karlowitz (1699) ended the conflict. To Austria the Turks surrendered Hungary, Croatia, and Transylvania. Venice got the Morea (southern Greece), and Poland received Podolia and part of the Ukraine. Although Russia won the port of Azov on the sea of that name, she failed to win access to the Black Sea. But she did move a step closer to a "window" to the south. The Ottoman Empire, although weakened and in decline, remained a great power, capable of revival.

The rise of Russia. It was at this time that Russia first began to take an important part in the international state system of Europe. This state, as has been seen, developed from the small Duchy of Moscow, which until the late fifteenth century had been subject to the Mongol (Tartar) Empire, and would become eventually the largest single mass of territory governed from one capital in the history of the world.

The heir of the Byzantine Empire. In their march to empire the Russians were sustained by the conviction that their country was the successor to the Byzantine Empire, which had been conquered by the Turks. This idea be-

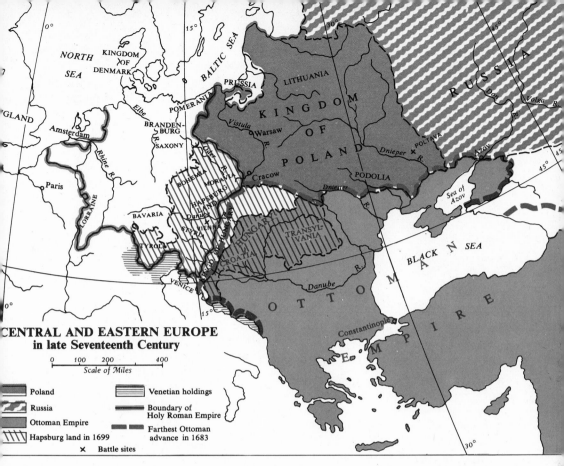

CENTRAL AND EASTERN EUROPE
in late Seventeenth Century

0 100 200   400
Scale of Miles

Poland
Russia
Ottoman Empire
Hapsburg land in 1699
× Battle sites

Venetian holdings
Boundary of
Holy Roman Empire
Farthest Ottoman
advance in 1683

came fixed during the long reign of Ivan III (1462–1505), who married Princess Zoë, niece of the last emperor of Byzantium.

The Czars. In 1589 the Metropolitan (or Archbishop) of Moscow took the title of Patriarch and became independent of the Patriarch of Constantinople. Russian leaders skillfully used the zeal of the Russian Church to lead Orthodox Christians, as a tool to facilitate expansion of their empire. Meanwhile the Duke of Moscow took the title of Czar, or Tsar, which meant Caesar, the title of Roman emperors.

A series of Czars gained absolute control over all Russia and rooted out dissension. Ivan IV (1533–1584) ruled the country with an iron hand. He

Ivan III of Russia, also called "Ivan the Great." His dominant traits are said to have been wisdom and prudence. (Library of Congress)

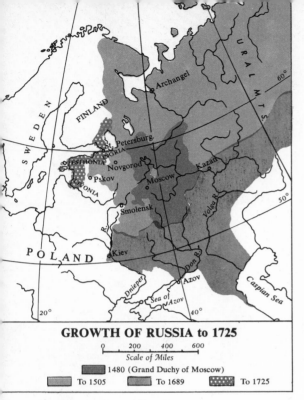

GROWTH OF RUSSIA to 1725

```
0      200     400     600
       Scale of Miles
```

██ 1480 (Grand Duchy of Moscow)

░░ To 1505   ▓▓ To 1689   ▒▒ To 1725

the Cossacks. Having acquired a huge land mass, the Great Russians turned to the goal of getting outlets to the sea. This desire for a port or "window" on the Baltic and a port on the Black Sea was not satisfied until the eighteenth century.

The Romanovs and Peter the Great. In 1613 a new dynasty began under Michael Romanov which governed Russia until the Russian Revolution in 1917. The most important early Romanov was Peter the Great (1689–1725), one of the strangest and cruelest rulers in history. Peter was a six-foot-eight-inch-tall giant of careless and unusual dress. His energy carried him without rest from one corner of Europe to the other in an effort to learn the arts and sciences that would strengthen Russia. His travels impressed him with the backwardness of his country and the necessity of Europeanizing it in order to brace his government for the tasks of rooting out traditional resistance to the government in Moscow and expanding the empire.

Peter the Great did not want the ideals or culture of Europe, but only Western strength. He forced Russians

Peter the Great of Russia, founder of the modern Russian state. (Hulton Picture Library)

even used a pike to pin the feet of offending noblemen to the floor! Convinced that Russia must copy Western countries, Ivan the Terrible built a port at Archangel on the White Sea where English and Dutch ships traded. After his death Russia underwent a "time of troubles" filled with civil war, peasant rebellion, and foreign intervention by Poles, Swedes, and Tartars. But other peoples were unable to exploit Russia's internal troubles for long. Her immense area was assurance that invading armies would be swallowed up by distance. In the seventeenth century the "White" and "Little Russians" were in the Polish Empire. Russia exploited Polish internal weakness by nibbling away at the edges of the empire. The Russians ran into serious difficulty in conquering the fierce horsemen of the southwest, to imitate European manners and customs, ordering them, for example, to cut their beards (for those who did not comply Peter pulled off their beards!) and to smoke tobacco. His reforms only touched the surface of Russian life. The majority of Russians were unimpressed and lived their lives as their ancestors had. But they were affected by the burden of taxes that Peter levied in order to achieve his objectives.

The Czar streamlined the organization of the government, browbeat the nobles, drove his advisers to frenzied activity, and put the Orthodox Church under his thumb. He turned his attention to the army and navy. From semi-oriental hordes, the Russian army became a modern professional force that served as Peter's right hand at home and his weapon against foreign foes. As for his navy, Peter copied the practices of the shipbuilders of Europe whom he had observed during his tour.

Fighting against the Turks, Peter gained new territory to the south, the port of Azov, in 1696. During the rest of his reign, as we shall see, he vastly expanded his empire in other directions.

70. GLORIOUS REVOLUTION IN ENGLAND AND WAR OF THE LEAGUE OF AUGSBURG

Meanwhile, far to the west events of the greatest historical importance had been taking place in the British Isles ever since the restoration of the Stuart dynasty in 1660. The reign of King Charles II (1660–1685) had been marked by new quarrels between crown and Parliament and by new

Titus Oates preyed upon anti-Catholic fears and invented the Popish Plot describing the Jesuit plan to assassinate Charles II. In 1685, Oates was convicted of perjury, severely flogged, and imprisoned. (Hulton Picture Library)

tension between the dominant Protestants and the Catholic minority in England. A Catholic at heart and married to a Catholic princess, Charles wished to protect his co-religionists but found that he could not succeed without inciting revolution. The hatred of Catholicism deepened, in part because of Charles's alliance in 1670 with Louis XIV. In 1678, Englishmen swallowed credulously the lies of Titus Oates about a "Popish Plot" to murder the King and restore the Catholic Church. In the panic that followed, innocent persons were convicted and executed, and Catholics were persecuted.

Tories and Whigs. During the Restoration modern political parties began. The supporters of the King and his Catholic brother and heir to the throne, the Duke of York, were called Tories. They defended the existing order, the Stuart dynasty, and the position of the Anglican Church. Their opponents, the Whigs, favored a

Protestant heir to the throne, a vigorous anti-Catholic policy, and more privileges for those Protestants who dissented from the Anglican Church. An important landmark in the Restoration was the passage of the Habeas Corpus Bill (1679), which guaranteed speedy trials of accused persons by means of court writs ordering that the accused be brought quickly into court.

Fall of James II. Charles II avoided serious trouble with Protestants and Parliament, but his brother and successor, James II (1685–1688), was not as fortunate. James wished to put England back in the Catholic fold and to enlarge royal power. In order to achieve these purposes, he established a standing army—which Englishmen feared as a result of the memories of Cromwell—placed Roman Catholics in high positions, and took a firm grip on the government. The birth of a son to his second wife seemed to assure him a Catholic heir and England a Catholic dynasty. English leaders thereupon invited William of Orange, *stadtholder* of the Netherlands, to land in England and help their cause. William was the husband of Mary, daughter of James II by an earlier marriage, and a Protestant. Deserted by his army, James II fled to France and awaited an opportunity to regain his throne. A national convention invited William and Mary to become joint sovereigns and occupy the vacant throne.

The Glorious Revolution. The replacement of James II by William and Mary in 1689 has been called the Glorious Revolution by those who admired it. It was generally free of bloodshed. A Bill of Rights was enacted as part of the revolutionary settlement. It ended absolute monarchy and established parliamentary regulation of succession to the throne. It marked the beginning of constitutional monarchy; that is, a governmental system headed by a king who is limited by law and acts with Parliament. After 1689 the king could not be a Catholic, he could not suspend laws or tax or raise an army without parliamentary permission. The Glorious Revolution resulted in toleration for all Protestants in England, but it increased the persecution of Catholics and of the Irish, who were conquered by William. English and Irish Catholics had generally supported James II; hence they suffered heavily from his defeat.

The Glorious Revolution did not weaken the crown. While it doomed absolute monarchy, it placed no restriction on what the king could do with the consent of Lords and Commons. Indeed, the crown as limited by Parliament controlled greater segments

James II of England (The National Portrait Gallery)

of national life in the following years.

The Glorious Revolution was a lesson that English-speaking peoples did not forget. The successful limitation of royal authority served as a reminder to later monarchs not to push the opposition too far. In the eighteenth century not only Englishmen and Americans recalled the example, but Frenchmen and other Europeans hoped that they could imitate the events of 1689. The important immediate result of the Revolution was to plunge England into war with France.

War of the League of Augsburg. About three years before William of Orange overthrew James II in Engand, a coalition of states called the League of Augsburg had been formed to resist the aggressive tendency of France. It included the emperor Leopold, Spain, the Dutch Republic (led by William of Orange), Sweden, and some of the German princes. Its declared purpose was to defend the Peace of Westphalia, but the real object was to reduce the power of France. Now that the war in the east was going against the Turks, it seemed to the members of the League that the time had come to face the menace of Louis XIV. The French king, however, took the initiative in 1688 by invading German territory across the upper Rhine, where his troops carried on a ruthless and systematic devastation. While this was happening, William won the crown of England and brought the resources of that country into the coalition against France. William was the archenemy of Louis XIV and put England at the head of the coalition, which aroused most of Europe against France. Protestants were enraged at the tyranny of the ruler who had driven the Huguenots into flight. On the other hand, Catholic countries also joined the coalition. Even the Pope favored the coalition headed by King William.

In western Europe fighting occurred along the Rhine and in the Low Countries, Italy, and Spain. War also raged on the mainland of North America, in the Caribbean, and in India. The American phase of the war was called King William's War. The French landed in Ireland and engaged the English fleet in the Channel and Irish Sea. With French aid James II of England tried to recover his power in Ireland but was defeated. In general, the coalition pressed back the French armies.

The Treaty of Ryswick. Although it looked black for France, by 1697 Louis XIV managed to divide his enemies. He then agreed to compromise terms in the Treaty of Ryswick, whereby he retained some territories taken in Germany but surrendered lands along the right bank of the Rhine. Louis, who had hitherto supported James II, now recognized William as King of England. Dutch troops won the right to garrison certain fortresses in the Spanish Netherlands in order to provide a "barrier" between France and Holland. The Treaty of Ryswick marked the emergence of Austria[1] and England as powers strong enough, when acting together, to stop France. With territories won from

---

[1] The Holy Roman Emperor was the hereditary ruler of Austria and was also King of Hungary and Bohemia. It was his hereditary possessions rather than the emperorship that made him strong. The word Austria, as used here, signifies the Hapsburg hereditary lands —Austria, Bohemia, Hungary.

Turkey, Austria was a great power on the middle Danube, within the basin formed by the Alps and the Bohemian and Carpathian mountains. The loss of French influence was reflected in the failure of Louis XIV to secure the Polish throne for his candidate after the death of King John Sobieski in 1696.

71. WAR OF THE SPANISH SUCCESSION AND GREAT NORTHERN WAR

France and the Spanish Empire. Louis was not crushed. His was a temporary setback. In a few years he made a new reach for power which was the cause for an even greater war, ending in French disaster. The Hapsburg King of Spain, Charles II, was dying and had no direct male heir. He willed his entire "estate" to a grandson of the French king and died in 1700.

The prospect of the dynastic union of France and Spain was terrifying to Europe. The rich Spanish territories in stronger hands would give their possessors staggering power. France could control the Spanish Netherlands, the port of Antwerp, and endanger Holland. The threat frightened England, whose policy it had been to prevent an aggressive power from dominating the coast of Europe opposite the British Isles, lest an invasion be launched from there. If a French king sat on the throne of Spain, Louis XIV would control southern Italy and the Mediterranean, monopolize the trade of the New World, and with a combined Franco-Spanish fleet sweep the English navy off the high seas and master European waters.

War breaks out. War was necessary to prevent such a consolidation of power. The Archduke Charles of Austria had a claim to the Spanish inheritance, and his father, the emperor Leopold, supported it. The War of the Spanish Succession (1702–1714) pitted the Grand Alliance (Austria, England,

The Battle of Blenheim in the War of the Spanish Succession, in which Eugene of Savoy and the Duke of Marlborough were victorious. (Hulton Picture Library)

most of the German states, the Netherlands, Sweden, and after 1703 Portugal and Savoy) against France, Spain, and several German princes. The allied generals, the Duke of Marlborough of England, and Prince Eugene of Savoy, who served the emperor, won striking victories in the Low Countries and Germany, but other allied generals failed in their invasions of Spain. Lack of unity among the allies brightened French prospects. France had difficulty supplying her armies, while England sustained her war effort and her allies with funds that Parliament supplied. The war developed two of England's most valuable assets, money and the navy. England used the royal navy to establish water communications between the British Isles and the continental allies and thus by-passed the French positions. More important, British statesmen learned the lesson that the island kingdom had to control the high seas in order to defeat a strong land power such as France. By the end of the war Britain had the largest fleet in the world. During the war England and Scotland were united (1707) and the King of England became officially the King of Great Britain. The two countries had had the same kings since James I succeeded Elizabeth in 1603.

Spanish Empire partitioned. By 1709 the French were in a state of exhaustion and seemed certain to lose the war, but the British were beginning to tire of the war too. In 1711 the Archduke Charles inherited the Hapsburg dominion in central Europe, and it became too much now for him to claim the Spanish inheritance. The resultant increase of the power of the Hapsburgs led to a virtual withdrawal from the war by Britain. This enabled the French to win a compromise peace, despite extremely heavy losses in both men and wealth.

The treaties of Utrecht and Rastadt, 1713 to 1714. The treaties of Utrecht and Rastadt brought the war to an end and marked a restoration of balanced power in Europe and the lowering of France from her previous dominant position. The vast territories of the former Spanish Hapsburgs were partitioned. A grandson of Louis XIV became King Philip V of Spain, with the provision that the crowns of France and Spain were never to be worn by the same ruler. The Austrian Hapsburgs received the Spanish dependencies in Europe: the kingdom of Naples, the Duchy of Milan, the kingdom of Sardinia, and Belgium (previously called the Spanish Netherlands, but afterward known as the Austrian Netherlands). The Duke of Savoy added Sicily to his European possessions. Later he exchanged Sicily for the island of Sardinia and became King of Sardinia. The Dutch Netherlands received a defensive position within the Austrian Netherlands as a barrier against future French invasion and a monopoly of trade along the Scheldt River—thus ending the possible threat of the port of Antwerp to Dutch commerce—and certain commercial concessions.

Great Britain gains. By the treaties Britain acquired Gibraltar and the Balearic island of Minorca, thus bringing the British permanently into the Mediterranean region. One English company was given the right to

Articles of Union being presented to Queen Anne, 1707, uniting England and Scotland and adopting the Union Jack as the national flag of Great Britain. (Hulton Picture Library)

trade in Spanish America, and another was granted the privilege of supplying Spanish America with Negro slaves. This privilege was known as the *asiento,* and by it British influence was to be strongly asserted in the Caribbean region and along the Gulf coast of North America, which then was in Spanish hands. In North America, where the conflict was called Queen Anne's War, there had been raids of English and French colonists against each other's settlements. By the peace Britain gained French Acadia (which was renamed Nova Scotia), as well as Newfoundland, the Hudson Bay region, and additional territory in the West Indies. France also renounced support of the fallen house of Stuart in England.

In 1714, Queen Anne, who had succeeded William twelve years earlier, died and the succession to the British throne passed to the nearest Protestant heir, George, Elector of Hanover. He was recognized by Louis

XIV. James II had died in 1701, but his son, who called himself James III, still aspired to return to England as king. In 1715 Louis XIV died.

The Great Northern War. Toward the end of the seventeenth century Sweden's enemies (Denmark, Russia, and Poland) had been waiting for an opportunity to challenge her supremacy in the Baltic. In 1696, when a fifteen-year-old boy became King Charles XII, his enemies judged that their moment was at hand. Poland wanted Livonia, Denmark sought Holstein and the mouths of the Elbe and Weser rivers, while Russia looked for a Baltic "window." But their hopes faded when Charles XII proved to be a brilliant general.

The battle of Poltava. In 1700, Charles XII swept down on Denmark and began the Great Northern War (1700–1721). Peter the Great was alarmed by the success of the Swedes because it spelled the end of his Baltic ambitions. Charles XII next moved against the Czar and inflicted a terrible defeat on the Russians at the battle of Narva (1700). But instead of marching on to Moscow and following up his victory, Charles turned to Poland. After he had defeated Poland he turned south in order to link up the Swedish army with the Cossacks who resisted the Czar's rule. This delay enabled Peter to tap his superior resources and manpower and thus prepare for battle. In 1709 at Poltava, Peter fell upon the weakened Swedish armies and destroyed in one blow Charles's Baltic empire.

Russian power waxes. The battle of Poltava was the first Russian victory over an important European power and marked the replacement of Sweden by Russia as the dominant power in northern Europe. Sweden surrendered to Russia Esthonia, Livonia, and other lands. Peter now had his "window." He had already begun to build a new city, St. Petersburg (now Leningrad) close to the Baltic. This became his capital.

The Russian victory hurt the peoples who lived between Germany and Russia. The Ukrainians were now at the mercy of the Russian Empire. Russia began to interfere in Polish affairs on the grounds of protecting Orthodox Christians. Peter the Great was also interested in Asiatic expansion. Russian settlement in Siberia reached the Pacific. Peter dispatched Captain Vitus Bering on an expedition (1724–1730) that resulted in Russian claims to the sea between Siberia and Alaska that bears his name. After the death of Peter the Great in 1725, Russia continued to press against the borders of Poland, Sweden, and Turkey.

The kingdom of Prussia. The period of the War of the Spanish Succession and the Great Northern War witnessed the appearance of a new kingdom that was destined to play an important part in world history. The name Prussia applied originally to the small country along the eastern Baltic that had been conquered by German crusaders, the Teutonic Knights, in the later Middle Ages. During the Protestant Revolt the Grand Master of the Knights, Albert of Hohenzollern, transformed himself into the Grand Duke of Prussia. He was a member of the family whose head was the Margrave of Brandenburg, a prince of the Holy Roman Empire. Early in the seventeenth century the Brandenburg Hohenzollerns had acquired several

Bringing Home the Dead King Charles XII of Sweden from His Last Battle in Norway, 1718, *painting by Gustae Cederström. (National Museum of Stockholm)*

additional principalities in western Germany, and in 1618 the Grand Duchy of Prussia fell to the Margrave of Brandenburg. Thus a loose, disconnected system of states was formed under one prince, who was known as the Elector of Brandenburg because he was one of the princes who elected the Holy Roman Emperor. Naturally the Elector of Brandenburg, who was also the Grand Duke of Prussia, desired to unite all his lands and thus augment his power.

The Great Elector. The person who led Brandenburg-Prussia to strength was the Great Elector, Frederick William (1640–1688). The devastation of Brandenburg during the Thirty Years' War taught him the necessity of having a strong army to defend a country without natural frontiers. The Great Elector's successor, William, managed to advance to the rank of royalty. In 1701 he struck a bargain with the Holy Roman Emperor whereby he received the title of king (in Prussia but not in Brandenburg) in return for giving aid to the emperor during the War of the Spanish Succession. Thereafter Brandenburg-Prussia was known as the kingdom of Prussia. Its capital was at Berlin.

Prussia grew strong during the reign of King Frederick William I (1713–1740), who set the military tone of Prussian life in the future by magnifying the importance of the army. He created the Potsdam Guard made up of soldiers between six and seven feet tall and increased the size of the army to eighty-three thousand. To supply his army and collect a war chest, Frederick William I ordered pinch-penny methods in government and social life. He taught civil servants and subjects not to waste money or resources that could be used for war. Later generations remembered that "Prussia had starved herself to greatness." The king strictly controlled economic life in the interests of the state. And to get obedience and co-operation of the nobles as officers in the army, he permitted them to regulate the lives of peasants on their estates. Every phase of Prussian life was under the royal thumb. As the king said, "Salvation belongs to the Lord, everything else is my affair." He insisted on iron discipline ("Prussian discipline") in his army, so that a soldier who disobeyed a corporal or sergeant had to run the gauntlet. It was said of Prussian soldiers that they feared the enemy less than they feared their officers.

Possessions of the PRUSSIAN HOHENZOLLERNS

REVIEW

STUDY SECTIONS IN REVIEW

66. Political Disunion of Europe and the Increased Power of Kings

A. How did the Protestant Revolt affect "Christian unity" in both a religious and governmental sense?

B. Why is the seventeenth century called an "age of monarchical absolutism"?

c. Explain the meaning of the theory of the divine right of kings.

D. Cite an example of a religious minority that disrupted the political unity of a country.

E. Indicate the significance of the Edict of Nantes (1598) and Cardinal Richelieu in French history.

67. Thirty Years' War and the Puritan Revolution

A. What were the three main causes of the Thirty Years' War (1618–1648)?

B. Mention four major results of the Peace of Westphalia (1648).

c. What were the major disputes between the Stuart kings and the English Parliament?

D. Identify: Charles I, Cromwell, Milton, the Restoration.

68. France under Louis XIV

A. Indicate at least four policies of Louis XIV that were aimed at improving the economic position of France.

B. Identify: Versailles, Corneille, Molière.

c. How did Louis attempt to gain "natural frontiers" for France?

D. What was the cause of the dispute between Louis XIV and Pope Innocent XI?

E. How did the revoking of the Edict of Nantes ultimately weaken France?

69. Repulse of the Turks and Rise of Russia

A. Identify: Kara Mustafa, King Leopold, Sobieski, Treaty of Karlowitz.

B. Why did the French hope for a Turkish victory over Austria and her allies?

c. Mention the principal achievement of each of the following: Ivan III (the Great), Ivan IV (the Terrible), Peter the Great.

70. "Glorious Revolution" in England and War of the League of Augsburg

A. Identify the following: Tories, Whigs, Habeas Corpus Bill, James II.

B. What was the "Glorious Revolution"?

c. Who were the members and what was the purpose of the League of Augsburg?

D. What were the results of the Treaty of Ryswick?

71. War of the Spanish Succession and Great Northern War

A. What were the causes of the War of the Spanish Succession?

B. Mention four major results of the· treaties of Utrecht and Rastadt.

c. What was the significance of the Battle of Poltava (1709)?

D. Identify the following: Frederick William (the Great Elector), Berlin, King Frederick William I.

THE CHAPTER IN REVIEW

A. Briefly describe the goals of Prussia and the resulting way of life of the people of the kingdom. Can you find similarities with states in much earlier history? Explain.

B. Discuss the major developments that resulted in the rise of the modern state. How did power within the state become "centralized"?

c. What effects did the Thirty Years' War have on Germany?

D. Describe the character of Louis XIV of France. What goals did he set for France during his reign? In general, did he attain these objectives?

E. Mention the major causes of the difficulties between the Stuart kings and Parliament. How did the concept of a "constitutional monarchy" enter into the ultimate solution of the disputes?

FOR YOUR NOTEBOOK

One of the most important developments in world history is the emergence of the national dynastic state. The first entry in your notebook for this chapter should be a list of factors that caused the modern state to emerge. Then list chronologically the steps involved in the emergence of a strong Spain, France, and England.

The Thirty Years' War is sometimes called "the last of the religious wars" and the first "international war." Make a summary of the results of the war with this statement in mind.

In parallel columns show the domestic

developments in England and in France through the seventeenth century.

Outline the steps involved in the emergence of Russia as a European power.

Summarize the constitutional accomplishments of the "Glorious Revolution."

In your notebook draw a political map of Europe before the Great Northern War and the War of the Spanish Succession. Then draw another political map of Europe after the Peace of Utrecht and the Peace of Nystadt.

SELECTED READINGS

Highly recommended for background reading of Europe between 1500 and 1830 is Carlton Hayes, *Political and Cultural History of Modern Europe,* Vol. I, (New York: The Macmillan Co., 1952).

Four interesting biographies will help round out your knowledge of statecraft in this period. C. V. Wedgwood's *Richelieu* *and the French Monarchy* (New York: The Macmillan Co., 1950) is an excellent short study by a scholar on seventeenth-century affairs. Robert Ergang, *The Potsdam Führer, Frederick William I* (New York: Columbia University Press, 1941), is both scholarly and absorbingly interesting. Nina Baker's *Peter the Great* (New York: The Vanguard Press, 1943) is easy to read; and John B. Morton, *Sobieski, King of Poland* (London: Eyre & Spottiswoode, 1932), deals with one of the most romantic and interesting figures in modern history.

Two complementary works will give you a good picture of western Europe in this period. The first is the Berkshire Series study by Laurence B. Packard, *The Age of Louis XIV* (New York: Henry Holt & Co., 1950); like all the books in this series, it is by a recognized scholar who does a simple 100-page condensation of the period. The second is Dorothy Hartley and M. M. Elliott, *Life and Work of the People of England* (New York: G. P. Putnam's Sons, 1929).

CHRONOLOGICAL REVIEW

1460 *Death of Prince Henry the Navigator*
1462 *Ivan the Great of Russia (to 1505)*
1486 *Diaz discovers Cape of Good Hope*
1492 *Columbus discovers America*
1519 Charles V, Holy Roman Emperor; Cortez begins conquest of Mexico (to 1521)
1521 Magellan reaches Philippines
1526 Babar founds Mogul Empire in India
1534 Henry VIII breaks with Rome
1543 *Death of Copernicus; Vesalius' book on anatomy*
1552 *Death of St. Francis Xavier*
1556 Abkar the Great in India (to 1605)
1558 Elizabeth I of England (to 1603)
1580 Union of Spain and Portugal
1598 *Edict of Nantes*
1602 Dutch East India Company founded
1607 Jamestown, Va., settled
1616 *Death of Shakespeare and Cervantes*
1618 Thirty Years' War begins (to 1648)
1620 *Bacon's* NOVUM ORGANUM

1628 *Petition of Right in England; Harvey's discoveries of blood circulation*
1642 Puritan Revolution in England; death of Richelieu
Death of Galileo
1643 Reign of Louis XIV (to 1715)
1649 Charles I of England beheaded
1660 Restoration in England
1662 *Royal Society founded in England*
1666 *Great Fire of London and Plague*
1679 *Habeas Corpus Act*
1682 *Turkish-Austrian War begins*
1683 Turks repulsed at Vienna
1687 *Newton publishes* PRINCIPIA
1688 Glorious Revolution
1689 War of League of Augsburg (to 1697); Peter the Great rules Russia (to 1725)
Locke publishes ON CIVIL GOVERNMENT
1694 *Bank of England founded*
1700 Great Northern War (to 1721)
1701 War of Spanish Succession (to 1714); Frederick I, King of Prussia

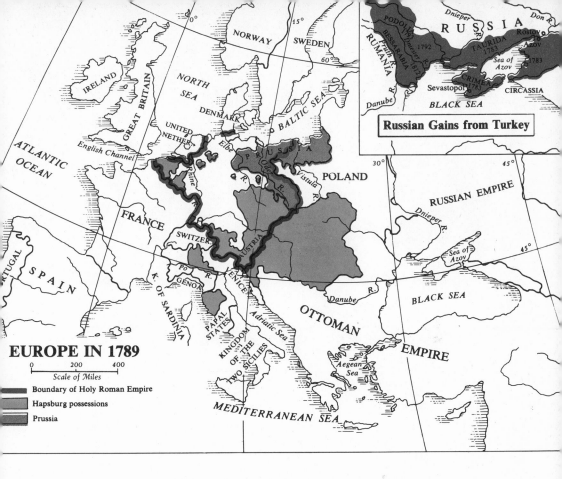

EUROPE IN 1789

| 0 | 200 | 400 |

Scale of Miles

Boundary of Holy Roman Empire

Hapsburg possessions

Prussia

UNIT EIGHT
Reason, Reform, and Revolution

The Age of Reason · The Reform Writers of the Age of Reason · Influence of the Enlightenment on Religion and Government · The Polish and Austrian Succession Wars · The Seven Years' War, 1756 to 1763 · Crown, Parliament, and the American Colonies · World War and American Independence · World Results of the American Revolution · The Old Regime and the French Monarchy · Outbreak of the Revolution · Europe vs. the French Revolution · The Directory and the Rise of Napoleon · The Empire at Its Zenith · The Downfall of Napoleon

Locke

Voltaire

Rosse...

Chapter 24. The European Enlightenment

72. THE AGE OF REASON

Introduction & Characteristics

p. 372

The progress in science, the increase in travel, and knowledge of other lands and peoples helped produce the "Age of Reason," or the "Enlightenment," in the eighteenth century. Newton's influence dominated the age. Just as he demonstrated that the universe was a vast machine subject to physical laws, other thinkers concluded that social and political life was similarly governed by "laws." The key that would unlock the secrets of these laws was "reason," a term that took on a meaning different from any in the past. "Reason" implied a doubting frame of mind and subjecting all ideas, beliefs, and institutions to test by natural human reason. Men of the Enlightenment had high confidence in the ability of "reason" to explain the principles that governed man, nature, and society.

Impressed by the achievements of explorers, artists, merchants, and kings, "enlightened" men praised man more than God. Many rejected the doctrine of original sin and were sure that human beings were naturally good. They were sure, too, that men and women would get progressively better and achieve undreamed-of progress. Many agreed with John Locke (1632–1704), who taught that man's mind at birth is like a sheet of blank paper whereon he may write anything. In effect, Locke meant that what man knows and does depends upon his experiences, from environment and reason. Therefore, according to this view, it would be possible to change the whole face of society in a single generation by shaping the minds of youth.

Faith in the future. The men of the Enlightenment believed that the future would necessarily be better than the past. Some persons went farther. Scrap the past, they recommended, and burn its records. Their trust was in the future and was based on the faith that knowledge brought wisdom and science led to happiness. They concluded that with the aid of knowledge and science —and with no reliance on Divine Providence—men could improve their lot on earth. Indeed, why wait for happiness in heaven, they exclaimed, if people can have it here?

Although the Enlightenment lauded the human personality, the rights of man, human freedom and equality, and the dignity of the person, all of which are honored by Christian democracy today, it exaggerated the natural virtues of man and undermined the religious foundations of Catholic Europe.

"Enlightened" persons accepted the Christian doctrine of the unity of the human race. Aristocrats, churchmen, merchants, scholars, scientists, and writers did not consider themselves as narrowly French, or English, or German, but as "citizens of the world." Their devotion was to European culture and civilization or what they called "the republic of letters." A man did not consider himself cultured unless he was familiar with the great books of the past and with learned men of his own day throughout the world. Young aristocrats and wealthier members of the middle classes took the "Grand Tour," visiting foreign capitals and cultural centers. Freedom of travel permitted a free exchange of persons and ideas. Those who had not the means to travel abroad read avidly the growing number of travel books, and became fascinated by accounts of lands

"Gulliver and the Brobdingnag Farmer," an illustration from Swift's Gulliver's Travels, *a political and social satire describing the hero's voyages to imaginary lands and peoples, published in 1726. (Hulton Picture Library)*

and peoples, such as the Chinese, Persians, and American Indians.

People swelled with pride over the excellence of their artists, scientists, and writers. When defenders of the past challenged the claim, a wordy "Battle of the Ancients and Moderns" followed. Yet the veneration of the art and literature of Greece and Rome continued. It seems at first sight inconsistent that an age that turned its back on the past nevertheless admired the ancient world. The men of the Enlightenment reasoned that the Greeks and Romans were free of "Christian superstition" and that they mastered the "natural laws." In the eighteenth cen-

St. Paul's Cathedral, London, whose unusual dome is made of wood and lead, was erected at the beginning of the eighteenth century. (British Information Services)

tury, the classical style dominated art and literature. Architects in Europe copied classical styles, while poems and plays observed classical balance, order, clarity, precision, and the "unities of time, place, and action."

Science. The Age of Reason showed great enthusiasm for science. For many, science was an interesting hobby, and for others a source of amusement. The public flocked to watch "scientific" demonstrations, for example, of brandy being ignited by a spark shooting from a man's finger. Pierre Simon de Laplace (1749–1827) proposed the "nebular hypothesis" to explain the origin of the universe; that is, that the

sun, moon, stars, and planets sprang from a fiery cloud. Although scientific progress was not as striking in the eighteenth as in the previous century, notable advances occurred. The outlines of the separate sciences became more distinct. This specialization rendered it more difficult for one person to master all the sciences.

Astronomy and physics progressed. William Herschel (1738–1822) improved telescopes and estimated the number of stars. In physics, Luigi Galvani (1737–1798) and Alessandro Volta (1745–1827) prepared an electric battery. Popular imagination, however, was caught by the famous kite experiment of Benjamin Franklin (1706–1790), undertaken to prove that lightning and electricity are the same. In 1752, Franklin flew a silk kite into a thunder cloud, where lightning struck it and raced down the wet string until deflected by a key in a Leyden-jar battery, charging the battery with electricity. The practical outcome of this demonstration was the invention of lightning rods to protect church steeples and tall buildings against lightning during electrical storms.

Chemistry. In chemistry, a knowledge of gases resulted from the experiments of an English clergyman, Stephen Hales (1677–1761), and a Scottish professor, Joseph Black (1728–1799). An eccentric genius, Henry Cavendish (1731–1810), broke down water into its components, oxygen and hydrogen. His discoveries in electricity were similarly remarkable, but Cavendish kept them to himself, with the result that a century later Michael Faraday (1791–1867) had to rediscover them. A major obstacle to chemical research in flame

Alessandro Volta, Italian physicist, became famous for his work in electricity. The volt, a unit of electrical measurement, is named for him. (Science Service)

Joseph Priestley, English theologian and scientist, produced "dephlogisticated" air, which Lavoisier named oxygen. (National Portrait Gallery)

and combustion was presented by the "phlogiston theory." Some investigators mistakenly pointed to a mysterious substance, called phlogiston, that caused a flame to burn and consume fuel. But they were challenged by two famous chemists, Joseph Priestley (1733–1804) and Antoine Lavoisier (1743–1794). Priestley isolated oxygen and undermined the phlogiston theory. He discovered the law of inverse squares (the attraction or repulsion between two electrical charges is inversely proportional to the squares of the distances between them). Lavoisier finally destroyed the phlogiston theory and made other advances that earned for him the distinction of being the "father of modern chemistry."

Biology and medicine. Biology and medicine progressed rapidly. Linnaeus (1707–1778) and Buffon (1707–1788) classified plants and animals by species and genus. A start was made in the control of disease. When a Boston preacher, Cotton Mather, read an account in the magazine of the Royal Society of London about a method of inoculating people with smallpox as a means of reducing the ravages of the disease, he decided to experiment in 1721. But it was not until the end of the century that an English doctor, Edward Jenner (1749–1823), invented a less dangerous method of vaccination. Observing that victims of cowpox, a less serious disease, were immune to smallpox, Dr. Jenner introduced the germs of the cowpox into the human body so that an immunity to smallpox could develop.

The Enlightenment was also characterized by a determination of authors to diffuse "useful knowledge"; that is, knowledge about farming, trade, history, and morality. Improvements in agriculture and manufacturing produced the agricultural and industrial revolutions that are discussed in a later unit. History was a "useful" study because it presented "horrible examples" of despotism and intolerance. Lord Bolingbroke (1678–1751), an "enlightened" Englishman, called history "philosophy teaching by example."

The press, the clubs, the salons. Books, popular newspapers and magazines, pamphlets, tours of authors and other influential persons, circulating libraries, and the meetings of salons, Masonic lodges, and other clubs all publicized "enlightened" ideas. Of course books were the principal channels of the new thought. The general abolition or relaxation of censorship led to a wider distribution of books to the reading public, which was, however, only a small but influential segment of the population.

The salons of Paris were another important means of spreading ideas. Authors, artists, noblemen, the rich, and foreign dignitaries met in the houses of leading hostesses for an afternoon or evening of conversation about fine arts, literature, philosophy, politics, or reforms. So important were the salons that foreigners visiting Paris vied with each other for invitations. To some degree, in England and Europe outside France, the place of the salon was taken by the coffeehouses, where men gathered not only to sip coffee but to exchange ideas and discuss the latest newspapers and pamphlets.

73. THE REFORM WRITERS OF THE AGE OF REASON

Philosophes. Reform writers were called *philosophes,* which is the French word for "philosophers." They were not philosophers in the true meaning of that word, but authors who used literature as reform propaganda. Their pens exposed the faults of political, social, and religious institutions and customs with a view to correcting them and thus improving mankind. Their study of certain unjust and absurd privileges of some classes led them to hold the past responsible for these inequalities. Hence the *philosophes* wanted to escape the past and mold society on entirely new lines. They took their cue from scientists. Had not scientists tested the ideas of Galen and other ancients and proved them to be

Lloyd's Coffee House in England. The coffeehouses were known as centers for literary and political discussion, often provoking government restrictions in the belief that they were meeting places of political rebels. The coffeehouses influenced the development of literature and were the forerunners of the modern clubs. (Hulton Picture Library)

wrong? In a similar way, they reasoned, the notions of the past on how to direct government, business, school, and church should be re-examined. If older ideas did not pass the test of "reasonableness," they were to be scrapped and replaced by "enlightened" institutions.

The vast majority of these reform writers were out of touch with practical politics, and they rarely saw the obstacles in the path of reforms. They failed to see that benevolent intentions and plans are not the only requirements. In some respects, they were naïve, believing that simple solutions could be found for all the problems of the world. Yet their influence was enormous.

John Locke. The reform of politics was a principal concern of such writers who had been influenced by John Locke (1632–1704). Locke had written that men, before the formation of civil society, lived in a state of nature and were reasonable and well disposed. Men agreed to establish society and government in order to protect their rights to life, liberty, and property. In other words, they had entered this "social contract" to safeguard their liberties. The king could not violate the liberties of the people without breaking the original contract between himself and his people. If he broke the contract, the people could overthrow him and resume their original rights. In short, the people make the state and remain the source of authority. Locke used these ideas to justify the Glorious Revolution in England which overthrew King James II. His views were influential not only in Britain and in the American colonies,

John Locke set down in his political theory the idea that revolution in some cases was not only a right but an obligation. The theorists of the American Revolution drew heavily upon Locke's philosophies. (Library of Congress)

where they were to be used against George III and the mother country, but also on the continent of Europe. Eager reformers read Locke to find the way of ousting tyrants.

Montesquieu. The Baron de Montesquieu (1689–1755), a French nobleman, was the eighteenth century's ablest and most influential political writer. His studies proved to him that no single type of government suited all countries at all times. But he pointed with pride to the English government because it had a limited monarch and permitted representation of the people in Parliament. He admired what he thought was the separation of powers among the legislative (Parliament), judicial (the courts), and the executive (the crown) branches which checked and balanced each other. Montesquieu had not really observed accurately. Yet his book, *Spirit of the Laws,* was devoured. American colonists would incorporate his suggestions about separation of powers and checks and balances in the United States Constitution.

Voltaire. The man who best typified the "enlightened" thinker was Voltaire (1694–1778). The son of a notary, Voltaire was educated by the Jesuits, who taught him to argue well. He turned to literature as a career, noting that "books rule the world" and that the pen is often mightier than the sword. Despite such faults as dishonesty and vanity, Voltaire was a hard worker who wrote witty novelettes, plays, histories, and poems. His works fill ninety-nine volumes. In these works he attacked the Christian religion, the Catholic Church, and the Jesuits. He poked fun at the Bible, monks, and St. Joan of Arc.

Rousseau. Born in Geneva, Switzerland, Jean Jacques Rousseau (1712–1778) went to France and there became a famous writer. He rebelled against all control and led an erratic life. His books are a mixture of silliness and wisdom. His book on the training of a boy, *Emile,* insists that children be educated according to nature and not by repression and custom. In his opinion, "everything is good as it comes from the hands of the Author of Nature: but everything degenerates in the hands of man." Therefore, he urged that the unspoiled nature of the child be given free play to develop. The child's own natural curiosity and interest, not the teacher's insistence, ought to determine what he should study. Rousseau opposed scolding, whipping, or punishing a child.

The writings of Jean Jacques Rousseau in the fields of politics and literature have had a profound influence on modern socialist thought. (Library of Congress)

Instead, he recommended, let the child suffer the "natural" results of his mistakes. Rousseau's *Emile* influenced educators. A Swiss educator, Johann Pestalozzi (1746–1827), adopted Rousseau's ideas in classroom practice.

Rousseau's political views have had as great influence as *Emile.* His book, the *Social Contract,* opened with the observation that "men are born free but are everywhere in chains." For him, man was the great victim and society was the villain. Through the centuries governments perpetuated and protected inequality and special privilege instead of recognizing the natural equality of all. John Locke was Rousseau's mentor in the doctrine that society is a contract. Unlike other *philosophes,* he had little faith in reason, which he accused of corrupting and perverting man. His faith was in the heart and in feeling, which he said led to virtue. Revolution did not frighten

Rousseau because the feeling of brotherhood that is part of human nature, he argued, was strong enough to keep society together even in perilous times.

Some observers today consider Rousseau a prophet of democracy because he raised the masses to social and political dignity and activity. They point to his beliefs that government is only an agency to carry out the supreme will of the people and that in the ideal state the people are bound in brotherhood by rights and duties for the achievement of the common good because it reflects the "general will." However, many other thinkers today conclude that Rousseau actually paved the way for dictatorship by seeing no limit on the power of government to give force to "the general will." In reality, the general will does not exist.

Prison reform. Enlightened writers sought to ease human suffering. They denounced the courts of law for relying on torture to get evidence. Terrible tortures—unparalleled until modern dictatorships exceeded any brutality known in the past—were employed by jailers to extract confessions from prisoners. Another sore spot in the judicial system was extremely severe punishment meted out to the guilty. Capital punishment for a variety of crimes took the form of hanging, mutilation, or being torn apart by teams of horses. After studying the problem of crimes and punishments, an Italian nobleman, Beccaria (1735–1794), opposed capital punishment and advocated more humane treatment of criminals.

Economic writers. During the Age of Reason, writers explored the relation-

Treadmill recommended by the Committee of the Society for the Improvement of Prison Discipline in England in 1817. Most treadmills served no useful purpose but were merely punitive in nature. (Hulton Picture Library)

ships between politics and economics. A group of French economists called Physiocrats rejected mercantilism because it paid too much attention to trade and money and because it slighted agriculture. They asserted that wealth was not a hoard of gold and silver but the surplus of farm, mineral, and other resources. In their view, a man's labor was his most sacred possession, more valuable than and prior to property, and hence a man ought to be free to use it as he wished. The Physiocrats attacked laws that tried to promote trade at the expense of farmers, and recommended that government keep hands off business.

A Scottish writer, Adam Smith (1723–1790), turned his attention to the relation of government and business in an important book, the *Wealth of Nations* (1776). Smith rejected the mercantilist argument that colonies were a source of wealth for the mother country by showing that colonies cost more than they were worth economically. He recommended that government cast aside unnatural controls of industry, especially the granting of monopolies to favorites of king or Parliament, which had the effect of artificially regulating supply and demand. Smith advocated economic freedom for moral as well as economic reasons.

The Enlightenment in America. The Enlightenment affected the New World. Benjamin Franklin and Thomas Jefferson moved in "enlightened" circles while in Europe and read widely in the books of the *philosophes*. Latin America also received the new ideas by means of books smuggled past colonial authorities, by personal contacts of Spanish and Portuguese Americans with the books of the *philosophes* during their schooling at Spanish and French universities, and by associations with foreign merchants and travelers. Spanish Americans were particularly impressed by the career of Benjamin Franklin, whom they regarded as a symbol of science and political liberty. The Enlightenment thus left its mark on thought and action in Latin America.

74. INFLUENCE OF THE ENLIGHTENMENT ON RELIGION AND GOVERNMENT

Protestantism had shattered Christendom into numerous sects and thus led some persons to conclude that truth in religion could not be attained and therefore one belief was as good as its rival. If no church had a monopoly of truth, they argued, then all

sects and religions ought to be tolerated. Many began to think that, since all forms of Christianity could not be true, perhaps they were all false. Besides, a serious threat was posed by the rise of science, which produced a climate of opinion that was hostile to the supernatural or mysterious. The explosion of many myths and superstitions, such as the fantasy that comets foretold plague or other public disaster, weakened religious belief—though most scientists believed in God, and many were devout Catholics.

Bayle. The tendency to doubt revealed religion was deepened by Pierre Bayle (1647–1706), the author of a biographical and philosophical dictionary, who has been called the "father of the eighteenth century." His book was an arsenal of arguments against the Bible, dogma, tradition, and in support of the opinion that society could exist without religion.

Pierre Bayle, French rationalistic philosopher. Bayle's radical opinions in his writings influenced the writers of the French and German Enlightenment and the English deists. (Giraudon)

Diderot and Gibbon. The sharpest attacks on religion and the Catholic Church came from Denis Diderot (1713–1784). Articles in his *Encyclopedia* attacked the Church and other old institutions for intolerance and superstition and advocated "enlightened" reform. Diderot was convinced that the earth would come into its own only when the notion of heaven was destroyed. Edward Gibbon (1737–1794), first a Protestant, then a Catholic, and finally a non-believer, wrote a monumental *Decline and Fall of the Roman Empire,* in which he attacked Christianity. His book, he said, described the triumph of barbarism and religion.

Suppression of the Jesuits. The attack on the Catholic Church not only took the form of ridicule of Catholic practice and beliefs but assaults on the Pope and the religious orders. One of the chief campaigns was waged against the Jesuits, who were influential not only in Europe but in countless foreign mission outposts. The Society of Jesus was suppressed in Portugal, then in France, Spain, Naples, and Parma. Under pressure of Catholic princes, Pope Clement XIV suppressed the Jesuits in 1773 for the sake of peace in the Church.

The attack on religion came also from within. The dissension among the French Catholics had repercussions elsewhere, because France set the tone for the rest of Europe. The quarrel over the Gallican Liberties and Jansenism divided France. Although they were rejected, they left a legacy of hatred, especially against the Pope and the Jesuits. The Pope's position was attacked in Germany by a German bishop who called himself

St. Paul of the Cross founded the Passionist Fathers in Italy in 1727.

Febronius and maintained that the Papacy was subject to the Church and not infallible. Febronius urged Catholic princes to resist him and advised bishops to request rulers to protect them against the authority of the Pontiff.

While the Church suffered in Europe, significant gains were won in the mission field. Among the saints, the period numbers St. Margaret Alacoque, St. Paul of the Cross (the founder of the Passionist Fathers), and St. Alphonsus Liguori (the champion against the Jansenist heresy and a famous theologian).

Deism. During the Enlightenment a new religion, deism, emerged. Some persons—who rejected Christianity because they could not accept divine revelation and because Christians fought among themselves concerning what God revealed—wished to devise a religion that all men of good will and intelligence could accept. Their suggestion was a "natural religion," worshiping God as a master engineer and scientist Who created the universe and let it run according to certain physical laws. The deist's God did not intervene in human affairs (thus denying Providence) and did not perform miracles, because miracles suspend natural laws. In an answer to the question: What must a person do to be saved? deists answered, "Follow reason—the God within you—and your nature will tell you what you must do to be saved."

Deists, however, could not agree among themselves as to what was "reasonable" and "natural" in religion! Some men went farther and threw aside all belief in God and became atheists. But they were a small minority, considered dangerous to society. Although many writers and social and political leaders were lukewarm in their attachment to Christianity and attended religious services only for the sake of appearances, they realized that Christianity was a beneficial force that kept society together and taught people to obey the law and respect their neighbor.

The Enlightened Despots. Benevolent or Enlightened Despots appeared as champions of the Age of Reason. The kings and princes were called benevolent because they desired the welfare of their people, and called despots because they brooked no opposition to their determination to enforce their will throughout the whole country and govern without any limitations to their power. They minimized the divine-right character of their thrones and emphasized instead the "reasonableness" and usefulness of their rule.

Mixed motives led them to request advice of the *philosophes* and to carry out some of their suggestions. Some rulers genuinely wished to ease human suffering; others took pride in associating with men of wit and talent, and still others saw in "enlightened" reforms the means of increasing their own authority and the economic prosperity of their country.

The Benevolent Despots tolerated minority religions, curbed the power of the Catholic Church, reformed the courts, abolished torture, encouraged schools and the arts and sciences, and restricted old privileges of towns, nobles, and clergy. But they did not permit popular participation in government. Indeed, the despots removed safeguards to local liberty and reduced things to a dead level of uniformity in their effort to increase royal authority throughout the land.

Catharine the Great of Russia. The careers of four Enlightened Despots

Catharine the Great of Russia, in reorganizing the local governments, relied heavily on the writings of political theorists such as Montesquieu. (Alinari)

are particularly interesting: Czarina Catharine the Great of Russia, Charles III of Spain, King Frederick the Great of Prussia, and Emperor Joseph II of Austria. Catharine (1762–1796) prided herself on corresponding with some of the celebrated writers of the world. She invited Diderot to be a guest at her court at St. Petersburg and requested advice from him and other Encyclopedists on how to govern her empire. When she convoked a commission to codify laws, the *philosophes* applauded her. But little came of her effort. Reform was welcome only as long as it did not reduce the Czarina's power. The reorganization of local government effected by Catharine actually strengthened her grip on the country and prevented rebellion.

Charles III of Spain. In Spain, Charles III (1759–1788) encouraged scientific studies, permitted the publication of the books of the *philosophes* and the establishment of clubs to discuss enlightened ideas.

Frederick the Great of Prussia. In an effort to compensate people for the sufferings caused by his wars, Frederick (1740–1786) built homes and lightened the financial burden of the peasants.

Joseph II of Austria. Joseph II of Austria (1765–1790) was in many ways the model of Enlightened Despots. The eldest son of Maria Theresa, Joseph was elected Holy Roman Emperor and co-regent with his mother in the hereditary Hapsburg lands at the death of his father in 1765. He determined to govern according to the new ideas. Unlike his mother, who was a devout Catholic, Joseph was anti-clerical. He suppressed certain monasteries and convents, especially

Joseph II of Austria attempted to create a powerful Austria by controlling the Church. (Austrian Information Service)

those of the contemplative orders, placed the wealth of the Catholic Church in a general fund, reorganized parishes on the basis of one parish for each seven hundred persons, and even regulated the number of altar candles to be used during Mass! The efforts of Pope Pius VI to have him retract these orders failed. Joseph's Church policy was imitated in Spain, Sardinia, Naples, and Venice. The emperor was energetic. He tolerated Protestants and Jews, freed the serfs on the grounds that serfdom was contrary to the dignity and liberty of man, declared the equality of all subjects before the law, and established a legal code in accordance with the suggestions of Beccaria. But he overreached himself. The effort to enforce uniformity in the complex Hapsburg system ignored local customs and feeling and hence met resistance, especially in Belgium and Hungary. Although he sighed at the end of his life that his reforms were in vain, Joseph had left his mark.

REVIEW

FOR YOUR NOTEBOOK

STUDY SECTIONS IN REVIEW

72. The Age of Reason

A. What was the eighteenth-century meaning of the term "reason"?

B. Why did the Age of Enlightenment turn to the classical Greek and Roman ages for its inspiration?

c. Mention the contributions to science of Laplace, Priestley, Lavoisier, and Jenner.

73. The Reform Writers of the Age of Reason

A. What were the objectives of the *philosophes?*

B. Cite the principal political contributions of John Locke and the Baron de Montesquieu.

c. How did Rousseau differ from other *philosophes* on the role of "reason"?

D. What were the views of the Physiocrats and Adam Smith in regard to governmental regulation of business?

74. Influence of the Enlightenment on Religion and Government

A. How did "enlightened" authors regard organized religion?

B. In what ways did Diderot and Gibbon attack religion?

c. What were the principles of deism?

D. What was meant by the term "benevolent" or "enlightened despot"?

THE CHAPTER IN REVIEW

A. The eighteenth century is called the Age of Enlightenment. Why did man feel that he was "enlightened" in this period?

B. How was the French author Voltaire typical of the "enlightened" authors of the eighteenth century?

c. Discuss the reasons for the rejection of revealed religion during the Age of Enlightenment. Why, having rejected Christianity, did "enlightened" men turn to deism?

D. Discuss the social contract theories of John Locke? What theory of governmental authority that you have previously studied was Locke trying to overthrow with his social contract philosophy?

Look up the following in your reference sources in the library and enter into your notebook a summary of each man's contribution to European intellectual history:

Locke	Beccaria
Bayle	Voltaire
Montesquieu	Adam Smith
Diderot	Rousseau

List four well-chosen adjectives to describe the general characteristics of the Age of Reason. Under each adjective write a paragraph to justify your choice.

Sum up the advances made in natural sciences during the period of the Enlightenment.

Summarize the reforms of the Benevolent Despots under the headings of (1) political, (2) social, (3) economic, (4) cultural. Use two specific examples to back each of your general entries.

SELECTED READINGS

The best general coverage of this chapter's material is given in the Berkshire Series book by Geoffrey Bruun, *The Enlightened Despots* (New York: Henry Holt & Co., 1929). Saul K. Padover has done two very readable biographies of rulers in this period: *The Revolutionary Emperor, Joseph the Second* (New York: R. O. Ballon, 1934), which describes a radical reforming emperor; and *The Life and Death of Louis XIV* (New York: D. Appleton-Century Co., 1939), which describes a king who failed to effect "enlightened reforms."

The ideas of the Enlightenment can best be seen in F. J. C. Hearnshaw (editor), *The Social and Political Ideas of Some Great French Thinkers of the Age of Reason* (London: George G. Harrap & Co., 1930); Kathleen O'Flaherty, *Voltaire, Myth and Reality* (Oxford: B. H. Blackwell, Ltd., 1945); and Thomas P. Neill, *Makers of the Modern Mind* (Milwaukee, Wis.: Bruce Publishing Co., 1952), Chapters 5–8.

Chapter 25. International Dynastic and Colonial Rivalry, 1715 to 1763

75. THE POLISH AND AUSTRIAN SUCCESSION WARS

The balance of power. In the eighteenth century national and dynastic rivalry continued to lead to wars and the reshuffling of the map. It was difficult for statesmen to determine how to satisfy national ambitions of rival powers so that all would share in the spoils and prestige without permitting any one country to become a menace to the others. A major source of friction was the rivalry of Hapsburg, Bourbon, and other royal and noble families for vacant thrones formerly occupied by princes related to them by blood or marriage. Rulers recognized no superior authority to settle disputes with their neighbors. In the last analysis, they adjusted their differences by war. Often a king formed a temporary alliance with another monarch against a common enemy. The alliance would end when the old enemy was humbled and the former ally had become so strong as to be a new threat. Then a reversal of alliances would take place. The purpose was to preserve the balance of power, so that one country could not single-handedly change the map of Europe to suit its ambitions.

France was still the mightiest power in western Europe. Her influence in Germany, Poland, Turkey, and in world commerce and in her own empire made her a power to be reckoned with. Although the Holy Roman Emperor, Charles VI, had a central place in European affairs, he was vulnerable. His possessions were widely scattered: the Austrian Netherlands, Milan and Parma in Italy, and the Hapsburg family possessions of Austria, Bohemia, and Hungary. Furthermore, the emperor had no son and he feared that the Hapsburg lands would fall into the hands of his enemies after his death. He therefore endeavored to prevent the division of Hapsburg lands by securing the recognition (the Pragmatic Sanction), by other rulers, of his daughter Maria Theresa as his heir. To secure the acceptance of the Pragmatic Sanction, he was forced to make concessions.

The Spanish threat. The treaties of Utrecht ending the War of the Spanish Succession did not mean peace everywhere in Europe. Fighting still continued in the Balkans between Austria and Turkey (ended in 1718) and along the shores of the Baltic between Russia and Sweden (ended in 1721). Peace in western Europe was threatened by the effort of Spain to supplant Hapsburg influence in Italy and to upset the succession of King Louis XV to the throne of France. Cardinal Alberoni, the adviser of King Philip V of Spain and his wife, Elizabeth Farnese, sought to replace Austrian power in Italy with Spanish influence and thereby secure a throne for their son, Don Carlos. Alberoni prepared to recapture the islands of Sicily and Sardinia and to act in concert with Sweden and Denmark in an attack on Britain for the purpose of deposing George I and restoring the Stuarts. However, Austria, Britain, France, and Holland determined to avoid another world war and checked

Philip V of Spain, with his wife Elizabeth Farnese, governed Spain almost absolutely. During the reign of Philip's son, Ferdinand VI, the government was in the hands of its ministers. (Library of Congress)

Alberoni's schemes by forming a Quadruple Alliance. A short war against Spain followed (1718–1720) in which Britain and France, only recently foes, joined together to stop Spain.

The War of the Polish Succession. The rivalry of the powers in Italy soon became interwoven with the problem of electing the King of Poland. Meanwhile the principal royal and noble German families were in the midst of a race to enhance their prestige. Some of them hoped eventually to win the first dynastic honor of Europe, the emperorship of Germany, then in the hands of the Hapsburgs. The Brunswicks of Hanover had gained the throne of Britain after the death of Queen Anne in 1714, and the Hohenzollerns of Prussia had enlarged Brandenburg-Prussia into a great state with a royal title. The Wettins of Saxony tried to "keep up with the Joneses." When the Wettin, Augustus the Strong, King of Poland, died in 1733, the Poles refused to pick his son as his successor (Augustus III) and elected instead Stanislaus Lesczynski, the father-in-law of King Louis XV of France. International complications occurred. Saxony naturally backed Augustus III and France supported Stanislaus. Austria stood behind Saxony in return for a Saxon promise to recognize Maria Theresa as the successor to Emperor Charles VI.

The War of the Polish Succession (1733–1735) followed. France declared war against the emperor in 1733 and was joined by Sardinia and Spain. The latter entered hostilities after the French and Spanish branches of the Bourbon family concluded a family pact. The war was waged mainly in Italy and in the upper Rhineland without decisive results. The Franco-Spanish-Sardinian allies failed to crush the emperor because Spain and Sardinia were at cross-purposes in Italy.

As a result of a peace treaty made at Vienna, Lesczynski renounced his claim to the throne of Poland but retained the courtesy title of king and was given the Duchy of Lorraine from its Hapsburg duke, who in turn was compensated by receiving Tuscany in Italy. Upon Lesczynski's death it was provided that Lorraine would go to his daughter (the Queen of France) or her heirs. In Italy the treaty produced an exchange of territories between the Spanish Bourbons and the Austrian Hapsburgs. Don Carlos became King of the Two Sicilies (Naples and Sicily) on condition that the kingdoms of Spain and of the Two Sicilies would remain separate. The Hapsburgs received the Spanish-held duchies of Parma, Piacenza, and Tuscany. Including Milan, the Austrian Hapsburgs now reigned over a well-knit area in northern Italy. With minor modifications, this territorial arrangement of Italy remained unchanged until the peninsula was unified in the nineteenth century.

Russo-Austrian war on Turkey. No sooner was the War of the Polish Succession over than Austria joined Russia in an attack on Turkey, who was then at war with Persia. A settlement with Persia allowed the sultan to throw all his might into a counteroffensive against the Russo-Austrian allies in the Balkans. But in 1739 they routed him. A Russian offensive into present-day Rumania succeeded and alarmed not only the French, who backed the Turks, but also the Austrians, who feared domination of the Balkans by the Czar. The emperor made separate peace with the sultan in 1739. Soon Russia also came to terms, surrendered almost all conquests (except Azov) and promised to demolish fortifications and to remove her fleet from the Black Sea. These developments enhanced the prestige of the King of France, who was cast in the role of the defender of the sultan, who now expressed his gratitude by granting to the French King the right to protect Christians in the Holy Land and to French subjects commercial privileges in the Turkish Empire. France thus became the principal commercial power in the Near East.

Anglo-Spanish friction. The problems of maintaining trade and the balance of power on the continent of Europe and in the colonies were interrelated. Britain was particularly eager to press her advantage over Spain in the Caribbean and along the Gulf coast of North America. Her aim was to despoil Spain of her rich colonial resources and commerce. Britain's task was made easier by the fact that Spain was unable to supply her colonies with goods in sufficient quantities and at suitable prices. British and American colonial merchants were engaged in widespread smuggling and evasion of Spanish mercantilist regulations. But Spanish authorities cracked down on this illegal trade by establishing a patrol on the Spanish Main (or Caribbean) and searching British vessels. A series of incidents and retaliations by British subjects led to war.

War of Jenkins' Ear. Protests of English and American merchants reached London. The incident that occasioned war concerned Captain Robert Jenkins, who alleged that in 1731 a boarding party from a Spanish gunboat had cut off his ear. Jenkins displayed his severed ear in London. Hatred against Spain increased, with the result that Prime Minister Robert Walpole yielded to popular pressure for war in October 1739. Noting the happiness of the English people at the news of war, Walpole remarked, "They are ringing their bells now; they will be wringing their hands soon." During the War of Jenkins' Ear, the British planned to paralyze Spanish commerce by attacking the colonial centers in the Caribbean at Porto Bello and Cartagena. This conflict merged later into a wider and more devasting fight, the War of the Austrian Succession (1740–1748), in which Britain and Spain were on opposing sides.

Sir Martin Frobisher, Sir Walter Raleigh, and Sir Francis Drake were England's famous "Sea Hawks," who engaged in daring and profitable raids on the Spanish Main. All three were knighted by Queen Elizabeth I, whose fancies were caught by their bold schemes to increase England's wealth and colonies and to rival the Spanish. (The Trustees of the National Maritime Museum, England)

FROBISHER　　　　　　　　　DRAKE　　　　　　　　　RALEIGH

Frederick the Great. The development of Prussia into a great power disturbed the European balance. As we have noted, Prussia's might increased during the reign of Frederick William I. That stern monarch despaired of his son, who became Frederick II (the Great), because "young Fritz" liked music and poetry and had no taste for war—and even tried to escape. The strong-willed king hardened the prince by forcing him to witness the execution of the friend who had helped him escape and by a rigid training schedule.

With this training, Frederick the Great (1740–1786) was prepared to advance Prussia's military career. Working hard from early morning to late at night—he called himself "the first servant of the state"—Frederick built up his army and government to a peak of efficiency. At the same time he conducted a busy correspondence with some of the most learned men of his day.

The War of the Austrian Succession. The death of Emperor Charles VI in 1740 and the accession of Maria Theresa to the throne provided Frederick with the opportunity to seize Silesia, a rich province of Austria, and thus to enlarge the kingdom of Prussia. Other princes also sought to satisfy their ambitions at the expense of Maria Theresa. The Elector of Bavaria claimed all the Hapsburg lands except Hungary, while the Elector of Saxony demanded Silesia, Bohemia, and Moravia. The King of Spain aspired to take Austrian possessions in Italy. The satisfaction of these ambitions depended in large part on the willingness of the King of France to permit the despoilment of Austria. He threw

Frederick the Great, upon accession to the throne of Prussia, showed superior qualities of militarism and cynical disregard for treaties. He vastly expanded Prussian territory and made Prussia Europe's foremost military power. (The Metropolitan Museum of Art)

in his lot with Frederick the Great. The conflict that broke out between France, Spain, Prussia, and Bavaria on one side and Austria on the other is called the War of the Austrian Succession (1740–1748).

With Prussian armies sweeping across Silesia, Maria Theresa eloquently appealed to Hungary for support. The bravery of Austrian and Hungarian troops was not equal to the task of recovering Silesia. At first sight the power of the Franco-Spanish, Prussians, and Bavarians was preponderant. But it did not bring Austria to her knees. As in other coalitions of the past, the conflicting ambitions of the major powers dimmed the prospects of a clear-cut decision over Austria.

In 1742, Maria Theresa conceded to Frederick the Great the province of

Silesia. This meant that Saxony, also interested in Silesia, was estranged from her Prussian ally and left the war. Austria could now face Bavaria and soon overwhelmed Bavarian forces. Maria Theresa sought Bavarian territorial gains as compensation for her loss of Silesia. In the meantime, Britain, already waging the War of Jenkins' Ear with Spain, came to the aid of Austria in alliance with many German princes (1743). What brought Britain and Austria together was their common interest in checking the ambitions of France. Frederick the Great of Prussia re-entered the war a second time in 1744. Austria, Saxony, Britain, and Holland joined against Prussia, but the chief opponents by this time were Britain and France.

Inconclusive fighting occurred. Austria and Prussia soon came to terms again. Accordingly, Prussia recognized Francis I, the husband of Maria Theresa, as Holy Roman Emperor.

War continued, however, between the Austro-British allies and the French. In Flanders, the French Marshal de Saxe won a resounding victory over British and Austrian armies at Fontenoy in 1745 and prepared the way for French control of Belgium. Meanwhile, the deposed Stuart dynasty of England and its Scottish and English supporters raised a rebellion that failed in 1745.

While the principal theater of operations was in Europe and the basic concern the European balance of power, the entry of Britain on the side of Austria meant another Anglo-French world war. In America this conflict was called King George's War. Colonial forces captured the fortress of Louisburg on Cape Breton Island, which was a French naval base guarding the gateway to the St. Lawrence and French Canada. In the East, the French and the British East India companies grappled for com-

HAPSBURG EMPI
c. 1740

Maria Theresa of Austria won the support of her subjects by her warm personality and strong determination. (Austrian Information Service)

mercial control of India. The French prospered with the capture of Madras in 1746 by Dupleix and La Bourdonnais. On the seas, the French and British destroyed each other's trade, but the heaviest losses were French.

Peace of Aix-la-Chapelle. Peace came in 1748 at Aix-la-Chapelle when Britain and France considered themselves on the brink of bankruptcy and victory too far away. The British gains at sea and in the colonies were offset by failures of their armies on the European continent. Statesmen at Aix-la-Chapelle sought to establish a balance of colonial power by restoring conquests made by Britain and France. As for the European balance, Austria confirmed the cession of Silesia to Prussia and of Parma in Italy to Don Philip, the son of Elizabeth Farnese of Spain, and in turn the powers acknowledged the Pragmatic Sanction. This peace settlement meant that Frederick the

Great of Prussia was able to retain Silesia and thus to defy the authority of the Holy Roman Emperor. The indecisive results of the War of the Austrian Succession showed that Britain and France would come to blows again over colonies and trade.

76. THE SEVEN YEARS' WAR, 1756 TO 1763

The diplomatic revolution. After the War of the Austrian Succession, a realignment of European powers occurred. Old allies separated; former enemies embraced each other. Austria and Britain, traditional friends, drifted apart.

Meanwhile Maria Theresa wanted to recover Silesia. Her minister, Prince Kaunitz, laid plans for an attack on King Frederick the Great of Prussia by driving a wedge between him and King Louis XV of France. Frederick realized that he was vulnerable and that Maria Theresa, in league with the Czarina of Russia and the Elector of Saxony, was preparing a blow against him.

The British, fearing war, wanted an ally who could defend the German principality of Hanover, whose prince was also King of Great Britain. In their view, Frederick the Great might defend Hanover if he were an ally. Thereupon they offered him an alliance in January 1756, which was accepted. Anglo-Prussian negotiations angered the King of France, who denounced what he considered to be double-dealing on the part of the King of Prussia. The way was now prepared for a complete reversal of alliances. Kaunitz convinced French ministers that Prussia threatened the peace of Germany and of Europe. The result was a defensive agreement between the King of France and Maria Theresa. The Czarina of Russia also resented Anglo-Prussian discussions and joined Austria against Prussia. This reversal of alliances, in short, brought Austria and France together in a "diplomatic revolution."

The outbreak of war. Frederick's invasion of Saxony in August 1756 touched off war. Soon Austria, and most of the members of the Holy Roman Empire, France (and after 1762 Spain), Russia, and Sweden were pitted in the Seven Years' War (1756–1763) against Prussia, Britain, Hanover, Brunswick, Gotha, and Hesse. Britain and France had already been waging an undeclared war over colonies and trade in the New World.

There were two main features of the war: the allied effort to crush Prussia in Germany and the Anglo-French struggle for commerce and colonies. Fighting in Germany was primarily centered in two fronts: between Prussian and Austro-Russian armies, and

William Pitt, one of England's greatest prime ministers, increased British world influence through his foreign alliances.

between the Anglo-Hanoverians and the French forces. Before the Austro-Franco-Russian allies could bring their superior manpower and resources to bear on the smaller Prussian forces, Frederick the Great struck lightning blows and disrupted the enemy. Because he did not possess the men or the supplies to crush his foes, he was compelled to employ the strategy of wearing them out. A number of times he was on the brink of disaster and only his daring and cunning use of his disciplined armies prevented the enemies of Prussia from toppling him and partitioning his kingdom. The allies failed to deliver the knockout blow. They were not united in purpose. The Czarina wanted territory from eastern Prussia and part of Poland, which frightened Maria Theresa of Austria and Louis XV of France, who concluded that Russian control of the Baltic and of Poland threatened the balance of power.

The war for commerce and colonies. British statesmen disagreed at first about the priority of their war effort. Some persons maintained that, since the campaigns in Germany proved that Frederick could protect Prussia but not Hanover, it would be foolish to pour men and money into the German war. They suggested that Britain concentrate on warfare against French commerce and colonies. William Pitt, who in effect became the dictator of the British war effort, believed, however, that the German battlefields and the colonial theaters of war were interrelated. Pitt urged Britain to "conquer America in Europe" by paying Frederick subsidies so that his enemies could not crush him.

Colonial trade in the East Indies, which included Borneo (shown above), was profitable to the mother countries because of the island's rich deposits of gold, iron, and other minerals. Borneo was settled by the Portuguese, Dutch, and English. (Hulton Picture Library)

Since the end of the War of the Austrian Succession, Britain and France had girded themselves for a life-and-death struggle for commerce and colonies, which were of pivotal importance in their economies. Among the most important colonies were the West Indies, the "sugar bowl" of the world. The African slave trade—in which Britain alone had over 150 ships transporting Negroes to the New World—and its bases along the west coast of Africa were similarly important. Besides, trade with India and the East contributed to British and French prosperity. The trade of the West Indies, Africa, and India was interrelated. From the West Indies came tropical products, precious metals, and money. The latter was sent to India to purchase cotton goods. In turn, these cottons were transshipped from England to Africa in exchange for slaves, or to the West Indies as clothes for the slaves.

The existence of rival empires ready to raid and trade illegally with each other's colonies prevented the enforcement of mercantilistic regulations that had been designed to give the mother country a monopoly of colonial trade. French and English colonies in North America discovered that they would mutually profit if they traded with each other directly in violation of regulations. For example, the French sugar islands of St. Dominque, Martinique, and Guadeloupe traded with New York, Massachusetts, and Rhode Island.

The battle for North America. Even before the outbreak of war in Europe, the struggle for the control of the mainland of North America had led to a race for the wilderness. Britain and France contested for the wide prairies and forests. The thirteen English colonies on the mainland developed rapidly and pushed against the thinly held frontiers of the French and Spanish empires. They felt hemmed in on three sides: in the north they were blocked by French Canada, in the west by a ring of French forts situated between the Great Lakes and New Orleans, and in the south by Spanish Florida and French Louisiana. Virginia wished to expand beyond the Alleghenies but found the path blocked by the French Fort Duquesne at the junction of the Allegheny and Monongahela rivers. Undeclared war began in 1754. A young Virginian, George Washington, was sent by the British governor to request the French to leave western Pennsylvania. To win the West, the British sent an expedition commanded by General Edward Braddock with the mission of driving out the French. Braddock's army met defeat in western Pennsylvania at the hands of the French and their Indian allies. However, the French were unable to pursue victory because a relief expedition sent out from France was intercepted on the high seas by the British fleet. In September 1755 the British fleet was ordered

to attack all French ships. These actions were the opening moves in the French and Indian War, as the Seven Years' War was called in the colonies. The conflict became a titanic struggle to determine whether North America would be British or French.

At first the British were unsuccessful against the French. Braddock's army was shattered, in India the French-aided Nabob of Bengal attacked Calcutta in 1756, and in the Mediterranean the French seized the British island of Minorca. But the tide soon began to turn against France. With greater resources and control of the seas, which cut off French Canada from the home base, the British and their colonial allies struck at the French forts in the wilderness and at Canada. In the meantime the British navy scoured the seas for French vessels and kept open the lines of communication and supply between the

A view of the storming of Quebec by British General James Wolfe. Fighting took place on the strategic Plains of Abraham, a level field adjoining upper Quebec. The British victory influenced the fate of Canada. (The Metropolitan Museum of Art)

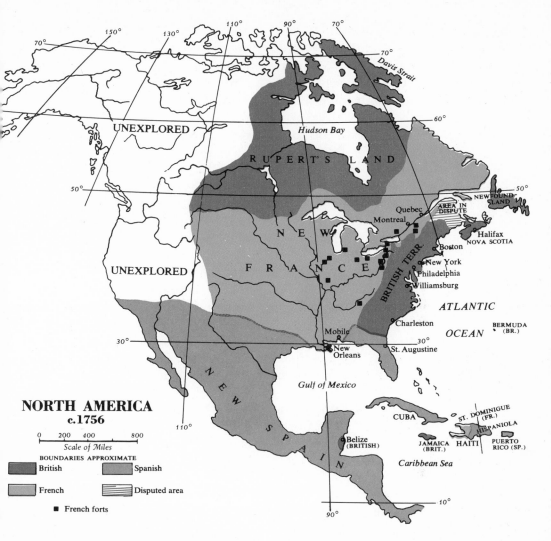

**NORTH AMERICA
c.1756**

0   200   400   800
Scale of Miles
BOUNDARIES APPROXIMATE

British   Spanish

French   Disputed area

■ French forts

British Isles and the colonies. The effort of the French to strike at the heart of the British Empire by launching an invasion of England was thwarted by the British destruction of a great French fleet in Quiberon Bay.

British victories. The fortunes of war smiled on Britain in 1759, the "wonderful year." In September, General James Wolfe stormed Quebec, which was defended by Montcalm. In the dramatic battle that followed, both gallant commanders fell, and Quebec surrendered to the British. In 1760

Montreal fell to the British. The fish, furs, and naval stores of North America were lost to the French. The British also moved against the French West Indies, taking the islands of Guadeloupe (1759) and Martinique (1762). French slave-trading stations on the coast of Africa were captured by the British. The loss of these posts was a severe blow to the French economy. Meanwhile British trade and manufactures prospered, so that Englishmen increased their share of the world and its trade. Events in India were similarly favorable to Britain. French forces had been cut off. Robert Clive, a servant of the British East India Company, warded off French threats. In 1757, as a result of bribing the Indian commander of a native army twenty times larger than his own, Clive won the battle of Plassey and thus became the master of Bengal. British forces a year later took the French base at Pondicherry.

Spain enters the war. France and Spain renewed the Family (Bourbon) Pact in 1761. The King of Spain cherished the hope of regaining Gibraltar and eliminating the British commercial invasion of his empire. He feared the vast increase in British power that had occurred during the war. Furthermore, the King of Spain wished to support France in return for French support of Spanish ambitions in Italy. War between Britain and Spain came in 1762. The British fought the Spanish in the Caribbean and captured Havana on the island of Cuba.

The fortunes of Frederick the Great. While Britain humbled France and Spain in the colonies and on the high seas, her ally, Prussia, hung on determinedly against Austrian and Russian armies. To make matters worse, Britain and Prussia fell out in 1762. At the darkest moment for King Frederick the Great of Prussia, when his enemies were preparing a mighty blow, Czarina Elizabeth of Russia died and was succeeded by Czar Peter III, a madman and admirer of Frederick. Peter III halted the advance of the Russian army, deserted Austria, and joined the King of Prussia! But this mad Czar had an obsession to play with toy soldiers. In his wife's opinion he had as much discretion as a cannon ball. Soon he was assassinated.

The Treaty of Paris. The campaigns in Europe and in the colonies exhausted the belligerents, who opened negotiations for peace. Although France had been severely defeated overseas, the French foreign minister shrewdly exploited the differences between Britain and Prussia and among the members of the British peace delegation. Frederick the Great of Prussia signed a separate peace with Maria Theresa at Hubertusburg. The Treaty of Paris (1763) represented a great victory for Britain. France ceded Canada and the territory east of the Mississippi (excluding New Orleans), together with the right of navigation on that river. Britain returned some French colonies and trading stations, while France restored Minorca to Britain. The French Empire was reduced to trading posts in India, some islands in the Caribbean and in the Gulf of St. Lawrence. For her defeat, Spain surrendered to Britain East Florida and her claim to a share in the Newfoundland fisheries. In addition, Spain permitted Britain a foothold in Honduras in Central America and agreed to renew commercial treaties. In order to maintain Spain's friendship, France ceded to her the Louisiana territory west of the Mississippi.

REVIEW

STUDY SECTIONS IN REVIEW

75. The Polish and Austrian Succession Wars

   A. Why was the Pragmatic Sanction important to Charles VI?

   B. Identify: Cardinal Aberoni, Quadruple Alliance, Stanislaus Lesczynski.

c. How did France benefit from the Russo-Austrian war with Turkey?

D. What difficulties arose between Britain and Spain in the New World during this period?

E. What were the results of the Peace of Aix-la-Chapelle, which ended the War of the Austrian Succession?

76. The Seven Years' War, 1756 to 1763

A. What steps were taken by Maria Theresa to recover Silesia from Prussia?

B. In what areas of the world did Britain and France battle during the Seven Years' War?

c. Identify: Braddock, Wolfe, Robert Clive.

D. Why did Spain enter the Seven Years' War on the side of the French?

E. Mention four consequences of the Treaty of Paris (1763), which ended the Seven Years' War.

THE CHAPTER IN REVIEW

A. What is meant by the "balance of power" when speaking of international relations? What did Britain's role seem to be in keeping the balance during this period?

B. Review the steps that led to the War of the Polish Succession so as to show the complicated dynastic and political relationships of this historical period.

c. In order to demonstrate the temporary nature of alliances in a struggle for a balance of power, name the allies on each side at the end of the War of the Austrian Succession (1748) and at the beginning of the Seven Years' War (1756).

D. Into what two major aspects can the fighting in the Seven Years' War be divided? What were the stakes in each? Were the results conclusive? Explain.

FOR YOUR NOTEBOOK

The wars and international rivalries of the eighteenth century can be most confusing. You should use your notebook in this chapter not so much to supplement the material of the text as to look at it from a new viewpoint and thus to understand it better.

1. Make a list of the wars of the eighteenth century. Line up the countries on each side for each war; list the most important battles and other military developments; show the results of each war in terms of the treaties concluding them.

2. Each of the European wars was also fought overseas. Thus the Seven Years' War is known in America as the French and Indian War. Prepare four parallel columns—for (1) Europe, (2) North America, (3) the West Indies, (4) India —and show the principal events in each area throughout the wars of the eighteenth century until 1763.

SELECTED READINGS

The French-British aspect of the eighteenth-century wars is well highlighted by Arthur H. Buffinton's Berkshire Series study, *The Second Hundred Years War* (New York: Henry Holt & Co., 1930), which carries the story from 1689 down to 1815 as far as overseas struggle is concerned.

Spain's big reason for greatness in the eighteenth century centers around the meteoric career of Elizabeth Farnese's adviser, Cardinal Alberoni. The story is dramatically told by Simon Harcourt-Smith, *Cardinal of Spain: The Life and Strange Career of Alberoni* (New York: Alfred Knopf, 1944).

The struggle between Prussia and Austria can be followed in biographies of Frederick II and Maria Theresa. Scholarly, well written biographies are Pierre Gaxotte, *Frederick the Great* (New Haven, Conn.: Yale University Press, 1942); and Constance Morris, *Maria Theresa: The Last Conservative* (London: Eyre & Spottiswoode, Ltd., 1938). A handy brief summary of the rise of Prussia is the Berkshire Series study by Sidney B. Fay, *The Rise of Brandenburg-Prussia to 1786* (New York: Henry Holt & Co., 1950).

Chapter 26. Great Britain and the American Revolution

77. CROWN, PARLIAMENT, AND THE AMERICAN COLONIES

The early Hanoverian rulers, George I and George II, were not strong kings. The fact that the son of the deposed James II possessed a better hereditary claim to the throne than the Hanoverians meant that there was a large element in the country who regarded the latter as usurpers. Furthermore, an important bulwark of the British monarchy, the Anglican Church, grew weak as a result of the religious indifference of many persons in the eighteenth century. The early Hanoverians undermined their own position by associating themselves closely with the Whigs, thus becoming "party kings," and by failing to win the hearts of the English people. George I was dull and immoral, more interested in his native Hanover than in England. His successor, George II, was no great improvement.

The House of Commons. The Commons came into its own in the eighteenth century, meeting regularly, protecting its members from arrest, and safeguarding their freedom of speech. The king depended upon it for taxes to run the government and to wage a series of wars against France and Spain. The Commons enforced ministerial responsibility by making it necessary for the ministers to receive parliamentary support in order to remain in office. Yet because of inadequate representation and election frauds, the House of Commons was hardly responsible to the people. Its importance led the king and his ministers to bribe members and control legislation.

The Cabinet. In the eighteenth century the cabinet began to resemble somewhat its modern form as a group of ministers who decide governmental policy under the chairmanship of the Prime Minister. Because he could not speak English, George I ceased attending cabinet meetings. The person who presided over them in his absence came to be the Prime Minister. In the absence of the king, his ministers were free to settle policy; and once their decisions were made, it was difficult for the king to reverse them. During the reign of George II, the cabinet grew under the leadership of Sir Robert Walpole, who may be called the first modern Prime Minister.

The Whig party leaders played a dominant role and considered themselves as defenders of the constitution. George I employed them exclusively to run the government. Unlike the situation in France, where the monarchs reduced the power of the nobility, in England the aristocrats enjoyed not only social but governmental influence. The British nobility had long experience in the affairs of local government and in the art of managing men. Although the Whig leaders were interested in place and prestige for themselves and their families and "connections," they were still motivated by the desire to serve their country.

George III. The English constitution was imperfect, to be sure, but it did work fairly well. In 1760, George III ascended the throne. The grandson of George II and only twenty-two years old, he was the first of his dynasty to be born in England and raised as an Englishman. He determined to play a

Robert Walpole, in effect England's first Prime Minister, began the rise in the influence of ministers and the decline in the power of the monarchs.

large personal role in the government and wished to unite all groups and factions around himself as a "patriot-king." He wished to abolish political parties. Thus he meant to end the influence of the Whig aristocrats, who had already weakened themselves by splitting up into many rival factions, each intent on advantages for its members. By means of patronage and royal influence he attracted followers known as the "King's Friends" to carry out his wishes in Parliament and government.

George either failed to appreciate or ignored the changes that had occurred since his ancestors took the throne in 1714. He underestimated the conviction of his opponents that his policies tended to destroy liberty. The king also overlooked the force of public opinion. Advances in education, the spread

George III, King of England, and America's last "king." He was determined to rule as well as reign and ended the control of the Whigs. (Library of Congress)

of literature, and the growth of towns led more and more people to realize the part they might play in politics. This political awareness was encouraged by pamphleteers and reformers who pointed to abuses and corruption in the British constitution. These writers advocated "common sense" and short cuts to reforming church, state, and society. They were doubtlessly influenced by European reform writers. Now the problem was how to bring this new force to bear on the House of Commons, which was rather unresponsive to the wishes of "the people." The Whigs flirted with this "extra-parliamentary opinion" in their struggles with George III.

Britain and America. Meanwhile the British government attempted to strengthen its control over the American colonies by means of closing the loopholes in the mercantilist laws, or the "old colonial system," which regulated the relationship of mother country and colonies. Earlier in the eighteenth century, British officials had made little effort to enforce the Navigation Acts and revenue laws or to prevent smuggling and illicit trade between America and the French and Spanish possessions. But when Americans traded with the enemy during the French and Indian War, Britain decided to crack down. General search warrants enabled British colonial officials to investigate suspected hiding places of smuggled goods.

The Stamp Act. Victory in the French and Indian War created new problems in the British Empire. Britain was saddled with a heavy debt. With the prospect of additional expenditures in the future in order to protect their empire in North America, British statesmen expected Americans to share the cost of a standing army. They planned two things, the strict enforcement of the trade and revenue laws to prevent smuggling, and the increase of revenue through new customs duties and a stamp tax on legal documents and newspapers. The Revenue or Sugar Act of 1764 caused discontent, and the Stamp Act of 1765 provoked violent American resistance. Subsequently Parliament modified the first act and repealed the second.

Taxation without representation. A renewed British attempt in 1767 to raise revenue in the colonies caused a new storm of protest. Americans demanded all the rights and liberties of natural-born Englishmen and attacked parliamentary taxes on the grounds that the colonists were not represented in the House of Commons.

Their motto was: "No taxation without representation." Again the British government moved toward conciliation. Neither the king nor his ministers meant to tyrannize over America or to provoke violence, but they were never able to understand the temper of Americans.

The Boston "Tea Party." For a few years after 1770 there was a period of calm in Anglo-American relations. Parliament had repealed some of the measures to which the Americans objected, and its chief attention was directed to the affairs of the East India Company. That company was guilty of misgovernment in India and had fallen into bankruptcy. An act was passed in 1773 placing the company under partial crown control, and another act was designed to help the company financially. The latter is known as the Tea Act. It authorized the East India Company to dispose of a vast surplus of tea imported from India by selling it in America. Hitherto the Americans had boycotted all tea from England because Parliament had put a tax on its importation into the colonies. When a ship arrived in Boston Harbor, angry Boston citizens disguised as American Indians boarded the ship and threw the tea into the water. This momentous event took place on the night of December 16, 1773.

The Intolerable Acts. The Boston Tea Party in turn provoked the British government to coerce the colonies by means of the Intolerable Acts of 1774. These laws closed the port of Boston for an indefinite period, reorganized the government and the courts of Massachusetts, limited the right of public meeting, and compelled Boston to supply barracks for British soldiers in needed locations. The London government also pushed through the Quebec Act, by which the boundary of Canada became the Ohio River and the Mississippi, thereby closing the West to settlers from English-speaking colonies. The Intolerable Acts stirred strong American resistance. The colonists established committees of correspondence to pass along information to patriots in all the colonies. Out of this activity came the first Continental Congress, which adopted measures to boycott all British goods and prevent their importation. The British replied by military coercion. Hostilities began at Concord, Massachusetts, in April 1775.

While most Americans opposed the pretensions of king and Parliament and the threat to their interests and liberties, they were reluctant to break with the mother country. When events forced patriots to take up arms against the British, some Americans (the Loyalists) supported the king. In a similar way, many English Whigs openly supported the Americans, but not for American independence. The

Newspaper cartoon of 1776, devised by Benjamin Franklin, advocates the unity of the American colonies in their fight for independence. (NYPL)

English friends of America thought that the colonists were fighting for English liberty everywhere against the royal oppression.

Declaration of Independence. Through the Continental Congress the patriots took up the armed challenge and selected George Washington of Virginia to lead their army. However, they were reluctant to sever their connections with the mother country. Independence appealed to them only after Parliament cut off all trade and hired German soldiers to help crush them. Sentiment against George III was well expressed in Thomas Paine's pamphlet, *Common Sense,* which labeled kings "crowned ruffians" and urged the colonists to separate from Great Britain. "The blood of the slain, the weeping voice of Nature cries, 'Tis time to part.'"

George Washington, portrait by Gilbert Stuart. Washington was named commander-in-chief of the Continental forces, an unorganized and poorly equipped militia. (National Gallery of Art)

On July 4, 1776, the Continental Congress, meeting in Philadelphia, declared the independence of the thirteen colonies. The Declaration of Independence asserted that all men are created equal, that they are endowed by God with certain inalienable rights, that among these are life, liberty, and the pursuit of happiness, and that governments are established to protect these rights and, failing to do so, may be altered.

Whether the Americans would be able to make good their claim to independence depended on their ability to fight and win in war.

78. WORLD WAR AND AMERICAN INDEPENDENCE

The French and Spanish allies nursed their wounds after their unsuccessful encounter with the British lion in the Seven Years' War and plotted for their moment of revenge. The bitter struggles between the British king and the Whigs and between the government and the colonies looked like promising opportunities for French-Spanish interference. Under the wily Duke of Choiseul, the French strengthened their army and navy and seized control of the island of Corsica (1768), to be used as a naval base for future operations against British-held Minorca and Gibraltar. In 1770 the Spanish showed their teeth by ousting a British garrison from the Falkland Islands off the coast of Argentina in South America.

While the American crisis was developing, events in eastern Europe occupied France's attention. The ambitions of Frederick the Great of Prussia

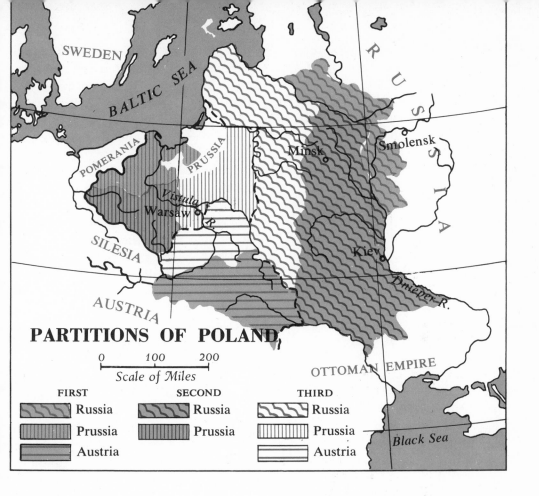

PARTITIONS OF POLAND

Scale of Miles
0   100   200

FIRST	SECOND	THIRD
Russia	Russia	Russia
Prussia	Prussia	Prussia
Austria		Austria

and Catharine the Great of Russia mingled. Catharine continued Russian ambitions of expanding at the expense of Poland in the west and Turkey in the south. She sought a solution of the "Eastern Question" favorable to Russia; that is, a division among the great powers of territories belonging to Poland and Turkey in eastern Europe.

Russo-Turkish War. Catharine intervened in Polish affairs and placed her friend on the throne. When the Poles rebelled later, she sent in troops and virtually reduced Poland to the status of a Russian province. Meanwhile France urged the Turks to declare war on Catharine for the purpose of de-

fending the Polish rebels. In the Russo-Turkish War (1768–1774) the sultan's armies were no match for superior Russian forces, which overran Moldavia and Wallachia (present-day Rumania) and conquered the Crimea. It seemed that the whole Turkish Empire would collapse. At this moment the great powers stepped in. Austria and France feared Russian designs on the Balkans; Austria especially dreaded Russian annexations along the Danube, which would make Russia her neighbor. They forced Catharine to moderate her gains. The peace treaty gave Catharine territory in the Crimea, free navigation for her merchant vessels in Turkish waters, and the right to protect Orthodox Christians in the Turkish Empire.

First Partition of Poland (1772). The Russo-Turkish War spelled the doom of Poland, because Russian gains excited the envy of Austria and Prussia. The German powers demanded equivalents to compensate them for the relative loss of power. Besides, Frederick the Great felt that Austrian resentment at Russia might lead to a general European war in which he would probably have to join. His argument was that peace could be maintained among the big three of central and eastern Europe by cutting up Poland and giving shares to Austria, Prussia, and Russia.

Weak, divided, and unable to resist, the Poles had to accept the surrender of about one-third of their land and people. This first partition of Poland had far-reaching consequences on world history. It destroyed one of the oldest countries in the world. For the first time in modern history a big country was divided among its enemies.

The Poles did not forget the dismemberment and they nursed the hope that they would regain their lost territories. France also suffered. As the traditional ally of Poland, France lost prestige for being unable to prevent the partition.

French intervention in America. What France lost in prestige in the East she gained in the West by extending aid to the American rebels which tipped the scales in their favor.

The Continental Congress had assumed the functions of central government, and patriot armies had taken the field against the British. British commanders, however, lacked the will or the skill to prosecute the war successfully. A series of British errors, coupled with American valor, led to the defeat of the armies of King George. A decisive battle occurred in 1777 at Saratoga, in New York, where the army of General John Burgoyne, which had marched from Canada to enter the Hudson Valley and cut the colonies in two, was defeated and forced to surrender.

The surrender of General Burgoyne to General Gates (1777). The battle of Saratoga was the first great American victory of the Revolution. Not only did it encourage the French to send official aid to the fighting colonies, but it also raised the morale of American patriots. (Library of Congress)

General Lafayette, enthusiastic over the cause of the American Revolution, left France to join Washington's army. Benjamin Franklin, one of the greatest statesmen of the American Revolution, won European respect through his diplomatic efforts. (French Embassy Press & Information Division)

The American victory at Saratoga convinced France that the time had come to take an active part. She had already aided the rebels unofficially, her purpose being to break the British Empire. Saratoga indicated to France that the Americans would not be conquered. It was followed by signs of a British desire for peace by conciliation. France feared a reconciliation between colonies and mother country that might be capped by a joint Anglo-American attack on her. Benjamin Franklin, who went to Paris to represent the American Congress, expertly played on French fears and obtained an alliance between the United States and France in 1778. The coming of France into the war converted the American Revolution into another world conflict.

In 1779, France and Spain concluded a military alliance in which France agreed to remain at war with Britain until Spain recovered Gibraltar and the Floridas. Spain entered the war in 1779, and Holland the following year. Britain now stood alone against many enemies. Much European opinion favored the Americans, in part because Benjamin Franklin pleaded their cause with skill and tact. Distinguished volunteers flocked to America: Lafayette from France, Kosciusko and Pulaski from Poland, and Steuben from Prussia.

British defeats. British sea power, weakened by the loss of American vessels, which had been an important segment of the commercial fleet, could not match the combined Franco-Spanish fleet that now dominated the English Channel in 1779, a year the British consider one of their darkest moments. The French foreign minister, Vergennes, lined up the European maritime nations against Britain in 1780 to safeguard the freedom of the seas against the British practices of searching neutral vessels on the high seas for goods of their enemies.

Britain was under attack everywhere: on the American mainland, in the West Indies, in the English Channel, the Mediterranean, the high seas. Even in India, France aided the ruler of Mysore, Hyder Ali, in league with the princes of central India and the Mahratta Confederacy, who made war against the British East India Company. The company almost lost its empire, but the governor general, Warren Hastings, successfully met the challenge.

Yorktown. General Washington's army, aided by French troops and ships, hemmed in a large British army under Lord Cornwallis in the Yorktown peninsula of Virginia in 1781. Cornwallis surrendered, and after that the British made no more efforts to conquer the colonies. In the Treaty of Paris of 1783, Britain recognized the thirteen United States as free and sovereign and ceded to them all the land west to the Mississippi, north to Canada, and south to Florida. Spain recovered Florida and the island of Minorca in the Mediterranean, while France got back trading posts in India and West Africa and two islands in the West Indies.

Eastern Europe. While the American Revolution raged on, the great powers of central and eastern Europe sparred for gain and prestige. Czarina Catharine of Russia aspired to carry out the "Grand Design"; that is, the effort to build on the ruins of the Turkish Empire a new Byzantine empire. The Czarina and the Holy Roman Emperor, Joseph II, signed a defensive alliance, which permitted Russia to execute the Grand Design and Austria to occupy the western Balkans. As the fighting stopped in America,

the Russians overran the Crimea, where later was built the city of Sevastopol, the Russian naval base on the Black Sea. The French advised the Turks to concede the Crimea and Kuban area to Russia, and thereby lost international prestige for having "let down" their allies.

79. WORLD RESULTS OF THE AMERICAN REVOLUTION

Effects on Britain. The American Revolution was a vast event in world history. Its effects on Britain and her empire were far-reaching. The military defeats and the taxes and hardships of war aroused public dismay. Committees sprang up and claimed to speak for the people of England. Many protesters directed their anger not only at king and government but also to the "unreformed" House of Commons,

Billy the Butcher's Advice to John Bull

Since Bread is so dear (and you say you must eat),
For to save the expence, you must live upon meat;
And as twelve pence the quartern you can't pay for bread,
Get a crown's worth of meat,— it will serve in its stead.
(NYPL)

and demanded an overhauling of the system of representation, even universal manhood suffrage. The doctrine of "no taxation without representation" thus appealed also to the people of England, who felt they were not really represented in the House of Commons.

Of primary importance, the American Revolution was a grave warning to Britain that she should never again permit discontent in her colonies to reach the point of rebellion and civil war.

Ireland. Since the Glorious Revolution, Ireland was a misgoverned province of the British Empire. National, religious, and economic freedom was denied. The Irish Parliament, which was exclusively Protestant (although the great majority of the nation was Catholic), was under the British thumb. Irish manufactures and exports could not compete with British goods. As a result of the American Revolution, however, the Irish partially achieved certain national political aspirations. Since the 1760's Ireland had been shaken by agitation against British restrictions on Irish trade and manufactures and heavy burdens placed on the Irish treasury to provide money for supporters of the London government. The war cut off trade between Ireland and France. Soon demands for commercial freedom were mingled with demands for religious and political freedom. The Catholic population, poverty-stricken and persecuted, saw an opportunity to improve its lot. The British government encouraged the Irish legislature to grant partial toleration to Catholics as a means of preventing the French and Spanish from appealing successfully to the Irish.

Leadership in obtaining commercial freedom came from the Protestant gentry, who formed the Volunteers, a sort of national guard, without the permission of the government. The Volunteers were a thinly veiled threat to Britain. To bring further pressure on Britain, the Irish began a boycott against English goods. Finally, in 1779–1780, in the throes of rebellion in America and elsewhere, the British government gave virtual commercial freedom to Ireland. Irish patriots wished to go farther and end the subordination of the Irish Parliament and government to the British. In 1782 the Irish Parliament passed a resolution asserting its legislative independence and noting that Ireland was a separate kingdom joined to Britain by means of a common crown. Britain conceded this; but Irish legislative independence ended in 1801 when the two kingdoms of Ireland and Great Britain were merged.

Canada. The effects of the American Revolution on Canada were also significant. Canadian numbers and influence increased, because American Loyalists fled to New Brunswick, Ontario, and other parts of Canada, which had remained loyal to Britain. Although the Loyalists had left their homes and properties for their convictions, they coupled their devotion to the crown and to Britain with a demand for rights as Englishmen. In 1791 the English-speaking element was permitted representative assemblies in Ontario and Quebec. The French Canadians remained second-class citizens until they broke out in rebellion in 1837, after which their position improved. Discontent never reached the proportions of revolution, because British officials were sobered by the existence of the United States just south of the Canadian border, a republic that regularly invited Canada to join.

India. Just before the American Revolution, Warren Hastings became governor general of India. While the British lost heavily throughout the world, Hastings actually enlarged British dominion in India on the ruins of the Mogul Empire. Indian events were viewed with interest in London, where some statesmen denounced the corruption of the East India Company officials and the treatment of the Indians. The loss of the American colonies shifted the balance of trade and interest within the British Empire to the East and to India. Public opinion was disturbed over the conduct of British officials in India and their enrichment at the expense of the natives. After their tour of duty in India, many East India officials returned to England and with their wealth bought seats in the House of Commons. These "nabobs," as they were called, generally supported royal influence.

The American Revolution had popularized lofty ideals and views of the nature and purpose of empires. These ideals were shown in the Whig attempt to impeach Warren Hastings in 1788. Hastings was tried before the House of Lords on charges that as governor general of India he had violated the moral law of justice. He was specifically charged with maltreating native princes and peoples, charges that were somewhat exaggerated. But the important issue in his trial was the idea that a Christian country was obliged to

govern according to Christian principles because God grants a conqueror a sacred trust to govern people according to justice. A leading prosecutor was Edmund Burke, who maintained that "all dominion of man over man is the effect of Divine disposition," which meant that the governor must not be a despot but must conform to the moral law. Hastings was eventually acquitted, but the ideas of imperial morality popularized during his trial remained alive.

Australia. Dutch explorers had entered Australia in the early seventeenth century, but it was the explorations (1768–1771) of the east coast by Captain James Cook that led to British settlement. At first the British considered Australia as a possible haven for American Loyalists and later as a site for convict settlements. Convicts had been transported to America, but of course this practice stopped when the United States won her independence.

Captain James Cook, greatest English explorer and navigator of the eighteenth century, explored the coasts of New Zealand and Australia. (British Information Services)

British officials decided to use New South Wales as a dumping ground for prisoners. In 1788, Captain Arthur Philip landed at Botany Bay with over seven hundred convicts and a marine guard. Five years later free settlers began to arrive in the new colony.

Downfall of the old colonial system. The American Revolution weakened mercantilism and the old colonial system. The principle that colonies existed solely for the benefit of national commerce was rudely jolted by American and Irish resistance. This opposition underscored arguments against mercantilist regulations in Adam Smith's *Wealth of Nations,* published in 1776. The British began to doubt the wisdom of colonies, reasoning that colonies broke off like ripe fruit when they were developed and left the parent with nothing for her efforts.

Suppression of Slave Trade. The African slave trade also felt the direct effects of the American Revolution. A strong moral opinion against the slave trade and slavery itself grew up in Britain. It is true that the British West Indies still demanded the continuation of the slave trade, but at home many petitions came to Parliament to abolish it. Finally in 1807 the British slave trade was suppressed.

France. The effects of the Revolution on France were immediate. The heavy expenditures to finance French and American forces led to national bankruptcy. The financial crisis of the 1780's in France occasioned the outbreak of the French Revolution. Furthermore, the American Revolution worked like an acid that corroded the foundations of the French absolute monarchy. French officers who served in America and the reading public which followed events in the New World demanded more political liberty in their kingdom. They felt that they too should enjoy the fruits of freedom.

The United States after the Revolution. When royal officials fled, the patriots in the American colonies established state governments based on written constitutions that guaranteed personal liberty, and extended the vote to more persons. In general, however, much of the old machinery of government was preserved and adapted to the new order of things. In many instances the Anglican Church, formerly established by law, lost its favored status and was disestablished. The fact that so many Loyalists who fled the country came from the higher and professional classes meant that aristocrats lost political and social influence. A more popular—or what is called today democratic—system became possible.

Articles of Confederation. The United States lacked unity. Americans during the war had established a loose central government under the Articles of Confederation. The Confederation (1781–1789) was really a league of states, for each of the states behaved almost like a separate country. The general government lacked the power to tax, and the states were reluctant to supply it with necessary funds.

The Philadelphia convention. The states agreed to revise the general government. In 1787 a convention met in Philadelphia, where the deliberations of the "Founding Fathers" produced a new Constitution. They established a republican form of government; that is, a system in which political power is

**THE THIRTEEN
UNITED STATES
1783**

0   100   200
Scale of Miles

■ States
▨ Claims of certain
states (dates ceded)

given to representatives of the people who act in their name and are responsible to them. A federal system was established, whereby the central and state governments shared political power. The "general government" received certain "enumerated powers," and the states retained the rest. This federal system ran counter to the European trend toward centralizing administration in the national capital and stripping provinces or local regions of autonomy.

The United States Constitution. The United States Constitution provided for a three-branch system of government. Congress consisted of a Senate (where each of the states would be equally represented) and a House of Representatives (where the people of the states would be represented in proportion to their numbers). Congress could raise revenue and regulate commerce. The executive was the Presi-

dent, elected indirectly for a four-year term, and possessing the power of veto. The national judiciary included a Supreme Court. In establishing a three-branch government, the Founding Fathers took their principle from the French writer, Montesquieu, who thought he had discovered it in the British constitution. By the tripartite system, a balance of power was secured in the government and tyranny was prevented.

REVIEW

STUDY SECTIONS IN REVIEW

77. Crown, Parliament, and the American Colonies

A. Identify: The British cabinet, Walpole, George III, Whigs.

B. What measures were adopted by the British to increase their revenue from the American colonies?

C. Did all the colonies originally want complete independence from Britain? Explain.

D. Identify: Edmund Burke, Intolerable Acts, First Continental Congress, Declaration of Independence.

78. World War and American Independence

A. What were the consequences of the First Partition of Poland (1772)?

B. Why did France aid the American colonists in their revolt against Britain?

C. Mention three factors that weakened the British position by 1780.

D. What were the result of the Treaty of Paris of 1783?

79. World Results of the American Revolution

A. Mention three domestic consequences in Britain after the American revolt.

B. How did American and Irish resistance affect the mercantile theories of Great Britain?

C. What immediate effects did the American Revolution produce in France?

D. Explain the following American constitutional terms: republican, federal, separation of powers.

THE CHAPTER IN REVIEW

A. What gains had the British Parliament made at the expense of the crown by the eighteenth century? Were these reversed under the first two Hanoverian kings? Explain.

B. What was the concern of France in the "Eastern Question"? What steps did she take in this matter?

C. Why is a knowledge of *world* history important for an understanding of the reasons for the success of the American Revolution?

D. What similarities can be found between the British form of government as of 1800 and the American form after the Constitution of 1787–1789? Note also three major differences.

FOR YOUR NOTEBOOK

It is held by many historians that the British policy of "salutary neglect" through the eighteenth century (until 1763) helped the American colonists develop ideas of independence and gave them political experience. Read your section in the text and appropriate entries in the encyclopedias (such as Walpole) to see precisely what "salutary neglect" meant and what effect it had on the colonists.

After looking up Walpole, George I, and George II in one of the encyclopedias or a standard history of England, write three or four reasons in your notebook to show why Walpole can be called the "first Prime Minister" of England.

Many Englishmen looked upon the American Revolution as an extension overseas of the "Glorious Revolution," or a victory for the Whig party. Show why the American Revolution could so appear to Englishmen.

Americans very often look on our Revolution as a local affair. By means of a diagram and a short summary, show how it was in many respects a "world war."

Outline the effects on world history of the American Revolution.

SELECTED READINGS

Two excellent books on the non-technical level on this subject are in the New American Nation Series intended for college students and the general public, but easily readable by high school students: Lawrence Henry Gipson, *The Coming of the Revolution* 1763–1775 (New York: Harper & Bros., 1954), and John Alden, *The American Revolution* 1775–1783 (New York: Harper & Bros., 1954). For the British side of the story of the American Revolution, students should consult the various biographies of such men as Edmund Burke, Lord North, King George III, Charles James Fox, John Wilkes, and William Pitt the Elder.

A popular survey of the world at the time is to be found in Genevieve Foster, *George Washington's World* (New York: Charles Scribner's Sons, 1957). Students will enjoy the novel woven around the life of John Paul Jones, *Captain Paul,* by Commander Edward Ellsberg (New York: Dodd, Mead & Co., 1951). Also of considerable interest for presenting the "Tory" point of view is the novel by Kenneth Roberts, *Oliver Wiswell* (New York: Doubleday & Co., 1940).

Chapter 27. The French Revolution

80. THE OLD REGIME AND THE FRENCH MONARCHY

As the American Constitution was being adopted, a great revolution broke out in France. It shook the political and social foundations of Europe by destroying the old Regime and replacing it with a new order; and plunged Europe and much of the world into a succession of wars for a quarter century.

The Old Regime. The Old Regime signifies the traditional way of life in Europe: absolute monarchy, privileged classes, established churches, and old social customs and habits. The head of the old Regime in France, the king, was the absolute master. Through the royal government he controlled public affairs. In each province an intendant acted in his name and managed every detail of government. Rigid control by the central government in Paris made the capital the economic, cultural, and political center of the country. In practice the king limited his authority by selling public offices, thereby restricting somewhat his appointing and dismissing powers. Other limitations on royal despotism included the easygoing temperaments of Louis XV and Louis XVI and the existence of French courts that generally settled legal disputes with justice.

The society of the Old Regime in France consisted of three classes, or orders: the First Estate, or the clergy; the Second Estate, or the nobility; and the Third Estate, or the commoners, which meant the people of the middle class.

The Third Estate. The Third Estate consisted of all commoners, ranging from wealthy bankers, contractors, tax collectors, treasury officials, bondholders, lawyers, doctors, and merchants to skilled and unskilled workers. In modern terms, it included the middle and working classes. Peasants were sometimes thought of as the Fourth Estate but were not officially recognized.[1] Now the middle-class merchants and professional people were jealous of aristocrats and complained of social inequality. Although the peasantry owned about thirty per cent of the land of the country, individual holdings were too small to support an increasing population. The peasants were subject to the police power of the aristocrats; they had to bake their bread in the lord's ovens, grind their grain in his mills, press their grapes in his winepresses, and of course pay rents for the lands they farmed wherever they did not own them. A special vexation was the hunting rights of noblemen who chased game through the peasant's fields and often ruined his crops. As for demands put on them by the government, peasants had to draw lots for military service. They had to work on the roads and supply their wagons for military transport. The *taille*, or direct tax, fell heavily upon them.

The Old Regime weakens. Before 1789 the Old Regime suffered a series of shocks that undermined its vitality. *First*, the prestige of monarchy declined as a result of the wars, scandals, and corruption of the reign of Louis XV (1715–1774). To the disgust of observers, his rule deteriorated into intrigues and "petticoat government"

---

[1] An estate may be defined as a political class, so recognized by the king.

Louis XV, King of France, inherited the corruption of Louis XIV's reign and was indifferent to the need for reform. (Giraudon)

of his friends, Madame de Pompadour and Countess du Barry. Promotion in Church and state usually depended upon privileged influence. Louis XV foresaw the collapse of the Old Regime and is supposed to have said, "After me, the deluge!" His grandson and successor, Louis XVI, though a courageous and upright man, did not possess royal qualities of authority and resolution. Interested more in locks and keys than in kingship, he was unsuited to reign in perilous times. His well-meaning efforts to improve the lot of the underprivileged only emboldened the critics of the Old Regime; and his lack of resolution permitted the financial crisis of the 1780's to issue in a revolution that cost him his throne and his life.

Second, the French monarchy lost the affection of many supporters by running roughshod over old rights and privileges. In building roads and public works, the kings sometimes seized private property. Charitable institutions in various parishes were abolished and the property of hospitals seized. Criminal justice was severely administered when the state was a party to the case. Biased judges and arrest without trial left the impression of tyranny.

Third, in centralizing the country and trampling down local liberties, the monarchy weakened important allies, the aristocrats. By depriving the nobles of local jurisdiction and leadership, the kings had left them with no natural function. Shorn of almost everything save their social privileges, great property, and prestige—which in turn alienated them from the people —the nobility flocked to Paris and other cities. The absence of political freedom for both aristocrats and middle-class people left them inexperienced in matters of government. This disposed them to accept the theories of reform writers, who despised the past and sought to remold society on entirely new lines. In welcoming reform, the aristocrats forgot that their own privileges came from the Old Regime.

Fourth, the attack on the Church by writers prepared the way for revolution. Irreligion was a passion in many Frenchmen. They scorned the Church because it respected tradition, authority, and Revelation, and because it had tried to censor their books. Above all, the Church was a privileged order, and its enemies dreamed of stripping priests and bishops of their tax exemptions and even of their property. In attacking the Church, they also attacked a powerful supporter of the Old Regime and the foremost force to make the Old Regime more tolerable.

Fifth, the ideas of the *philosophes* were acids that ate away the foundations of the Old Regime. The beliefs that all men are equal, that all privileges ought to be leveled, and that the people make the state and are therefore sovereign were destructive of the Old Regime.

Sixth, the wars of the eighteenth century weakened the prestige of the government. The defeat in the Seven Years' War discredited the monarchy and lessened French influence in international affairs. The partition of Poland in 1772 measured the decline of France, for Austria, Prussia, and Russia annexed large parts of that country without reference to France, who was a historic ally of Poland. France's participation and victory in the American Revolution did not help her in the long run. Indeed, the aid given to the American rebels was the main direct cause of the French Revolution. The government fell into bankruptcy. What is more, by supporting a fight for freedom in the New World, Louis XVI whetted the appetites of Frenchmen who also sought the fruits of liberty.

And last, economic conditions encouraged discontent with the Old Regime. As a result of the general prosperity of the eighteenth century, the commercial and professional middle classes increased their proportional share of national wealth and prestige and now wanted a share in the privileges of the nobility. In addition, workers grew restless because wages lagged far behind prices. Another feature of the economic picture was the failure of the government to tax the new wealth. Although the country grew more prosperous, the government became bankrupt and in debt to international moneylenders because it used a tax system that rested on persons least able to pay. Yet the French national debt was only half that of the British and less than that of the Dutch. One-fourth of the French budget went for the armed forces, one-twentieth for the upkeep of Versailles and the government, and one-half for interest on the debt.

81. OUTBREAK OF THE REVOLUTION

The Estates-General. In the 1780's, the French government was very nearly bankrupt. Louis XVI took several measures to restore the government to financial stability, but all these measures failed. Finally he decided to present the problem to the people of France, and he convened the Estates-General for May 1789. This French parliament was an assembly representing the three orders, or estates, of French society; it had not met since 1614.

Each of the estates picked its own deputies. Local assemblies that selected the deputies also drew up *cahiers,* or grievance lists, to accompany the representative to Paris. The *cahiers* denounced absolute royal power, infringements on personal liberty, and unjust taxation. However, no cry was yet heard against monarchy or the union of Church and state. Nevertheless, the elimination of many of the grievances would have involved a thorough overhauling of political and social customs. France thrilled with excitement. Peasants, for example, were optimistic, confident that the "good king" meant to do justice because he asked them to state their grievances. The Estates-General assembled on May 5, 1789, at Versailles, about twelve miles from Paris. The splendor of the king's court at Versailles convinced many deputies that the public money was being wasted.

The National Assembly. Prospects for success in solving France's problems were not bright. The twelve hundred deputies were politically inexperienced. They received no direction or program from the king or his advisers, with the result that their meetings became noisy debates. The first big question before them was the proposal to form a single assembly of the three-branch Estates-General. To this the nobles, clergy, and king were opposed. On the motion of Abbé Siéyès, the Third Estate declared itself the only national representative body, or National Assembly. When their meeting hall was closed by the king, the deputies of the Third Estate met on a nearby tennis court on June 20, 1789, and swore not to disband until France had a new and written constitution. Count Mirabeau, a renegade nobleman and spokesman for the Third Estate, exclaimed, "We are here by the will of the people, and . . . only bayonets can drive us out." Although the king had troops to crush the National Assembly, he hesitated. After some of the nobles and clergy joined the Third Estate in the National Assembly, he consented to this arrangement.

Fall of the Bastille. Meanwhile revolutionary agitators were active among handicraft workers, shopkeepers, and the wage-earning people of Paris. A wheat shortage (which raised the price of bread), scarcity, unemployment, and an increase in the number of beggars played into their hands by creating an atmosphere of insecurity and fear. Hope was aroused by the National Assembly, and fear spread that it might be dissolved. Crowds barricaded the streets in fear that royal troops would crush them. Gun shops were seized by the mob. A rumor spread that arms were stored in the ancient fortress, the Bastille, then being used as a prison. There, agitators claimed, many persons were imprisoned without having been brought to trial. In reality, the Bastille contained only seven prisoners. The Bastille seemed a symbol of the Old Regime. A crowd gathered before it on the morning of July 14 to demand arms and the removal of cannon that had been trained on the city. Soon the mob stormed the Bastille and murdered its garrison. This event marked the triumph of the Parisians over the authorities and has since been celebrated in France as a national holiday, commemorating symbolically the great revolution.

Reforms of the National Assembly. Louis XVI appeared before the National Assembly on the day after the storming of the Bastille to announce the removal of troops around Paris and the recall of Necker. At this point the tricolor flag—the blue and red colors of Paris and the white of the monarchy—was adopted. Revolution gathered momentum. Crowds captured stores of grain. National guards were formed throughout France to maintain order. Contact between the National Assembly and the provinces was established by means of committees of correspondence. Emboldened by want and opportunity, the peasants turned against the aristocrats and landlords, burning castles in order to destroy records of manorial dues and rents. A terrible fear gripped the whole country. This "Great Fear" lasted from July 20 to August 6, during which people became panicky in the imaginary belief that "brigands" had been hired by aristocrats.

The storming of the Bastille by the people of Paris, July 14, 1789. The Bastille, fortress and state prison in Paris, was bitterly hated because it was a symbol of the absolutism of the Old Regime. (French Embassy Press & Information Division)

The National Assembly sought to meet the crisis by vast, far-reaching measures of reform. On the night of August 4–5, in an emotional scene, many aristocrats voluntarily renounced all their privileges. The Assembly agreed to abolish all feudal rights and privileges, serfdom, game laws, the *gabelle* (or salt tax), and the tithe (or tax for the Church), and to substitute equality of taxation and equal opportunity in public service.

The Declaration of the Rights of Man. Later in these "August days" the Assembly adopted a *Declaration of the Rights of Man and of the Citizen*. This document has been called the death certificate of the Old Regime. Written in the spirit of the Enlightenment, the Declaration said that "ignorance, forgetfulness, or contempt of the rights of man are the sole causes of public misery and the corruption of governments." Acknowledging God (the "Supreme Being"), it declared that "men are born and remain free and equal in rights" and that social distinctions could be based only on common utility. The natural rights of man were liberty, property, security, and resistance to oppression, rights which the state was formed to preserve. The Declaration defined liberty as the freedom to do all that does not injure others, and advocated equality of all citizens before the law, religious toleration, freedom of speech and press, taxation according to means, sacredness of property, and an end to arbitrary arrest.

The National Assembly then proceeded to adopt comprehensive reforms in the whole royal administration and to write a new constitution for the kingdom, much to the displeasure of the king and his court. At the same time, extreme revolutionary factions grew strong and exploited discontent caused by hunger and fear. The driving forces behind the radicals were popular clubs and newspapers. Two of the numerous clubs were the Cordeliers and the Jacobins. Deputies, writers, and agitators met in the clubs to discuss questions of the day and plan future moves. The Jacobins extended their influence beyond Paris by means of branches in the provinces.

The march of women to Versailles. Events moved quickly in the fall of 1789. The fear that troops would be used against the Assembly spread in Paris. On October 5 the mob of Paris, principally the women, marched to Versailles to demand the end of hunger and high prices. The national guard, commanded by Lafayette, adopted a tolerant attitude toward the marchers. The mob invaded the palace and threatened the lives of Louis and his queen, Marie Antoinette. They were forced to accompany the mob back to Paris, escorted by the national guard. With them went their little son. As the crowds returned to the city, they chanted that they had "the baker, the baker's wife, and the baker's boy," and soon they would have bread. The historian, Thomas Carlyle, described this event as "the funeral march of the French monarchy." The National Assembly followed the king to Paris, where its deliberations were influenced by the mobs who filled the galleries and applauded or hooted.

The Church is attacked. In order to prevent bankruptcy, the National Assembly confiscated the property of the

The flight of Louis XVI and the royal family was stopped at Varennes. (French Embassy Press & Information Division)

Catholic Church. It promised to support priests, provided they took an oath to accept the "Civil Constitution of the Clergy" (1790). This document, drawn up by Gallican lawyers, provided for the election of priests and bishops by the people. Religious communities were disbanded and the monks and nuns were "liberated" against their wills. Less than half the clergy took the required oath, while the rest remained "non-jurors." The Pope condemned the Civil Constitution of the Clergy and prohibited priests from taking the oath. In the succeeding years, religion fared badly in France.

The National Assembly abolished the hereditary nobility and the *parlements,* overhauled the legal system, introduced juries, and replaced the old system of provinces by eighty-three approximately equal departments. Its principal achievement was the Constitution of 1791, which provided for limited monarchy. Under this system the king could neither make laws nor

levy taxes, but he could delay legislation by means of a suspensive veto and conduct foreign affairs subject to the approval of the legislature. The new constitution reserved the dominant role for a one-house legislature, the Legislative Assembly, consisting of 745 members. It was a completely novel and theoretical system unrelated to the social and political habits and customs of the French people.

The flight of the king. Louis XVI had tried to stem the tide of revolution and now he sought to escape from Paris, call faithful men to his side, and restore order in the country. In June 1791 the royal family fled Paris and attempted to reach the northeast of France, where loyal troops awaited. The king's carriage was stopped at Varennes, just short of freedom, and was brought back to Paris. The king was first suspended and then reinstated. His position was shaky because radicals openly charged him with disloyalty. Many aristocrats made good their escape, pouring into the east of France and to foreign countries, where they mobilized opinion against the revolution.

82. EUROPE VS. THE FRENCH REVOLUTION

Burke's Attack. Europeans and Americans generally rejoiced at the early news of the French Revolution. The leader of the English Whigs, Charles James Fox, exclaimed, "How much the greatest event it is that ever happened in the world, and how much the best!" In the United States, many persons compared it to their own rebellion against George III. But the opinion of many changed as a result of the violence and crimes of the revolutionists. The most effective attack on the revolution was made by Edmund Burke in his *Reflections on the Revolution in France,* published in 1790.

Burke's primary purpose was to warn Englishmen against the principles of the revolutionaries, who were carrying into practice the worst doctrines of the *philosophes.* The British statesman viewed the French Revolution as a threat to all Europe. His argument was that Europe was one society, and if France was degraded, then other countries as well would be affected. Burke predicted that the confusion in France would give rise to a military dictator. The *Reflections* began a pamphlet war in England and America in which one of Burke's main opponents was Thomas Paine, who had left America for England. In later books Burke continued to attack the revolutionists because they destroyed property, morality, religious institutions, and warred upon all that he deemed valuable in European society. Burke was not only a powerful thinker but a writer of great eloquence. His books formed an arsenal of political and moral weapons against all that was evil in the revolution.

The French Legislative Assembly. The Legislative Assembly, elected for two years, met in October 1791 and at once was torn by party differences. The deputies who sat in the upper benches on the left side of the hall constituted the "Mountain" and were the most radical. Their principal support came from the radical clubs, such as the Jacobins and the Cordeliers. The Girondists, so called because their

Edmund Burke

leaders came from the Department of the Gironde, were aggressive and doctrinaire republicans. The "Plain," or center, composed of moderate republicans or lukewarm monarchists, was overwhelmed first by the Girondists and then by the Mountain, which was dominated by Jacobins. The weakest faction in the Legislative Assembly was made up of the "right," or royalists, and rapidly lost strength.

War begins. In August 1791, Emperor Leopold II (brother of the Queen of France, Marie Antoinette) and Frederick William II of Prussia had threatened to interfere in France. The Legislative Assembly reacted indignantly to this and subsequent menacing gestures on the part of these powers. The Girondists, in temporary control of the Legislative Assembly, wished for war because they believed war would bring the overthrow of the monarchy. The emperor and the Prussian king concluded a defensive alliance to meet the French threat. In April 1792, France declared war against Austria.

The Austro-Prussian allies believed that the revolution would be crushed easily. Their commander-in-chief, the Duke of Brunswick, issued a manifesto warning all Frenchmen to lay down their arms or be treated as rebels against Louis XVI. This warning only strengthened the determination of the revolutionists to resist the invaders at all costs and to end the monarchy. Rowdies crowded into the galleries of the Legislative Assembly and filled the deputies with fear. On August 10 the mob attacked the royal palace and massacred the King's Swiss guards. The Assembly suspended and imprisoned the king. In the excitement that followed—aroused by the news that revolutionary armies were falling back —the Legislative Assembly went into the background. Real power went to the Jacobins, who seized control of the government of the city of Paris and terrorized the Assembly. Jacques Danton emerged as the leader. In the "September Massacres" mobs butchered priests, nobles, and other prisoners and launched a house-to-house search for enemies of the revolution. The failure of the revolutionary armies to halt the invasion led the radicals of Paris to take extreme measures. Danton recruited soldiers and urged "audacity" for the salvation of France. On September 20, French revolutionary soldiers turned back the Prussians at Valmy in one of the decisive battles of world history. Enthusiasm for war grew in France and found expression in a marching song of troops from Marseilles, the *Marseillaise,* which became the French national anthem.

From monarchy to republic. A new convention elected by manhood suffrage

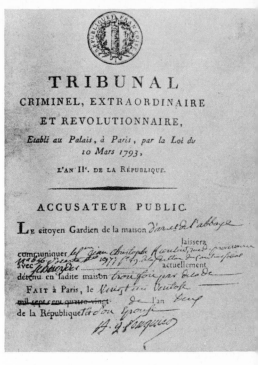

This visiting permit, signed by the warden of the "extraordinary and revolutionary" Criminal Court of the French Republic, allows communication with a prisoner three times every ten years! (Ullstein)

met to draft a republican constitution. It consisted of 749 radical republicans. The Girondists, who had been the "left" in the old Legislative Assembly, now became the right! Three urgent tasks faced the National Convention immediately: to decide the fate of the imprisoned king, to create a provisional government, and to carry on the war.

On September 21, 1792, the Convention cast aside the Constitution of 1791, dethroned Louis XVI, and proclaimed France a republic. Louis XVI was tried and executed by guillotine, a new instrument of death, in January 1793.

This grim and somber event made a profound impression in France and

Europe. Moreover, it had been preceded by the French conquest of Belgium and other military successes for the revolutionists.

The First Allied Coalition. Spain declared war on the French to avenge the killing of Louis XVI. French aggression against the Dutch Republic added that country and Great Britain to the list of states at war with France. Thus a coalition, or alliance, developed that included the emperor, Prussia, the other German states, Great Britain, the Netherlands, Sardinia, and Naples. For a time it seemed that these powers must surely prevail against the French revolutionary government. They were not sufficiently united in purpose and policy, however, to pursue a common aim or strategy. On the other hand, the French mobilized large conscript armies, fought with fanatical fury, and turned their enemies back.

Revolutionary extremes. During 1793–1794 the revolution was carried to its wildest and worst extremes. Foreign danger led the Jacobins to cruel persecution of their opponents and to foster a fanatical patriotism whose aim was not merely the defense of France but the conquest and "conversion" of the enemy to revolutionary principles. The Jacobin brand of patriotism or nationalism possessed the zeal of missionaries in spreading the creed of revolution and rooting out the past. They sought to destroy Christianity and substitute for it a Cult of Reason and a fanatical faith in "the people" as embodied in the nation. In 1793 they crowned an actress as "Goddess of Reason" on the high altar of the Cathedral of Notre Dame. They even adopted a new calendar, in which the creation of the French Republic marked the beginning of a new era and was deemed of greater importance than the birth of Jesus Christ.

Such measures inevitably aroused the wrath of genuinely patriotic and Christian Frenchmen in France. Civil war broke out. Royalists rose in rebellion in the Vendée, Lyons, Marseilles, and Toulon. Besides, the revolutionaries quarreled among themselves. A purge of Girondist deputies left absolute control in the hands of the Jacobins, led by Robespierre, who entrenched themselves in the Committee of Public Safety, which now ruled with dictatorial power.

Robespierre. Maximilien Robespierre had been an influential lawyer in Arras before the revolution. Election as deputy to the Estates-General led him to Paris, and soon he became a leader of the radical Parisian mobs. With the ouster of the Girondists, Robespierre became a dictator in a Reign of Terror, during which almost two thousand persons, including Queen Marie Antoinette and Jacques Danton, lost their lives.

Jealous of his authority and fearful of his ambitions, Robespierre's colleagues worried and plotted. They feared that at any moment he might order them to the guillotine. The common people also detested his dictatorship, which was associated in their minds with the guillotine, scarcity of goods, arbitrary arrests, abolition of gambling, and a religion that offended their religious sense. The conspirators denounced him while he spoke before the Convention. Amid shouts of "Outlaw him!" the Convention ordered the arrest of the dictator and his friends and his execution. The death of Robespierre (July 28, 1794) marked the beginning of the end of the Terror.

Triumph of the French. Enthusiasm and bravery, meanwhile, carried the revolutionary armies from French soil into foreign conquests. Thus the French went from defense to conquest. They believed they could break the encirclement of France only by conquering Europe. The war went badly for the allies. British losses led to strong anti-war sentiment at home. In 1794 the French again overran Belgium and conquered Holland, annexing the first and establishing the revolutionary Batavian Republic in the second. Prussia about the same time withdrew her troops from the front and in the following year dropped out of the Coalition. Saxony, Hanover, and Hesse-Cassel in Germany followed suit. Spain came to terms and surrendered her half of the island of Santo Domingo to France. By the end of 1795 only Austria and Great Britain remained at war with republican France, and even they were ready to consider peace terms. The French revolutionaries had shattered the Coalition.

The discontented of all countries now looked to the French for support and inspiration. The success of French armies was due in part to their sympathetic reception by the credulous people in invaded countries who at first imagined them to be bearers of liberty, equality, and fraternity. Although the causes of discontent varied from country to country, there was a general grumbling against old governments and institutions that did not recognize the natural rights of the people and maintain justice.

Conduct of the allies. Neither their creed nor their fanatical courage, however, can explain the success of the French. Much was due to the foolish or criminal conduct of their enemies. Immediately after the war began in April 1792, Russia had invaded Poland. Both Austria and Prussia had been forced to turn their attention to that country to prevent its being swallowed up by Catharine the Great. In 1793, Russia and Prussia annexed large parts of Poland. Two years later Austria joined them in partitioning what remained of Poland, which thus disappeared from the map of Europe. Such actions were in a sense as revolutionary an attack on the law and public order in Europe as the French themselves had made. Great Britain had shown more zeal in capturing French colonies in the West Indies than in fighting against Jacobinism. Spain discovered that she had more grievances against Britain than against France. All members of the Coalition had followed their own selfish purposes instead of uniting effectively against the revolution. Had they acted differently, the French might easily have been defeated.

REVIEW

STUDY SECTIONS IN REVIEW
80. The Old Regime and the French Monarchy

A. What was the meaning of the "Old Regime"?

B. Identify the three estates or classes of French society under the Old Regime.

C. Mention four factors that had weakened the position of the French monarchy.

D. How did the Age of Enlightenment weaken the Old Regime?

E. What was the economic condition of France in this period?

81. Outbreak of the Revolution

A. Why was it necessary for Louis XVI to convene the Estates-General in 1789?

B. Identify: Abbé Siéyès, National Assembly, Mirabeau, the Bastille.

C. Mention four reforms adopted by the National Assembly in August 1789 to cope with the "Great Fear."

D. Note the significance of the following: women's march on Versailles, Civil Constitution of the Clergy, Constitution of 1791.

82. Europe vs. the French Revolution

A. Identify the following: Jacobins, Girondists, Danton, "September Massacres," battle of Valmy.

B. Why was the first allied coalition unable to crush the French revolutionary government?

C. Describe the purpose and the methods of Jacobin nationalism during 1793–1794.

D. What successes had the French armies achieved by 1795?

THE CHAPTER IN REVIEW

A. Briefly summarize the places of king, aristocracy, and the Third Estate under the Old Regime in France.

B. The decline of the Old Regime by 1789 set the stage for the revolution. What seven reasons are given in the text for this decline?

C. Discuss the importance of the *Declaration of the Rights of Man and of the Citizen.* Were the principles of this document observed during the "Terror"? Explain.

D. Summarize Edmund Burke's objections to the French Revolution as expressed in his *Reflections on the Revolution in France.*

FOR YOUR NOTEBOOK

The Old Regime—France from about 1750 to 1789—has been called both a "tyranny" and an "anarchy." Enter into your notebook a list of reasons for both appellations.

What was accomplished in promoting the French Revolution by each of the following:

> The Events at Versailles of May and June 1789
> Bastille Day in Paris
> The "August Days," or renunciation of social privileges
> The Civil Constitution of the Clergy
> The Constitution of 1791

Robespierre and many other Frenchmen believed that the French Revolution was finished when the Constitution of 1791 was adopted. Enter into your notebook all the reasons you can think of to explain why it continued and went to extremes in the following two years.

SELECTED READINGS

There is a tremendous number of books on the French Revolution. From them the following have been selected as factually sound and most likely to convey the interest and excitement of the times. Leo Gershoy, *The French Revolution* (New York: Henry Holt & Co., 1945), in the Berkshire Series, is an excellent textbook that covers the subject. The historian William Stearns Davis covers the French Revolution in story fashion for young people in *The Whirlwind* (New York: The Macmillan Co., 1929). Interesting insights into the revolution can be obtained from Charles Dickens' famous novel, *A Tale of Two Cities,* which is available in many editions.

Also helpful for understanding the French Revolution are biographies of its leading actors. Some of the most readable and helpful are the following four: Louis R. Gottschalk, *The Youngest General* (New York: Alfred A. Knopf, 1949), on Lafayette; Hilaire Belloc, *Marie Antoinette* (New York: G. P. Putnam's Sons, 1924); Belloc's *Robespierre* (New York: G. P. Putnam's Sons, 1927), and his *Danton, A Study* (New York: G. P. Putnam's Sons, 1928).

Napoleon   Bernadotte

Chapter 28. The Napoleonic Empire

83. THE DIRECTORY AND THE RISE OF NAPOLEON

After the fall of Robespierre, the Committee of Public Safety lost its dictatorial powers. The Convention then completed a new constitution for France. The Constitution of 1795 restricted the vote to property owners and established a two-house legislature consisting of a Council of Ancients and a Council of Five Hundred. A five-man Directory made up the executive.

The Directory, though corrupt, clung to power by suppressing plots of royalists and extreme radicals. It faced grave economic problems, arising largely from a wild inflation of the currency and from war. More conquests were needed, not only to force an end to the war, but to obtain wealth by plunder. Hence a great army was sent into Italy in 1796 to defeat the Austrians and establish French domination of the Italian states. The commander of that army was General Napoleon Bonaparte.

Early life of Bonaparte. Napoleon was born in Corsica in 1769. France had annexed Corsica the year before his birth. Because his father was a petty nobleman, young Napoleon obtained a scholarship to the military academy at Brienne established for the sons of the French nobility. There he was a brilliant student of mathematics and military science. But his poverty, melancholy nature, and his dreams of freeing Corsica from France won him few close friends. Upon his graduation from Brienne, he received a commission in the artillery corps.

The French Revolution opened to

the Corsican patriot an opportunity to play a great part in France. In his youth he had studied the ideas of the Enlightenment and hence was disposed to accept the destruction of the Old Regime. Meanwhile he continued his military career and received thorough training as an officer. He made his mark during the allied siege of the city of Toulon in 1793, forcing the enemy to evacuate French territory. In February 1794 he became a brigadier general at the age of twenty-four! In the following year he achieved national importance when he dispersed a mob attack on the Convention and became commander of the Army of the Interior.

Napoleon's success in Italy. In 1796 and 1797 he won many brilliant victories in Italy. First he crushed the Sardinians, who had to agree to ceding

Bust of Napoleon Bonaparte, by Corbet. (French Embassy Press & Information Division)

Nice and Savoy to France; then he turned on the Austrians, whom he severely defeated.

As a result of his victories, Austria made peace with France in the Treaty of Campo Formio (1797). The emperor abandoned all claim to Belgium, recognized the French absorption of all former imperial lands west of the Rhine, and partitioned with Bonaparte the territories of the Republic of Venice. The treaty left France dominant in Italy and in western Europe.

The Egyptian expedition. Bonaparte returned to France a popular hero. His next assignment was in Egypt, then part of the Ottoman Empire. French writers in the eighteenth century had already excited interest in the land of the Nile. He proposed to take Egypt as a base for an attack on British India. In May 1798, a French expedition sailed from Toulon with thirty-eight thousand troops in four hundred ships, and a Commission of Arts and Sciences of over one hundred and fifty scholars, engineers, and scientists. On the way across the Mediterranean, Bonaparte captured the island of Malta, then in the hands of the Knights of St. John, a military order dating back to the crusades. The French ships slipped by the British fleet of Admiral Horatio Nelson but were sighted after the landing in Egypt. Outside Cairo, in the Battle of the Pyramids, Bonaparte won control of Egypt, but Nelson destroyed the French fleet in the battle of the Nile and thus cut off his communication with France. It was a crippling blow. The Indian state of Mysore, in league with the French, attacked the East

India Company but was defeated. Bonaparte's plans for Indian conquest were dashed. He invaded Syria and plunged into war with the Turks, but his position became hopeless. In August of 1799, Napoleon left his troops in Egypt and slipped through the Mediterranean to return to France.

French defeats in Europe. Then the Directory was facing a political storm because the domestic and military situations had deteriorated. The French had invaded the Papal States and established a satellite republic there, making a political prisoner of Pope Pius VI. Thus the revolution further outraged Europe. The British, moreover, had won other important naval victories in the North Sea and the Atlantic and were besieging Malta. Austria had declared war again on France, so that a new coalition was rising against the revolutionary republic. It consisted of Austria, Britain, Naples, Portugal, Russia, and Turkey. An Austro-Russian force under General Suvorov occupied Milan and Turin in Italy, and French domination of the peninsula had been undone. Americans were waging an unofficial naval war against France.

Napoleon becomes dictator. Conditions were made to order for a strong man of Napoleon's caliber. Every faction in the government courted his support. Finally he sided with a faction in the Directory that wished to strengthen the constitution. The politicians and the general both schemed to use each other for personal ends. With the help of his brother Lucien and other politicians, the thirty-year-old Bonaparte seized power. Soldiers drove out protesting members of the legislature.

Under the new government called the "Consulate" (1799–1804), certain republican institutions were retained in order to mask Bonaparte's absolute dictatorship. Napoleon was made First Consul with a ten-year term, a development accepted by the people of France in a plebiscite.

New French successes. As First Consul, Napoleon took the field against his enemies and recovered control of Italy but agreed to restore the Papal States. Lack of unity doomed the Second Coalition. Russia withdrew from alliance with Austria and Britain. Napoleon defeated the Austrian army in Italy at the battle of Marengo (1800). As a result, Austria signed the Treaty of Lunéville (1801), which confirmed the terms of the Treaty of Campo Formio and recognized France's satellite republics in the Netherlands, Switzerland, and northern Italy. Then France and Britain came to terms in the Treaty of Amiens (1802). Britain agreed to evacuate the Mediterranean islands of Elba, Malta, and Minorca, as well as the French islands in the Caribbean. France was then not only at peace but the dominant power in Europe.

The empire. In 1802, Napoleon became First Consul for life with the powers of an absolute monarch, and two years later became emperor of the French with a hereditary crown. In the Cathedral of Notre Dame he followed the example of Charlemagne by being crowned Emperor Napoleon I in the presence of Pope Pius VII. But the Pope did not crown him; Napoleon did that with his own hands. This step was approved by the French people in another plebiscite. The French had now gone through the full cycle of political development: from absolute monarchy, to limited monarchy, to a democratic republic, and under Napoleon to a democracy enslaved by a dictatorship, to a new monarchy.

A strong government characterized his regime. His dictatorship was based on popular approval as expressed in plebiscites in which all men voted. His government machinery and police spies rooted out internal opposition. The presence of mighty armies made it unlikely that royalists or radicals would rise against him.

Code Napoleon. One of his principal achievements was the codification of French law. Out of the welter of laws, a uniform code emerged, called the Code Napoleon. It swept away remnants of feudalism, recognized the legal equality of all, permitted government a firm control over subjects, and abolished the old guilds and other obstacles to economic freedom of the middle classes. The legal uniformity it brought to France helped unify the country. The Code followed his armies into conquered territories and satellites. The Code forms the basis not only of French civil law but of Italian, Belgian, Dutch, and German law.

Religion. Napoleon valued religion as a political weapon, realizing its importance to stable society. As he said, "Men who do not believe in God— one does not govern them, one shoots them." However, he was hardly a believer himself. He said, "I was Mohammedan in Egypt; I shall be Catholic [in France], for the good of the people."

When he came to power he found religion in a sorry state. Only about half of the priests at the beginning of

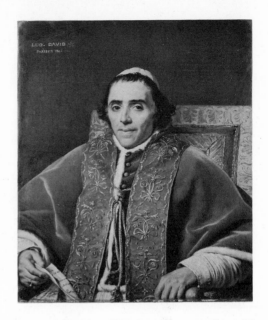

Pope Pius VII signed a concordat with Napoleon to re-establish the Church in France.

the revolution remained ten years later. The rest were dead or had fled for their lives. Catholics were at odds with the radicals and other enemies of the Church.

Concordat with the Church. Napoleon wanted to heal the breach in France between believers and non-believers. Toward this purpose he negotiated a concordat, or treaty, with Pope Pius VII, much against the wishes of anti-clerical generals and politicians. The Concordat of 1801 provided for the nomination of bishops by the French government and their institution by the Pope. The government promised to support the clergy, while the Pope waived the rights of the Church to its lands that had been confiscated during the revolution. Napoleon now appeared to be the protector of Catholic Europe. The Concordat of 1801 remained in force until 1905.

The Battle of Trafalgar, fought on October 21, 1805, assured Britain's naval supremacy and ended Napoleon's power on the sea. This famous British naval victory is attributed to Admiral Nelson, whose strategy was to divide his own fleet and penetrate the Franco-Spanish line in two places, engaging the enemy in two battles simultaneously.

(British Information Services)

84. THE EMPIRE AT ITS ZENITH

With the establishment of peace in 1802, Napoleon dreamed of a new French colonial empire in America, in which Haiti would supply tropical products while Louisiana (returned by Spain to France in 1801) provided wheat. But the French Revolution had already touched off a revolt of the Negroes of Haiti under Toussaint L'Ouverture, the slave grandson of an African king. Napoleon then changed his mind about Louisiana. President Thomas Jefferson of the United States feared French possession of Louisiana and considered making an alliance with Britain to safeguard America's interests. Napoleon decided to sell Louisiana to the United States in order to get needed money and prevent an Anglo-American combination. More important, he realized that he could not hold that vast territory in the event of war, which came again in 1803.

Third Coalition. The Peace of Amiens was only a lull in the struggles between Napoleon and Great Britain. In 1803 they were again at war because of violations of the treaty. By 1805, Austria, Russia, and Sweden were banded together with Britain in the Third Coalition to restore the balance of power and to end French mastery of Europe.

Napoleon had hoped to invade Britain. Success depended on his controlling the English Channel long enough to transport his armies in barges. Franco-Spanish fleets, however, were not able to control the waters off England, and in 1805 Napoleon turned to meet Austrian and Russian armies to the east. The Franco-Spanish naval forces were ordered to the Mediterranean but were caught and destroyed by Admiral Nelson in the battle of Trafalgar (1805) off the coast of Spain. As a result, Bonaparte's naval power was permanently broken.

Napoleonic Empire at its zenith. On land, the emperor of the French was still supreme. In a dazzling display of genius he shattered an Austro-Russian army at Austerlitz (1805). This devel-

The battle of Jena, 1806. Although supported by the Russians, the Prussian army met with defeat at the hands of Napoleon, who advanced to Berlin and occupied Prussia. (Library of Congress)

opment alarmed Prussia, who had collaborated with France since 1795. Prussia now declared war, only to receive a terrible beating on the field of Jena. Napoleon whipped Prussian armies, which had a reputation of being unbeatable since the days of Frederick the Great. The French rubbed salt in Prussian wounds by occupying Prussia as a base of operations against Russia. Napoleon then befriended the Poles and pursued the Russians. His defeat of Czar Alexander I of Russia led not only to a peace settlement but to a Franco-Russian alliance in 1807.

The French Empire was now at its zenith. It had partitioned Europe with Russia, and as long as this alliance endured, Great Britain—which remained steadfastly at war with Napoleon—could do little that was effective. Spain was the ally of France. A new order was established in Germany called the Confederation of the Rhine

under Napoleon's protection. The Holy Roman Empire ceased to exist in 1806, and the emperor had taken the title of Emperor of Austria.

Napoleon's might was imposing. He dominated all of Europe except Russia and the Balkans. His "Grand Empire" consisted of the French Empire (France, Belgium, after 1810 the Dutch Netherlands, and much of Italy) and satellites such as the Confederation of the Rhine, Switzerland, Naples, Spain, and the Polish Duchy of Warsaw. In addition, he counted as allies Austria, Denmark, Prussia, Russia, and Sweden. He used his empire to provide wealth and position for his brothers and relatives. For example, his brother Louis was King of Holland (1806–1810), Jerome became King of Westphalia, and Joseph was first King of Naples and later King of Spain. In order to make his empire hereditary, Napoleon wanted an heir.

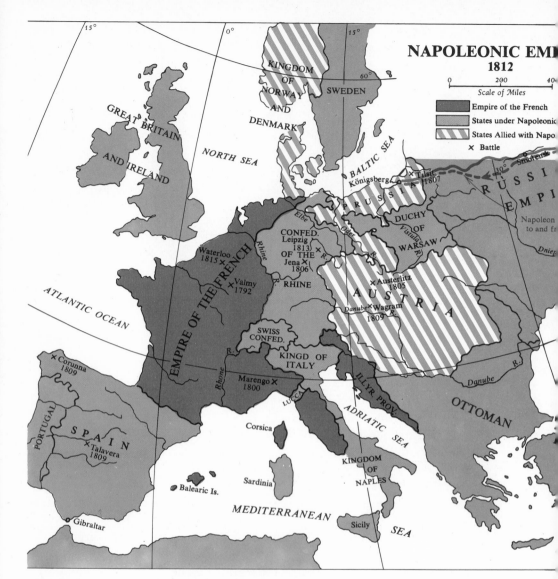

0	200	40

Scale of Miles

Empire of the French
States under Napoleonic
States Allied with Napo.
× Battle

In 1810 he divorced his wife Josephine and married Marie Louise, an Austrian archduchess and niece of former Queen Marie Antoinette.

Napoleonic propaganda. He taught the modern world the power of propaganda by shaping public opinion to serve the needs of the Napoleonic state and to consolidate victories he had won on the battlefield. He talked to Frenchmen directly and personally by means of bulletins and orders of the day, and he marshaled the whole machinery of government to conduct systematic propaganda. In order to bolster confidence in his abilities and in the mission of France, Napoleon encouraged Frenchmen to take pride in their achievements and to glory in belonging to the mightiest nation on earth.

To ensure the loyalty of youth, Napoleon ordered a new catechism with questions about the duties of Catholics toward him. The catechism said that "to honor and serve" the emperor is "to honor and serve God himself." And it answered the question, "Are there not special motives which must attach us more strongly to Napoleon, our emperor?" with this statement:

Yes: for he is the one whom God has given us in difficult times to re-establish the public worship of the holy religion of our fathers and to be the protector of it. He has re-established and maintained public order by his profound and active wisdom; he defends the State with his powerful arm; he has become the Lord's anointed through the consecration which he received from the pontifical Sovereign, head of the universal Church.[1]

Britain stands alone. As Napoleon and the Czar Alexander in alliance dominated Europe, Great Britain refused all peace overtures and with her maritime supremacy continued at war with Napoleon. She could move at will in the waters all around Europe but did not possess the military power to strike an effective blow against her enemy. Napoleon sought to force Britain to come to terms by developing what was called the Continental System: he declared a paper (or theoretical) blockade of Britain and determined to close every European port to British trade. He expected to be obeyed, because Europeans generally resented the high-handed methods of the British navy in destroying the maritime trade of France and her allies. He was not obeyed, because continental peoples needed British goods, and his efforts to enforce his

system drew him on to new acts of tyranny that in the end caused his downfall.

Clash with the Pope. Early in 1808 French troops seized Rome in an attempt to force Pope Pius VII to join the Continental System. A few months later a great uprising of the Spanish people broke out against the usurpation of the throne of Spain by Napoleon's brother, Joseph Bonaparte. This event resounded in the New World, where it sparked the beginning of the revolt of Spanish America against its mother country. Britain came to the aid of the Spanish insurgents, landing an army in Portugal under the command of General Arthur Wellesley, who later was made Duke of Wellington. Napoleon brought large French forces into Spain and continued to hold the main positions there, but he was never able wholly to stamp out the revolt or to dislodge the British from the Iberian Peninsula. While guerrilla war raged in Spain, Austria in 1809 struck for the liberation of Germany from French control, and Britain sent an army to attack the French in Holland. Napoleon again completely defeated these powers, but to secure himself went on to new outrages. He forced a treaty of the utmost severity on Austria and annexed the Papal States to France. For this the Pope excommunicated him. In savage retaliation, Napoleon made the Pope a state prisoner of the French government.

The empire undermined. From 1809 to 1812, Napoleon's empire appeared all-powerful, but the forces that would overthrow it were working steadily. The British navy systematically de-

---

[1] Quoted in Robert Holtman, *Napoleonic Propaganda* (Baton Rouge: Louisiana State University Press, 1950), p. 141.

The passage of the Grand Army across the Berezina River. Napoleon arrived at Moscow to find the city devastated and his supplies overextended. The retreat from Russia began on October 19, 1812. Now only a fifth of its original strength, the army crossed the Berezina at a terrible sacrifice, after which Napoleon's retreat became a race with starvation and the cold. (French Embassy Press & Information Division)

stroyed all its overseas trade and nibbled at territorial positions in the Mediterranean, notably in the Ionian Isles. The Spanish guerrillas remained active, and the anger of subject peoples grew ever greater. Moreover, Franco-Russian relations went from good to bad and then from bad to worse. These two mighty powers could not agree on a common policy in the Ottoman Empire, with which Russia had been engaged in war since 1806. The Czar wished to have Constantinople; Napoleon would not agree. The Russians, moreover, found no advantage but only disadvantage in maintaining the Continental System. Napoleon at length resolved to impose his will on Russia and prepared to attack her. The Czar made peace with the Turks in 1812 and braced his forces for the impending invasion.

85. THE DOWNFALL OF NAPOLEON

Invasion of Russia. In June 1812, Napoleon led an army of six hundred thousand men—the greatest army the world had yet known—into Russia. It was French, German, Italian, and Polish in composition. The kingdom of Prussia and the empire of Austria were whipped into line as allies, although they would rather have been against Napoleon than with him.

The Russians refused to give battle and retreated eastward in a "defense in depth." As they retreated across the vastness of Russia, they burned and destroyed whatever the invaders could use. Apparent success thus greeted Napoleon at first. Smolensk fell. But difficulties multiplied. Heavy rains at the beginning of July and unbearable heat in August slowed down the invaders. Finally the Russians made a stand at Borodino and were defeated. Moscow lay open. But the capture of Moscow by the Grand Army was no triumphal entry, for the Russians had set the city afire and deserted it.

Retreat from Moscow. Napoleon soon had no choice but to return to Smolensk, where he hoped to reprovision his troops. His hopes were disappointed: there were no supplies in Smolensk. The only course was retreat. Hounded by "Generals" November and December (the temperature fell to 30 degrees below zero) and by fierce Russian attacks, the remnants of the once-proud Grand Army staggered back to Europe with less than one hundred thousand. Austria withdrew into neutrality, and Prussia switched to an alliance with Russia.

Britain and America at war. The French emperor had suffered a colossal military disaster, but he was not at the end of his resources. He still held control of most of Germany, all Italy, and his armies had chased the Duke of Wellington out of Spain into Portugal as the march on Russia had begun. Moreover, his major enemy, Britain, had been seriously embarrassed by the outbreak of war with the United States in June 1812. The main cause of that war had been the British navy's activity against the French: restricting the freedom of the seas, halting American ships and impressing alleged British sailors into the Royal Navy. In going to war against Great Britain, the United States was in no sense allied with Napoleon, but its action may well have encouraged him.

Battle of the Nations. Napoleon gathered new troops to meet the Russo-Prussian forces, which soon were joined by the Austrians, and fought the great Battle of the Nations at Leipzig in October 1813. Overwhelming defeat sent the French in flight across the Rhine as German patriots rose to hasten the downfall of a tyrannical and alien rule over their country.

The Chaumont Alliance. The next decisive step was for the allies to invade France. Some of them were reluctant to do this lest they arouse a French resistance like that of 1792. At length, however, they moved into eastern France, while the Duke of Wellington effected the liberation of Spain and entered France from the south. Napoleon fought some of his most brilliant maneuvers to repel the invasion, but the allies were too much for him. They united in a four-power pact (Austria, Prussia, Russia, and Great Britain) in March 1814, at Chaumont, in eastern France. This was the first time during the whole revolutionary and Napoleonic era that these four powers were simultaneously joined together in war against France.

Allied victory. Marching on Paris, they found the French people exhausted and almost indifferent. French political and military energies were at a low ebb after nearly a quarter century of revolution and war. The allies were not vindictive; they sought peace rather than revenge on France. They took the advice of Prince Talleyrand, who had been a Catholic bishop before the revolution and had served in several political offices under the Directory, the Consulate, and the Empire.

Restoration of the French monarchy. Talleyrand was sure that the French people would agree to the restoration of their monarchy under the Bourbon dynasty and the ending of all revolutionary politics. To this the allies assented, and Louis XVI's brother returned to rule as Louis XVIII.[2] A generous peace was made with

---

[2] The young son of Louis XVI had died in prison years earlier. The dynasty recognized him, however, as Louis XVII, but he never ruled.

France, and allied troops were quickly evacuated. The victors were even generous to Napoleon after his surrender at Fontainebleau, near Paris. He was exiled to the island of Elba off the coast of Italy, where he was to be a hereditary ruler confined to a tiny country and lacking, as a British wit said, "Elba-room."

The role of Czar Alexander I. The major military burden in the last war against Napoleon had been borne by the Russians, and their Czar was the hero of the hour in the spring of 1814. There was something dramatic and heroic about him. His country had suffered a terrible invasion and then harried the enemy back to western Europe. The Czar was the first of the victorious sovereigns to arrive at Paris. He seemed to take the lead in making all the great decisions at the end of the war. He was handsome, dashing, and young. He appeared wise and generous, devoted to peace and to good principles of government. He would play a great part in the resettlement of Europe.

End of the Anglo-American war. The Americans, meanwhile, had not been very successful in their war against Great Britain. They had tried and failed to take Canada, and the British invaded the Chesapeake region and burned Washington. By the end of 1814 both nations desired peace and signed a treaty at Ghent.

The Napoleonic age in world history. It would be difficult to exaggerate the impact of Napoleon and his wars on world history. In Germany his rule aroused a new nationalism that was to have revolutionary consequences of great dimensions. He stirred British energies to develop new technological devices, to establish a maritime supremacy that was not seriously challenged for nearly a century. In Italy, where he was more popular than in France, Napoleon stirred hopes and desires for national unification. His use of Spain as an ally, and the campaigns of his army in that country, largely ruined it and provoked the revolt of its colonies in America. His tyranny and appetite for power taught

The storming of Fort Oswego on Lake Ontario in North America on May 6, 1814. Because of its strategic position, the fortifications of Oswego were much contested in the colonial wars. (The Metropolitan Museum of Art)

Europe anew the necessity of preserving a balance of power among the nations. Having established a strong centralized state in France, he spread that kind of government wide over Europe. It continued to exist and to grow after he was no more. To some extent he conferred great benefits on Europe. Wherever he conquered, he abolished serfdom. As a soldier he was unequaled, and military schools and academies for generations were to study his battles, his tactics and strategy.

He had always professed to be the Son of the Revolution and the continuator of it. He arose from Jacobin politics and considered himself a democrat, even though he was an emperor. By seeking to level all men before himself, he promoted social equality.

REVIEW

STUDY SECTIONS IN REVIEW

83. The Directory and the Rise of Napoleon

A. Describe the legislature and the executive established by the French Constiution of 1795.

B. Cite three military victories that established Napoleon as a popular hero.

C. Cite five reforms introduced in France by Napoleon.

D. What was Napoleon's policy toward religion?

84. The Empire at Its Zenith

A. Why did Napoleon abandon his hopes of an American empire?

B. Identify: Third Coalition, Trafalgar, Austerlitz, Jena.

C. What was the extent of the Napoleonic empire in 1810?

D. What were the purposes and the results of the "Continental System"?

85. The Downfall of Napoleon

A. What defensive tactics were used by the Russians against Napoleon's invasion?

B. What caused the War of 1812 between Britain and the United States? How did this aid Napoleon?

C. Which nations entered into the Chaumont Alliance?

D. What were the results of the allied victory over Napoleon?

E. Identify: Talleyrand, Czar Alexander I, Treaty of Ghent.

THE CHAPTER IN REVIEW

A. In a paragraph summarize Napoleon's achievements in the following fields: military science, law, education, propaganda.

B. Cite at least six influences that Napoleon's wars exerted on world history.

C. Explain the following statement by identifying the stages: "When Napoleon was crowned emperor, France completed the cycle: from absolute monarchy to limited monarchy, to a republic, to a dictatorship, to a new imperial monarchy."

FOR YOUR NOTEBOOK

The sorry state of affairs in France under the Directory made Napoleon an even greater hero for his exploits abroad. In parallel columns trace the domestic history of the Directory and Napoleon's accomplishments as a general abroad. To do this, you will have to use one of the standard college histories of the French Revolution and Napoleonic Empire, which you can find in almost any library.

Read the sketch of Napoleon in any encyclopedia. Then list in your notebook his qualifications as a military and a political leader.

Use your reference materials in the library to see what tactics Napoleon employed to win his astounding victories. If your search of standard reference materials does not give you sufficient material, consult Hilaire Belloc's or one of the other lives of Napoleon.

Napoleon's accomplishments as an administrator have been more lasting than his military exploits. In your notebook summarize the religious, social, political, and legal settlement he bequeathed to France.

The Napoleonic Empire collapsed quickly. Enter into your notebook the reasons for this collapse. Be sure to list more than the obvious military reasons, such as the failure of the invasion of Russia.

SELECTED READINGS

An excellent book on the material of this chapter is James M. Thompson, *Napoleon Bonaparte* (New York: Oxford University Press, 1952). A smaller and somewhat livelier account is Hilaire Belloc, *Napoleon* (Philadelphia: J. B. Lippincott Co., 1932). Alfred Hoyt Bill has done a study for young people on Napoleon's downfall, *The Clutch of the Corsican* (Boston: Little, Brown & Co., 1925). Even more exciting is Eugene Tarlé's *Napoleon's Invasion of Russia, 1812* (New York: Oxford University Press, 1942).

Biographies of other important persons in this period will help the student understand its developments. Among these, the following are most helpful and interesting: Crane Brinton, *The Lives of Talleyrand* (New York: W. W. Norton & Co., 1936); Philip Guedalla, *The Duke* (London: Hodder & Stoughton, Ltd., 1931), a biography of Wellington.

CHRONOLOGICAL REVIEW

1714 Hanoverian dynasty begins in Britain
Farenheit's thermometer
1715 Louis XV of France (to 1774)
1719 *Defoe's* ROBINSON CRUSOE
1733 War of Polish Succession (to 1738)
Kay invents flying shuttle
1735 Russia and Austria fight Turkey
1739 War of Jenkins' Ear
1740 Frederick the Great in Prussia; War of Austrian Succession (to 1748)
Captain Bering discovers Alaska
1748 Treaty of Aix-la-Chapelle
Montesquieu publishes THE SPIRIT OF THE LAWS
1752 *Franklin's kite experiment*
1756 Seven Years' War (to 1763)
1759 British defeat French in Canada
1760 George III of Great Britain (to 1820)
1762 Catharine the Great rules Russia (to 1796)
Rousseau publishes EMILE *and* THE SOCIAL CONTRACT
1768 Russo-Turk War
Explorations of Cook in Australia
1772 First partition of Poland
1773 *Suppression of the Society of Jesus*
1774 Louis XVI of France (to 1793); 1st Continental Congress
Priestley discovers oxygen

1776 United States declares independence
Adam Smith publishes WEALTH OF NATIONS
1778 Franco-American alliance
Death of Rousseau and Voltaire
1780 *Galvani's discoveries in electricity*
1789 Washington becomes President of U.S.; French Revolution begins
1790 Civil Constitution of the Clergy
Burke's REFLECTIONS; *Goethe's* FAUST
1793 Reign of Terror in France; 1st Coalition; 2nd partition of Poland
Whitney invents cotton gin
1799 Napoleon seizes power in France
1803 Jefferson buys Louisiana
1804 Napoleon becomes French emperor
Death of Kant; Code Napoleon
1806 Napoleon ends Holy Roman Empire
1807 *Fulton's steamboat* Clermont *(N. Y. to Albany); slave trade abolished in British Empire*
1812 War of 1812 between Britain and France; Napoleon's invasion of Russia
1814 Napoleon defeated at Leipzig and is exiled; restoration of Louis XVIII
Stephenson adapts steam engine to railroad; Scott's WAVERLY
1815 The Hundred Days in France; Napoleon's defeat at Waterloo

1. Mecklenburg   6. Württemberg   11. Lucca
2. Holstein   7. Baden   12. Tuscany
3. Oldenburg   8. Luxembourg   13. Lombardy
4. Hanover   9. Parma   14. Venetia
5. Saxony   10. Modena

━━━ German Confederation

UNIT NINE
Nationalism and Liberalism

The Restoration in Europe and the Treaty of Vienna · Forces of Reform and Revolt ·
Upheaval in Europe in the 1830's · The United States, the British Colonies, and Latin
America · Romanticism · Revival of Religion · Industrial and Agricultural
"Revolutions" · Results of Changes in Industry and Agriculture · Outbreak of
Revolution in Europe, 1848 · Failure of Revolutions in Italy and Central Europe ·
Crimean War and the Unification of Italy

Metternich

Chapter 29. Restoration, Reaction, and Revolt

86. THE RESTORATION IN EUROPE AND THE TREATY OF VIENNA

The period following the defeat of Napoleon is called the Restoration. The old rulers were restored to the thrones from which they had fled in terror, or been deposed, years before. Some of them tried to resume their old ways and to blot from memory what had happened since their exile. Victor Emmanuel I, King of Sardinia, for example, re-entered his capital city of Turin in the same old-fashioned clothes he had worn when he had escaped the revolution, and even destroyed gardens planted by the French conquerors during his exile. Yet in general the basic aim of the rulers was not to restore the abuses of the Old Regime, but its good features, such as orderly government and an interna-

tional system that would prevent one country from overwhelming the others.

The Napoleonic wars left the peoples of Europe weary and disillusioned. Many were broken in spirit by the failure of their hopes to create a new order of freedom by means of revolutionary principles, which had brought instead only war and sorrow. There was a universal yearning for peace. Yet it was a difficult task to restore national and international order. First, the great powers had to establish safeguards against any future French aggression and restore the balance of power. Through the Treaty of Chaumont, Austria, Britain, Prussia, and Russia had agreed to unite to prevent further French aggression and to safeguard the peace settlement they were about to make. Second, the great powers had to cope with the problem of the mighty Czar Alexander I of Russia, who had grown strong in the war against Napoleon and wanted to keep Poland and Finland.

The powers gather at Vienna. When the great powers sent their representatives to the Congress of Vienna, they realized that satisfactory solutions could not be reached on all issues and that little could be done to change certain steps already taken. Thus the allies had promised to cede Norway (hitherto Danish) to Sweden as the price for Swedish aid against Napoleon in 1812. Certain other important decisions were made.

Francis I, Emperor of Austria, was host to the leaders of Europe who flocked to Vienna. Among the many present, four men possessed commanding voices—Alexander I, Viscount Castlereagh for Britain, King Frederick William III of Prussia, and Prince Metternich of Austria.

Louis XVIII was restored to the throne of France in 1814 by the allies after their entry into Paris and the abdication of Napoleon. (Alinari)

Metternich. The last-named was perhaps the most remarkable, and he was to bulk large in European history for the next thirty years. Born in 1773 of a noble family prominent in the Austrian government, Metternich had gained much experience in various diplomatic posts. He was an intelligent and uncompromising enemy of the principles of the French Revolution, which he feared had not been destroyed by the downfall of Napoleon. What Europe needed, he reasoned, was a long period of peace so that people could recover from the unsettling effects of war and revolution. Like Castlereagh, Metternich stressed the importance of co-operation among the allies. Only if they remained alert and united, he warned, could peace be preserved.

Poland and Saxony. The two thorny problems of Poland and Saxony illustrated the difficulties in the problems facing the statesmen at the Congress of Vienna. The Czar had already occupied the larger part of Poland with a large army and wished to be recognized as King of Poland. But Russian domination of all Poland threatened central Europe and the balance of power, to the alarm of Austria and Prussia. At first the Czar was supported by the King of Prussia, who in turn had received Russian support for his annexing Saxony. Castlereagh, Metternich, and many German princes were alarmed at the possibility of a Prussian-Russian combination that would threaten peace in eastern Europe. The wrangling among the allies provided Talleyrand, who represented France, with an opportunity to exploit their differences to French advantage. In exchange for his support of Austria and Britain, Talleyrand received a main voice in the negotiations. The opposition of the great powers forced Czar Alexander to compromise.

Return of Napoleon: Waterloo. The spirit of compromise among the allies was encouraged by the return of Napoleon to France. Believing that the French were dissatisfied with the regime of Louis XVIII and that the allies were quarreling at Vienna, Napoleon fled Elba and governed France from March to June 1815 (the "Hundred Days"). But the odds were against him. His hopes were crushed on the battlefield at Waterloo in Belgium. With his armies shattered and the morale of the people crushed, Napoleon surrendered to the British, who exiled him to the lonely isle of St. Helena in the South Atlantic. He remained there with a few devoted followers until his death in 1821.

Before the Hundred Days, the allies had given the French lenient peace terms on the ground that the French themselves had been wronged by "General" Bonaparte, who was not the rightful ruler. But in the second Treaty of Paris in 1815, the allies were harsher. France was reduced to her 1790 boundaries, was required to support an army of occupation until an indemnity was paid, and to restore works of art carried away from other countries by French troops.

The Vienna Treaty. By June 1815 a comprehensive treaty for the resettlement of all parts of Europe disturbed by the French Revolution was signed by the diplomats at Vienna. The main outlines of the Vienna treaty remained the basis of European political and international affairs until World War I, though parts of it would be materially modified during those intervening years. The treaty embodied the principles of balance of power, legitimacy, and compensation.

First, the treaty restored the balance of power, which had been overturned by the French revolutionaries and Napoleon. The allies tried to make it impossible for France to become a threat again. A barrier was thrown up by strengthening the neighbors of France. Holland received Belgium (then known as the Austrian Netherlands) and received her rich colony of Java back from Britain. Prussia acquired all the German territories on the left, or west, bank of the Rhine, in addition to some Polish and Saxon territories. In the south, the Kingdom of Sardinia was strengthened by the cession of Nice, Savoy, and Genoa. And the Swiss Confederation gained three new cantons, or provinces.

Second, the treaty opened the way to

The surrender of Napoleon Bonaparte to the British at Waterloo, the last action of the Napoleonic Wars. His hopes had lain in attacking the enemy, which was gathering on the eastern front, before they could attack him. (Giraudon)

The Congress of Vienna (1814–1815) met to reconstruct Europe after the fall of Napoleon Bonaparte. Metternich (standing in the foreground) was the Austrian negotiator and presided over the Congress. (Ullstein)

restoring a number of monarchs who were in power before the French Revolution. However, the pre-war political map could not be fully restored. Germany was reorganized in a confederation consisting of thirty-eight states (but dominated by Austria and Prussia) with headquarters at Frankfurt. With Austrian princes seated on the thrones of Modena, Parma, and Tuscany, Austria was the dominant power in Italy as a result of her recovery of Lombardy and Venetia (to compensate her for giving up Belgium to Holland and Rhine territories to Prussia).

Lastly, the principle of compensation meant that the powers who had made great sacrifices to defeat Napoleon deserved rewards. Thus Russia acquired Finland and most of Poland, while Sweden received Norway. Britain enlarged her colonial empire by the ac-quisition from Denmark of the island of Heligoland in the North Sea, Malta, and a protectorate over the Ionian Islands in the Mediterranean, Cape Colony in South Africa, the islands of Ceylon and Mauritius in the Indian Ocean, and the islands of Santa Lucia, Tobago, and Trinidad in the Caribbean.

The Holy Alliance and the Concert of Europe. Now that a European settlement had been made, the powers determined to prevent further French aggression, to maintain the treaties of Vienna, and to preserve order against Jacobin democrats and nationalists who threatened it. Toward these ends, two efforts had already been considered during the Congress—the Holy Alliance and the Quadruple Alliance. The Holy Alliance was the brain child of Alexander I, who asked the rulers of Europe to pledge to follow Christian principles in domestic and foreign affairs. In deference to the mighty Czar, all Europe's rulers (except the Pope, the sultan, the British regent,[1] and the president of the Swiss Confederation) signed the Holy Alliance. Although they considered the Holy Alliance a noble gesture, many statesmen realized that it was a potential tool for Russian imperialism. Since the sultan as a Mohammedan could not subscribe to Christian principles, the Czar could isolate him and interfere in the Ottoman Empire without fearing European intervention. Then, too, these statesmen saw that the Holy Alliance mixed the religious and political spheres in circumstances that would injure both. It is little wonder that the Pope refused to join. At any rate, the Holy Alliance became a weapon in the hands of the Czar and his fellow monarchs to stifle the growth of liberty and national freedom.

In November 1815 the Quadruple Alliance (often confused with the Holy Alliance) was formed by Austria, Britain, Prussia, and Russia in order to maintain the second Treaty of Paris. In effect, the four principal signatories of the Vienna settlement formed an international body to preserve peace against "the revolution." The periodical meetings of these four powers to discuss matters of general European concern were called the "Concert of Europe."

Alexander I, Czar of Russia, claimed that he was "inspired" to convert Europe to the true Christian faith. The Holy Alliance was the product of his religious zeal.

87. FORCES OF REFORM AND REVOLT

To conservatives, the revolution stood for the guillotine, an attack on Christianity, aggressive wars, and general ruin. And they believed that in their own day liberalism, democracy, and nationalism embodied the revolution. A great part of the history of Europe following the Congress of Vienna is the story of the conflict between these political forces and the forces of European conservatism. Before proceeding it is necessary to examine the meaning of liberalism, democracy, and nationalism. Liberalism stressed the liberty of the individual and democracy the rule of the people, while nationalism meant the freedom of nations to establish independent governments.

Liberalism and democracy. Liberals were fervent admirers of liberty. They be-

---

[1] The later George IV, who at this time was regent, George III being insane.

lieved that only free men could govern and control themselves. Consequently, in such matters as voting and the conduct of business, they demanded the removal of abuses and privileges, that restricted the freedom of individuals. Many varieties and degrees of liberalism existed. In politics, some liberals favored British-type parliaments and governments elected and dominated by the middle classes; these liberals were not democrats, for they opposed extending the vote to men without property. In economics, liberalism meant for many a policy of *laissez-faire,* a hands-off attitude on the part of government that would ensure equality of opportunity for every businessman to advance as far as his abilities and resources carried him against his competitors. Now many European liberals, especially French, Italian, and Spanish reformers, went much farther than British reformers. Drawing their inspiration from the Encyclopedists and Rousseau, these continental liberals believed in "progress," the doctrine that man is naturally good and could achieve indefinite improvement if he used scientific knowledge and industry. And, more important, they believed that man was self-sufficient, that he had no standard outside or above himself. In their view, the enemies of progress and reason were restrictions on individual liberty imposed by Church or state. Hence they demanded the right of absolute freedom of thought, conscience, speech, and press. Most of these liberals wished to deprive kings, aristocrats, and priests of their power, prestige, and position.

There was also, however, a Christian liberalism inspired by a love of liberty under law and a hatred of despotic or arbitrary government. Christian liberals respected the dignity of human nature and saw that good morality and freedom were inevitably linked. They knew that good government implied restraints on power and organs of representation. Conservatives often opposed the views of Christian liberals, not from dislike of them, but from fear that they might weaken the power of government to such an extent that the door would be opened to democratic and nationalist revolution.

Democracy in Europe in the age of the Restoration meant the arbitrary government of "the people," which in practice appeared to lead to dictatorship or mob rule. Democracy was understood to be nothing other than the French Revolution, with all that it implied in the looting of property and attack on the Church. Not until democracy was united with the rule of law could it become a tolerable and even good kind of government.

Nations and nationalities. The word *nation* has a variety of meanings. As it was used in the Gospels ("teach ye all the nations"), it meant a tribe or group of people possessing similar race and language. Its meaning changed in the course of centuries until it meant an independent country. In the nineteenth century, the word *nation* signified a people who shared all or most of the following characteristics: a certain geographical area, common race and language, similar religion and traditions. To avoid confusion, the word *nationality* was substituted for nation as it was used in the last meaning. An eminent historian has defined nationality as "a group of people who

The Sorbonne, first endowed college in the University of Paris, which, after the French Revolution, was the seat of the faculties of theology and of the Académie de Paris.

speak either the same language or closely related dialects, who cherish common historical traditions, and who constitute or think they constitute a distinct cultural society." [2] This definition of nationality omits political independence. Many nationalities in Europe in the early nineteenth century hoped for independent or united political existence. These latter nationalities have been termed "oppressed" or "subject nationalities." The great historic states and empires—the Austrian, British, Russian, and Turkish—

were shaken by the stirrings of the nationalities within their boundaries. In the Austrian Empire, for example, Croats, Czechs, Italians, Magyars, Poles, Slovenes, etc., and the dominant German nationality were held together only by their common allegiance to the Hapsburg emperor. An awakening of nationality occurred, and many nationalities strove to free themselves. To justify their struggle for independence, subject nationalities appealed to the "principle of nationalities": the idea that a nationality had the moral right to free itself from alien governors and to establish a national state.

Nationalism. Perhaps the most important "ism" of the nineteenth century was nationalism. It was the exaggerated and emotional devotion to the combination of nationality and patriotism. Nationalism implies that the ultimate duty and loyalty of every person are to his nationality—whether the nationality has already become or hopes to become a national state—and its special mission or role in history. The welfare and interests of the nationality come before all other persons and institutions.

Nationality and patriotism are as old as Europe, but their union in nationalism was born of the French Revolution. That is why nationalism was associated in the minds of the Vienna statesmen with another "French idea," democracy. The French Revolution furnished nationalism with the belief that the people were the source of law and that all nations had the right to govern themselves.

Napoleon encouraged national feel-

[2] Carlton J. H. Hayes, *Essays on Nationalism* (New York: The Macmillan Co., 1937), pp. 6–7.

ing not only in France but everywhere in Europe. In Italy, Napoleon was greeted as a liberator who wiped away local jealousies and proclaimed the kingdom of Italy. But his aggressions turned other nationalities—Germans, Portuguese, Russians, and Spaniards— against him and provoked national resistance. Nationalism also grew in the nineteenth century as a result of the writings of Fichte, Herder, and Humboldt in Germany, Mickiewicz in Poland, and Alfieri, Foscolo, and Mazzini in Italy—to choose only a few examples. The study of national customs, legends, history, language, music, and art filled many Europeans with a sense of pride in their nationalities.

Repression of popular movements. The rulers of Europe sought to repress popular movements that threatened to upset peace. Metternich established a system of spying on liberals and nationalists and then ruthlessly suppressing them. Even in Great Britain, where the tradition of personal liberty was established, harsh measures curtailed the freedom of the person. In spite of repression, liberals, democrats, and nationalists fought back, especially in Germany, where the press and the universities demanded political freedom. National disturbances in Belgium, Lombardy-Venetia, Poland, and Ireland convinced many statesmen that the "revolution" was again rearing its ugly head.

A wave of popular disorders, which occurred from 1817 to 1820, met a strong wall of repression. In England, unemployment and political unrest led Tory statemen to suspend the writ of habeas corpus, to censor the press,

and forbid the possession of firearms. In 1819, political agitation in the German states culminated in the murder of Kotzebue, a friend and agent of Czar Alexander of Russia. Meanwhile, in southern Europe, repression only increased demands for constitutional government and freedom of press and speech. Ferdinand VII, King of Spain, was compelled to grant a constitution, while the regent of Portugal was overturned in favor of John VI (recently returned from Brazil), who granted a constitution. In Naples, the agitation of secret societies, such as the Carbonari (literally "charcoal burners"), compelled King Ferdinand I to confer a constitution. But Ferdinand appealed to Metternich for assistance against the Carbonari, and in turn, Metternich convened the Concert of Europe at Troppau.

Ferdinand VII, King of Spain, was forced to grant a liberal constitution after a revolution by the Carbonari. (Library of Congress)

At Troppau the problem of the revolts in Naples and Spain were discussed. The Czar—by now purged of any liberal tendencies and convinced of the need to repress revolution—volunteered to send his armies across Europe to suppress popular movements. But Metternich and his colleagues felt that Europe would be safer if Alexander's Cossacks remained behind the Russian frontier. Hence the statesmen persuaded the Czar not to aid the King of Spain against his rebellious subjects.

Austrian and French interventions. While Metternich blocked Russian intervention in Spain, he desired Austrian intervention to suppress the Neapolitan revolt. Italy was vital to Austria. Hence when the Concert of Europe met again at Laibach, Metternich asked for European approval of Austrian intervention in Naples. He justified this intervention on the grounds that an internal disturbance that had international effects could be suppressed by another country. Moreover, in 1815 Austria had made a treaty with the King of Naples which gave her a right to intervene for such a cause. Over the objections of Britain, Austrian troops marched into Naples in 1821 and re-established autocratic government. Metternich also crushed a similar revolt in Piedmont.

Maintaining that the Vienna treaties were endangered by a host of new and old problems, the Concert of Europe in 1822 met at Verona in Italy. Three issues stood out: the democratic revolt in Spain, the revolution of the Spanish colonies in the New World, and the rebellion of the Greeks against the Turks. France was eager to intervene on behalf of King Ferdinand VII of Spain against his revolutionary subjects. Her aim was to regain military and international prestige. Over British objections, the great powers permitted French intervention to suppress revolution. A French army crossed the Pyrenees and restored Ferdinand VII. Britain opposed the use of force in the domestic concerns of another country and feared French domination of Spain. In her view, intervention was justified only if the clear danger existed that war would follow an internal revolution.

The Greek Revolution. In Greece, nationalism was on the rampage. Although the modern Greek differed in race and culture from the Athenian and Spartan of old, he readily identified himself with his illustrious ancestors. He was filled with pride in their achievements and was chagrined that the Greek people were under Turkish rule. In 1821 the Greeks revolted. Enthusiasm for Greek nationalism was shared by many persons throughout the world. They had studied and loved the Greek classics and they now concluded that the modern Greek was fighting for the freedom the ancient Greeks cherished. Some persons, including Lord Byron, the famous poet, rushed to enlist in the Greek rebel forces.[3]

Striving to suppress the Greek revolt, the Turks employed excessive

---

[3] Even Americans were affected by "Greek fever" and sympathized with the victims of Turkish terror (the cruel Turks, Americans were told, gathered Greek ears by the bushel!). Some persons wished the government to intervene on behalf of the Greeks.

cruelty. Their hanging of the Patriarch of Constantinople in public shocked the Christian world. Savage warfare damaged British trade and aroused French crusading zeal against the Turks. The great powers failed to unite on a policy. Meanwhile, Mohammed Ali of Egypt agreed to help the sultan. After the conquest of Crete (1822–1824) by the Egyptians, and threatened with other defeats, the Greeks in 1827 appealed to the great powers of Europe. Russia proposed aiding the rebels but was opposed by Austria and Prussia, who argued that the Greeks were setting an example for other suppressed nationalities to follow. But Britain and France agreed to join naval forces with Russia in order to head off Egyptian interference. Finally, in 1829, the Greeks won their independence, and in 1832 Greece was recognized as a sovereign kingdom.

Nicholas I of Russia used the motto "Orthodoxy, autocracy, and national unity" in bringing the administration, the press, and universities under rigid control. (Ullstein)

88. UPHEAVAL IN EUROPE IN THE 1830'S

The conservatives had tried but had failed to halt the growth of reform and revolutionary forces. In the years immediately following the defeat of Napoleon, they could rely on the fear of war among the people to repress popular movements that threatened peace. But as the memories of the horror and destruction of the French wars became fainter, liberalism, democracy, and nationalism (which had been discredited with the revolution) rallied.

In dealing with their enemies, two courses were open to European statesmen. They could either repress them, as Alexander I and then his successor, Nicholas I, did in Russia by erasing personal liberty; or they could satisfy some of their demands by a step-by-step correction of specific abuses. The second path was followed in England. It was easier to deal with reformers in England than it was on the Continent, because British liberals did not demand the overthrow of all social and political institutions.

Parliamentary reforms of 1832. Demands for the reform of the House of Commons pointed to "rotten" and "pocket" boroughs. Rotten boroughs were generally small towns or villages with sparse populations that nevertheless retained the right to return members to Parliament. Old Sarum, for example, was an open field with no inhabitants, yet was entitled to send two members to the House of Commons, the same number assigned to crowded Westminster in metropolitan

The Reform Bill of 1832 as it was presented in the House of Lords. (Hulton Picture Library)

London. A pocket borough was the property of a great landlord who could therefore select the representative for it.[4] The "unreformed" House of Commons represented property rather than persons. Less than two hundred landlords or royal ministers appointed more than half the membership. The economic and social changes that were transforming the face of Great Britain, altering the distribution of the population, and magnifying the power of the middle classes made the basis of representation in the House of Commons obsolete. The center of population shifted away from southern England to the new northern towns, such as Leeds, Manchester, and Sheffield, which were not represented. At the same time, manufacturers and merchants demanded a voice in the

_____
[4] Certain other boroughs were controlled by the government.

government and agitated for the reform of the rotten and pocket boroughs. The Whigs, who came to power in 1830, were prepared to sponsor this reform but were confronted with stiff opposition. Only when the king and such persons as the Duke of Wellington concluded that the rejection of the Whig Reform Bill might cause a revolt as had occurred in Paris in 1830 were the abuses of the electoral system corrected in 1832.

The Reform Act of 1832 abolished most of the rotten boroughs by redistributing seats in the House of Commons with a view to providing for representation for new towns such as Birmingham and Manchester. Second, the act increased the number of voters from approximately five hundred thousand to about eight hundred thousand (but as yet only one out of eight persons could vote). This benefited the upper middle classes. Although the landed classes now shared their influence with the middle classes, they still retained considerable power in elections and in Parliament.

Other reform measures. The Reform Act broke down resistance to change, and statesmen soon turned to other reforms. Slavery was abolished in 1833, and about eight hundred thousand Negroes throughout the British Empire were made free. In the same year some of the worst abuses of the factory system were corrected; in 1834 the care of the poor was reformed, and in 1835 town government was modernized. But more important than any of these changes was the influence the Reform Act exerted in Europe and the British colonies. European reformers hastened to imitate the

Factory scene in England employing child labor, from Life and Adventures of Michael Armstrong, the Factory Boy, *by Frances Trollope. (Hulton Picture Library)*

English system of government, which permitted the acceptance of liberal reform without revolution. For British colonies the Act was a favorable sign that self-government would be expanded throughout the empire.

French Revolution of 1830. French liberals and republicans, who took their inspiration from the revolution, had sought to establish or promote a new order based on individual liberty. They were opposed by conservatives who stood for the preservation of a stable system like that which existed before 1789. The government of France during the Restoration failed to satisfy either group. When Louis XVIII died in 1824, the crown passed to his reactionary brother, Charles X, whose ministers were hostilely received by liberals. These liberals were daily growing stronger. Under Charles X, France asserted herself again as a great power and took the first step toward conquering Algiers. At home his policy of strengthening monarchy and improving the position of the nobility and the clergy was climaxed by the Ordinances of July 1830. These attacked the freedom of the press and the system of voting and representation. The July Ordinances really overturned the constitutional system and struck at a growing liberalism.

The people of Paris rose almost immediately against the king. Charles X abdicated and fled. The problem of forming a new government divided the rebels. Republicans, supported by students, secret political societies, and the mob, opposed monarchy. On the other hand, liberals, led by Adolph Thiers, wished to preserve monarchy because they realized that the great powers of Europe would never tolerate another French republic. The two parties almost came to blows. But General Lafayette (famous in the American Revolution) used his influence to reach a compromise: a liberal king with popular institutions. Louis Philippe, Duke of Orleans—of a branch of the royal family that had sided with the French Revolution—was chosen as "King of the French." The revolutionary red, white, and blue tricolor replaced the Bourbon flag. The main idea of the "July Revolution" was to establish a government clearly modeled on the British government, which was widely admired as a balance of liberty and authority.

Belgian independence. The French revolt exerted an immediate effect on

Louis Philippe, favored by the discontented upper bourgeoisie and finding approval of Lafayette, who commanded the national guard, was chosen as "King of the French." His reign was known as the July Monarchy, which favored the wealthy bourgeoisie and the business class and lacked understanding of the poor conditions of the workers. (Alinari)

Belgium. In August 1830, French-speaking Belgians fought for their independence from the Dutch. Dutch rule was hateful to Catholic and democratic groups alike. Belgians resented Dutch Protestant slights to the Catholic Church, the supremacy of the Dutch language and of Dutch officials in the government. When they drove off the Dutch, the King of the Netherlands appealed to the Concert of Europe to restore him in Belgium, but the great powers did not intervene. France openly sided with the Belgians, and Britain objected to foreign intervention that might start a European war. Although Prussia and Russia wished to intervene, they were prevented from doing so by a Polish revolt against Russia. This probably saved both Belgium and France from being invaded by the Czar's armies. The great powers met in London in 1831 and recognized the independence of Belgium, which chose Leopold of Saxe-Coburg as king. He was related to the British royal family. The great powers recognized the neutrality of Belgium in 1839.

Russia and Poland. The Polish rebellion mentioned above broke out when infantry cadets feared that Polish troops would be employed to crush revolts in France and Belgium. The army revolted and the Polish parliament dethroned the Czar as King of Poland (the November Insurrection). Although supported by French and British sympathy, Polish valor was unequal to the task of defeating the Czar's mighty armies. In 1831, Warsaw was captured and the Polish cause failed. The "Congress Kingdom" was abolished and became a mere Russian province.

Revolts in Germany and Italy. Elsewhere in Europe riots and demonstrations of liberals and democrats forced princes to grant constitutions in the German states of Brunswick, Hanover, Hesse-Cassel, and Saxony. In Italy revolts occurred in Modena and Parma (expelling Hapsburg rulers from their thrones) and in the Papal States, where the revolutionists repudiated the rule of the Pope. Austrian armies crushed the Italian revolts.

On the whole, the revolutions in

western Europe were liberal triumphs. Belgium and France boasted parliamentary governments and freedom for the individual, and Britain had secured her constitution by reforms. Belgium, Britain, and France were limited monarchies, where personal rights were respected and members of the middle classes participated in government. Liberal agitation in 1830 did not, however, achieve similar changes in southern, central, and eastern Europe.

Europe divided. The Concert of Europe was split now into two groups: liberal France and Great Britain vs. the autocratic powers of Russia, Austria, and Prussia. Louis Philippe's France supported the Belgians and encouraged the Poles. Austria, Prussia, and Russia wondered how far France might go in challenging the old order. They were apprehensive of Paris as a European capital of revolution. Political refugees —German, Italian, and Polish nationalists and liberal students and professors from many lands—flocked to Paris because they felt a sense of solidarity and security.

89. THE UNITED STATES, THE BRITISH COLONIES, AND LATIN AMERICA

Viewing America's abundant and fertile lands and the political and social system that respected liberty and encouraged equality, Europeans saw a promised land. Three thousand miles separating America from the Old World convinced many Americans that they could lead their lives heedless of the struggles they or their ancestors had left behind in Europe.

The growth of the American population was striking. When the century opened, the United States numbered only five million. Large families and heavy immigration swelled population from twenty to thirty-six per cent every ten years. The lure of good farmland, personal liberty, and favorable opportunities attracted thousands of settlers from the British Isles. Political oppression and poverty—aggravated by great depressions in 1837 and 1847—brought Europeans to the northeastern states and the bustling cities of Boston, New York, Philadelphia, and Baltimore.

Expansion of the United States. Americans began to settle the lands beyond the Appalachian Mountains in greater numbers after the War of 1812. Settlement was so rapid that by 1820 one-fourth of the population lived beyond the mountains. The purchase of the Louisiana Territory from France in 1803 had provided the new nation with ample room for expansion, in addition to control of the Mississippi

The building of the railroads across the Great Plains began in the 1840's and spurred on the settlement of the Midwest. The railroads encouraged homesteading by selling land along their routes at low prices. (The New-York Historical Society)

The storming of Chapultepec by the Americans under General John Quitman. This great fortress was one of the strong points defending the Mexican capital. The victorious Americans proceeded to Mexico City, where they remained until peace was restored. (Library of Congress)

and New Orleans. In 1812 the United States annexed West Florida and in 1819 East Florida—both formerly Spanish. New states filled the vast area between the Appalachians and the Mississippi, so that by 1837 twice as many states were in the Union as in 1790. Up to this time westward expansion was accomplished without serious friction among Americans. Once admitted to the Federal Union, the new state enjoyed all the privileges of the older ones.

The United States wished to add the Oregon Territory. Spain had transferred to the United States her rights to the area. But both Britain and the United States wished to settle the rich Northwest, which included present-day Washington, Oregon, Idaho, and parts of British Columbia, Montana, and Wyoming. In the 1840's, Americans believed in "manifest destiny," that the United States was destined to expand from sea to sea through an empty continent. Manifest destiny

supported the pleas of American settlers in Oregon for the annexation of the Northwest to the American Republic.

The Mexican War. American expansionists set their eyes also on Texas. When American settlers in Texas defied Mexican authorities and in 1836 established the Lone Star Republic, Americans rejoiced. Although Britain and France tried to prevent Texas from going to the United States, they failed to prevent annexation in 1845. A dispute over the southern boundary of Texas led to the invasion of Mexico. Victory in the Mexican War (1846–1848) won for the United States Arizona, California, New Mexico, and other territories, an area exceeding that of France and Germany. In settling the West, Americans did not meet many powerful neighbors. Britain and European countries were dismayed at the gains of the United States but did not interfere. Rivalry among the great powers almost ensured a free hand for Americans in westward settlement.

The British colonies. The white colonies of Britain also advanced in population and self-government. A steady flow of immigrants, from the end of the Napoleonic wars to 1837, swelled the populations of Canada, South Africa, and Australia. In that period about four hundred thousand left the British Isles as a result of working conditions that were bad in England, worse in Scotland, and unspeakably hard in Ireland. Britain controlled her colonists less rigidly than she had before the American Revolution. The existence of the United States was a daily reminder that, unless Britain governed her subjects wisely, they might follow the American example of rebellion. This cautious attitude toward the colonists was encouraged by the movement for political reform in Britain, which led them to expect some self-government in the near future.

Canadian development. Canada had been British since 1763. The loss of the thirteen American colonies made Canada more important to the British. Thousands of British loyalists—clergymen, lawyers, and merchants—fled from the United States to Canada. These people, however, cherished the traditions of self-government and personal liberty.

French Canadians also were discontented and rebelled in 1837. The revolt led to the appointment of a commission under Lord Durham to investigate Canadian conditions. The Durham Report, called by some the Magna Carta of the "second" British Empire, recommended the introduction of considerable self-government in British North America. Durham suggested that British (Upper) and French (Lower) Canada be joined in order to give the English element control and thus prevent the French population from falling under the influence of the United States. The Canada Reunion Act of 1840 carried out some of Durham's ideas.

South Africa and Australia. Cape Colony in South Africa fell to Britain as a result of the Vienna treaties. The area south of the Zambezi River, possessing a temperate climate, was settled by Dutch farmers, the Boers. These courageous Boers were conservative by instinct and wished to preserve their own liberties and beliefs. Proud of their Dutch and Protestant heritage, they were antagonized by Britain's decision to make English the official language of South Africa. They left

One of Australia's many penal colonies was established at Port Arthur on the island of Tasmania. The British took possession of the island in 1803 for convict settlement. (Australian News & Information Bureau)

the British colony in the "Greak Trek" of 1835–1837 and established the independent Orange Free State and the Transvaal to the north.

Australia assumed importance when the loss of the American colonies deprived Britain of colonies to receive convicted criminals. Although Australia was regarded at first as a colony of convicts, it soon attracted other immigrants. Large areas were opened for sheep grazing from 1810 to 1820, and efforts were intensified to attract more settlers. The expansion of the population and the area of Australia led in 1850 to the granting of self-government. Missionaries first called attention to the possibilities of settlement in New Zealand, and its development paralleled that of Australia. A private expedition of British settlers forced the hand of the British colonial office to annex the islands in 1840.

Latin American Independence. Spanish colonies of Central and South America had rebelled against the mother country in 1808. Many Spanish Americans were influenced by eighteenth-century philosophers; they admired the ideals of liberty, natural rights, equality before law for all men, and popular government denied to them in the Spanish colonial system. The example of free America to the north made the Spanish colonists envious. Contact with the English-speaking world was maintained by visits to the United States of Simón Bolívar, Francisco Miranda, and other leaders, and by illegal trade with England and America. Spanish colonists felt they could count on the help of English-speaking peoples if they sought independence. The immediate occasion of rebellion

James Monroe, fifth President of the United States, met the threat of European encroachments in the New World with the Monroe Doctrine. (Library of Congress)

was the invasion of Spain in 1808 by Napoleon. When Napoleon created his brother King of Spain, he stirred up Spaniards not only at home but also in Spanish America. The return of the Spanish Bourbon king, Ferdinand VII, after the defeat of Napoleon, did not restore the pre-war situation. The colonists had tasted freedom and refused to submit to a royal rule that would deny it to them.

A civil war was fought in Latin America. The rebels were opposed by a third of the population, including many influential persons, who remained loyal to Spain. The rebels prevailed because of the courage, perseverance, and genius of leaders such as Bolívar, O'Higgins, Páez, San Martín, and Sucre. They were aided by foreign soldiers and sailors, especially by the British admiral Lord Cochrane, by English loans, and moneys paid as custom duties by British and American merchants.

The Monroe Doctrine. Britain and the United States gave the Spanish colonists diplomatic support. Britain extended commercial relations but delayed political recognition. Her hope was that independent kingdoms instead of republics would emerge from the confused political picture in Latin America. Meanwhile the balance of power and trade dictated the British policy of preventing the Holy Alliance from interfering with the New World. Toward this purpose, George Canning, the foreign secretary, invited President Monroe of the United States to co-operate. President Monroe refused to join in a warning to the European powers unless Britain first recognized the independence of the new countries of Latin America. Advised by his secretary of state, John Quincy Adams, he issued the "Monroe Doctrine," in which he bravely warned the Old World that the Western Hemisphere was no longer open for colonization and that the two worlds must remain separate.

Simón Bolívar. One of the greatest figures in South America, Simón Bolívar worked toward the establishment of a small number of strong countries linked in a federation. Although he succeeded in bringing together areas that now include Bolivia, Colombia, Ecuador, Peru, and Venezuela, his "Great Colombia" fell apart. Bolívar believed that Latin Americans were not ready to govern themselves. "An ignorant people is a blunt instrument for its own destruction," he said. He recommended, therefore, a strong government as a

Simón Bolívar, liberator and elected president of Greater Columbia, organized the government of Peru and created Bolivia. (Library of Congress)

compromise between a republic and a monarchy. Liberals opposed strong government and forced his retirement, which opened the dykes to a flood of anarchy and war in northern South America.

Dictatorships. After the Wars of Independence, the new Latin-American republics suffered from chronic political disorders, dictatorships, and foreign intervention. Latin Americans[5] were unprepared for self-government, having been accustomed to obey the Spanish king as children obey their

---

[5] Spanish-blooded (or Creole) persons constituted one-fifth of the population, Indians one-half, Indian-white mixtures (mestizos) one-third, Negroes, mulattoes, and Indian-Negro combinations the remainder.

father. Spain could scarcely have prepared them for popular government when she did not possess it herself. Despite the absence of a political tradition of self-government, some Latin-American statesmen deluded themselves that good laws and a worthy constitution copied from the United States or Britain would produce stable politics and enable the people to govern themselves. These statesmen wrote constitutions that were excellent on paper but did not meet the needs and experience of the people. When these constitutions proved unworkable, strong men (*caudillos*) found loopholes in the laws and seized power.

Geographical conditions retarded political development. High mountains, deserts, and jungles isolated the population centers. The absence of easy access to their own countrymen bred local jealousy and destroyed national unity. The central government often exercised little authority in outlying regions, where local strong men reigned supreme. What was true of domestic life was characteristic of international affairs. Central America, for example, was a federal republic from 1824 to 1839; but local jealousies and dictators dissolved it into the republics of Costa Rica, El Salvador, Guatemala, Honduras, and Nicaragua. Furthermore, economic conditions provided shaky foundations for stable government. Poverty was widespread. Lack of capital prevented Latin-American republics from exploiting their natural resources. Trade and industry were dominated by foreign capitalists and were hindered by unskilled labor, poor communications, and unsteady politics.

LATIN AMERICA
AFTER THE WARS
FOR INDEPENDENCE

0   200 400   800
Scale of Miles

United Provinces of Central America
Portuguese territory
Spanish territory

REVIEW

STUDY SECTIONS IN REVIEW

86. The Restoration in Europe and the Treaty of Vienna

A. Mention the basic purposes of the great powers during the Restoration.

B. Identify: Congress of Vienna, Czar Alexander I, Metternich, Talleyrand.

C. What was the significance of the Vienna Treaty of 1815?

D. Distinguish between the Holy Alliance and the Quadruple Alliance.

87. Forces of Reform and Revolt

A. Mention three basic principles of the liberalism of this period.

B. Identify: nation, nationality, nationalism.

C. What was the reaction of the great powers to the rise of liberalism and nationalism?

D. Cite three instances of liberal or nationalistic revolt during this period.

88. Upheaval in Europe in the 1830's

A. What two courses of action were used by European rulers in dealing with the forces of reform or revolt?

B. Cite four specific reforms introduced into Great Britain.

C. Note three areas of Europe that followed France into revolution after 1830.

D. What division within the Concert of Europe appeared after 1830?

89. The United States, the British Colonies, and Latin America.

A. Why did large numbers of Europeans emigrate to the United States?

B. Name four areas added to the territory of the United States by 1848.

C. Identify: the Durham Report, the Boers, Simón Bolívar.

D. What was the significance of the Monroe Doctrine?

E. List three reasons why Latin-American republics experienced difficulty with self-government.

THE CHAPTER IN REVIEW

A. What lesson was learned by the British as a result of the American Revolution? How did this affect their treatment of Canada?

B. Explain how the Vienna Treaty of 1815 put into practice the principles of "balance of power, legitimacy, and compensation."

C. What caused the revolution in France in 1830?

D. Discuss the causes and general results of the widespread revolutions of 1830.

FOR YOUR NOTEBOOK

Imagine yourself a diplomat-at-large at the Congress of Vienna. List the problems you think confront you and the Congress in securing a lasting peace. Put down your ideas on how each problem should be settled. Then put down the actual settlement made by the Congress of Vienna on each problem.

Write down the various ideas you believe can be put under each of the following terms: liberalism, democracy, nationalism. Now read through the text again and look up each term in one of the standard encyclopedias to find what other ideas you should put down.

Devise a diagram running from "reaction" to "revolution," and then trace the process of events in Britain and France to contrast developments in the two countries.

To keep track of the way events move in this period, prepare four parallel columns for France, Britain, the United States, and Latin America, and enter the principal happenings in each column.

SELECTED READINGS

A very good study of the Congress of Vienna is Harold Nicolson, *The Congress of Vienna: A Study in Allied Unity* (New York: Harcourt, Brace & Co., 1946). Insight into the politics of the period can be obtained from two excellent biographies of Metternich and Czar Alexander I: Algernon Cecil, *Metternich, 1773–1859: A Study of His Period and Personality* (London: Spottiswoode, Ballantyne & Co., 1933); and L. I. Strakhovsky, *Alexander I of Russia* (New York: W. W. Norton & Co., 1947).

The flavor of the age in England is well portrayed in Charles Dickens' *Oliver Twist,* which is available in many editions. For the Catholic revival in this part of the century, Albert Paul Schimberg, *The Great Friend: Frederick Ozanam* (Milwaukee, Wis.: The Bruce Publishing Co., 1946).

Chapter 30. Cultural, Religious, and Economic Trends

90. ROMANTICISM

Before the French Revolution, many persons were sure that science and reason alone could produce an era of peace, progress, and prosperity. If reason were only followed, they argued, ignorance and misery would be banished from the face of the earth. To many minds the French Revolution was the acid test of the value of such "enlightened" ideas. The occurrence of the Reign of Terror, the dictatorship of Napoleon, and world war disillusioned many thinkers about the Enlightenment. Critics blamed it for what had gone wrong and for poisoning the European mind. Many turned away from the ideals of the eighteenth century, especially from its exaggerated confidence in reason; they stressed the importance of feeling and sentiment,

faith and tradition, personality and nationality.

Meaning of the word. This new way of thinking, feeling, and acting is usually called *romanticism*. That word derives from a certain kind of literature in the Middle Ages—tales and ballads of love, chivalry, and heroism. It was now used generally to characterize the new and widely prevalent spirit of the early nineteenth century. Romanticism had a great variety of forms, but mainly it was a reaction against what was called *classicism*, which had been culturally dominant in the seventeenth and eighteenth centuries. Classicism was an exaggerated and almost slavish following of the patterns of literature, art, and architecture that were drawn from the models of ancient Greek and Roman culture. The Renaissance, it will be recalled, had been marked by a revived interest in classical antiquity, and in the age of classicism the ideas from classical studies had hardened into rigid forms dominating literature and art. This cultural rigidity had been reinforced by the court life of the eighteenth century, so that manners, attitudes, and even ways of dressing had become standardized. Classicism and rationalism were closely related, for the classical writers most widely read were calm, reasonable men whose souls had never been touched by mysticism.

The "Romantic Revolt." Romanticism was a bursting through these old rules and standards, and an affirmation of the values of sentiment, imagination, folkways (against court ways), of movement against rigidity, of revolution against authority. The way had been prepared for the "Romantic Revolt" in the eighteenth century, when some writers had ignored classical standards and sought inspiration in natural scenery, folk customs, and primitive peoples. Thus the English poet Thomas Gray sang of the "simple annals of the poor," and the Scottish bard Robert Burns wrote of the common man and the commonplace. The German writer Johann Herder urged the study of folk literature and customs and sought to discover national "souls." Perhaps the strongest single influence for romanticism had been Rousseau. He praised the value of the imagination and feeling in literature, and noted the importance of primitive peoples in the "natural state" who were "uncorrupted" by the conventions and rules of civilized society. Both the liberal-democratic and romantic movements were inspired

William Wordsworth and Lord Byron, two of the most representative English Romantic poets. Their temperaments were quite different—Wordsworth being sensitive to the beauties of nature and Byron reflecting his stormy and revolutionary character in his satirical poetry. (National Portrait Gallery, London; British Information Services)

by Rousseau; both involved rebellion against the authority of precedent and the past.

The romantic movement took many forms. The romantics discarded not only the classical rule of meter and rhyme in poetry and the "unities" of time, place, and action in drama, but also the frills, knee breeches, and wigs of eighteenth-century costume. In music, for example, Ludwig van Beethoven turned away from the formal rules of musical composition and adopted original rhythms, tones, and melody. Composers of opera rejected classical models and took their themes from a variety of subjects in history or the lives of the common people.

Romantics stressed the dignity and integrity of the individual. Every man, they believed, had the right to develop his potentialities. The American poet and thinker, Ralph Waldo Emerson, advocated self-reliance and self-respect for the individual. Neither church nor state nor any agent of human society, in his view, had the right to infringe personal rights, unless the individual interfered with the rights of others. His fellow New Englander, Henry Thoreau, went farther by maintaining that society had no right to restrict the individual, and spent several years in the woods.

The romantics charged that the Enlightenment had placed excessive emphasis on reason and intelligence to the detriment of feeling and sentiment. They believed that in the eighteenth century human experience had been explained too narrowly in terms of reason to the neglect of the human heart. Romantic artists and writers prized faith, sentiment, and emotion.

They took their cue from Rousseau, who opened his heart to his readers. Franz Schubert and Felix Mendelssohn and other composers wrote music that expressed their inner thoughts and feelings. Romantics also took delight in the fantastic, the exotic, and the imaginative.

Nature idealized. Romantic artists and writers were inspired by nature in its varied aspects—majestic mountains, rolling seas, placid lakes and countryside, or delicate flowers. Romantics rejected the eighteenth-century conception of nature as a vast machine that obeyed definite physical laws in favor of the idea that nature is a living force in which men and women live and take their source.

Romanticism and the past. Another characteristic of romanticism was love of the past. Again this was a reaction to the eighteenth-century thinkers and the French Revolution, which had swept away traditions and age-honored institutions. In preparing for a new society and mobilizing for war, the French revolutionaries ran roughshod over human affection for old institutions. Influenced by Edmund Burke and Joseph de Maistre, romantics considered tradition natural to man and harmonious with liberty. The novels of Sir Walter Scott (*Ivanhoe, Kenilworth, The Talisman,* etc.), with their setting in English and Scottish history, enjoyed European popularity. The Italian writer Alessandro Manzoni used seventeenth-century Italy as the setting for his famous novel, *The Betrothed.* In similar manner, composers selected historical themes for operas. Thus Gioacchino Rossini based his opera *William Tell* on the deeds of the legendary Swiss hero.

In architecture, the medieval Gothic style was revived.

The romantic love of the past stimulated the rediscovery of past cultures and the study of history. Interest in common folk and ordinary things led to the study and praise of folk legends, folk customs, and folk music. In turn, this contributed to nationalist history. Many writers described with feeling the history of their own country, especially the medieval period. In Germany, Baron vom Stein sponsored the collection and publication of source materials for the history of medieval Germany. The study of history was encouraged by the conviction of many romantics that in order to understand any idea, ideal, or institution (e.g., liberty, the French nation, etc.) it was necessary to study its gradual growth or history.

Romanticism and revolution. Many romantics were discontented with the real world and desired to change it. Hence they were at odds with the established order. In their anxiety to free the individual from restrictions, many romantics (such as Samuel Coleridge and William Wordsworth) greeted the French revolution enthusiastically. Its excesses, however, led them to welcome the Restoration and turn their backs on reform. But by 1830 many of them forsook monarchy and the Church and agitated for reform. The career of the great French writer, Victor Hugo, illustrates this. From a staunch defender of the old order, Hugo became its enemy. For him romanticism was "liberalism in literature." Younger writers sought to identify their literary aspirations with new and sometimes revolutionary movements. The British poets,

Lord Byron and Percy Shelley, denounced authority and went into open rebellion. The romantic writers urged respect for and recognition of individual rights and the common people. They attacked censorship.

91. REVIVAL OF RELIGION

Christianity had been attacked in word and deed by "enlightened" writers and by French revolutionaries. They attacked all revealed religion as superstition and ignorance that created a "priest-ridden" society. In place of traditional Christianity, some eighteenth-century writers recommended deism, a "natural" religion honoring a supreme being who had created the universe and then left it alone. The French revolutionaries confiscated Church lands and persecuted priests. Deism and persecution brought in its train religious indifference and the corruption of morals.

The reaction to the atheistic rationalism and the French Revolution was accompanied by a revival of faith. A quarter century of war and revolution profoundly affected European souls. The atrocities, battle casualties, and confiscation of properties revived in many a sense of the reality of sin. Romantic writers turned to religion as a source of inspiration, while conservative statesmen depended on religion to help them preserve order. They recalled Edmund Burke's dictum that "religion is the basis of civil society."

Both Protestant churches and the Catholic Church were affected by the religious revival. Among Protestants the revival took the form of Pietism in

Joseph de Maistre, most powerful literary enemy of eighteenth-century rationalism, advocated that the world should be ruled by the Pope as the spiritual ruler. (Giraudon)

Germany and Methodism in the British Isles. Both directed attention to the problem of personal salvation and to the religion of the heart. John Wesley, the eighteenth-century founder of Methodism, had stressed a "virtuous heart, producing a virtuous life."

The Catholic revival. The revival became apparent in the pontificate of Pius VII (1800–1823), whose sufferings at the hands of Napoleon evoked sympathy of Christians everywhere. The revival was heralded by an important book, *Genius of Christianity,* by René de Chateaubriand. He maintained that Christianity created European culture and cradled art and learning. Chateaubriand emphasized the unity of the Church and the rule of the Pope. Another influential writer, Joseph de Maistre, advocated the return of Europe to obedience to the Pope:

There is no public morality or national character without religion, no European religion without Christianity, no Christianity without Catholicism, no Catholicism without the Pope, no Pope without the supremacy which belongs to him.

Those who shared Maistre's ideas that Catholics ought to accept papal guidance and leadership in all things were called *ultramontanes,* persons who looked beyond the Alps to Rome.

Catholic liberalism. One group of ultramontanes looked to Rome to save the Church in France from bondage to the state. Led by the Abbé de Lamennais, these Catholics sought to combine ultramontanism and liberalism in France, where the Church had traditionally sided with authority. Lamennais was influenced by faith in the natural goodness of man and the revolutionary ideals of liberty, equality, and fraternity. He urged the Church to ally herself with the people and thus safeguard liberty against the menace of the state. His program included separation of Church and state, freedom of education from state control, freedom of press and association, extension of the vote and of local liberties. In his view, the Church would always prevail in a free society because truth always triumphed. He was supported to a certain extent by a great Dominican preacher, Henri Lacordaire, and by the Count of Montalembert in France, and by many influential Italians. However, Pope Gregory XVI disapproved Lamennais' extreme views, which seemed to regard the state as evil. Moreover, the Pope held that freedom of conscience had been misinterpreted to mean that one belief was as good as another, all being a matter of personal choice.

Catholicism in Great Britain. The fortunes of the Catholic Church improved in Great Britain. A long persecution dating from the days of Queen Elizabeth I had placed on the statute books a series of laws designed to outlaw Catholicism and deprive Catholics of normal civil, political, and religious rights. Mass was forbidden. A priest caught saying Mass might receive life imprisonment. Catholics could neither vote for nor sit in Parliament. The legal, medical, and military professions were closed to them. They could neither attend non-Catholic schools nor maintain their own schools and seminaries. Their property was taxed heavily. Only the lax enforcement of the penal code saved Catholics from extinction. While Catholics formed only a small minority in England and Scotland, they constituted the bulk of the population of Ireland.

The spirit of persecution had declined in the eighteenth century. Toleration had then been extended to Catholics. Although they were permitted the exercise of their religion, they were not yet allowed to serve the state. During the French Revolution, English public opinion regretted the anti-religious campaign of the French revolutionaries and sympathized with thousands of French priests and nobles who fled to England for safety. In 1791 full legal security was given to Catholic rites and to priests who took a loyalty oath. Catholics were admitted to the legal profession, but they could not yet sit in or vote for the House of Commons.

In Ireland the French Revolution resulted in the growth of a pro-French party, the United Irishmen, which sought to unite Protestants and Catholics in an Irish republic free of English control. In order to offset the influence of the United Irishmen, the British-controlled Irish government gave the vote to Irish Catholics and also removed some other disabilities. As in England, toleration for Ireland was not accompanied by full equality for Catholics. High positions in government, the armed forces, and the legal profession were still monopolized by the "Protestant Ascendancy."

Catholic Emancipation. The Irish refused to accept the status of second-class citizens. In 1823 the Catholic Association was formed to conduct propaganda and to weld the Irish Catholics together. The association threw its influence behind Daniel O'Connell, who was elected to Parliament in 1828, despite the fact that no Catholic was eligible. The English government was startled at the demonstrated strength of the Catholic Association. It faced the alternatives of changing the laws to enable O'Connell to take his seat in the House of Commons or risking civil war in Ireland. Under the leadership of the Duke of Wellington the British govern-

Daniel O'Connell, Irish political leader. Before his election to the House of Commons, which forced Parliament to change its laws, Catholics were excluded from Parliament by inability to take the oath of office.

ment grudgingly passed the Catholic Emancipation Bill in 1829. But the British then discriminated against Irish Catholics by raising voting requirements, which reduced the electorate from two hundred thousand to twenty-six thousand.

The Church in Ireland and the English-speaking world was affected by Maynooth College, founded in 1795 to prepare Irish youths for the priesthood. Before the foundation of Maynooth, Irish seminarians studied in France or Spain, but the outbreak of the French revolutionary wars interrupted this practice. Under these circumstances the British government extended financial support to Maynooth. Thousands of Maynooth-trained priests served in Ireland, England, and the British overseas possessions.

John Henry Newman. The growth of the Catholic Church in England was aided by the Oxford Movement, originated by John Henry Newman and other young scholars of Oxford University in order to inject new life and enthusiasm into the Anglican Church. The Oxford scholars insisted on the spiritual independence of the Anglican Church and on its sharing the rich religious heritage of the Catholic Church before the Protestant Revolt. Studies in Catholic history and dogma led Newman to conversion to Catholicism. The conversion of a man as influential as Newman in turn moved others to follow him. The addition of Newman and his followers enhanced the prestige of the Church in England and for the first time in modern history enabled Catholics to influence British public opinion. About thirty years later Newman was made a cardinal.

Although the restoration of English Catholic bishops in 1850 provoked bitter attacks on Catholicism, by 1851 England had one million Catholics, an increase of a hundred per cent in ten years. Under the direction of Cardinal Wiseman and then Cardinal Manning, the Church prospered. The progress of the Church was aided also by Irish immigrants. To escape poverty and persecution at home, thousands of Irish families flocked to the new English and Scottish cities and swarmed across the seas to the United States, Australia, and other British possessions, carrying with them their traditional faith.

The Church demonstrated immense vitality throughout Europe. New religious orders and congregations were formed, many of them teaching brotherhoods or congregations of women. Lay groups were established to work among the poor and the underprivileged in the cities. Thus the Society of St. Vincent de Paul was founded in 1833 by Frederick Ozanam. The growing vitality of the Church was mirrored in the conversion of many prominent scholars and writers.

John Henry Cardinal Newman

92. INDUSTRIAL AND AGRICULTURAL "REVOLUTIONS"

James Watt, Scottish inventor, invented a new type of engine. The watt, a unit of power, was named after him. (British Information Services)

In the early nineteenth century most people still lived very much as their ancestors had. Farm and village were the center of life, just as they had been hundreds of years before. Although towns and cities grew, and trade dealt more and more in articles of general use such as tea and tobacco, these economic developments did not really change the tempo of life. Most people still spent their whole lives where they were born. For the most part, they supplied their own food and clothing or bought them from neighbors, who produced the goods by hand. Restrictions on freedom of travel and trade, coupled with poor roads, discouraged movement of persons and products.

Beneath the surface, however, the old way of life was slowly being altered, so that by the middle of the nineteenth century Europe had changed. First, there was a demand for more goods and services. People's minds were turned from the idea that this world is a vale of tears and a preparation for the world to come. Instead they were encouraged to look for happiness, comfort, and liberty to sweeten life on earth rather than look for rewards only in the next life. Second, the steady growth of population[1] increased markets and the labor force. This growth in numbers was due to a decline in the death rate caused by improved sanitation and care for newborn babies and mothers. Last, the rise of modern science taught

men basic mechanical principles and methods of making precise measurements. Scientific experiments required accurate instruments. The skill and technical knowledge acquired in the production of instruments enabled inventors to transform an idea for a machine into a working model. Thus James Watt (1736–1819), an instrument maker for a Scottish university, possessed the technical skill to invent the modern steam engine in 1765.

The machine. The changes in the ways men and women earned their living constitute the industrial and agricultural revolutions. The symbol of change is the machine. Men perfected machines to do jobs they had formerly done by hand or with the aid of simple tools and animals. Machines enabled people to do what had been impossible earlier: to produce huge quantities of steel and textiles, and to travel long distances quickly.

Now some machines were used long before the nineteenth century. The

---

[1] The population of Europe increased from 140 million in 1750 to 266 million by the middle of the nineteenth century.

The spinning frame, built by Samuel Slater in Pawtucket, Rhode Island, in 1790. Spinning, once a household industry, went into the factory with the invention of the spinning frame, which was powered at first by horses, then by steam. Samuel Slater was an American pioneer in the cotton textile industry, becoming prosperous by establishing mills throughout New England. (Smithsonian Institution)

clock, the windmill, the blast furnace, and the printing press were products of the Middle Ages. By the beginning of the eighteenth century simple machines were widely employed in grinding grain, stamping coins, mining coal, and cutting wood. Even within these fields, however, hand labor was necessary, for machines did their work imperfectly and required costly repairs. Until machine tools were produced to turn out accurate parts for machines, the old difficulties remained. The celebrated spinning jenny, the water frame, and the steam engine possessed only limited importance until the 1780's. It was the use of coal in making iron and the application of the steam engine to manufacturing and of power machinery for spinning yarn that quickened industrial change.

Textile industry. Important improvements characterized the textile industry. Weaving was the big bottleneck in clothmaking. Edmund Cartwright's power loom, patented in 1785, helped but did not end the weaver shortage. Weaving was still done at home by hand until the 1840's. Finally the improvement of Cartwright's loom ended the shortage and ushered in the factory system. Home weaving could not compete with the steam-powered loom of the factory. Another important development in textiles was the improvement of the sewing machine by an American, Elias Howe, in 1846. His invention led to rapid and inexpensive manufacturing of clothing and shoes.

Coal and iron. The inventions in the coal and iron industries were even more important than those in textiles for Belgium, Britain, and France. The perfection of the steam engine for pumping water from mines rendered mining safer and cheaper. Sir Humphry Davy's safety lamp (developed in 1809) for coal miners lessened the frequency of explosions set off in the pits by the old-type open lamps and candles. Iron remained the basic metal until the 1840's, though steel was considered superior. The use of steel was limited by its prohibitive cost and production difficulties. Henry Bessemer in England in 1857 overcame these drawbacks by inventing a converter capable of producing large quantities of steel at a saving of over seventy-five per cent.

Gas, rubber, oil. Improvements and new inventions followed each other with amazing rapidity. Artificial lighting, essential for modern industry and

Charles Goodyear (1800–1860), "father of the rubber industry." Goodyear, in the face of poverty and debt, carried on his experiments with rubber. (Goodyear Rubber Co.)

cities, was proved feasible when illuminating gas was used commercially to light Baltimore, Maryland, in 1817. Soon other American and European cities followed suit. In 1844, Charles Goodyear invented the process for vulcanizing rubber (eliminating the stickiness of natural rubber by heating it with sulfur). Astounding developments transpired in printing and papermaking, clearing the way for mass-circulation of newspapers and books. Industrial development was facilitated by the production of lubricants. The discovery of petroleum in Pennsylvania in 1859, and in the Russian Caspian Sea area later, provided the necessary lubricants for the world's machines.

The railroads. In 1825 the world's first railway was opened in England, a short line connecting Stockton and Darlington. Soon major British centers were linked by a network of rails, and railroads were introduced into Continental Europe and the United States. In the latter, where vast distances hampered the exchange of goods, the railroad was a blessing. From 1850 to 1860 a period of furious railway construction linked together the northern and western states. Other areas of the world were the scene of construction. By 1876 even China and Japan boasted of trains.

The telegraph. Inventors sought to make rail travel faster and safer. In the 1850's they applied hydraulic brakes to trains, and in 1868 George Westinghouse patented the air brake. Closely associated with the railroad was the telegraph, perfected in the United States by Samuel Morse in 1844. At first the telegraph was used to carry news from city to city; later it was adopted by railways to co-ordinate train movements; and still later it became a handy method of communication for businessmen.

Steamships. Water travel also was revolutionized. In America, inland waterways (the Great Lakes, the Mississippi, the Ohio, and other great rivers) were often the only convenient highways of travel and commerce. Naturally, Americans followed with great interest the application of the steam engine to ships. In 1807, Robert Fulton's steamboat, the *Clermont,* sailed the Hudson River from New York to Albany and back in sixty-two hours. By 1840 over four hundred paddle-wheel steamboats were operating on the Mississippi and its tributaries, carrying passengers and freight to New Orleans, the commercial

The Clermont, *built by Robert Fulton in 1803, was the first commercially successful steamship in American waters.* The Clermont *was 150 feet long, 13 feet wide, and 9 feet in depth. It ran from New York to Albany in 32 hours and made the return trip in 30 hours, using pine wood as fuel. (Smithsonian Institution)*

depot of the New World. Transportation on the Great Lakes was eased by the opening in 1825 of the Erie Canal, which linked the Hudson and Lake Erie. Its success led to the construction of about thirty-two thousand miles of canals by 1850.

Ocean-going vessels were improved. The trip of the *Savannah* in 1819 from America to England demonstrated the practicality of the paddle-wheel steamship. Inventors turned their talents to replacing wooden vessels with iron ships; they were ridiculed by many who laughed at the idea that iron could float. The grand effect of steamdriven ocean vessels was to shorten traveling time between ports and to lower freight charges. The time of an Atlantic crossing was reduced from four to twelve weeks to a few weeks, and the lengthy journey between Britain and India or Australia no longer lasted from four to seven months. Distance was reduced not only by ships but also by oceanic cables. In 1866, Cyrus Field finally succeeded in laying down a submarine

cable between Britain and America. The world was knit together by telegraphic cables and by steamships plying the seven seas.

Electricity and water power. The industrial revolution was characterized by the invention of power machinery. Although the steam engine had been applied to a number of machines, it was inefficient and faulty. Later the

The first permanent transatlantic cable was laid in 1866 by Cyrus W. Field aboard the Great Eastern.

production of machine tools permitted the manufacture of more accurate steam-engine parts. The improved engines not only pumped water from mines effectively but drove machinery, railways, and ships. New sources of energy were utilized. For example, rapid-flowing rivers and streams were harnessed in England to provide water power. The disadvantages of steam and water power caused engineers to search for other forms of energy. The basic research of Franklin, Galvani, and Volta and the experiments of Faraday demonstrated that electricity could be produced mechanically. It was not until 1873 that a dynamo capable of steady operation was produced. Attention was centered on the use of water power to produce electricity (hydroelectricity). In the 1860's, paper mills in Grenoble, France, were powered by hydroelectricity, and in 1861 a village in Savoy, France, was illuminated by electricity.

Great Britain leads. Britain led industrial expansion. Enjoying unique advantages over her European and American rivals, she pulled ahead of the field between 1830 and 1870. She was conveniently situated at the window of Europe, close to Belgium, France, Germany, the Netherlands, and Scandinavia, and closer to the New World than her competitors. A mild climate favored industry. Well-located deposits of coal and iron ore assisted the metals industries, while abundant water power aided textile manufacturing. Britain had skilled labor, experienced inventors and engineers, many able scientists, and a prosperous middle class that was eager to invest in new industries. What is more, the British government not only encouraged manufacturing and trade at home and in the empire but also encouraged national economic interest throughout the world. At the same time, the mighty British navy protected commerce on the high seas. Some of the profits flowing from English industry were reinvested by British capitalists in Europe and the New World. Often not only money but British technicians and engineers went abroad to build railways and supervise mines.

The industrial revolution presently reached the United States and Europe and eventually much of the world. At the opening of the nineteenth century only fifteen small factories were in New England. Agriculture was the principal source of support for Americans, whose products, such as cotton and wheat, were marketable in Europe. After the War of 1812, however, manufacturing developed rapidly, especially between 1840 and 1860, and was accompanied by construction of railways and canals (financed by European investors).

Although Britain led the industrial march, she had competitors. France boasted of inventors who did basic work in mechanical and technical fields, but old habits in manufacturing, lack of credit, poor communications, few skilled workers, and limited natural resources for long handicapped France. Above all, French strength was sapped by the revolution and Napoleonic wars. Industries developed after 1830 as a result of the encouragement of the July Monarchy. Manufacturing never replaced farming as the nation's principal industry, nor did France approach Belgium, Britain, and Germany in degree of industrialization.

Belgium's progress in manufacturing and transportation was astounding. It converted the tiny country into one of the most densely populated and industrialized areas of the world. In 1850 her neighbor, Germany, was still predominantly agricultural, but the tempo of industrial change quickened in Germany. The opening of the coal fields of Silesia about 1840 was the prelude to rapid development. Elsewhere in Europe, industry was unimportant, being about a hundred years behind Britain.

Advance in agriculture. Much of rural Europe in the early nineteenth century looked the same as it had in the Middle Ages. Fields surrounded a village. Individual farmers owned strips of land but shared the crop and stock with other villagers. Everybody had certain rights in the "common" or undivided lands. The peasant rarely manifested interest in the stirring political and social changes; instead he was attached to traditional things, to king, to Church, to country. Similarly, his farming methods were unchanged through the centuries. He sowed his seed broadcast, with the result that birds ate much of it. As the rhyme said:

Sow four grains in a row,
  One for the pigeon, one for the crow,
  One to rot and one to grow.

Crop and animal yields increased in the eighteenth century. In England, Viscount Townshend, Jethro Tull, Arthur Young, and other gentlemen-farmers improved the breed of cattle and discovered new farming techniques. The belief was widespread in England that farmland could be exploited effectively if small farms were consolidated and "common" lands enclosed; that is, to replace the open-field system and "common" lands by individually owned farms. Enclosure had been in progress since the end of the Middle Ages, and between 1760 and 1840 some seven million acres were enclosed in England. Although enclosure contributed to increased crop yields, it had harmful effects on the independent farmer or yeoman. Small owners lost their independence and self-respect, becoming hired workmen on large farms or going to the city for work. Although the condition of English farmers worsened, European peasants generally improved their lot. From 1848 to 1860, peasants of central and eastern Europe were freed from payments to the lord, a custom that dated back to the Middle Ages, and they were free to leave their villages either for the new cities or the New World.

Just as the machine revolutionized manufacturing, it changed agriculture. Big landowners who profited from enclosure turned to machinery for larger yields and greater efficiency. Farm machinery was not as widely used in Britain as it was in the United States, however. Great tracts of fertile land and a relatively small laboring force invited the use of labor-saving devices in the New World. Americans improved the cast-iron plow and invented machines for preparing the seedbed and for seeding and planting. Some asked, "Can the traditional way of cutting wheat with scythes be im-

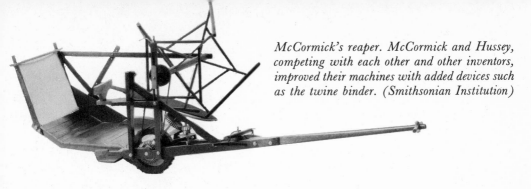

McCormick's reaper. McCormick and Hussey, competing with each other and other inventors, improved their machines with added devices such as the twine binder. (Smithsonian Institution)

proved?" The answer was the mechanical reapers of Obed Hussey and Cyrus McCormick, patented in 1834. After initial reluctance to employ it was overcome, the reaper was adopted on American and European farms. The adoption of new farm machinery was slower in Europe than in Britain and the United States. The wide distribution of land in France, for example, resulted in many small farms that were unsuitable for expensive machinery.

93. RESULTS OF CHANGES IN INDUSTRY AND AGRICULTURE

The industrial revolution further ensured the supremacy of Europe over the rest of the world. Non-European countries that lagged behind in farming and manufacturing imported new products and techniques from Europe. Often these countries relied upon European engineers and technicians to develop their industries and European capitalists to lend them money. South American countries, for example, employed British engineers and capital to build railways. While Europe generally reigned supreme, Britain enjoyed a special position. Britain's early lead won her prestige and power. Her industries earned for her the title, "workshop of the world."

British steamships carried British and foreign manufactures to distant African and Asiatic ports and returned with raw materials. London became the money center of the world.

The changes in farming and manufacturing knitted together the economic life of all nations. Just as regions within a country depended on one another, so nations became interdependent. Raw materials of one country were vital to another. Thus American cotton supplied British mills, while British machinery served American factories. The steamship, the railroad, the cable, and the telegraph virtually made the world one economic unit. So interdependent were the nations that a local disturbance in trade or industry affected all countries. Financial panic or depression in New York foreshadowed similar trouble in Antwerp, London, Milan, and Paris.

Interdependence was also demonstrated by the movements of European peoples within their own and neighboring countries or to lands across the seas. Bad harvests, unemployment, and political instability led millions of Germans, Englishmen, and Irishmen to leave their homes.

Effect on war. The machine revolutionized warfare. Large armies were now feasible because the machine provided weapons and clothing. Military necessity stimulated inventors to find better weapons for their country. Bessemer's studies in steel were begun in order to produce cannon capable of firing more powerful shells; and Eli Whitney, the inventor of the cotton gin, tried to speed up the production of rifles at the armory at Springfield, Massachusetts. Whitney saw that if rifle parts were standardized—that is, if they were machine-produced—they could be made more cheaply. Robert Fulton, who built the first successful steamboat, experimented with warships; and John Ericsson, one of the inventors of the screw propeller, produced the warship *Monitor,* used by the Union forces in the American Civil War. The importance of industrial change in warfare was demonstrated in that conflict. Union forces employed three silent allies: McCormick's reaper freed thousands of farmers for military service; the sewing machine produced huge quantities of uniforms; and railways ensured rapid movement of men and supplies to the battle zones.

Nationalism stimulated. The industrial and agricultural changes helped to destroy the old society that Metternich and other conservatives were trying to save. These changes strengthened nationalism, one of that society's enemies. The railway, telegraph, and cheap newspaper ended local isolation and turned people's attention away from their neighborhoods to the country at large. Better communications tended to popularize national feeling.

Increase of wealth. The most obvious result of the industrial revolution was material prosperity. A staggering variety of goods was produced. For

The four-hour, close-range combat between the Monitor *and the* Merrimac *showed the value of ironclad warships. (United States Navy)*

the most part, life became easier. Comforts unknown even to kings and emperors of old were now enjoyed by an increasing number of people. Although at first the richer classes improved their standard of living most, the poor later shared a greater variety of food and clothing. Greater abundance of food and goods, together with the advances in medicine and public health, reduced epidemics and famine.

Effect on cities. Before the industrial revolution, cities had derived their importance as cultural, commercial, political, religious, or strategic centers. By modern standards their population was small. Ancient Athens contained about one hundred and fifty thousand persons, and Rome at her peak, about a million. At the beginning of the nineteenth century even London had less than a million. However, cities developed side by side with industry when people deserted the countryside for coal fields, iron mines, or cotton mills. The population of England, which was previously centered in the farming areas of the south, now moved to the north, where new industries found the necessary coal and iron. By 1855, Britain had thirty-one cities with populations of over fifty thousand.

Evils of industrialism. The scene of manufacturing shifted from the home to the factory. In the eighteenth century, middlemen or subcontractors purchased raw material and "put it out" to workers who produced finished goods in their own homes. Under this "domestic system" the worker was practically his own master and could hire others to help him. A personal tie existed between master and laborer who worked side by side. Despite poor conditions, workmen preferred the domestic system to the new factories. They feared being thrown together in a barracks-like building and being disciplined as soldiers by unfriendly foremen. Yet inventions in clothmaking rendered it impossible for small-scale spinners or weavers to survive. The factory system spread from the textile industry to other fields in Britain and then throughout Europe and the United States.

Working conditions in factory and mine for a long time were very bad. Women pulled coal carts in dark mine tunnels, and boys mined coal side by side with their fathers for twelve to sixteen hours daily. In cotton mills and other factories, children under fourteen toiled from fourteen to sixteen hours a day. For this difficult work wages were meager, despite the fact that national income rose sharply. The lion's share of income went to capitalists, who then reinvested much of their profits in industry. The factory destroyed normal family life. Both parents and children were away from home from sunrise to sunset. In England, for example, a typical home was one of hundreds of dingy buildings clustered about the mill or mine entrance. It is not difficult to understand why so many persons were broken in health and spirit. Perhaps the worst effects on the worker were not long hours, poor wages, accident risk, and monotony, but the loss of independence and self-respect. A new social class of men and women arose —those who owned nothing. They owned neither tools nor raw materials nor even their homes. They were completely dependent upon their wages. Unemployment was their nightmare, because they could be "fired" or "laid off" at the will of their employers. They were the proletariat.

Economic liberalism. Those who led and largely profited from industrial changes—capitalists, merchants, manufacturers—coveted the power and prestige of the old landed classes. Their ambitions were only partially realized by the Reform Act of 1832 in Britain and the regimes established in Belgium and France after the revolu-

Children carrying clay in an English brick field. With the introduction of the factory system in England, child labor became a social problem. (Hulton Picture Library)

tions of 1830. They now had a share in government. However, while British merchants and manufacturers profited from political reform and economic change, they did not monopolize the government. The older aristocrats still mistrusted them and often refused to accept them as social equals. The opposition of the aristocrats in Britain and on the European continent did not prevent the business classes from enhancing their position and eventually dominating government. Businessmen aimed to free business from state control; they demanded the repeal of old regulations so that they could conduct their affairs without governmental interference. In general, they advocated economic liberalism.

Economic liberals sought to set aside protective tariffs and other mercantilistic measures. Their goal was free trade. British manufacturers did not require tariff protection, because their industrial superiority enabled them to compete successfully against foreign competitors without government help. What they wanted were cheaper raw materials, which would lower production costs, and cheaper food, which would permit a reduction in wages. They urged the government to allow foreign wheat, cotton, and other raw materials to enter without high tariffs. In the 1820's some commercial restrictions were lifted, and by the 1840's tariffs on raw materials were lowered. Free traders also attacked the mercantilist assumption that colonies were outposts of national commerce, on the grounds that they were expensive to defend and unnecessary for trade.

The biggest obstacles to free traders were the Corn Laws, which shut out foreign wheat in order to protect English-grown grains. Led by John Bright and Richard Cobden, prosperous manufacturers attacked the Corn Laws. The failure of the Irish potato crop supplied them with the argument that these laws prohibited the importation of wheat into Ireland to ease famine. In 1846, after a hard fight, the Corn Laws were repealed and soon the whole protective system was swept away. The European business classes considered commercial freedom, like representative government, to be a desirable goal. In 1819 a movement for a customs union was begun by Prussia, who established uniform tariffs for all her territories. By 1834 seventeen German states (not including Austria) formed a customs union (or *Zollverein*), which abolished internal customs duties and permitted raw materials to be imported into the union duty-free and manufactures to enter with moderate tariffs.

Social reform. A host of critics attacked the business classes and their *laissez-faire* system. Certain writers denounced free competition and free trade on economic grounds, while religious leaders denounced evils of the industrial system in the name of God and humanity. Some critics resented capitalists and merchants on the grounds that they had no appreciation of the finer things of life and that they valued only comfort, practicality, and money.[2] Romantic novelists and poets

---

[2] The attitude of some merchants and manufacturers exposed them to criticism. After having visited Rome, Richard Cobden said that the only monuments of the Eternal City worth preserving were the aqueducts!

increased discontent among the under-privileged by their descriptions of the contrast between the wretched lives of the poor and the elegant comfort of the rich. A few factory owners attempted to improve the condition of workers. Robert Owen, a Scottish manufacturer, believed that misery and evil could be banished by a form of socialism. Taking his cue from Rousseau, he charged that misery and suffering were due to ignorance. Owen established a model community and factory at New Lanark, where he outlawed child labor and drunkenness and provided adequate food and housing. His influence was strong in British and American reform circles.

Chartism. Social reformers had expected improved working conditions in England with the enactment of the Reform Bill of 1832. But this primarily aided the middle classes. Many workers were disillusioned and considered violence as their only path to improvement. Nevertheless, a majority of workers and reformers adopted peaceful political agitation as the most effective method of curbing the evils of the factory system. Reformers believed that if workers were represented in the House of Commons their lot would be improved. Toward this purpose an alliance of political radicals and workers was formed in the 1830's and 1840's to demand political rights. They advocated what was known as the "People's Charter" and called for:

1. Votes for all men
2. Annual elections for the House of Commons
3. No property qualifications for representatives
4. Salaries for members of Parliament
5. Secret voting
6. Equal electoral districts

Riots and agitation followed, but they did not persuade Parliament to accept the "People's Charter." This movement was called Chartism.

The upper and middle classes were not prepared to yield to Chartism. They held that the Reform Act had settled for all time the question of extending the vote. The liberal middle classes believed that only those persons who owned property ought to have a stake in government. But despite opposition, the Chartists persisted and for the second time submitted the Charter (containing over three million signatures) to Parliament in 1848. It was rejected. Meanwhile workers had turned to other methods of improving their condition, such as trade unions and co-operatives.[3] Also, the government began to enact laws to eliminate the worst evils. Mills and factories were inspected, working hours were regulated, and food was cheaper after the repeal of the Corn Laws. The 1850's brought prosperity to Britain.

Beginnings of socialism. The loudest critics of the upper classes were socialists, who saw in industrialism the way to a new form of society in which all productive property might be owned and operated by society for the benefit of all the members. Early socialists attacked the liberal program of the business classes by charging that fac-

---

[3] The example of some English weavers who established a co-operative grocery store in Rochdale in 1844 was followed by others groups in the British Isles, western Europe, and the United States.

Louis Blanc (1811–1882), French socialist (Photo Viollet)

tory owners and their supporters had captured governments and parliaments in order to promote private business interests. Like liberals, socialists drew their belief in man's goodness, in his ability to progress without the aid of religion, from the Enlightenment. Socialists believed that the only things that mattered were material things. However, where liberals desired to free the individual of government control, socialists hoped for regulation of the individual. Early socialists rejected violence to achieve their ends.

France, the home of the great revolution, was also the birthplace of the modern socialist movement. The Count de Saint-Simon wrote voluminously in favor of the total organization of society under the direction of engineers and intellectuals. Another French socialist, Charles Fourier, recommended the establishment of self-sufficient communities of persons who owned lands and tools in common. Louis Blanc, a practical political leader, urged government to alle-

viate poverty by instituting national workshops where the unemployed could be hired for public projects. Socialists successfully planted the idea in the minds of French workers that the wealth of capitalists had been stolen from the laboring classes. During the 1840's socialist ideas spread wide in that country.

REVIEW

STUDY SECTIONS IN REVIEW

90. Romanticism

A. What was the nineteenth-century meaning of "romanticism"?

B. Note five authors or composers who contributed to the romantic movement.

C. How did romanticism affect the writing and study of history?

D. Did romanticism have any political aspects? Explain.

91. Revival of Religion

A. How did romanticism contribute to a revival of religion?

B. Identify: Methodism, Chateaubriand, ultramontanes.

C. What was the significance of the work of Lamennais during the romantic period?

D. List three improvements in the position of Catholics in Britain in this period.

92. Industrial and Agricultural "Revolutions"

A. Name three factors that greatly changed economic life in the nineteenth century.

B. List five inventions of the period that stimulated the industrial revolution.

C. Mention four factors that helped Britain take the lead in industrial expansion.

D. What was the effect of "enclosure" on agriculture in Great Britain?

93. Results of the Changes in Industry and Agriculture

A. How did the industrial revolution affect the cities of the world?

B. List four evils that resulted from the growth of industrialism.

C. What were the goals of the economic liberals of this period?

D. Identify: Robert Owen, Chartism, Saint-Simon, Fourier.

THE CHAPTER IN REVIEW

A. What were the basic principles of nineteenth-century romanticism? How did romanticism represent a reaction to the thought of the Enlightenment?

B. What was the industrial revolution? Mention at least five major results of this revolution.

C. What evil effects were produced by the industrial revolution? Mention the social reform movements that arose to combat these evils.

D. Review the origins of socialism. What were the similarities and differences between socialism and the liberalism of the period?

FOR YOUR NOTEBOOK

Analyze two works of one of the romantic writers, such as Wordsworth or Shelley, to illustrate the characteristics the authors of your text consider typically romantic.

After thinking about this subject and re-reading the appropriate section of this chapter, write a paragraph in your notebook to show the connection of romanticism with the political and social history of the early nineteenth century.

From reference works in your library and perhaps from one of the standard Church histories, prepare a list of prominent Catholics in the first half of the nineteenth century—both clerical and lay—indicating those who were converts, and showing the historical contribution of each. For example, Frederick Ozanam founded the St. Vincent de Paul Society and the Notre Dame Conferences and wrote a number of important works in literary and cultural history.

Prepare a chronological list of important industrial inventions and show the connections between them. Improved methods of weaving, for example, made it necessary for more rapid methods of spinning thread.

The effects of the industrial revolution were momentous. Summarize them under the headings of (1) political, (2) economic, (3) social, (4) military, (5) cultural. Some effects are quite obvious, such as the social effect on large cities, but do not overlook less obvious results, such as the possibility of universal literacy and the changing of "day and night" because of artificial lighting.

SELECTED READINGS

The industrial revolution is best covered in summary fashion by the Berkshire Series study of Frederick Dietz, *The Industrial Revolution* (New York: Henry Holt & Co., 1927). Gauged more for young people is Gertrude Hartman, *Machines and the Men Who Made the World of Industry* (New York: The Macmillan Co., 1939). Two novels succeed in presenting vivid pictures of the social effects of the industrial revolution: D. M. Mulock (Mrs. Dinah Maria Craik), *John Halifax, Gentleman* (New York: E. P. Dutton & Co., 1950), tells of a young man who made good in the industrial world, whereas the unfair labor practices of the time are portrayed vividly by Charles Dickens, *Hard Times,* in many different editions.

Volume II of Carlton Hayes, *Political and Cultural History of Modern Europe* (New York: The Macmillan Co., 1952) provides excellent background reading for the period 1830 to 1939. The most readable account of the Oxford Movement is by Shane Leslie, *The Oxford Movement* (Milwaukee, Wis.: Bruce Publishing Co., 1933), and a good popular biography of Cardinal Newman is John Moody, *John Henry Newman* (New York: Sheed & Ward, 1945).

Chapter 31. International Crises, 1848 to 1860

94. OUTBREAK OF REVOLUTION IN EUROPE, 1848

For three decades liberals and nationalists attacked the Vienna settlement in Europe. They wanted in its place constitutional government, economic liberty, and freedom for the subject nationalities. In the late 1840's liberals and nationalists judged that the old order was on its way out. Just as emperors and kings were united to resist change, reformers everywhere felt they had something in common. They were encouraged by British Whigs (in power after 1846), who declared that only parliamentary government respected personal liberty and welfare and therefore recommended its adoption in Greece, Italy, Spain, and Portugal. The July Monarchy also encouraged liberalism. The

French minister François Guizot, though opposed to revolution or disorder, encouraged liberals to resist the old system. Liberals and democrats became bolder at the moment that Metternich and other defenders of the Vienna settlement were losing their grip.

Metternich vs. Mazzini. Metternich was threatened in Italy and Germany, where liberal and national hopes merged. The treaties of Vienna had left Austria the dominant power in Italy.[1] The Carbonari, a secret society, plotted against all Italian princes and Austria in order to achieve a liberal Italy. The desire for a democratic and

---

[1] Italy was composed of the Kingdom of Sardinia-Piedmont, Lombardy and Venetia (both Austrian provinces), Parma, Modena, Lucca, Romagna, Tuscany, the Papal States, and the Kingdom of the Two Sicilies (Naples and Sicily).

unified Italy was best expressed by Giuseppe Mazzini, who had joined the Carbonari in his youth. Mazzini dedicated his life to inspire Italians to unify their country and lead the regeneration of the whole world. He urged them to ignore popes and princes and to place their faith in a popular revolution that would produce a republic of Italy. By forming a republic, Italians could help Europe and the world to achieve democracy and freedom. To achieve his purpose he founded the society of Young Italy in 1832, and later Young Europe. Although Mazzini was imprisoned and exiled for conspiracy and agitation, he was a great revolutionary strategist.

In 1831, Charles Albert had become King of Sardinia-Piedmont. He had patriotic leanings, wished to expel Austria from Italy, and then place his family, the house of Savoy, on the throne of a united Italy. His cause was helped by writers and statesmen such as Massimo d'Azeglio, who advocated attack on Austria. Some devotees of Italian unity urged the Pope to lead Italy. A Piedmontese priest, Vincenzo Gioberti, suggested that the Pontiff head an Italian confederation.

Pope Pius IX. The greatest encouragement to Italian nationalists came in 1846 with the election of Pope Pius IX. Influenced by Gioberti, the Pope was an Italian patriot and reformer. He introduced a series of notable reforms in the Papal States, such as the reform of administration, tariffs, and the criminal code. The papal reforms were interpreted as approval of the "revolution," and Pius IX was hailed throughout Italy as a liberal and nationalist. Italian nationalism was on

Pope Pius IX (Library of Congress)

the rampage. Fearing for Austrian security, Metternich strengthened his Italian garrisons. His action was met with boycotts and revolts. Early in 1848 a revolution erupted in Sicily and soon spread to Naples and Salerno. When Metternich sought permission to march Austrian troops across papal territory in order to suppress the rebels in southern Italy, he was rebuffed by Pius IX and suffered a loss in prestige. Meanwhile liberal-nationalist agitation compelled the Duke of Tuscany and the King of the Two Sicilies to grant constitutional government. These concessions were hard blows for Metternich and the system he wished to preserve in Italy and in Europe.

German nationalism. Like Italian nationalism, German nationalism strove to assert itself but was stifled by the Metternich System which divided Germany. Herder, Fichte, and other writers popularized a love for Germany. Scholars who studied the German language, folklore, and history urged Germans to be proud of their achievements. Many nationalists felt that German achievements were not appreciated by other peoples because Germany was divided. Arguing that if their fatherland were united, German superiority would be universally acknowledged, they spurred a great national movement for union and liberal reform.[2]

Cracow. Metternich's hands were full. In order to nip an expected rebellion within the Polish free city of Cracow (whose independence as a republic was guaranteed in the Vienna treaties), Metternich wiped out the Republic of Cracow in 1846. This act was denounced by liberals and viewed suspiciously by conservatives who thought Metternich inconsistent as simultaneous champion and violator of the Vienna treaties. The Austrian minister also lost prestige by his unsuccessful interference on behalf of the losing side in the Swiss civil war of 1847[3] and his failure to crush the Neapolitan revolt noted above. Besides, the liberals and nationalists of Hungary posed a dangerous threat to Austria. The first blows against the old order were not struck against Metternich, however, but against the king in France.

The situation in France. Louis Philippe, who was King after the July Revolution of 1830, never won the hearts of Frenchmen. Some of them longed for the Bourbon kings of the Old Regime, others for the First Republic or Napoleon's empire. Democrats and socialists charged that Louis Philippe's government promoted business only to enhance the prestige and wealth of the upper classes. Pointing to the fact that only 250,000 out of a population of 35,000,000 were eligible to vote, the radicals demanded an extension of the franchise. Louis Blanc, the socialist, wanted the government to organize major industries as national workshops that would offer work to those who needed it.

The Paris revolt, February 1848. Guizot, the king's chief minister, had to cope with these demands. Insisting that the first aim of government was the maintenance of order at home and peace abroad, he rejected the democratic and socialist demands on the grounds that they would produce disorder. Opposition to Louis Philippe and Guizot unexpectedly came to a head in February 1848. A mob in Paris called for reform and the resignation of Guizot. Without staunch supporters or the will to fight, the seventy-five-year-old king decided to abdicate, saying, "I've seen enough blood spilled." The mob seized control of Paris. A Committee of Public Safety assumed the task of carrying through the revolution. Soon a provisional government proclaimed the establishment of the Second Republic. At first the radicals had their way and it appeared as if they would outlaw private property and capitalism and replace the tricolor with the red flag of socialism.

The June Days. Their program, how-

---

[2] Prussia took the lead in establishing a German customs union (*Zollverein*), which excluded Austria, so that by 1848 Prussia enjoyed economic superiority in central Europe and laid the economic groundwork for German unification.

[3] Seven Catholic cantons voted in 1845 to secede from the Swiss Confederation and formed the Sonderbund. Their defeat in a war in 1847 compelled their return to the federal system.

ever, was opposed by the business class and peasants. For a time the danger of civil war existed, but a famous poet (and politician), Alphonse de Lamartine, conciliated moderates and radicals. The former regained power at the expense of conceding the radical demand for national workshops for the unemployed. Within four months about one-hundred thousand unemployed and idlers flocked to Paris to enroll in the workshops. Socialists and radicals were not satisfied with the moderate regime and were angered at the victory of their opponents in the elections of April 1848. From June 24 to 27 ("the June Days") they rose in rebellion in Paris. The army closed in on the workers behind street barricades and suppressed the revolt at the cost of thousands of lives. The red terror frightened the government into dissolving the workshops.

The Second French Republic. With the radicals vanquished, moderates laid the groundwork for a republic. A new constitution provided for a government composed of a president and a legislature. The chief candidates for the presidency were Ledru-Rollin, a socialist; General Cavaignac, the hero of the June riots; and Louis Napoleon Bonaparte, nephew of the great Napoleon. The name Napoleon was magic. Millions believed the emperor had fought for nationality, democracy, and the tricolor, and that Europe had misunderstood his intentions. They had demonstrated deep reverence when Napoleon's remains were returned in 1840 for reburial in Paris. Riding on his uncle's reputation, Louis Napoleon was elected president of the Second French Republic.

95. FAILURE OF REVOLUTIONS IN ITALY AND CENTRAL EUROPE

Impact of the French Revolution on Europe. News that King Louis Philippe had fallen traveled quickly via the railways and telegraphs. Newspapers were filled with accounts of the Paris revolt. Liberals rejoiced. The English magazine *Punch* printed these lines:

> Louis Philippe
> Has lost his sheep
> And never again will find them
> The people of France
> Have made an advance
> And left their king behind them.

Conservatives shuddered at the unexpected turn of events. They recalled that the last time France had a republic all Europe plunged into war. So great was the impact of the 1848 disturbance that all governments staggered. Not until the twentieth century were so many governments threatened by a universal radical movement.

Fall of Metternich. The Austrian Empire bore the brunt of liberal-nationalist revolts. Opposition to Metternich culminated in an uprising in Vienna. On March 13, 1848, he fled for his life, going to London, where he joined his fellow exiles, Louis Philippe and Guizot. His flight opened the dykes of revolution, which he had held back for over thirty years. As in France, the Austrian rebellion was led by the middle class. Leaders were authors, professors, students, and minor government officials. Although Emperor Ferdinand I agreed to meet their demands for a new constitution and a parliament, he was forced to flee the capital.

Nationalist movements. Metternich's fall encouraged Croats, Czechs, Ger-

Francis Joseph, Emperor of Austria, and the empress on a drive through Vienna prior to the uprising in 1848. Ferdinand I abdicated in favor of his nephew, Francis Joseph. (Austrian Information Service)

mans, Italians, Magyars, Poles, and other nationalities in the Austrian Empire to reach for personal liberty, constitutional government, and, above all, national self-government. Satisfying their aspirations would involve the collapse of the Austrian Empire. The Hungarians, the most powerful nationality, demanded and won national autonomy. Liberal leaders, Francis Deák and Louis Kossuth, dominated Hungary and sponsored a series of sweeping reforms in the government which ignored the Austrian emperor, who was King of Hungary.

In June 1848, Croats, Czechs, Poles, Slovenes, Slovaks, and other Slavic peoples of Austria and Hungary convened a Pan-Slav Congress at Prague to consider ways and means to develop their own national life within the Austrian Empire. Central Europe was a patchwork of rival nationalities. If one nationality formed a national state, it would include sizable minorities of other nationalities living in the same area and equally desirous of self-government. By failing to respect each other's hopes and by bickering, they eventually checkmated nationalism.

Revolution in Germany. Meanwhile local uprisings, not specifically directed against Austria, occurred throughout Germany. Several princes agreed to establish liberal governments. Prussia was also affected; after wavering, King Frederick William IV promised reforms. With demands for liberal government were heard louder cries for a strong and united Germany. Frederick William was moved to declare that Prussia was now merged into Germany.

Frankfurt Assembly. Throughout Germany, liberals and nationalists took up the task of replacing the German Confederation (established by the Vienna treaties) with a unified Germany. From Austria, Prussia, and the other German states, popularly elected delegates met at Frankfurt in May 1848 for the purpose of establishing a federal Germany. Delegates were professional people, professors, lawyers, clergymen, and minor government officials who had little political experience. Well-meaning and idealistic, they wished to establish a liberal and greater Germany by peaceful means.

Should the new Germany be an empire or a republic? Was Austria or Prussia to lead it? To draw up a constitution for a united Germany that would please German liberals and princes and Prussia and Austria was a near-impossible task. While the Frankfurt Assembly wrestled with the problems for over a year, the European picture changed. Austria recovered from the initial shocks of revolution and was prepared to resist liberalism and nationalism. Eventually the Frankfurt liberals decided to exclude Austria from the new Germany and to offer the crown to the King of Prussia. Frederick William, however, was not prepared to challenge Austria, and he therefore refused the offer of a crown. He followed up his refusal by cracking down on Prussian liberals. Liberal-nationalist hopes, which had risen high during the Frankfurt Convention, were shattered.

War and revolution in Italy. The situation in Italy was explosive. Metternich's fall stirred the Milanese in 1848 to expel the Austrian garrison under Marshal Radetzky. The Austrians were also driven out of Venice, where Daniele Manin established the Venetian Republic. Riots and nationalist agitation encouraged Charles Albert of Sardinia-Piedmont to march his army against the Austrians in Lombardy on March 24. When the French offered aid, he explained that Italy would make herself. A war of liberation against Austria ensued. The King of the Two Sicilies and the Duke of Tuscany sent their armies to help Sardinia. A papal army was sent to the north to defend the Papal States, but its commander supported the Sardinian troops. This led Pius IX to recall the papal army and repudiate the war against Austria.

The tide turned against Italian na-

Joseph Mazzini, Italian patriot and revolutionist, was an inspiring leader but incapable of organization and practical statesmanship. (Library of Congress)

tionalism. In late July 1848, Radetzky seized the military initiative and defeated Charles Albert at Custozza. Sardinia was now out of the war. This defeat converted Italian enthusiasm and hopes into despair and disunity. Mazzini and the radicals gloated over Charles Albert's predicament, because they believed that now the people instead of princes would take up the fight.

Papacy and Roman Republic. Liberal-nationalist agitation continued to rock the Papal States. The Roman Constitution of 1848 did not work out because it was alien to the nature of the Papal States. There was a contradiction in the dual role of the Pontiff as constitutional monarch of the states of the Church and as Head of the Universal Church. Pius IX directed Count Pellegrino Rossi to restore order, reform the government of the city of Rome, and negotiate with other Italian princes in order to unify Italy by means of a league. Mob violence led to the murder of Rossi and the flight of the Pope from Rome on November 25, 1848. Under the leadership of General Garibaldi and Mazzini, the Roman Republic was proclaimed; its leaders hoped to extend it throughout Italy. Now the Catholic princes of Italy and Europe were anxious to crush the Roman Republic. Spain, France, Naples, and Austria came to the aid of the Pope against the Roman revolution, the French taking the leading part. After much fighting, the republic came to an end in July 1849, and soon afterward the papal government was restored.

Defeat of Charles Albert. Charles Albert reopened his war against Austria in another attempt to unify Italy under Sardinian auspices. His armies were defeated at Novara in March 1849. The Sardinian king abdicated in favor of his son, Victor Emmanuel II. Everywhere in Italy the revolution failed.

Failure of revolution in central Europe. The tide turned decisively against revolution also in central Europe. The mass of people were generally not politically interested and hence remained loyal to the throne, the Church, and country. Likewise, the armies were equally loyal and executed orders to suppress violence. Austria suppressed revolutionaries step by step. The Czechs were subdued and the city of Prague taken. Next, with the help of Jellachich, a Croatian general, Austria turned on Hungary. When radicals in Vienna attemped to prevent troops from being sent against Hungarian radicals, the Austrian army captured

its own capital city of Vienna. Government affairs were put into the hands of Count Felix Schwarzenberg, an iron-willed statesman and disciple of Metternich. In 1848, Emperor Ferdinand abdicated because his name was associated with concessions to liberals. His successor was young Francis Joseph (1849–1916), who withdrew concessions to the liberals. However, some reforms were not rescinded, such as abolition of feudal services and emancipation of serfs.

Russians in Hungary. Hungary refused to submit to Austria without a fight. Louis Kossuth, the Hungarian leader, proclaimed a republic, dethroning the Hapsburg dynasty. Francis Joseph called upon Czar Nicholas of Russia for help against the Hungarians. Anxious to prevent the revolution from spilling over into the Balkans, Poland, or Russia, Nicholas had his Cossacks strike from the east as Austrian armies invaded Hungary from the west and south. By August 1849, Hungary was back in the Hapsburg Empire, and Kossuth and other liberals were in flight.

Reaction in Germany. The defeat of liberals and nationalists became a rout. Last-ditch attempts to establish republics in Baden and other German states failed. In 1850 the Prussian king still hoped to create a German union under his leadership. However, Schwarzenberg rallied support for Austria in Germany and received Russian aid, so that he shattered the Prussian dream. In 1851, Prussia agreed to the restoration of the old German Confederation and recognized the emperor as its president. Austria momentarily regained her position as dominant German power. She had met and blunted the challenge of liberalism and nationalism in central Europe, and she had resisted Prussia's plan to reorganize Germany. However, the necessity of calling in Russian help during the Hungarian revolution was a humiliation for Austria. She lost respect and the reputation of being a moderate power and henceforth was regarded as the ally of despotic Russia.

The fate of the liberals. Liberals and democrats were in flight. To escape arrest, some German and Hungarian revolutionaries went to the United States. After all their efforts, it seemed that nothing had changed. Germany and Italy were neither liberal nor unified. What was especially depressing to them was the might of the Russian Czar. The Czar declared, "I firmly believe Providence has given me a mission to deliver Europe from constitutional government."

The results of the revolutions of 1848–1849 proved that the impulse for national unity was stronger than the desire for constitutional government. The failure of the nationalist uprisings led to a loss in prestige of liberal reformers and idealists. Nationalists concluded that liberal ideas were unable to achieve unification; they regretted that they had pinned their hopes on men of ideas rather than on men of action. The idea that Germany or Italy *ought* to be united was worthless without the *power* of achieving it. The will to be united was not enough for Italians or Germans, nationalists included.

Reaction not complete. All liberal traces of the revolutions of 1848–1849, of course, were not swept away. Small countries retained liberal forms of government adopted during the revolutions. Thus Switzerland kept a democratic constitution, Sardinia a constitutional government modeled on the English system. Prussia retained a conservative constitution granted by the king in 1850. Under liberal pressure and revolutionary outbreaks, Denmark and Holland moved toward parliamentary government. Chartist agitation stirred Great Britain in 1848.

Failure of Irish Revolt. In Ireland, congestion, famine, and oppression prompted violent opposition to British control. The death of Daniel O'Connell in 1847 removed a leader who had avoided using violence as a means of gaining freedom for Ireland. The stage was set for Young Ireland, a society that advocated quick and violent methods to free Ireland. Encouraged by the Paris revolution of February 1848, Young Ireland rebelled. But the attempt failed and the leadership of Young Ireland soon fled or was captured.

96. CRIMEAN WAR AND THE UNIFICATION OF ITALY

Napoleon III. The Second Republic in France, created in 1848, did not last long. Soon a quarrel arose between President Bonaparte and the parliament, or National Assembly. With the support of the army, Louis Napoleon seized all power in the early hours of December 2, 1851. Many were convinced that he had saved France from disorder and voted him president for life in a national plebiscite. A year later he was proclaimed Napoleon III,

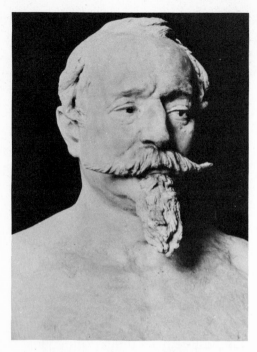

Bust of Napoleon III by Carpeaux. As president of the Second Republic, Napoleon III pretended to defend French democracy while preparing for his eventual seizure of dictatorial powers.

Emperor of the French.[4] The Second Empire was a dictatorship based on the will of the people expressed through the plebiscite. The presence of a Bonaparte on the throne of France violated the Vienna treaties. Nevertheless, the European powers recognized Napoleon III because they were assured that "the empire means peace." In a short time Napoleon improved French finances, education, and the condition of workers and farmers. But as the heir of his great uncle, his eyes were set on glory in foreign lands. Hence it was inevitable that France,

---

[4] Napoleon I's son, who never reigned and who died in 1832, thus was recognized as Napoleon II.

under his rule, should become again a disturbing force in Europe.

The state of the Ottoman Empire. In the nineteenth century the Ottoman Empire (often called Turkey) was a loose collection of territories in Africa, the Near East, and Balkan Europe. The sultan at Constantinople—once the scourge of Europe—retained but little of his former power. A measure of his weakness was his failure in the 1830's to prevent Mohammed Ali, the ruler of Egypt, which was nominally under the sultan's jurisdiction, from seizing Palestine and Syria. The future was dark for the Ottoman Empire. Corruption and inefficiency in government increased the heavy burdens of administering a far-flung empire. The empire still possessed Constantinople and the straits—the keys to the Black Sea—Asia Minor, and the Balkans. There were millions of subject Christians in the latter: Albanians, Bulgarians, Macedonians, Montenegrins, Rumanians, and Serbs. Generally they were Orthodox Christians whose churches did not acknowledge the authority of the Pope. Although the Balkan Christians were divided in race and religion, they shared a common dream of liberation from the Turks. The example of the successful Greek revolt and the knowledge that the Turks were feeble raised their hopes of independence.

Russia and the Ottoman Empire. Russia wished to exploit the weakness of the Ottoman Empire. Czar Nicholas called it the sick man of Europe who was about to die, and coveted his rich possessions. In 1844 the Czar suggested to Britain a plan for partitioning Turkish territories. Britain became alarmed at Russian ambition, because Constantinople or other Turkish possessions along the Mediterranean in Russian hands might upset the European balance of power and cause war.

Nicholas, as head of the greatest Slav state in the world and champion of Orthodox Christians, was bent on helping the suppressed Christians in the Balkans. He claimed a treaty right to insist on good treatment for his coreligionists. But if the sultan recognized his claim as champion of Balkan Christians, he would simultaneously acknowledge Russian domination in the Balkan peninsula. Neither Austria nor Britain welcomed Nicholas' pretensions which would upset the European balance of power. France also disliked them, and Napoleon III had been angered by Nicholas' effort to prevent the revival of the empire in France. Besides, Napoleon III was eager for an opportunity to win glory for France by taking the lead to block Russian moves against Turkey.

Dispute over the holy places. What the issue came down to was this: Would the Western powers permit Russia to take exclusive advantage of the impending collapse of the Ottoman Empire? Britain and France answered in the negative. The immediate cause of war was the question of supervising the holy places in Palestine, where all Christians wished to pray. Orthodox priests and monks, supported by the Czars, had encroached on the rights of Latin Christians. When Louis Napoleon became Emperor of the French

he decided to win Catholic approval by becoming the champion of suppressed Christians in the Ottoman Empire and defending Catholic rights in the Holy Land. His efforts were successful. Napoleon's victory was a blow to the Czar in eastern Europe.

War breaks out. No doubt religious conviction motivated Nicholas to send an ambassador to Constantinople to demand the right of supervising the holy places and protecting the Balkan Christians. The British urged the sultan to resist Russian pressure. Meanwhile the Czar ordered the occupation of Turkish-held Wallachia and Moldavia[5] and the sultan declared war on

Florence Nightingale, the "Lady of the Lamp" and courageous English nurse in the Crimean War. (Hulton Picture Library)

---

[5] These two Ottoman principalities were later united to form Rumania.

his ancient enemy. To the delight of liberals, Britain and France declared war on the Czar, the autocrat who had crushed the revolutions of 1848. Soon Sardinia joined the alliance against Russia. Sardinia's principal reason for 'fighting was to gain European prestige and to win a seat at the peace conference where the Italian question might be raised.

Siege of Sevastopol. The major campaigns occurred in the Crimean peninsula in the Black Sea. In the fall of 1854 the allies attacked the Russian naval base of Sevastopol. Although battered by a large army and navy, Russian defenders held out for a year.[6] Disease, wounds, severe weather, and

lack of supplies took an enormous toll in lives, especially Russian. The horrors of military hospitals were partly alleviated by the work of the volunteer English nurse, Florence Nightingale. By insisting on cleanliness and good care for the wounded, she saved many lives.

Treaty of Paris, 1856. The Crimean War disturbed the international system that had been established by the Congress of Vienna. Under the auspices of Napoleon III, the signatories of the Vienna treaties sat in Paris as

---

[6] The heroism of British troops was immortalized in Alfred Tennyson's poem, *The Charge of the Light Brigade.*

The Concert of Europe met in 1856 to discuss and settle the problems of eastern Europe. The conference was attended by representatives of France, Great Britain, Turkey, Sardinia, Russia, Austria, and Prussia. The conference issued an agreement concerning the rules of maritime warfare, restored the boundaries of Russia and Turkey in Asia to their pre-war limits, and made the Ottoman Empire a member of the European concert. (Giraudon)

the Concert of Europe and settled the problems raised by the war. The Treaty of Paris of 1856 had important provisions. First, the powers renounced the right to intervene in the affairs of the Ottoman Empire. The Czar was thus prevented from becoming the protector of Balkan Christians. Second, the Black Sea was neutralized, which meant that Russian warships could not threaten Constantinople. Third, the sultan recognized the autonomy of Wallachia and Moldavia. Modern Rumania emerged from the union of these principalities in 1861. Fourth, Serbia was guaranteed her autonomy. Other Balkan peoples remained restless and yearned for liberation from Turkish tyranny. In short, the Crimean War gave the Ottoman Empire another lease on life. It halted for the moment the Russian threat to Turkey and to British influence in the eastern Mediterranean. And Napoleon III, who had led the alliance against Russia, won the glory he coveted.

Effect of war on Russia. Russia's reputation as the colossus of the East suffered. The war converted Russia from a mighty guardian of the treaty system of 1815 into a revisionist power anxious to regain lost prestige. Russia resented the failure of Austria to help in the hour of need, and she repaid Hapsburg ingratitude for Russian participation in suppressing Hungary by backing Prussia in German affairs. In 1859, when Austria was attacked by France and Sardinia, and again in 1866 by Prussia and Sardinia, Russia stood by and permitted the map of Europe to be altered at Austrian expense.

Defeat precipitated debate in Russia between those who wished to introduce Western reforms (the "Westerners") and those who urged Russians to scorn the West and develop the distinctive features of national life (the "Slavophiles"). The Westerners attributed the defeat in war to serfdom, which stifled initiative among brave Russian soldiers. Alexander encouraged discussion of plans for emancipating serfs. Serfs lived on the estates of the Czar and members of his family or of the nobility; they owed their masters labor, rents, and obedience, and they could not leave without permission. Alexander effected a series of reforms in the 1860's that reflected Western influence. In 1861 he abolished serfdom and permitted the free men to purchase their lands from the nobles, who were compensated by the government for property losses. The abolition of serfdom made necessary changes in local government that had been dominated by landowners. In 1864, therefore, the Czar established councils (*zemstvos*) in the provinces to levy taxes, supervise schools, public health, and other concerns of local government. Another reform altered the courts. All citizens were made equal before the law. Open and public trials, the jury system, and justices of the peace (with authority formerly exercised by nobles on estates) were introduced. Next, the press and the universities received more freedom, and Russians were permitted to travel abroad. Thus many Russians tasted freedom and they continued to agitate for it even in the face of later ruthless repression.

Suez Canal. The victory of the Anglo-French allies lent prestige to liberal

Camillo di Cavour (1810–1861), Italian statesman and premier of Sardinia, was more responsible than any other man for the unification of Italy. (Library of Congress)

ideas in government and economics. Egypt, for example, fell under Western influence. Mohammed Said modernized his government, removed internal tariffs to permit goods to move freely within the country, and encouraged French engineers and capitalists to build canals, ports, and railways. In 1859 they began the construction of the Suez Canal.

Sardinia and Cavour. France, like Russia, desired a revision of the European treaty system in order to enhance her prestige. The Crimean victory put Napoleon III at the pinnacle of influence. He favored liberation of Italians,

Poles, and other submerged nationalities, realizing that the application of the principle of nationality would weaken Austria and increase the influence of France in Europe. Britain still promoted liberal reform on the Continent and followed a policy of nonintervention when nationality and reform threatened the old order. Austria, the natural guardian of the system of 1815, was busy solidifying her position in the German Confederation, or *Bund,* in rivalry with Prussia.

Sardinia, like France and Russia, had more to gain by changing the map of Europe than by preserving the status quo. Her object was to expel Austria from Italy and unify Italians. Count Camillo di Cavour, an able statesman, was now Prime Minister of Sardinia, and he was dedicated to the task of making the King of Sardinia the king of a united Italy. His first goal was to convert Sardinia from a backward and weak country into a modern state. He promoted industry and transportation and encouraged the construction of railways in order to help unify Italy and bring the peninsula closer to Europe.

Cavour permitted nothing to block his objective. He was bold and ready to gamble. Realizing that he could not make Victor Emmanuel King of Italy without the aid of Napoleon III, he involved Sardinia in the Crimean War without just cause so that he could claim British and French support and sit at the conference table at the end of hostilities. At the Congress of Paris of 1856, he won the sympathy of many diplomats and planted the idea in their minds that Austria was Italy's oppressor.

The Battle of Magenta (1859), in which the French and Sardinians won a decisive victory over the Austrians, opening the way to Milan. The military and political weakness of the Austrian empire was displayed in the Italian War. Austria lost possession of Lombardy to Italy. (Compagnie des Arts Photomécaniques)

War against Austria. Cavour translated Napoleon's sympathies for Italian nationalism into a promise of help. In the summer of 1858, Napoleon III and Cavour came to an understanding. In return for French aid, Napoleon was promised Savoy and possibly Nice, which belonged to Sardinia. Statesmen realized that war was coming and attempted to head it off. As a result of these efforts, Napoleon hesitated, but Cavour put pressure on him. Finally he found a handy excuse to force the Emperor of the French to go to war by trapping Austria into sending an ultimatum to Sardinia to demobilize. France and Sardinia went to war with Austria in 1859. Cavour had really plotted the war. As he once

remarked, "If we did for ourselves what we do for our country, what rascals we would be!"

While Cavour incited the peoples of central Italy to revolt against their Austrian-supported princes, French and Sardinian troops crushed the enemy at the battles of Magenta and Solferino. But the mobilization of Prussia and her threat to join Austria induced Napoleon to stop. Without his ally he negotiated an armistice with Emperor Francis Joseph at Villafranca. There was nothing for Victor Emmanuel to do but stop fighting. A treaty provided for the cession to Sardinia of Lombardy (but not Venetia) and the establishment of an Italian confederation. This was a settlement Cavour and Italian nationalists refused to accept.

Sardinia absorbs most of Italy. When the princes of central Italy fled, nationalists seized control and prepared the way for the annexation of their small states to Sardinia. Before the European powers could supervise the establishment of an Italian confederation in accordance with the terms of the Villafranca armistice, Italian nationalists forced annexation. Sardinia could not accept annexation without Napoleon's consent, which Cavour bought by agreeing to give Nice and Savoy to France. This was a high price to pay for the annexation of central Italy, because Savoy was the original home of the Sardinian royal family, and Nice was the birthplace of the popular general, Garibaldi. In order to justify the transfer of these provinces, Cavour arranged for a plebiscite. The results of the voting favored ceding them to France.

Meanwhile Garibaldi, who was a military adventurer, organized a force of a thousand men (called "Red Shirts") and set out to carry the revolution to the Kingdom of the Two Sicilies. Cavour was aware of his expedition and planned to exploit it if Garibaldi succeeded and to repudiate it if he failed. In 1860, Garibaldi conquered Sicily and set his sights on Naples. Lacking the firmness needed to halt the march of Garibaldi's thousand, now swelled in numbers, Naples fell. Garibaldi was master of southern Italy. Fearing that he might become more popular than Victor Emmanuel and that he might attack Rome and the city's French garrison, Cavour ordered Sardinian troops to invade

the Papal States (but to stay out of Rome) and thus block Garibaldi. In October, Garibaldi turned over Naples and Sicily to Victor Emmanuel, who was proclaimed King of Italy. The Italian dream of unification had nearly come true. Still nationalists were disappointed. For the capital of a united Italy they would have Rome, and Rome alone. In 1861, before Cavour could move toward that objective, he died.

Effects on Europe. The Italian war of 1859 and its aftermath were disastrous for the old treaty system. Austria was shaken, and the loss of prestige weakened her position in Germany, where Prussia was ready to follow Sardinia's example. The old system had been based on the idea of legitimacy (princes had a hereditary right to govern their countries). The Italian war, however, popularized the principle of nationalities. Not the wishes of princes and kings, but the will of the nation, expressed through a plebiscite, deter-

UNIFICATION
OF ITALY
1857-1870

× Battle sites

mined whether an old state (e.g., Parma or Tuscany) was to be destroyed and a new country created (e.g., kingdom of Italy). The old system was also based on the idea that the Concert of Europe ratified changes in the treaties of 1815. But in 1859 the great powers failed to restrain Sardinia and later did not get the opportunity to block the disappearance of the small Italian principalities and the establishment of the kingdom of Italy. Finally the Italian war of 1859 and the creation of Italy disturbed international order. War had been deliberately planned; treaties were broken. Cavour's career seemed to prove that limited, carefully planned violence was practical. Other statesmen were ready to imitate him.

REVIEW

STUDY SECTIONS IN REVIEW

94. Outbreak of Revolution in Europe, 1848

A. Identify: Mazzini, Charles Albert, Pius IX.

B. What three events around 1848 caused losses in prestige for Metternich?

C. What were the factors that caused the Paris revolt of 1848?

D. Discuss the form of government of the Second French Republic.

95. Failure of the Revolutions in Italy and Central Europe

A. What caused the fall of Metternich?

B. Identify: the Pan-Slav Congress, Kossuth, Frankfurt Assembly.

C. What was the fate of the Roman Republic of 1849?

D. Cite two reasons for the failure of the revolutions in central Europe.

E. Mention three results of the liberal revolts of 1848.

96. Crimean War and the Unification of Italy

A. What was the form of government in France during the Second Empire?

B. What were the causes of the Crimean War?

C. Mention three results of the Treaty of Paris of 1856.

D. What internal reforms were adopted by Russia after the Crimean reverses?

E. List three results of the Italian war of 1859 and the events that followed:

THE CHAPTER IN REVIEW

A. Why did Europe seem ripe for revolt in 1848? How were liberalism and nationalism involved in the revolutionary movements?

B. List the causes and results and trace the course of the French revolution of 1848. What other areas were inspired to revolt by the French example?

C. In general, why were the revolutions of 1848 failures? Mention at least three such failures.

D. How did the results of the wars of Italian unification and independence upset the treaty system and the European status quo?

FOR YOUR NOTEBOOK

The year 1848 was one of general revolution throughout Europe. Imagine yourself an American making a quick circuit of the major European countries early in January. Under the heading of each country enter the words or phrases that best describe social and political conditions in the country.

The revolutions of 1848 seemed everywhere successful at first. But in the end they all failed. Go through your text carefully to find all the reasons that account for their ultimate failure. Enter these into your notebook.

Each of the four states engaged in the Crimean War entered for a different set of purposes. You will clarify your knowledge of this war if you list the different purposes of each country engaged in the war.

Outline the steps Cavour took to unify Italy. Indicate on a tracing of the textbook map how much of the Italian peninsula had been incorporated into Sardinia after each step.

SELECTED READINGS

This chapter covers a large number of developments, and we can suggest only one or two readings for each.

The revolutions of 1848 are handled in stimulating fashion by Priscilla Robertson, *Revolutions of 1848* (Princeton, N.J.: Princeton University Press, 1952), and a somewhat easier account is Arnold Whitridge, *Men in Crisis: The Revolutions of 1848* (New York: Charles Scribner's Sons, 1948).

Italian unification is the theme of the novel by Anne D. Kyle, *Red Sky over Rome* (Boston: Houghton Mifflin Co., 1938). Interested students will find this subject excellently handled by the two outstanding biographies of E. E. Y. Hales, *Pio Nono* (New York: P. J. Kenedy & Sons, 1954), and *Mazzini and the Secret Societies* (New York: P. J. Kenedy & Sons, 1956).

The most interesting information available on the Crimean War are the recently published letters of Henry Clifford in *Henry Clifford, v.c., His Letters and Sketches from the Crimea* (New York: E. P. Dutton & Sons, 1956). The Berkshire Series study of Michael Karpovich, *Imperial Russia, 1801–1917* (New York: Henry Holt & Co., 1950), is helpful for this period, as well as for the rest of Russian history in the nineteenth and early twentieth centuries.

France in this period is excellently covered by James M. Thompson, *Louis Napoleon and the Second Empire* (New York: Noonday Press, 1955), especially in chapters 4 to 7.

CHRONOLOGICAL REVIEW

1815 Congress of Vienna; Holy Alliance; Quadruple Alliance
Large scale emigration from Britain begins
1818 Congress of Aix-la-Chapelle
1819 Congress of Troppau
S. S. Savannah crosses Atlantic
1821 Death of Napoleon; Greeks revolt against Turks
Champollion deciphers hieroglyphics
1823 Monroe Doctrine; Mexico becomes republic
1825 Portugal recognizes independence of Brazil
1829 Catholic Emancipation in Britain; Greece becomes independent
1830 Revolts in France, Belgium, and Poland; Belgian independence
Apparition of Our Lady to Catherine Labouré
1832 Great Reform Bill in Britain; Mazzini founds Young Italy
1833 *Slavery abolished in British Empire; German Zollverein*
1837 Queen Victoria of Britain (to 1901)
Dicken's OLIVER TWIST
1844 *Morse's first telegraph message*
1845 Annexation of Texas by U. S.
Famine in Ireland
1846 U. S.-Mexican War; Corn Laws abolished in Britain; Pope Pius IX (to 1878)
Howe's sewing machine; rotary printing press
1848 Revolutions in France, Italy, and Central Europe; fall of Metternich; Frankfort Assembly
COMMUNIST MANIFESTO *of Marx and Engels; death of Chateaubriand; gold discovered in California*
1849 Austro-Sardinian War; Russia helps Austria crush Hungarian revolt
1850 *Restoration of Catholic hierarchy in England; death of Wordsworth*
1851 Coup d'état of Louis Napoleon in France
1852 Louis Napoleon becomes emperor; *Stowe's UNCLE TOM'S CABIN*
1853 Crimean War (to 1856)
1854 Perry opens Japan
Dogma of Immaculate Conception
1856 *Bessemer invents steel converter*
1857 Sepoy Mutiny in India
1858 *Apparition of Our Lady at Lourdes*
1859 France and Sardinia fight Austria
Construction begins on Suez Canal
1860 Garibaldi seizes Sicily and Naples

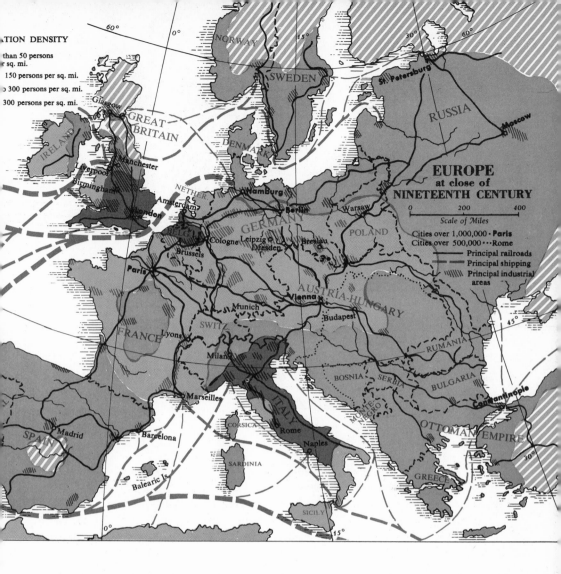

POPULATION DENSITY

less than 50 persons per sq. mi.

50-150 persons per sq. mi.

150-300 persons per sq. mi.

over 300 persons per sq. mi.

EUROPE
at close of
NINETEENTH CENTURY

Scale of Miles
0   200   400

Cities over 1,000,000 · **Paris**
Cities over 500,000 ···**Rome**
———— Principal railroads
———— Principal shipping
〰〰〰 Principal industrial areas

UNIT TEN
Internationalism and Imperialism

Great Britain and the United States · Prussia Creates a New German Empire · Relations of the Great Powers in Europe, 1871 to 1894 · Imperialism and the Scramble for Africa · The United States and Latin America · The Great Powers and India, Southeast Asia, and China · Japanese Imperialism and War with China · Russian Imperialism and War with Japan; Revolution in Russia and China · The "New" Industrial Revolution · Science and Religion · The Pressure of the Masses

527

Gladstone   Bismarck   Lincoln

Chapter 32. The Great Powers in the Latter Half of the Nineteenth Century

97. GREAT BRITAIN AND THE UNITED STATES

From 1860 to 1880 the middle and professional classes rose high in western Europe. Their liberal parties guarded their interests and above all their personal liberty. Liberals cherished freedom of speech, press, and conscience; and they adored science, which they believed had demonstrated that man could progress indefinitely. Progress could be achieved by science, by free men who were unhampered by any restrictions, and by popular education that was free of Church influence. Material prosperity, it appeared, could be ensured by the alliance of industry and science.

Growth of government. Liberals unknowingly prepared the way for the loss of personal liberty, which they cherished. Having considered the state as a giver of liberty, they forgot that the state could take away what it gave. They surrendered supreme authority to the state by recognizing no authority above it. Duties that were once performed by churches or local authorities, such as caring for the poor, educating children, or regulating marriage, were assumed by modern governments in Europe. The mightiest emperors and kings of old never affected the daily lives of people as regularly as did governments in the latter part of the nineteenth century.

The central government—in Paris, London, Rome, or Berlin—possessed broad powers over the whole country.

These powers had steadily increased from the days when medieval kings began to assert a measure of authority over local areas. In modern times the might of king and minister multiplied many times. Still the king's government did not dare to deprive provinces of certain functions until the nineteenth century. Then local areas lost real authority and were reduced to the role of carrying out the wishes of the government that was located in the national capital. Even in the United States, where the national government only exercised certain enumerated powers (to conduct foreign affairs, to wage war, to regulate commerce among the states, etc.), we see the gradual growth of the national government at Washington at the expense of the states that compose the Federal Union.

The Pre-eminence of Britain. Great Britain was the center of the liberal world. She enjoyed popular government, a parliamentary system, material prosperity, and free trade. So great was her prestige that the British system of government and industry was copied widely. The belief was widespread that a parliamentary system and economic liberty were enough to bring prestige and prosperity to any nation that followed the British example.

During the sixty-four-year reign of Queen Victoria (1837–1901), monarchy, although greatly transformed, became solidly established. When she died, she left monarchy popular, strong, vital, and a symbol of British patriotism. Although Britain was a monarchy, real power was in the hands of Parliament. Two major parties rivaled each other in Parliament, Conservatives and Liberals. Both parties agreed about the fundamental questions of government: preserving the monarchy and the parliamentary system of government. What especially attracted attention throughout the world was the extension of the vote beyond the limits of the Reform Act of 1832. Prime Minister Benjamin Disraeli, a Conservative, in 1867 sponsored a measure giving city workers

Prime Minister Gladstone, Queen Victoria, and Prime Minister Disraeli were able to bring to Great Britain more popular government in which the franchise was extended and the government increased its intervention for the benefit of the workers. (Hulton Picture Library and British Information Services)

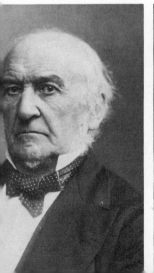

the vote. As a result, a million more men participated in the election of Parliament. In 1872, William E. Gladstone, Britain's greatest Liberal Prime Minister, introduced the Australian or secret ballot, which enabled people to cast their votes without fear of having their choices known. In 1885, he induced Parliament to give the vote to farm workers. Public sentiment as well as opinion was now immediately felt in the affairs of government. The growth of popular education and of cheap newspapers helped to interest Englishmen in public affairs.

Trade and industry gave Britain a strong foundation for power and prestige. By the 1870's Britain became an industrial nation in the sense that the majority of her people derived their living from industry and commerce instead of farming. She was the chief workshop, banker, and shipper of the world. Her mills produced the cloth and her mines the coal and iron for much of the globe. English vessels far exceeded in number those of any other country. British brokers wrote insurance and British merchants supplied markets with goods from the four corners of the world. And, more important, the bankers of England invested the profits earned by British industry in faraway lands. Since opportunities for investing money in mines or railways or factories were promising, British bankers poured a steady stream of capital into foreign enterprises. By 1914 about one-fourth of Britain's national wealth was invested abroad. Half of this was in the British Empire.

English manufacturers and bankers were eager to invest money in foreign

Advertisement of an English textile mill's cotton thread from "The Official Descriptive and Illustrated Catalogue of the Great Exhibition, 1851." (Hulton Picture Library)

lands not only because investment brought profit but also because it increased foreign customers for English goods.

Free trade vs. protection. British manufacturers and traders favored the policy of free trade so that their goods could move without restrictions. But world events undermined the foundation for free trade. The '60's and '70's brought to the fore a strong United States, a mighty Germany, and a united Italy. When industry began to grow in such countries, especially in the United States and Germany, manufacturers urged their governments to erect high tariffs that would shut the door on British goods and thereby protect home industry. By 1890 the United States and the countries of Europe had abandoned free trade and adopted protective tariffs. They were serious competitors of Great Britain in manufacturing.

The gold standard. Nevertheless, Britain still dominated international trade. An indication of her importance was the adoption of the gold standard by other countries. In 1816, Britain had adopted the gold standard, which meant that the pound or unit of English money was defined as a certain weight and fineness of gold. When other countries also valued their money in terms of gold, the British pound sterling became international currency.

Britain depended on imports to supply her factories with raw materials and her people with food and necessities. Since she did not export enough manufactures to pay for her imports, she made up the difference by supplying the world with special services, such as maritime insurance, shipping, technical assistance, or money invested in foreign lands. These "invisible items" of trade produced the sums needed to offset the costs of imports.

British colonies. British influence was also extended by her colonies, despite the fact that many Englishmen considered colonies as needless expenses that returned little for the huge expenditures necessary to administer and defend them. Free traders taught that world commerce would supply Britain with all the advantages of colonies without any of the disadvantages. But, as we have seen, free trade declined. Moreover, the British colonies themselves protested against the lack of interest shown by the mother country. They wanted neither separation nor independence, but they did want home rule.

Canada, which continued to hold first place among English colonies, was given control over home affairs, while Britain retained control over foreign affairs and war. By 1855 these ideas were applied to all the British colonies in North America and later to New Zealand and the Australian settlements. The British North America Act of 1867 formed a federal union, called the "Dominion of Canada," consisting of the provinces of Nova Scotia, New Brunswick, Ontario, and Quebec. This federation permitted the free development of the English and French peoples without the hostility that characterized their earlier association, and the settlement of the vast areas of the Canadian west.

The improvement of transportation and communication that was highlighted by the laying of the Atlantic

Statue of Ferdinand de Lesseps in Port Said. De Lesseps formulated plans for the Suez Canal, organized the canal company, and supervised the work on the canal. (Suez Canal Company)

Samuel F. B. Morse (1791–1872), American inventor of the telegraph, received world acclaim for his invention which transmitted messages over a wire. (Library of Congress)

cable in 1866 and the opening of the Suez Canal in 1869 helped to bring the parts of the British Empire together. Englishmen became less willing to cast their colonies adrift when they realized that other nations would reach out for them. With the development of British patriotism and nationalism, books and newspapers showed the pride of Britain in those Englishmen who had planted the British flag all over the world. As the nineteenth century came to a close, Englishmen renewed their interest not only in the older colonies, such as Canada and Australia, but in newer lands in Africa and Asia. Considerable discussion took place about plans to allow self-governing colonies to send representatives to an imperial parliament that would be entrusted with the duties of defense, war, and foreign relations.

Slavery question in the United States. Since the Louisiana Purchase (1803), the southern states desired to extend Negro slavery in the western territories over the objections of the North. North and South settled their differences temporarily by compromises in 1820 and 1850 because the statesmen who led the country during the trying days of the founding of the Republic were eager to settle the differences among the sections so that they could safeguard their beloved Union. After the 1830's, however, the younger statesmen would not compromise. Some of them were abolitionists, who considered slavery a moral wrong that had to be wiped out. In 1854 a new party, the Republican, announced its intention of ending slavery. On the other hand, many Southerners loudly proclaimed that slavery was a social system that brought prosperity and civilization and therefore should be preserved and extended. The clash of these two extremes filled the country with hate.

Northern and southern tempers flared up over the issue of permitting slavery in the territories of Kansas and Nebraska. A series of unwholesome incidents culminated in the execution of John Brown, a half-crazed abolitionist. It was clear now that numerous issues divided North and South, only one of which was slavery. Basically, the South feared that her proud position in the country was endangered. Southerners looked back to the "good old days" of the Republic when they had given their greatest sons to the nation as presidents, statesmen, or generals. Southerners saw a dark future. The growth of population in the northern and western states and the admission of new free states threatened to deprive them of an influential voice in national affairs. The other sections were threatening not only the South's "peculiar institution" of slavery but its political and economic position.

When Abraham Lincoln, the Republican candidate, was elected in 1860, Southerners called state conventions to dissolve the Federal Union. In reality, the South was relying on the right of self-determination, the same principle that led Italians and other nations to declare that they had the right to decide for themselves under what government they would live. It is not difficult to understand why many liberals like Gladstone applauded the efforts of the South to become a separate nation.

United States Civil War. War broke out in April 1861. The northern, or Union, forces strove to preserve the Union. Twenty-three states with twenty-two million people faced the rebellious South, which counted only eleven

Abraham Lincoln intended to heal the wounds of his country after the Civil War with a generous policy of amnesty and reconstruction.

(The Metropolitan Museum of Art)

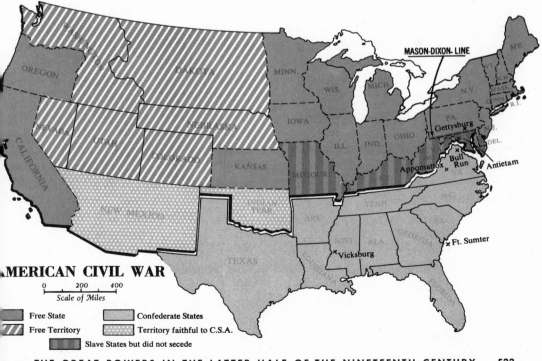

MERICAN CIVIL WAR

0   200   400
Scale of Miles

Free State
Free Territory
Slave States but did not secede
Confederate States
Territory faithful to C.S.A.

MASON-DIXON-LINE

states and nine million people. Although outnumbered and outgunned, the South had able generals and the advantage of fighting for its own soil. While the Union navy blockaded southern ports and cut off outside help, the northern armies launched a series of campaigns that cut up the South and broke its fighting spirit.

The American Civil War aroused the interest of the world. Not only were the European powers interested in the struggle of the South to make good her claim for independence, but they wanted southern cotton for their factories. The attempt of the Union navy to cut off foreign trade from the South aroused the anger of Britain and France, who came near to recognizing the southern Confederacy. The campaigns of the Civil War were studied carefully by foreign military experts, who sought information for future wars. Never before in history had such huge and well-equipped armies been thrown into battle. Prussian generals examined the tactics of the southern military geniuses, Generals Lee, Jackson, and Stuart. Furthermore, the war was of world importance because it showed the advantages that a nation would possess if it had modern industries supplying its armies and navy with weapons and ammunition.

Results of the war. The victory of the Union forces was a powerful lesson to the rest of the world. When Lee surrendered to Grant at Appomattox, disunion lost. The lesson was not wasted on Britain, who now became anxious for Canada. The Civil War strengthened the American federal government and settled the question of whether or not a state could withdraw from the Federal Union.

The Civil War was followed by the development of American nationalism. The bravery of war heroes filled young people with pride, while the exploits of soldiers, and of pioneers who after the war opened up the West, provided future generations with materials for stories that gloried in America. In a single lifetime men and women saw the American Republic expand from the Mississippi to the Pacific and establish railways, mines, cities, and free government. And Americans were convinced that the future held even greater prospects for them. They were encouraged by the amazing expansion of manufacturing and agriculture that provided the country with economic power.

98. PRUSSIA CREATES A NEW GERMAN EMPIRE

We noted in the last unit that Prussia failed to unify Germany in the revolutions of 1848–1849 when the conservative forces rallied to prevent major changes in the status of Germany. We shall now see that Prussia overcame these obstacles by using German nationalism and her army. If the unification of Italy shook international life, the union of the German states under Prussian leadership would change the direction of history.

The earlier defeat of German unification prepared the way for Prussia's eventual success. The failure of German liberals in 1849 pushed them into the background and brought to the fore hard men who were ready to face hard facts. Germans were determined to achieve national unity at any cost.

They admired the methods that Cavour employed to unify Italy. In their view, only a great and powerful nation commanded respect among the nations of the world. Furthermore, German manufacturers and traders realized the advantages that union would bring. They noted that the *Zollverein* that Prussia organized promoted industry and trade. How much more effective would a political union be at a time when German industry was making huge strides to overcome a slow start!

Prussia was the hope of nationalists, who admired her toughness and determination. Despite meager resources and unfavorable conditions, Prussia became a great state. Her power was based on her kings and an efficient army. The state was the main concern of Prussians. The "Prussian system" permitted the operation of the government on a small budget so that large sums could be set aside for a big army, which was recruited by compulsory military service. Prussia had "starved herself to greatness." Although she had a consti-tution that appeared to be liberal, real power was in the hands of the king.

Bismarck's policy and wars. In 1862 the Prussian parliament blocked the plans of Prussian generals to strengthen the army. Otto von Bismarck, a bold and astute statesman, was appointed chief minister to force the army bill through parliament. He was dedicated to the purpose of making the King of Prussia the ruler of a united Germany. He had only contempt for liberals. German unity, he thought, would not be won by speeches and majority resolutions but only by "blood and iron." From 1862 to 1866, Bismarck, with the support of King William I, defied parliament and carried through the military program.

Prussia could become master of Germany only after Austria was humbled, and Bismarck set out to accomplish that step by step. In 1864 the King of Denmark wished to strengthen his authority in the duchies of Schleswig and Holstein, which were connected with Denmark and possessed a partly Ger-

The reign of William I, King of Prussia (1861–1888), was important in the history of Europe because it saw the rise of Germany as the first power of continental Europe. (Library of Congress)

Otto von Bismarck (1815–1898), the "Iron Chancellor," was the creator of the new German Empire by means of a strong military program and skillful propaganda.

man population. Prussia drew Austria into an attack on Denmark, after which the victorious Austro-Prussian allies quarreled over the disposition of Schleswig-Holstein. Bismarck used this quarrel as a pretext for provoking war with Austria.

He had prepared the way for war with Austria by getting a promise from Italy and France to help. Italian nationalists considered unification of their country incomplete until Venetia and Rome were annexed. But they could not be annexed without opposing Austria again. Since Austria also stood in the way of Prussia's ambitions in Ger-

many, Bismarck offered Venetia to Italy in exchange for help.

War broke out in 1866. Before the Austrians could catch their breaths, the Prussians had unleashed a lightning attack. Prussian discipline, new weapons, and competent leadership by General von Moltke broke Austrian resistance in seven weeks! The Italians attacked Austria from the south.

North German Confederation. Prussia annexed not only Schleswig-Holstein but also Hanover and the duchies of Nassau and Hesse-Cassel and the city of Frankfurt. Italy received Venetia. Bismarck had achieved his objective of

General Helmuth von Moltke, Prussian field marshal, worked tirelessly to perfect Prussia's efficient and powerful war machine. Moltke's military genius led to complete Prussian victory. After the Prussians' decisive battle at Sadowa (July 3, 1866), King William I visited the scene and was cheered by his victorious soldiers. (Historisches Bildarchiv)

humbling Austria, but the shrewd statesman did not wish to embitter a country whose support he would need in the future. Still the results of the war were a hard blow to Austria. Bismarck organized the small states north of the Main River into the North German Confederation, which replaced the German Confederation established by the treaties of Vienna.

The dual monarchy, Austria-Hungary. The defeat convinced Emperor Francis Joseph that Austria had to rid herself of weakness, derived from the lack of unity among the populations of the Hapsburg Empire. To strengthen the empire, Joseph conceded to the demands of the Hungarians. In 1867 the *Ausgleich* (or Compromise) created the dual monarchy, known as Austria-Hungary. Francis Joseph was Emperor of Austria and King of Hungary. The two states were separate, but a joint Austro-Hungarian ministry was in charge of finances, foreign affairs, and war. This partnership between the Austrians and the Hungarians strengthened the Hapsburg Empire but in the long run alienated such peoples as the Croats and Czechs, who had hoped that the empire would give all the subject nationalities equal rights.

Prussia vs. France. Prussia now held two-thirds of Germany and was ready to add southern Germany. Before Bismarck could bring the south Germans under Prussia he had to come to grips with Napoleon III, the mighty Emperor of the French, who did not desire a united Germany on his eastern flank.

After 1860 Napoleon's fortunes had suffered. Although he proudly said that his regime stood for democracy and na-

Francis Joseph I, Emperor of Austria and King of Hungary under the dual monarchy. (Ullstein)

tionality, he suppressed liberal agitation. The emperor's troubles multiplied. He had said that the "empire means peace," but he involved France in a costly war to place Archduke Maximilian, the brother of Francis Joseph, on the throne of Mexico. The defeat of his Mexican venture in 1867 came on top of his failure to help the Poles, who tried to win independence in 1863. But the emperor still was master of France and meant to force Prussia to stay in her place.

Napoleon demanded compensation for Prussia's recent victories which had upset the balance of power. He wanted Bismarck to support his claim for Belgium or lands along the Rhine or in southern Germany. But the Prussian minister ignored these demands. Meanwhile he stripped Napoleon of his allies. The Russian Czar was friendly to Prussia. The princes of southern Germany were convinced that Napoleon was a menace. The King of Italy

After losing the battle at Sedan on September 1, 1870, Napoleon III and 100,000 of his men were captured by Bismarck's army. (Historisches Bildarchiv)

was ready to support the Prussian king in return for help in annexing Rome, which was still protected by French troops.

The Franco-Prussian War. The pretext for war was supplied when a prince of the Hohenzollern house, the royal family of Prussia, was nominated as King of Spain. Napoleon III objected to an extension of Prussian influence to Spain, but he was not content in merely preventing the Hohenzollern candidacy. He demanded a Prussian promise that no member of the Prussian royal family would ever be a candidate for the Spanish throne. The refusal of Prussia to give that guarantee led to a French declaration of war in July 1870. In taking up Napoleon's challenge, Bismarck posed as the defender of the liberty of Germany, which he wished to protect against the French.

The Prussian army was ready to march. Within six weeks the French were shattered and Napoleon III was captured with his army at Sedan. The news of the collapse led to the overthrow of the Second Empire and the creation of a provisional government, which stubbornly defended Paris against Prussian troops until January 1871.

"Prisoner of the Vatican." When the war compelled Napoleon to recall the French garrison from Rome, the Italians occupied the papal city and proclaimed Rome the capital of a united Italy. Pope Pius IX withdrew behind the walls of the papal palace to become the "prisoner of the Vatican." The Pope's self-imposed prisonment was a protest against the lawless seizure of Rome and much property of the Church. By taking Rome, the Italian government put an end to the temporal power of the Pope, a development hailed by European liberals who saw the end of papal authority as a victory for religious freedom.

Treaty of Frankfurt. Franco-Prussian peace terms were settled in the Treaty of Frankfurt of 1871. France surrendered the rich provinces of Alsace and part of Lorraine and paid an indemnity of a billion dollars. Alsace was a rich manufacturing district, while Lorraine contained important reserves of coal and iron ore. Germany now was the strongest state in Europe, for Prussia by her victory had created a new German Empire.

German Empire. During the war the four independent states of southern Germany joined the northern union. With a flair for the dramatic, Bismarck arranged to have the King of Prussia, William I, proclaimed *Kaiser* or German emperor in the Hall of Mirrors in the Palace of Versailles. Bismarck's work was a triumph for German nationalism but was a setback, however, for other nationalities. Large numbers

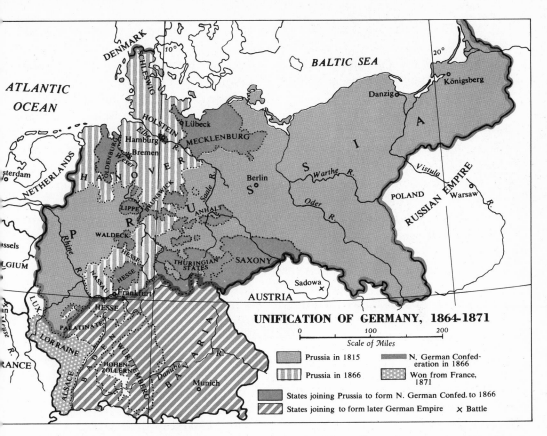

UNIFICATION OF GERMANY, 1864-1871

Scale of Miles
0   100   200

- Prussia in 1815
- Prussia in 1866
- N. German Confederation in 1866
- Won from France, 1871
- States joining Prussia to form N. German Confed. to 1866
- States joining to form later German Empire
- × Battle

of Danes in Schleswig agitated for union with Denmark, while millions of Poles scattered throughout eastern Germany wished to be joined to Poland. And the populations of Alsace-Lorraine, especially the Alsatians, were not content. But Bismark tolerated no disunion. To enforce German unity, he discriminated against the use of the Polish and French languages.

Bismarck and the Church. Having unified Germany, Bismarck saw his next task as the elimination of threats to the autocratic system of government. He saw three main enemies: liberals, Catholics, and socialists. He left no doubt in the minds of Germans that he distrusted liberalism, and he did his utmost to divorce liberalism from German nationalism. He won middle-class sup-

port for his policy of strengthening the empire, the army, the state Protestant Church; and won the nobility by showing that Prussian power, rather than liberal ideas, achieved German unification.

The German chancellor turned against German Catholics because they had been sympathetic to Austria, Poland, and Alsace. In 1872 the German government began to repress Catholics in what was called the *Kulturkampf* ("battle for civilization"). The Jesuits were expelled, religious orders were forbidden to teach, clergymen were made state officials, civil marriage was decreed, and the state controlled education. But German Catholics struck back by organizing the Center Party to defend the interests of the Church.

In 1877, Bismarck called off the fight because he saw that his third enemy, the socialists, were a greater menace to his regime than were conservative Catholics.

Socialism in Germany. The Socialist Party was outlawed in 1878. Bismarck then attempted to reduce socialism's attraction of the working class by extending welfare benefits to laboring classes. Sickness and accident insurance, old-age pensions, and free education laws were enacted to "kill socialism by kindness." Although workers eagerly accepted these benefits, they continued to support the socialists, or Social Democrats, as they called themselves. Bismarck's social policy is usually called *state socialism.*

The development of the Socialist Party in Germany was an index of the extent of German industry. In the latter half of the nineteenth century the output of coal and iron ore was evidence that Germany had taken giant strides in industry. The application of scientific knowledge to industrial prob-

lems gave Germany a leading position in the production of chemicals and dyes. With an intelligent and adequate labor force and with a government that supported home industry by shutting out foreign goods, the Germans prospered.

The humiliation of France. As Germany rose to great power, France sank low. After the surrender of Paris in 1871, that city erupted in a short but fierce civil war. The task of providing France with a permanent government to replace the empire was difficult. Many wished to restore a king but could not agree on the person of the new king; hence republicans were able to establish the Third Republic in 1875.

France was a divided country: republicans, Bonapartists, socialists, and monarchists vied for support. An influential part of the French nation, especially Catholics, royalists, and the army, looked to the day when a more favorable government would be established. The fact that no one party could gain an absolute majority led to the

William is proclaimed Emperor of Germany at Versailles. The new Reich included twenty-five states, four kingdoms, five grand duchies, thirteen duchies and principalities, and three free cities. (Library of Congress)

formation of blocs, or temporary political alliances of two or more parties, to control the Chamber of Deputies and the cabinet. These blocs were not stable, with the result that the life of many cabinets was a few months or even weeks.

Troubles of France. A series of crises shook the French Republic. In 1886–1887, General Georges Boulanger, the war minister, advocated a war of revenge on Germany. For a while it looked as if he would become dictator and declare war on Germany, but at the crucial moment he lost heart. A second threat to the republic was the discovery of financial scandals that implicated leading politicians. In 1892, French investors in a company that was digging a canal through Panama, under the supervision of Ferdinand de Lesseps, lost three hundred million dollars in a swindle. Perhaps the greatest crisis was posed in 1894 by the trial of Captain Alfred Dreyfus, a French Jew, on a charge of handing over secret documents to a foreign power. He was convicted and sentenced to penal servitude for life on Devil's Island. The army, royalists, and anti-Semites were convinced that the Jewish captain was guilty, while republicans and anti-clericals were convinced that he was innocent. By 1906, Dreyfus was proved innocent. His vindication was a triumph for the republic, which was now in the control of anti-clericals. A series of strict laws deprived the Church of many of her historic functions. Oddly enough, while the activities of the Church were restricted in France, the government encouraged Catholic missionaries to evangelize China, Indo-China, and islands of the Pacific.

99. RELATIONS OF THE GREAT POWERS IN EUROPE, 1871 TO 1894

International co-operation. In the late nineteenth century the nations of Europe were in many ways drawn into closer relations. Scientists and scholars from every country exchanged information and help. Trade unions in one country encouraged the development of the labor movement in other lands. Radicals and revolutionaries ignored national boundaries in spreading their doctrines. Distances were shrunk by fast ships and trains that encouraged tourists to vacation away from their own country. Religion also helped to knit the peoples of Europe and the world together. Beginning in 1881, Eucharistic Congresses brought together thousands of Catholics from the four corners of the earth. Societies dedicated to the promotion of peace sprang up and were heartened by evidences of international co-operation: the establishment of the international Red Cross in 1864, the Telegraph and Postal Unions in 1875 and 1878 respectively, and agreements on uniform patent and copyright laws in the 1880's. Industry and capital were strong links because they created an international economic society. It is true, as we have said, that practically all countries erected high tariffs to keep out foreign goods. Nevertheless, money and goods crossed national boundaries. French wines went to Germany, British textiles to Italy, and German steel to Russia. A world market for the special products of different countries existed. As the white European reached out to conquer or dominate economically Africa and Asia, Negro and yellow races began supplying European and American industry with raw materials. Rubber, cotton, jute, tin, gold, Manila hemp, and palm oil fed industry, while sugar, tapioca, coffee, tobacco, and spices improved the standard of living in the Western world. In return for these products, Europe exported manufactured goods.

Since so much of the world became an economic unit, the rise and fall of prices affected men and women in the far corners of the globe, so that a depression that started in one country could be felt everywhere. The world became so interdependent in trade, agriculture, and manufacturing that a change in one part of the world soon affected others. For example, the opening of the rich prairies of the United States and Canada in the 1870's and 1880's enabled American-grown grains to be exported to Europe. At the same time Russia became a great exporter of wheat. Because of the resulting surpluses Europe staggered into a serious agricultural depression.

Bankers and capitalists ignored national boundaries. Englishmen, Frenchmen, Dutch, Belgians, Swiss, and Germans invested money in railways, mines, or other enterprises located in each other's country or in America, Africa, or Asia. Often capitalists reached understandings on sharing opportunities for investment or markets and patents.

Great power rivalries. National rivalries threatened to wipe out the effects of international co-operation. With the growth of the state, men seemed to be more divided than ever before in history. Although fewer political units existed in the nineteenth century than in the Middle Ages, they behaved as if they had no ties with the rest of the world. As the great powers strove to strengthen themselves by adding other territories, conflict occurred. Six great powers dominated the European picture—Britain, France, Italy, Austria-Hungary, Germany, and Russia.

Although trade and industry helped to make these powers interdependent, they also stimulated their rivalry and ambition. Industrial development enabled the great powers to maintain mass armies and modern navies, to move troops rapidly, and to develop deadlier weapons. Modern war required long-range preparation. Supplies had to be stored, and plans for transporting soldiers and equipment had to be made long before war was declared. This meant that general staffs laid their plans for battle in peacetime so that armies and navies could move on short notice.

All the great powers, except Britain, maintained large standing armies that were recruited by universal military service. From 1871 to the outbreak of general war in 1914, great armies were ready to march at the command of their governments. As Bismarck said,

Inspection of the crew by the captain of a British merchantman. Rivalry among nations stimulated the growth and development of armies, navies, and merchant marines. (Hulton Picture Library)

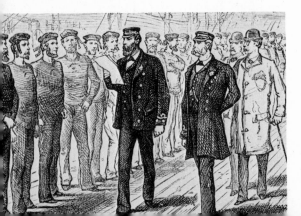

"The great powers of our time are like travelers, unknown to one another, whom chance has brought together in a carriage. They watch each other, and when one of them puts his hand into his pocket, his neighbor gets ready his own revolver in order to be able to fire the first shot."

Furthermore, the series of wars for German unification that ended in the Franco-Prussian conflict had shown that might brought results. The sword could do what years of peaceful effort failed to accomplish. The victory enabled Prussia to bring southern Germany into the union. To many this was proof that war *did* pay. In those years it was believed widely that war was an instrument of progress and even a blessing to mankind! As Herbert Spencer, an English social theorist, declared, "Without war the world would have been inhabited only by men of feeble types sheltering in caves and living on wild food."

Pre-eminence of Germany. We shall now see how the great powers of Europe clashed. Bismarck had realized his ambitions. Prussia had expanded into Germany. Austria was eliminated from German leadership, and France was no longer the leading power of Europe. It was Germany who had the loudest voice in the affairs of Europe. No single country could dare attack her. Yet the thought of another war with France sent chills up Bismarck's spine, because it would endanger the fruits of the victory of 1871. He was sure, however, that France would not attack without the help of an ally. Therefore, the object of his diplomacy from the end of the Franco-Prussian War to his retirement in 1890 was to isolate France

Fëdor Dostoevsky, Russian novelist, journalist, and short-story writer.
(Ullstein)

so that she could not get an ally. He wished to prevent war, and the task of preserving peace was difficult.

Austria-Hungary and Russia. Austria, banished from German leadership, now turned to the Balkans as a field for influence and expansion. But Austrian ambition conflicted with Russia's. Russian efforts to dominate the Balkans at the expense of the Ottoman Empire had been temporarily blocked in the Crimean War. However, Russian ambitions remained. Moscow was the "Third Rome." Russian nationalists believed that Russia had a mission in the world. This idea is expressed by the famous novelist Fëdor Dostoevsky: "Do you know who are the only God-bearing people on earth, destined to regenerate and save the world in the name of a new God, and to whom are given the keys of life and of the new world?" The answer was "Russia." Dostoevsky believed that Russia should unite all Slavs. Now the Czars cleverly exploited such sentiments in getting support for their ambitious schemes.

The Congress of Berlin, of which Bismarck was chairman, reconsidered and deeply modified the terms of the Treaty of San Stefano. In the photo, Disraeli is sixth from left; Bismarck is shaking hands with Russian Count Shuvalov. (Hulton Picture Library)

Balkan upheaval. Conditions in the Balkans supplied Russia with opportunities for intervention. The suppressed Christian peoples chafed under Turkish rule. Having achieved partial home rule, Bulgars, Serbs, and Rumanians now demanded complete independence. And they looked to Russia for help. The Balkans exploded in July 1875, when the Christian populations of Bosnia and Herzegovina rebelled against the Turks. After Serbia and Montenegro joined the fight in 1876, the Turks moved to prevent Bulgaria from interfering by terrorizing the country. Russia prepared to intervene and sought an Austrian promise to stand aside in exchange for a Russian assurance that Bosnia and Herzegovina would be given to Austria.

Russo-Turk war and Treaty of Berlin. The Czar's insistence that the sultan mend his ways led to a Russo-Turk war in 1877. Turkish troops were no match for the Czar's armies, which overran the Balkans. The victorious Czar then imposed the Treaty of San Stefano on the sultan, who was forced to pay a big indemnity to Russia and to surrender lands that placed Russia at the mouth of the Danube River. The sultan was also compelled to recognize the independence of Serbia, Montenegro, and Rumania. Bulgaria was enlarged and made autonomous while remaining loosely connected with the Ottoman Empire. The extent of the Russian victory startled the other powers, who did not relish the idea that the Czar alone should determine the fate of the

Balkans. The other powers forced Russia to come to negotiate with them in a conference at Berlin so that the treaty could be revised. At this meeting Bismarck played the role of the "honest broker," trying to smooth over the differences between Britain and Austria on one side and Russia on the other. The Treaty of Berlin (1878), which resulted from these discussions, fell short of what Russia had gained in the Treaty of San Stefano. Bulgaria, over which Russia now held a protectorate, was reduced in extent. It was agreed that Austria should occupy and pacify Bosnia and Herzegovina. This was a clear indication of Hapsburg interest in the Balkans and of Austrian determination to regulate the affairs of the southern Slavs. Soon afterward Serbia placed herself under Austrian protection.

Russian nationalists were angry at having to pare down their victory over the Turks. They had conceived the war as a crusade for liberating their fellow Slavs and Orthodox Christians in the Balkans from the control of the infidel Turks. And they felt that the great powers, especially Germany, had robbed Russia of the fruits of victory.

Austro-German Alliance. Bismarck did not rule out the possibility that Austria and Russia might still go to war. In such a war Austria would probably be defeated. In that event her subject nationalities would revolt and Russia would aid them, thus becoming dominant in central-eastern Europe. In 1879, Germany and Austria-Hungary negotiated an alliance, in which each power promised to help the other in case of war. This alliance was not aimed directly against Russia but

Die besorgte Erzieherin.

The anxious governess (Bismarck) exhorts her charges (Tisza of Austria-Hungary and Crispi of Italy) not to step out of line (the Triple Alliance).

(Ullstein)

against a possible alliance of France and Russia.

League of Three Emperors. Bismarck judged that peace could best be preserved if Austria, Germany, and Russia were allied. Toward this purpose he sponsored the Three Emperors' League, by which the emperors of Austria, Germany, and Russia promised to cooperate to settle questions in certain defined regions. By bringing Austria and Russia together, Bismarck made sure that neither could move against the other without first consulting Germany. This would enable Bismarck to keep the Austrians and Russians from going to war over the Balkans.

Italy joins German-Austrian alliance. Bismarck wished to improve the prospects of peace in Europe by diverting the attention of the powers from European affairs to colonial expansion. He encouraged France to occupy Tunisia in North Africa. Italy, who had considered Tunisia a natural field for Italian expansion, was embittered and sought German support. In 1882, Italy became the ally of Germany and Austria. Thus the Triple Alliance was born. Austria, Germany, and Italy formed a mighty bloc, and they were joined by Serbia and Rumania, who were afraid of Russian domination of the Balkans. Their Triple Alliance continued until 1915.

In 1887, Britain and Italy reached an agreement concerning the Mediterranean. Since Austria and Spain also subscribed to the Mediterranean agreement, France was isolated.

Franco-Russian Alliance. Bismarck's diplomatic efforts to isolate France failed. His Triple Alliance forced France and Russia together. When he made it difficult for Russia to borrow German money in 1887, the French eagerly supplied the necessary funds. Thereafter events drifted toward a Franco-Russian alliance, although the movement was slow because the Czar distrusted the French Republic. It was an accord between Germany and Great Britain that finally forced the Franco-Russian alliance. In exchange for ceding the island of Heligoland in the North Sea to Germany in 1890, Britain was compensated with African territories. The Czar suspected that a British-German alliance had been hatched. As much as he detested the French—who had overthrown monarchy and were atheists in his opinion—the Czar came to terms with the French Republic in 1894.

The Franco-Russian allies seemed to be on the offensive. The Russians were pushing out in the direction of Persia and China, while the French were on the move in Siam and North Africa. These developments worried Britain. Germany was willing to support Britain for a price, but the British refused to meet the large price of the Germans, which amounted to joining the Triple Alliance. Soon both countries drew apart.

With the great powers now poised for further rivalry, the international picture became more critical than before. France was no longer isolated. In the 1870's and 1880's, Bismarck had preserved European peace by skillful diplomacy. In the 1890's, however, peace was kept by a balance of power between two camps, the Triple Alliance and the Franco-Russian combination. Britain stood outside these camps and was sought by both because she could tilt the balance one way or the other.

REVIEW

STUDY SECTIONS IN REVIEW
97. Great Britain and the United States

   A. Describe the developments in Britain's form of government at the end of the nineteenth century.

   B. Mention three factors that helped Britain lead the world in trade and shipping.

   C. What issues divided the North and the South in the United States?

   D. Why was the rest of the world interested in the American Civil War?

   E. Cite two results in the United States of the American Civil War.

98. Prussia Creates a New German Empire

A. What three wars were instigated by Bismarck to unify and strengthen Germany?

B. What steps did Bismarck take against Catholics? How did he deal with Socialists?

C. What were the terms of the Treaty of Frankfurt, which ended the Franco-Prussian War?

D. Identify: the "dual monarchy," the Third Republic, the Dreyfus Affair.

99. Relations of the Great Powers in Europe, 1871 to 1894

A. List four factors that made European nations more interdependent in this period.

B. Why did Bismarck aim at separating France from her potential allies?

C. Why were other nations alarmed by Russia's victory over the Turks in 1877?

D. Identify: Treaty of Berlin (1878), League of Three Emperors, Triple Alliance.

E. Did Bismarck finally succeed in isolating France? Explain.

THE CHAPTER IN REVIEW

A. What internal difficulties weakened France in the period 1871–1900?

B. Discuss the economic and political position of Great Britain in the world during the late nineteenth century.

C. Review the steps by which Bismarck unified the German nation.

D. Discuss the membership and purposes of three major power alliances in the period 1880–1900.

FOR YOUR NOTEBOOK

Under the headings of (1) industrial, (2) commercial, and (3) political, list in your notebook the reasons why Great Britain was the wealthiest and in certain respects the most powerful nation in this period.

Your authors point out that slavery was one issue dividing the North and the South. They also tell you that other basic differences developed between these sections. You can understand how these differences grew stronger by putting down the following data for the "free states" and the "slave states" for 1820, 1830, 1840, 1850, and 1860: number of states, population, miles of railroads, principal products or industries.

List chronologically the steps Bismarck took to unify Germany. Under each step—for example, the Franco-Prussian War—list reasons why Bismarck took the step and also list the results of each step.

Sum up the international relations covered in this chapter under the headings of "Co-operation" and "Competition." Now look at your lists and decide which kind of relationship predominates in this period.

This chapter covers internal developments in Britain, the United States, and Germany, as well as international relations. You will get a better view of the progress of events in this period if you draw up parallel columns for these four topics and enter into them the important events in each development.

SELECTED READINGS

Interesting books on Victorian England are G. M. Young, *Victorian England* (New York: Doubleday & Company, Inc., Anchor Books, 1954), and David Thoreson, *England in the Nineteenth Century* (Baltimore: Penguin Books, Inc., 1950).

Friedrich Darmstaedter, *Bismarck and the Creation of the Second Reich* (London: Methuen & Co., 1948), is an excellent study of this subject. Chapter 23 in Richard M. Brace, *The Making of the Modern World* (New York: Rinehart & Co., 1955), is a good short summary of Bismarck's unification of Germany.

Genevieve Foster, *Abraham Lincoln's World* (New York: Charles Scribner's Sons, 1957), is a good description of things throughout the world in the first half of the nineteenth century. The Civil War and its making are well described by Arthur Cole, *The Irrepressible Conflict, 1850–1865* (New York: The Macmillan Co., 1934).

Chapter 33. The Western Nations and World Power

100. Imperialism and the Scramble for Africa

While the Europeans and Americans had strengthened themselves economically by industrialization, many Asiatic and African countries were weak and disorganized. The great powers took advantage of the weakness. In a short time Europe and America extended their power influence throughout the world.

Imperialism means empire-building. It is the policy followed by stronger countries when they compel weaker or economically backward peoples to submit to their military, political, or economic control. As we have seen, from the dawn of history powerful countries have conquered their weaker neighbors or even crossed the seas to subdue distant lands. Thus Macedonians marched south to conquer the

weaker (though scarcely backward!) Greeks, and the Romans sailed across the Mediterranean to add Egypt to their empire.

After 1500, Portugal, Spain, England, France, and Holland established overseas empires. Their empires were primarily interested in extending national trade and power. After the 1880's there developed a "new imperialism" that sought more than trade and goods. Backward areas of the world were carefully controlled in order to provide the great powers with military or naval bases, national prestige, and extensive opportunities to invest capital in overseas railways, industries, and mines.

Forms of imperialism. European powers exercised varying degrees of control over weaker peoples. When they annexed an area or exercised full control over its government, they established a *colony*. If they controlled an area through a native chief who was kept in power by foreign troops and ships and told what to do by a foreign commissioner, they enjoyed a *protectorate*. Next, when two or more world powers divided a backward country among themselves for the purpose of exploiting its natural resources or commerce, they had a *sphere of influence*.

In the early part of the nineteenth century little interest in colonies existed. Liberals had then considered colonies unnecessary, and nationalists were more concerned with the problems of unifying their own country than in what Bismarck called expensive luxuries. Having unified their countries and consolidated their power, many nations now felt that they must expand farther so that they could fulfill a mission to civilize backward peoples. Patriotic writers, professors, statesmen, workers, and farmers took pride in their country's accomplishments and shared a wish to extend national influence. They founded societies to promote colonial development. Enthusiastic persons spread their country's influence in Africa and Asia and demanded that the home government back them up. They included merchants like Adolf Woermann of Germany, explorers like Savorgnan de Brazza of France and Karl Peters of Germany, capitalists like the Englishman Cecil Rhodes, soldiers like the British generals Gordon and Kitchener, and writers like Sir John Seeley of Britain and Josiah Strong of the United States. Even the common folk gloried in the accomplishments of their nation. For example, the millworker in Manchester, who lived a drab life, identified himself through the patriotic poems of Rudyard Kipling with the British soldier in India or Africa who experienced danger and adventure in order to raise the Union Jack throughout the world.

A *second reason* was economic. Fast-

Rudyard Kipling, England's first Nobel Prize winner in literature, described life and adventures of India. (British Information Services)

Lord Kitchener, British field marshal, was idolized by many British as a leader of British imperial expansion. (British Information Services)

growing industries required additional markets to dispose of goods manufactured in Europe, raw materials for industry, food for millions of Europeans, and opportunities to invest surplus funds. Capitalists and merchants enjoyed many privileges in areas annexed by the mother country. In some countries the rise of protective tariffs restricted markets for European goods and therefore drove capitalists to seek colonial markets. However, Italy and Russia—who had no surplus manufactured goods to sell—were in the forefront of the imperialist movement. Italy sought land for her surplus population, and Russia sought power.

Third, modern imperialism was aided by the widespread belief that there were superior races and nations—especially the Anglo-Saxon and Teutonic peoples —that had a natural right to rule weaker members of the human race. This was the view expressed by Josiah Strong when he declared that the Anglo-Saxon was "divinely commissioned to be . . . his brother's keeper." Many persons combined the motive of being their brother's keeper with the idea that the white men were superior to the Negro and yellow races and therefore had an obligation to raise them to civilization. This is the meaning of Rudyard Kipling's poem, *The White Man's Burden.*

> Take up the White Man's burden—
> Send forth the best ye breed—
> Go bind your sons to exile
> To serve your captives' need;
> To wait in heavy harness,
> On fluttered folk and wild—
> Your new-caught, sullen peoples,
> Half-devil and half-child.

Doubtless many colonial officials, teachers, doctors, and missionaries were sincere in sharing these sentiments. And they did much to raise the standard of living of the native peoples.

Fourth, religion encouraged the extension of European control. Protestant and Catholic missionaries wished to convert the heathen in Africa and the Far East, and they called upon their home governments to support their work. Thus French missionaries urged the Paris government to occupy the island of Madagascar off the coast of south Africa and Indo-China in the Far East. The reports of missionaries to benefactors at home described the customs and problems of China, Siam, and Samoa, and generated interest in these faraway lands.

Lastly, strategic considerations encouraged imperialism. The great powers of the world wanted naval bases where their cargo vessels and warships could refuel and take on supplies. They also wanted colonies in Africa, Asia, and the Pacific islands so that they could enjoy world-wide prestige and power.

The scramble for Africa. Africa south of the equator was a wilderness thinly inhabited by primitive Negro tribes whose economy was based on cattle and simple farming. Progress was hindered by the slave trade, which had reduced the population. Even after European countries one by one put an end to the enslavement of Negroes, Arabs continued to capture Negroes and march them to bases on the east coast of Africa. No unity existed among the Negro tribes, a fact that is easy to understand if we remember that over seven hundred different dialects were spoken.

Before 1880, Europeans had demonstrated little interest in colonizing Africa. They had landed on the coast to engage in the slave trade or to establish bases for ships sailing around Africa on their way to the East. And of course many Europeans had long been interested in Egypt and North Africa. Yet most of Africa was inaccessible. Little was known about the interior of the "Dark Continent." Few of its rivers were navigable because cataracts, rapids, or sand bars blocked entry. Overland travel was rendered dangerous by tropical disease and by hostile tribes. Moreover, the climate was generally too hot for white men.

Not long before 1875 a group of brave men explored the rivers and jungles of Africa. Two of the most famous explorers were John Hanning Speke and Richard Burton. Speke found Lake Victoria, a great inland sea of twenty-six thousand square miles, and Burton discovered Lake Tanganyika. Others fanned out in all directions: some traced the course of the great rivers, the Nile, Congo,

The meeting of Dr. Livingstone and Mr. Stanley. (British Information Services)

Niger, and Zambezi; others traveled inland from Red Sea ports, Zanzibar, or South Africa.

Livingstone and Stanley. David Livingstone (1813–1873), a British medical missionary, perhaps did more than any other single individual to arouse interest in Africa. He explored the regions around the Congo and Zambezi rivers and discovered Victoria Falls. His ultimate purpose was to free East Africa from the horrors of the slave trade. By opening Africa to British trade and Christian missions, he reasoned, the traffic in Negroes could be halted. He believed that the expansion of the British Empire into Africa meant the extension of Christendom. When no word of Livingstone reached the outside world after many years, an American newspaper sent Henry M. Stanley to find him. In 1871, Stanley found the great man in the heart of Africa, greeting him with the famous phrase, "Dr. Livingstone, I presume?" The medical missionary continued his labors among the Negroes until his death. So devoted were his African friends that when he died they carried his embalmed body fifteen hundred miles to the British consul in Zanzibar.

Effects of Suez Canal. The opening of the Suez Canal in 1869, linking the Mediterranean and Red seas, hastened the settlement of Africa by European nations. The east coast of Africa could now be reached more easily. But more important, the Suez Canal created more interest in the Mediterranean coast of Africa; that is, in all the vast territories stretching from Morocco in the west to Egypt in the east. You will recall that the Mediterranean basin had been the center of world history before the New World was discovered and the Atlantic powers of Portugal, Spain, England, and France became strong national states. It then faded into the background. The canal now converted the Mediterranean into a great highway between Europe and the Orient.

With her empire in India and commercial interests in China, Britain considered the Suez Canal as a short cut to India and the jugular vein of her empire. It became British policy to prevent any other strong country from dominating the eastern Mediterranean and thus threatening the British "life line." This meant that the Dardanelles and Bosphorus straits, the water links between the Black and Aegean seas, had to be closed to Russian warships that might threaten the Suez Canal in the event of war. And it also meant that France, who from the days of Napoleon Bonaparte, had hoped to control the Nile Valley, had to be kept out of Egypt. Any country annexing Egypt was a threat to Britain.

In 1875, Prime Minister Disraeli purchased for the British crown forty-four per cent of the capital stock of the Suez Canal Company from the Khedive (viceroy) of Egypt. The company that built and owned the canal had been largely French, although it was chartered by Egypt.

British in Egypt. Britain's next step was the occupation of Egypt. Because European bankers had made large loans to the Egyptian government, which was unable to pay the interest, Egypt fell into great financial difficulty. This led to much foreign med-

dling in Egyptian affairs. Egyptian nationalists resented the foreign influence. Disturbances in Egypt convinced British statesmen that European control was necessary, and in 1882 a British expedition occupied Egypt.

Equatorial Africa. The great powers of Europe had already engaged in a scramble for central African territories. In 1879, Leopold II, King of the Belgians, employed Henry Stanley to carve out an empire in the Congo. This formed the basis of the Belgian Congo Free State, an area rich in rubber and ivory but unfortunately the scene of terrible exploitation of the natives. Captain Lugard of the British Royal Niger Company took the Borgu and the right bank of the Niger just a week before the arrival of a French force. A German force claimed the Cameroons five days before the arrival of a British group with the same intentions. From November 1884 to

Leopold II, King of the Belgians, created social and political unrest in the Congo by building up his personal fortune through exploitation and forced labor. (Belgian Government Information Center)

February 1885 the great powers and the United States met in Berlin to establish rules for annexing African territories. It was agreed that any country that wanted to annex land should first inform the others, conclude a treaty with the native chiefs, and then occupy its claim. The Berlin agreement meant: "Take what you want in Africa, but don't go to war with your neighbors."

Britain, France, Belgium, Germany, Portugal, Spain, and Italy annexed large segments of Africa (see map). Their methods were similar. Having received gifts of liquor and toys, African chieftains were prevailed upon to sign treaties (which they could not read), turning over their lands to the European power. By means of such treaties, Karl Peters secured for Germany about sixty thousand square miles of African territory in ten days.

British and French clash. African colonization led to further international rivalry. The French dreamed of creating an east-west African empire extending from the Atlantic coast to the Red Sea. But their dream brought them into conflict with Germans, Italians, and British. The French and Germans settled their differences over equatorial Africa in 1894. The Germans gave the French a free hand for an empire on the upper Nile because they wished to play off France and Russia against Britain. They would then be able to throw their support to one side or the other in exchange for advantages to Germany.

The French also opposed Italian aspirations in Africa. Italy wished to make a triumphal entry on the stage of world history by conquering African territories and in part re-creating the

Menelik II, King of Abyssinia, astonished the world by his great victory over the Italians, forcing the Italians to concede Ethiopia's absolute independence.
(Library of Congress)

glories of the Roman Empire. After annexing Eritrea and Italian Somaliland, Italy was tempted to occupy Abyssinia. However, an Italian expeditionary force was defeated by the Emperor Menelik, who was aided by the French. The two Latin countries, Italy and France, became bitter competitors. When at length they came to terms in 1896 the Italians recognized the French conquest of Tunisia in exchange for French approval for the future annexation by Italy of Tripoli.

France planned to push Britain out of Egypt by placing herself on the upper Nile in the Sudan, from which she could threaten to divert the course of the Nile and deprive Egypt of water. The Nile supplies Egypt with life-giving waters, without which that country would be a desert. In July 1898, the French sent Captain Marchand with a small force from equatorial Africa to the upper Nile at Fashoda. Meanwhile a joint Anglo-Egyptian force subjugated the Sudan. (The Sudan is an area one fourth the size of Europe!) The commanding general, Sir Herbert Kitchener, continued up the Nile to Fashoda, where Marchand had raised the French tricolor. The two forces faced each other. Neither withdrew. War was threatened and the French yielded. Divided at home by the Dreyfus case and uncertain of support by Russia, the French were compelled to retreat.

France presently realized that she could not push Britain out of Egypt and that she had no alternative but to come to terms with her archrival. In 1899 the rivals agreed on the boundary between the Sudan and French Equatorial Africa. Britain and Egypt jointly controlled the Sudan, but since Britain controlled Egypt the rule was British.

Imperialism in South Africa. In 1854, Great Britain had recognized the independence of the Orange Free State and thirty years later recognized the autonomy of the Transvaal. These small South African states had been created by people called Boers, who were descendants of the early Dutch settlers. The hardy Boers fought to maintain their freedom and subdue the tribes of Bushmen, Hottentots, and Bantus. The last included the dreaded Kaffir and Zulu peoples. British settlers in Cape Colony, which had passed to Britain in 1815, cast envious glances in the direction of Boer territory in the north, where they hoped to share in great riches. In 1868 a Boer farmer bought a small stone from a native witch doctor for five hundred sheep, ten oxen, and one horse. The farmer sold it for £11,000 to a trader, who in turn resold it for £25,000. The small stone was the eighty-three-carat diamond, "Star of South Africa." In 1867 diamonds were discovered at Kimberley, a little to the north of Cape Colony. News that gold also was discovered in Boer territory sent adventurers from Cape Colony and Britain. The Boers heartily despised these "outlanders" and discriminated against them. The protests of the outlanders were heard by Cecil Rhodes.

Rhodes was Britain's greatest empire-builder in Africa. As a young man he went to South Africa to regain his health and soon became a millionaire and a leading figure in the Cape Colony. His dream was for a British railway from South Africa to Egypt (the "Cape-to-Cairo" railroad). To realize his dream he occupied Rhodesia and attempted to annex the territory that was later called German East Africa. Although he failed to obtain for Britain an unbroken strip of land from South Africa to Egypt, he did succeed in annexing the Boer republics. Rhodes hoped that Britain would dominate the world. As he said, "We are the first race in the world and . . . the more of the world we inhabit, the better it is for the human race."

The Boer War. When the outlanders asked for help from the Cape Colony, Rhodes felt the time had come to establish a single government for both Boers and British in South Africa. In 1895 some British settlers led by Dr. Leander Jameson made a raid into the

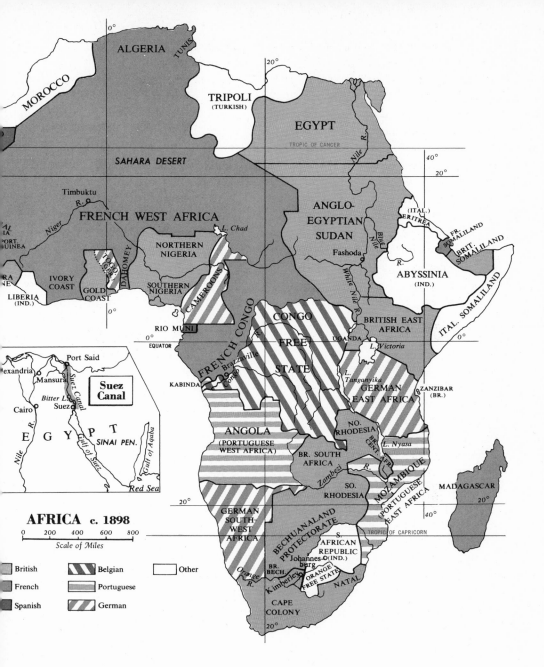

AFRICA c. 1898

Scale of Miles
0   200   400   600   800

British   Belgian   Other

French   Portuguese

Spanish   German

Transvaal. They were defeated. Urged on by Rhodes, the British government decided to subdue the Boers. War broke out in 1899. As expert marksmen and outdoor men, the Boers proved themselves tough fighters. Using guerrilla tactics, barbed-wire

entanglements, camouflaged uniforms, and displaying great personal courage, they held off for a time the numerically superior British troops.

The Boer War greatly strengthened British imperial patriotism, because it was supported not only by Englishmen but by Canadians, Australians, and New Zealanders, who sent contingents of troops to a foreign war for the first time in their history. By 1902 the British mopped up remaining Boer resistance. Britain proved to be a generous victor and soon introduced responsible government in South Africa. Boer leaders were permitted to hold public office, and South Africans drew up their own constitution.

The Boer War was a glaring reminder to Britain that she was friendless. Germany had encouraged the Boers to resist, and the Kaiser had telegraphed his congratulation to President Kruger on the occasion of the suppression of the Jameson raid. Germany went so far as to suggest the formation of a European coalition against Britain.

It was at this time that Germany resolved to build a strong navy. Under the influence of a famous book, *The Influence of Seapower on History,* written by an American, Captain Alfred Mahan, Kaiser William and Admiral Tirpitz planned a German navy that would be strong enough to threaten the British in the North Sea. The Germans believed that the threat of a powerful German navy would force Britain to come to terms. Conversations about conditions for an Anglo-German alliance took place but broke down, and Germany continued her naval building program. Britain then began to draw her forces to home waters in the North Sea and strengthen her empire by diplomacy. In the Far East she concluded a treaty of alliance with Japan in 1902, and in the New World she reached an informal understanding with the United States. In 1904 she settled her disputes with France.

Benefits to Africa. European imperialism conferred substantial benefits on the natives of Africa. The white men wiped out the frightful ceremonies of cannibalism and human sacrifices, witchcraft, slave raiding, and tribal warfare. Life became easier for the African natives. Tropical disease was checked. Schools and churches were established. Christian missionaries not only preached the gospel but taught the natives how to read and write. They nursed them when they were sick and showed them the importance of hygiene for good health. However, the natives could not forget that they were held down by the sword and that the white man's tyranny and greed often exceeded his generosity.

101. THE UNITED STATES AND LATIN AMERICA

Western expansion. For thirty years following the Civil War, American expansionist energies were absorbed in building and developing the West. Western expansion was highlighted in 1869 by the completion of a transcontinental railroad. By cutting the plains in half, the railway prevented the Indian, who had been roaming the vast area between the Canadian border and the Rio Grande, from blocking permanently the advance of white settlers. A series of Indian wars eliminated the red men from their western home. Settlement by white men was often preceded by railways. Aided by generous grants of public lands, railways connected the Midwest and plains states with the East. Attracted

East meets West in the dramatic completion of the first transcontinental railroad on May 10, 1869. The occasion of the joining of the Union Pacific from Omaha with the Central Pacific from Sacramento was marked by the driving of a golden spike. (Library of Congress)

by the abundance of rich lands, settlers poured into the West not only from the older states in the East but also from northern Europe. They took advantage of the Homestead Act (1862), which made available large tracts of free land. Railways also offered lands to settlers at market prices. The rapid western advance was reflected in the admission of new states to the Union. In 1889 the admission of four western states brought the total to forty-four.

Expansion of industry. Just as spectacular as the march to the Pacific was the expansion of industry. Conditions for rapid expansion were favorable. The United States contained vast stores of well-located natural resources, especially coal, iron ore, petroleum, timber, and various other minerals. The Great Lakes and the Mississippi River system, together with canals and railways,

afforded rapid movement of men and products. Inventors such as Thomas A. Edison, George Westinghouse, and many others turned out an endless stream of inventions and machines that continued to revolutionize industry. Besides, a large group of aggressive business managers and "captains of industry" utilized the resources, transportation, inventions, and intelligent workers to multiply their own and their country's wealth. The federal and state governments encouraged the expansion of industry.

Pacific acquisitions. Americans turned also to overseas ventures. In 1867, they took an important preliminary step when they purchased Alaska from Russia and occupied the Midway Islands. Next, the navy was interested in the excellent harbor of Pago Pago in the Samoan Islands, situated about six thousand miles from San Francisco. After the completion of the transcontinental railroad, many anticipated an increase in trade between the Pacific coast of the United States and the Far East, in which the Samoan Islands would be a natural stopover. But more than one country had imperial designs on the islands. Their rivalry almost caused a violent collision of Britain, Germany, and the United States. It was settled in 1899 when the islands were divided between Germany and the United States, with the latter annexing Pago Pago. An American interest arose in the Hawaiian Islands, and by 1875 the islands were virtually an American protectorate. Hawaii was annexed to the United States in 1898.

The Caribbean regions. Strategic and commercial considerations converted the Caribbean into an American sea.

The defense of the Caribbean islands was vital for the defense of the Gulf coast of the United States, and the resources of the Caribbean were useful for American industry. The Monroe Doctrine, issued in 1823, reflected American interest in the whole Western Hemisphere. The withdrawal of French troops from Mexico in 1867 added new laurels to the Monroe Doctrine. The United States declared that it would not tolerate the transfer of territory in the New World from one European power to another or any further colonization. In 1895, when a boundary dispute arose between Venezuela and British Guiana, the Monroe Doctrine was put to another test. Informing Britain that a forcible settlement of the dispute would violate the Monroe Doctrine, Secretary of State Olney declared that the "United States is practically sovereign on this continent, and its fiat is law upon the subjects to which it confines its interposition." In the interests of Anglo-American friendship, which she

Trenches at El Caney in the Spanish-American War. The successful Santiago campaign (in which Theodore Roosevelt won popular acclaim) in effect ended the war. (National Archives)

greatly needed, Britain submitted the dispute to arbitration.

Spanish-American War. Americans were especially concerned with Cuba, where Spain was unsuccessfully trying to stamp out a native revolution. The use of harsh methods shocked the American public, which urged the government at Washington to prevent Spain from subduing Cuba. Tension between Spain and the United States was heightened by exaggerated newspaper accounts of Spanish cruelties, which inflamed public opinion. When the battleship *Maine* was mysteriously sunk in Havana Harbor in Cuba, Americans cried, "Remember the Maine!" and demanded war. The Spanish-American War (1898) brought victory to the United States. Spain withdrew from Cuba; and Puerto Rico, Guam, and the Philippines were annexed by the United States.

The Spanish-American War heralded the entry of the United States on the stage of world politics. America gained prestige, territories, and influence in the Caribbean and Pacific. The acquisition of the Philippines at the doorstep of China intensified American interest in China and brought the United States into close association with the countries that had Asiatic interests.

Asserting the Monroe Doctrine. The United States continued to develop a Caribbean empire. The Caribbean was the route to a possible interoceanic canal that could link the Atlantic and Pacific coasts of the United States by means of inexpensive ocean-going transportation. America's dominant position in the Caribbean was clear to the world. In 1902, when

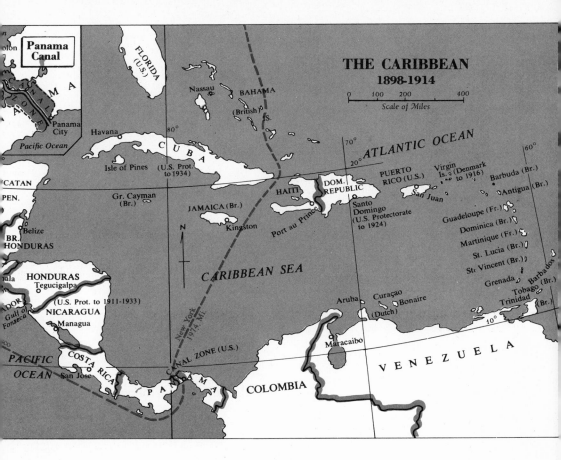

THE CARIBBEAN
1898-1914

0   100   200   400
Scale of Miles

Britain, Germany, and Italy blockaded Venezuela to enforce the collection of unpaid debts, President Theodore Roosevelt forced them to lift
their blockade and announced that the
United States would exercise an international police power in the Caribbean. The United States would inter-
cede in the affairs of Latin-American
countries in order to stabilize their
finances, thereby preventing European
nations from stepping in to collect their
debts. Cuba, the Dominican Republic,
Haiti, and Nicaragua were at least
partly controlled by Washington.

Panama Canal. One of Roosevelt's
objectives was the construction of a
canal through the Isthmus of Panama

within the territory of the Republic of
Colombia. This project had been
abandoned by a French company
under Ferdinand de Lesseps. When
Colombia demanded a high price to
permit Americans to build the canal,
Roosevelt was enraged and thereupon
encouraged a revolution to detach
Panama from Colombia. In 1903, a
rebellion was staged in Panama. An
American vessel prevented Colombian
troops from landing to suppress the
rebels. The new Republic of Panama
granted the United States a zone
through the isthmus for the projected
canal, which was completed in 1914.

Dollar diplomacy. Active interest in
the Caribbean continued under Presi-

Theodore Roosevelt (Library of Congress)

dent William Taft. As a result of the policy of "dollar diplomacy," the government encouraged American bankers and industrialists to secure favorable opportunities in this area. The purpose of dollar diplomacy was to prevent European governments from interfering in the affairs of Central American governments and to promote the security of the United States. This meant American capital in lieu of European money and influence. This policy was followed also in China, where the American government encouraged American bankers to invest capital in the construction of railways in order to strengthen China's resistance to the imperial ambitions of Europeans powers.

British-American relations. America's entry into world politics was marked by growing friendship with Great Britain, whose isolation during the Boer War and Fashoda crisis taught her the value of allies. And she deliberately courted the United States. It seemed natural at the turn of the century that the so-called "Anglo-Saxon" countries should become friends. Britain returned American sympathy during the Boer War by supporting the United States during the Spanish-American War and the Philippine rebellion that followed. Anglo-American friendship was helped by the peaceful settlement of many disputes that had embittered their relations. Beginning with the disputes occasioned by the Civil War down to the controversy over the boundary between Canada and Alaska, Britain and the United States resorted to arbitration. In 1902–1903 they reached an unofficial naval understanding concerning the protection of the Caribbean.

An "Atlantic community," consisting of Britain, Canada, and the United States, was being formed. Strong links held these countries together. Their language, their history, and their similar political traditions formed invisible yet powerful, ties. Common interests also brought them together. Canada's welfare and resources were a bond of interest for the United States and Britain. Canada and the United States shared the Great Lakes, vital communications for both their industries. Goods and people moved freely across the Great Lakes and through bridges and tunnels and railways that crossed Canadian and American boundaries. Canadian and American industries were interlocked.

Latin America and Europe. After the wars of liberation that cut it free from Spanish control, Latin America continued to be a "new Europe" overseas. European literature and philosophy dominated the cultural life of the former Spanish and Portuguese colonies. The Catholic Church linked Latin America with Latin Europe. Throughout the nineteenth century a steady stream of Portuguese, Spanish, and Italian emigrants to Latin America forged further ties between the two continents. In turn, the sons of noblemen or of rich merchants sailed across the Atlantic to study in Spain or France. The exchange of students between Spain and the Latin-American republics produced mutual sympathy and understanding. Indeed many thinkers on both sides of the Atlantic considered the possibility of uniting all peoples of Spanish race.

Economically the republics of the New World were dependent on Europe and the United States. Argentina and Uruguay were virtually economic protectorates of Great Britain. British loans and technicians developed railways, copper mining, and petroleum refining. This influence on the economic life of Latin America did not lead to military control by European powers. Such designs would have been opposed not only by the United States but by the determination of the Latin-American peoples to remain free.

Failure to confederate. Many Latin Americans hoped for the day when large parts of the former Portuguese and Spanish colonies would form some type of confederation. But ambitions of rival politicians and warfare deepened existing differences and shattered these hopes. Two wars were very destructive. The first was the Paraguayan War (1865–1870), the bloodiest conflict in the history of South America. It was touched off by the dictator of Paraguay, Francisco Solano López, who aspired to be the Napoleon of South America. His intervention in an Uruguayan civil war brought him to blows with Uruguay, Argentina, and Brazil. Despite the fact that López drafted every available man into his army, his forces were no match for the allied armies. Yet he persisted until the bitter end and lost nearly every able-bodied man in Paraguay.

The second conflict was the War of the Pacific (1879–1883), provoked by the expansion of Chile into the rich nitrate area that lay between her and Bolivia and Peru. With a strong army and navy Chile easily defeated the Bolivian-Peruvian allies. Victory permitted Chile to extend her northern boundary at the expense of Bolivia, who lost her coastline on the Pacific, and to become the dominant power on the west coast of South America.

After 1890 the republics of Latin America co-operated in some fields. A

Christ of the Andes, the symbol of peace, stands on the Argentine-Chilean boundary. (Wide World)

series of conferences discussed scientific, social, legal, cultural, and economic problems. In 1899 a happy chapter in the relations among the republics of South America was written. Argentina and Chile peacefully settled their boundary line in the Andes Mountains. To commemorate this success, they erected a huge statue high in the mountains called "Christ of the Andes." Central American republics established a court of justice to preserve peace, which functioned from 1907 to 1917.

United States and Latin America. Latin Americans were not enthusiastic about the Pan-American movement inaugurated by the United States in 1889. They were reluctant to place themselves under the tutelage of their northern neighbor, whom they called "the Colossus of the North." They resented the American protectorate of the Caribbean and were angered by the high-handed manner of Theodore Roosevelt in obtaining the Canal Zone from Colombia and Panama.

Politically the nations of Latin America kept aloof from world politics. Interest in world affairs increased, however, and at the second Hague Conference in 1907, all the Latin-American republics except Costa Rica and Honduras were present. Not until after World War I would their voice be heard in international councils.

102. THE GREAT POWERS AND INDIA, SOUTHEAST ASIA, AND CHINA

India contained over three hundred million people of diverse religions, languages, and races. Politically India was a complex mass. British India, the area directly controlled by Britain, formed the greater part of the country, while native states, governed by rajahs (Hindu) or nabobs (Moslem), comprised more than one-third of the area. Economically India was a rich prize. She imported English cotton goods and railway equipment and was an excellent field for investment and a source for raw materials. Nevertheless, the cost of holding her was high. Britain had to maintain a large fleet to protect the sea lanes to India and wage a number of wars in order to ward off invaders and pacify rebellious native princes.

The Mutiny. In 1857 a great military mutiny of native tribes seriously shook British rule. First, rumors of British losses in the Crimean War (1854–1856) had weakened the belief that English armies were invincible, and the necessity of transferring troops from India to the Crimea both offended native feelings and weakened British power in India. Matters came to a head when the British introduced among the sepoys, or native troops, a new type of rifle cartridge that was greased with the fat of beef and swine —things that were repulsive to Moslem and Hindu alike. The native soldiers refused to use the new cartridges and rebelled. The mutiny was suppressed, but it compelled Britain to re-examine the problem of governing India. Before this time it was ruled by the East India Company. In 1858, India passed directly under the control of the British crown, and in 1877, Queen Victoria was proclaimed Empress of India.

British rule. Under the control of the British government internal conditions in India were improved. Famines were lessened, health was improved, farmlands were reclaimed, and railways and factories were built. Under the stern control of the British, petty wars among native princes that had previously ravaged the land were eliminated.

British control was followed by the extension of Western influence in India. These influences entered through schools, through the machinery of government, from commerce, and from Christian missionaries. The impact of Western culture on the older Hindu civilization was not very apparent, however, and the village (the center of Indian life), the caste system, and religious observances remained the same. But changes had occurred. Many Christian and Western ideas reached the higher classes, who were influenced by Western culture, which they studied in British and European schools and universities.

Indian nationalism. These leaders returned from Britain with Western liberalism and nationalism. Cherishing the ideal of freedom and national self-government, in 1886 they formed the Indian National Congress to demand a system of home rule. Unintentionally, by knitting the country together, Britain had prepared the way for Indian unity. Railways, the telegraph and postal systems enabled Indians from scattered areas to meet and discuss their mutual problems. The English language became the common tongue of the educated. Furthermore, by familiarizing young Hindus who were studying in England with free government, Englishmen unwittingly encouraged these youths to introduce the parliamentary system in India. On their return home, these students were angered by the haughty attitudes of certain British officials, who believed that they had to help the less fortunate Indians to achieve prosperity, freedom,

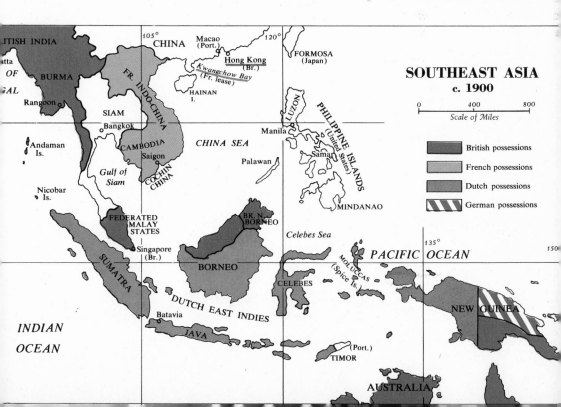

SOUTHEAST ASIA
c. 1900

0   400   800
Scale of Miles

British possessions
French possessions
Dutch possessions
German possessions

and culture. The natives were quick to point out that India was civilized when England was still a wilderness. Arguing that materialism and the concern for physical comfort that had captured the minds of Europeans were unsuitable ideals for India, the native leaders said that India had a mission to show the world that Indian spirituality and philosophy could teach people how to lead a good life.

Southeast Asia. The urge for power, prestige, raw materials, and markets carried Europeans into Southeast Asia. The Suez Canal enabled them to reach this area more easily and exploit its natural resources. Tropical climate made possible the cultivation of rice, sugar, rubber, kapok, hemp, quinine, teakwood, coconuts, palm oil, tapioca, tea, coffee, tobacco, pepper, nutmeg, and other spices.

The great powers strove to control the great river valleys, which were the principal centers of civilization in Southeast Asia: the deltas of the Mekong and Red rivers in Indo-China, the Irrawaddy in Burma, and the Menam in Siam (Thailand). From the 1860's to 1885, Britain conquered Burma and expanded her interests in Malaya. She had occupied parts of Malaya since 1795 and the vital port of Singapore, just north of the equator, since 1819. By 1895, Britain had established a protectorate over the Malay States. Malaya supplied Britain with tin and rubber. Meanwhile France carved out an empire in Indo-China. Napoleon III had detached Cochin China from the Chinese Empire (1858–1863). By 1893, the French Republic occupied all of Indo-China (Annam, Tonkin, Cambodia, Cochin China, and Laos), an area approximately the size of Texas. In Southeast Asia only Siam preserved her independence, though she fell under Western political and economic influence. Siam remained a buffer between British-held Burma and French Indo-China.

Chinese in Southeast Asia. Chinese customs and influence had been spread throughout Southeast Asia and the Pacific islands by the emigration of millions of Chinese subjects. For centuries the Chinese had settled Malaya, Singapore, and neighboring countries and had filtered into the Philippines, Hawaii, and even North America. But in the late nineteenth century, emigration increased, especially to Malaya. These emigrants retained their attachment to China because of the necessity of worshiping their ancestors in their home villages. Their first duty was to their parents, whom they left behind in China and to whom they sent part of their earnings.

The Chinese Empire in the nineteenth century entered into a long period of troubles. These troubles were due to many causes, among which was the use of the drug opium, imported by Europeans into China from India. Political disorders, arising from remote and obscure causes, chronically affected China. Her weakness was a temptation to imperialist powers, who turned eager eyes toward China. British, French, Russian, and American merchants urged their governments to secure privileges to trade in China. This was difficult to achieve because the Chinese were hostile and regarded all who were not influenced by Chinese culture as barbarians; they expected everyone to be subordinate to the sacred emperor.

The Opium War. Britain forced China to throw open her doors to trade. The attempt of the Chinese government to prohibit British merchants from exporting opium to China led to the first Anglo-Chinese or Opium War (1839–1842). More than opium was at stake. Britain wanted commercial opportunities. The successful operations of the British fleet revealed at a glance the weakness of China and the superiority of industrialized countries with modern weapons and ships. The peace treaty revealed the extent of China's inferiority. She ceded Hong Kong to Great Britain and had to bear the cost of the British war effort and permit British merchants to trade in five "treaty ports," which included Canton, and Shanghai. Similar privileges were soon sought by other countries. The biggest country in the world fell partly under European economic influence.

China and Western influence. Western ideas entered China not only through merchants but also through missionaries. In the nineteenth century, missionaries came to China in greater numbers: Catholic missionaries primarily from France, Protestant missionaries from Britain and the United States. However, they were scarcely tolerated by the Chinese government. The troubles of the Chinese Empire multiplied when the Taiping Rebellion (1850–1864) broke out. The leader of the rebels, who had been influenced by Protestant missionaries, wanted to establish what was called the Heavenly Kingdom of Great Peace. The aim was social reform on a grand scale. The government finally put down the rebellion at the cost of twenty million lives. During this great turmoil Britain again went to war with China, in 1856–1860, and was joined by France, who protested the murder of a missionary. These Western powers defeated China and won eleven new ports for merchants and a promise that missionaries and converts would not be molested. In the years that followed, China submitted to other demands. Russia was ceded the lands north of the Amur River, rounding out Siberia. China was "wide open" to the European west.

Europeans and Americans were exempt from observing Chinese laws or justice. Instead, they were tried by their own courts, which China was forced to permit them to establish. The outlook was dark for China. She fell under increasing Western influence as her government was unable to meet expenses and was obliged to go into debt. After 1870, even China's political independence was threatened. Under pressure from their merchants and bankers, European governments sought opportunities to develop China's resources or to finance railways, factories, and mines.

103. JAPANESE IMPERIALISM AND WAR WITH CHINA

Across the Yellow Sea from China, Japan lived in isolation. Since 1638 Japan had kept her doors closed against foreigners, allowing only the Dutch in the East Indies and Chinese to trade in Japan, on a very limited basis. Nevertheless, Western ideas in medicine, warfare, geography, and

Interior of a Yokohama Commerce House *shows the various business activities that were increased considerably by the introduction of foreign trade to Japan. Woodcut by Utagawa Sadahide. (The Brooklyn Museum Collection)*

science crept in. Meanwhile the emperor or Mikado was a sacred figurehead, believed to be descended from a god. The *shogun,* or the head of a powerful clan, was the real ruler of Japan. By the nineteenth century a revival of learning stimulated a revival of the national religion, Shintoism, and also stimulated a new devotion to the Mikado.

The opening of Japan. Europeans and Americans saw great commercial opportunities if Japan opened her doors. The development of rapid transportation and communication made desirable a station in Japanese waters where their ships could be refueled and reprovisioned. Americans were particularly interested in securing a coaling station on the way to China and in receiving assurances from Japan that shipwrecked sailors would no longer be maltreated as "foreign devils" by Japanese authorities. Although Russian and British efforts to

open the doors of Japan had failed, the United States commissioned Commodore Matthew Perry to secure from the Mikado the following: protection for shipwrecked sailors, permission to use Japanese ports for provisioning and repairing ships, and the establishment of trade with the United States. In July 1853, Perry sailed into Tokyo Bay, where the appearance of American steam vessels frightened the Japanese. Although Perry emphasized his peaceful intentions, he said that the United States would not tolerate the cruel treatment of American sailors. Allowing Japanese officials an opportunity to think it over, he returned in 1854. Japan agreed to open two ports to the United States, and later to Britain, Russia, and Holland. The United States sent a representative to Japan in 1856 to negotiate a commercial treaty. In 1860 Japan sent an ambassador to Washington.

The opening of Japan had momentous results in world history. It introduced to the world stage a vigorous people who soon played a dominant role in the affairs of Asia. The Japanese learned quickly from their Western friends. They modernized their government and modeled their army, navy, and industries on those of the West. Indirectly the opening of Japan weakened the power of the *shogun*. A political revolution restored the Mikado to supreme power.

Japan and Western culture. On the surface, the Japanese were eager to adopt the customs of their Western teachers. Yet they did not fully accept Western ideas about government and culture. Accustomed to bow before authority, they were religiously devoted to the Emperor. Although they copied the parliamentary system of government, they scarcely appreciated the spirit of a constitution and parliament. Japan learned the lesson from the West about the importance of schools but established popular schooling in order to teach millions of children absolute loyalty to the state. The use of Western methods increased Japanese strength. Few persons believed, however, that Japan could become a powerful nation.

War with China. The event that changed world opinion was the Sino-Japanese War (1894–1895). The immediate cause of war was a clash between Japan and China over Korea, where intrigues, murders, and ruinous taxation reflected disregard for life and property. Korea was a part of the Chinese Empire in name, but China could exercise only token authority over the peninsula. Both Japan and Russia were interested in this strategically situated country. Japan feared that the occupation of Korea—located only a few hundred miles away—by a strong power would be a dagger pointed at her heart. Korean rice was vital for Japan's growing millions, while Korean resources could provide Japanese shipping and commerce with excellent opportunities for profit.

War between Japan and China seemed to be a battle between David and Goliath. China had large armies, while her adversary had fewer but better trained troops. While Chinese power was destroyed by graft and incompetence, the Japanese people solidly backed their government.

Before the world could believe that little Japan had dared to challenge the Chinese Empire, the Japanese destroyed the Chinese navy and crushed the enemy in Korea. By the Treaty of Shimonoseki, China was obliged to grant to Korea her independence and to turn over to Japan the Liaotung peninsula, Formosa, and the Pescadores. In addition, China had to pay an indemnity and open four new ports to trade. France, Germany, and Russia forced Japan to moderate her demands on China by surrendering the Liaotung peninsula. Nevertheless, Japan had won the respect of the great powers for her thumping victory, while China invited new aggressions by concession-hungry countries who realized the extent of her military ineptness and disunity.

Effect on China. European nations now moved in to "slice the Chinese melon." They cut up China into spheres of influence, where capitalists from a single country received concessions to finance construction of railways, mines, and other industries. From 1895 to 1902, Russia launched a sustained drive to extend her influence in China. Russian influence became dominant at Peking, the imperial capital. Supported by her French ally, Russia planned to make China a vassal state and almost achieved this purpose by a treaty of alliance in 1896. In exchange for the right to extend a branch of the Trans-Siberian Railway across northern Manchuria in a short cut to Vladivostok, Russia pledged to protect China from Japanese aggression. This treaty placed northern Manchuria in the Russian sphere of influence.

Russia extracted a 25-year lease from China giving her control over the Liaotung peninsula and its ice-free harbor of Port Arthur. Germany soon demanded the naval base of Kiaochow in the Shantung peninsula, and Britain wanted a lease of the port of Weihaiwei. France, who wished to dominate southern China, leased Kwangchow. The great powers staked their claims in the event of the dismemberment of the Chinese Empire. Russia eyed Manchuria, Germany the Shantung peninsula, Britain the Yangtze Valley, and France the area south of the Yangtse.

The fear that the European powers would erect high tariff walls in their respective spheres of influence led Britain and the United States to ask them to pledge equal commercial opportunities for citizens of all countries. This was the aim of John Hay, the American secretary of state, who asked that the "Open Door" policy be kept in China (1899). A year later the American government proclaimed its policy to favor not only commercial equality but the territorial integrity of China.

Boxer Rebellion. Meanwhile the defeat in the Sino-Japanese War shook the authority of the imperial Chinese dynasty. Increased foreign encroachment led to the formation of patriotic societies that aimed to revive China. One of these societies was called Righteous Patriotic Fists, nicknamed

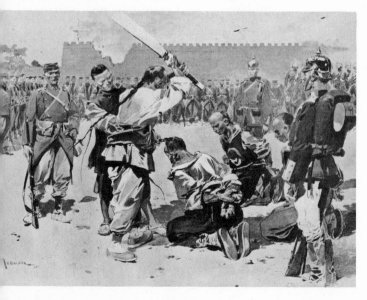

The execution of three pro-foreign officials during the Boxer Rebellion. Strong feelings against foreigners and Christians caused the war. (Hulton Picture Library)

the "Boxers" by Western journalists. The Boxers even attacked Chinese Christians, whom they regarded as renegades for adopting a foreign religion and ignoring the worship of ancestors that was an intimate part of village life. Most violently opposed to the foreigners who were cutting up their country, they broke out in rebellion in 1900. Western merchants and diplomats took refuge in the British legation at Peking. An international expedition, sent to relieve the beleaguered Europeans at Peking, crushed the Boxer Rebellion. The Chinese government was loaded down with an indemnity of a third of a billion dollars to compensate Westerners for loss of life and property. The American government used its influence to moderate the demands of the other powers and to prevent them from using the Boxer Rebellion as a convenient opportunity for carving up China. The Boxer movement convinced the Chinese that the country would have to be reformed or else the dynasty would be swept away by war and revolution.

104. RUSSIAN IMPERIALISM AND WAR WITH JAPAN; REVOLUTION IN RUSSIA AND CHINA

Russia had been growing larger for over four hundred years. Unlike other conquerors who had to cross the seas to expand their empires, the Russians pushed back their frontiers and incorporated a variety of territories and peoples.

Expansion in Siberia. What the West was for the United States, Siberia was to Russia. The conquest of this vast area had begun in 1581, and then gradually, against only light opposition of semi-barbarian peoples, the Russians pushed toward the Amur River and the Pacific. With the Chinese no longer able to resist, Russia began the settlement of Siberia from the Amur to the Pacific in the 1840's and 1850's, and Vladivostok was founded in 1860.

Russia then mopped up the troublesome Mohammedan tribes of central Asia, whose ancestors had launched terrifying invasions of Europe under Attila and Tamerlane. In 1865, Russia absorbed Turkestan and advanced toward the borders of Afghanistan. Her ambitions to absorb Afghanistan were resisted by Britain, who regarded the independence of that mountainous country as necessary to the security of India.

Siberia was soon colonized. Between 1823 and 1887 about seven hundred thousand exiles left Russia for Siberia. They included prisoners and peasants, the latter being free to leave their homes after the emancipation of the serfs. Colonization was hastened by the construction of the Trans-Siberian Railway in 1891–1903.

Russia, as we have seen, next acquired from weakened China a dominant influence in Manchuria and the possession of Port Arthur. She had been actively interested in Korea, but here she came up against the rising power of Japan. In order to ward off a collision, Japan suggested a compromise. Since Korea was of greater strategic value to her than Manchuria, Japan proposed Japanese supremacy in Korea and Russian domination of Manchuria. But Russia rejected this

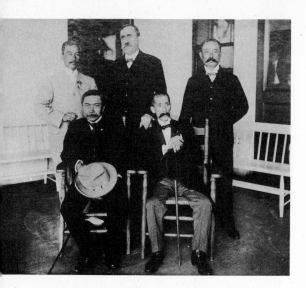

The Japanese Peace Commission. The meeting at Portsmouth, New Hampshire, in 1905 marked the end of the Russo-Japanese War. (Library of Congress)

navy dominated Korean waters and destroyed the Russian Baltic fleet, which traveled halfway around the world only to be sunk in Tsushima Strait off Korea.

Having achieved their objective of driving the Russians out of Korea and Manchuria, the Japanese sought peace. They knew that a long war would exhaust them and bring a Russian victory. Through the efforts of President Theodore Roosevelt, Japan and Russia met at Portsmouth, New Hampshire. Japan attained the southern half of Sakhalin Island, the Russian leaseholds of Port Arthur and the Liaotung peninsula in China, and a Russian promise to stay out of Manchuria and Korea. Korea was now within the Japanese sphere of influence and was finally annexed by Japan in 1910.

Russia in Revolution. The Russian defeat had important consequences. Russian prestige tumbled throughout the world. The Russian threat to Afghanistan, Persia, and Tibet was reduced. Having been repulsed in the Far East, Russia turned her attention to the Balkans, where she calculated her efforts might be more fruitful. Within Russia the existence of graft, corruption, and incompetence during the war brought resentment against the Czar and his advisers. The feeling was widespread that they had let down the soldiers who had fought bravely.

Not only were Russian nationalists disillusioned, but political reformers were disappointed that the reforms of Alexander II had not seemed to accomplish much. Convinced that the Czar would never reform Russia, many turned to revolution and vio-

plan. She fortified Port Arthur, sent troops into Manchuria, and set her sights on Korea.

Russo-Japanese War. Japan's attempt to prevent her rival from annexing Korea and thereby holding the dagger pointed at her heart led to the Russo-Japanese War (1904–1905). As in the case of the Sino-Japanese War of 1894, Japan was considered no match for her mighty adversary. Once again Japan demonstrated to the world that her people were solidly behind the emperor and his government and that her army and navy were prepared. Through the Anglo-Japanese alliance of 1902, Japan had gained Britain as an ally who would be obligated to support her if another power sided with Russia. Japanese troops seized the initiative and drove back the Russian armies in Manchuria and then laid siege to the Russian fort at Port Arthur. The Japanese lence. The Czar was also opposed by nihilists: persons who were so sure everything in Russia was rotten that they believed in nothing—not in the Czar, or the Orthodox Church, or in any other traditional institution. Clear away everything and start anew, they recommended. Emboldened reformers and revolutionaries incited street demonstrations and fomented a wave of strikes. Demands for a representative assembly and civil liberties were echoed all over Russia. On January 22, 1905, a procession of workers under Father Gapon, an Orthodox priest, marched on the Czar's winter palace in St. Petersburg to present a petition to the "Little White Father," as Czar Nicholas II was called. As the people reached the palace, singing "God Save the Czar," troops opened fire. "Red Sunday" began the Revolution of 1905.

Nicholas II, last emperor and Czar of Russia, with his wife. Nicholas tried in vain to preserve the foundations of autocracy. (Library of Congress)

Bombs were thrown at leading officials. Socialists organized industrial workers and spread violence. Liberals demanded parliamentary government and universal suffrage. In the face of strikes, disorders, and mutinies, the Czar agreed to call an Imperial Duma, or assembly, to be elected by a small number of voters for the purpose of advising him. These concessions were deemed too little. In October 1905 a general strike tied up the whole country. The workers of St. Petersburg formed a soviet, or council, to direct the strike. The Czar was now forced to yield. He granted Russia a constitution, which provided for a Duma with legislative powers and guarantees for personal liberties. These concessions still failed to satisfy the radicals. Workers threw up barricades in the cities, while peasants burned the houses of noblemen. Street fighting in Moscow was drowned in a bath of blood.

The Czar soon recovered from the initial shocks and cracked down on the extremists, who became more desperate than ever. The government divided the opposition. By making some concessions, it detached the moderates, who shrank from bloodshed and revolution. The use of police agents and spies provided the government with the plans of terrorists. Despite the Revolution of 1905 and liberal concessions, Russia was still an autocratic country. Real power remained in the hands of the Czar. The Duma had no real power, for it could not control the army, navy, or foreign affairs.

Prestige of Japan. The Japanese victory erased all doubts that Japan was

FAR EAST
-1914-

0   200   400
Scale of Miles

Railroads
Russia
Japan

the major non-white power in the world. Her victory was a tonic for the peoples of Asia, who for the first time in modern history saw the spectacle of the hitherto invincible white men defeated by Orientals. Nationalists in India and Indonesia were encouraged to strive for their independence from foreign control. Asians learned the lesson that Japan had mastered: Western science, warfare, and industry are the keys to power. Nationalist revolutions—aimed at the introduction of Western-type schools, industries, and governments—occurred in Persia (1906), Turkey (1908), and China (1911).

Western ways in China. The fact that Japan defeated Russia suggested to the Chinese that the Western forms of culture, adopted by Asian peoples, nourished their strength. Many Chinese had demanded Western reforms in government, in the army, and in the schools. The old system of selecting candidates for government service—by means of examinations that tested the candidate's knowledge of the old Confucian classics—was scrapped in 1905. Steps were taken also to centralize the government by encouraging the establishment of railways and communications, which would break down regional isolation and strengthen the hands of the central government at Peking.

Western education and industry combined to upset Chinese traditions. Chinese students went abroad to absorb Western learning, which was now considered the key to a career and public office. Many students went to Europe and to the United States, but many more sailed to Japan, where they took "quickie" courses. While abroad, these students associated with revolutionaries. When they returned to China and failed to receive the positions they sought, they were disillusioned and ready for revolution. Modern industries in China also worked for revolution; they broke up village and guild life and disrupted families.

In 1910–1911 floods in central China brought famine and disease. Heavy taxes, levied to pay the Boxer indemnity and for the reforms in government, added to distress. The death in 1908 of the Empress Tzu Hsi, who had ruled China since the 1860's, left the government without firm direction.

Republic and chaos in China. Under the leadership of Dr. Sun Yat-sen and his Young China movement—composed of thousands of disappointed students —the revolutionaries sought to overthrow the dynasty. Improved communications enabled them to spread their doctrines, and in 1911 the dynasty was overthrown and the Chinese Republic was created. Sun Yat-sen was elected provisional president.

The Chinese Republic never realized the expectations of its founders. The idea of a republic was foreign to the people, who had been led to believe that it meant the end of taxes. Representative government was unknown to China. The vexing problems of finance also weakened the republic. The decline in the authority of the central government and the lack of national unity complicated matters even more. China sank into chaos.

REVIEW

STUDY SECTIONS IN REVIEW

100. Imperialism and the Scramble for Africa

A. Cite four reasons why European nations sought colonial empires.

B. Why was the control of Egypt important to the British Empire?

C. What were the purposes and the results of the Congress of Berlin of 1885?

D. Identify: Cecil Rhodes, General Kitchener, Captain Alfred Mahan.

101. The United States and Latin America

A. Why was the Caribbean region important to the interests of the United States?

B. Describe two occasions on which the United States invoked the Monroe Doctrine during this period.

C. What were the results of the Spanish-American War?

D. Identify: "dollar diplomacy," Paraguayan War, War of the Pacific.

102. The Great Powers and India, Southeast Asia, and China

A. What was the value of India as a colony?

B. List two ways by which British rule aroused Indian nationalism.

C. What did Britain gain from China as a result of the Opium War?

D. What nations, other than Britain, made imperialistic gains in China?

103. Japanese Imperialism and War with China

A. How was Japan "opened" to Western trade?

B. Why was Korea considered to be important by the Japanese?

C. What were the results of the Sino-Japanese War (1894–1895)?

D. List three imperialistic goals European nations hoped to win from China.

104. Russian Imperialism and War with Japan; Revolution in Russia and China

A. List the causes and the results of the Russo-Japanese War (1904–1905).

B. How did the Czar deal with the Revolution of 1905?

C. How did Japan's victory over Russia affect Asian nationalism?

D. Cite three factors that made republican government difficult in China after 1911.

THE CHAPTER IN REVIEW

A. Why did nations embark upon imperialistic ventures during the nineteenth century?

B. Review the position of China, Japan, and Russia in the world as far as power and prestige were concerned in the year 1905.

C. How did Great Britain come to control the Suez Canal? What was the importance of this waterway?

D. How did imperialism after the 1880's differ from the imperialism of previous history?

E. Is there evidence that the United States was affected by the imperialistic fever that swept the world of the late nineteenth century? Illustrate with examples.

FOR YOUR NOTEBOOK

This chapter covers the "Age of Imperialism," in which European countries extended their influence and political control over much of the world. Because so much material must be included, you should use your notebook in this chapter not to supplement the text so much as to review its content. Each of our entries is designed to achieve this latter purpose.

The test gives five reasons for imperialism. Under each of these reasons list the groups supporting it. Can you list any groups who opposed imperialism?

Africa was partitioned among the European powers in thirty years. You can clarify these swift-moving events by two sets of chronologies. First, divide a page into parallel columns headed "North Africa" and "South Africa." In each column enter the principal events mentioned in the text. Second, prepare parallel columns under "Great Britain," "France," "Italy," and "Germany." Enter the steps each took in Africa according to date.

Make a chronological list of acquisitions made by the United States during this age.

Your authors explain how Indian leaders learned about nationalism and liberalism when studying in English universities. Look back through your text to make a list of some authors and some specific ideas or theories they might have read while in England, as, for example, John Locke or the Magna Carta.

Outline the developments in China from the Opium War to the Russo-Japanese War.

You will get a good over-all view of the material of this chapter by making three parallel columns for Africa, China, and Southwest Asia (including India) and then entering into these columns the principal events as the story of imperialism unfolds simultaneously in all three areas.

SELECTED READINGS

There are two standard books on imperialism. They are Parker T. Moon, *Imperialism and World Politics* (New York: The Macmillan Co., 1926), and Mary Evelyn Townsend and Cyrus Peake, *European Colonial Expansion Since 1871* (Philadelphia: J. B. Lippincott, 1941). Both are big books, but the student will find various chapters good for handling one or another aspect of imperialism. Brief coverage of the subject is made by the Berkshire Series book of David Edward Owen, *Imperialism and Nationalism in the Far East* (New York: Henry Holt & Co., 1929).

Additional insight into imperialism can be obtained in *Cecil Rhodes,* a biography of an outstanding South African capitalist and statesman by J. G. Lockhart (New York: The Macmillan Co., 1933). The famous Cardinal Lavigerie founded a society, The White Fathers, to work in Africa during the age of imperialism. Their history is interestingly told by Glenn D. Kittler, *The White Father* (New York: Harper & Bros., 1957).

Marx

Pope Leo XIII

Chapter 34. An Age of Material Progress

105. THE "NEW" INDUSTRIAL REVOLUTION

Greater changes occurred in industry and agriculture in the late nineteenth century than ever before in history. Machines and inventions described in the previous unit now appeared awkward and primitive when compared to newer models. The tempo of industrial and agricultural change was so accelerated that a period of ten years brought more radical changes in industry and agriculture than the entire preceding century. A great number of improved machines and tools multiplied the efficiency of the older machines and increased the productivity of labor. For example, between the Civil War and the turn of the twentieth century, shoe machinery could produce eight times as many shoes as before, and looms could turn out

eighty times as many yards of gingham cloth as before. As in manufacturing, so in agriculture, the replacement of hand tools by power-driven machinery resulted in dramatic labor savings. In 1830, fifty to sixty man-hours were required to farm an acre of wheat, but in 1890 only eight or ten man-hours were needed. These great changes have been called the new or second industrial revolution.

The new industrial revolution was in large measure the result of German and American efforts. German scientists applied the findings of chemistry to industry and agriculture, while American industrialists developed mass production. Technical superiority and scientific knowledge gave the Germans a virtual world monopoly of the production of certain chemicals and dyes. Getting a late start in the

Thomas Alva Edison (1847–1931), a genius in practical applications of scientific principles, held over 1,300 U.S. and foreign patents for his inventions.

industrial race and consequently having less old-fashioned machinery, they used the best and the most modern equipment of Britain and France and improved upon it. The system of mass production uses the assembly line and combines a variety of men and machines to produce huge quantities of a single product. In the manufacture of shoes, for example, the production process is divided into a number of separate tasks or steps performed by different persons and machines. This increased "division of labor" means that a single worker or machine performs only a fraction of the work necessary.

Electric power. New types of power were applied to manufacturing, mining, agriculture, and transportation. A wider and more efficient use was made of steam. Discoveries in the properties of electricity enabled inventors to develop the electric motor. Electricity as a source of light and power was advanced by Thomas A. Edison. In 1879 he invented a practical electric lamp and shortly afterward put into operation a large dynamo capable of supplying electric power to eighty-five buildings in New York City. By the end of the century the development of electric power was the most prominent feature of economic advance throughout Western civilization.

Transportation and communication. Mechanical transportation was revolutionized. Improvements in local and long-distance land and sea transportation staggered the imagination. The Suez Canal (1869) and the Panama Canal (1914), transcontinental railways in the United States, Canada, and Siberia shrank distances in terms of time. Steel ships, powered by screw propellers and with marine turbine engines, proved a boon to ocean-going traffic. Local transportation was speeded by widespread use of bicycles, trolley cars, and the automobile. The last was aided by, and in turn helped, the development of the oil and rubber industries. The automobile revolutionized ground warfare by making available vehicles for the transport of soldiers and supplies. The most ambitious development in transportation was the airplane. Man achieved his fondest dream in flying like the birds. Count Zeppelin of Germany experimented with dirigibles, while the Brazilian Santos-Dumont, and the Americans, Wilbur and Orville Wright, developed the airplane. The first dramatic use of the airplane was a flight across the Strait of Dover, from France to England, by Louis Blériot in 1909.

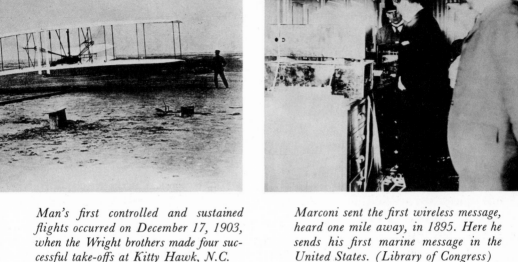

Man's first controlled and sustained flights occurred on December 17, 1903, when the Wright brothers made four successful take-offs at Kitty Hawk, N.C.

Marconi sent the first wireless message, heard one mile away, in 1895. Here he sends his first marine message in the United States. (Library of Congress)

Progress in communications was similarly amazing. Alexander Graham Bell in 1876 invented the telephone, which was soon used throughout the world. The next step was the wireless or radio, invented by the great Italian scientist, Guglielmo Marconi, in 1895.

Industrial consolidation. The new industrial revolution was characterized by the consolidation and integration of industry after 1880. Big corporations developed in steel, oil, chemicals, and retail commerce. Individually owned firms or partnerships could no longer provide the capital to build new factories and purchase modern machinery. Some firms grew so large that they controlled all the materials and processes that were needed for manufacturing their products. For example, the great steel companies owned or controlled mines for iron ore and coal, quarries for limestone, railway cars for the transportation of these raw materials, blast furnaces for smelting ore, and rolling mills for producing steel girders or rails.

Finance capitalism. Another feature of the new industrial revolution was finance capitalism. Since the amounts of capital required for industries were greater than individuals or even large corporations could raise, investment bankers stepped in to supply money by underwriting large issues of stocks and bonds. In lending huge sums to expand or modernize industry, the great banking houses of the world—J. Pierpont Morgan of New York, the Baring Brothers of London, and the Dresdener Bank of Berlin—were able to control a great deal of industry. The career of Morgan illustrates the power of the finance capitalist. By controlling banking houses, trust companies, and insurance companies that possessed money for investment, Morgan became the dominant power in American industry. The capital he controlled was the lifeblood of the great industries.

Hundreds of brilliant scientists from many lands were almost daily enlarging man's knowledge of his own body and of the world around him. This knowledge was taught by specialized institutes that were established to train scientists and by those colleges and universities that gave greater attention to natural science in their courses of study. Scientists made their knowledge available to the rest of the world by describing their experiments in scientific journals or at scientific conventions.

As scientific knowledge grew, it became impossible for one man to master all the sciences as had been possible during the Renaissance, when the great Leonardo da Vinci understood all that was known of natural science. When the main outlines of astronomy, biology, chemistry, geology, and physics emerged, scientists began to specialize in one science, and often in a single phase of a science. Thus a physicist might specialize in electricity or magnetism.

Charles Darwin (1809–1882) shocked Victorian England with his theory of evolution. (British Information Services)

Theory of evolution. Interest in natural science gave rise to much explanation about human nature. The most important was the theory of evolution developed by Charles Darwin. In 1859, Darwin's famous book, *The Origin of the Species,* explained similarities that exist among plants, animals, and men on the grounds that they evolved from earlier and less complex species. Darwin contended that in all species some individuals differ from the rest; that if they are strong enough to adjust themselves to their environment and outlast others in a struggle for existence, these "mutations" transmit their peculiar characteristics to their offspring. Thus evolution occurred by means of "natural selection," Darwin explained. In the struggle for existence among plants and animals, the weak fell by the wayside and only the strong survived.

Darwinism and religion. The theory of evolution (which has never been proved) disturbed many Christians, especially Protestants, who interpreted the Bible literally. They could not reconcile the biblical account of Creation—that God created everything in the universe in six days—with Darwin's theory that everything evolved over a long period of time. Catholics were less disturbed. St. Augustine, more than a thousand years before, had declared that God created the whole of nature at the beginning but permitted some species of animals and plants to evolve or develop later. On the whole, Darwin's theory of evolution struck religion a hard blow by leaving God and religion out of his view of nature.

Medicine and biology. Giant steps were taken in these sciences during the nine-

...och
...bacteriologist
...anisms

Joseph Lister
English surgeon
Antisepsis

Louis Pasteur
French chemist
Pasteurization

Wilhelm Roentgen
German physicist
X-ray

(Library of Congress)

teenth century. The invention of the stethoscope enabled physicians to diagnose heart and lung conditions. The discovery of painkillers such as chloroform and ether permitted surgeons to operate without inflicting the unbearable pain that usually accompanied surgery in the past. While the use of painkillers facilitated surgery, it did not remove a menace greater than pain: infection that generally followed surgery.

Three men made singular contributions to medicine: Louis Pasteur, Joseph Lister, and Robert Koch. Pasteur (1822–1905), a French chemist, disproved the theory of spontaneous generation (that bacteria and other microscopic organisms originated spontaneously from water or from decaying matter); he showed that maggots came from living organisms and did not spring up from spoiled meat, as was generally believed. Pasteur's researches on bacteria saved the French wine and silk industries. But more important, he proved that microbes cause disease. His next step was to learn how disease could be checked. Pasteur developed

serums for chicken cholera and rabies. In developing a serum for rabies, he injected a boy who had been bitten by a mad dog with a substance he had prepared from the dried spinal cords of animals that had withstood that disease. Joseph Lister (1827–1912) developed antiseptic surgery. To Robert Koch (1843–1910) belongs credit for definitely proving that infectious diseases *are* caused by bacteria or other germs. Koch also discovered the microbes that caused tuberculosis and cholera.

The work of Pasteur, Lister, Koch, and other bacteriologists was eagerly followed by public health authorities. Governments began to regulate water supplies, the disposal of waste materials, the preparation of milk, meat, and other foods, and sanitary conditions in schools, factories, and hospitals. From 1880 to the turn of the century, scientists identified the bacteria that cause many of the most important diseases. The task of finding antitoxins (substances, derived from the disease itself, that could fight the disease) was not easy. Scientists were enabled to study the human body more carefully as a result of the accidental discovery in 1895 of the X-ray by Wilhelm von Roentgen (1845–1923).

Pierre and Eva Curie's experiments in extracting radium from pitchblende in 1895 led to the study of radioactivity. There were hundreds of other important developments. The experiments of Gregor Mendel (1822–1884), an Austrian monk, discovered the possibility of improving the breeds of plants and animals. Mendel laid the foundation for the scientific study of heredity by studying the inheritance of characteristics in garden peas. Although his work was unknown during his lifetime, "Mendel's laws" were hailed after his death.

The state of religion. Until the end of the nineteenth century most Europeans and Americans still believed that a personal God exists in Three Persons, that He created all things, and that He became man. Most people did not doubt that man is a creature, made to the image and likeness of God, that his mind can arrive at truth, and that after death he will be called upon to account for his life, thereby meriting heaven or hell. In social life people considered the family as the foundation of the state, and believed that parents are responsible to God for the education of their children. Divorce was condemned. Of course writers often attacked Christian beliefs, but they could not count on a receptive audience, because the vast majority of men and women on both sides of the Atlantic still cherished Christianity. By the latter part of the nineteenth century, however, Christianity began to lose its hold over the minds and hearts

of some. Many scientists, businessmen, artists, and writers either denied supernatural religion or acted as if they did. They left the impression that Christianity was obsolete and was going to be replaced by faith in reason, science, progress, and humanity.

Some governments struck at religion by curtailing the independence of the churches, removing education and marriage from religious jurisdiction and controlling both. Religious orders were forbidden to teach. State-supported schools largely ignored religion and fostered religious indifference. This was especially the case in France.

Pius IX and the Church. The pontificate of Pius IX (1846–1878) was a critical era for the Catholic Church. As we have seen in Unit Nine, liberals and nationalists established the Roman Republic in 1849 and forced out the Pope. Although the Roman Republic was crushed and the Pope returned to Rome, papal lands were later seized by Sardinia-Piedmont. The seizure of papal territories and many Church properties outraged Pius IX, who saw nationalism and liberalism as forces destructive of the interests of the Church. In the eyes of the Church, the "Patrimony of St. Peter," as the Papal States were called, was given to the Church by God in order to fulfill her spiritual duties more effectively. Now the anticlerical program of the Italian government did not improve church-state relations. Although Italian nationalists said that they favored a "free church in a free state," their actions convinced the Pontiff that what they meant was a church at the mercy of the Italian government. Pius IX cast his lot with the conservative forces, who welcomed the Church as a powerful ally against revolution and disorder.

Syllabus of errors. In 1864, Pius IX clearly committed himself against liberalism in his encyclical *Quanta cura* and the accompanying *Syllabus of Errors,* which listed dangers to the Faith. The *Syllabus* condemned eighty propositions, including absolute rationalism, socialism, communism, secret societies, and errors concerning the Church and civil society. In condemning the eightieth proposition, which stated: "The Roman Pontiff can and should reconcile himself with progress, with liberalism, and with recent civilization," the Pope caused the greatest wonder. What the Pope condemned in this proposition was not the present meaning of the words progress, liberalism, and modern civilization. In back of his mind was his recent experience with anti-Catholic liberals and nationalists. The words, as he used them, implied closing monasteries and convents, removing religious influences from education, and the seizure of the Papal States. In short, he meant secularism and anti-clericalism. However, the *Syllabus of Errors* was much misunderstood.

Papal infallibility. The outlook was dark. The Church was attacked and ridiculed. Nevertheless, in Pius IX's reign the Papacy gained new strength. Catholic journalists, typified by Louis Veuillot of France and Wilfrid Ward of England, were formidable allies. And the Vatican Council (1869–1870), the first general council of the Church since Trent, (1545–1563), defined carefully the Church's long-held teaching concerning the authority of the Pope. The result was the famous infallibility dogma. The Roman Pontiff was infallible when he spoke *ex cathedra;* that is, when, as pastor and teacher of all Christians, he defined with his supreme apostolic authority a doctrine concerning faith or morals to be held by the Universal Church. There was nothing new in this belief, but only in its authoritative definition. Nevertheless, it angered many people, especially those who held that the state possessed authority over the Church.

Catholic achievements. As the difficulties of the Church increased in southern Europe, they decreased in northern Europe and elsewhere in the world. English-speaking countries experienced remarkable progress. In 1850 the Catholic hierarchy was restored in England after an absence of three hundred years. In 1878 the hierarchy was also restored in Scotland. In the United States the steady influx of immigrants from Ireland and other Catholic lands increased the Catholic population and made necessary the establishment of many new dioceses. The progress of the Church in English-speaking countries is shown by the fact that out of seven hundred bishops attending the Vatican Council, one hundred and twenty came from English-speaking countries. The growth of the Church was similarly rapid in the Netherlands (where the hierarchy was restored in 1853), Switzerland, and in Germany. During the pontificate of Pius IX, Franciscan, Jesuit, Salesian, and other missionaries labored fruitfully in the Near East, Africa, China, Japan, and Central America. This was one of the great missionary ages of the Church.

Leo XIII. The pontificate of Leo XIII (1878–1903) was glorious and brilliant. A great scholar himself, Leo XIII en-

Pope Leo XIII (Library of Congress)

couraged the revival of the philosophy of St. Thomas Aquinas to combat the effects of modern philosophies. He demonstrated sympathy for sound civil reforms. By his actions he demonstrated that the Church could thrive under any form of government that respected its liberty. He advised French Catholics to rally to the Third Republic, and he praised the Constitution of the United States. At the same time he repeated the condemnation of liberalism made by Pius IX. By liberalism, Leo XIII meant (as Pius IX had meant) the doctrine that makes man self-sufficient, answerable only to himself and not to the will of God and lawful authority.

Leo XIII turned to the problem of restoring and nourishing the faith of industrial workers who had been alienated earlier in the century. His encyclical *Rerum novarum* (1891) has been called the Magna Carta of Labor. He upheld private property and the family, and he condemned the exploitation of workers by employers. Leo XIII stressed the dignity of labor and warned that workers must receive a living family wage. To achieve this end, the Pope urged workers to form trade unions and co-operatives. In supporting the claims of workers, Leo XIII denounced socialists, who, in order to help the workers, would abolish private property, place production in the hands of the state, and pit workers against employers in class war. The Pope's encouragement of social reformers led to the establishment of democratic Catholic parties in Belgium, Austria, and Germany.

Pius X. Another remarkable Pope followed. Saint Pius X (1903–1914) strengthened the interior life of the Church, condemned modernism (the doctrine that watered down religious truths), and began the important task of codifying canon law. His holy life was an inspiration to Catholics everywhere.

107. THE PRESSURE OF THE MASSES

Growth of population. Europe underwent a remarkable increase in population, from 175,000,000 in 1800 to 450,-000,000 by 1914. This increase in numbers went hand in hand with the expansion of European influence throughout the world. While there were more than four non-Europeans for every European in 1650, there were only two non-Europeans for every person of European extraction three hundred years later. Although the total number of Europeans continued and

Pope St. Pius X (Religious News Service)

still continues to increase, the *rate of increase* had already slackened by the end of the nineteenth century. The countries to feel the decrease first were France, Sweden, and Britain. Large families, which were the rule rather than the exception in the nineteenth century, became rarer.

Only one out of every seven persons added to the population of Europe stayed on the farm. One emigrated overseas and the remaining five flocked to the cities. The major part of the population of Britain lived in cities. And one Englishmen out of seven lived in London. After 1871 the growth of cities in France, Germany, and European Russia accelerated. A wide variety of recreation, and better living conditions—good water, sanitation, paved and lighted streets, entertainment facilities—attracted new residents. Cities set the tone of society. In rural areas people imitated the ways of the city. The city was the dream of young farm people, who longed for the lights and amusements the city offered.

Emigration. The desire to find a better and easier life in the period from 1871 to 1900 caused the emigration of about twenty-five million Europeans to Argentina, Australia, Brazil, Canada, Siberia, or the United States. Half of that number went to the United States, which was considered to be a promised land where an industrious person could improve his position. European emigration was made possible by the removal of laws that had prevented the free movement of people. Moreover, countries such as Argentina and the United States welcomed immigrants as a source of labor needed in the expanding factories, farms, and mines. Steamship companies and railroads advertised the benefits of lands beyond the seas and encouraged many Europeans to leave their old homes.

Popular education. One of the most remarkable features of the nineteenth century was the development of popular education. Never before in history did as many people of all classes receive an opportunity to go to school. No longer was education regarded as the privilege of a small group of persons who could afford it. The masses now demanded equality of opportunity to attend school. Liberals believed that schooling gave everyone equality of opportunity: all persons could progress in social and economic life if they were given the opportunity to receive an education. If all persons attended school, some liberals argued, the world would be a better place in which to live. This idea was expressed well by Guizot, the French statesman, who remarked that "the opening of every school closes a jail."

Universal suffrage. The extension of the vote to all men was a sign that political power was passing from the aristocratic and middle classes to the masses. The affairs of government were no longer the exclusive concern of the well-born and the wealthy. Britain extended the vote to all men as a result of a series of reforms from 1832 to 1918. France had universal manhood suffrage in 1848, and the German Empire had adopted it by 1871. By the twentieth century voting was widespread and general over the greater part of Europe and the Europeanized world. The extension of the vote was followed by the adoption of the secret or Australian ballot and by the granting of the vote to women in a few countries.

Women reformers were now demanding equal political rights for men and women. This movement made few gains, however, until after World War I (1914–1918). Women also were beginning to demand equality of opportunity with men to enter colleges and universities to prepare for careers in law, medicine, and

The suffragettes toured London in 1913 with sandwich boards advertising their publication. (Hulton Picture Library)

teaching. The number of women who entered colleges and universities was only a small fraction of those who entered business and industry, which were once the exclusive places of men. Very often women went to work to help support the family or to earn money to purchase luxuries. Unfortunately women substituted drudgery of office or factory for the work of raising a family. The "emancipation" of women contributed to the weakening of the family.

Marxian socialism. Socialists continued to profess their devotion for the working classes, but they had changed from the days of Owen and Fourier, who believed that benevolence and co-operation could bring about socialism. The new or "scientific" socialists advocated unremitting class conflict and the conquest of the state by strictly organized socialist parties. The scientific socialists were sure they had discovered the laws of social development and that the future lay with their cause.

Karl Marx, born in Prussia of a middle-class family of Jewish descent, was the prophet of the new socialism. After studying history and philosophy, Marx wrote fiery articles against the government and was therefore forced to leave Prussia. He went to Paris, where he met Louis Blanc and other radicals. Later he went to England, where he spent the rest of his life studying, writing, and plotting revolution. In 1848 he and Friedrich Engels published the *Communist Manifesto* and appealed to workers to rise against their governments.

The class struggle. Marx was a materialist; for him nothing existed but

Karl Marx and Friedrich Engels, the founders of modern communism. The two men had a lifelong association, during which they collaborated on several works, notably the Communist Manifesto *in 1848. (Library of Congress; Ullstein)*

matter. Religion was not only untrue but the enemy of socialism; it turned attention away from harsh conditions and taught people to concern themselves with getting to heaven and accepting poverty and oppression as roads to salvation. Marx explained all history in terms of economics. According to his "economic interpretation of history," all human life—political, cultural, religious, and social— was basically determined by existing systems of producing and distributing goods. Further, he said that class conflict was the inner principle of history. In the Middle Ages the class struggle was between the nobility and the middle classes, and in the modern era between capitalists and workers (the proletariat). Workers were denied the full value of what they produced and thus were oppressed by capitalists and their "bourgeois institutions." Marx advocated sweeping away all private property in production and substituting a communist system in which all productive property was owned by society as a whole. Under this system all railroads, mines, factories, banks,

and public utilities would be social property, not private property. Workers were growing stronger, he assured his followers, and would rise against their capitalist masters and capture control of society. Depression and war, which he believed were inevitable results of capitalism, only hastened the day of revolution. Workers could hurry the day when the old governments would fall and the "dictatorship of the proletariat" would follow by violence and revolution. Marx's battle cry was, "Let the ruling classes tremble at a Communist revolution. The proletarians have nothing to lose but their chains. They have a world to win. Working men of all countries, unite!"

The revolutions of 1848–1849 convinced Marx that the capitalist or bourgeois state could not be toppled easily. Before the workers could take over all property, they had to be trained for revolution. To foment communist revolution all over the world and to train agitators, he established the First International in London in 1864. But the communist movement

Anti-union feeling is shown in this British cartoon of the nineteenth century. Most of the caricatures are supposed to be Irish, who were often degraded in this way. (Hulton Picture Library)

failed to attract warm support from workers; instead, it enlisted ambitious revolutionary middle-class persons. Sharp differences of opinion among communist leaders split the movement. Marx died in 1883, not having achieved his goal of world revolution. Yet his influence was tremendous, especially in the twentieth century.

Anarchists and syndicalists. Communists had rivals for revolutionary action. Anarchists wished to do away with the state—which they said corrupted man and perpetuated private property—so that people could live in peace and harmony and co-operate spontaneously to establish justice. Syndicalists urged labor unions to wage constant warfare against capitalists by means of boycott, strike, and sabotage for the purpose of seizing control and ownership of industry. Like the communists, the anarchists and syndicalists used violence to attain their ends.

Trade Unions. The last half of the nineteenth century was marked by the progress of the trade-union movement throughout the Western world. By this means workingmen sought higher wages and better working conditions from their employers. Strikes were the principal weapon to gain these ends, but the vote was equally powerful.

The strength of the labor vote led many politicians to compete for their support. In Britain, for example, the Liberal Party flirted with the Labor Party, whose support it needed. And the Conservative Party contained some leaders who supported "Tory democracy," the idea that the government should take steps to improve the condition of the working classes. The idea that governments must help the poor to achieve a richer life had captured the imaginations of many people by the twentieth century.

REVIEW

105. The "New" Industrial Revolution

A. What factors enabled Germany and the United States to become leaders in the second industrial revolution?

B. List four technical developments that stimulated this industrial expansion.

C. Explain the terms "industrial consolidation" and "finance capitalism."

D. Identify: Baring Brothers, J. P. Morgan, Marconi, Edison.

106. Science and Religion

A. What was Darwin's theory of "natural selection"?

B. How was Darwin's theory of evolution received by various religions?

C. What was the *Syllabus of Errors?* What was condemned by the eightieth proposition?

D. List three achievements of the pontificate of Leo XIII.

107. The Pressure of the Masses

A. What was the argument put forth in behalf of "popular education?"

B. List two examples of extensions of suffrage during this period.

C. Explain the "economic interpretation of history" of Karl Marx.

D. What was the importance of "class conflict" in the Marxian doctrines?

E. Identify: First International, anarchism, syndicalists.

THE CHAPTER IN REVIEW

A. Explain briefly Darwin's theory of evolution.

B. What was the meaning of the "welfare state" according to the Fabians? Cite four social reforms in Britain during the period that followed this welfare principle.

C. What was the effect of the rise of science on the religious environment of the nineteenth century?

D. How did Marxian socialism differ from previous socialist theories? Was the Marxist movement a political success in the nineteenth and early twentieth centuries? Explain.

FOR YOUR NOTEBOOK

Make a list of the developments in this period in transportation and communication. Under each development put down two or three obvious results that are important historically. For example, under the "internal combustion engine" you could list automobiles and gasoline-powered machines.

Look up the following in one of the standard encyclopedias and list each man's contributions to practical science:

Bell	Pasteur
Marconi	Lister
Edison	Koch

The Catholic Church made remarkable progress during the pontificates of Pius IX (1846–1878) and Leo XIII (1878–1903). Use one of the standard one-volume histories of the Church, such as Neill and Schmandt, *History of the Catholic Church* (Milwaukee: Bruce Publishing Co., 1957), to list the principal accomplishments of each pontificate.

During this period the "masses" emerge from obscurity onto the scene of history. Prepare a list of events and developments promoting this emergence of the common man under these headings: (1) political, (2) economic, (3) social, (4) theoretical or ideological. Under "political," for example, you will list the coming of universal suffrage in many countries, and under "social" you will list widespread, state-supported education and the coming of inexpensive newspapers and journals.

In 1899 most Europeans felt the greatest century in history was drawing to a close and that the twentieth century would be even better. List all the reasons they had for optimism. Now list all the reasons that might justify pessimism instead of optimism in 1899 or 1900.

SELECTED READINGS

Paul de Kruif describes the work of Pasteur, Koch, and others in his *Microbe*

Hunters (New York: Harcourt, Brace & Co., 1939), and Floyd L. Darrow does the same thing for inventors in *Masters of Science and Invention* (New York: Harcourt, Brace & Co., 1938). A firsthand story of a "captain of industry" is the *Autobiography of Andrew Carnegie* (Boston: Houghton Mifflin Co., 1957), and both good and bad aspects of big industry are presented in the "Problems in American Civilization" book edited by Earl Latham, *John D. Rockefeller, Robber Baron or Industrial Statesman?* (Boston: D. C. Heath & Co., 1949).

The accomplishments of Pius IX and Leo XIII are handled satisfactorily in Neill and Schmandt, *History of the Catholic Church* (Milwaukee, Wis.: Bruce Publishing Co., 1957), Chapters 33 and 34, and somewhat more briefly in parts of Chapters 9 and 11 in Philip Hughes, *A Popular History of the Catholic Church* (Garden City, N.Y.: Doubleday & Co., 1954).

Perhaps the best books for American students on Marxian communism are Francis J. Sheed, *Communism and Man* (New York: Sheed & Ward, 1938), and Fulton J. Sheen, *Communism and the Conscience of the West* (Indianapolis: Bobbs-Merrill Co., 1948).

CHRONOLOGICAL REVIEW

1859 *Darwin publishes* ORIGIN OF SPECIES
1861 American Civil War begins; kingdom of Italy proclaimed; emancipation of serfs in Russia
Gatling's machine gun
1862 Bismarck becomes Prussian chancellor
1864 Austria and Prussia defeat Denmark
Pius IX issues SYLLABUS OF ERRORS
1866 Prussia defeats Austria; Italy gets Venetia
Cable laid, Ireland to Newfoundland
1867 Dual monarchy in Austrian Empire; North German Confederation; Maximilian of Mexico executed; restoration of emperor in Japan
Marx publishes DAS KAPITAL
1869 Suez Canal; Union Pacific R. R.
1870 Franco-Prussian War; defeat of Napoleon III; Italy takes Rome
Papal Infallibility proclaimed
1871 German Empire
Stanley finds Livingstone; trade union legalized in Britain
1873 Three Emperors' League
World depression
1876 *Bell invents telephone*
1877 Queen Victoria becomes empress of India; Russo-Turk War
Edison invents phonograph
1878 Congress of Berlin
Pontificate of Leo XIII (to 1903)
1881 Death of Disraeli; League of the Three Emperors renewed

1882 Triple Alliance; British occupy Egypt
Koch discovers tuberculosis germ
1885 Indian National Congress founded; Leopold of Belgium established Congo State
Gold discovered in Transvaal
1890 Bismarck dismissed
Death of Cardinal Newman; Mahan's INFLUENCE OF SEA POWER
1894 Japan attacks China; Franco-Russian alliance; Dreyfus trial in France
Germ of bubonic plague discovered by Kitasato
1895 Jameson raid into Transvaal
Roentgen discovers X-ray; Marconi's radio; death of Pasteur
1896 Russo-Chinese treaty; Italian defeat in Abyssinia; France annexes Madagascar
1898 Fashoda incident in Africa; Spanish-American War; European rivalry in China
The Curies isolate radium; zeppelin invented; diesel motor
1899 Boer War begins; 1st Hague conference
1900 Boxer Rebellion in China
Gold standard in U. S. A.
1902 Anglo-Japanese Alliance
1904 Russo-Japanese War
1905 "Red Sunday" in Russia; Norway becomes independent
Einstein publishes his special theory of relativity

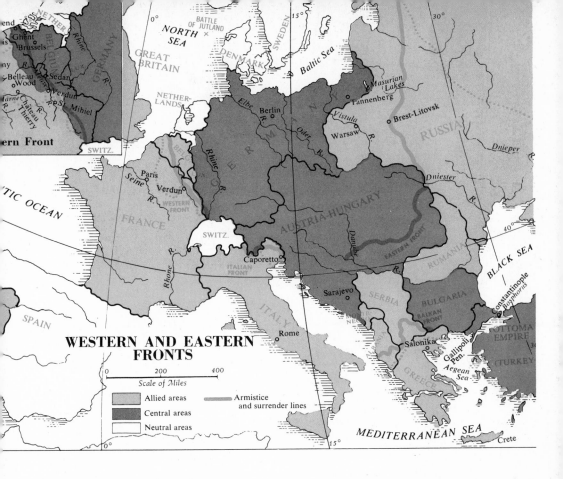

WESTERN AND EASTERN
FRONTS

Scale of Miles

0   200   400

Allied areas   Armistice
                            and surrender lines
Central areas
Neutral areas

UNIT ELEVEN
The World Catastrophe of
the Early Twentieth Century

Diplomatic Crises and Antagonisms in Europe, 1894 to 1911 · The Balkan Crisis Leads
to General War, 1911 to 1914 · The Great Stalemate, 1914 to 1916 · American
Intervention and the Collapse of Russia · Allied Triumph and Collapse of the Central
Powers · The Measure of Disaster and Chaos · The Peace of Paris and the League of
Nations · Communism and Soviet Russia, 1918 to 1924 · Intensified Nationalism

Chapter 35. The Outbreak of World War I

108. DIPLOMATIC CRISES AND ANTAGONISMS IN EUROPE, 1894 TO 1911

The dawn of the twentieth century gave promise to a golden age of peace and progress. It seemed that the future must be happier and more progressive than the past. There had been no great general war involving many nations since the fall of Napoleon in 1815. Although the Crimean, Franco-Sardinian, and Franco-Prussian wars had broken the peace, they were short and local in character. The greatest war of the nineteenth century had been the American Civil War. Hope was widespread that somehow a reasonable way would soon be discovered for blotting out war, which Europeans thought did not belong in their progressive society. Some statesmen recommended applying to international affairs the methods of conciliation used in settling disputes between workers and employers.

A yearning for peace was found among kings and emperors such as Czar Nicholas II of Russia, who wished to reduce armaments and lift the fear of war from the hearts of people. In 1899 he convoked a peace conference of twenty-six nations at the Hague, in the Netherlands, to consider ways and means of reducing armaments and avoiding the causes of war. The attempt to limit armaments failed, but an international court of arbitration was established at the Hague. The Hague Conference also established rules of warfare for all civilized nations to follow; it banned the use of poisonous gases, poisoned and dumdum bullets. In 1907, at the second Hague Conference, forty-four countries met to limit armies and navies. And again the attempt failed, but it showed how strong was the disposition of nations to meet together and work to remove causes of war.

International disorder. We know that the closing years of the nineteenth century and the early years of the twentieth were marked by a number of localized wars in many parts of the world. The Japanese fought the Chinese (1894–1895); the United States went to war with Spain in 1898, and the British made war upon the Boers of South Africa from 1899 to 1902. The Russo-Japanese War followed in 1904–1905. These wars were signs of deep-seated disorder in the world of nations. The disorder was to grow worse until a great war broke out in Europe in 1914 and then spread to other parts of the world. This war was not really the first world war, but it was the first world war of the twentieth century. Hence it is usually called World War I.

The war was not started by wicked men ambitious to conquer the world. It resulted from a complex chain of events and circumstances that put certain European powers in a predicament from which they saw no escape except through war. Let us therefore try to understand this predicament.

Germany and the Triple Alliance. We have already seen that imperial Germany, led by Prince Bismarck, formed a Triple Alliance in 1879–1882 with Austria-Hungary and Italy. At that time the Balkan kingdom of Serbia leaned for protection upon Austria-Hungary, and in 1883 the kingdom of Rumania entered the Triple Alliance system. Bismarck conceived of this system of alliances as what he called "Our League of Peace." The alliances were not for aggression but for defense. They served, however, to make Germany the strongest power in Europe. To lessen French and Russian resentment of this fact, Germany encouraged France to expand in Africa and Russia to expand in Far East Asia. In Africa, French imperialism collided with British interests. Russian imperialism in Asia alarmed both the British in India and the rising power of Japan. It was then natural that France and Russia should at length, in 1894, conclude an alliance.

Franco-Russian alliance. This was a military defense pact in which each power agreed to come to the aid of the other if either was attacked by *two* major powers. That is to say, if Germany and Austria-Hungary attacked Russia, France would come to Russia's aid; and if France were attacked by Germany and Italy, Russia would be obligated to go to war. Neither France nor Russia meant to start a war against Germany; each was seeking greater security, and each hoped to gain the diplomatic support of the other in clashes with Great Britain. In a certain sense the alliance was designed to work against Great Britain too. The British indeed were more alarmed by the Franco-Russian alliance that were the Germans.

Anglo-German relations. If the Franco-Russian alliance tended to draw Britain and Germany together, other factors worked more powerfully in the opposite direction. Germany did not remain content with security and military pre-eminence in Europe; she wished to become also a world power. In Africa and the Pacific islands she had acquired the beginnings of a colonial empire. She had become so thoroughly industrialized that she needed a secure supply of raw materials and large export markets. Hence she developed a large merchant marine and by the end of the nineteenth century determined to become a first-class naval power. These developments brought her into a lively rivalry with Great Britain.

While the British were fighting the Boers, the German government in 1900 laid down a warship-building program that was designed to create a navy strong enough to threaten British naval superiority in the North Sea. As soon as the Boer War was over, Great Britain began a revolution in her naval and foreign policies. This meant concentrating her fighting ships in the North Sea while seeking new security for her imperial interests through diplomacy. In 1902 she concluded an alliance with Japan; under the terms of it each power, if attacked by two major powers, could call upon the full support of the other. About the same time Great Britain came to an informal naval understanding with the United States. It became a basic principle of the British Foreign Office to avoid at all costs a serious dispute with the United States. The new British policy was highly advantageous to the United States, especially in the Caribbean region, and to Japanese imperialism in the Far East. It was necessitated by the German menace in British home waters.

The Entente Cordiale. The next step in Britain's new policy was to reach a settlement of all differences and conflicts with France. This was accelerated by the outbreak of the Russo-Japanese

War in 1904. Since Britain was allied with Japan and France with Russia, both might have been drawn into the war if another major power had come to Russia's aid. With good will on both sides, they now came to an *entente cordiale* (or cordial understanding) by resolving all their disputes in all parts of the world. The most important details of the entente concerned Egypt and Morocco. Ever since 1882 France had contested Britain's protectorate in Egypt; this she now recognized and gave Britain a free hand in that country. On the other hand, Britain had previously opposed French ambitions to establish a protectorate over Morocco; now France received from Britain a free hand in Morocco.

Germany and the Anglo-French entente. Imperial Germany sensed a danger in the new relations between France and Great Britain. Taking advantage of Russia's preoccupation with war against Japan, the German government in 1905 challenged French penetration of Morocco and even threatened France

German policy temporarily triumphed in Morocco when Emperor William II influenced the sultan to reject French reforms for the country. However, at the Algeciras Conference in 1906 (below) Britain supported France's claims to a privileged position in Morocco. (Ullstein)

with war. The German aim was to bulldoze the French into depending on German favor instead of British. The crisis was overcome by an international conference at Algeciras on the Moroccan question. With strong British diplomatic support, the French obtained recognition of their special interests in Morocco. Germany failed to disrupt the Anglo-French entente; indeed her conduct only made the British and French more determined to maintain it. The entente was not an alliance, but the Germans knew it established a community of Anglo-French interest that might develop into an alliance.

Germany and Russia. In that part of Europe which stretches from the Baltic Sea to the Balkan pensinsula lay the greatest dangers to the peace of the world. Four great empires ruled over many different nationalities, which were growing ever more restive. Imperial Germany possessed parts of Poland; the rest of Poland was divided between Russia and Austria. Russia included Finland, Latvia, Esthonia, Lithuania, and the Ukraine. Austria included Bohemia, which was populated mainly by the Slavic Czechs, and also held Italian lands, which Italy hoped one day to annex. Most of the Jugo-Slav (south Slav) peoples—Croats, Slovenes, and Serbs—were under the government of Austria-Hungary. There were Slovaks and Rumanians in Hungary. The Ottoman Empire still possessed Bulgaria and most of the country south of the lower Danube, except little Greece. The Ottoman Empire had long been declining, but since the latter part of the nineteenth century Germany had been developing its railways and training its soldiers. Hence German influ-

William II, Emperor of Germany
(Library of Congress)

ence was dominant in that empire. Austria-Hungary, too, had become seriously weakened by internal discords and depended heavily on German support. The great powers that directly or indirectly dominated all eastern Europe were the German and Russian empires. If they plunged into war, great revolutions were certain to sweep the whole region.

As long as Bismarck directed German policy he sought to maintain good German-Russian relations. These were supported also by the fact that the German emperor, William II (1888–1918), and Czar Nicholas II (1894–1917) were cousins and friends. However, after Bismarck retired in 1890, and still more after the Franco-Russian alliance was made, German-Russian relations deteriorated. William II tried to improve them during the Russo-Japanese war, but soon afterward they took a new turn for the worse. Defeat in the war with Japan caused Russia to turn to Britain and France for loans and to seek compensation in Europe for losses in the Far East. Russia sought to restore her influence in the Balkans, thus threatening both Austria-Hungary and the Ottoman Empire. Inevitably Germany opposed such threats.

Anglo-Russian convention. The British government had long been eager to pin down Russian imperialists from encroaching through central Asia and the Middle East on India. It was now eager also to bring the diplomatic weight of Russia into Europe to counter Germany. The Russian government, with its attention centered on the Balkans and the problem of persuading the Turks to open the Constantinople straits (long closed to all ships of war) to the Russian navy in the Black Sea, saw an advantage in negotiating with Great Britain. In 1907 these powers concluded a treaty to settle their differences. Both agreed to keep their forces out of Tibet; Russia recognized Afghanistan as within the British imperial sphere of interest, and Britain promised not to annex it. Persia (Iran) was divided into three spheres of influence, Russian, British, and a neutral zone. As in the case of the Anglo-French entente, the convention of 1907 was in no sense an alliance. However, Britain's new friendly relations with both France and Russia, together with the Franco-Russian alliance, brought into existence what was known as the Triple Entente. Increasingly the Triple Entente appeared as a rival combination to the German-headed Triple Alliance.

Germany witnessed the Triple En-

Following the successful rebellion of the Young Turks, a strongly nationalist group, Turkish Parliament was opened in 1908. (Year, Inc.)

tente with dismay and began to fear what the Germans called "encirclement." If war broke out it seemed possible, even likely, that Germany might have to fight on two great fronts, in the East and in the West.

The crisis of 1908. This year a revolution broke out in the Ottoman Empire. It was launched by a party known as the Young Turks, who hoped to reform and strengthen the Ottoman Empire by introducing a parliamentary constitution; but the immediate effect was further to weaken the Ottoman state. Austria-Hungary chose this crisis as an opportunity to annex the Ottoman provinces (Serb in population) of Bosnia and Herzegovina, which had been under Austrian occupation since 1878. Bulgaria declared its independence of Turkish rule. Russia protested the Austrian annexation and sought to get the support of the great powers for opening the straits to her fleet. Neither Great Britain nor France was willing to give such support. The small state of Serbia, which since 1903 had broken free from Austrian control, was most enraged at Austria's annexation. Serbia had hoped ultimately to annex Bosnia and Herzegovina. She threatened to fight, and Russia seemed disposed to support her; but early in 1909 Germany sternly demanded that Russia back down. Disappointed by France and Britain and unprepared for war, the Russian government gave way. It was a great diplomatic triumph for Germany.

The Young Turk regime in the Ottoman Empire had at first opposed German influence in Turkish affairs and looked for support from Britain and France. They turned to Germany after 1909, and German influence became stronger than ever in the Ottoman Empire.

The Moroccan crisis of 1911. Having browbeaten Russia, Germany in 1910 lured that power into an agreement that seemed for a time to destroy the Triple Entente. Russia gave up all diplomatic opposition to the German construction of a railway, called the Bagdad Railway, through the heart of the Ottoman Empire; and Germany agreed to support Russian plans in Persia. The next year, 1911, Germany threatened France in a new move to rupture the Entente Cordiale.

France was about to establish a protectorate over Morocco when Germany sent a warship to the Moroccan Atlantic port of Agadir and indicated by military moves in Europe that France would have to come to terms. Once again Germany meant to force France into a dependence on her instead of Great Britain. A strong British reaction indicated that the London government would go to war rather than tolerate German dictation to France. This threat caused the Germans to moderate their tactics. Presently a Franco-German compromise agreement was reached. Germany was to allow the French to establish a protectorate over Morocco and received in exchange a slice of French colonial territory in equatorial Africa.

Italy attacks Turkey. When the tension between Germany on the one hand and Britain on the other was at its height in the Moroccan crisis of 1911, the Italian government suddenly started a war. Italian leaders had long been eager to found an empire in Mediter-

The Bagdad Railway was a dream of the Germans, who planned the road in 1889. Considered a menace to British, Russian, and French interests, it was highly contested until in 1914 an agreement between Britain and Germany settled most difficulties. But World War I unsettled everything, and the railway has been considered a major cause of Turkey's joining the Central Powers. (Ullstein)

ranean Africa. It seemed to them that Tunisia had been snatched away from them by France, and nothing was left but the largely desert lands between Tunisia and British-controlled Egypt. These were part of the Ottoman Empire, but that state was too weak to defend them. In September 1911, Italy sent an expedition to Tripoli and began to seize coastal regions. Turkey declared war, but Britain would not permit Turkish troops to pass through Egypt to fight the Italians.

Italy's allies, Germany and Austria-Hungary, deeply disapproved her behavior. It was embarrassing to Germany's interests in Turkey for her ally to seize Turkish territory. Austria feared that Italy's success might go to her head and lead next to an effort to annex the Italian provinces of the Austrian Empire. Hardly less feared was an Italian attack on the Ottoman Empire in the Balkans, which could easily provoke the Balkan states to make a similar attack. To Austria, Italy seemed like a firebrand who might set fire to her house. To force the Turks to yield satisfactory peace terms, the Italians early in 1912 seized the Dodecanese Islands.

In the critical state of international relations, neither France nor Britain wished to oppose Italy lest a general war be started. Germany did not wish to antagonize Italy lest Italy break her alliance and go over to the entente powers. Russia actually encouraged Italy and used the crisis as an opportunity to demand that the Turks open the straits to Russian warships. The Turks, supported on this point by Germany, Austria-Hungary, and Britain, refused the Russian demand.

109. THE BALKAN CRISIS LEADS TO GENERAL WAR, 1911 to 1914

The weakness displayed by the Turks when the Italians attacked them excited the nationalist ambitions of Bulgaria, Greece, and Serbia. They were tempted to strike in order to partition among themselves what remained of the Ottoman Empire in Europe. The Greeks wished also to acquire numerous Turkish-held islands in the Aegean and to annex Crete. In March 1912, Serbia and Bulgaria made an alliance directed against the Turks. It was followed by a pact between Bulgaria and Greece; so that a sort of Balkan league came into existence, and it was joined, in effect, by the little Serb principality of Montenegro.

Balkan states attack. No sooner had the Italo-Turkish war been brought to an end than Montenegro went to war with the Turks. Quickly the Balkan league joined in the attack (October 1912). The aggressors justified themselves by charging the Turks with barbarous tyranny and oppression over the subject peoples of Macedonia. Rapidly the Balkan allies overran almost the whole of Turkish territory in Europe.

The Concert of Europe acts. These events raised the greatest alarms in Europe, for all statesmen knew that the fall of the Ottoman Empire in Europe might produce a clash between the major powers. The success of the Serbs and Bulgars appeared as a triumph of Russian interests, and the failure of the Turks was a reverse for German interests. Austria-Hungary felt that she could not tolerate the growth of Serbia, which was well known to have territorial ambitions in Bosnia and Herzegovina. Neither Austria nor Italy was prepared to see Serbia acquire an outlet on the Adriatic.

In this Balkan crisis, Great Britain and Germany found a large measure of agreement. Both wished to prevent a clash of major powers; hence they took the lead in assembling the Concert of Europe at London. Under Concert supervision a treaty of peace was at length made in May 1913. It provided for the creation of an independent Albania and the partition of Macedonia by Serbia, Bulgaria, and Greece.

Second Balkan war. Less than a month after the Treaty of London, a new war broke out. The Serbs were embittered at being denied a port on the Adriatic and felt that Bulgaria had acquired more Macedonian territory than was due her. The Greeks disliked Bulgarian annexations that reached to the Aegean coast. Hence Greece and Serbia formed an alliance against Bulgaria. The Bulgars, who had borne the brunt of the fighting against the Turkish army, suddenly on June 29 attacked the Serbian army. The Greek-Serb alliance became operative, and these two states fiercely drove back the Bulgarians. At the same time, Rumania, which had hitherto remained at peace, joined in the war against Bulgaria. Even the Turks re-entered the fight and won back some territory previously lost to the Bulgars.

Bulgaria was completely defeated and forced to sign the Treaty of Bucharest (August 1913). Rumania gained a large strip of Bulgaria, called the Dobrudja, south and east of the lower Danube River. The Greeks obtained most of southern Macedonia. Soon afterward they were allowed by the great powers to annex the island of Crete. Serbia had now doubled her former size by the acquisition of western Macedonia. Montenegro, too, was enlarged and obtained a common frontier with Serbia. Since the people of both these states were Serb, it had always been Ottoman and Austrian policy to prevent their having a common frontier. Montenegro had a small Adriatic coast but no good port; Serbia's strenuous efforts to acquire an Adriatic port had not succeeded. Nevertheless, Serbia and Montenegro were now in effect united and Serbia had become much larger and stronger. This feature of the peace was very alarming to Austria-Hungary. Weakened from within by her discontented nationalities, the Hapsburg monarchy feared the influence of a swollen Serbia's nationalist agitation among the Serbs of Bosnia and Herzegovina. Austria-Hungary was only a little less disturbed by the growth of Rumania, which was drifting toward closer relations with Russia, for Rumanian nationalists had designs on Transylvania, a part of Hungary.

Anglo-German relations improve. Diplomatic co-operation between Great Britain and Germany was greatly developed during the Balkan wars. Although their efforts to come to a naval agreement did not succeed, they continued to seek bases of agreement. Both powers supported the aspirations of Greece, whose King Constantine was a brother-in-law of the German emperor. They came to an understanding for partitioning the Portuguese colonies in Africa in the event that Portugal, a state gravely weakened by revolution in 1911, failed to retain them. Britain and Germany also came to a complete harmonizing of their previous rival interests in the Ottoman Empire. The British had long striven to prevent the completion of the Bagdad Railway; now they abandoned opposition to that in return for valuable economic concessions in Ottoman Mesopotamia. So far had Anglo-German differences been smoothed out by 1914 that both the French and Russians feared Britain was about to abandon the Triple Entente. The grand object of German diplomacy in negotiating with Britain had been to ensure that the British would remain neutral in the event Germany became involved in war with the Franco-Russian allies. Official Germany was almost persuaded that this had been gained.

Early in 1914 the Russian government put the weakened Triple Entente to the test. A German general, Liman

THE BALKAN COUNTRIES 1914

von Sanders, had been placed by the Turkish government in command of its troops at Constantinople. Russia energetically protested and sought diplomatic support from Great Britain and France to force the Turkish government to remove Liman. Such support was not given. The Russian foreign minister, Baron Sazonov, remarked bitterly that the Triple Entente had "no more reality than the sea serpent." Despite her success in drawing Rumania away from the Central Powers and her rejoicing in the enlargement of Serbia, Russia in 1914 was seized by fear of drifting into political isolation from her Entente partners.

Sarajevo. It was the misfortune of Europe and the world that the government of the Balkan kingdom of Serbia lacked the power to control its own subjects. A nationalist secret society, called the Black Hand, which included officers of the Serbian army, was able to terrorize Serbian political leaders and aspired to carry out a revolution to unite all Serbs in a Greater Serbia. Membership in this society extended into the Serb lands of Austria-Hungary. The Black Hand feared nothing so much as the possibility that Austria-Hungary might allow the formation of a South Slav state under Hapsburg rule, since that would dash the hopes of Serbian nationalists. It was widely rumored that the heir to the Austrian Empire and kingdom of Hungary, Francis Ferdinand, favored such a South Slav policy; and he was likely soon to succeed to the throne, since Emperor Francis Joseph was eighty-four years old.

In June 1914, Francis Ferdinand visited Bosnia. The Serbian government, fearing something awkward might take place, warned the Austrian government, but the warning went unheeded. A young Serb named Gavrilo Princip, a member of the Black Hand, shot and killed Francis Ferdinand and his wife in the streets of Sarajevo on June 28. This crime started World War I.

The Austro-Hungarian government resolved to hold Serbia responsible for the crime: to seize, discipline, and reduce that state to the status of a satellite. It was well known that Russia would strongly object and seek to defend Serbia, but the Vienna government counted on strong German support to ward off Russian military intervention. On July 23 a severe note was sent from Vienna to Belgrade, demanding in effect that Serbia place herself under Austrian police control. In little more than a week most of Europe was at war.

The fateful chain of events. The Serbs determined to defend themselves and mobilized their army; Austria-Hungary did the same. Russia demanded that Austria-Hungary refrain from attacking Serbia. Great Britain sought to convoke the Concert of Europe to negotiate a settlement of the crisis. Germany proposed that Austria-Hungary and Russia reach a settlement by direct negotiations. On July 28, Austria-Hungary declared war on Serbia, and the next day Russia ordered a general mobilization of her armies. Imperial Germany saw this mobilization as a threat to both Austria-Hungary and herself and demanded that the Russians stop it. When Russia disregarded the German demand, the Berlin government on August 1 declared that

Archduke Francis Ferdinand and his two sons. (Wide World)

Russia had placed itself in a state of war with Germany.

Reason for German declaration. It is of the utmost importance to understand why Germany chose to declare a state of war with Russia. The first reason was strategic. Russia was a very large country with a vast manpower; she could not manage her military movements as fast as Germany could. German military leaders had long planned, in the event of war with Russia, to ensure themselves against the danger of having to fight simultaneously in the West and in the East. They planned to obtain a guarantee of French neutrality, or a quick military knockout of

France before the Russian menace could reach its full dimensions. In declaring war on Russia, therefore, the German general staff did not mean to move at once against Russia, but to attack France first. The civil government, headed by Chancellor von Bethmann-Hollweg, had, however, to consider German public opinion, which was not inclined to support an aggressive war against France. Assuming war to be inevitable, the government thought it necessary to convince the public that Russia was forcing war on Germany, so that attack on Russia's French ally might be understood as an unfortunate necessity. Bethmann-Hollweg hoped that the British would see the situation that way too.

Germany vs. France. Germany now confronted France with a demand to know whether she would fulfill her alliance with Russia. René Viviani, the French Premier, replied that France would consult her own interests. Having seen clearly what was coming, the French government had for some days been imploring Great Britain to declare a stand against Germany, but the British cabinet was divided in opinion and could not come to a determination. On August 2, Germany occupied Luxembourg and demanded passage of its armies through Belgium. The following day Germany declared war on France.

Intervention of Great Britain. The leading men of Prime Minister Herbert Asquith's cabinet had long been convinced that it would be disastrous for Great Britain to allow western Europe to fall under German control. They were not less eager to defend France against a warlike Germany than to

come to an understanding with a pacific Germany. But public and parliamentary opinion was not ready to support war until after Belgium was invaded. Belgium was a neutral country and had enjoyed that status since 1839. All the Great Powers, Germany included, had committed themselves to respect Belgian neutrality. Now the Germans had broken their word. The British cabinet found strong support for demanding that Germany withdraw from Belgium. This demand was rejected by Germany, and at midnight on August 4 the British government declared war.

The British dominions rapidly followed with declarations of war against Germany, so that Canada, Australia, New Zealand, and South Africa became involved. Before a month had passed Japan declared war on Germany and began to move against German colonial bases and possessions in the Pacific. Thus a war between the major powers of Europe rapidly became global in its dimensions. The United States, however, immediately declared neutrality.

Herbert Asquith, Prime Minister of England during the early years of World War I, was bitterly attacked by the press for his conduct of the war. He was succeeded by Lloyd George in 1916. (Hulton Picture Library)

George V succeeded to the throne of his father Edward VII in 1910. A sound but unimaginative ruler, he reigned until 1936. (Hulton Picture Library)

110. THE GREAT STALEMATE, 1914 TO 1916

The intervention of Great Britain, although dismaying the Germans, caused no change in their strategy, which aimed at a quick military victory in the West before massing their forces to settle with Russia. Britain had only a small army to send to the Continent, and the Germans believed it could not seriously affect the course of military events. The German plan was to swing through Belgium and eastern France, around Paris, and take the French army from the rear. At the same time the Austrian forces were to take the offensive against the Russians in Russian Poland and keep them busy until France was beaten.

The Marne and Ypres. The Germans did not swing wide enough to destroy the Belgian army or prevent the first British divisions from landing against their flank. Moreover, the Germans fell behind their timetable in breaking through Belgium. Before the swing

around Paris could be attempted it became necessary to transfer four divisions of troops to East Prussia to meet the Russians, who moved more rapidly than had been expected. In East Prussia the German generals Hindenburg and Ludendorff, in late August–early September, won the great battles of Tannenberg and the Masurian Lakes: battles that cost Russia a quarter million men and cut the first great wounds in that empire. In the West, however, the Germans chose to swing before Paris instead of around it. The French, commanded by Marshal Joffre, counterattacked and threw back the enemy in what is called the first battle of the Marne River (September 6–12, 1914). Then came a German tactical change: a push for the English Channel ports to sever Anglo-French lines of communication. This drive was stopped at Ypres, chiefly by the small British forces. Antwerp, Zeebrugge, and Ostend were captured by the Germans, but Dunkirk and Calais were held by the

French soldiers on guard at the Marne with an anti-aircraft gun mounted in a shallow well. (Wide World)

Field Marshal Paul von Hindenburg (center) is shown with members of his general staff in the historic market place of Brussels during the German occupation of Belgium. (National Archives)

Allies. The shortest line of Anglo-French communications remained secure.

The battle of Ypres (which the French called *eepr* but the British called *wipers!*) and the first battle of the Marne meant failure of the German strategy for a quick victory in the West. Winter settled down upon a deadlocked trench war destined to continue four years. The barbed-wire line that extended from the North Sea to the Swiss frontier would bend and bulge, hammered now to one figure and then to another, but it would not be broken until the last days of the war. The military historian, Major Liddell Hart, wrote: "The power of modern defense had triumphed over attack, and stalemate ensued."

British blockade. The Germans had not risked throwing their North Sea fleet into action in 1914; as a result, the superior British naval forces with some help from the French fastened a blockade upon Germany that cut her off from the Atlantic. All over the waters of the world, except in the Baltic, German ships were captured, sunk, or driven to internment in neutral ports.

Austrian reverses. To the east, German fortunes were much better, although by no means as good as the Central Powers wished. Western (Russian) Poland had come under German control, but the Russians still held Warsaw, and the Austro-Hungarian armies had sustained terrible losses. It became necessary for them to recruit large numbers of new officers from the doubtfully loyal subject nationalities of the Austro-Hungarian Empire. That empire was still more weakened and became dependent for survival on Germany. The war against Russia forced General Conrad von Höetzendorff, commander of the Austrian armies, to neglect fighting the Serbs. In the early days of fighting, the Serbs had been forced to give up their capital, Belgrade; now they recaptured it and by the end of 1914 had pushed their foes back over the frontier.

Turkish intervention. On August 1 the Ottoman Empire signed a defensive alliance with Germany, which was directed primarily against Russia. After the British declared war, two powerful German cruisers, the *Goeben* and the *Breslau,* were driven for refuge to Constantinople, still a neutral port. The Germans sold these ships to the Turks, who were then emboldened to challenge Russia. On October 29, 1914, the Turks shelled Russian Black Sea ports. The Turks were at this time sure that Germany would defeat Russia. Their intervention was of vast importance. Russia was forced to open a new front in the Caucasus. The British and French, fearful that Russia might make a separate peace with her enemies, at once declared war on the Turks for Russia's sake. The British had to divert forces to defend the Suez Canal against Turkish attack. The necessities of the war against Turkey caused divisions of opinion between the French and English over questions of high strategy. The French wished to concentrate all Allied strength against the Germans in France. The British had important imperial interests in Egypt and India to consider. Many Frenchmen came to feel that they were bearing the brunt of fighting the Germans while the British were making their empire safe.

The Gallipoli expedition. The German general staff planned a great offensive against Russia for the spring of 1915, hoping to win in the East such a victory as had been denied them in the West the year before. At the same time the British navy resolved to break through the Dardanelles and Bosphorus, gain the alliance of the Greeks, capture Constantinople, and open communications with Russia through the Black Sea. This plan was conceived and pushed forward by Winston Churchill, at that time First Lord of the British Admiralty. However, the naval expedition was halted by Turkish mines in the Dardanelles and the Greeks did not enter the war. It became necessary to raise an Allied military force to land on the Gallipoli peninsula (April 1915). By that time

Infantrymen pick their way through shell craters in "no man's land." This zone between opposing trenches was sometimes only a few yards away. Men were pinned down by machine-gun fire and had to "go over the top" at great risk in order to advance.

(National Archives)

the Turks, under a German commander, were able to establish strong defenses and the Allies were pinned down. The effort thus failed.

Italian intervention. For a short time it appeared that the Gallipoli expedition would succeed, and Italy chose that moment to enter the war on the side of the Allies. The Italian government had seen the military weakness of Austria-Hungary and thought the Allies would ultimately win the war. Although allied with Germany and Austria-Hungary, Italy denounced that alliance and made the Treaty of London (April 1915) with Britain and France, who promised to support Italy's aspirations to gain Austria's Italian provinces in the Alps and along the Adriatic. In May, Italy declared war against Austria, but not against Germany until the following year. Weakened Austria now had three war fronts: Serbian, Russian, and Italian.

German victories in Eastern Europe. During the spring and summer of 1915 a vast German offensive in Russian Poland almost knocked Russia out of the war. Warsaw fell to the Germans, and the Russian armies were driven behind the Pripet Marshes. They ran short of ammunition and suffered such great casualties that it was doubtful if they could ever mount another offensive. Then German-Austrian forces moved down upon the Serbs; Bulgaria saw her chance for revenge on the Serbs and entered the war against them in alliance with the Central Powers.

In the fall of 1915, Serbia was conquered and occupied; her government went into exile on the Greek island of Corfu. Bulgaria as a belligerent bridged the territorial gap between the Central Powers and Turkey. Thus was completed the building of a great fortress of German power that reached from Antwerp to Mesopotamia. It remained standing until the fall of 1918. Everywhere it was sustained by German energy, efficiency, and arms.

Western front in 1915. There was little change in the position of the front in France and Belgium. The Germans stood mostly on the defensive here, although it was at this time that they introduced the use of poison gas against their foes. Navally they launched a submarine campaign in the waters around the British Isles and in the shipping lanes of the Mediterranean and Atlantic. In May 1915 a German submarine sank the British passenger liner *Lusitania* in the Atlantic Ocean west of Ireland, with the loss of many American lives. This barbarity of war was strongly protested by the President of the United States, Woodrow Wilson, and did much to arouse an American opinion favorable to aiding the Allied cause. Presently the Germans promised the United States to limit their submarine warfare. Great Britain, the world's leading mercantile nation, suffered terrible losses from the German U-boats. The Germans, of course, were trying to weaken Britain's naval blockade and to cut off war supplies from British industries.

Verdun. Victorious in the East, the German general staff, in February 1916, opened a mighty offensive against the French fortress of Verdun. The tactic was psychological as well as military. The purpose was to force the French armies to bleed to death. Verdun guarded the gateway to the upper Meuse Valley. For centuries the French had thought of it as an indispensable and impregnable bastion of defense; national morale seemed to require that it be held lest the country plunge into despair and defeatism. The Germans knew how widespread were French complaints over Britain's failure to send enough troops to the front. They knew, too, that the British would not be able to take the offensive until midsummer. Hence the Germans chose to make the French fight to the death with little British military aid. The French Marshal Henri Pétain held Verdun from February to July at the cost of half a million men—a cost too great for the French nation to bear. But Verdun was held.

While the battle of Verdun continued, a British army that had advanced against the Turks in Mesopotamia was bottled up and forced to surrender. About the same time (Easter, 1916) Irish nationalists attempted to make an armed revolution against the British government of Ireland. German Zeppelin balloons were dropping bombs almost nightly upon London. To compound the Allied peril, the Austrians in mid-May launched a powerful offensive against Italy that for a time threatened to cave in the Italian lines. While this danger was at its height the German high-seas fleet boldly met the British in open waters off the Danish coast in what is known as the battle of Jutland (May 31–June 1). The Germans inflicted heavier damages than they suffered but chose to break off the fighting.

Russian and British offensives. Relief for the French at Verdun and for the Italians came from two quarters. In mid-June the Russians suddenly began a massive offensive against the Austro-Hungarian army on a three-hundred-mile front. Under a brilliant commander, General Brusilov, the Russians kept up their advance until September, piercing the Carpathians, taking four hundred thousand prisoners, and bringing Rumania into the war as an ally. During this advance the Allied army, which had been moved from Gallipoli to Salonika in Greece, launched an offensive against Bulgaria. On the Western front the British began a well-prepared offensive in the Somme Valley, which persisted until November, giving the Germans the most severe punishment they had yet received on that front. It was during the battle of the Somme that the British introduced a new weapon of war, the tank. It was hoped that this weapon would have the offensive power to break through the trench and barbed-wire lines. Not yet, however, had it been adequately developed.

Germany's peace offensive. Although the Germans managed to rescue Austria-Hungary from the Russian advance and to conquer Rumania in the winter of 1916, they decided upon a peace offensive in the West. In December the German government informed the American government that it was willing to negotiate a peace if the Allies would state their war aims. Wilson sounded out all the belligerent powers, and the Allies declared for aims that the Germans were unwilling even to consider. Hence the war continued. At this time a new administration was formed in Great Britain: David Lloyd George, a fiery Welshman, replaced Herbert Asquith as Prime Minister and called for a supreme war effort to

Lloyd George, Prime Minister of England, during whose ministry the British Parliament passed the Compulsory Military Training Bill, which was urgently needed to step up mobilization. (Hulton Picture Library)

strike "a knockout blow" against Germany. Under Lloyd George, British men and resources were more effectively mobilized.

Austria-Hungary's emperor-king, Francis Joseph, died in November 1916 and was succeeded by his grandnephew, Charles. The new ruler and his wife, Zita, tried hard to get out of the war by negotiation during the

Gun crew in action aboard a German submarine during World War I. In the last months of 1916, German submarines were sinking 300,000 tons of shipping a month. By October 1917, the Germans had destroyed 8,000,000 tons of shipping. (National Archives)

winter of 1916–1917, but Italian territorial demands prevented their aims from succeeding.

Fateful German decisions. In Germany, the victor at Tannenberg, General von Hindenburg, had been made chief of the general staff during the battle of the Somme. He and General Ludendorff, quartermaster general, now dominated the state. They resolved upon a new strategy for 1917 which they were confident would win the war. It called for a retreat to shorter lines on the Western front and a campaign to put Russia out of the war. At the same time an unrestricted U-boat campaign was launched against Great Britain: the sinking without warning of every surface vessel, British or neutral, that approached the British Isles. Britain was thus to be cut off from overseas raw materials and food: reduced to industrial and human starvation. The German leaders knew this policy was likely to bring the United States into the war, but they did not believe such an event could prevent their victory.

REVIEW

STUDY SECTIONS IN REVIEW

108. Diplomatic Crises and Antagonisms in Europe, 1884 to 1911

A. What factors increased rivalry between Germany and Britain in the period around 1900?

B. What was the significance of the Anglo-French Entente Cordiale?

C. How did Germany attempt to weaken the Triple Entente in 1910–1911?

D. What caused the Moroccan crisis of 1911?

109. The Balkan Crisis Leads to General War, 1911 to 1914

A. List three results of the second Balkan war (1913).

B. Why did Germany seek to improve relations with Britain in this period?

C. Identify: the "Black Hand," Francis Ferdinand, Gavrilo Princip.

D. Why did Germany declare a state of war with Russia?

E. What reasons were used to justify the entry of Britain and France into the war?

110. The Great Stalemate, 1914 to 1916

A. What caused the failure of the German strategy on the Western front?

B. Identify: Dardanelles offensive, the *Lusitania*, Verdun.

C. Explain the German "peace offensive" of 1916.

D. Discuss the significance of the Russian offensive of 1916 and the British drive in the Somme Valley.

E. Note two objectives of the new German strategy of 1917.

THE CHAPTER IN REVIEW

A. What were the causes and the consequences of the second Balkan war (1913)?

B. Review the attitudes of each of the members of the Triple Alliance and the Triple Entente toward Italy's invasion of Turkish lands in 1911.

C. List the steps that led to a world war following the assassination of Francis Ferdinand in 1914.

D. What was the military strategy of Germany at the outset of World War I? Why did it fail?

FOR YOUR NOTEBOOK

The period from 1894 to 1911 is one of changing alliances and shifting international relations. Use a column for each of the "Big Five": Great Britain, France, Germany, Russia, and Austria-Hungary. Then show the relationship of the country to each of the other four by using one of five words: allied, friendly, neutral, unfriendly, hostile. Enter into the column each change of relationship. Thus you will find Britain's relationships neutral in 1894 but friendly with France after 1904 and with Russia after 1907.

Make a chronological list of the crises and wars from 1908 until 1914. Under each entry put its results in a phrase or two. Thus under "Balkan Crisis of 1908," you would put down "great diplomatic triumph for Germany."

Outline the "fateful chain of events" from June 28 until the outbreak of general war. It is absolutely necessary to know these events in detail and in sequence to understand how the local Serbian affair became a world war.

The World War is a seesaw affair, with first one side and then the other taking the offensive. Draw a three-colored time line in your notebook, indicating month by month whether the Central Powers or the Allies are on the offensive or whether there is a stalemate.

Enter into your notebook the names and dates of the most important battles in World War I, such as the first battle of the Marne, and Verdun.

SELECTED READINGS

The Berkshire Series book by Bernadotte E. Schmitt, *Triple Alliance and Triple Entente* (New York: Henry Holt & Co., 1934), is an excellent brief treatment of international relations before World War I. Also helpful in understanding the genesis of the war is Chester M. Tobin, *Turkey: Key to the East* (New York: G. P. Putnam's Sons, 1944).

Good summary coverage of the war is Basil Liddell Hart, *The War in Outline 1914–1918* (London: Faber & Faber, Ltd., 1936), and it is graphically shown by Laurence Stallings (editor), *The First World War: A Photographic History* (New York: Simon & Schuster, 1933).

Of the novels and plays dealing with the war, the best are probably Erich Remarque, *All Quiet on the Western Front* (Boston: Little, Brown & Co., 1929), and Robert Cedric Sheriff and Vernon Bartlett, *Journey's End* (New York: Frederick A. Stokes Co., 1930).

Chapter 36. War Releases Revolutionary Forces

When war broke out in Europe, the American government declared neutrality. Fearing that the passions aroused in the Old World would be stirred in the United States, President Wilson urged that Americans be neutral "even in thought." But the United States had become too great a power to be unaffected by an immense world war. Soon the British were interfering with American neutral commercial rights on the high seas; but what outraged Americans far more was the German submarine warfare. Moreover, the Allied powers, having command of the sea, were able to purchase large supplies of war material from the United States. To facilitate this business, American bankers extended large loans to the British and French govern-

ments. Hence there gradually developed a considerable American financial stake in an Allied victory.

Yet these links were not strong enough to pull the United States into the war. The presidential campaign of 1916, which earned for Woodrow Wilson a second term in the White House, was conducted with the slogan, "He kept us out of war." The result reflected America's desire to remain at peace. However, on January 31, 1917, the German government announced its intention to resume unrestricted submarine warfare, which meant sinking without warning every ship that approached the British Isles and the coast of France. The United States could not tolerate this total disregard of neutral rights at sea. Germany tried to divert the United States by attempting to negotiate an alliance with Mexico. The United States retaliated by breaking diplomatic relations with Germany, and soon U-boat sinkings brought an American declaration of war (April 6, 1917). Wilson called the submarine campaign a "warfare against mankind" and painted imperial Germany as a militaristic autocracy seeking to dominate the world. Maintaining that the United States had no quarrel with the "German people," the President said America would fight for the "right of nations great and small and the privileges of men everywhere to choose their own way of life and obedience. The world must be made safe for democracy."

Immediate results of American intervention. No one foresaw in April 1917 that the United States would raise an army of four million men and send half of them to western Europe within the next year and a half. Several months passed before the American government began to raise an army by drafting men. The most important immediate achievement was to aid the Allies overcome the U-boat peril, which had come close to starving out Great Britain, and to reinforce the surface blockade of enemy ports. The American navy provided the Allies with escort ships for convoy duty and destroyers for anti-submarine patrols. The German U-boat campaign had to be defeated before vast American armies could be sent to Europe. By the end of 1917 the submarine danger was greatly reduced, and in the meantime the American Expeditionary Force (AEF) was gathering in Europe under the command of General John J. Pershing.

Revolution in Russia. In the early months of 1917 the German leaders were convinced that they would lose the war if they did not soon succeed in knocking out their enemies either in the West or in the East. They resolved upon a new supreme effort against Russia, the most severely wounded of the powers at war. Hence, in February 1917, the German army was suddenly withdrawn to a new and shorter defense line in France, the "Hindenburg line," which was believed to be impregnable against the Western Allied forces. Soon afterward, in mid-March, events began to unfold in Russia that led to her collapse.

President Woodrow Wilson (Library of Congress)

General John J. Pershing (Library of Congress)

Nikolai Lenin (Library of Congress)

The first phase of a long-preparing revolution overthrew the Russian imperial monarchy. The opportunity for revolution was prepared by the failure of the imperial government to carry on the war successfully and by the terrible sufferings of the Russian people because of the war. Discontents were voiced in the Duma (parliament). There were small and ill-organized political parties, such as the Kadets (Constitutional Democrats), who were supported by progressive landlords and the middle and professional classes. The Kadets wanted a limited monarchy or a republic. Another party was called the Social Revolutionary Party, whose leaders professed to stand for improving the condition of the peasantry. The most energetic and well-disciplined party was that of the Bolsheviks, militant Marxian socialists who were soon to call themselves communists. They aimed at establishing a dictatorship in the hands of professional revolutionists. Their influence was greatest among the urban workers. The leader of the Bolshevik Party was Nikolai Lenin, who had long been banished from Russia and was living in Switzerland in 1917. He was probably the most determined and ruthless revolutionist the world had yet seen.

In March 1917, strikes and troop mutinies in the Russian capital, St. Petersburg (called Petrograd by the Russians) forced the abdication of Czar Nicholas II and the establishment of a provisional government that was soon followed by the creation of a republic. Control passed into the hands of Kadets and Social Revolutionaries. At first these great events were regarded hopefully in the Western world: Russia seemed to be on the road to democracy. Her revolution made it easier for President Wilson to paint the great struggle against Germany as a war for democracy. In reality, Russia was going to pieces. Her new government could not maintain order or carry on the war effectively. Peasants seized lands and livestock from their landlords, whose houses were pillaged and burned. Bolshevik influence swelled, and the soldiers lost the will to fight. The dominant personality in the Russian government of this period was Alexander Kerensky, a Social Revolutionary, who failed to recover public confidence in the government.

Germany and the Russian Revolution. The German army took full advantage of the deteriorating political and military situation of Russia. Since the Bolsheviks were known to desire an end to the war, Germany allowed Nikolai Lenin to make his way from Switzerland through Germany to Finland. From there he entered Russia. With his ruthless colleagues, notably Leon Trotsky and Josef Stalin, he set himself to organizing a new revolution. Meanwhile the Germans maintained a steady pressure against the failing Russian army.

Bolshevik tactics were to organize revolutionary councils or committees, called soviets, throughout the working class, the army, and the navy. On November 7, 1917, an All-Russian Congress of Soviets met in Petrograd, and Lenin concluded that the right moment for communist revolution had come. Seizing all transportation and power centers in the capital, Lenin and his colleagues forced the overthrow of Kerensky's government and themselves took full control. The Russian armies disintegrated, and on December 15 the Bolshevik government concluded an armistice with Germany and Austria-Hungary.

The war on other fronts in 1917. The fall of their Russian ally ended a year marked by many ups and downs for the British, French, Italians, and Americans. In April 1917 a French offensive from which much had been expected failed badly on the Western front. As a result, the French army became sullen and mutinous, until morale was restored by General Henri Pétain. During the summer the British opened a series of heavy attacks known as the battle of Passchendaele. By the fall little ground had been gained and the attackers had lost four hundred thousand men. During these months the French resumed the offensive in the second battle of Verdun, and the battle of Malmaison. At Cambrai the British penetrated German lines with the first large-scale tank raid of the war. But nothing decisive was accomplished. In October an Austro-German attack on the Italian front proved a near-total disaster for the Allied cause. The Italian armies at Caporetto were thrown back in defeat and demoralization. French and British soldiers had to be rushed to their aid. A spirit of desertion and surrender had swept through the Italian army. Under a new commander, General Luigi Cadorna, order and morale were restored and the front was stabilized.

Benedict XV's peace effort. One reason for the collapse of Italian morale was the failure of a notable effort Pope Benedict XV (1914–1922) made to end the war in the summer of 1917. On August 1 he put proposals before the warring powers. Foreseeing that dangerous revolutionary forces were being liberated in Russia and might engulf

American infantry guard German prisoners after the capture of St. Mihiel during the second drive at Verdun. (National Archives)

Pope Benedict XV (Fototeca Unione, Roma)

other countries, the Pope proposed that the war be ended by negotiation according to right moral principles. He urged the evacuation of Belgium and the conciliatory settlement of such national disputes as that over Alsace-Lorraine; also the reduction of armaments and the renunciation of claims for war indemnities. However, neither the Central Powers nor the Allies were willing to yield to the Pope's proposals. This failure was a crushing disappointment to millions of Italians.

Other states enter the war. In June 1917 the kingdom of Greece was virtually forced by Allied pressure to enter the war. It became the base for large Allied forces facing the Austrian-German-Bulgarian positions to the north. In August, China, then falling under Japanese influence, declared war on Germany. Chinese laborers were sent to help build fortifications in France, while German ships and other properties in China were seized. In October, Brazil declared war on Germany. A number of other Latin-American states did the same.

Allied successes against the Turks. Since the failure of the attack on the Dardanelles and the Gallipoli campaign in 1915, the principal war effort of the British imperialist forces against the Turks had been in promoting Arab nationalist insurrection against the Ottoman Empire. Colonel T. E. Lawrence, the famed "Lawrence of Arabia," organized guerrilla warfare among the desert Arabs. The British and French governments agreed to promote new Arab states, freed of Turkish rule and under British and French protection. Thus the Allies aimed at breaking up the Ottoman Empire. In the fall of 1917, from his base in Egypt, the British general, Allenby, launched an offensive that resulted in the capture of Jerusalem and the firm possession of Palestine. At this time British Foreign Secretary Balfour issued what became famous as the *Balfour Declaration* (November 2, 1917). It announced the intention of the British government to establish "a national home for the Jewish people in Palestine." Since the latter part of the nineteenth century there had been a Zionist movement among the Jews of central and eastern Europe who had suffered repression and persecution. They desired to have their ancient biblical homeland. The Balfour Declaration was both a gesture in behalf of Zionism and a piece of psychological warfare. It was designed to turn Jewish sentiments in central-eastern Europe away from Germany and away from the Russian Revolution.

Position of the Powers at end of 1917. Russia's withdrawal from the fighting against the Germans was an enormous disaster for the Allied cause. It raised at once the specter of a German concentration against the Western Powers, who were approaching exhaustion. It seemed that nothing but the arrival of massive American reinforcements could turn the tide and bring Allied victory.

112. ALLIED TRIUMPH AND COLLAPSE OF THE CENTRAL POWERS

Wilson's "Fourteen Points." In November 1917 the Central Powers and the Bolshevik government of Russia, having made an armistice, invited all the warring nations to a peace conference at Brest-Litovsk in eastern Poland. At the conference the following month, the Germans and Bolsheviks proposed that peace be made "without annexations or indemnities." Had the Allied Powers accepted this offer and this principle for peace, they would have stopped fighting without achieving anything. Hence they refused the German-Bolshevik proposal. President Wilson made an effective counterproposal by calling for peace on the basis of Fourteen Points. These included the abolition of secret diplomacy; international freedom of the seas; reduction of armaments and barriers to trade; an impartial adjustment of colonial claims; German-Austrian evacuation of Russian territory and freedom for Russia to determine her own policies and development; German evacuation and restoration of Belgium; the return of Alsace-Lorraine to France; satisfaction of Italy's national claims against Austria-Hungary; autonomy for the subject nationalities in the Austro-Hungarian and Ottoman empires; evacuation and restoration of Serbia, Montenegro, and Rumania; establishment of an independent Poland; the creation of a general association of nations to preserve the peace of the world.

Wilson's pronouncement of his Fourteen Points was an act of psychological warfare as much as it was a plan for peace. One can see in it the following:

1. An effort to draw the Bolshevik rulers away from collaboration with Germany and to hold before the Russian people a vision of their land freed from the German invasion, so that they might renew their war effort.

2. An effort to weaken the Central Powers by associating the Allied cause with the hopes of their subject nationalities.

3. The identification of the Allied cause with the aspirations of all peoples for peace, security, prosperity, and national independence.

4. An effort to fortify the flagging spirits of France and Italy by holding before them the prospect of gaining desired territories.

Peace of Brest-Litovsk. The Central Powers now proceeded to force their own kind of peace on defeated Russia. The Bolsheviks were compelled to recognize the independence of a number of small states formerly part of the Russian Empire: Poland, Latvia, Lithuania, Esthonia, and Finland—all now dependent on German protection. An independent Ukraine also was established under German control. Large Russian territories were ceded to Turkey. Russia thus lost about a third of her population and farmland, half her industry, and almost all her coal and oil. The Bolshevik leader, Lenin, agreed to this peace so that he and his fellow revolutionists might be free to carry out the communist revolution in what remained of Russia. The Germans recognized the Bolshevik republic and entered into diplomatic relations with it. As a result, Bolshevik doctrines were to spread into Germany.

The last German offensives in the West. With no enemy front to the east and the prospect of large food supplies and raw materials from the conquered Russian lands, the German High Command determined to launch a massive "win-the-war" offensive against the Western Allies. To meet this expected drive, the United States hurried hundreds of thousands of soldiers across the ocean to France during the winter. On March 21 the German offensive broke through the British lines, and from then on to July repeated offensive actions carried the Germans again to the banks of the Marne

A procession of American tanks goes into action as the Americans advance in the Forest of Argonne, September 1918. The fighting in the difficult terrain was fierce. (National Archives)

River. But victory eluded them; their energies were spent. The terrible danger to the Allies that spring induced them at last to place all their forces under one supreme commander, General Ferdinand Foch, a Frenchman of great military skill and heroic character. Foch turned the tide by counterattacking on July 18. Thrown off balance, the Germans began a retreat. Soon many were throwing away their arms or surrendering, and by September their retreat was turning into a rout. On the Italian front an Austrian offensive in June had failed and soon the Austrian government determined to seek peace. In September the Allied forces—French, British, Greek, Serb, Italian—broke through the Bulgarian front and reached the lower Danube.

The end of the war. Early in October 1918 the imperial German government proposed to negotiate peace on the basis of Wilson's Fourteen Points, but more than a month passed before the Allies were willing to consent to an armistice. Austria-Hungary had asked for an armistice, indicating assent to the program of President Wilson; but the Allies wished to allow her subject nationalities to establish new independent governments. Revolutions were now taking place that would give rise to an independent state of Czechoslovakia, a Hungary separated from Austria, and a Croatia joined with Serbia. Little territory remained in Austria when that state accepted armistice terms on November 3. Four days earlier the Ottoman Empire had signed an armistice in defeat.

In the last days of the war, socialist and communist revolutions broke out in various parts of Germany, and the High Command saw that further resistance to the Allies was impossible. On November 6, German armistice commissioners met General Foch in Compiègne Forest and received terms that required little short of military

Marshal Ferdinand Foch assumed the unified command of the British, French, and American armies in March 1918. (Library of Congress)

surrender. On November 9, socialist leaders established a provisional republican government at Berlin and Emperor William II fled to Holland. On November 11 the great war came to an end in western Europe with the acceptance of Foch's armistice terms by the German High Command.

Dead empires and new states. On November 12 the Austrian emperor, Charles, fled his dominions, leaving behind a small revolutionary republic that hoped to unite with Germany. The two great central European empires had passed away in military defeat and internal revolution. As the British, French, Belgians and Americans moved to occupy the German Rhineland, the Italians occupied former Austrian territories in the Alps and at the head of the Adriatic. A new state, called the Kingdom of the Serbs, Croats, and Slovenes, and later known as Yugoslavia, sprang into existence. It included Serbia and all the Slav-inhabited southern lands of Austria and Hungary. Another Slav state, Czechoslovakia, came into being in the northern parts of Austria and Hungary. Rumania had re-entered the war on the winning side at the last moment in order to appropriate a large part of Hungary. At Warsaw, a Polish general, Joseph Pilsudski, seized control of the Polish government the Germans had created in 1916 and proclaimed the restoration of his country's independence. This new Poland identified itself with the successful cause of the Allies and aspired to rule over vast territories that formerly were Austrian, German, and Russian.

Ottoman Empire in defeat. The end of the war found the Allied forces in occupation of Constantinople, the Ottoman capital, while the Arab provinces were in successful revolt, assisted by the British. Although the sultan, Mohammed VI, did not abdicate his throne until nearly four years later, the historic Turkish empire was at an end. During the war Britain, France, and Italy had reached agreements for creating spheres of interest in this empire; and Britain, as we have seen, had agreed to support the establishment of independent Arab governments. The Greeks, who belonged to the winning alliance, hoped to acquire large annexations of former Turkish territory in the Aegean region.

The plight of Russia. Ever since the Bolsheviks had seized power in November 1917, a civil war had raged between these revolutionaries and those Russians who wished to save their country from communism. This conflict was intensified after the Bolshevik government signed the peace of Brest-Litovsk with the Central Powers. The Western Powers gave aid to the anti-Bolshevik forces in an effort to re-establish a Russian front against the Germans. When Germany gave up the fight in November 1918, she was ordered to withdraw all her forces from Russian territory. Large quantities of German arms and munitions fell into the hands of the Bolsheviks. What the outcome of the Russian civil war would be, no one could tell at the end of 1918. It was one of the most merciless wars the world had ever known; each side sought the total extermination of the other. An example of the ruthlessness may be seen in the murder on July 16, 1918, of the former Czar Nicholas II, his wife, and all their children. Captives of the Bolsheviks, they were put to death in a cellar at Ekaterinburg.

The spirit of the Allied victory. The entry of the United States into the war and the decisive part that American ships, weapons, and manpower played in the defeat of Germany greatly influenced the spirit of the triumphant Western Powers. President Wilson had repeatedly emphasized that the war was fought *for* democracy and *against* autocracy. Connected in his mind with the idea of democracy was the idea of national self-determination, which meant that politically discontented peoples should have the right to secede from empires and form national states of their own. The British and French leaders did not always agree with President Wilson's idealistic views but felt it necessary to go along cautiously with them. His utterances had encouraged the Germans to overthrow their Kaiser and to blame the war on their imperial government, in order to obtain generous peace terms. His words had also helped to persuade the Czechs, Slovaks, Croats, and Poles (who had fought on the side of the Central Powers) to form new states and thus to get out of the ranks of the defeated and join the winning side.

113. THE MEASURE OF DISASTER AND CHAOS

Before the twentieth century, wars had rarely involved whole populations. Soldiers and sailors fought and died and civilians in the vicinity of the fighting suffered, but most people lived very much as in peacetime. The development of nationalism, centralized governments, and industrialism in the

Captain Eddie Rickenbacker, commander of the 94th Pursuit Squadron in France in World War I, poses with the members of the squadron after the war. Rickenbacker is credited with bringing down twenty-five German planes in the days when small forces of fighter planes were engaged in "dog fights." (United States Air Force)

more advanced countries had now, however, made it certain that war would touch everyone. The "home front" had to produce enormous supplies of costly weapons and feed and clothe the largest armies that ever had gone to war. At least sixty-five million men had been mobilized for fighting! To maintain such forces, almost everybody in the chief belligerent countries had to work to aid the war effort.

Weapons and economies. The main weapons of World War I were machine guns, rifles, and artillery. Airplanes were used in war for the first time, chiefly for reconnaissance and strafing enemy troops; they were not yet sufficiently developed to carry bombs large enough to destroy enemy supply lines, assembly areas, and civilian populations. The Germans, however, repeatedly sent Zeppelin airships to bomb London. Poison gas was used by both sides from 1915 onward and tanks after 1916. Motor trucks by the scores of thousands were used for movement of men and war supplies; hence enormous quantities of gasoline also had to be produced. Rubber consumption soared. The seas, especially the Atlantic Ocean and the Mediterranean, became graveyards for sunken ships that had to be replaced, and thousands of additional ships were needed. War necessitated the rapid creation of new steel plants, the opening of new mines, expansion of factories and farms.

Total war. Whole national economies had to be mobilized to serve the war effort. Governments controlled business and planned production. A maze of boards, bureaus, and new offices sprang up to direct war industries. Profits were limited and prices were controlled. The production of civilian goods was either reduced or stopped; hence government rationing was near universal. In the principal countries the life of almost everyone was directly affected by an economic mobilization for "total war."

During World War I, Herbert Hoover was U. S. Food Administrator and chairman of the Interallied Food Council. Many food drives were conducted in this country, such as the one above in California. At the time, the popular expression hooverize *meant to conserve food. (National Archives)*

Propaganda. To retain the loyalty and endurance of the people for the immense sacrifices they were called upon to make, belligerent governments restricted freedom of speech and press and mobilized public opinion. Every effort was made to prevent the circulation of information harmful to the war effort. Those who opposed war or conscription often were thrown into jail. It was not enough to silence opposition; it was even more important to arouse a passion for fighting until the enemy was defeated. The peoples of the world were flooded with wave after wave of propaganda designed to convince them that their cause was just and that their enemies were criminal.

With the American entry into the war and Wilson's declaration that it was being fought to end all wars and to make the world safe for democracy, the Allied peoples began to feel that they were crusading for lofty ideals and principles. This rendered them less willing to compromise or accept any settlement with the enemy that did not mean his total defeat. Allied propaganda nursed and exploited the hope that the unconditional defeat of the Central Powers would bring a peaceful and prosperous world.

Suffering and death. The peoples of Europe naturally groaned under the weight of war as never before in history. The movement of mass armies across Belgium, northern France, Luxembourg, East Prussia, Poland, Austria, the Balkans, and Italy carried the horrors of war close to millions. Scarcities of food and clothing were daily reminders. Little remained for civilians after the needs of the army and navy were filled. War was felt even more personally by millions of men conscripted into armies and by women who left home to take the place of their husbands, sons, or brothers in factories and offices. If this did not touch families intimately, battle casualties did. By 1916 almost every family had lost a dear one. By the end of that year Germany alone counted one million dead. Even the French island of Corsica, whose sons went off in large numbers to fight for France, counted forty thousand dead out of a population of 280,000—or one death out of every seven persons—by the end of the war!

During the four and half years of fighting, at least ten million men had died in action or from wounds sustained in action. Twice that many had been wounded, and a third of these were permanently disabled. Five million had simply disappeared. The Russians, Germans, French, and British had the greatest numbers of casualties. Since most of the men killed were young, important effects were produced on the social system: notably an excess of widows and unmarried women. The high proportion of officers killed in the Austro-Hungarian army weakened the dominant social class and helped to pave the way for the breakup of the empire. British society was weakened in the same way for the same reason; so, too, was Germany. In Russia the war produced the greatest social revolution in history.

Emotional Derangement. The war was a terrible emotional experience that left millions (especially in the defeated countries) without faith in the future. The order of things they knew and loved had been shattered. Many found it difficult to believe in anything; they denounced the past for bequeathing international disorder, imperial rivalry, and social injustice that brought so much sorrow and death. They despaired of the future. For the ex-soldier, four years spent under the fear that a rifle bullet or a shell fragment would snuff out the candle of life; and for the civilian, the fear that the meager food supply might be cut off—or, more terribly, that news might come that a father, son, or brother died in action—all these had a severe physical and psychological effect.

Normal life had been shattered during the war years. The old safeguards that the home and neighborhood provided were loosened. The war brought women out of the home to work in factories and offices, to replace the men who were called to the colors. The absence of both mother and father from the home weakened family discipline and authority. The end of the war in 1918 did not restore law and order. Violence had run wild on the battlefields for four years, and almost without thinking, people acted as if force were the solution to their problems and quarrels.

Central and eastern Europe continued to be plagued by unrest, civil war, and revolution long after the armistices of 1918. The moment the restraining hands of the great empires were removed, national and revolutionary groups pulled in different directions. Political life became so disordered that it was easy for ambitious men to seize control of governments under the pretext that they were restoring order and liberty.

The victors in the war—at least the British and French—had suffered almost as much as the losers. Eastern France was totally devastated. A vast part of British wealth had been consumed. Both nations were convinced that Germany had started the war and therefore was responsible for all the damage; hence she should pay the full cost of the war, which was an economic impossibility. The spirit of vengeance against Germany was strong. The British Prime Minister, Lloyd George, publicly called for the hanging of the German emperor. Few people were sufficiently cool and candid to understand and declare publicly that the war had been a great human tragedy growing out of causes and circumstances for which all nations bore some share of responsibility.

The spirit of justice, not vengeance, and the highest statesmanship were needed if a durable peace was to be made. With new nations coming into existence and civil war continuing to rage in Russia, Europe was by no means under the control of the victor powers. Hence the greatest problems that ever confronted peacemakers faced the world's political leaders at the end of 1918.

REVIEW

STUDY SECTIONS IN REVIEW

111. American Intervention and the Collapse of Russia.

A. What were the causes of the United States' entry into World War I?

B. What was the immediate result of the American entry?

C. What were the results of the first phase of the Russian Revolution?

D. Why did the Germans allow Lenin to return to Russia?

E. Identify: General Pétain, Benedict XV, the Balfour Declaration.

112. Allied Triumph and Collapse of the Central Powers.

A. List five proposals contained in President Wilson's "Fourteen Points."

B. Note three results of the Brest-Litovsk Treaty between Germany and Russia.

C. Discuss the final German offensive on the Western front.

D. How did Yugoslavia and Czechoslovakia come into being?

113. The Measure of Disaster and Chaos

A. List three new weapons introduced during World War I.

B. Explain the term "total war."

C. Summarize the total casualties suffered by both sides during the war.

D. List three social effects of the war.

E. What was the financial condition of Europe at the conclusion of World War I?

THE CHAPTER IN REVIEW

A. List the causes and the results of the entry of the United States into World War I.

B. What caused the revolution in Russia? Discuss the two phases of the revolt. Why did the Germans hope for a Bolshevik victory in the Russian Revolution?

C. Explain the following statement: "Wilson's pronouncement of his Fourteen Points was an act of psychological warfare as much as it was a plan for peace."

D. Review the physical, social, and psychological conditions of Europe at the conclusion of World War I.

FOR YOUR NOTEBOOK

In one of the standard United States histories in your library, such as that by Smelser and Kirwin or the one by Hicks, read the chapter covering this country's entry into World War I. Now list in your notebook the events from 1914 that led us to declare war.

List the reasons why revolutions occurred in Russia in 1917. Make a second list of reasons why the first revolution failed and a second one occurred later in the year.

In any standard reference work or United States history get a list of Wilson's Fourteen Points and put them in your notebook. Now indicate how, if at all, each point is related to one of the four headings of "psychological warfare" given in the text.

Look back through the last two chapters to find all the reasons you can why the Central Powers lost the war. List these in your notebook in brief phrases, such as "British control of the seas," or "American industrial production."

Section 113 gives "the measure of disaster and chaos." Make an itemized list of the factors you consider important and —as with a grocery bill—put the quantity lost. Your list will certainly include human lives and various types of property. Perhaps you can list other less tangible but important losses.

SELECTED READINGS

Many interesting and true stories have been written about experiences in World War I. Reading some of these will increase your knowledge of that war. A set of short biographical sketches is found in Mary Rosetta Parkman, *Fighters for Peace* (New York: Appleton-Century Co., 1919). Another set of contemporary stories is *Tales of the Great War,* by John Henry Newbolt (New York: Longmans, Green & Co., 1916). The exploits of aviators in the war is told in *Falcons of France,* by Charles Bernard Nordhoff and James N. Hall (Boston: Little, Brown & Co., 1929). The war is seen from a different point of view in John Joseph Pershing's, *My Experiences in the World War* (New York: Frederick A. Stokes Co., 1931).

A good account of the tremendous destruction caused by the war is E. L. Bogart, *Direct and Indirect Costs of the Great World War* (New York: Oxford University Press, 1919).

The most readable story of the Russian revolutions is Father Edmund A. Walsh, *Fall of the Russian Empire* (Boston: Little, Brown & Co., 1928), but also useful is the Berkshire study for students by George Vernadsky, *The Russian Revolution, 1917-1931* (New York: Henry Holt & Co., 1932).

Wilson

Chapter 37. World Pacification, 1919 to 1924

114. THE PEACE OF PARIS AND THE LEAGUE OF NATIONS

On January 18, 1919, a great world peace conference met at Paris. None of the defeated states was allowed to take part in the negotiations. The plan of the principal victor powers (Great Britain, France, Italy, the United States, and Japan) was to reach agreement among themselves on treaties that would then be submitted to Germany, Austria, Hungary, Bulgaria, and Turkey. Since none of the powers had recognized the Bolshevik government in Russia and a civil war was going on there, no Russian representatives took part in the peace conference.

The leading personality among the statesmen at Paris was the American President, Woodrow Wilson, whose main interest was in the creation of an international association to prevent future wars. His Fourteen Points had called for such an association, and the decisive role the United States had played in the war made him appear to European peoples as the prophet of a new and better world. His eloquence and idealism corresponded to this conception. Moreover, since the United States alone was in a position to grant large loans for European reconstruction, the Allied statesmen were bound to cultivate his good will. He succeeded in persuading them to make the drafting of the Covenant (or treaty) of the League of Nations the first business of the peace conference.

Other leading figures at the conference were Prime Minister David Lloyd George of Great Britain, Prime Minister Georges Clemenceau of France, and Prime Minister Vittorio Orlando

Meeting of the Big Four: Prime Minister Orlando of Italy, Prime Minister Lloyd George of Great Britain, Prime Minister Clemenceau of France, and President Wilson of the United States. (National Archives)

of Italy. These men and President Wilson were known as the Big Four. Japan took little part in settling European questions; her interests lay in Asia and the Pacific. On many important questions the Big Four had sharp differences. France and Britain during the war had made secret treaties with Italy and Japan to support territorial annexations which Wilson disapproved as being inconsistent with the principles of the Fourteen Points. To win the support of the Allies for the League of Nations, Wilson was compelled to make a number of compromises.

The League of Nations. The peace conference in full session on January 25, 1919, adopted a resolution declaring that "it is essential to the maintenance of the world settlement . . . that a League of Nations be created," and that the League "should be treated as an integral part of the general treaty of peace." A commission presided over by Wilson quickly prepared the Covenant, and on April 28 it was accepted by the conference. The governments sponsoring the League were the thirty-two states that had placed themselves at war with the Central Powers between 1914 and 1918, with the exception of Russia. The thirty-two included not only European states but the Latin-

American countries that had followed the United States into the war; four British Dominions and British imperial India, in addition to Great Britain; three Asiatic nations—Japan, China, Siam; the new states of Poland, Czechoslovakia, Yugoslavia, and the Arab kingdom of Hejaz; and, last, the little African Negro republic of Liberia. Thirteen other nations that had remained neutral in the war were invited immediately to accede to and become sponsors of the League.

The purpose of the League was to maintain peace and to promote international co-operation and welfare. All members had one vote each in the Assembly, which was to meet at certain stated intervals or on any occasion that required a meeting. At such meetings it could deal "with any matter within the sphere of action of the League or affecting the peace of the world." It was not, however, a world legislature; it could do little more than discuss and recommend actions to its members. A smaller executive body called the Council was created, consisting of five permanent members (United States, Great Britain, France, Italy, Japan) and certain other members elected for fixed terms by the Assembly. The Covenant provided for permanent headquarters of the League at Geneva in Switzerland and created a body of permanent civil officials known as the Secretariat. They were directed by the Secretary-General, who was chosen by the Council.

Nations joining the League obligated themselves "to respect and preserve as against external aggression the territorial integrity and existing political independence of all Members of the

League." They agreed to submit their disputes with other nations to arbitration, or to judicial settlement before the Permanent Court of International Justice. This tribunal was provided for in the Covenant. If such methods did not lead to settlement of a dispute, the nations involved were obligated to take it to the Council; and if the Council could not agree, they were bound not to go to war until at least three months afterward. If any member of the League went to war against another member in violation of the Covenant, certain punitive, economic, or even military measures (sanctions) might be voted by the Council or the Assembly against the offending member.

Instead of annexing outright the former colonies of the German Empire in Africa and the islands of the Pacific, the statesmen provided that these should be assigned to various victor nations as mandates of the League of Nations. They would be governed as trusts, and the ruling power would report on them regularly to the League Mandates Commission. The first aim of mandate rule was to promote the welfare of the native peoples. Some of the Arab lands taken from the Ottoman Empire were likewise to be placed under mandate rule by Britain and

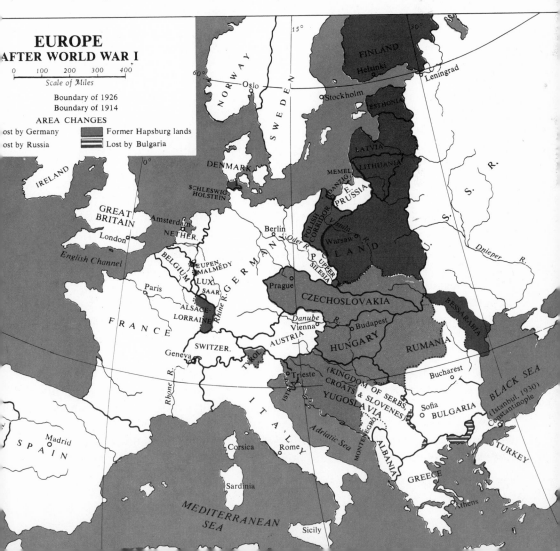

EUROPE
AFTER WORLD WAR I

0   100   200   300   400
Scale of Miles

Boundary of 1926
Boundary of 1914
AREA CHANGES
ost by Germany   Former Hapsburg lands
ost by Russia   Lost by Bulgaria

France until the people were ready for self-government.

The League Covenant committed the members to carry out a general reduction of armaments; to secure and maintain fair and humane conditions of labor for men, women, and children; to treat fairly the native inhabitants of territories under their control; to suppress slavery and the illicit drug traffic; and to take steps in matters of international concern for the prevention and control of disease. All international welfare bureaus and organizations were invited to place themselves under the general direction of the League.

The Treaty of Versailles. While the work of preparing the League Covenant was still continuing, the Allies began to settle the terms of a treaty of peace with Germany. After many fierce debates, they agreed upon a very harsh treaty. It stripped Germany of her colonies, transferred Alsace-Lorraine to France, the little region of Eupen-Malmédy to Belgium, and a large part of eastern Germany to Poland. It drastically limited the right of Germany to possess arms, and gave to the Allies the right to occupy all German territory west of the Rhine River for fifteen years. The Saar region, a part of this occupied territory, was prized by France because of its rich coal mines; and the treaty provided that fifteen years hence the people of the Saar should vote to decide whether to be French or German. France hoped to retain that land permanently. Germany lost her navy and most of her merchant fleet. She was required to admit responsibility "for causing all the loss and damage to which the Allied and Associated Governments and their

nationals have been subjected as a consequence of the war imposed upon them by the aggression of Germany and her allies." On this basis, Germany was to be assessed for colossal war reparations—greater by far than she ever could pay. Only by the maintenance of the Allied war blockade of her ports and the threat of military coercion was the German Republic induced to accept these harsh terms. The German people were convinced that the treaty was a great injustice. It is known as the Treaty of Versailles because it was presented to the Germans at a great ceremony in the palace built at Versailles by King Louis XIV of France. In the same room—the Gallery of Mirrors—the German Empire had been proclaimed in 1871 during the Franco-German War. To the French, who thought the treaty too lenient, revenge had come at last.

The other treaties. The treaties for Austria, Hungary, Bulgaria, and Turkey were gradually prepared and named after the French palaces in which they were presented. For Austria, the Treaty of St. Germain required the renunciation of all claim to her former territory now organized into Poland, Czechoslovakia, Italy, and Yugoslavia. From a great empire, Austria was reduced to a small state not much larger than Switzerland. Her instinct was to federate with the new Germany, but this was prohibited by the treaties of Versailles and St. Germain. Hungary, by the Treaty of Trianon, recognized large annexations of her territory in the north and south by Czechoslovakia and Yugoslavia. She was compelled also to cede the large region of Transylvania to Rumania. By the Treaty of Neuilly,

Bulgaria was forced to give up territory to Greece, Yugoslavia, and Rumania. Reparations and limitation of armaments were imposed by the treaties on Austria, Hungary, and Bulgaria.

The Allies and the Turks. Turkey was the only one of the defeated states who succeeded in defying the will of the Allies. The Treaty of Sèvres designed for her was long delayed owing to the revival in 1919 of conflict between the Greeks and Turks and to the difficulties of the British and French in coming to agreement on their interests in the Arab lands formerly under Ottoman rule. By the time (1920) the Treaty of Sèvres was presented to the Ottoman sultan, a Turkish nationalist movement of a very stubborn character had got under way. The Turks, although losing the Arab lands, succeeded in defeating the Greeks and defying the Allies. In a few years they were able to negotiate a more favorable peace than had been designed for them.

Japanese acquisitions. During the war Japan had seized the German naval base of Tsingtao on the Shantung peninsula of China and captured Germany's central Pacific colonies, the Marshall, Caroline, and Mariana islands. In 1917, Great Britain and France secretly agreed with Japan to support her permanent acquisition of these territories. The United States government did not wish to see Japanese power so increased, but American eyes were riveted upon Europe. The Japanese had, moreover, adopted a very dictatorial attitude toward China, which was weak and disunited. It seemed then likely that great parts of the former Chinese Empire would fall under Japanese control. At the Paris Peace Conference, President Wilson contested Japan's claim to annex the former German possessions in the Pacific and defended the interests of China. Australia also opposed Japan. The Allied Powers, however, were bound to Japan and in the main she vindicated her claims. China was so angry that her government refused to sign the Treaty of Versailles. The German Pacific islands north of the equator were assigned to Japan as a mandate from the League of Nations. The islands to the south of the equator were entrusted on similar terms to Australia.

The United States and the peace. The American government had professed a lofty altruism and renounced all territorial ambitions. Its aim was idealistic: to promote democracy, national self-determination, and the League of Nations. Nothing of material value was gained by the United States, although she had played a decisive role in winning the victory. Because of Japan's Pacific acquisitions, the strategic security of the United States in the Philippines and Hawaii was weakened. Both the Treaty of Versailles and the League of Nations were to be rejected by the United States Senate, while Japanese-American relations became increasingly dangerous after the war and the peace.

115. COMMUNISM AND SOVIET RUSSIA, 1918 TO 1924

We have already seen that the Bolsheviks seized power in Russia and made peace with Germany. In the midst of their violent struggle for power, a civil war and foreign intervention occurred. Many Russians, who opposed the revolution and wished to fight both the Central Powers and the communists, organized "White" armies. They received Allied support in preventing the Germans from transferring troops from the Russian to the Western front and in ending the threat of communist revolutions elsewhere in Europe.

In 1918 the Allies landed troops at Murmansk and Archangel in northern Russia with the double purpose of creating a new front against the Germans and of preventing the Bolsheviks from seizing valuable war materials. There the Allies fought the communists until the fall of 1919, when they withdrew. Another Allied army occupied Odessa in southern Russia, but it was turned back by the Bolsheviks. An international army that included a large Japanese contingent moved into eastern Siberia.

The anti-Bolsheviks lacked unity and steadiness of purpose. Quarrels, inefficiency, looting, and errors of political judgment ruined their cause. They failed to secure the loyalty of the peasants, who concluded that a White victory would not improve their lot, or of townspeople, who were under strong Red domination. On the other hand, the Bolsheviks were determined fighters, prepared to commit any outrage in order to win. They used terror and hostages to break the will to resist of relatives and friends of soldiers in the White armies. Their political police, the "Cheka"—"the eye, ear, and mailed fist of the revolution"—searched, arrested, and executed all suspects or enemies in a brutal reign of terror that made the crimes of the French revolutionaries pale into insignificance. The Red armies, guided by the daring Leon Trotsky, were motivated by revolutionary zeal and were supported by thousands of young people.

Communist uprisings in central Europe. While the civil war and foreign intervention raged on in Russia, communists in other parts of Europe sought to overthrow their governments. The breakup of the German and Austro-Hungarian empires gave radicals the opportunity to rebel. And the presence of communist Russia, who stood ready to encourage and aid, emboldened them. In Germany the extremist Marxist group known as the Spartacists rose in Berlin in January 1919 under the leadership of Karl Liebknecht and Rosa Luxemburg. But the German army rallied to the defense of the government. Communist uprisings occurred also in Bavaria, where a short-lived Soviet republic was established, and in the Ruhr Valley and in Saxony. Communist disorders plagued Austria and Hungary. An associate of Lenin, Béla Kun, established a communist dictatorship in Hungary in 1919 and declared war on Czechoslovakia for the purpose of seizing Slovakia. Rumanian troops then invaded Hungary. This action gave the counterrevolutionary forces in Hungary the opportunity to oust Kun, who fled in August 1919. In the following year Admiral Nicholas Horthy became regent and head of the new government. A Red peril also gripped Italy. In the new Italian parliament of December 1919 many Marxian socialists waved the red flag of revolution and called for Lenin and the Bolsheviks. Strikes and violence by communists frightened many Italians into believing that their country, too, would imitate Russia.

Poland vs. communist Russia. The communist triumph in the Russian civil war left many former political leaders, military officers, and professional or religious leaders with the alternatives of remaining in Russia and facing the wrath of the Reds with possible death or imprisonment, or of fleeing to another country. Thousands chose the second course. Priests and bishops escaped to Yugoslavia; some scholars made their way to Czechoslovakia; some officials emigrated to Germany and France and a few to England. Others chose Manchuria and China, where they formed colonies of White Russian exiles.

After mopping up the Crimea, the communists turned against the Polish armies in the Ukraine. From Kiev they drove back the Poles almost to the gates of Warsaw in Poland, but there the Polish armies made their stand. Under the leadership of General Pilsudski and the French general, Maxime Weygand, the Poles turned back the Red tide from Europe. By the Treaty of Riga of 1921, Poland and the Russian communists made peace. The communists then abandoned for a time all effort to expand westward in Europe.

Russian communism. Communism is a materialistic way of life that is based on the socialist ideas of Karl Marx and Friedrich Engels. Its immediate aim is a dictatorship in the name of the working class, and an economy in which the state owns and operates the means of production for the common benefit. Its ultimate end is a classless society and the replacement of the state by voluntary councils of workers. Marxian socialists had hoped to apply their theories in industrialized countries such as Britain and Germany. Lenin's task was to adapt Marxian socialism to Russia, a rural country that before the revolution was only slightly affected by capitalism. Lenin doubted that the workers alone possessed the ability to lead a communist revolution, and therefore he believed that they had to rely for guidance and leadership on a group of professional agitators and intellectuals.

The soviet system. The communists established a strong centralized state in the tradition of the Russian Czars. Local soviets of soldiers and workers sent representatives to the All-Russian Congress of Soviets, the body that selected the central committee of some two hundred persons. But dictatorial power remained in the hands of the Communist Party, whose members were hand-picked and who seldom exceeded two million persons out of a population of about 160 million.

The communists sought to change the habits and customs of Russia. At first they undermined the family by

Ignace Jan Paderewski (1860–1941), Polish pianist and patriot, represented his country at the Versailles Peace Conference and was premier of a coalition ministry in 1919. (Ullstein)

permitting easy divorce, but after weighing the consequences they reversed themselves. They did not relent in their hostility to religion, and sought to prevent the instruction of the rising generation in religious truths. The communists realized the propaganda value of schooling and they undertook a mammoth program to eradicate illiteracy.

The U.S.S.R. In 1923 the name of the Russian state was changed to the Union of Socialist Soviet Republics (U.S.S.R.). Of the four states in the original union (Russia, White Russia, the Ukraine, and Siberia), the largest and most important was the first, or the Russian Soviet Federated Socialist Republic. In theory, each member of the Soviet Union was autonomous and could secede from it at will. Communist propaganda boasted that the U.S.S.R. rejected imperialism and colonialism as practiced by the capitalist countries of western Europe and America, and instead encouraged the languages, literatures, and customs of each of the federated units. But in reality the various non-Russian nationalities lacked political power; they were in the iron grip of local communist leaders who took their orders from party headquarters in Moscow, the new capital of Russia.

The foreign policy of the communists fitted the needs of the Soviet Union and the anticipated world revolution. On the surface, the Soviet Union became correct and peaceful in its relations with foreign countries and was quick to suggest non-aggression pacts.

The Comintern. Beneath the surface of Soviet foreign policy lurked communist plots of espionage and revolution.

The organization entrusted with the task of world revolution was the Third International, or *Comintern.* It sponsored the training and indoctrination in Russia of foreign communists and students from Europe, Asia, and America for the purpose of stirring up revolution. One of its principal functions was to exploit colonial discontent in Asia and Africa against the Western Powers and to paint Russia as the enemy of capitalism and imperialism. In 1920 a congress of "oppressed Eastern peoples" assembled at Baku to win over the peoples of Asia. The Comintern attempted to exploit nationalist feeling in Afghanistan, Persia, India, and elsewhere in order to undermine the economic and political influence of the Western Powers.

Moscow's foreign policy and the plottings of the Comintern worked together. For example, the Soviet Union concluded a treaty with China in 1924 in which it recognized Mongolia as part of China and renounced the special concessions acquired by the Czars. Its purpose was to persuade the Chinese and other Asians that the Soviet Union favored the national unity and independence of China. Meanwhile, agents of the Comintern infiltrated the Kuomintang, the party of Dr. Sun Yatsen. Russian communist advisers and agents helped train the Chinese army and organize the Kuomintang.

116. INTENSIFIED NATIONALISM

The Weimar Republic. After the defeat of the German armies in France, a serious danger existed that Germany might go the way of Russia and become communist. Although the Red peril passed, the new German government established at Weimar in 1919—the so-called Weimar Republic—had an uneasy life. For a few years private armies of demobilized soldiers roamed the countryside and revealed the inability of the government to ensure civil security. It lacked the confidence of the people, who associated it with the dictated and humiliating Treaty of Versailles. Especially offensive to them were the treaty clauses that saddled Germany with the sole guilt of causing the war and with the duty of paying reparations. Their national pride prevented them from accepting the fact of military defeat and they readily believed instead the legend that the German army was not defeated on the battlefield but was mortally wounded by a "stab in the back"; that is, by the treason and disloyalty of socialists and communists. Germans were thus angry and unrepentant and they vowed revenge. Some persons recommended that Germany should shun the West, which had committed the outrage of

The meeting of the German and Russian signatories of the Treaty of Rapallo in 1922. The Allies viewed their treaty with great suspicion. (Ullstein)

the Treaty of Versailles, and embrace the East, and they applauded the Treaty of Rapallo with Russia.

In the meantime the Allies fixed the amount of reparations at thirty-three billion dollars, a sum Germany could not pay. The French were determined, nevertheless, that Germans must pay for the damages caused by their aggression. When the Germans defaulted on reparations payments, French and Belgian troops in 1923 occupied the great German industrial region in the Ruhr Valley.

Adolf Hitler. The course of German history was to be changed by the appearance of Adolf Hitler. He was born in 1889 in Austria, but he volunteered for service in the German army at the outbreak of World War I. After the war, Hitler joined the German Workers' Party (later called the National Socialist German Workers' Party) and in 1921 became its chairman and Fuehrer (leader). The program of his "Nazi" Party appealed to the discontented nationalists and veterans and to the poverty-stricken middle classes who sought a new creed by which to live. The Nazis sought to unite the ideals of socialism with those of nationalism. Hitler's fiery speech-making attracted large crowds in southern Germany. In 1923, with the aid of General Ludendorff, he staged an armed uprising in Munich. He was arrested, tried, and sentenced to prison, where he wrote *Mein Kampf* ("My Battle"), a book that was widely read and won him a nationwide audience. But Germany was not yet ready for Hitler. The political situation improved temporarily. When General Hindenburg became president of the republic in 1925, it appeared that revolution was unlikely to occur.

The Rise of Benito Mussolini. As a result of World War I, Italy, too, was the scene of inflation, poverty, unemployment, strikes, and communist disorders. Although the Italians were on the winning side, they felt that their allies had denied them the fruits of victory. Italian nationalists were disappointed that territorial ambitions in Fiume and the Dalmatian coast and in Asia Minor were unsatisfied. In this atmosphere of nationalist agitation and communist plots emerged a powerful figure, Benito Mussolini, who had been a socialist before the war but was converted to militant nationalism. In March 1919, Mussolini founded the Union of Combat in Milan and later planned similar *fasci,* or clubs, in important cities of Italy. He urged Italians to use revolutionary violence to achieve their nationalist ambitions and to overturn the present system. His semi-military "Black Shirts" broke up socialist and communist meetings and strikes. A virtual civil war in 1922 pitted communists and other radicals against the Fascists, as Mussolini's followers were called. When the disorders increased and the government was unable to stop them, the Fascists organized a march on Rome. King Victor Emmanuel asked Mussolini to form a cabinet on October 31, 1922. Mussolini aspired to dictatorial powers and by 1924 had a firm grip on the country and no intention of releasing it. His Fascists won a majority in the Italian parliament in April of that year and enabled him to move more decisively against his enemies. The enemies of the Fascist regime, both socialists and Christian Demo-

crats, became victims of outrages committed by gangs traveling in trucks.

The disunion of the Allies. The victorious Allied coalition of Britain, France, Italy, and the United States was dissolved by mutual suspicion and rivalry. Russia had already divorced herself from her former allies by the Treaty of Brest-Litovsk, and the Bolsheviks made no secret of their hostility to what the Western powers stood for. The United States separated itself from the allies by refusing to sign the Versailles Treaty and become a member of the League of Nations. Italy remained disgruntled and at odds with Britain and France. And the latter countries quarreled over German reparations, their aspirations in the Near East, aid to the Poles and Baltic peoples fighting the Bolsheviks, and over disarmament. The prospects for the success of the League of Nations were dim. Outside its ranks were two of the biggest world powers, the United States and Russia, and the most extensive European nation, Germany.

The nations that had sprung up on the ruins of the old empires of Austria-Hungary, Germany, and Russia were intent on pursuing their own national ambitions regardless of dangers to

King Victor Emmanuel III (1869–1947). (Library of Congress)

peace or the rights of others. The League of Nations was weakened by the disputes over the boundaries of these new nations. For example, Poland and Lithuania were at odds over the city of Vilna, which was seized by a Polish force. Poland and Czechoslovakia quarreled over the Teschen area, Poland and Germany over Upper Silesia, and Italy and Yugoslavia over the city of Fiume. The League managed to settle some disputes and to restore the financial health of Austria and Hungary, where runaway inflation had paralyzed economic life.

France and her alliances. France sought the security of her boundaries against German attack by means of military alliances outside the League of Nations. In 1921, France and Poland signed a treaty providing for mutual aid in the event of attack. Rumania was attached to the French security system by an alliance with Poland. The French supported the "Little Entente," an alliance formed by mutual assistance treaties between Czechoslovakia and Yugoslavia (1920), between the former and Rumania (1921), and between Rumania and Yugoslavia (1921).

The United States returns to "normalcy." The Senate's rejection of the Versailles Treaty because the Covenant of the League was part of it reflected the fatigue of the American people with world political responsibilities, the disillusionment with Wilson's idealism, and distrust of Europe. The election of the Republican Warren G. Harding as President in 1920 represented, in the words of the campaign slogan, a "return to normalcy." In 1921 the United States signed separate peace treaties with Germany and with Austria.

Many Americans took great pride in their victory over Germany, which they interpreted as proof of the superiority of the "American way of life." And they sought to protect it from the Red peril by a campaign against radicals, from a flood of cheaper foreign goods by a protective tariff in 1922, and from foreigners by restricting immigration. The anti-foreign prejudice was increased by the reluctance of the Allies to repay the war debts amounting to about ten billion dollars.

The British dominions. Australia, Canada, New Zealand, and South Africa came of age in the post-war period. They were proud of their role in Britain's victory over the Central Powers and they were confident of their future role in history. The League of Nations accorded them separate membership and assigned mandates to Australia, New Zealand, and South Africa. Fearing European entanglement, some of the dominions tended to draw Great Britain away from her close involvement in European politics.

Ireland. Irish nationalism had forced Great Britain to grant home rule to Ireland in 1912, but the carrying out of the law had been delayed because of the war. The Irish nationalists were impatient and rose in rebellion in 1916 (the Easter Rebellion) and later fought a fierce guerrilla war (1919–1920) against British security forces. In December 1920 the British Parliament established home rule for two separate and partially self-governing sections: Northern Ireland (the six counties of Ulster) and Southern Ireland (the remaining twenty-six counties). This settlement was opposed by Irish nationalists, who desired independence for a united Ireland. In 1922, Britain recognized the existence of Southern Ireland, or Irish Free State, as a dominion. Northern Ireland, or Ulster, chose to remain with the United Kingdom of Great Britain. The new Irish Free State resented the partition of the country. Irish nationalism continued intense and has never ceased to strive for a union of all Ireland.

Colonial discontent. The war helped to undermine colonialism. Although Britain and France acquired new colonies in the form of mandates, they had been weakened by the loss of wealth and lives. Their colonial subjects had taken seriously the ideals of democracy and self-determination diffused throughout the world by Allied propaganda. Many persons in Europe and America thought it inconsistent for Britain and France to wage war to permit each nation to rule itself, and still retain colonies. Communist agitators posed as friends of colonial peoples and stirred opposition to Britain and France.

India. Britain found the problem of governing India difficult, for the war had magnified the importance of that vast sub-continent and contributed to the restlessness of the natives. India had made a vital contribution to the British victory in men and matériel. By the end of the war India was on the verge of revolution as anti-British riots broke out. In 1919, Britain granted a measure of self-government but did not satisfy Indian nationalists. The opposition to British rule was spearheaded by the Indian National Congress, in which rich landlords and capitalists joined with socialists. Mohandas K. Gandhi, called the Mahatma, or Holy One, became the dominant figure in Indian

Mohandas Gandhi (the Mahatma), India's political leader, with Vallabhbhai Patel, Indian statesman. The title Mahatma reflected such a high personal prestige that Gandhi could exact political concessions by threatening "fasts unto death." (Government of India Press Information Bureau)

resistance. He advocated self-government for India and the revival of the old handicraft industries of the villages as the answer to the evils of Western industrialism. Gandhi denounced the use of violence and recommended passive resistance, civil disobedience, and the boycott. To dramatize his cause, he went on hunger strikes. He opposed any participation by Indians in the government established by Britain. In 1922 the British put him in jail.

China. We have seen that in 1911 Chinese nationalists overthrew the Manchu dynasty and established the Chinese Republic. In the years that followed, Dr. Sun Yat-sen, the Western-educated nationalist leader, stirred up Chinese nationalism. Although he was influenced by Marxist ideas and admired Lenin, Sun did not want

China to copy Russia. In his view, China needed a benevolent dictatorship and a planned society that would seek the welfare of all Chinese citizens. His views were summarized as democracy (political democracy), nationalism (national democracy), and livelihood (economic democracy). His party, the Kuomintang, sought to nullify the "treaty system" that since 1842 had subordinated China's welfare to the advantage of Western nations, and to eliminate foreign influence. Sun welcomed Chinese communists and invited Russian instructors to train the army. There was no real political unity in China. Various generals or "war lords" ruled different regions with almost complete independence.

Arab nationalism. The dissolution of the Ottoman Empire permitted Arabs to establish nationalist states and the British and French to acquire mandates and enhance their influence in that part of the world. The aspirations of Arab nationalists and the interests of the Western powers were often at odds. In Egypt, for example, a country Britain had administered since 1882, nationalists rebelled in 1919. Three years later the British hoped to end the riots and demonstrations of the Nationalist or Wafd Party by recognizing the independence of Egypt under King Fuad. But their concern with the defense of the Suez Canal led them to retain control of the country.

Spurred on by Colonel T. E. Lawrence, Arab nationalists aspired to establish a united kingdom under Feisal, then King of the Hejaz with his capital at Damascus. But these hopes conflicted with a secret agreement signed by Britain and France in 1916 for partitioning this area. Arab nationalists then decided to limit their ambitions and proclaimed Feisal King of Syria and Palestine but France ejected him when the League assigned the mandate for Syria to France. 1n 1921 the British placed Feisal on the throne of Iraq (Mesopotamia), their mandate, and made his brother, Abdullah ibn Hussein, the emir (or prince) of the new autonomous state of Transjordania (later called Jordan). Nationalist resistance soon compelled Britain to grant virtual independence to Iraq.

Zionism. Another British mandate, Palestine, was the scene of bloody encounters between Jewish nationalists, or Zionists, who sought to found a homeland promised to them by the British in the Balfour Declaration of 1917, and the Arabs, who feared that Jewish immigration was the first step in the formation of a Zionist state in the Holy Land. The Jews in 1917 formed only ten per cent of the population.

Mustapha Kemal and the Turkish nationalists. Turkey, the heart of the old Ottoman Empire, was transformed by nationalism. As we have seen, the defeat of Turkey in World War I enabled the Allies to consider plans for dividing Asia Minor and to impose the Treaty of Sèvres on the sultan (1920). But Turkish nationalists demanded a revision of the treaty. In the meantime an invasion of Turkish lands was launched by the Greeks, Italians, and French. When it seemed that Turkey was in her darkest hour and at the mercy of the Allies, Mustapha Kemal, an army officer, rallied Turkish national resistance. With the aid of the Bolsheviks, Kemal drove the Greeks from Asia Minor in 1922. Soon he was strong enough to gain a more favorable treaty from the Allies (the Treaty of Lausanne, 1923). The Turks and the Greeks agreed to settle the minorities problems by exchanging the populations concerned. Thus many Greeks whose ancestors had lived in Asia Minor for almost three thousand years were forced to leave their homes and take up residence in Greece.

Persia. A counterpart of the Turkish nationalist upheaval occurred in Persia. When the British attempted to secure a treaty in 1919 that would make Persia a British protectorate, nationalist

The Palace of the League of Nations at Geneva, Switzerland. In April 1946, the League was dissolved and its services and real estate (including the huge palace) were transferred to the United Nations. (Swiss National Tourist Office)

opposition opposed the step. In 1921, Riza Pahlevi, in command of an army in the capital city of Teheran, established a new government, in which he was minister of war. In 1923 he became Prime Minister and received extensive powers independent of the shah, or king, whom he deposed two years later. Riza Pahlevi established a dictatorship and became the shah with the title Riza Shah Pahlevi. Like Mustapha Kemal, he westernized the country, introduced European dress, the Gregorian calendar, secularized the nation, and of course encouraged nationalism. The name of the state was officially changed to Iran in 1935.

REVIEW

STUDY SECTIONS IN REVIEW

114. The Peace of Paris and the League of Nations

A. What was the purpose of the peace conference at Paris? Which nations participated?

B. What was to be the purpose of the proposed League of Nations?

C. List three obligations which nations assumed upon joining the League.

D. Cite four of the conditions of the peace treaty for Germany.

115. Communism and Soviet Russia, 1918 to 1924

A. What factors weakened the cause of the "White," or anti-Bolshevik, forces?

B. What other European countries experienced communist uprisings in the post-war period?

C. What were the aims of Russian communism?

D. Identify: Trotsky, "Cleka," soviets, the Comintern.

116. Intensified Nationalism

A. List three factors that weakened the Weimar Republic in Germany.

B. What was the program of Hitler's Nazi Party and to whom did it appeal?

C. How did Mussolini come to power in Italy?

D. Cite three causes for the breakup of the Allied coalition.

E. List three instances of nationalistic disputes in this post-war period.

THE CHAPTER IN REVIEW

A. Discuss the terms of the Versailles Treaty for Germany. How did this treaty plant the seeds of future French-German conflicts?

B. Explain the purpose, make-up, and obligations of membership in the League of Nations. Did the United States become a member?

C. Discuss the theoretical basis of Russian communism.

D. What conditions under the Weimar Republic seemed to make Germany ripe for the rise of a "strong man" like Adolf Hitler?

FOR YOUR NOTEBOOK

In our notebook entry for the period covered in this chapter we should try to clarify the events as much as possible.

List the purposes of the League of Nations. Make a chart to shows its organization.

Summarize the terms of the Versailles Treaty under territorial, military, and financial. After each piece of territory surrendered, put down when Germany obtained it and from whom. For example, after Alsace-Lorraine you would write "1871, from France."

Review the biographical sketch of a leading communist, such as Stalin, Lenin, or Trotzky, in one of the encyclopedias to learn what he was doing in the 1918–1924 period. In your notebook list the positions he held and the problems he faced.

After reading the appropriate chapter in one of the standard college texts, such as Chapter XXII in Langsam's *The World Since 1914*, summarize what happened in the Far East between 1918 and 1924.

SELECTED READINGS

An interesting account of the "inside" of political life before and during World War I is that by an active Democratic politician, Josephus Daniels, *The Wilson Era* (Chapel Hill, N.C.: North Carolina University Press, 1946). An outstanding authority on American diplomatic history, Thomas Bailey, has written a popular work, *Woodrow Wilson and the Lost Peace* (New York: The Macmillan Co., 1945). Some students will find the biography of *Woodrow Wilson* by Alden Hatch (New York: Henry Holt & Co., 1947) somewhat easier reading.

Two good studies of the Treaty of Ver- sailles are Varian Fry, *The Peace That Failed* (New York: Foreign Policy Association, 1939), and Paul Birdsall, *Versailles, Twenty Years After* (New York: Reynal & Hitchcock, 1941).

Russian developments can most easily be followed in the discerning biography, *Lenin*, by Christopher Hollis (Milwaukee, Wis.: Bruce Publishing Co., 1938), or in the study written expressly for younger people by Nina Baker, *Lenin* (New York: The Vanguard Press, 1945). The important happenings in China are related in Stephen Chen and P. S. R. Payne, *Sun Yat-sen: A Portrait* (New York: John Day Co., 1946), as well as in Nina Baker, *Sun Yat-sen* (New York: The Vanguard Press, 1946).

CHRONOLOGICAL REVIEW

1903 *Pontificate of St. Pius X (to 1914); flight of Wright brothers*

1904 Entente Cordiale; Russo-Japanese War

1905 First Moroccan crisis; Sein Fein party in Ireland

1907 Triple Entente formed

1908 Young Turk Revolution

1909 *Peary reaches North Pole; Blériot flies across English Channel*

1910 Japan annexes Korea; Portuguese Republic

1911 Second Moroccan crisis; Italy invades Libya
Amundsen reaches South Pole

1912 China becomes a republic; First Balkan War; Wilson is President of U. S.

1913 Second Balkan war

1914 World War I begins (to 1918); invasion of Belgium; battle of Marne

1914 *Pontificate of Benedict XV (to 1922); opening of Panama Canal*

1915 Allied campaign at Dardanelles

1916 Easter Rebellion in Ireland

1917 Revolution in Russia; U. S. enters war
Apparition of Our Lady at Fatima

1918 Collapse of Central Powers

1919 Versailles Peace Conference; Communist revolts in Germany, Hungary; civil war in Russia

1920 Bolsheviks stopped by Poles at Warsaw; Weimar Republic in Germany; League of Nations
Commercial radio broadcasting

1921 Little Entente formed

1922 Irish Free State proclaimed; Mussolini in power in Italy; Britain recognizes Egyptian independence
Pontificate of Pius XI (to 1939)

1923 Hitler fails to seize power in Germany; U. S. S. R. established

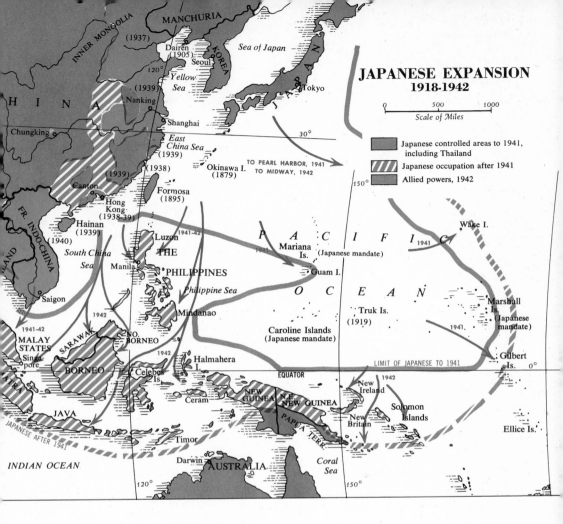

JAPANESE EXPANSION 1918-1942

Scale of Miles
0 — 500 — 1000

■ Japanese controlled areas to 1941, including Thailand

▨ Japanese occupation after 1941

░ Allied powers, 1942

MANCHURIA (1937)
INNER MONGOLIA
Dairen (1905)
Seoul
KOREA
Sea of Japan
Yellow Sea (1939)
Nanking
Shanghai
Chungking
CHINA
East China Sea (1939)
Okinawa I. (1879)
TO PEARL HARBOR, 1941
TO MIDWAY, 1942
(1938)
Canton (1939)
Formosa (1895)
Hong Kong (1938-39)
Hainan (1939)
(1940)
Luzon 1941-42
THE
PHILIPPINES
Manila
South China Sea
Saigon
FR. INDO-CHINA
THAILAND
Mindanao
Philippine Sea
Tokyo
JAPAN
PACIFIC
Mariana Is. (Japanese mandate)
Guam I.
OCEAN
Truk Is. (1919)
Caroline Islands (Japanese mandate)
Wake I.
1941
Marshall Is. Japanese mandate
1941
LIMIT OF JAPANESE TO 1941
Gilbert Is.
1941-42
MALAY STATES
Singapore
SARAWAK
BORNEO
NO. BORNEO
1942
Celebes Is.
Halmahera I.
Ceram
NEW GUINEA
N.E. NEW GUINEA
PAPUA TERR.
New Ireland
New Britain
Solomon Islands
Ellice Is.
SUMATRA
JAVA
JAPANESE AFTER 1941
Timor
Darwin
AUSTRALIA
Coral Sea
EQUATOR
INDIAN OCEAN

UNIT TWELVE
The Origins, Course, and Aftermath of World War II

The Organization of Peace · Economic and Technological Advances · Religious Life: Catholic Revival · The Breakdown of World Capitalism · The State and the Economic Crisis: Growth of Totalitarianism · The Crumbling of Peace and the Rupture of Treaties · How Europe went to War Again in 1939 · The Tide of German Success in War, 1939 to 1940 · The World-wide Spread of the War · Reversing the Fortunes of War · Victory of the United Nations · Weakened Empires and New Independent Nations · The Communist Threat and the Reversal of Alliances · Some Contemporary Trends of World History

Chapter 38. An Interlude of Peace, Progress, and Prosperity

117. THE ORGANIZATION OF PEACE

The wave of war and revolution that had swept over such a large part of the world since 1914 had so unsettled the minds and habits of peoples that it was not likely peace would be long preserved. The spirit of justice had not animated the peace treaties of 1919, and without that spirit there could be no durable peace. The basic principles of civilization are religion and morality, the security of property, and the rule of reason over the passions. These principles had been violated and weakened. In communist Russia they had been completely overthrown.

Moreover, the principal European states which had been the main props of international order were now seriously weakened, while great revolutionary forces were stirring in Asia. In China and India, whose populations make up nearly half the human race, nationalist movements were directed against European influence and domination. The British and French colonial empires were never again to know security in their rule over Indians, Chinese, and Arabs. Japan had shown that an Asian people could become a great power and succeed in war against Europeans, as she had done first against Russia and then against Germany. The communists in Russia were dedicated to a world revolution against capitalism, and they believed that a mortal blow could be struck against it by stirring up Asian peoples against European colonial powers. Long before World War I there had been pessimistic prophets who foresaw the coming of a revolutionary upheaval in the largest and most densely populated of the continents. Such signs were easier to discern after the war.

Nevertheless, the world was to enjoy a brief period in which turmoil and commotion gave way to comparative quiet. By 1924 the economic reconstruction of war-torn Europe was well advanced. The bankers of the United States—now the world's richest nation and chief lending power—had begun to supply large loans for European economic development and would continue to do so until 1929. As a result, the European governments that owed heavy war debts to the United States arranged schedules for the gradual payment of principal and interest. A period of general economic prosperity opened, and in such times political discontents always tend to diminish.

Lenin, the Soviet dictator, died in 1924, and a prolonged contest for power developed between Leon Trotzky and Josef Stalin. This situation weakened the world communist movement, and the Soviet Union for a number of years showed little disposition to violate flagrantly the rules of international conduct. Hence during 1924, Great Britain, Italy, and France established normal diplomatic relations with the Moscow government. Japan did the same in 1925 and withdrew the last of the Japanese troops who had entered Russian territory in 1918 to support anti-communist forces. In China, it is true, Soviet communist agents at this time were aiding the Chinese nationalist party, the Kuomintang, to unify that chaotic country. Before long, however, the nationalist leader, General Chiang Kai-shek, realized that the Russian agents' real purpose was to push him into conflict with Great Britain and Japan and to increase the strength of the Chinese Communist Party. In 1927, Chiang Kai-shek turned against the communists and forced the Russian agents to leave the country. Meanwhile Stalin had defeated Trotzky in the struggle for power in the Soviet Union. The issue that had divided them was whether to press forward with the world revolution or to concentrate upon the development of communism within the Soviet Union. Stalin favored the latter course, so that the country might be made powerful enough to resume revolutionary actions in other countries later and more effectively. In 1928 he launched the first of a series of five-year-plans to transform Russia into a great industrial power.

In India, by 1924, better relations were temporarily achieved between the nationalists and the British imperial government. Gandhi, who had been jailed by the British in 1922, was now released. Signs pointed toward peaceful development of a larger measure of self-government for India.

The League of Nations at work. Although the United States continued to remain outside the League, it had become the practice by 1924 for an American "observer" to attend the sessions at Geneva. The League was larger in membership. Ethiopia was admitted in 1923, and also the new Irish Free State. Three of the nations defeated in the war—Austria, Hungary, Bulgaria—had been admitted; and it was evident by 1924 that Germany soon would enter. The League had assisted in the economic reconstruction and contributed to solving a number of small international disputes. Responsible statesmen were forming the habit of meeting together at Geneva, and many political leaders regarded the League hopefully. By 1929, Winston Churchill described the League as a "granite block" on which would ultimately be built "a dwelling place and palace to which all the men in all the world will sooner or later resort."

The Locarno treaties. In 1925 the British, French, Belgian, Italian, German, Polish, and Czechoslovak governments held a conference at Locarno in Switzerland and negotiated a number of treaties that gave added security to the peace and opened the way for Germany to join the League of Nations. A five-power treaty (Britain, France, Germany, Belgium, Italy) guaranteed Germany's western frontier, and in return Germany agreed to the permanent demilitarization of the Rhineland. Germany entered into arbitration treaties with France, Belgium, Poland, and Czechoslovakia. Although Allied troops were still in occupation of the Rhineland, a more amicable spirit was produced in European international relations by these Locarno treaties. The following year, 1926, Germany was elected to the League of Nations as a permanent member of the Council. She took the seat that had been left vacant by the United States. In the same year the League's commission to prepare for a disarmament conference met for the first time to begin work on a plan for reducing armaments. In this activity even non-members of the League, such as the United States, Turkey, and the Soviet Union, participated.

The British Empire and Commonwealth. Another great international system was meanwhile forming in the British Empire. The British dominions (South Africa, Canada, Australia, New Zealand), which had long enjoyed self-government, were no longer willing to allow Great Britain to exercise more than a moral influence in the conduct of their foreign relations. In 1926 an Imperial Conference took place in London, attended by the prime ministers of Canada, Australia, New Zealand, South Africa, Newfoundland, the Irish Free State, and Great Britain. The conference declared that Britain and the dominions were "autonomous communities within the British Empire, equal in status, in no way subordinate one to another in any aspect of their domestic or external affairs, though united by a common allegiance to the crown, and freely associated as members of the British Commonwealth of Nations." After a few years this declaration was embodied in statute law in all the dominions. The process was completed in 1931 when the British Parliament enacted what is known as the Statute of Westminster.

The whole of the British Empire was not absorbed into the Commonwealth of Nations. Many British colonies were neither ready nor willing to become independent dominions; hence they remained closely attached to Great Britain. Later some would leave the empire to be numbered in the Commonwealth of Nations. Since all the members of the Commonwealth were also members of the League of Nations, these two international systems existed side by side and mutually strengthened each other.

The United States and the international world. The American government in these years refused to enter a collective security system but can hardly be said to have been isolationist, since it strove in its own way to promote and secure world peace. President Warren G. Harding, who succeeded Wilson in 1921, called an international conference for the reduction of naval armaments and the improvement of conditions in the Far East. It was held at Washington during the winter of 1921–1922. The United States, Great Britain, Japan, Italy, and France signed a treaty agreeing to postpone building new battleships for ten years and to limit the size of their battleship and aircraft carrier fleets. Another treaty to safeguard the freedom and territorial integrity of China was signed by the same powers and all other European states with possessions in the Far East. After the Washington Conference, Japanese-American relations improved and peace seemed more secure than it had been.

The American government was convinced that peace, and the prosperity that nourished peace, could be strengthened by removing the costly burden of heavy armaments. On the initiative of the United States, another naval conference was held at Geneva in 1927 in the hope of extending limitation to small naval craft; but no agreement was reached. Again in 1930 the naval powers met at London, where they accomplished little more than to prolong to 1936 the obligations of the Washington naval treaty.

The United States also sought to strengthen peace in the Western Hemisphere by improving relations with the Latin-American countries. Almost all of these had now become members of the League of Nations, so that they had "come of age" in international affairs. All, from their Spanish cultural inheritance, were devoted to the principles of international law. In the Caribbean and Central American countries the United States often had interfered with armed force to preserve order. American marines were withdrawn from Santo Domingo and Nicaragua in 1924 and 1925. Mexico since 1911 had been the scene of repeated revolutionary disorders that were of great concern to the United States. In 1916–1917 the United States sent an army into Mexico to pursue a revolutionary general, Francisco Villa, who had raided over the frontier into New Mexico. Relations between the two countries improved as Mexico became more orderly in the 1920's, but deteriorated again after Plutarco Calles became president in 1924. He seized foreign property and persecuted the Catholic Church. In 1927, American Ambassador Dwight Morrow won him over to reason and conciliation.

The Pact of Paris. During 1927 an agitation developed in the United States for an international treaty to outlaw war. Although President Calvin Coolidge dryly remarked that there was "no short cut to peace or any other kind of salvation," his administration responded to the agitation and sponsored a treaty that was signed at

Paris by fifteen nations in August 1928. The treaty obligated the signers to renounce war "as an instrument of national policy in all their relations with one another," and to settle "all their disputes or conflicts of whatever nature . . . by pacific means." The original signers of this treaty, in addition to the United States, were Great Britain and her dominions, France, Italy, Belgium, Poland, Czechoslovakia, and Germany. Thus the principal victors in World War I and their principal enemy resolved to act according to a higher code of international conduct. A little later the Soviet Union adhered to the treaty.

118. ECONOMIC AND TECHNOLOGICAL ADVANCES

Soon after the end of World War I a general economic depression became widespread in the world. It was due in part to unemployment resulting from the cessation of production of war materials. Other causes were political disorders in the new European state system, which retarded business. Russian economic recovery was long delayed by political leaders who were more interested in promoting revolution than in the welfare of the people. Germany, the industrial heart of Europe, faced reparations obligations that were too heavy for her to pay. All the countries that had been at war incurred enormous debts and by spending far more than their revenues had lowered the value of their currencies. Before the war, currencies were stable and interchangeable at a fixed rate with gold, but now much of Europe's gold had

gone to the United States for loans and purchases. Governments had suspended the exchanging of paper money for gold coins, and the value of the paper money had declined. Hence prices had risen; this is known as inflation. It was worse in the defeated countries. Until currency was stabilized, no one could tell what money would be worth in real goods a year, a month, or even a week later. This condition retarded economic recovery.

Conditions in Germany. Before the war the German mark had been worth about a quarter of a dollar in American money. Between 1919 and 1923 the value of the mark dropped until one American dollar could be exchanged for five trillion. German money thus ceased to be worth the paper it was printed on. There were a number of reasons for this astronomical inflation, some of which are too complex to mention here. One reason, of course, was that Germany lost so much of her real wealth: her colonies and markets, some parts of her territory in Europe, her merchant marine

Charles Dawes (1865–1951) initiated the Dawes Plan, which reduced reparations payments and stabilized German finances. (National Archives)

had been largely confiscated by the victor nations. Another reason was that the bill presented to her for war reparations was far beyond her capacity to pay. When the French and Belgians invaded and occupied the industrial region of the Ruhr in 1923, the German workers in that area went on strike. For nine months the Berlin government supported them in idleness, while the German economy lost the Ruhr production. In the fall of 1923 the government ceased to support the strikers, and the victor powers agreed to create a commission to inquire into Germany's capacity to pay reparations. The commission was headed by an American banker, Charles G. Dawes, and produced a plan that lightened the German burden and opened the way for American gold loans to stabilize the German currency. The paper money was called in and exchanged at the rate of one trillion marks in old money for one mark in new money. Then vast sums of American and British capital were borrowed by the Germans, who thus were able to build many new industries and enjoy a period of flourishing prosperity.

European recovery. The restoration of German economy stimulated recovery throughout all Europe. In 1925, Great Britain restored the gold standard for the pound sterling at its pre-war value. Everywhere business confidence revived. The most striking feature of the whole development was the investment of American capital in almost all the countries of Europe. If the United States government sought to remain aloof from European politics, American capitalism did exactly the opposite in European economic life. Prime Minister Mussolini of Italy remarked in 1928:

The Republic of the Stars and Stripes has played since the war a very great role, a preponderant role in the history of the world. The center of finance has shifted from Europe to America. The United States are creditors of all nations, especially of those on our old continent, to the extent of twelve thousand million dollars. American initiative seems to be preparing for the conquest of Europe.

Capitalism, socialism, communism. European and world economic recovery under the stimulus of American capitalism was in striking contrast with the continued impoverishment of the peoples of the U.S.S.R. under the control of communists. Hence the prestige of capitalism was high and that of communism diminished. Even that milder form of anti-capitalism called socialism, or social democracy, seemed to go somewhat into decline. Nowhere in Europe was a socialist party able to capture control of a government during this period, although in many countries socialist parties gained office by coalition with liberal parties. In Great Britain the Labor Party, which is socialist, created an administration in 1924 but had to depend on the Liberal Party for its measures in Parliament. Turned out by the Conservatives before the end of the year, the Laborites regained office in 1929, but still without sufficient strength in Parliament to enact socialist legislation.

Technical progress. A great spur to industry was the enormous expansion of motorcar production. This industry had far-reaching effects on society. It produced many new mechanical jobs and made people more mechanical-minded. It vastly stimulated the production of petroleum and the search for new supplies of that precious commodity. It promoted suburban residential development. It caused governments to spend greatly increased sums on roadbuilding.

Although radio (wireless telegraphy) had been invented in 1895, its development was long hampered by technical problems and difficulties. During the war it was used extensively, but the public knew little about it until, in 1920, the first commerical broadcasting on regular schedule was started in Pittsburgh. With the utmost rapidity improvements were achieved, and receiving sets and broadcasting stations spread round the world. The rate may be indicated roughly by the fact that in 1930 there were nearly four million receiving sets in the United States. Here was another great industry; production of its instruments flourished in every industrial country. From this time nothing of public interest could happen in any country that was not swiftly known everywhere. A new power was available for international communication, for public knowledge, for advertising men, and for use by political leaders.

Aviation. In this period aviation developed from the stunt-flying stage to that of regular commerical air lines and thus inaugurated the greatest of all revolutions in transportation. In 1919, Commander Albert C. Read and his crew flew a U.S. navy airplane from Newfoundland to the Azore Islands and then on to Lisbon. In the same year two Englishmen, John Alcock and Arthur Brown, made the first non-stop flight across the Atlantic from Newfoundland to Ireland. Soon short commercial air lines were carrying passengers and mail in Europe and America. In 1927 young Charles A. Lindbergh astonished the world by flying alone in a single-engine plane from New York to Paris. It was perfectly done. He took off from an airport on Long Island and landed gracefully on another three thousand miles away. The achievement opened new horizons for aviation and stirred people to an awareness of the air age and its possibilities. From this time aviation pioneers all over the world became busy charting lines of aerial communication with regions hitherto remote from populous centers. Thus new frontiers were opened. In 1928, Captain Charles Kingsford-Smith made

The Spirit of St. Louis, *the single-engine plane used by Charles Lindbergh on his solo transatlantic flight, is on exhibit in the Smithsonian Institution, Washington, D.C. (The Smithsonian Institution)*

the first flight over the Pacific, stopping in Honolulu and then going on to Java in the East Indies in one jump.

Not yet, however, were the planes developed sufficiently for transoceanic and transcontinental commercial flights. For a time it appeared that this field would belong to the dirigible balloon, first developed by the German Count Ferdinand von Zeppelin in 1906. Before the war these flying machines, called Zeppelins, were in use in Europe for passenger service; and the Germans used them to bomb London. In 1929, Hugo Eckener circumnavigated the earth in one of them, and soon afterward a regular Zeppelin passenger service was started between Europe and South America. Zeppelin development was to come to an end, however, in 1937 when the *Hindenburg* caught fire at its moorings and burned with many of its passengers at Lakehurst, New Jersey.

Aviation and exploration. The wonderful utility of aircraft stimulated geographic exploration over previously uncharted regions, the Brazilian, African, and Australian jungles, and the earth's polar caps. In 1926, Commander Richard E. Byrd and Floyd Bennett flew from Spitzbergen to the North Pole and back. They were the first men of our civilization to reach the pole whose achievement was not disputed. Other flights followed and made possible for the first time an accurate map of the Arctic zone. The Antarctic had been far better known than the Arctic. Since the eighteenth century many expeditions had gone there and partially explored the great continent of Antarctica. Various national claims had been made to parts

of it. Aviation now was a wonderful aid to expeditions by ship. In 1929, Commander Byrd flew over the South Pole (discovered in 1911 by the Norwegian Captain Roald Amundsen). About the same time Byrd established the base of Little America on this continent, which is larger than Australia.

Other advances. It would be difficult to indicate any field of technology or science in which great progress was not accomplished. Atomic physics, which really began with the discovery of radium by the Curies in 1898, broke new frontiers. In medicine, the use of extract of insulin was developed for the treatment of diabetes, and liver extract for pernicious anemia. Scientific studies became ever more popular. It was plain that the whole civilized world was moving into an age of apparently limitless frontiers of knowledge and power.

119. RELIGIOUS LIFE: CATHOLIC REVIVAL

Two opposing trends in religious life appeared distinctly in the decade following World War I. On the one hand, the pre-war trend of growing disbelief in supernatural reality was accentuated, and there came a widespread collapse of old religious beliefs and loyalties. Many could not comprehend how a loving Divine Ruler of the universe could allow such a horror of hate and killing as the war had been, and lost all faith in God. In the Soviet Union atheistic materialism was being promoted by the rulers of the state, who were bent on the total destruction of religion in Russia and everywhere else. In many parts of the world, especially in eastern Europe and Asia, religion had seemed to peoples so much a part of their way of life that a disturbance of long-settled social and political arrangements produced religious doubts and denials. Islamic faith was struck a hard blow by the breakup of the Turkish Empire and by the Turkish abolition of the caliphate (spiritual leadership) of Islam in 1924. The new Turkish republic turned to Western ways; it was "modern," secularist, and actively combated the old sacred Mohammedan way of life. The Turkish dictator, Mustapha Kemal, even forbade wearing the red "fez," an emblem of the Islamic religion. Other Mohammedan countries were feeling the impact of European interference and control, which unsettled the old ways of life.

The state of Protestantism. Among Protestant Christians, religious certitudes and church attendance were visibly in decline. Some Protestant churches were disturbed by sharp controversies between those who held firmly to the old faith and those who wished to water it down and modernize or "liberalize" it. The defeat of Germany, homeland of the Protestant Revolution, and the apparent decline of Great Britain weakened a certain confidence that had long been in Protestant minds. These two countries had been at the very head of nineteenth-century progressive civilization, and it had been widely believed that this was due in large measure to the moral and intellectual superiority of Protestant Christianity. This belief lost much of its force. Protestantism was in a crisis of doubt and self-examination.

Decline of the West. Countless thousands of people who lost their faith in Christianity began to look for another religion, and there was a great interest in Asian cults. The stirring of Asian peoples, the rise of Japan, the movement led by Gandhi in India, the communist revolution in Russia, and the apparent decline of great European states from a position of world power caused a loss of faith in the durability of Christian European civilization. A German philosopher of history, Oswald Spengler, in 1918 published a book entitled *The Decline of the West*. It was a massive treatise on the rise and decline of cultures, which he conceived as analogous to physical organisms. A culture was a way of life and the sum of beliefs and values of a particular society; it was born, came to maturity, passed through old age to death and disintegration. Spengler believed that a certain culture had been born in the European Middle Ages; he called it Western culture and gloomily announced that it was dying. His book appealed to the mood of those who had lost their faith in Christianity and the leadership of European civilization in the world.

Catholicism. A counter-trend to Spenglerian pessimism and the decline of strong religious faith among Protestants was to be seen in the renewed vitality and appeal of the Catholic Church. It appeared as a citadel of unchanging doctrine and firmly held faith; it aroused a new kind of interest on the part of many perplexed Protestants and a disposition to examine it. As a result an unusually large number of conversions to Catholicism took place. The Papacy was an important cause of this development. For more than a half century before the war, the popes had been warning the world against extreme nationalism, materialism, and indifference to the natural moral law; now these warnings were vindicated. Pope St. Pius X (1903–1914), a saint recently canonized, had tried to prevent the outbreak of the war; and his successor, Benedict XV, had tried to induce the belligerent powers to end it by just conciliation. The victor powers purposefully excluded him from having any voice in the peacemaking, and the peace had not been just. The Papacy thus appeared as the one voice of reason and justice raised above international quarrels: the one voice speaking for the permanent good of all mankind. Millions who never before had paid any attention to papal utterances now began to listen to them.

Significant political changes. Certain Catholic peoples enjoyed a larger freedom. The Poles and Lithuanians, predominantly Catholic, had long suffered oppression of their religious life by Russia and Germany; now they were free and independent. Catholic Ireland, by the establishment of the Free State in the greater part of the country, had gained a larger liberty from Protestant Britain. In republican Germany there were fewer Catholics because of territorial cessions to France and Poland, but the Church in the new German civil order was less cramped by state restraints and interference.

A great change was visible in France. In the early years of the century French politics had been dominated by a spirit of intense hostility to the Church. Anti-Catholic liberals, viewing the Church as a conservative force and Catholics as politically hostile to the republic, had outlawed religious orders and sought to destroy Catholic schools. In 1905 the French government had denounced the concordat (or treaty) with the Papacy and proclaimed the "separation of Church and state." In effect if not in purpose this meant placing Catholic institutions at the mercy of the state. The spirit of persecution was in these measures; they aimed at abolishing the Catholic religion in France. Pope St. Pius X courageously opposed them, and the loyal resistance of the French clergy and laity frustrated enforcement of them. By 1914 the failure of the persecution was evident. During the war French Catholics demonstrated a wonderful devotion to their country's cause, and the priests were outstanding battlefield heroes. Marshal Foch, supreme commander of the victorious armies, was a devout Catholic. The canonization of St. Joan of Arc in 1920 quickened French religious life. The republican government, once so hostile to the Church and still not friendly, restored its embassy at the Vatican. In 1926 the Pope condemned a French political movement, *Action Française,* which professed to favor the Church but was hostile to the republican form of government; in its agitation for the revival of monarchy it advocated certain wrong principles of morality. Occasional flare-ups of anti-Catholic activity continued to occur in France, but as the years passed the Catholic revival became steadily more evident.

English Catholicism. Catholics formed but one-twentieth of the population of

Distinguished converts: Msgr. Ronald Knox (modern English translation of the Bible), G. K. Chesterton and Hilaire Belloc (prominent literary figures), and Father Martin D'Arcy, S. J. (English philosopher). (The Sign)

England, and about half of them were Irish. Their position was unique: a small minority in a strongly anti-Catholic country that had been Catholic for a thousand years before the Protestant Revolution. Among them were an unusually large number of talented writers and thinkers whose works commanded much attention among non-Catholics. Some of these brilliant persons were converts from the Church of England; for example, Father Ronald Knox, whose father had been the Bishop of Manchester, and Gilbert K. Chesteron, one of the wisest, wittiest, and most popular writers in the country. Father Martin D'Arcy, a Jesuit at Oxford, was a great intellectual force in university circles. Hilaire Belloc, a half-French Englishman who had sat for a few years in Parliament, was an outstanding poet, essayist, journalist, biographer, and a militant defender of the Catholic faith. At a time when Protestantism seemed shaken and England had come upon difficult times, these and other gifted Catholic thinkers appealed to an older religious tradition and made it appear modern and attractive. Conversion to Catholicism became a rather prominent feature of English society. Because of overindustrialization and a chronic unemployment problem, there was an intense interest among Catholics in social and economic questions. The Catholic Social Guild, founded in 1919, did much to promote the principles of social justice set forth by Leo XIII in the encyclical *Rerum novarum*. The Catholic Truth Society and Catholic Evidence Guild carried on a highly intelligent apostolate, not arguing against Protestantism but simply spreading knowledge of the Catholic Church. Because of the world-wide spread of the British Empire and Commonwealth and the prevalence of the English language in the United States, the English Catholic activity was a development of universal importance.

The United States. This country, too, experienced the Catholic revival. The Church now embraced about one-third of all the regular church-going population in the United States. American Catholics were devoted to the Holy See and provided the main financial support for its many missions. Nowhere in the world did the Church enjoy a larger liberty for developing its schools and charitable institutions. Some of the younger generation of non-Catholics who had served in the armed forces in Europe became more aware of the Catholic tradition, and many conversions took place.

Pope Pius XI. In 1918, after Germany had imposed the Treaty of Brest-Litovsk on Bolshevik Russia, Pope Benedict XV commissioned the scholarly Vatican librarian, Monsignor Achille Ratti, to survey the whole ecclesiastical scene in Polish-Lithuanian lands now separated from Russia. For the first time in a century some twenty million Catholics in this part of the world were enabled to have direct communication with Rome. Many ancient bishoprics had lapsed under Russian rule. Monsignor Ratti directed a vast work of ecclesiastical reconstruction in this long-oppressed and now war-torn region. It was facilitated by the defeat of Germany and the resultant complete independence of Poland. In 1919 he was made papal nuncio (ambassador) to Poland. He remained at Warsaw and gave encouragement to the Poles when it seemed in 1920 that their country would be conquered by the Bolsheviks. The next year he was made Archbishop of Milan in Italy, and in 1922 he succeeded Benedict XV as Pope Pius XI. He governed the Church for seventeen years.

Every force of Catholic revival was stimulated by him. Vividly aware of the changing character of society and the dechristianizing forces at work, he laid the greatest stress on Christian education. "There can be," he said, "no true education which is not wholly directed to man's last end, and in the present order of Providence . . . there can be no ideally perfect education except that which is called Christian education." Pius XI has been called the "Pope of Catholic Action" because of his zealous effort to organize the laity of the Church for participation in the apostolate of the bishops. There was a militant energy in the spirit of this scholarly priest. During the first ten years of his reign the mission territories of the Church were enlarged by one-third in their extent.

The Lateran treaties. Pius XI brought to an end the unhappy era in which the popes were commonly called "prisoners in the Vatican." Since the years 1860–1870, when the Italian state confiscated vast Church properties and usurped the Pope's sovereignty in the old Roman state, there

Pope Pius XI (1922–1939)

had been unhappy relations between the Papacy and monarchy, Church and state, in Italy. The Pope would not leave the Vatican Palace, preferring to maintain the role of "prisoner" rather than recognize the usurpations of the state, while throughout the kingdom the Church suffered from anti-clerical state policies and arbitrary political regulations.

This situation grew worse during the early years of the Italian Fascist Party rule in Italy. Fascists were violent and lawless men who dealt brutally with all who opposed them. The Pope said in 1926: "We have recently seen a new storm breaking over Italy. We have seen Catholics attacked and Catholic institutions . . . The boldness and impudence of some of these rascals has broken all the limits, profaning churches and the very persons of the Catholic episcopate." But the Catholic revival gradually convinced the dictator Mussolini that he could not establish order and unity unless he stopped attacking the religion of the people. His government then turned toward an understanding with the Holy See, and negotiations were opened. They touched upon all questions growing out of the events of 1860–1870, the legal status of the Church, and the territorial independence of the papacy. They resulted in 1929 in the Lateran Treaty, by which Italy recognized papal sovereignty over what is called Vatican City and made a financial settlement for confiscated Church property. At the same time a concordat was concluded between the Papacy and the kingdom of Italy. It removed all political obstructions from the normal life of the Church and ex-acted from the state an extension of Catholic religious instruction to secondary schools under teachers approved by the bishops. The state also agreed to respect the freedom of Catholic Action organizations and to uphold the canon law on marriage. The Pope announced "that we have given God back to Italy and Italy to God." He ceased to be the "prisoner of the Vatican" and recognized the kingdom of Italy.

Unfortunately the fascist government of Italy proved unwilling to observe strictly the terms of the concordat; and indeed Mussolini, in making the treaty, had no higher aim than to overcome Catholic opposition to his dictatorial rule. Soon he showed that he was ready to violate the concordat at his convenience. Nevertheless, the concordat was not denounced and the sovereignty of the Pope in Vatican City was not violated. Pius XI stood up manfully against Fascist bullying and warned against the totalitarian claims of the fascist state. He told the students of a Jesuit college in 1929: "It is not the function of the state to absorb, to swallow up, to annihilate the individual and the family. This would be absurd, contrary to the nature of things, for the family existed before the state, as it existed before society."

Those words were spoken on the eve of a new universal social and economic crisis that would lead to a swelling of state power and growth of political tyranny far beyond anything the world had yet known.

REVIEW

STUDY SECTIONS IN REVIEW

117. The Organization of Peace

A. Identify: Stalin, Chiang Kai-shek, Gandhi.

B. What was accomplished by the treaties of Locarno (1925)?

C. Explain the status of a "dominion" within the British Commonwealth of Nations.

D. What was the purpose of the Pact of Paris of 1927?

118. Economic and Technological Advances

A. Note three causes of the world-wide economic depression after the war.

B. How did American capitalists and the American government differ in their approaches to European affairs?

C. What effects on society followed from the invention of the automobile?

D. What was the importance of the development of radio as a means of communication?

119. Religious Life: Catholic Revival

A. Cite three factors that caused a loss of religious faith in the period after World War I.

B. Identify: Spengler, *Action Française*, G. K. Chesterton.

C. List two achievements of the Papacy under Pius XI.

D. What was the significance of the Lateran treaties (1929)?

THE CHAPTER IN REVIEW

A. Explain the nature of the British Commonwealth of Nations. How did this differ from the previous British Empire?

B. What was the status of the League of Nations in 1929? Were European leaders disappointed in its achievements?

C. Explain the following statement: "As early as the 1920's there were indications that world peace was only temporary."

D. How did Oswald Spengler explain the apparent decline of Christian and European influence in the post-war world? Did this theory apply to Roman Catholicism in this period? Explain.

In this last unit we move into the period called "contemporary history." Your parents can probably remember many of the events discussed in this and the succeeding chapters. Talk these happenings over with them and your grandparents or other older relatives to learn what their reactions were at the time these things were occurring.

Make a list of reasons why many persons were optimistic in 1925 or 1926.

Four new and booming industries at this time were (1) automotive, (2) aviation, (3) radio, (4) movies. Under each make a list of its social, political, and economic effects. Under the automotive industry, for example, one social effect is to promote the growth of suburbs, and one economic effect is to promote such allied industries as steel and petroleum.

Use one of the one-volume Church histories, such as Neill and Schmandt's *History of the Catholic Church*, to make a list of the major accomplishments of Popes St. Pius X, Benedict XV, and Pius XI.

SELECTED READINGS

A readable account of this period in America is Frederick Lewis Allen, *Only Yesterday: An Informal History of the Nineteen-Twenties* (New York: Harper & Bros., 1957). A good general treatment of the rise of the automobile industry is E. D. Kennedy, *The Automobile Industry: The Coming of Age of Capitalism's Favorite Child* (New York: Reynal & Hitchcock, 1941), and the growth of a specific company is sketched out in Arthur Pound, *The Turning Wheel* (Garden City, N. Y.: Doubleday & Co., 1934), which traces twenty-five years' growth of General Motors.

Of the many biographies of Popes St. Pius X and Pius XI, the most readable are probably Kathleen Burton, *The Great Mantle: The Life of Giuseppe Melchiore Sarto* (New York: Longmans, Green & Co., 1950), and Lillian Browne Olf, *Pius XI, Apostle of Peace* New York: The Macmillan Co., 1938).

Chapter 39. World Economic and Political Crisis, 1929 to 1937

120. THE BREAKDOWN OF WORLD CAPITALISM

The great business prosperity of the 1920's came to a sudden end and was followed in the 1930's by a world-wide commercial and industrial depression. Banks failed, markets shrank, money became scarce, credit contracted, factories shut down or reduced production, and millions of men could find no way to earn a living. The result was a revival of political discontents throughout the world, a mounting fever of revolution, and stupendous new problems for statesmen.

Causes of the depression. The catastrophe that struck world capitalism resulted from a variety of causes. Perhaps no one could understand it completely

but the great main causes can be indicated.

First, there had been "pockets" of depression in the midst of the prosperity. Agriculture throughout the period suffered from surplus production that dragged down food prices. This made it difficult for farmers to buy the industrial goods they needed. The prosperous industrial and business world simply could not consume what agriculture produced. Thus the peasants of eastern Europe and the farmers of the United States did not share in the great prosperity, and their inability to buy ultimately depressed the market for industrial goods. Great Britain, overindustrialized and unable to employ all her workers, was a pocket of depression. The same could be said of the American cotton-growing region.

Second, too many governments were too much influenced by manufacturers bent on protecting their home markets against competition from rival producers in other countries. In time this led to overproduction of manufactures and the blocking of international trade. The situation became especially acute in Europe. New small nations, eager to develop their own industries, adopted high tariffs (import duties) and even prohibitions against certain goods of other nations. As early as 1926 the ill effects of this condition were such that a group of European and British business leaders published an appeal for the removal of such restrictions on international trade. Little was done, however, to correct these economic follies. The high-tariff policy of the United States contributed much to this general world condition. Supported by loans to foreign countries, the American export trade expanded to great dimensions; but the United States government protected the home market against European competitors.

Third, business corporations had not yet come to realize that workers were also consumers and that high wages helped to sustain the market. When manufacturing methods were improved so that production costs were lowered, too much of the savings went into lowering prices and raising shareholders' dividends and not enough into raising wages. Wherever the trade-union movement was weak, this tendency was strong.

Fourth, an overextension of international lending of capital took place, especially American and British lending to Germany. The Germans were paying war reparations by means of loans from American bankers; by the same means they were modernizing their industries and greatly increasing their industrial productive capacity. If American lending stopped or slowed down, Germany would be unable to meet her reparations obligations and a credit crisis would strike her business structure. This happened, and the effects were world-wide.

The *fifth* main cause was the great stock-market speculation craze that developed in the United States. People came to believe that business prosperity was permanent, that it would go on swelling ever more. Thousands, even millions, saw easy fortunes to be made in buying and selling stocks. They borrowed money, mortgaged their real estate, expanded their obligations in every way, in order to raise money to gamble on the Stock Ex-

The economic crisis in England caused a demonstration in Trafalgar Square, London, in 1934. The so-called "hunger" marchers came from Manchester to demand work and to protest unemployment. (Wide World)

change. For a few years before October 1929 the value of stocks kept soaring skyward; vast sums of European money were invested in American stocks. Money that previously had been used to buy the bonds of European governments and industries now was used to speculate in American industrial stocks. As a result, the source of the loans Germany needed began to dry up, and during 1929 her economic situation entered the danger zone. In October the great stock-market bubble burst. The wise investors had already sold out their holdings at top prices, and now a selling wave began that drove values down and down. Billions of dollars in the form of paper credits simply vanished. Banks that had extended credit to persons who now could not pay sold out their loan securities for what these could bring. Many banks failed. Those who had money were reluctant to lend, and those who needed it could not borrow it. Buying contracted and business firms could not sell their goods; people were thrown out of their jobs. The whole international world of banking and commerce went into a tailspin. World capitalism sank steadily during the year of 1930.

The German crisis. Political developments struck a further blow to make everything worse. In 1930 the French, British, and Belgian occupying troops were withdrawn from Germany. An election that fall showed that the National Socialist (Nazi) Party led by Adolf Hitler had become a powerful force in the country. It was loudly committed to repudiating the Versailles Treaty, rearming Germany, and uniting with Austria to make a Greater Germany. In order to enlarge the Ger-

man economy and to "steal the thunder" of the Nazis, the government headed by Chancellor Heinrich Bruening negotiated a tariff union with Austria. The French, Belgian, Polish, and Czechoslovak governments feared this as a step toward German-Austrian political union, which was forbidden by the Treaty of Versailles. They determined to prevent it. A tense situation arose. Many creditors of German and Austrian banks withdrew their loans and deposits, and a financial panic forced several great banks to close their doors. The German government could not meet its war-reparation payments without getting new loans, and these were not to be had. Other states felt they could not meet their war-debt payments to the United States without receiving the sums due them from Germany. The American President, Herbert Hoover, gained international agreement for a year's moratorium (emergency suspension) of reparation and debt payments. The French and their allies did not agree to this until after they had forced Germany to abandon the tariff treaty with Austria. From this time international insecurity discouraged the confidence needed to restore the international lending of capital to make the capitalist system work as it should.

Collapse of the gold standard. Prior to 1914 all the leading currencies in the world were based on a legally fixed price of gold. Paper money circulated because people knew they could go to a bank and exchange it for gold if they so desired. It was easy to exchange French francs for American dollars, or English pounds for German marks because all were backed by gold, which could be carried freely from one country to another. If a government lacked sufficient gold to back its currency and suspended paying gold for it, the value of that currency went down. This happened during the war because belligerent governments had to raise so much money by borrowing that their currencies were expanded far beyond their gold reserves. In the 1920's, however, there was a gradual restoration of the gold standard; but the depression destroyed it, and it has not been restored. The British government in the fall of 1931 found itself in financial trouble and suspended payment of gold for paper money. Immediately the value of the pound fell in terms of other currencies. A number of other governments quickly followed the British example.

To many politicians and shortsighted businessmen in industrial countries there seemed an advantage in cheapening the value of their currencies. For example, a British merchant with goods to sell abroad could undercut the price of his competitor, because the foreigner who bought the goods would pay less money in *his* currency to obtain the pounds needed to settle with the British merchant. On the other hand, the British manufacturer who had to import raw materials from, say, the United States had to pay more pounds to buy the dollars to settle his account. Thus an advantage gained on the one hand was balanced by a disadvantage on the other. When other countries entered (as they did) into this sort of competition by devaluing their currencies, all foreign trade suffered. It became necessary to protect currencies from falling too far, and this led to new

government regulation of foreign trade lest the "hard" or gold-backed currencies gain too powerful a purchasing advantage in "soft currency" countries.

In 1933–1934 the United States joined in the competition by recalling all gold coins to the Treasury and then lowering the gold value of the dollar by forty-one cents. The aim was to encourage business domestically by raising prices, while making it easier for foreign countries to get the dollars needed to buy American goods. The United States stopped coining gold but went on buying it from foreign and domestic producers of it, paying thirty-five dollars an ounce instead of the previous twenty dollars an ounce. The advantage given to new gold producers over former owners of gold coins was designed to stimulate the purchase of American products and to revive business and employment.

Increased tariffs. In spite of cheapened currencies, international trade did not revive. New efforts to protect home markets from competitive cheap imports resulted in more and higher tariffs and other forms of trade barriers. The United States in 1930 raised its tariff. In 1932 Great Britain and her dominions formed an economic arrangement by which special tariffs were adopted to promote trade within the Commonwealth while protecting that trade against competition from without the Commonwealth. Both of these developments further harmed international trade.

Reparations and war debts. In 1932, Germany succeeded in negotiating an end to the payment of war reparations, and the governments owing World War I debts to the United States made

Debtors: "Please will you give us a little more time, Sir?"
Creditor: "What, again? I'll be hanged if I do!"
Debtors: "Well, you'll be hanged if you don't!" (The Daily Express, London, November 16, 1932)

mere token payments instead of the installments that were due. Thus they acknowledged their obligations without fulfilling them. These debts never were paid. The failure to pay what was owed put an additional damper on international lending of capital.

World Economic Conference. A commission of economic experts was appointed by the League of Nations in January 1933 to prepare for a great international monetary and economic conference. The objects aimed at were the restoration of an effective international money standard and the removal of barriers to international trade. By the time the world conference met at London in June, however, there were new administrations in Germany and the United States. Hitler and the Nazis were in power in Germany. Franklin D. Roosevelt had succeeded Herbert Hoover as President of the United States. Both countries had committed themselves to national rather than international measures to overcome the depression. Both were seeking to create employment and help business by government policies of expanding internal credit; such policies were not consistent with an international approach to the world economic problem. Hence the conference broke up in complete failure.

The restoration of international capitalism was not achieved and the nations continued in varying degrees of economic distress. Conditions in Great Britain improved somewhat. In the United States vast taxing and spending by the government provided work for those who could find no other employment, and relief for those in distress, while agricultural decline was arrested. In Germany the unemployment problem was presently solved by the resumption of arming. All governments afflicted by a large unemployment problem tried to overcome it in various ways, all of which were expensive and swelled pubic debt. The capitalist system, therefore, continued to be in serious trouble.

Soviet development. Meanwhile, the Soviet Union completed its first five-year plan and started on another. Its ambitious programs were so large that it had a manpower shortage, and both men and women were forced to work.

Communist Russia was being fast transformed into a sort of slave society; hence it had no unemployment problem. In contrast with the capitalist world, the Soviet system seemed to be making great advances. Soviet propaganda, never truthful, made much of this. By 1933 there was a growing fear —and also hope among many in Europe—that the future might belong to communism.

121. THE STATE AND THE ECONOMIC CRISIS: GROWTH OF TOTALITARIANISM

Wherever the great depression reached, there was intense suffering among those whose savings were gone and who had to rely upon daily labor for their bread but could find no work. Everywhere men asked what had happened, what was wrong, who was responsible for the sorry state of affairs. They speculated and theorized about it and demanded that their political leaders act to correct what was wrong. Governments, therefore, were called upon to take new responsibilities and experiment with new theories and methods for promoting the welfare of society. Not only capitalism, but liberalism and its philosophy of economic individualism had broken down.

Liberal - democratic governments that worked through parliaments and elective representative institutions had relied too much on the business world to look out for itself and now they faced problems for which they could find no solutions in the doctrines of economic liberalism. Hence new political and social ideologies came to the front. The commonly accepted meaning of the word *ideology* is a connected system of ideas forming a theory that its holders believe can explain the present state of society and show the direction in which it should be developed. Intelligent and informed men never have accepted ideologies, but ambitious and unscrupulous men have sometimes found them to be useful instruments for gaining and holding onto power. This is because the credulous can be led to believe them. They *seem* to explain even though they do not explain. Socialism and communism, while differing in political practice, had almost identical ideologies. They had, therefore, easy and simple explanations for the crisis of capitalism which they had long predicted and hoped for, and they had theoretical plans for creating a new economic and social order.

Socialism and liberalism. Since the latter part of the nineteenth century there had been socialist political parties in most countries. In their earlier days these parties held to Karl Marx's theory of social development which affirmed that capitalism contained the seeds of its own destruction. The idea was that capitalist owners of the means of production were exploiting and increasing the number of the propertyless wage earners (the proletariat). Hence a day would come when the wage earners would seize the great instruments of production and socialize them for the equal benefit of all. The seizure would be violent, bloody revolution would occur, and the task of the socialists was to hasten that event. The belief in an inevitable and desirable socialist revolution through violence was now held only by the communists. The socialist parties envisaged the coming of socialism as a gradual process taking place without violence within the general constitutional framework of liberal-democratic states. Many of the more moderate socialist ideas had long been adopted by democratic political leaders and embodied in various forms of social welfare legislation. Hence democracy, while remaining liberal, had gone far in the socialist direction. This trend was to be speeded up in the 1930's, but the advance of socialism showed less in the growth of socialist parties than in the adoption of socialist measures by democratic governments. As the old liberalism fell into discredit, a new socialistic democracy became more prominent and showed itself in increased state regulation of economic life for the purpose of guarding the general welfare.

Fascism. A lively interest was stirred by the new political order Benito Mussolini and his Fascist Party were shaping in Italy. They called it the totalitarian state, which meant that the authority of the state over society was total: the state assumed the direction of every department of life. It forbade all political parties except the Fascist Party, which formed a sort of civil militia at the service of the Duce, leader of the movement and dictator of the state. The state controlled the schools, the press, and all economic institutions. Its policy was "everything in the state, nothing outside the state, nothing against the state." It rejected the French revolutionary motto of "liberty, equality, fraternity," and called for "order, authority, and justice." There was a superficial efficiency about this system that led many people to admire Mussolini as an energetic man who for the first time made the Italian trains run on time. The state showed an interest in social welfare which won the general approval of the common people, but the leaders were corrupt and squandered public money. All opposition was terrorized into silence or banished from the country, and order depended largely on fear of the secret police. There was almost constant friction between the Church and the state.

Although Italian fascism was intensely nationalistic and Mussolini said that it was "not an article for export," the Italian political example was widely imitated. Spain had been ruled from 1923 to 1929 by a dictator, Primo de Rivera, who admired Mussolini as a model. Primo fell from power and soon afterward a revolution against the monarchy brought a republic to Spain. Then other fascist developments took place. Poland had a semi-dictator, Marshal Joseph Pilsudski, from 1926 to 1935, and displayed moderate fascist tendencies. In Yugoslavia, King Alexander assumed dictatorial power in 1929. In 1932 a dictatorial form of government with certain fascist tendencies was established in Portugal with Antonio de Oliveira Salazar as its chief. None of the states mentioned here went nearly to the extremes that the Italian state reached under fascism. The essence of fascism was dictatorship and the totalitarian state. It resembled communism in its political methods, but did not aim at the abolition of private property and socialization of the means of production. It offered security while taking away political and civil liberty.

National socialism. Far and above the most revolutionary movement of a fascist character was that which gained control of Germany in 1933. The National Socialists (or Nazis), led by Adolf Hitler, for a decade had been a disturbing force in the national life. They had massive uniformed organizations that committed many acts of terrorism. They were sworn to destroy the large Communist Party in Germany, to do away with the Versailles Treaty, to reclaim lost German territories, to annex Austria to Germany, to solve the unemployment problem, and to wipe out Jewish influence in Germany. They blamed most of the misfortunes of their country on international capitalism, which they held to be dominated by wealthy Jews; and on communism, which they imagined was still another aspect of the hidden power of the international community of Jews. The Jews, so the Nazis professed to believe, were mortal enemies of Germany and all other nations. This was a fantastically untrue belief; yet it proved a powerful political force because people, when they are suffering, easily become credulous and are on the lookout for a scapegoat.

Hostility to Jews was an expression of a strange Nazi ideology of race. The Nazis held that the most important thing in human society was race; that there were superior and inferior races, the Jews being among the latter. Nazis wished to purify their race from all debasing contact with the Jews and urged other nations to take similar measures against inferior races. They boasted that a solution of the race question would facilitate a solution of all other problems.

The Nazis came to power by constitutional procedures in coalition with the German Nationalist Party. Hitler was appointed Chancellor (Prime Minister) by President von Hindenburg in January 1933. Then, by a series of violent and illegal moves, Hitler's followers rapidly established a dictatorship, abolished all other parties, drove all Jews from public office, schools, universities, professions, and confiscated Jewish property. Nazi control was established over newspapers and every social, economic, and political institution in the country. The labor unions were forced into one great organization under Nazi direction and forbidden to strike. The only resistance to the Nazis was shown by the churches, Catholic and Protestant, but this was beaten down. Thousands of Germans fled the country rather than submit to terror and tyranny. Many more thousands, even millions, rejoiced at what they imagined to be a resurrection of vitality and power in Germany. The Nazis displayed great zeal for relieving the economic distress of all but Jews and persons deemed enemies of the state. Before a year had passed, the unemployment problem had been mastered by starting armament industries in violation of the Versailles Treaty. The Nazi triumph in Germany gave an impetus to this kind of politics in other countries.

The New Deal in the United States. Franklin D. Roosevelt, candidate of the Democratic Party for the presidency in 1932, campaigned in the midst of business stagnation and unemployment. He promised the American nation a "New Deal." It proved to be

President Franklin D. Roosevelt (1882–1945) (National Archives)

state for the guidance of governments the basic laws of justice in social-economic life. He issued the encyclical letter *Quadragesimo anno* (After Forty Years), which recalled Leo XIII's *Rerum novarum* of 1891 and made new applications of that "Magna Carta of the Social Order."

The Pope said that "the earthly goods so abundantly produced in this age of industrialism" were "far from being rightly distributed and equitably shared among the various classes of men." The basic cause of this condition was moral: violation by both capital and labor of the law of the common good.

This sacred law is violated by an irresponsible wealthy class who, in the excess of good fortune, deem it a just state of things that they should receive everything and the laborer nothing; it is violated also by a propertyless wage-earning class who demand for themselves all the fruits of production as being the work of their hands.

Rejecting both economic individualism and collectivism in all its forms, he defended the right of private property and called for a mutual concord between capital and labor. He stressed the moral responsibility of business firms to pay the workers a just wage so that they might be able to provide honorably and decently for their families and acquire some property. He commended trade unions, provided they acted on right moral principles, and also gave a guarded approval to certain forms of economic organization the Italian fascist state was promoting. These were corporations, or syndicates, of employers and workingmen in the same trade or profession. Such organizations might make possi-

neither fascist nor socialist, but a unique American political effort to save capitalism and provide work for the unemployed. Businessmen were encouraged to adopt higher standards of social responsibility. New laws were enacted to strengthen the trade unions. Large sums of government money were spent for relief and the building of public works. The money was raised by "deficit financing"; that is, spending more than the revenue brought in and allowing the public debt to grow. Agriculture was restored to some degree of prosperity by subsidizing the farmers. The federal government assumed a much larger control of the country's economic life, but the aim was merely to restore economic prosperity. The New Deal had no ideology. It aroused great interest all over the world and exerted considerable influence on French politics in 1936.

Pius XI and the social question. Early in the depression the Pope saw that the time had come for the Church to reble "peaceful collaboration of the classes, repression of Socialist organization and efforts." The Pope saw, however, a danger in their taking on "an excessively bureaucratic and political character . . . and serving particular political aims rather than contributing to the initiation of a better social order." Pius wished to see employers and employees co-operating voluntarily for mutual welfare and the common good; he did not wish to have the state impose the new forms of organization on them by force.

Pius recognized that the disorders and distresses of society called for an enlargement of the functions of the state, but warned against believing that "all salvation" was "to be hoped from its intervention." The state had the duty to maintain social justice, but it ought not to become involved in "an infinity of affairs and duties." It was, said the Pope, "a grave evil and a disturbance of right order for a higher organization to arrogate to itself functions which can be performed efficiently by smaller and lower bodies. This is a fundamental principle of social philosophy, unshaken and unchangeable, and it retains its full truth today."

Quadragesimo anno aroused great interest among non-Catholics as well as Catholics and influenced the thinking of many practical political leaders. An effort was made in Austria to reorganize the national life so as to embody some of the papal principles. The encyclical had an influence on the thinking of some of the American New Dealers. The Irish Free State tried to develop policies in harmony with the encyclical; so did Portugal, and in spite of the to-talitarian state the papal doctrines made a strong impression on Italians. Spanish Catholics attempted to promote the papal principles of social justice. Nowhere was the great encyclical received with warmer admiration than among the English Catholics. Even the Nazis pretended for a time in the Catholic regions of Germany to be inspired by papal principles of social justice.

122. THE CRUMBLING OF PEACE AND THE RUPTURE OF TREATIES

Between 1930 and 1937 a series of international crises demonstrated that peace organization through such institutions as the League of Nations and the British Commonwealth and Empire was too fragile and weak to prevent local wars or stop a dangerous drift toward renewal of world war. The first clear signs of this deterioration of international security appeared in Asia.

British India. In the midst of Anglo-Indian conferences aimed at the establishment of India as a self-governing dominion in the British Commonwealth of Nations, the extremists in the Indian National Congress overwhelmed the moderates and voted for complete independence. A new period of conflict was opened, and it became evident that British ability to maintain authority in India was growing steadily weaker.

Japan vs. China. While India was in new turmoil, the Japanese government became gravely alarmed at the course of events in China. The nationalist movement led by Chiang Kai-shek was advancing far toward the reunification of China, and the Japanese became concerned for the security of their economic and political interests in Manchuria, the northeast province of China. With a dense and growing population and a dependence on Chinese markets for the sale of her manufactures, Japan could be seriously hurt by the unification of China, for China was developing rival manufactures and might shut out those of Japan. As Chinese-Japanese relations went from bad to worse, a boycott of Japanese goods was started in China. In September 1931 a Japanese army moved from Korea into Manchuria and established complete control over that country.

Japan quits the League of Nations. China appealed to the League of Nations, which appointed a commission to inquire into the seizure of Manchuria; and the United States protested to Japan, reminding her of her obligations under the Washington Treaty to respect the territorial integrity of China. Japan defied both the League and the United States, and in order to teach the Chinese a stern lesson bombed the city of Shanghai early in 1932. When the League commission of enquiry in 1933 produced a report that was unfavorable to Japan, the Assembly of the League voted that Japan had violated her obligations under the League covenant. Japan countered by resigning from the League of Nations.

The League lost more than Japan; it lost credit and prestige by failing to protect a member state, China, which from this time was unable to resist the further rise of Japanese power. None of the Great Powers of the League was willing to agree to the use of armed force or economic sanctions against Japan; nor was the United States willing to do more than protest and refuse to recognize the Japanese rule in Manchuria. The influence of Great Britain was strongly exerted to prevent action against Japan, because Britain had so large a stake in the trade of the Far East. The British preferred to appease the Japanese in the hope that they would moderate their ambitions and refrain from interference with

The Disarmament Conference convened sporadically from 1932 to 1937 and was deadlocked by the opposition of France (in the interest of its own security) to any plan that would strengthen Germany. (National Archives)

British commerce with China. Moreover, the British government was preoccupied by the difficulties in India and by the dangerous tensions the Nazi revolution in Germany was producing in Europe.

Failure of Disarmament Conference. In February 1932 the long-prepared conference for the reduction and limitation of military armaments opened at Geneva. All the Great Powers, including both the United States and the Soviet Union, were represented. Quickly it became deadlocked because of the inability to reconcile the differing views of France and Germany. The Germans insisted on a recognition of their equal rights; that is, abolition of the unequal status imposed on them by the armament clauses in the Treaty of Versailles. The French would not assent to this unless the League of Nations was strengthened by broader authority and an international army. The French feared that, without a stronger international security system, if they agreed to German equality of right the Germans would break through any treaty agreement and become militarily superior to France. Belgium, Poland, Czechoslovakia—all Germany's neighbors—agreed with the French view. All efforts by Britain and the United States to moderate the French stand failed.

Germany leaves the League. The Disarmament Conference continued to meet, while accomplishing nothing, for several years. Meanwhile the Nazis came to power and showed that they did not mean to waste time and talk at Geneva. In October 1933, Hitler ordered the withdrawal of the German delegates at Geneva and announced Germany's resignation from the League of Nations. Plainly he meant to open a new foreign policy entirely outside the framework of the League. Poland proposed to France that they take joint military measures to break up the armed and uniformed Nazi military organizations, but France did not agree. Whereupon the Poles lost faith in their alliance with France and made a non-aggression treaty with Germany. The French at this time were engaged in bitter internal disputes over public policies and measures.

The Austrian crisis. The small state of Austria, bereft of its former empire, had serious difficulties in maintaining its economic existence. It was German in language and culture, and a large part of the population had long desired to unite with Germany. This union was one of the great aims of the Nazis, and there was a large branch of the Nazi Party in Austria. On the other hand, the Austrian government at this time was headed by Chancellor Engelbert Dollfuss. A devout Catholic, he was sincerely outraged by the lawless conduct of the Nazis and was determined to maintain the independence of his country. In June 1933 he suppressed the Austrian Nazis as a party and turned to Italy for help in warding off a German seizure of Austria. Mussolini was strongly opposed to such an enlargement of Germany and agreed to support Austrian independence. When Hitler went to Italy in June 1934 to see Mussolini, the two leaders parted on very cool terms. The Italian dictator had strong support from both France and Great Britain for his policy of preserving Austrian independence. On July 25 the Austrian Nazis attempted

Engelbert Dollfuss (1892–1934), Chancellor of Austria, never wavered in his firm stand against Nazism. He was assassinated in an unsuccessful attempt by the Austrian Nazis to seize power. (Bildarchiv)

a revolution. They murdered Dollfuss but failed to gain control of the state. Mussolini sent an army to the Austrian frontier to counter the threat of German invasion, and Hitler saw that the time was not yet ripe for him to invade and annex Austria. So strong was the impulse to do so among the German Nazis that, shortly before the attempt in Austria, Hitler found it necessary to purge and discipline his own party. On June 30, 1934, he murdered many who were not obedient to his will in what was known as the "Blood Purge."

Soviet Russia joins the League. If Nazi Germany continued on its course, war in Europe seemed certain. Soviet Russia feared Germany would ally with Poland and lead other states in an attack on the communist empire. Hitler often talked of Germany's need for *Lebensraum,* or "living space," which meant undeveloped lands for exploitation, and indicated that this might be found in Russia. Hence, as Germany

rearmed, Stalin and the Bolshevik masters of the U.S.S.R. looked for possible allies in the West. At the same time France considered coming to some defensive understanding with the Soviet Union. The French took the lead in electing the Moscow government to the League of Nations in 1934. The Soviet Union became a permanent member of the League Council in the seat vacated by Germany. The communists hoped to make use of the League as a collective security instrument against the German menace. There was, however, a profound incompatibility between the League of Nations and the Soviet Union. The aim of the League was to protect peace; the aim of the Soviet Union was to defend and promote communism. Poland, Rumania, the Baltic States, and Turkey all took alarm at the thought that one day the Red Army might enter them to protect them against Germany.

German triumphs. Early in 1935 a plebiscite (popular vote) took place in the Saar region, under the auspices of the League of Nations, to determine whether the people wished to be under French or German rule. The Treaty of Versailles, which had placed this region under League administration for fifteen years, provided for a vote of the people at this time. The people had three choices: to be French, to be German, or to continue under the rule of the League. They voted overwhelmingly (by nine to one) to join Germany. Thus Germany recovered the first of the territories she had lost in 1919. It was a great triumph for the Nazi government and heightened its prestige. Two months later, on March 16, the

Hitler regime announced the introduction of a military draft (conscription) and Germany's repudiation of the Versailles limits on her armed forces. It was an open secret that she had long been violating the treaty's armament clauses; in fact, she had built the largest air force in the world. The former Allied Powers protested Germany's acts but did nothing to enforce the treaty. France's reply to this menace was to make a defensive alliance with the Soviet Union, which alarmed all Europeans who dreaded communism. The British government disapproved the French alliance with the communists and quickly made a treaty with Germany on naval armaments. The Germans interpreted Britain's action as indicating that she had no desire to join in any hostile combination against Germany. The British, in fact, were greatly alarmed at the power of the German air force and saw that they could not risk war with Germany until they had vastly increased their own power to strike from the air.

Italy attacks Ethiopia. Mussolini desired to enlarge Italy's colonial empire in East Africa and had designs on the state of Ethiopia, which was a member of the League of Nations. France, desiring to remain on good terms with Italy and to have Italian support against Germany's ambitions, indicated that she would place no obstacles in Mussolini's way. Great Britain, however, at this time held control of Egypt and was opposed to Italy's moving into Ethiopia; moreover, Italy could not do so without clearly violating her obligations as a member of the League. Nevertheless, Mussolini ordered Italian armies to advance into Ethiopia in October 1935. The resultant war lasted until the following spring, when the Ethiopian emperor, Haile Selassie, fled to Europe and Italy annexed the country. The League of Nations condemned Italy for her aggression and even voted to apply economic sanctions against her; this meant that most members of the League cut off or greatly reduced their commercial relations with Italy. Even the United States assisted this effort to some extent. But it did not succeed because the sanctions were not carried to the point of shutting off Italy's supply of oil. The failure of the League to restrain Italy was another disastrous blow to its prestige.

End of Locarno treaties. In March 1936,

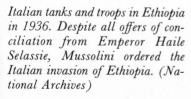

Italian tanks and troops in Ethiopia in 1936. Despite all offers of conciliation from Emperor Haile Selassie, Mussolini ordered the Italian invasion of Ethiopia. (National Archives)

while the war in Ethiopia was in its final phase, Germany violated both the Locarno treaties of 1925 and the Versailles treaty clauses that had committed Germany to the permanent demilitarization of the Rhineland. Hitler sent regular army troops into that region, but might have backed down and recalled them if France had defended her treaty right by armed force. The French, however, did not know that he was bluffing and shrank from "calling his bluff." They protested, as did other states, but nothing was done. Quickly the Germans began building powerful defensive fortifications that came to be known as their Siegfried Line or West Wall. Their purpose was to assure themselves against a French invasion when they moved to expand eastward. The French thus failed to make use of their last chance to check the rise of German power in Europe. French prestige

sank still lower. Mussolini now saw that he could no longer count on French or British aid in defending the independence of Austria and advised the Austrian Chancellor, Schuschnigg, to come to an understanding with Hitler.

Civil war in Spain. During 1935 the Soviet government, which dominated all communist parties in the world, decided to promote what were called "popular fronts." These were temporary combinations of all liberal, democratic, socialist, and communist parties for the defense of democracy against "fascism." The communists promoted the idea that all such parties had one common enemy, which was fascism; and fascism—so said the communists —was capitalism defending itself by means of violence. In Spain early in 1936 a popular-front organization won a victory in the national elections. The result was a government

Benito Mussolini, Count Ciano (Mussolini's son-in-law and one of the engineers of the Rome-Berlin Axis), and Adolf Hitler upon the occasion of Mussolini's state visit to Germany in 1937. (Ullstein)

made up of discordant political elements that failed to preserve civil order in the country. Violent anti-Catholics attacked and burned churches and monasteries, and the government did not even try to prevent these crimes. As a result, Spaniards who loved their country and were loyal to their religion revolted against the popular-front government of the republic. An able general, Francisco Franco, put himself at the head of the revolt, which began in July 1936. A terrible civil war raged in Spain for three years between Franco's nationalists and the forces of the popular front.

The Rome-Berlin Axis. The Italian and German governments gave aid to the Spanish nationalists, even to the extent of sending troops to fight for them. The Soviet Union sent aid and political advisers to the other side. France, where another popular-front government had been formed in 1936, was opposed to the nationalists but did not intervene. The British government sought to prevent all powers from intervening. The Italian and German governments painted the Spanish war as a great struggle against communism. In the fall of 1936 these two governments formed what was called the Rome-Berlin Axis. It was not yet an alliance but a declaration of their community of interest in promoting a new order of international relations in Europe. About the same time Japan and Germany signed an agreement to co-operate against international communism and to oppose the activities of the Communist International, which was the federation of communist parties under Moscow's direction. The

new treaty was known as the Anti-Comintern Pact. Italy adhered to it and later other states were brought into this strange alliance, which appeared to be pointed against the Soviet Union. At the end of 1936 it was clear that the world was on the way to war.

REVIEW

STUDY SECTIONS IN REVIEW

120. The Breakdown of World Capitalism

A. How did the protective tariff affect trade during the post-World War I period?

B. How did the American stock-market boom affect the economy of Germany?

C. What immediate advantage could be gained if a nation abandoned the gold standard?

D. What caused the failure of the London economic conferences of 1939?

121. The State and the Economic Crisis: Growth of Totalitarianism

A. Why did the depression bring about increased governmental responsibility for the common welfare?

B. What is the meaning of the term "socialistic liberalism"?

C. Note three objectives of the program of the National Socialists in Germany.

D. What were the purposes of the New Deal in the United States?

E. What was the proper role of the state according to the encyclical *Quadragesimo anno?*

122. The Crumbling of Peace and the Rupture of Treaties

A. Why did the Japanese invade Manchuria in 1931?

B. On what issues did Germany and France differ at the Disarmament Conference of 1932?

C. Why did Mussolini oppose Hitler's designs on Austria?

D. How did Hitler defy the Allied powers in 1935?

E. How did the Italian invasion of Ethiopia weaken the prestige of the League of Nations?

F. Identify: Franco, Rome-Berlin Axis, Anti-Comintern Pact.

THE CHAPTER IN REVIEW

A. Discuss the causes of the world depression of the post-World War I period.

B. Discuss the program and rise to power in 1933 of Hitler and his National Socialist Party.

C. Explain the gradual adoption of socialistic measures by democratic governments. How was this stimulated by the depression?

D. Trace the major steps taken by Hitler between his rise to power and the formation of the Rome-Berlin Axis of 1936.

FOR YOUR NOTEBOOK

Make a list of the causes of the depression as they are given in your text. Now consult your older relatives about what they remember. Were they aware of the causes given in the text? Does their knowledge in any way modify your list? (You will probably learn from this project that it is easier to see causes and effects *after* things have happened than when they are happening. This is one of the great values of history.)

The disruption of international trade was a complicated development. Enter into your notebook the factors that promoted it, such as higher tariffs and devalued money. In a single sentence explain each entry.

List five ideas or practices that each of the following *advocated,* and five each *opposed:* fascism, national socialism, liberalism, socialism, *Quadragesimo anno.* Fascism, for example, advocated a totalitarian state, and it opposed democracy.

Section 123 is called "Crumbling of Peace and Rupture of Treaties." Write down in one or two sentences how each of the following promoted this process:

Japanese seizure of Manchuria
Failure of the Disarmament Conference of 1932
Italy's attack on Ethiopia
Hitler's march into the Rhineland in 1936
The Spanish Civil War

SELECTED READINGS

The depression is brought home to the reader by Frederick Lewis Allen, *Since Yesterday* (New York: Harper & Bros., 1943), which is an informal history of the 1930's. Philip H. Gibb's novel, *The Cross of Peace* (New York: Doubleday & Co., 1934), deals with the tragic failure of World War I to secure peace, as seen by a French war veteran.

Stephen H. Roberts, *The House That Hitler Built* (London: Methuen & Co., 1938), is a very readable account of how Hitler came to power and consolidated Nazism in Germany. A lively study of Mussolini is George Seldes, *Sawdust Caesar* (New York: Harper & Bros., 1936), which tends to underrate the fascist leader's ability. Father Edmund Walsh analyzes the first Soviet Five-Year Plan in *The Last Stand* (Boston: Little, Brown & Co., 1931), and Joaquin Arrarás gives a sympathetic portrayal of the Spanish leader in *Francisco Franco, the Times and the Man* (Milwaukee, Wis.: Bruce Publishing Co., 1938).

Chapter 40. The Second World War

123. HOW EUROPE WENT TO WAR AGAIN IN 1939

A mighty whirlpool of forces over which statesmen lost all control drew Germany and Poland, France and Britain, into war in 1939. The war lasted nearly six years and spread until almost all the nations of the world were drawn into it.

By the end of 1936 most acute observers of the international scene regarded the coming war in Europe as virtually inevitable, for three reasons: *first,* the reckless and aggressive spirit of the Axis powers, Germany and Italy. *second,* the inability of France and Great Britain to agree on a common political strategy for restraining the Axis powers; *third,* the fear of communism, which made it impossible for the western Euro-

pean powers to come to a reliable defensive agreement with the Soviet Union.

During 1937 the Spanish Civil War continued without coming to a decision. It inflamed all political passions in Europe, partly because of the German-Italian and Soviet intervention and partly because it bore the appearance of a war between Catholics and anti-Catholics. Everywhere people tended to favor one side or the other, so that the French and the British peoples were divided in sentiment. Even in the United States the Spanish war was a subject of hot debate and argument. This kind of partisanship in a conflict that seemed to many a miniature of a greater war likely to come had a bewildering and paralyzing effect on the policies of Western democratic nations.

Resumption of war in China. Meanwhile, Japan in the summer of 1937 began large-scale military operations against the Chinese. The spirit of military aggression and determination to make their power dominant over China had entered into the Japanese army, which dominated the political government. Japan did not declare war on China, because she had renounced war as an instrument of policy by signing the 1928 Pact of Paris; Japan simply made war. Her aim was not to annex Chinese territory but to crush the Chinese nationalist movement and take control of Chinese economic life by means of a political protectorate. All of China's ports were placed under Japanese naval blockade, except a few that were left open out of consideration for other foreign powers; although these ports, too, were at the mercy of Japan. In 1936 the naval treaties of Washington, Geneva, and London terminated, and the Japanese had resumed a completely free hand in enlarging their forces. No power seriously challenged this Japanese aggression in China, although the United States was very seriously alarmed and sent a series of notes of protest to Tokyo.

The United States and the international scene. Fearful of a new war in which the United States might be involved, the Congress had passed a Neutrality Act in 1935 and re-enacted it with some changes in 1937 shortly before the Japanese resumed their warfare in China. These laws laid down various procedures whereby the country might isolate itself, although it was impossible for a world power as great as the United States to remain indifferent to the whirlpool of forces that were drawing the world into war. On October 5, 1937, President Roosevelt made a speech at Chicago recommending the "quarantine" of aggressors, which meant the severance of all economic and political relations with nations that made aggressive war. He compared lawless aggression (with veiled reference to Japan) with a physical disease, saying that "when an epidemic . . . starts to spread, the community . . . joins in a quarantine of the patients in order to protect the health of the community against the spread of the disease." However, the United States took no effective move to stop the war in China or in Spain. Even the deliberate sinking by the Japanese of the American gunboat *Panay* in the Yangtse River did not arouse anything more than an American demand for apology and damages. To this demand the Japanese government assented.

British policy of appeasement. During 1937, Neville Chamberlain became Prime Minister of Great Britain and

Neville Chamberlain (1869–1940), Prime Minister of Great Britain and signatory of the Munich Pact. The period of "appeasement" reached its apex with the signing of this agreement. (British Information Services)

conceived a policy which he hoped would reverse the trend toward war in Europe. He called the policy *appeasement*. It was an effort to moderate Hitler by a show of willingness to consider peaceful revision in Germany's favor of some of the territorial clauses of the Treaty of Versailles. Since Italy, with her new Ethiopian conquest and her forces fighting in Spain, was aspiring to dominate the Mediterranean, Chamberlain hoped to draw Germany away from Italy, to isolate Mussolini and induce him to behave in a manner more respectful to important British strategic interests; e.g., Gibraltar, Malta, and Egypt.

The fall of Austria. Hitler interpreted Chamberlain's policy as a sign of British fear and weakness and resolved to take advantage of it. He encouraged Italy to keep the British government alarmed in the Mediterranean while he pushed forward the project of union with Austria. Nazi agents, in the guise of "tourists" and "commercial travelers," swarmed into Austria during the winter of 1937–1938. Austrian Nazis created a turbulence of illegal activities, and Hitler made it plain that Germany would protect them. The Austrian Chancellor, Kurt Schuschnigg, in a last effort to preserve the independence of his country, announced on March 9 that a plebiscite would be held on this issue. Two days later German troops entered Austria to "restore order," and Hitler announced the union of the two countries. A brutal persecution was launched against all who opposed the union, and many thousands fled for their lives to other lands. No government offered any effective protest against this breach of the

treaties of 1919. Mussolini, who had defended Austrian independence four years earlier, publicly announced his willingness to accept the event that had happened. France and Britain filed formal protests at Berlin, but it was plain they did not mean to make a serious challenge. By all visible signs, union with Germany was overwhelmingly popular among the mass of Austrians at the time it occurred. None of the second-rank states of central-eastern Europe—Poland, Czechoslovakia, Hungary, or Yugoslavia—dared act to prevent Germany's aggression, although the result of it was to make them virtually helpless if Germany chose to strike again to the east. It was clear that the only conceivable combination of powers that might be able to check the ascent of Germany to dominance in Europe was a defensive alliance between France, Britain, and the Soviet Union. From this, however, the British shrank.

Renewed British appeasement. The next step in Chamberlain's policy of appeasing the ambitious and discontented Axis powers was the conclusion on April 16 of an agreement with Italy. It was generally expected that the Spanish Civil War would soon end. Italy agreed to withdraw her troops from Spain when the war was over, and Britain agreed to recognize Italian sovereignty in Ethiopia. This agreement was to take effect after the conclusion of the Spanish war. The British government was hopeful that such conciliation of Italy would draw her away from close collaboration with Germany. Mussolini, uneasy over the German acquisition of Austria, which made Italy and Germany territorial neighbors, at the time welcomed improved relations with Britain; but this disposition did not endure for long.

Czechoslovakia and the Munich Pact. Soon after the fall of Austria, Hitler directed his aims against the state of Czechoslovakia, which contained about three and a half million German-speaking inhabitants in the Sudeten region. Among them a powerful Nazi movement flourished and the leaders looked to Germany for support. Hitler championed their demands for "national self-determination" and threatened war against Czechoslovakia, which stood in alliance with both France and the Soviet Union. Great Britain attempted to mediate but without success. The crisis came to a head in late September 1938, when the German armies were poised to strike Czechoslovakia. Neville Chamberlain made two trips to Germany to confer with Hitler, and both the British and French governments advised the Czechs to seek conciliation with Germany. War was avoided when Hitler

Thomas Masaryk (1850–1937), first President of Czechoslovakia. After the collapse of the Austro-Hungarian monarchy, Masaryk served as President of the new republic until succeeded in 1935 by Eduard Beneš, who resigned after the dismemberment of the republic by the Munich Pact. (Wide World)

accepted a proposal from Mussolini for a four-power conference (Britain, France, Germany, Italy), which met at Munich on September 29 and allowed Hitler to have his way with Czechoslovakia. Germany annexed the Sudeten lands and acquired certain important privileges in what remained of Czechoslovakia. Poland was allowed by Germany to become an accomplice in this dictatorial violence and seized some four hundred square miles of former Czechoslovak territory around Teschen. Hungary, too, made territorial demands, which soon were granted. Thus during October the Czechoslovak state, which arose out of the dissolution of the Austro-Hungarian Empire in 1918, was reduced to little more than half of its territorial extent and could exist only on terms defined by Nazi Germany. All this took place in spite of Czechoslovakia's alliances with both France and the Soviet Union. These alliances and also the Franco-Italian alliance of 1935 were now considered to be dead. Hitler was master of central Europe and could proceed to further aggressions. The Munich conference and its decisions were a terrible blow to the prestige of Great Britain and France, who revealed no will whatever to stand up against Nazi lawlessness in Europe. Italy now drew closer to Germany and soon was agitating demands upon France for Corsica and Tunisia.

New Axis aggressions. In March, 1939, Hitler demonstrated beyond all doubt that he meant to make war. He seized the whole of what remained of Czechoslovakia and put it under a tyrannical protectorate. He took the city of Memel from Lithuania by threat of

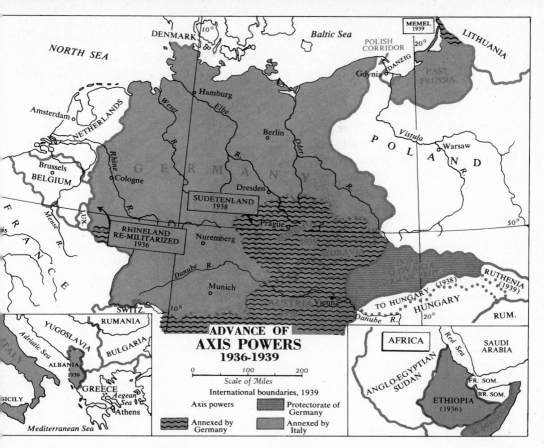

ADVANCE OF AXIS POWERS 1936-1939

Scale of Miles
0   100   200

International boundaries, 1939

Axis powers

Annexed by Germany

Protectorate of Germany

Annexed by Italy

armed force and submitted a list of demands to Poland. These included Polish approval of Germany's annexing the former German city of Danzig, which had been under administration by the League of Nations yet was closely linked to Poland economically, and the cession of a belt of territory through western Poland to give Germany overland communications with East Prussia. By the Treaty of Versailles, Poland had been awarded a large part of former eastern Germany in order to gain access to the Baltic Sea; thus a Polish "corridor" to the sea had severed East Prussia territorially from the rest of Germany. Through this "corridor" Hitler meant to have a German-controlled highway. Poland rejected all of the German demands.

With the eyes of the world on the German-Polish crisis, Italy in early April invaded and conquered Albania.

These grave events worked a change on the British and French governments. The policy of appeasement was cast aside by Chamberlain, who was convinced that Germany meant to dominate all Europe by force. France revitalized her alliance with Poland. Britain, having by this time vastly increased her air power, now began to enlarge her army by conscription and made a defensive alliance with Poland. Both Western powers began a feverish effort to create new alliances in eastern Europe and opened negotiations for a security pact with the Soviet Union.

Enraged at meeting unexpected obstructions, Hitler, on April 28 denounced the 1934 German-Polish non-aggression pact and the 1935 Anglo-German naval treaty. On May 22, Germany and Italy announced the formation of a military alliance which they called the "pact of steel."

Both Axis powers, moreover, had gained that spring what appeared to be a great triumph in Spain, where the civil war ended on March 28 in the complete victory of General Franco's forces. Italian and German military forces took part in a victory parade in Madrid, and in their propaganda the Axis powers claimed to have played a decisive part in the war.

Soviet policy. From 1934 to 1938, the Soviet Union had been periodically shaken by a series of Communist Party purges and treason trials, which Stalin instigated in order to destroy suspected disloyalty and consolidate his despotic power. In the summer of 1938 there was a brief undeclared war between Soviet and Japanese forces along the Siberian-Manchurian frontier. The Moscow government was greatly frightened by the threat of a German-Japanese military combination, especially after the Munich Pact, from which the Soviet Union had been excluded. That pact was interpreted at Moscow to mean that the British and French would give the Germans a free hand to pursue their expansion in eastern Europe. This circumstance, so reasoned the Soviet dictator, would lead to a German attack on the Soviet Union. Stalin resolved to ward off the threatened blow. When the British and French proposed a military alliance with the Soviet Union in 1939, the Russians feared a trap. They asked the Western powers to persuade Poland,

Rumania, and the Baltic States to admit Soviet forces to defensive positions; but all of these nations were as much afraid of communist protection as of German attack. Hence the negotiations were stalled.

German-Soviet Treaty. Meanwhile the German government resolved to seek an agreement with Soviet Russia to ensure Soviet neutrality when force was used against Poland. Stalin sensed that a German attack on Poland would probably involve Germany in war with Britain and France and decided to accept the German offer of a non-aggression pact. It was signed at Moscow on August 23, 1939, and announced to the world. It meant that the Poles could expect no support from the Soviet Union. There followed a frenzied week during which Hitler bore down on Poland, and the British and French governments exerted all possible pressure to stay the march of the German forces. The Polish government stood firm, confident that Britain and France would be faithful to their alliances. On September 1 the German army invaded Poland, piercing the Polish lines with armored divisions that moved

The people of Poland fought bravely although in vain to protect their country from German invasion. In Warsaw, women and children helped to dig trenches. (Wide World)

with great speed, while a mighty air attack caught most of the Polish aircraft on the ground and destroyed them. On September 3, Great Britain and France declared war on Germany. Canada and all the British dominions, except the Irish Free State, soon followed the example of Great Britain.

124. THE TIDE OF GERMAN SUCCESS IN WAR, 1939 TO 1940

The fall of Poland. The Poles were a brave and confident people and their military leaders believed their troops could hold their own against the Germans. Also, the Poles were counting on an Anglo-French attack to divert German forces to the west. This was an illusion. Poland was conquered in less than a month, and as she fell the Soviet forces, in agreement with Germany, invaded and occupied the eastern half of the country. The British and French created no diversion in the West. The former were not ready to do more than begin a naval blockade, and the latter had no spirit for starting an offensive. Although the French army was reputed to be the best in Europe, the French people were reluctant to go to war, and this spirit made itself felt in the army. During the 1930's France had constructed what was believed to be an impregnable line of defensive fortifications (the Maginot Line) along her eastern frontier. On this the French depended for security, and the instinct of the army was to man the Maginot Line instead of attempting an invasion of Germany. Hence the Western powers failed to aid the Poles, whose country was quickly partitioned by

Germany and the Soviet Union.

Hitler then announced that he saw no reason why the war should continue, and urged the British and French to make peace. As yet no other nation had entered the conflict. Italy, not yet ready for war, announced a state of "non-belligerency"—which seemed to mean that although she would maintain her alliance with Germany she was not prepared to fight. Spain, although under some obligations to the Axis powers, declared neutrality; and since the Germans had undertaken no aggression in the West, both Belgium and the Netherlands remained at peace. If the British had been willing to end the war, it is likely that the French would have agreed; but the British government was determined to remain at war until "Hitlerism" was abolished in Germany. The United States remained at peace, but the sympathies of the people and of the Roosevelt administration were with the Anglo-French cause against the Nazis. Hence it was likely that American aid would be given to that cause if the Germans launched a successful attack in western Europe. Japan was rudely shocked by the German policy of collaboration with the Soviet Union, and during the winter there was some vain expectation that Japan would associate herself with the Western powers.

The Russo-Finnish war. In the fall of 1939 the Soviet Union exacted by threat of force special rights to establish military, naval, and air bases in Latvia, Lithuania, and Esthonia. Hitler disliked this development, which plainly indicated Soviet distrust of Germany, but with Britain and France allied against him he could not afford to protest. When Moscow made similar demands on Finland they were refused. As a result Soviet troops invaded Finland. The Finns stoutly resisted until March of 1940, when they were compelled to cede the extensive region of Karelia to the Soviet Union. It was exasperating to the Germans to be compelled by the war with Britain and France to refuse the challenge of Soviet aggression in these Baltic countries, which had owed their very existence to German victories over Russia in World War I. At the time, however, it appeared to the world that the Soviet Union was acting in alliance with Germany. Officially and outwardly the Berlin government approved Soviet conduct. Had the Finnish war lasted a little longer, Franco-British aid would have reached the Finns. As it was, they fought alone, their neighbor Sweden refusing aid and keeping to a strict neutrality.

The Germans pounce on Denmark and Norway. In order to prevent the shipment of Swedish iron ore in German vessels from Narvik in northern Norway through Norwegian territorial waters to the Baltic and thence to German ports, Britain and France decided to lay mines in Norwegian waters. The Germans suddenly reacted on April 9, 1940. Quietly their troop transports were sent into Norwegian ports where surprise attacks were launched. At the same time the Germans seized the small state of Denmark. British and French troops went to Norway to aid in the fight against the Germans, but the latter quickly got the upper hand. The Norwegian royal family was forced to take refuge in England, and the Germans created a new government headed by a pro-Nazi Norwegian traitor, Major Vidkun Quisling. In Denmark, King Christian X remained with his people and helped to moderate their suffering under German occupation. Strategically, the seizure of Denmark and Norway was of great advantage to the Germans. They acquired new bases for their submarines and forced the British navy to undertake additional defense measures which dispersed its strength. If the Soviet Union were to become hostile to Germany and seek an alliance with the Western powers, the Baltic was barricaded against a British penetration. The success of the pounce on these Scandinavian countries, especially Norway, was very disheartening to the Western powers. It created an awesome sense of German skill and ruthlessness.

The blitzkrieg in the West. On May 10 the Germans opened an action that was designed to bring a quick end to the war. Powerful armored divisions supported by overwhelming air superiority struck into Holland, Belgium, and through Luxembourg into France, swinging around the northern end of the Maginot Line. They moved so swiftly that the action was compared to lightning; hence it was known as a *Blitzkrieg,* which in German means "lightning war." The Low Countries were paralyzed in a few days. The main French and British armies were separated. The whole of the British forces and a large body of French were driven to the beaches of the French port of Dunkirk, where they were heroically rescued by transport vessels, cruisers, destroyers, and every craft that could be mobilized in England (May 28–June 4). The German armies moved on Paris, from which the French government, headed by Paul Reynaud, fled. On June 10, Italy, sure that France was falling and that Britain must sue for peace, declared war on those countries in order to have a share in the victory. A new French government was formed to treat with the Germans. At its head was Henri-Philippe Pétain, the aged marshal who had held Verdun against the Germans in 1916 and was a national hero. On June 22, France surrendered to humiliating armistice terms. They were signed in exactly the same spot (Compiègne) and in the same railroad car in which, twenty-two years before, Marshal Foch had received the surrender of the Germans. Hitler had that car brought from Les Invalides, a Paris military museum, for dramatic emphasis. He was photographed dancing a jig on the scene of this great reversal of the fortunes of war. By the armistice of 1940, the French army was totally disarmed and about three-fifths of France was placed under German occupation.

The Position of Britain. On the day the Germans began their blitz in western Europe, a cabinet crisis occurred in

Sir Winston Churchill (1874–) (Cecil Beaton for British Information Services)

London. Parliamentary attacks on Chamberlain's cabinet for incompetence in conducting the war led to the formation of a new administration headed by Winston Churchill. He had been the outstanding advocate of re-arming in the years before the war and had entered the Chamberlain government, first as head of the Admiralty and then as defense minister. A descendant of John Churchill, first Duke of Marlborough, the new Prime Minister had long been a brilliant and eloquent political leader—perhaps the most talented one of the century, and certainly the "man of the hour" in 1940. As France was giving up the fight, he told the British people:

The whole fury and might of the enemy must very soon be turned upon us. Hitler knows he will have to break us in this island or lose the war.

If we can stand up to him all Europe may be freed and the life of the world may move forward into broad sunlit uplands; but if we fail, the whole world, including the United States and all that we have known and cared for, will sink into the abyss of a new Dark Age made more sinister and perhaps more prolonged by the lights of a perverted science.

Let us therefore brace ourselves to our duty and so bear ourselves that if the British Commonwealth and Empire last for a thousand years, men will say "This was their finest hour."

Hitler announced now that he was ready to make peace with Britain, but it was clear that such a peace would place Great Britain under a German political protectorate. Churchill rallied the nation for a defense that to many appeared completely hopeless. The army rescued from Dunkirk had abandoned all its tanks, armored vehicles, and artillery, and there were not enough rifles and machine guns in the country to defend it against invasion. The navy, however, was intact and, although the world did not suspect it, the British had a powerful air defense.

The German dilemma. Had Hitler's forces been ready to mount an invasion of England in June 1940, the British might have been conquered, but they were not ready for such an undertaking. Moreover, events in eastern Europe were causing the Germans a serious concern. The Soviet Union at this time annexed outright the three Baltic States and forced Rumania to yield the territory of Bessarabia, which had once been part of the Russian Empire. Stalin clearly was taking up positions that would better enable the Soviet Union to defend itself in the event of a breach with Germany; he also was using an opportunity to enlarge the spread of communist power. These developments made it strategically necessary for Germany to bring the war in the West to an end. Hence Hitler rejected a Spanish proposal to enter the war against Britain, and refused to allow Mussolini to appropriate French territory in Africa, and displayed comparative moderation toward defeated France. Such a policy was aimed at inducing the British to quit the war without further fighting.

The Battle of Britain. During the early summer of 1940 the United States reinforced the British with large quantities of small arms that would be useful in the event of an attempted German invasion. Churchill heroically rejected every German suggestion for peace, defied Hitler to do his worst, and encouraged the Soviet Union to worry him in the East. Hence Hitler had no choice but to try to smash the British if he was to free himself for a move against the Soviet. Before the Battle of Britain began, he had already resolved to make war against the communist empire. To Air Marshal Hermann Goering, creator and commander of the German air force (*Luftwaffe*), he assigned the task of pulverizing the industries, railways, and cities of Great Britain—to destroy the ability of Britain to continue the war, to beat her flat. This campaign started during July, was stepped up in August until a thousand bombing planes daily were over the British Isles, and continued in full force into November. At the same time German submarines attempted to maintain a blockade of Britain and succeeded in taking a dreadful toll of her shipping. The Royal Air Force (R.A.F.), however, proved itself a match for Goering's bombers—in fact, more than a match. Although a large part of London was destroyed and almost every industrial city in Britain was terribly gutted by blast and fire, the British flyers succeeded in shooting down three times as many German planes as they lost of their own. By November the Battle of Britain had been lost by the Germans, and Hitler saw that his master problem now had been reversed. It was no longer the problem of knocking out Britain in order to deal with Russia, but of removing the growing Russian menace in order to concentrate anew against Britain.

The United States and Great Britain. The American government was firmly committed to the proposition that Great Britain must not fall. In September 1940 the British were enabled to ac-

The effect of Hitler's invasion in Britain is shown in the damage caused to Westminister Abbey in 1941. Led by the inspiration of Churchill, the English won their battle. (British Information Services)

quire fifty American destroyers to fight the submarine menace, in exchange for giving the United States a lease of air bases in Newfoundland, Bermuda, and the British West Indies and Caribbean colonies. The United States also began to prepare for possible entry into the war by passing a conscription law to enlarge the army and by vastly increasing its production of tanks, guns, ships, and airplanes. A large part of this production was earmarked for British purchase. The Germans were well aware of the vast industrial capacity of the United States. If, as seemed likely, it was put at the service of Britain, Hitler knew that he must destroy that country's ability to fight, or lose the war. But to succeed, the Russian menace had first to be removed.

125. THE WORLD-WIDE SPREAD OF THE WAR

The failure to knock the R.A.F. from the skies was not the only reverse the Germans suffered before the end of

1940. General Franco of Spain sensed that the war might ultimately go against Germany and shrank from joining her even when Hitler changed his mind and urged Spain to become an active ally against Britain. The Italians, moreover, suffered humiliating defeats that were highly embarrassing to Germany. Their forces in North Africa advanced against the British in Egypt during September 1940, with the capture of the Suez Canal as their aim. In December, however, the British counterattacked and drove them back in disorderly retreat. Also, Mussolini in October made demands on Greece, a country that leaned on Britain for support. The demands were rejected; as a result, an Italian army attempted to invade Greece from Albania. The Greeks not only repulsed the invaders but pursued them into Albania. In November, British naval aircraft attacked the Italian naval base at Taranto and destroyed or disabled the most important units of Mussolini's navy. It was plain from the start that the Italians had no appetite for fighting an aggressive war; they would require German aid to accomplish anything valuable to the Axis alliance.

Early in 1941 the British took over Italian East Africa, restoring Haile Selassie to the throne of Ethiopia. Everything that had been gained by Italy in the Ethiopian War was now lost.

Germany prepares to attack Soviet Russia. As the air battle over Britain remained undecided and the Italians were advancing upon Egypt, Germany in October took control of Rumania, which was the principal source of oil for the Axis. The act was a warning to the Soviet Union. The next month the Soviet foreign minister, Molotov, was invited to Berlin, where Hitler unfolded before him a plan for the Soviet to join the Axis. The plan was for a combination of Germany, Italy, Japan, and Soviet Russia to partition the British Empire and jointly to dominate the world. Molotov and his master, Stalin, viewed this proposal suspiciously, fearing a German trap; they neither accepted nor rejected it, but chose to prolong negotiations. As a result, Hitler on December 18 issued a fateful order to the German army: to prepare for an attack on the Soviet Union. "The German armed forces," said Hitler, "must be prepared to crush Soviet Russia in a quick campaign even before the conclusion of the war with England." The preparations were kept in the deepest secrecy. Stalin and Molotov were so deceived that they did not know what the Germans were up to until the very eve of the German attack, which came in the following June.

Subjugation of the Balkans. Before invading Russia, the Germans deemed it necessary to establish control of the Balkans. During the winter of 1940–1941, Hungary, Bulgaria, and Yugoslavia were compelled to join the Axis and admit German troops. Hitler sent an expedition of troops under the command of General Erwin Rommel early in 1941 to spearhead a new Italian advance against the British in North Africa. In March, however, Hitler's plans were rudely upset by a revolt in Yugoslavia against the Regent Prince Paul and his ministers, who had slavishly bowed to the German dictator's will. Enraged at this defiance and at the Greeks for their defeat of the Italians, Hitler sent his armies from Hungary and Bulgaria into Yugoslavia and Greece. During April and May of 1941 both countries passed under Axis control. Even the island of Crete, which most military experts were sure the British navy could protect, was captured by German parachute troops. German success in the Balkans might have been prevented or at least delayed if Turkey, a British ally, had entered the war. The Turks now were compelled by dangerous circumstances to put on their best behavior for the Germans; Turkey did not, however, join the Axis alliance. The British sent military aid to the Greeks and thereby weakened their own men in North Africa. This fact enabled General Rommel to drive them back. Such was the general position of things when the German armies, on June 22, began the invasion of Russia.

American Lend-Lease Act. Franklin D. Roosevelt had been re-elected President in November 1940. Confident of public support, he resolved to give additional support to Great Britain, which was running short of the dollar credits needed to buy war materials in the United States. Proclaiming America as "the Arsenal of Democracy," he proposed to Congress a bill to authorize the President to lend or lease its weapons to any country willing to fight the Axis alliance. Congress passed the bill in March 1941. The reason was not mere pro-British sentiment but the conviction of political leaders that defeat of Britain by Germany would imperil the security of the United States. The British Empire and Commonwealth would dissolve and great parts of it would be thrown into dependence on the United States. Europe, Asia, and Africa would fall under control of powers unfriendly to the United States. South America would lie open to economic and political penetration by a German-dominated Europe; while the mastery of the Pacific might be seized by Japan. The Lend-Lease Act, in reality, marked the end of American neutrality and the beginning of participation in the war.

President Roosevelt and Prime Minister Churchill on the occasion of the signing of the Atlantic Charter. In 1942 the United Nations Declaration pledged adherence to the principles of the Atlantic Charter. (British Information Services)

The Atlantic Charter. As German armored divisions were cutting their way through western Russia, Churchill and Roosevelt met aboard a warship off Newfoundland on August 14 and drafted a set of written aims that were known as the Atlantic Charter. The document won the admiration of the civilized world. The two leaders renounced all desire of annexations, defended the right of all peoples to determine their own form of government, called for restoring conquered peoples to independence, and restated the fundamental principles of international morality. The Charter was understood to be a definition of the great purposes of policy on the part of Great Britain and the United States.

The fighting in Russia. The tactics of the blitzkrieg were employed by the Germans, but the vast expanse of Russia rendered them futile. One army broke through the Baltic States toward Leningrad; another advanced straight toward Moscow; a third burst into the Ukraine. The whole German operation was aided by the Finns in the north and the Rumanians in the south. The grand aim was to pierce, cut up, drive the Red army into pockets by various pincer-like maneuvers, and destroy it; but the main body of that army was far to the east along the line of the Dnieper River. Thus the Germans during the first month encountered only frontier guards and advance posts. Great indecisive battles were fought in July and August on the upper Dnieper in the region of Smolensk and Gomel, and the German advance on Moscow was stopped; but to the north a siege of Leningrad was begun and in the south the whole of the Ukraine was conquered by the Germans. By October 1941 the Germans were able to mount a new offensive on the center of the front several hundred miles from Moscow. That city was not only the Soviet capital but the communications center of Russia, the railways going out from it like spokes from the hub of a wheel. The Germans pressed forward until they were only thirty miles from Moscow, but could get no farther in the severity of the Russian winter. On December 6 the Soviet forces took the offensive and Hitler's army went into winter retreat. Although Hitler announced to the world that the Soviet Union was beaten, the fact was that German strategy had failed. It had aimed at smashing the Red army in one campaign and capturing Moscow. This had not been accomplished.

Britain, America, and Soviet Russia. When the attack on the Soviet Union started, Prime Minister Churchill, although a militant enemy of communism, announced that Great Britain would ally herself in war with any nation that fought against Nazi Germany. Soon an Anglo-Soviet war alliance was made. Soon, too, the United States adopted the policy of extending material aid to Soviet Russia by authority of the Lend-Lease Act. These developments marked a political defeat for Hitler, who had painted his attack on Russia as a great European anti-communist crusade in the hope that Western sentiments would become less hostile to Nazi Germany American and British leaders, however, feared Hitler's power far more than that of communist Russia.

The Japanese Attack. The Tokyo government had been watching the war in Europe with an eye to seizing opportunities for its own advantage. Japanese leaders at first were gravely alarmed at the apparent Nazi-Soviet collaboration, since they had seen in Soviet Russia their most dangerous enemy. This fear did not prevent them, however, from forcing their occupation on French Indo-China after the fall of France in 1940. In September of that year a German-Japanese-Italian alliance was announced; by it Japan agreed to recognize the New Order the Nazis were creating in Europe, and the Axis powers agreed to allow Japan a free hand to create a new order in "Greater East Asia." This development gravely alarmed the government of the United States, which had long been doing what it could to obstruct Japanese territorial expansion. It was evident that the Japanese had designs on the Philippines and the rich archipelago of the East Indies. Since the end of World War I they had held the central Pacific islands lying between Hawaii and the Philippines and had heavily fortified them. In this whole region the United States had only three small weakly defended islands, Guam, Wake, and Midway. Britain was too heavily engaged with Germany to be able to defend Malaya and British Borneo against Japanese attack, and the Dutch East Indies lay equally open to such danger. Nor did Australia possess the means to beat off a Japanese attack on New Guinea and the Bismarck archipelago. Thus the way lay open to the capture of a vast empire by Japan, while all fear of Soviet Russia was banished by the German invasion. On December 7, 1941, the Japanese be-

In the surprise attack of the Japanese on Pearl Harbor, eight battleships and other warcraft were seriously damaged or sunk. "Remember Pearl Harbor" became the battle slogan of the Americans. (Official U. S. Navy Photograph)

gan their new aggressions with a surprise attack on the United States fleet at Pearl Harbor in Hawaii. At the same time they moved against the Philippines and Malaya. The strategy of the attack on Pearl Harbor was to cripple or destroy the only force that appeared able to interfere with their designs. The United States at once declared war on Japan. The German leaders rejoiced; it appeared that the attention of the United States would be directed away from the war in Europe. Both Italy and Germany kept faith with Japan by declaring war on the United States a few days after the Japanese attack.

New British-American strategy. Instead of meeting the Japanese challenge by quick offensive retaliation, the American and British governments formed a common strategy that aimed at merely holding defensive positions as long as possible, while concentrating first against the European Axis powers. This meant aiding the Red army with all manner of supplies and weapons in order to force the Germans to waste

their strength on the Russian front. The strategy proved effective. Although the Philippines, Malaya, most of the East Indies, Burma, Guam, and Wake fell to the Japanese in the first half of 1942, a great naval disaster was inflicted upon them by U. S. naval and air units in the waters around Midway Island (June 4–7), and a little later American marines opened what was to prove a successful effort to save the Solomon Islands. Meanwhile the Soviet Union was massively reinforced.

The United Nations. Prime Minister Churchill and his staff went to Washington to plan this strategy with President Roosevelt in December 1941. A close British-American war alliance, with combined chiefs of staff, was formed. On January 1, 1942, the United States, Great Britain and her dominions, the Soviet Union, China, and all the Central American and Caribbean states that had followed the United States into the war signed the Declaration of Washington. They pledged themselves to make no separate peace with their enemies, to prosecute the war to a successful conclusion, and to accept the principles of the Atlantic Charter. In this general war alliance they described themselves as the United Nations. Such was the origin of that great association, although it was nothing more than a war alliance at the beginning.

126. REVERSING THE FORTUNES OF WAR

During 1942 the vast industrial power of the United States was rapidly geared for war in East and West, and this power was to prove decisive for the military success of the grand alliance. Not until the fall of the year, however, did events make it plain that the fortunes of war had been reversed in favor of the United Nations.

Stalingrad, El Alamein, French North Africa. During the summer the Germans launched a new offensive on the Russian front. It was aimed at capturing the Soviet oil resources in the Caucasus and shutting off the flow of American aid that passed through Iran to Russia. Hitler's forces failed to hold Stalingrad on the Volga River in Novem-

ber and never recovered the initiative on this front. At the same time the contest on the deserts of North Africa took a decisive turn. During May and June, Rommel led his German-Italian army in a sweeping drive into Egypt, but on October 23 the British Eighth Army, commanded by the brilliant General Bernard Montgomery, defeated Rommel at El Alamein and drove him out of Egypt. While Rommel was retreating westward, an American-British expedition directed by General Dwight D. Eisenhower invaded French North Africa. This

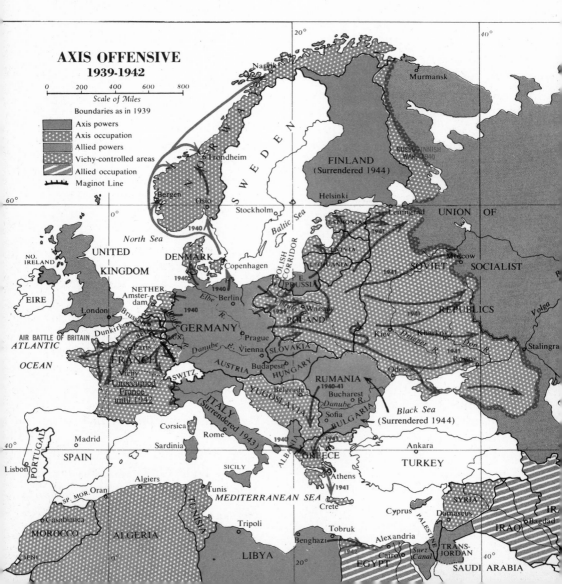

AXIS OFFENSIVE
1939-1942

Scale of Miles
0   200   400   600   800

Boundaries as in 1939

Axis powers
Axis occupation
Allied powers
Vichy-controlled areas
Allied occupation
Maginot Line

region—Morocco, Algiers, Tunisia—at the time was under the rule of officials responsible to the French government that had surrendered to Germany. In Morocco and Algiers they quickly capitulated to Eisenhower; but the invaders failed in Tunisia, which was rapidly reinforced by German-Italian troops. Also, the Germans used this occasion to extend their occupation to the whole of France in Europe, thus adding another burden of defense to their already dangerous position.

Unconditional surrender. Roosevelt and Churchill met at Casablanca in Morocco in January 1943 to develop further war plans. Stalin was invited to join them but refused to come. The American and British war leaders announced that their countries would prosecute the war until their enemies surrendered unconditionally. During the next nine months Tunisia was conquered, clearing Africa of Axis troops, Sicily was conquered, and southern Italy was invaded. Perceiving that his country had lost the war, King Victor Emmanuel dismissed Mussolini and placed him under arrest. A new Italian minister, Pietro Badoglio, then negotiated an unconditional surrender (September 3, 1943). The American and British forces, however, were unable to receive what they had demanded. The Germans seized control of almost the whole of Italy and rescued Mussolini, who created a puppet government under Hitler's protection. The Germans also captured Italy's Dodecanese islands at the mouth of the Aegean Sea. The British fought for them but failed. The Italian king and his Prime Minister took refuge with the British-American armies in south-

General of the Army Douglas MacArthur (1880–) (U. S. Army Photograph)

ern Italy. Thus only the Italian government—not the country itself—was surrendered.

As these Mediterranean campaigns were developing, the German Sixth Army at Stalingrad was surrounded, isolated, and forced to surrender (February 2, 1943). Thereafter the Russian front moved steadily westward. A steel net was closing against German-held Europe.

Japanese defeats. In the Pacific theater, too, the reversal in the fortunes of war was evident. The Japanese were decisively beaten in a great naval battle in the waters off the Solomon Islands about the same time French North Africa was being invaded (November 1942); and in New Guinea offensive military operations against Japan were under way. They were directed by General Douglas MacArthur, the outstanding soldier of World War II. He had commanded the small American and native forces in the Philippines when Japan attacked.

Early in 1942 President Roosevelt had ordered him to turn over his besieged troops to his subordinate, Jonathan Wainright, and make his way to Australia. He was then made Supreme Allied Commander of the whole South Pacific war theater. In 1943 he directed combined military, aerial, and naval offensives, by-passing Japanese-held positions and cutting their communications. At the same time American naval forces and marines took the Gilbert Islands from the Japanese. Their newly won empire was slipping from their possession.

Teheran and Cairo conferences. As the tide turned against the Axis powers, fear arose that the Soviet Union and the Western powers would fall into disagreement over war aims. Dictator Stalin was not only a ruthless communist but a man whose ways were secretive and mysterious to British and American officials. Some wondered if, when the Germans were forced from the Soviet Union, Stalin might not choose to make a separate peace with them, thus returning to the policy of 1939. This fear explained to a considerable degree why the Western powers showed such generosity in aiding the Soviet Union without exacting any conditions for it. They sought to accommodate Stalin in every possible way, but he showed no such disposition toward them. In November 1943, Roosevelt and Churchill went to confer face to face with Stalin at Teheran in Iran. There Stalin agreed that no peace would be made until Germany was totally conquered and the Western armies met the Red army on German soil. Stalin agreed also to make war on Japan after the conquest of Ger-

Pope Pius XII (1876–) (Fototeca Unione, Roma)

many; while the Western leaders agreed to increase the flow of aid to Russia and to launch a massive assault on the Germans in Europe in the spring of 1944. Churchill had serious misgivings about the coming of communist armies to the heart of Europe, but Roosevelt confidently believed he could exert a beneficent influence on Soviet policy.

From Teheran, Roosevelt and Churchill went to Cairo to meet the Chinese leader, Chiang Kai-shek. They agreed to enlarge military aid to China and, when Japan was brought to unconditional surrender, to dismember her empire. It was stipulated that China should be totally freed of Japanese domination and should gain back Manchuria and Formosa; that the Japanese should be removed from all Pacific islands acquired in World War I, and that an independent Korea should be established.

The papal appeal for peace. Pope Pius XII, who had succeeded Pius XI in 1939 and done everything within his power to prevent the war, saw clearly that no good was likely to result from fighting the war to the bitter end of unconditional surrender. He saw, too, the terrible danger to Christian civilization that must come with a complete victory of the Soviet Union in eastern and central Europe. In his Christmas broadcast, 1943, he urged the statesmen of the world to set themselves at "the task of securing agreement and concord between the warring nations." This wise appeal was ignored by the United Nations alliance.

The liberation of France. The Soviet armies, which were accustomed to winter fighting, in the early months of the year 1944 moved steadily westward toward the Polish and Rumanian frontiers. Hard fighting on the front in southern Italy culminated in the capture of Rome on June 4 by an international army of Americans, British, Free French, and Polish soldiers. Two days later the long-prepared invasion of German-held France was launched from England under the supreme command of General Eisenhower.

This was the greatest military offensive across the sea in the history of the world. To make it possible, more than a million and a half American troops were assembled in Britain, and every other war theater was skimped in materials. Nothing could guarantee its success, for the Germans had left nothing undone to fortify the Atlantic coast of France, Belgium, and Holland. Had it failed, the outcome of the war might have been very different. Soviet Russia might have decided to make a separate settlement with Germany, and the Germans were developing new and more terrible weapons of war that might have prevented another assault from Great Britain. General George Marshall, the American Army Chief of Staff, later defined the necessity of the great attack: "These conclusions seemed inescapable: France must be invaded in 1944, to shorten the war by facilitating the advance westward of the Soviet forces. At the same time German technological advances such as in the development of atomic explosives made it imperative that we attack before these terrible weapons could be turned against us."

The attack succeeded. The beaches of Normandy were gained and held and massively reinforced. Next came the break-through of American armored divisions and the second Battle of France. By August 25, Paris

American assault troops landing on Omaha Beach during the Normandy campaign. The Allies used 4,000 troop transports, 800 warships, and more than 11,000 airplanes in their efforts to liberate France. (U. S. Army Photograph)

was entered by Allied forces. By September, all France and Belgium were cleared of the Germans. During the same summer months the Germans were driven from central Italy to new defense positions in the north, while the Red army advanced into Rumania, Finland, and the pre-1939 lands of Poland.

Attempted revolution in Germany. In the midst of this general cave-in of German military positions to the west, east, and south, a conspiracy of German patriots who had long hated the Nazi regime came to a head in an effort to murder Hitler, seize power, and negotiate an end to the war. High-ranking generals and other military officers as well as many civil officials were enlisted in this effort. They hoped to ward off total ruin of their country and to surrender to the Western powers in order to prevent a Russian invasion. Secret contacts with these powers failed to win any aid or encouragement. When the bomb planted in Hitler's headquarters failed to kill him, the conspiracy failed and the leaders of it were executed.

Soviet conquests in the Balkans. Instead of driving straight against Germany through Poland, the Red army in the fall of 1944 moved for the conquest of Hungary and the Balkans. Rumania and Bulgaria surrendered. Contact was made with revolutionary Yugoslav forces, known as partisans, who were fighting the German occupying forces in their country and emerging as its rulers. Their leader was Joseph Broz, who called himself Tito. He was a militant communist revolutionary who had been trained in Russia. The only Balkan country that did not pass from

German to Soviet control was Greece. Churchill made an agreement with Stalin in October 1944 for British troops to go to that country. Nevertheless, Greek communists tried to get control and would continue to fight for it until several years after the end of World War II.

Germany invaded. On the Western front, the tide of advance was slowed in September. At a few points British, American, and French troops were on German soil, confronting the strongly defended West Wall. The Germans, however, were still holding Holland and barring passage by the Scheldt Estuary to the port of Antwerp. General Eisenhower was convinced that no further advance should be made until Allied supplies could be brought by sea to that port. General Bernard Montgomery, second-in-command, believed it possible to mount a rapid invasion north of the West Wall right on to Berlin and end the war. Eisenhower overruled him in favor of more cautious tactics because of the supply difficulties. Not until these were overcome could a general advance be made into Germany.

Last German counterattacks. During the second Battle of France the Germans introduced new terrifying weapons—rocket bombs—which were launched from bases in Belgium and Holland to fall upon London and other places in Great Britain. Flying faster than the speed of sound, they dropped and exploded without warning that they were on their way. Apart from inflicting additional horrors on the war-wearied British, this weapon did not influence the result of the fighting. In mid-December, however, the Western

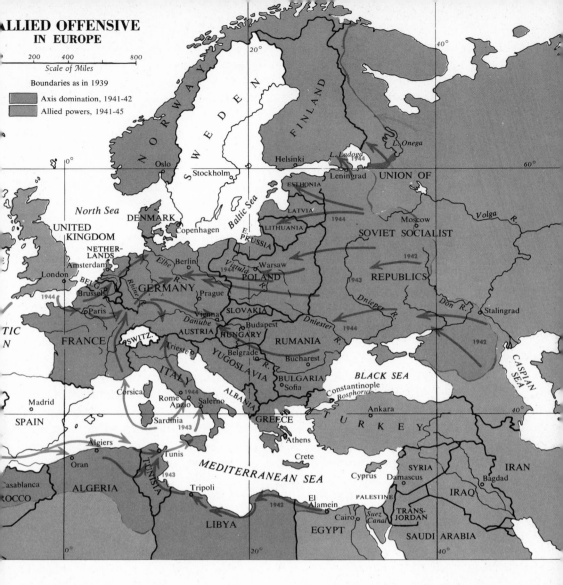

200 400   800
Scale of Miles
Boundaries as in 1939

Axis domination, 1941-42
Allied powers, 1941-45

forces were struck a reeling blow when the Germans broke through the lines in Luxembourg. For ten days they pushed forward, penetrating fifty miles and making a great bulge in the Allied lines. The effort was doomed from the start, for complete German defeat was now inevitable. By the end of December the Battle of the Bulge, as it was called, ended in German retreat. Early in January 1945, with the Red army at Warsaw and threatening a break-through across flat country to Berlin, the Germans counterattacked the Soviet forces in Hungary in one more unsuccessful maneuver to delay the inevitable.

MacArthur returns to the Philippines. Throughout 1944 the war went steadily against Japan. American naval forces continued their steady advance through the central Pacific, and General MacArthur's island-hopping campaign brought the Americans to the Philippines on October 19. The reconquest of those islands was thus started.

127. VICTORY OF THE UNITED NATIONS

On January 12, 1945, the Red army began a powerful drive through western Poland and by mid-February penetrated Germany to within thirty miles of Berlin. When this advance started, the Western armies were still recovering from the Battle of the Bulge and hence were not yet ready for the final actions against Germany. The onward movement of Soviet forces was at once applauded and feared by Western leaders. Stalin was supporting a new government for Poland: a communist regime that was deeply disapproved by the West. It seemed likely that throughout central-eastern Europe communist power would be established.

The Yalta Conference. In order to renew agreements and understandings, Roosevelt and Churchill traveled to Yalta in the Soviet Crimea to meet Stalin. That they went to him instead of his going to them indicated that his negotiating position was the stronger. The meeting occurred February 7–12. A plan to partition Germany into zones of military occupation by Britain, the United States, Soviet Russia, and France was made. Stalin promised that the peoples of Soviet-dominated eastern Europe would be allowed free elections to form "democratic" governments friendly to Soviet Russia. Roosevelt made far-reaching concessions to Stalin in order to win his good will and a promise to enter the war against Japan not later than three months after the final defeat of Germany. At

this time the President and his advisers believed that a massive invasion of the Japanese homeland would be necessary in order to exact an unconditional surrender. Hence a Soviet attack on Japan seemed then desirable. The "Big Three"—as they were popularly called—pledged themselves to call an international conference at San Francisco on April 25 to establish a new permanent international organization in place of the defunct League of Nations.

The fall of Germany. In the three months following the Yalta Conference military events moved fast. The Western armies broke through the West Wall and ran almost at will through Germany, seeking, however, to keep within the territorial zones determined at Yalta. The Red Army closed in upon Berlin. One impulse seemed to pervade the German people: to surrender to the Western armies and escape from Soviet conquest. The Yalta agreements

Eduard Beneš (1887–1948), second President of Czechoslovakia. Beneš headed a provisional government during the war and in 1945, he was confirmed in office. Beneš served until 1948 when he refused to sign the new constitution under the communists. (Wide World)

were kept, however, and Eisenhower held back his forces so that Berlin would fall to the Russians. Hitler remained at Berlin, where he took his own life on April 30. The Red army had by then surrounded the capital and was shelling it. A German effort to create a new non-Nazi government to treat with the conquerors failed. Military leaders surrendered unconditionally to Eisenhower at Reims in northeastern France on May 7, and to the Soviet commander, Marshal Zhukov, in Berlin on the following day. Shortly before these surrenders, the German-Italian defenders in northern Italy gave up the fight. Mussolini attempted to escape to Switzerland but was caught and murdered by antifascists. The European Axis powers were defeated, conquered, and occupied by their enemies. Early in June an Allied Control Committee composed of the principal military commanders assumed supreme power over the affairs of all Germany. Wholesale arrests of Nazi military and civilian leaders took place, preparatory to trying them for crimes.

The Potsdam Conference. Early in July the Big Three met again at Potsdam (near Berlin) to settle a variety of questions touching the occupation of Germany and the levying of war reparations. By this time President Roosevelt had died (April 12) and was succeeded by Harry S. Truman. During the conference a general election in Britain swept Churchill and his Conservative Party from office and brought in a Labor (Socialist) Party government headed by Clement Attlee. Thus new and less experienced leaders spoke for Britain and America. They found in

The Big Three—Prime Minister Churchill, President Truman, and Premier Stalin —as they relaxed in the palace garden before the meeting of the Potsdam Conference. (U. S. Army Photograph)

Stalin and Molotov hard and determined negotiators, interested only in consolidating Soviet control in eastern Europe, in stripping Germany of her machines and factories, and in adding much German territory to the new communist-dominated Poland. Not wishing to quarrel with Soviet Russia while the war against Japan continued, the Western leaders agreed to more severe treatment of Germany than they might otherwise have done. Split into zones of military government, that country was subjected to far-reaching political, civil, social, economic, and educational reforms. These were aimed at the ultimate establishment of "democracy." With their cities in ruin, their economic life crushed, their vast armies held as prisoners of war, Germans had paid a terrible cost for having submitted to the Nazi dictatorship.

No greater disaster has fallen upon a nation in modern times.

The last campaigns against Japan. During the winter and spring of 1944–1945 Japan experienced nothing but reverses. MacArthur completed the reconquest of the Philippines. The American navy achieved mastery of the western Pacific and made possible continuous bombing of the Japanese homelands from aircraft carriers. In April, U.S. marines and army forces began the conquest of Okinawa in the Ryukyu Islands, which lie between Japan and Formosa. Everywhere, but especially on Okinawa, the Japanese fought with tenacity and fury. During the prolonged Okinawa battle British imperialist forces based in India, with Chinese and American aid, liberated Burma and broke the Japanese army's great stronghold in Southeast Asia. Late in the spring came a change of ministry in Japan, and peace feelers were put out by the new ministry. Japan was ready to negotiate in defeat but not to surrender unconditionally.

Atom bombs on Japan. While attending the Potsdam Conference, President Truman learned that scientists and engineers working secretly in the United States had made successful experimental tests with an atomic bomb. He resolved to hasten Japan's surrender by means of it. First he sent an appeal to Japan to lay down her arms unconditionally. Despite their hopeless position, the Japanese leaders were reluc-

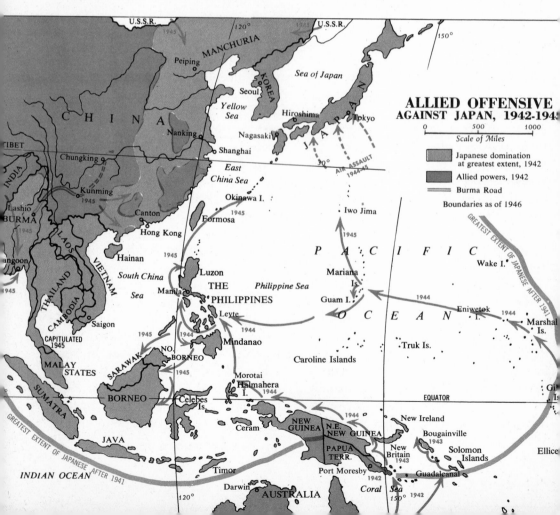

ALLIED OFFENSIVE AGAINST JAPAN, 1942-194

Scale of Miles
0 — 500 — 1000

Japanese domination at greatest extent, 1942

Allied powers, 1942

Burma Road

Boundaries as of 1946

tant to deliver themselves without condition to the mercy of conquerors. On August 6, American airman dropped a bomb with an explosive power of twenty thousand tons of TNT on Hiroshima. Two days later the Soviet Union declared war on Japan —to be "in on the kill"—and began an invasion of Manchuria. On August 9 another atomic bomb was dropped, this time upon the city of Nagasaki.

Surrender of Japan. On August 14 the Japanese government surrendered "unconditionally," but not until after assurance from President Truman that they might retain their emperor if they desired. The emperor was, however, required to obey the orders of an Allied commander. General Mac-Arthur was appointed to this command and he flew with a small military guard to Tokyo to resume his duties. The Japanese proved as obedient to MacArthur in defeat as they had been tenacious against him in war. Allied troops, almost all American, occupied the Japanese homeland. Although the victors intended an extensive reorganization of Japanese political, economic, and social life, they preserved the state. From the start a moderation, unlike the spirit of the occupation of Germany, was shown. The United States was in effective command of the scene, and MacArthur proved himself a wise and just provisional ruler.

The Charter of the United Nations. Meanwhile representatives of the United Nations had gathered at San Francisco on April 25 to draft the constitution of a new international organization. It had been decided not to revive the League of Nations but to create another bearing the name United

Emperor Hirohito of Japan (1901–) was deprived of all but ceremonial powers under the new constitution of 1947. (National Archives)

Nations Organization. The very name of the League was unpopular in the United States, and the Soviet leaders hated it because almost its last act had been to expel Soviet Russia for attacking Finland in 1939. Moreover, the United Nations aimed at a stronger organization that might be better able to preserve the peace which was expected to be made soon. It was not easy to reconcile the ideals of the Atlantic Charter with the habits and disposition of the Soviet communist state. Nevertheless, a treaty of organization called the Charter of the United Nations was drafted. It provided for an Assembly in which all member nations would have one vote each. This body could discuss and recommend collective UN policies and measures, but no real power was conferred upon it. Executive power was to reside in the Security Council, a body of eleven members, of whom five were permanent and six elected periodically by the Assembly. The five permanent members were the so-called "great powers" of the victorious alliance: the United States, Soviet Russia, Great Britain, France, and China. All decisions of the Security Council, except on merely procedural questions, required the affirmative vote of seven members, including the five permanent members. Thus each permanent member possessed what was popularly called a power of veto. The authors of the Charter accepted this principle for two reasons: first, an attempt to coerce a major power was likely to lead to war; second, no major power was willing to permit the UN to interfere with its defense of its vital interests. There was an unfounded but widespread hope that no "great power" would abuse the veto and that all would co-operate to preserve and promote peace. It even was expected that the Security Council would have international military, naval, and air forces at its disposal—to check aggression everywhere in the world. The Charter provided for an Economic and Social Council to consider and promote international social welfare. A Trusteeship Council was created to concern itself with colonies such as those taken away from Italy and Japan. It was hoped that all nations having colonies would agree to regard them as "trusts" for the well-being of the people and agree to administer them under regulations of the Trusteeship Council. The World Court of International Justice was adopted by the U.N. The United Nations Charter provided also for a Secretariat, or Secretary-General and staff, to administer the day-to-day business of UN offices and headquarters. In 1946 these headquarters were established in New York.

During the summer and fall of 1945 the various nations that attended the San Francisco conference ratified the UN Charter. Thus they pledged themselves—in the words of the document —"to establish conditions under which justice and respect for the obligations arising from treaties and other sources of international law can be maintained, and to promote social progress and better standards of life in larger free-

Trygve Lie (1896–), Norwegian statesman, was installed as the first Secretary-General of the United Nations on February 2, 1946. (United Nations)

Dag Hammarskjöld (1905–), Swedish statesman, succeeded Trygve Lie as Secretary-General of the United Nations on April 10, 1953. (United Nations)

dom . . . and to unite our strength to maintain international peace and security, and to ensure, by the acceptance of principles and the institution of methods, that armed force shall not be used, save in the common interest, and to employ international machinery for the promotion of the economic and social advancement of all peoples . . . "

The Charter stated that membership in the UN was "open to all other peace-loving states which accept the obligations contained in the present Charter and, in the judgment of the Organization, are able and willing to carry out these obligations."

No peace, no war. It was one thing for the nations that had been victorious in war to form a new international organization and pledge themselves to higher rules of conduct. It was something else to make a genuine peace. This was not achieved. No peace conference such as that which followed World War I was held. A main reason was that the Western powers and the Soviet Union were not able to agree on principles to be followed in making treaties. No German state existed with which a treaty of peace could be made, and it was soon evident that the Soviet Union would not accept joint Allied administration of Germany as a whole. Hence the country was, in effect, partitioned. Throughout eastern Europe the Russians were in control and would neither keep their Yalta promises nor allow the Western powers the slightest influence there. Thus not only Germany but Europe was partitioned, and what Winston Churchill called an "iron curtain" was raised by Soviet Russia across the heart of Europe. When Soviet and American

forces entered Korea to disarm the Japanese there and establish an independent nation, the same thing happened: partition and a Soviet "iron curtain." A second and perhaps more fundamental reason why no general peace was made lay in the way the war had been fought. Had the Allies fought for limited purposes instead of for "unconditional surrender"—that is, to defeat their enemies without conquering and occupying them—treaties of peace might have been negotiated. In 1947 treaties were at length made with Italy, Bulgaria, Hungary, and Rumania. Not until 1951 did the United States and most of the other nations make a treaty of peace with Japan. The Soviet Union refused to have any part of it. With a united Germany no general treaty of peace has ever been made, because Germany is still partitioned.

REVIEW

D. What dilemma faced Hitler after the defeat of France?

125. The World-Wide Spread of the War

A. How did Hitler divert the Russians while he planned war on them?

B. What Balkan countries came under Hitler's domination during this period?

C. Note the significance of the Lend-Lease Act and the Atlantic Charter.

D. Where were Hitler's armies stopped in the Russian campaign of 1941?

E. What were Japan's goals in entering World War II?

126. Reversing the Fortunes of War

A. Identify: Rommel, Stalingrad, Casablanca Conference, Badoglio.

B. What was the American strategy after 1942 in the war in the Pacific?

C. Indicate the significance of the Teheran and Cairo conferences.

D. Why did the Western democracies feel that it was necessary to invade France in 1944?

127. Victory of the United Nations

A. List three of the agreements reached at the Yalta Conference.

B. What policies toward Germany were concluded at Potsdam?

C. Identify: Okinawa, Hiroshima, General MacArthur.

D. What were the purposes of the United Nations Organization?

E. Explain the "veto power" of a permanent member of the Security Council of the UN.

THE CHAPTER IN REVIEW

A. Review the foreign policies of the United States, Great Britain, and Russia in 1937.

B. What were the immediate causes of World War II? What areas or countries had Hitler absorbed prior to this?

C. Summarize the foreign policy of the United States in the period 1939–1941.

D. Review the purposes and the organization of the United Nations.

FOR YOUR NOTEBOOK

List in your notebook the chain of principal events from 1937 to the outbreak of World War II. After each event write a sentence to indicate its results. For example, after Germany's seizure of Austria, you might write: "Enveloped part of Czechoslovakia and exposed the Balkan countries to Hitler's grasp; acceptance by Western countries encouraged Hitler to grab more."

Find a firsthand account describing an air raid on England. These can be found in many novels and in reporters' stories from London. From what you have read in this chapter and previous ones, put down reasons why the British survived the air raids without "cracking."

Make a chronological list of the great German victories. Indicate when their peak of success was reached. Now make a chronological list of Allied victories in the European theater of action.

Make four parallel columns in your notebook for (1) North Africa and the Western front; (2) the Eastern or Polish-Russian front; (3) the war in the Pacific; (4) the conferences of the Allied statesmen. In these columns enter pertinent principal events with their dates so that you can see more clearly how the war was progressing on all fronts and how the Allied statesmen met to plan over-all strategy.

SELECTED READINGS

The war, as seen by the average G.I., is vividly described by E. T. Pyle, *Here Is Your War* (New York: Henry Holt & Co., 1943). Underground activity in Europe was an important factor in the war and in post-war politics. Such activity in France is the subject of Howard Pease's *Heart of Danger* (Garden City, N.Y.: 1946).

The most authoritative accounts of the war are George C. Marshall, *Report: The Winning of the War in Europe and the Pacific* (New York: Simon & Schuster, 1945), and Dwight D. Eisenhower, *Crusade in Europe* (Garden City, N.Y.: Doubleday and Co., 1948).

Chapter 41. Years of Fragile Peace

128. WEAKENED EMPIRES AND NEW INDEPENDENT NATIONS

As a result of defeat in World War II, the Japanese empire ceased to exist as a great power ruling subject peoples. It remained an empire only in the sense that its monarch continued to style himself as an emperor. The Japanese were forced to abandon Korea, Formosa, all Pacific islands acquired during both world wars of the twentieth century, and to cede part of the island of Sakhalin as well as the Kurile Islands to the Soviet Union. Their power and influence in China were totally destroyed. Until 1951, Japan remained under American military occupation, and since then American military forces have been stationed there by treaty agreement. The principal American military and naval base in this part of the world is on the Japanese island of Okinawa. Formerly the greatest power in eastern Asia and the western Pacific region, Japan is no longer a great power in any sense of the word.

France tried to recover and maintain her colonial rule in Indo-China against native resistance aided by Chinese communists; but after ten years she faced the fact that her power in Asia was gone. In Syria, where the French had ruled as mandatory of the League of Nations, they were compelled after World War II to recognize the political independence of the country. Next they had to retreat before similar forces in Tunisia, and for the past few years they have been fighting to retain Algeria. Morocco, formerly under French and Spanish protectorates, achieved its complete independ-

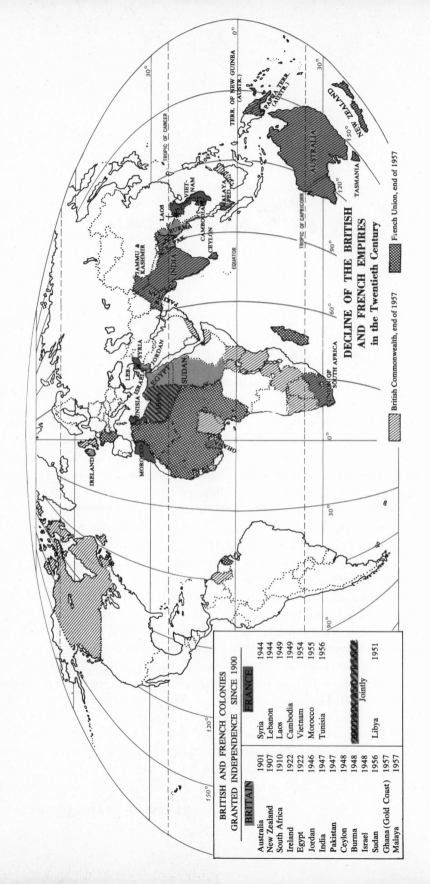

**DECLINE OF THE BRITISH
AND FRENCH EMPIRES
in the Twentieth Century**

British Commonwealth, end of 1957

French Union, end of 1957

BRITISH AND FRENCH COLONIES GRANTED INDEPENDENCE SINCE 1900			
BRITAIN		**FRANCE**	
Australia	1901	Syria	1944
New Zealand	1907	Lebanon	1944
South Africa	1910	Laos	1949
Ireland	1922	Cambodia	1949
Egypt	1922	Vietnam	1954
Jordan	1946	Morocco	1955
India	1947	Tunisia	1956
Pakistan	1947		
Ceylon	1948		
Burma	1948	**BRITAIN AND FRANCE**	
Israel	1948	Jointly	
Sudan	1956	Libya	1951
Ghana (Gold Coast)	1957		
Malaya	1957		

ence after World War II. Thus France lost control of the greater part of her overseas territory. Although French troops both before and after the liberation of France from German rule in 1944 played some part in the defeat of Germany and Italy, the story of that great country in the last twenty years has been one of misfortune and decline. Bitter internal conflicts in French politics had long existed, but in this period they were sharpened by the growth of a powerful Communist Party and by popular hatred of the large number of Frenchmen who had "collaborated" with the Germans from 1940 to 1944.

Italy in defeat was compelled to give up her whole colonial empire in Tripoli, Libya, and East Africa. Thus Ethiopia, which had been conquered by Italy in 1936, regained independence and even acquired some former Italian colonial territory. Italy not only ceased to possess an empire but turned out her king and became a republic in 1946. Within five years after the war, defeated, shrunken, and partitioned Germany evolved into two new states: the German People's Republic under Soviet control, in the eastern part; and in the west, the Federal Republic of Germany, which was allowed to develop under the guardianship of the United States, Great Britain, and France. All these Western nations continue to maintain military forces in the Federal Republic to protect it against a possible attack by the Soviet Union.

The decline of the British Empire. Although Great Britain had played a great and heroic part in the victory of the United Nations over the German-Italian Axis, her position in the world was gravely undermined and weak-

ened. She had suffered more heavily from aerial bombing than any country except Germany. Much of her navy and merchant shipping was at the bottom of the sea. Most of her overseas investments had been sold to pay war costs. She was deeply in debt to various parts of the British Empire and Commonwealth, as well as to the United States. Having for five years mobilized all their economic energy for war production, British manufacturers and merchants had lost most of their foreign markets. In every way Britain's plight was painful and her outlook dark. To make matters worse, an election in 1945 gave the socialist Labor Party control of the government. The Labor Party leaders were more interested in building socialism in Great Britain than in maintaining its great position in the world. In 1948 the British abandoned completely the government of India and paved the way for two new independent states, Pakistan and India; afterward other imperial positions

David Ben-Gurion became the first Premier of the new Free State of Israel, established May 14, 1948, after the termination of the British mandate. (Israel Government Tourist Office)

were given up in Burma and Ceylon. In 1948 the British withdrew from Palestine, thus opening the way for the Jews to establish an independent state there. In the last few years British imperial rule over Malaya, Gold Coast (Ghana), and Nigeria has ended. British political leaders have proceeded rapidly and almost with enthusiasm in abandoning most of the great empire that had reached its zenith in the days of Queen Victoria. The process has been for the most part peaceful, and all the new states that have arisen in the wake of the empire have joined the British Commonwealth of Nations. This is a loose international association in which all or most of the member nations recognize the British crown and co-operate to an undefined extent. Not all of the British Empire, however, has been liquidated. The British still hold Gibraltar, Malta, Cyprus, Aden, various islands in the Indian, Atlantic, and Pacific oceans, British Guiana, and some undeveloped regions of Africa. In the retreat from empire they have sought to retain naval, military, and air bases. Britain is still an important power in the world. Where her

rule disappears, her influence often continues; but she has sought to cut her responsibilities in the world and to transfer many of them to the United States.

The United States and the Soviet Union. The American Republic emerged after 1945 as the principal naval, air, and military power in the world and the possessor of the greatest industrial economy the world had ever seen. American arms played the decisive role in the defeat of both the European Axis and Japan, and American war supplies sustained the fighting forces of all the United Nations, including Soviet Russia. After the war the United States fed the hungry in devastated regions and provided the means—largely by free gifts—for restoring the economic life of western Europe. Until 1949 the United States was the only nation possessing atomic bombs.

The Soviet Union, having been the decisive victor in the war against Germany in eastern Europe, was able to enforce its will throughout a vast region extending from Finland to the frontier of Greece. The former Baltic states of Latvia, Lithuania, and Es-

NEW NATIONS OF AFRICA AND 1945-1958

0   1000   2000
Equatorial Scale of Miles

Independent since 1945   Colonial

tonia, together with part of pre-1939 Rumania and Poland, were annexed by the Soviet Union. Poland fell under Soviet control, and part of eastern Germany was added to it. Czechoslovakia, Hungary, Rumania, Bulgaria, and Albania came under pro-Soviet governments. In Yugoslavia a Communist dictatorship under Marshal Tito arose but curbed Soviet domination and diverged somewhat from the policies and interests of the Soviet Union. By maintaining large military forces in eastern Germany, Red Russia threatened to dominate central Europe and to threaten the West. Although much of their industry had been wrecked in the war, the communist Russians under the dictatorship of Stalin rapidly rebuilt it. They stripped the conquered lands of machinery, even of whole factories, and put their former enemy war prisoners at forced labor. This practice continued for many years after the war. Helped by the knowledge of how to build atomic bombs, which Soviet spies in the United States managed to obtain, the Soviet Union in 1949 exploded its first one. In the Far East, Soviet Russia dominated northern Korea and Manchuria and between 1945 and 1949 assisted the Chinese communists to defeat the Chinese Nationalists in a great civil war. So great had become the power of the Soviet Union and international communism that all free nations in Europe and Asia became gravely alarmed for their survival in independence.

Thus it was that World War II had produced a vast revolution in the distribution of political power in the world. Japan, Italy, and Germany were eliminated from the ranks of the

Josip Broz (Marshal Tito), President of Yugoslavia since 1946. Titoism, a brand of independent and nationalist communism, is the political philosophy of the government of Yugoslavia. (Yugoslav Information Center)

great powers, France and Britain declined, while the United States and the Soviet Union rose as "super-powers."

Small nations and new nations. With the dissolution of so great a part of the British, French, Japanese, and Italian colonial empires, a large number of new independent nations came into existence in Asia and Africa: India, Burma, Pakistan, Vietnam, Malaya, the Philippines, Indonesia, Syria, Lebanon, Libya, Israel, Tunisia, Ghana. This development was not caused merely by the decline of empires but by the spirit and ideals that had charged the war effort of the victorious alliance. The British and American governments had sponsored the Atlantic Charter, which advocated the right of all peoples to self-government. Moreover, the communists in Russia and China gave strong support to the nationalist aspirations of peoples who desired to free themselves from Western imperial rule. So powerful was the trend toward completely independent national life that the Irish Free State in 1949 withdrew from the British Commonwealth in order to cut the last links with the crown of Great Britain. The United Nations encouraged the trend and in recent years has admitted new nations to its body with amazing rapidity. Thus the number of small nations in the world has grown greatly, and they have come to exercise a great and active influence in the United Nations.

Israel and the Arab nations. In some instances the new nations have had to fight to establish themselves. The most striking case was that of Israel. After the fall of Hitler and the Nazi rule in Europe, the Jews who had survived Hitler's terrible persecution faced the alternative of living under communist rule in communities from which most of their friends and relatives had disappeared, or making their way to other countries to start new lives. A mass migration from central and eastern Europe struck Palestine, which was ruled by Great Britain until 1948. The coming of the Jews in such large numbers was bitterly resisted by the Arabs in Egypt, Syria, Lebanon, Iraq, Jordan, and Saudi Arabia as well as in Palestine. The British attempted to hold down the numbers of immigrants, and prevent fighting between Jews and Arabs, but after the British departed a bitter war broke out. The Jews were animated by the ideal of re-creating the ancient kingdom of Israel in the form of a progressive democratic republic. Although far outnumbered by their enemies, they won a complete victory and established their independent national existence. Not yet, however, have the Arab neighbors of Israel been willing to make a definite peace and recognize her existence.

129. THE COMMUNIST THREAT AND THE REVERSAL OF ALLIANCES

The failure of the Western powers, led by the United States, and of the government of the Soviet Union to reach agreement in settling the peace after World War II quickly gave rise to what the whole world has called the "cold war." The words and acts of the Soviet Union indicated, as early as 1946, that Dictator Stalin meant to establish communism and Soviet control in eastern Germany and the greater part of eastern Europe. That is to say, he meant to establish a "Soviet empire," despite the fact that he accused the Western governments of striving to maintain imperialism and "colonialism" in their former colonies. The Soviet Union gave aid to the

Hans Christian Andersen, the famous storyteller, looks down upon Nicolai Bulganin and Nikita Khrushchev in The New York Times *cartoon. After a series of purges following Stalin's death in 1953, Bulganin and Khrushchev emerged as the Soviet's top rulers.*

communists in a civil war in Greece that raged for some years after the war. Moscow directed the political strategy of the large communist parties in France and Italy; it threatened Turkey and Iran. By far the greatest military power in Europe, Red Russia threatened the freedom and independence of all the nations of Europe. Victory over the Germans seemed to turn the heads of the Soviet leaders and to stimulate the spirit of militant communism.

The Truman Doctrine. The United States government, although maintaining an army in western Germany, was slow to realize that the Soviet government would not be persuaded to co-operate peacefully with other nations. The British government was even slower. Early in 1947 the British informed the United States that they could no longer continue aiding the Greeks to fight against the communists. A sudden change came over the American government. President Harry S. Truman boldly announced to the world that the United States would give military aid to nations threatened by communist conquest and ordered the immediate dispatch of arms and military advisers to Greece and Turkey. The President's policy was known as the Truman Doctrine. It produced immediate good results. The Greek communists were defeated, and for some years the Soviet menace to Greek and Turkey declined. A few months after the Truman Doctrine was announced, the United States launched what was called the Mar-

Through the co-operation of the Italian government and America's Economic Co-operation Administration, a new housing project was built in Matera, Italy. (International Cooperation Administration)

shall Plan[1] for aiding the restoration of the economic welfare of European free nations. The Soviet Union forbade the receiving of American aid by the countries under its control, but the Marshall Plan was carried out in the rest of Europe with great success. By the early 1950's the communist menace on the free side of the "iron curtain" was much diminished.

The NATO Alliance. In 1948 the Soviet military forces committed two acts of aggression in Europe. They violently interfered in the state of Czechoslovakia, overturning a Czech government that showed certain independent tendencies. They forced a completely communist government on the country. Next they attempted to compel the Western troops of occupation to leave Berlin. By an absurd military arrangement at the end of the war the Americans, British, and French had

---

[1] Named for Secretary of State George C. Marshall, who started the plan.

agreed to the inclusion of the whole territory around Berlin in the Soviet zone of occupation; hence the Western powers had no access to their troops in that city except through or over Soviet-controlled land. Now in 1948 the Soviet forces shut off western railway and automobile routes to Berlin. The United States, almost singlehandedly, met this challenge by providing for all the needs of the allied troops and the civilian population of more than half of Berlin by means of air transport. This so-called Berlin "airlift" continued for nearly a year and was one of the most extraordinary engineering and technical feats in history. The Russians were amazed and confounded.

It was during this crisis that the United States, Great Britain, Canada, France, Belgium, Holland, Luxembourg, Italy, Denmark, Norway, Iceland, and Portugal negotiated a twenty-year alliance (1949). They agreed upon plans for co-operative defense against the threat of Soviet Russia. The alliance was soon expanded to include other nations, including Greece and Turkey. Thus arose NATO, the North Atlantic Treaty Organization. It has grown steadily stronger and now includes the Federal Republic of Germany. It is coherent and practical; it is the main instrument for defense of the free world against the Soviet menace. The formation of NATO was followed quickly by the Russians' abandonment of the Berlin blockade.

Red Russia and Red China. After the fall of Japanese power in China, civil strife broke out between the Chinese nationalist government headed by General Chiang Kai-shek and the Chinese communists. The latter were aided by the Soviet Union. The United States, although favorable to the nationalists, tried to mediate for peace between the opposing sides, but this policy proved a complete failure. From 1945 to 1949 the civil war continued until the communists, led by Mao Tse-tung, drove Chiang Kai-shek from continental China to take refuge on

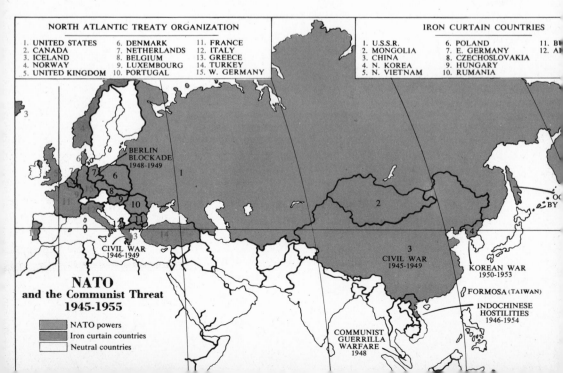

NORTH ATLANTIC TREATY ORGANIZATION

1. UNITED STATES
2. CANADA
3. ICELAND
4. NORWAY
5. UNITED KINGDOM
6. DENMARK
7. NETHERLANDS
8. BELGIUM
9. LUXEMBOURG
10. PORTUGAL
11. FRANCE
12. ITALY
13. GREECE
14. TURKEY
15. W. GERMANY

IRON CURTAIN COUNTRIES

1. U.S.S.R.
2. MONGOLIA
3. CHINA
4. N. KOREA
5. N. VIETNAM
6. POLAND
7. E. GERMANY
8. CZECHOSLOVAKIA
9. HUNGARY
10. RUMANIA
11. B...
12. A...

BERLIN BLOCKADE 1948-1949

CIVIL WAR 1946-1949

NATO and the Communist Threat 1945-1955

NATO powers
Iron curtain countries
Neutral countries

CIVIL WAR 1945-1949

KOREAN WAR 1950-1953

FORMOSA (TAIWAN)

INDOCHINESE HOSTILITIES 1946-1954

COMMUNIST GUERRILLA WARFARE 1948

The difficulty of solving the puzzle of western Europe defense is shown in The New York Times *cartoon, "Not Easy to Fit In."*

Formosa and other nearby islands. Thus a new Chinese state arose: the People's Republic of China, dominated by a communist political organization that looked to Moscow for alliance and support. Here was a world-shaking development; with the six hundred millions of China added to the peoples of the Soviet Union and its satellites in eastern Europe, international communism held control of nearly half the world's population. It became sternly necessary for the free nations of the world, led by the United States, to combine and co-operate in common defense against so great a menace to their safety, for the communists made no secret of their determination to revolutionize and dominate the entire world. As the Soviet Union appeared to threaten the nations of western and southern Europe, communist China imperiled the security of Southeast Asia, the Philippines, Japan, and the Republic of Korea.

The Korean War. Korea after 1945 was divided into two zones. In the north the Soviet Union supervised the new order of things and in time sponsored a communist People's Republic of Korea; in the south, the United States and the United Nations aided the creation of the Republic of Korea. Both the Soviet Union and the United States favored the formation of a unified Korea, but since they could not agree on what sort of government should exist, no union was possible. Moreover, the people of South Korea, who were led by an able and good man, Syngman Rhee, would not accept communism. The outcome of the Chinese civil war had a profound effect on Korea, partly because it generated a sense of triumph and confidence among Asian communists, and partly because it brought about a serious difference between the United States and Great Britain. The British, hoping to preserve long-established business relations with China, recognized the new communist government; the United States did not, but continued to recognize the government of Chiang Kai-shek on Formosa as the legitimate government of China. A dominant American opinion held that Chiang, if effectively aided, would be able to return to mainland China and defeat the communists. This Anglo-American difference in the Asian region seriously weakened the free world. Such was the situation when the North Koreans, armed by Soviet Russia, launched an invasion of the Republic of Korea in June 1950.

President Truman immediately ordered General Douglas MacArthur, who still commanded the American occupation forces in Japan, to aid the South Koreans. During the summer most of South Korea fell to the invaders, but in September MacArthur's forces landed at Inchon, well to the north on the west coast of the Korean peninsula, and took his enemy from the rear. Quickly the whole position changed; South Korea was freed and North Korea was invaded. By the late fall of 1950 MacArthur's forces were advancing in complete triumph to the northern boundary of Korea. The unification of that country seemed at hand. Suddenly a massive invasion of Korea by hordes of Chinese communist forces took place. The war was enlarged and lasted for three years.

The United Nations and the Korean War. When the war began, the United States called upon the UN to defend the Republic of Korea. The Soviet delegate to the UN Security Council was not present to cast a veto vote against such action, and the Security Council asked all UN members to help the South Koreans. Many of them sent small token forces, and General MacArthur directed the war as a United Nations activity, although the burden of the fighting was carried by the South Korean and American armies. By the end of the fighting the United States had sent five hundred thousand troops to Korea and suffered more than a hundred thousand casualties.

The Korean stalemate. MacArthur probably could have won the war, but he was not allowed to do the things that were necessary to win it. Fear of Russian intervention and a Soviet attack in western Europe inspired Great Britain, France, and other allies of the

United States to persuade President Truman to limit MacArthur's action to merely defensive moves. The general's discontent with this policy led to his removal by President Truman in 1951. Thereafter the war settled into a stalemate. In 1953 a truce was negotiated. American troops remain in South Korea, and no peace has ever been made. The failure of the United States to win the Korean War caused a great decline in American prestige in Asia and an increase in the prestige of Russian and Chinese communism.

During the war the United States extended its protection to Chiang Kaishek's government on Formosa. In 1955–1956 an alliance was concluded between the United States and the nationalist Chinese regime, and the American Congress by almost unanimous vote approved President Eisenhower's declaration that the United States would go to war with Red China if that power attacked Formosa.

Syngman Rhee, President of South Korea, had urged the United States to join Asian forces in a war against Communist China. (Korean Consulate)

Meanwhile other defensive moves have been made in Southeast Asia. In 1954 the new nations of that region, together with the United States, Australia, New Zealand, France and Great Britain, concluded a long-term military alliance known as the Southeast Asia Treaty Organization (SEATO). With the SEATO alliance, the American protectorate over Formosa, the American forces in Korea and Okinawa, and the American-Japanese alliance—all backed by American naval and air power—a dike has been erected against the tide of communism in eastern and southeastern Asia. It would, however, be difficult and risky to estimate how strong this dike is.

The co-existence ideal. In 1953 important changes occurred in the governments of the United States and the Soviet Union. Dwight D. Eisenhower had been elected President in 1952 on the Republican Party ticket and had barely taken office the following year when Joseph Stalin died. This dictator was succeeded by no single man but by a collective dictatorship of leading Soviet politicians. The principal one, as it presently appeared, was Nikita Khrushchev, secretary of the Communist Party. Eisenhower was willing to try to strengthen the fragile peace by meeting the Soviet leaders halfway, and they began to replace their frowns with smiles and promote the ideal of "peaceful co-existence" of the communist and capitalist-democratic forms of state and society. In 1955, President Eisenhower went to Geneva and met the Soviet leaders. He sought to convince them that the United States would never launch an unprovoked attack; he even proposed an "open-

British soldier, wearing gloves to protect his hands against knives and to avoid accusations of theft, searches civilians in Suez to guard against riots following Britain's refusal to recognize Egyptian sovereignty over the Sudan in 1951. (British Information Services)

sky" plan whereby each side would be allowed to make aerial inspection of the other, thus removing mutual fears of a sudden attack. All, however, was illusion. The antagonism of communism and the free world was not to be negotiated away. Prolonged subsequent efforts to reach agreement on disarmament and mutual inspection have failed.

The Middle East crisis. To strengthen the defense of western Asia (often called the Middle East) against possible Soviet attack, Great Britain in 1955 entered into an alliance with Turkey, Pakistan, Iran, and Iraq. It is known as the Bagdad Pact. The United States encouraged this pact but did not join it lest the Russians consider such action provocative. About the same time the British withdrew their troops that had long been stationed in the Suez Canal Zone, which is part of Egyptian territory. They left primarily because Egyptian nationalist resentment at their presence had grown very menacing. Within a short time thereafter the Egyptian government, headed by President Nasser, began to receive large shipments of arms from the Soviet Union. Nasser was intensely ambitious to put himself at the head of the several Arab nations. He gave aid and comfort to the Algerians fighting against the French. He threatened Israel; he became the champion of Arab nationalism throughout western Asia and Africa. Meanwhile the Republic of Syria began a perhaps closer political flirtation with the Soviet Union. The American government tried to moderate Nasser by offering to build a great Nile dam at Aswan but then withdrew the offer; whereupon Nasser seized the Suez Canal and nationalized it. The Canal had been built and operated by an international company which, though chartered in Egypt, was owned by shareholders in many countries. The largest owner was the British government. Through the Canal passed the tankers that brought oil from the great Middle East wells to Britain and Europe. Thus free access to this all-important commodity might be impeded by Egypt, which appeared to be drawing close politically to Soviet Russia.

In the fall of 1956 Nasser threatened to attack Israel, but the bold-spirited Israelis anticipated him and struck swiftly at Egyptian forces east of Suez. The British and French governments, long angry and now out of patience with Nasser, moved to seize the Suez Canal. They were not well prepared, and they badly bungled the operation,

although the Israelis easily defeated the Egyptians and captured most of their arms. Egypt appealed to the United Nations Assembly, where feeling was bitter against the British, French, and Israelis, who were denounced as aggressors. The United States did not support the action of its allies but joined with—indeed led—a large number of small nations in condemning by assembly vote the British, French, and Israelis and demanding their withdrawal from Egypt. The UN Assembly had no authority to order such a withdrawal; nevertheless, the British and French agreed to withdraw their troops, and soon afterward the Israelis did likewise.

Results of the crisis. These were bad developments indeed for the security of peace and for the relations of the United States with Great Britain and France. The Arab-Israeli antagonism was deepened. The Suez Canal was blocked by ships the Egyptians sank in it in order to make it unusable in the event of its capture. More than six months were required to clear it. Nasser's prestige soared. Syria drew still nearer to the Soviet Union, which had threatened to intervene in the crisis. Millions of Arabs were convinced that the Russian threat, rather than the actions of the United States and the United Nations, was the cause of the British and French withdrawal. A large part of the public in Great Britain blamed the United States, and these great allies for a time seemed at the parting of their ways.

The Hungarian revolt. One of the sorriest features of the international crisis was that just as it came to a head the people of Hungary revolted against Soviet

The Hungarian revolt as seen in the actions of this insurgent mob in Budapest on October 24, 1956. The overturned streetcar bears the slogan, "Ruskies, go home!" (Wide World)

control. For a short time they won their freedom; then Soviet armored divisions rolled into the country and reconquered it with hideous brutality. No nation in the free world moved to help the brave people of Hungary. Many of the small Asian nations that called for military sanctions against Britain and France were unwilling to consider the plight of Hungary, although Hungary, too, was a member of the United Nations. To aid Hungary meant risking war with Soviet Russia; from that the Western powers shrank.

The Eisenhower Doctrine. The humiliation of Great Britain and France, the dangerous rift in the NATO allies, and the subjugation of Hungary brought a new and more vivid awareness to the Western nations of the threatening power of the Soviet "empire." It had long been plain that a breakup of the NATO alliance would lay Europe helpless before Red Russia. Now Soviet activities in Egypt and

Syria imperiled the Middle East oil fields, which are indispensable to the economy of Europe. Hence President Eisenhower asked and obtained from the Congress the authority to declare an American guarantee of the independence and security of the nations of the Middle East. The powerful American Sixth Fleet with great aircraft carriers and jet planes capable of carrying atomic and hydrogen bombs patrols the eastern Mediterranean as the principal instrument of the American guarantee. The year 1957 also saw a tightening of the bonds of the NATO alliance. International tension, however, was higher than at any time since the Korean War.

Alliances reversed. Reviewing international political history since the end of World War II, one sees that a great reversal of alliances occurred. In 1945, Great Britain, the United States, and the Soviet Union were in military alliance against Germany and Japan. Now the United States is allied with Japan against the Soviet Union and is joined by Great Britain and France in alliance with Western Germany. To the historian there is nothing very surprising in this. After the other great wars of the past, such reversals of alliances usually took place. The reason is that nations that win wars are likely to abuse their victories and become too powerful for the security of others.

130. SOME CONTEMPORARY TRENDS OF WORLD HISTORY

"One World." During World War II a prominent American political and business leader, Wendell Willkie, flew

round the world and wrote a book called *One World*. The title became a phrase on men's tongues to signify the ideal of universal co-operation by all peoples in establishing a peaceful and progressive world; and this ideal sprang from a recognition that the human race is one great family whose members are mutually interdependent. There was nothing new in the recognition or in the ideal, but the practical need for a new advance toward inter-

THE WORLD
1958

0   500 1000   2000
Equatorial Scale of Miles

• Capitals of countries

national co-operation and understanding was felt as never before. The Charter of the United Nations was designed to meet this need.

The UN has disappointed millions of persons who credulously believed that, almost overnight, it could remove national jealousies, suspicions, hatreds, rivalries, and secure the peace of the world. The conflicting interests of great powers possessing "veto" rights has rendered the Security Council

Headquarters of the United Nations in New York, showing the Secretariat, Conference, and General Assembly buildings. (United Nations)

completely unable to carry out any executive actions; and the Assembly has no authority to do anything but pass resolutions and make recommendations. The UN, therefore, is not an effective international instrument for *enforcing* peace. It is, however, a permanent center for discussion and even for negotiation, and it exerts an important influence. The fact that Britain, France, and Israel bowed to an Assembly resolution and withdrew from Egyptian territory in 1956 was proof of that influence. No nation has withdrawn from the United Nations, and no major power can be expelled. A variety of international social and economic agencies are constantly at work, quietly strengthening the habit of international co-operation. The debates and discussions in the Assembly command increasing attention throughout the world. However imperfectly the United Nations organization may function, it does to some extent embody the "one world" ideal. Its membership takes in both the communist world and the "free world" and thus is a narrow bridge that crosses the "iron curtain." The UN is likely to continue.

Racial antagonisms. One of the most serious evils that stands in the way of international co-operation and social peace within nations is the upsurge of strong racial passions. In Asia brown- and yellow-skinned peoples continue to attack "white colonialism," even though the British and French empires in that part of the world have all but disappeared. Angry racial passions have been reflected in the voting of a number of the new nations in the UN Assembly. What is true in Asia is true also in Africa among the Negro peoples. To many Africans and Asians the days of "white man's rule" are over and the new age is to be dominated by the colored races. The communists have tried with studied purpose to excite these racial passions against Europe and the United States. In the latter country very dangerous racial hatreds have been aroused by the aspirations of a progressing Negro element in the population to gain complete social and civic equality with the white majority and by an ill-tempered and ungenerous attitude toward the Negroes on the part of many whites. Far graver racial antagonism exists in the Union of South Africa, a member of the British Commonwealth of Nations and the principal state on the African continent: there, absolute white supremacy prevails over a large Negro population. The problems generated by racial conflict seem not to be soluble by legislative action but only by improvement in manners and morals.

Industrial society and the state. The techniques of producing goods by machinery, the improvement of machinery, the application of science to economic production have now become almost world-wide. The process continues at a constantly accelerated pace. Countries such as Brazil, Argentina, Australia, South Africa, China, Canada, and India have become extensively industrialized, so that this type of economy is no longer to be found only in Europe, the United States, and Japan. Many are the consequences of this development: labor unions, increase of schools, costly road construction, airports, bigger governments levying higher taxes, and a variety of problems for the state. How to keep the machines running so that the workers are employed; how to stimulate the production of food so that they may be fed; how to secure necessary supplies of raw material; how to find the revenue to do all these things; how to adjust the national economy to the world of international economic exchange—these are the great problems of industrialized countries.

During the war the governments of the belligerent countries greatly extended their regulation of economic life. The American, British, German, Japanese, and Soviet governments assumed almost complete control in order to direct all economic energies toward serving the war effort. There was no unemployment; instead there were not enough hands for the jobs to be done. Hence the idea arose among millions of workers that the state which had maintained full employment in war ought to be able to do the same in peace. The industrial workers recalled the unemployment that had followed World War I and had bitter memories of an even more painful scarcity of jobs during the great depression of the 1930's. They and their leaders demanded that measures be adopted by the state to guard against renewed unemployment; they demanded, too, that government undertake to provide cheaper medical service for all and a variety of other social services. In Great Britain these demands resulted in the establishment of a socialistic "welfare state," in which the most powerful forces are the

Queen Elizabeth II and President Eisenhower upon the queen's visit to the United States in October 1957. (Wide World)

trade unions and a vastly expanded body of government officials. The United States, Canada, Australia, Argentina, and several other countries moved toward the welfare state.

This development, together with the increased police measures to protect society against communist spies and political agents, has made the state more powerful than ever before. In many places over the world the individual person and the family have less independence and freedom than they had fifty years ago. Here, then, is one of the principal problems of the human race in this century: how to revive, preserve, and strengthen freedom in the all-powerful state.

There has been considerable reaction against the dominance of government over society. Western Germany, having tasted to the dregs the bitter cup of national socialism, has elected to follow policies of limited government activity, private enterprise, and economic freedom for individuals. So far this choice has been rewarded by great material progress and prosperity. Italian politics has veered away from socialism. The British people in 1951 voted against the socialist Labor Party and brought in the Conservatives, who without dismantling the welfare state have sought to revive within it the principles of economic freedom and capitalist enterprise. In 1953 the Republican Party in the United States returned to power and moved even more actively in the conservative direction of more economic freedom and less state control. In Australia, Canada, and several other countries the same trend has been visible. No modern state, however, is prepared to abandon all economic controls or to do away with social security, unemployment insurance, and old-age pensions. All these appear permanently established in industrialized societies.

The main reason for the conservative reaction against socialism and the thoroughgoing welfare state is the widespread discovery that they are not compatible with personal freedom and that they cause soaring taxes and inflation of prices. These evils fall ultimately upon the mass of people who make up the main body of the voters.

The international foreign-aid system. During World War II the United States gave vast aid not only in weapons but in food and a great variety of goods to the nations fighting against the European Axis powers and Japan. This was known as the "Lend-Lease" program. It stopped at the end of the war. Soon, however, it was revived under the name of foreign aid in the Marshall Plan and in other forms. Almost all countries outside the Soviet-dominated regions received some aid, although at

Solar energy, used to boil the water in the kettle, is studied by Korean and American professors taking part in a United States foreign-aid contract involving an exchange of professors and scientists under the International Cooperation Administration. (International Cooperation Administration)

first it went only where it was needed for restoring economic life. By 1951 the United States was supplying arms to allies in Europe, and since then has extended arms and economic aid to more than twoscore countries in order to strengthen them against the communist danger. In addition, vast shipments of goods go abroad constantly to maintain the numerous troops and bases the United States has established in Great Britain, Germany, Spain, Japan, Okinawa, and many other countries. The American economy is geared to a large export trade; to keep up the volume the United States sends out agents to assist the technical advance of undeveloped countries. Apart from defensive purposes and generous benevolence to the needy, American foreign aid aims at developing the kind of economic world in which the American people can prosper economically.

Recently the Soviet Union began to develop a comparable foreign-aid system, and in certain regions, particularly Asia, an American-Soviet competition in giving economic aid has arisen. Great Britain seems likely to follow the same course, and it may be that other heavily industrialized countries will do so likewise in order to promote their export trade and keep their workers employed.

There would be less need for the international foreign-aid system if there were fewer barriers to free international trade. The strict control of all trade by the state in the communist world, protective tariffs and national controls over the movement of currencies in many other parts of the world have so far barred the way to

The Eucharistic Congress, held annually, is one way in which the universal Church speaks to the world. Shown above is the formal opening of the Congress held in Rio De Janeiro, Brazil, 1955. Over 20,000 foreign pilgrims attended the ceremonies. (Wide World)

re-establishing what used to be regarded as normal international trade.

Religion and education. The mid-twentieth century forms part of a great age of Christian martyrs. The Christian religion has been and continues to be despised, rejected, and persecuted by the communists. There have been unnumbered martyrs in eastern Europe, Russia, and Red China. Churches and missions have been destroyed. Little news reaches the world at large of the sufferings of Christians under this persecution, but enough is known to say that nothing like it has occurred since the agonies suffered under the pagan Roman emperors. The heaviest attacks have come upon the Catholic Church.

Although many people of the Protestant world display a continued falling off in the practice of religion, notably in church attendance, the present age is one of great growth for the Catholic Church. The only universal church, it alone is able to speak to "one world."

Never was there so great a growth of schools as in our times. The whole civilized world is convinced that popular education is an imperative social necessity. Every government is deeply concerned with the schools, in which the next generation of citizens will be formed. Industry, technology, science, civil service constantly recruit men and women who have learned special skills. The result is that education undergoes considerable change as it becomes universal and is drawn into the service of such special interests. The study of the liberal arts tends to decline as scientific and technical subjects expand. Thus many reflective persons fear that, the more complex society becomes in its technological and economic aspects, the less the coming generations may understand the principles of religion, morality, and liberty which lie at the foundation of civilization.

Giant missiles stand guard in a U. S. air defense center. The urgency of national defense felt by all countries encouraged scientific developments and launched the world into the present space age. (Wide World)

Our revolutionary age. The historian surveying the times in which we live recognizes that they are part of a great revolutionary era that opened in the early years of the twentieth century and has not yet terminated. The spread of democracy and communism are only details of the revolution. More significant features transpire in the laboratories of the scientists and in the vast engineering enterprises of governments and business corporations. The ability of men to harness natural forces and alter the scene of life grows at an ever more rapid pace. Only about fifty years have passed since men learned to fly in an airplane; now there are jet-propelled craft that fly faster than the speed of sound, and men are beginning to investigate the world of outer space. Not a century has passed since the telephone was invented; now television spreads fast through human society. In the United States, Great Britain, and Soviet Russia there are atomic and hydrogen bombs capable of blasting away islands, mountains, and cities; while an international race has started in the production of guided missiles—gigantic rockets directed electronically to chosen targets thousands of miles away. Such awesome things can be produced only where there is a vast scientific and industrial development that restlessly pushes forward to new frontiers of knowledge and power. The skies are laced with global airlines. No place on earth is more than sixty hours distant by air travel. A great part of mankind seems utterly fascinated by speed and power, and all human society feels the impact of them.

REVIEW

FOR YOUR NOTEBOOK

128. Weakened Empires and New Independent Areas

A. List three difficulties faced by Great Britain in the post-World War II period.

B. What areas came under the domination of the Soviet Union following the war?

C. In general, what was the fate of colonial empires in the post-war world?

D. List three factors that encouraged the rise of new nations in this period.

129. The Communist Threat and the Reversal of Alliances

A. What was the Truman Doctrine, and what were its immediate effects?

B. Identify: the Marshall Plan, the "Berlin airlift," NATO alliance.

C. What brought an end to hostilities in Korea?

D. Cite three results of the Suez crisis of 1956.

130. Some Contemporary Trends of World History

A. List three beneficial results of the work of the United Nations organization.

B. Cite two reasons for the increase in power of the state over the individual in recent years.

C. What are three purposes of American foreign-aid programs?

D. What change of emphasis is noticeable in modern education? What are the possible dangers in such change?

THE CHAPTER IN REVIEW

A. Again to illustrate the changing nature of international alliances, compare the alliances of the major powers during World War II with those of the year 1957.

B. What is meant by the "cold war"? Cite four events that demonstrate this modern conflict.

C. Briefly describe the condition of each of the following nations after World War II: Japan, France, Great Britain, the United States.

D. Discuss the weaknesses and advantages of the UN as revealed in its efforts to preserve world peace.

Now that we have finished our course in world history we see that history can be read in two ways: (1) for the practical purpose of helping us to understand better the present world; (2) for the enjoyment that can be had in studying the story of mankind here on earth. Although not mutually exclusive, these two ways tend to adjust the way we look at historical developments. The first purpose, for example, will make us look at the French Revolution to see how it furthered modern developments, whereas the latter purpose will make us look at the French Revolution as a dramatic story full of interest independent of its consequences.

A review of our notebook and of our text should reveal a number of conclusions about history:

1. It is something like a "five-ring circus," in that developments are going on simultaneously in various countries and continents. These stories must be told one at a time, and the student is apt to overlook their simultaneity unless he reviews his parallel-column and time-line assignments.

2. "Causes" and "effects" for any big event in history, such as a war, are many and complex. Thus we remember that there were economic and social as well as religious causes of the Protestant Revolt from the Catholic Church, and that there were moral and social as well as political effects of World War I.

3. History is a continuous story. Each chapter flows from the preceding one and leads to the following one. But nothing in the story is absolutely determined before it happens, for it is a story of human persons reacting to certain conditions—people whose actions are "conditioned" but not "determined."

Your final notebook assignment is to review the entries you have made for each chapter with three things in mind:

1. See which entries supplement material in the text and thus help you get a fuller story of the past.

2. See which entries make you do something with material in the text, such as rearranging it, in order to help you review, summarize, and remember the material of each chapter.

3. See how each entry you have made in your notebook, just like each of the 131 sections in the text, is a part of the whole story called "World History," and how each section is related to those before and after it.

SELECTED READINGS

In this chapter we come down to "contemporary history," and our selected readings might well be taken more from periodical publications than from books. An excellent journal the history student should know is *Current History.* You will find articles in this monthly on almost every subject covered in this chapter. Another way of keeping "up to date" on recent developments is to use the yearbooks published by the various standard encyclopedias. Look through one or two of these yearbooks to see how developments in various countries are summarized annually.

Among the recent books summarizing historical developments since World War II, a handy and reliable volume is the paperback *The Present in Perspective,* by Hans W. Gatzke (Chicago: Rand McNally & Co., 1957). Also useful but more extensive are J. Hampden Jackson, *The Postwar Decade* (Boston: Houghton Mifflin Co., 1956), and Louis Fischer, *This Is Our World* (New York: Harper & Bros., 1956).

CHRONOLOGICAL REVIEW

1921 Washington Conference
1924 Death of Lenin; Dawes Plan
1925 Locarno treaties
1926 Germany enters League of Nations
General strike in Britain
1927 *Lindbergh flies across Atlantic*
1928 Pact of Paris
1929 *Lateran treaties; world depression*
1930 London Naval Disarmament Conference; Statute of Westminster
1931 Spanish Republic created; Japan invades Manchuria
1933 F. D. Roosevelt President of U. S. (to 1945); Hitler is German chancellor
World Economic Conference
1935 Italy invades Ethiopia; Saar restored to Germany
1936 Civil war in Spain; Rome-Berlin Axis
1937 Japanese invasion of China
1938 Munich Pact
1939 Russo-German pact; Hitler invades Poland; World War II
Pontificate of Pius XII
1940 Germany conquers Denmark, Norway, and France

1941 Germany invades Russia; Pearl Harbor
Television broadcasting begins
1943 Allied victory in North Africa; Mussolini falls; Stalingrad relieved
1944 New Allied offensives
1945 Yalta Conference; Germany, Japan collapse; atom bomb; U. N. founded
1946 Italy becomes a republic; independence of Philippines
1947 Communists seize power in eastern Europe; India and Pakistan become dominions; Truman Doctrine; Marshall Plan
1948 Israel founded; death of Gandhi
1949 Communists conquer China; NATO established
1950 Korean War (to 1953)
1952 *Hydrogen bomb*
1953 Eisenhower President of U. S.; death of Stalin
1954 *Dogma of Assumption proclaimed*
1956 Israel-Egypt War; Hungarian revolt
1957-58 International Geophysical Year; U. S. S. R. and U. S. A. launch earth satellites

Genealogical Tables

KINGS OF ENGLAND 1066–1485

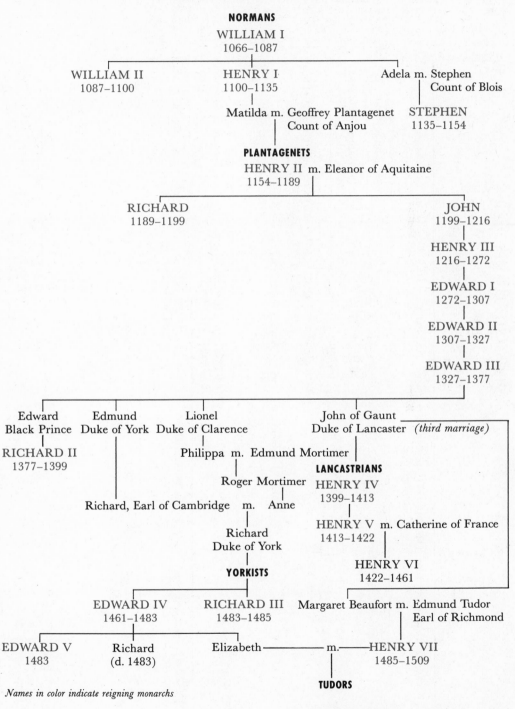

NORMANS

WILLIAM I
1066–1087

WILLIAM II
1087–1100

HENRY I
1100–1135

Adela m. Stephen
Count of Blois

Matilda m. Geoffrey Plantagenet
Count of Anjou

STEPHEN
1135–1154

PLANTAGENETS
HENRY II m. Eleanor of Aquitaine
1154–1189

RICHARD
1189–1199

JOHN
1199–1216

HENRY III
1216–1272

EDWARD I
1272–1307

EDWARD II
1307–1327

EDWARD III
1327–1377

Edward
Black Prince

Edmund
Duke of York

Lionel
Duke of Clarence

John of Gaunt
Duke of Lancaster *(third marriage)*

RICHARD II
1377–1399

Philippa m. Edmund Mortimer

LANCASTRIANS

Roger Mortimer

HENRY IV
1399–1413

Richard, Earl of Cambridge   m.   Anne

HENRY V m. Catherine of France
1413–1422

Richard
Duke of York

HENRY VI
1422–1461

YORKISTS

EDWARD IV
1461–1483

RICHARD III
1483–1485

Margaret Beaufort m. Edmund Tudor
Earl of Richmond

EDWARD V
1483

Richard
(d. 1483)

Elizabeth————— m.————**HENRY VII**
1485–1509

Names in color indicate reigning monarchs

TUDORS

TUDORS AND STUARTS

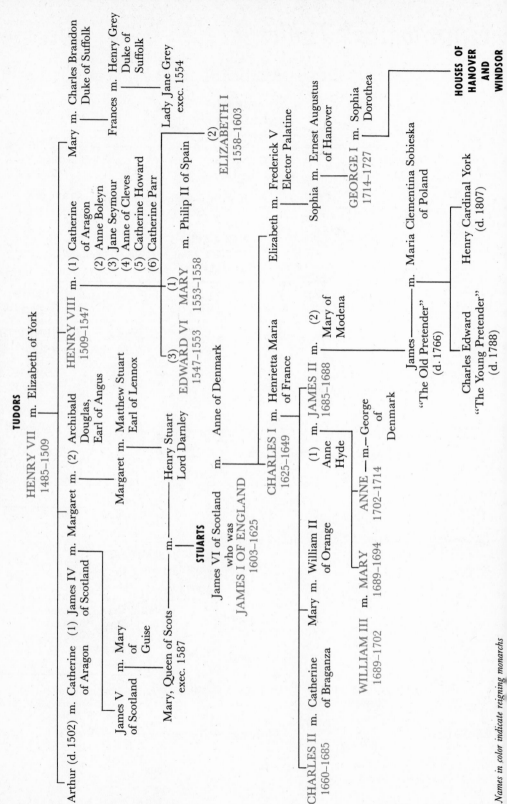

TUDORS

HENRY VII m. Elizabeth of York
1485–1509

Arthur (d. 1502) m. Catherine   (1) James IV m. Margaret m. (2) Archibald   Mary m. Charles Brandon
                      of Aragon   of Scotland   Douglas,   Duke of Suffolk
                                                                        Earl of Angus
                                                                                                  Frances m. Henry Grey
James V   Margaret m. Matthew Stuart   Duke of Suffolk
m. Mary   Earl of Lennox
of   Lady Jane Grey
Guise   Henry Stuart   exec. 1554
                              Lord Darnley

Mary, Queen of Scots ——————————— m. ———————————

exec. 1587

HENRY VIII m. (1) Catherine   EDWARD VI   MARY   m. Philip II of Spain
1509–1547   of Aragon   1547–1553 1553–1558
                 (2) Anne Boleyn   (3)   (1)
                 (3) Jane Seymour   (2)
                 (4) Anne of Cleves   ELIZABETH I
                 (5) Catherine Howard   1558–1603
                 (6) Catherine Parr

STUARTS

James VI of Scotland   m.   Anne of Denmark
who was
JAMES I OF ENGLAND
1603–1625

CHARLES I m. Henrietta Maria   Elizabeth m. Frederick V
1625–1649   of France   Elector Palatine

CHARLES II m. Catherine   Mary m. William II   (1)   (2)   Sophia m. Ernest Augustus
1660–1685   of Braganza   of Orange   Anne — JAMES II m. Mary of   of Hanover
                                                          Hyde   1685–1688   Modena
                                                                                                GEORGE I m. Sophia
WILLIAM III m. MARY   ANNE — m. — George   1714–1727   Dorothea
1689–1702   1689–1694 1702–1714   of   James m. Maria Clementina Sobieska
                                           Denmark   "The Old   of Poland   HOUSES OF
                                                            Pretender"   HANOVER
                                                            (d. 1766)   AND
                                                                                                      WINDSOR
                                                           Charles Edward   Henry Cardinal York
                                                           "The Young Pretender"   (d. 1807)
                                                           (d. 1788)

Names in color indicate reigning monarchs

HANOVERIANS OF GREAT BRITAIN

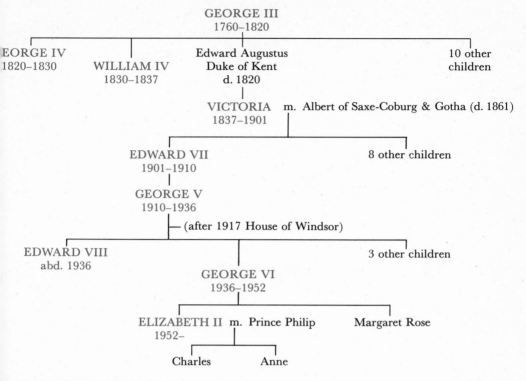

GEORGE III
1760–1820

EORGE IV
1820–1830

WILLIAM IV
1830–1837

Edward Augustus
Duke of Kent
d. 1820

10 other
children

VICTORIA   m. Albert of Saxe-Coburg & Gotha (d. 1861)
1837–1901

EDWARD VII
1901–1910

8 other children

GEORGE V
1910–1936

— (after 1917 House of Windsor)

EDWARD VIII
abd. 1936

3 other children

GEORGE VI
1936–1952

ELIZABETH II m. Prince Philip
1952–

Margaret Rose

Charles   Anne

mes in color indicate reigning monarchs

Hanover

Stuart

THE CAROLINGIANS

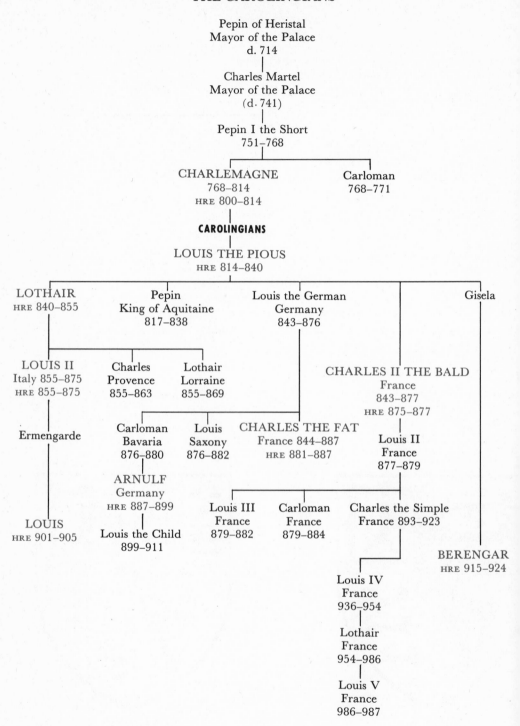

Pepin of Heristal
Mayor of the Palace
d. 714

Charles Martel
Mayor of the Palace
(d. 741)

Pepin I the Short
751–768

CHARLEMAGNE
768–814
HRE 800–814

Carloman
768–771

CAROLINGIANS

LOUIS THE PIOUS
HRE 814–840

LOTHAIR
HRE 840–855

Pepin
King of Aquitaine
817–838

Louis the German
Germany
843–876

Gisela

LOUIS II
Italy 855–875
HRE 855–875

Charles
Provence
855–863

Lothair
Lorraine
855–869

CHARLES II THE BALD
France
843–877
HRE 875–877

Ermengarde

Carloman
Bavaria
876–880

Louis
Saxony
876–882

CHARLES THE FAT
France 844–887
HRE 881–887

Louis II
France
877–879

ARNULF
Germany
HRE 887–899

LOUIS
HRE 901–905

Louis the Child
899–911

Louis III
France
879–882

Carloman
France
879–884

Charles the Simple
France 893–923

BERENGAR
HRE 915–924

Louis IV
France
936–954

Lothair
France
954–986

Louis V
France
986–987

Names in color indicate Holy Roman Emperors

CAPETIAN HOUSE TO 1328

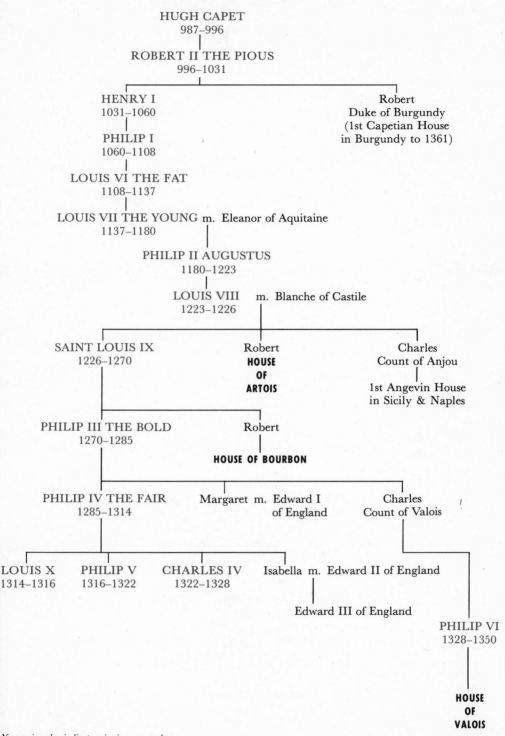

HUGH CAPET
987–996

ROBERT II THE PIOUS
996–1031

HENRY I
1031–1060

Robert
Duke of Burgundy
(1st Capetian House
in Burgundy to 1361)

PHILIP I
1060–1108

LOUIS VI THE FAT
1108–1137

LOUIS VII THE YOUNG m. Eleanor of Aquitaine
1137–1180

PHILIP II AUGUSTUS
1180–1223

LOUIS VIII   m. Blanche of Castile
1223–1226

SAINT LOUIS IX
1226–1270

Robert
**HOUSE
OF
ARTOIS**

Charles
Count of Anjou

1st Angevin House
in Sicily & Naples

PHILIP III THE BOLD
1270–1285

Robert

HOUSE OF BOURBON

PHILIP IV THE FAIR
1285–1314

Margaret m. Edward I
of England

Charles
Count of Valois

LOUIS X
1314–1316

PHILIP V
1316–1322

CHARLES IV
1322–1328

Isabella m. Edward II of England

Edward III of England

PHILIP VI
1328–1350

**HOUSE
OF
VALOIS**

Names in color indicate reigning monarchs

HOUSE OF VALOIS TO 1515

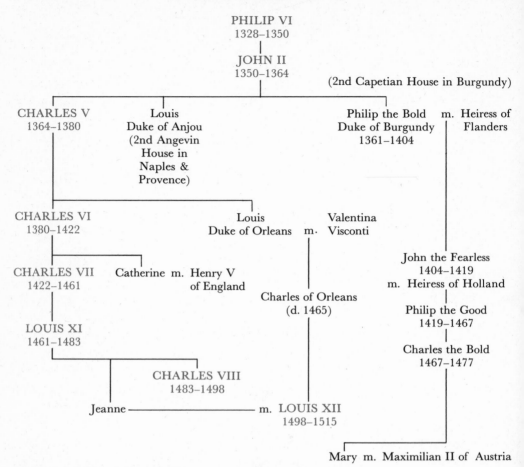

PHILIP VI
1328–1350

JOHN II
1350–1364

(2nd Capetian House in Burgundy)

CHARLES V
1364–1380

Louis
Duke of Anjou
(2nd Angevin
House in
Naples &
Provence)

Philip the Bold
Duke of Burgundy
1361–1404

m. Heiress of
Flanders

CHARLES VI
1380–1422

Louis
Duke of Orleans

m. Valentina
Visconti

John the Fearless
1404–1419
m. Heiress of Holland

CHARLES VII
1422–1461

Catherine m. Henry V
of England

Charles of Orleans
(d. 1465)

Philip the Good
1419–1467

LOUIS XI
1461–1483

Charles the Bold
1467–1477

CHARLES VIII
1483–1498

Jeanne ——————— m. LOUIS XII
1498–1515

Mary m. Maximilian II of Austria

Names in color indicate reigning monarchs

Bourbon

HOUSE OF BOURBON

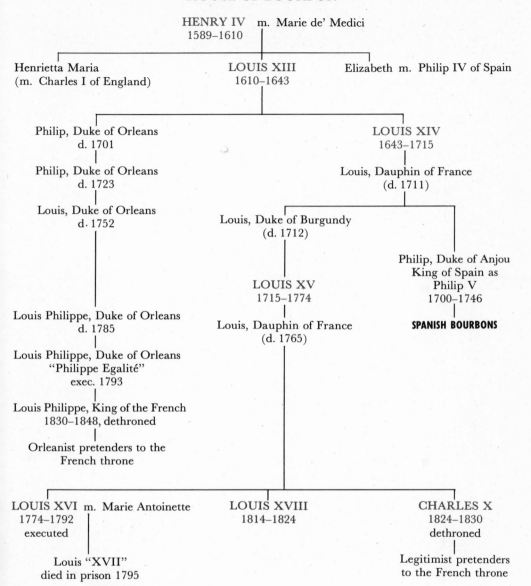

HENRY IV   m. Marie de' Medici
1589–1610

Henrietta Maria   LOUIS XIII   Elizabeth m. Philip IV of Spain
(m. Charles I of England)   1610–1643

Philip, Duke of Orleans   LOUIS XIV
d. 1701   1643–1715

Philip, Duke of Orleans   Louis, Dauphin of France
d. 1723   (d. 1711)

Louis, Duke of Orleans   Louis, Duke of Burgundy
d. 1752   (d. 1712)

                                                    Philip, Duke of Anjou
                                                    King of Spain as
                                                    Philip V
                                                    1700–1746

                                     LOUIS XV
                                     1715–1774

Louis Philippe, Duke of Orleans Louis, Dauphin of France   **SPANISH BOURBONS**
d. 1785   (d. 1765)

Louis Philippe, Duke of Orleans
"Philippe Egalité"
exec. 1793

Louis Philippe, King of the French
1830–1848, dethroned

Orleanist pretenders to the
French throne

LOUIS XVI m. Marie Antoinette   LOUIS XVIII   CHARLES X
1774–1792   1814–1824   1824–1830
executed   dethroned

Louis "XVII"   Legitimist pretenders
died in prison 1795   to the French throne

Names in color indicate reigning monarchs

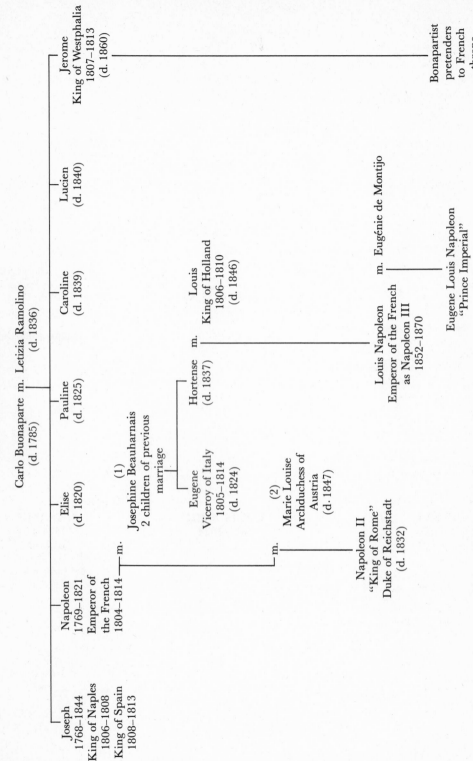

BONAPARTE FAMILY

Carlo Buonaparte m. Letizia Ramolino
(d. 1785)   (d. 1836)

Joseph
1768–1844
King of Naples
1806–1808
King of Spain
1808–1813

Napoleon
1769–1821
Emperor of
the French
1804–1814 m.

Elise
(d. 1820)

(1)
Josephine Beauharnais
2 children of previous
marriage

Pauline
(d. 1825)

Caroline
(d. 1839)

Lucien
(d. 1840)

Jerome
King of Westphalia
1807–1813
(d. 1860)

(2)
Marie Louise
Archduchess of
Austria
(d. 1847)

m.

Eugene
Viceroy of Italy
1805–1814
(d. 1824)

Hortense
(d. 1837)

m.

Louis
King of Holland
1806–1810
(d. 1846)

Bonapartist
pretenders
to French
throne

Napoleon II
"King of Rome"
Duke of Reichstadt
(d. 1832)

Louis Napoleon
Emperor of the French
as Napoleon III
1852–1870

m. Eugénie de Montijo

Eugene Louis Napoleon
"Prince Imperial"

HOUSE OF HOHENSTAUFEN

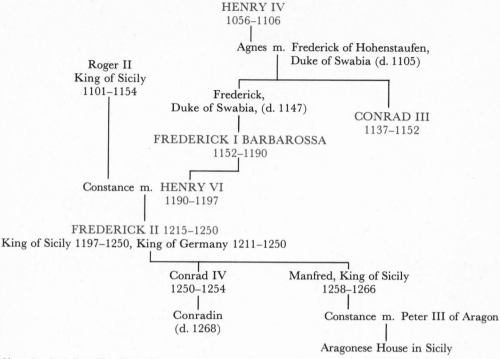

Names in color indicate Holy Roman Emperors

THE HAPSBURG FAMILY

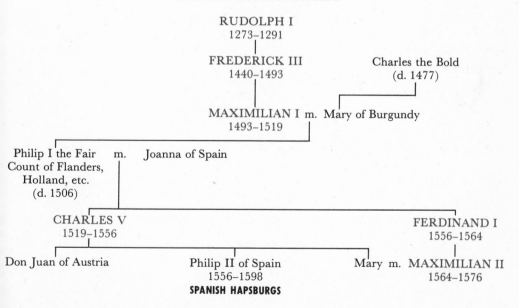

Names in color indicate Holy Roman Emperors

HOHENZOLLERN RULERS OF PRUSSIA AND GERMANY

Joachim I (Elector)	1499–1535	Frederick William I	1713–1740
Joachim II	1535–1571	Frederick II (the Great)	1740–1786
John George	1571–1598	Frederick William II	1786–1797
Joachim Frederick	1598–1608	Frederick William III	1797–1840
John Sigismund	1608–1619	Frederick William IV	1840–1861
George William	1619–1640	William I	1861–1888
Frederick William	1640–1688	(after 1871 Emperor of Germany)	
Frederick William III	1688–1713	Frederick III	1888
(after 1701 King as Frederick I)		William II	1888–1918

Romanov

Hohenzollern

IMPORTANT RULERS OF RUSSIA

HOUSE OF RURIK

Ivan I (Moneybag)	1325–1340	Basil III	1505–1533
Simeon I	1341–1353	Ivan IV (the Terrible)	1533–1584
Ivan II (the Red)	1353–1359	Theodore I (or Fëdor)	1584–1598
Demetrius III	1359–1389	Boris Godunov	1598–1605
Basil I	1389–1425	Basil IV	1606–1610
Basil II	1425–1462	(Interregnum, civil war, 1610–1613)	
Ivan III (the Great)	1462–1505		

HOUSE OF ROMANOV

Michael Romanov	1613–1645	Elizabeth	1741–1762
Alexis	1645–1676	Peter III	1762
Theodore II	1676–1682	Catharine II	1762–1796
Ivan V & Peter I	1682–1689	Paul	1796–1801
Peter I (alone)	1689–1725	Alexander I	1801–1825
Catharine I	1725–1727	Nicholas I	1825–1855
Peter II	1727–1730	Alexander II	1855–1881
Anna	1730–1740	Alexander III	1881–1894
Ivan VI	1740–1741	Nicholas II	1894–1917

The Papacy

Adapted from "The New List of Popes," prepared by Msgr. Angelo Mercati for the *Annuario Pontificio* (1947) and translated with additional notes in *Mediaeval Studies*, Vol. IX, 1947 (Toronto: Pontifical Institute of Mediaeval Studies).

St. Peter (M)[1] 42 to 67
45–67 Missionary journeys of St. Paul
  51 St. Peter presides at the Council of Jerusalem.
  64 Emperor Nero persecutes Christians.
  67 Martyrdom of SS. Peter and Paul.
St. Linus (M) 67 to 76[2]
St. Anacletus (M) 76 to 88
St. Clement (M) 88 to 97
  95 Emperor Domitian persecutes Christians.
  96 Pope Clement admonishes the Corinthians, whose church was split by controversy, to make peace among themselves.
St. Evaristus (M) 97 to 105
  100 Death of St. John, apostle and evangelist.
St. Alexander I (M) 105 to 115
106–117 Emperor Trajan persecutes Christians.
St. Sixtus I (M) 115 to 125
St. Telesphorus (M) 125 to 136
St. Hyginus (M) 136 to 140
St. Pius I (M) 140 to 155
St. Anicetus (M) 155 to 166
161–180 Emperor Marcus Aurelius persecutes Christians.
St. Soter (M) 166 to 175
St. Eleutherius (M) 175 to 189
  180 St. Irenaeus *Adversus Haereses* ("Against Heretics"), in which he upholds primacy of the popes.
St. Victor I (M) 189 to 199
  196 Pope Victor orders bishops of Asia to adopt Roman date for Easter.
St. Zephyrinus (M) 199 to 217
202–211 Emperor Septimius Severus persecutes Christians.
St. Callistus I (M) 217 to 222
  220 Pope Callistus upholds the truth (then under attack by heretics) that there are three distinct persons in God.
St. Urban I (M) 222 to 230
St. Pontianus (M) July 230 to September 235

---

[1] Abbreviation M stands for Martyr on this and subsequent pages.
[2] Up to Eleutherius, the years of the beginning and end of the pontificate are not absolutely sure.

St. Anterus (M) November 235 to January 236
235–238 Emperor Maximinus persecutes Christians.
St. Fabian (M) January 236 to January 250
249–251 Emperor Decius persecutes Christians.
St. Cornelius (M) March 251 to June 253
St. Lucius I (M) June 253 to March 254
St. Stephen I (M) May 254 to August 257
  256 Pope Stephen teaches that baptism, provided right form and intention are observed, may be administered even by heretics.
St. Sixtus II (M) August 257 to August 258
257–260 Emperor Valerian persecutes Christians.
St. Dionysius July 259 to December 268
  260 Upholds the truth (under attack by heretics) that the God of the Old Testament and the God of the New Testament are one and the same person.
St. Felix I (M) January 269 to December 274
274–275 Emperor Aurelian persecutes Christians.
St. Eutychianus (M) January 275 to December 283
St. Caius (M) December 283 to April 296
St. Marcellinus (M) June 296 to October 304
  303 Council of Elvira declares indissolubility of marriage.
303–311 Emperors Diocletian and Galerius persecute Christians.
  305 St. Anthony of Egypt founds first community of hermit monks.
St. Marcellus (M) May 308 to January 309
St. Eusebius April 309 to August 309
St. Melchiades July 311 to January 314
  313 The Edict of Milan
St. Sylvester I January 314 to December 335
  318 St. Pachomius of Egypt founds first cenobitic monastery.
  325 First ecumenical council (Nicaea I)
St. Mark January 336 to October 336
St. Julius I February 337 to April 352
350–361 Arian emperor, Constantius, persecutes Catholic Christians.
Liberius May 352 to September 366
361–363 Emperor Julian fails to re-establish paganism.
St. Damasus I October 366 to December 384
  379 Death of St. Basil
  381 Second ecumenical council (Constantinople I).
  382 Pope Damasus commissions St. Jerome to translate Bible into Latin.
St. Siricius December 384 to November 399
  390 St. Ambrose forces Emperor Theodosius to do public penance.
  392 Emperor Theodosius forbids celebration of pagan rites.

St. Anastasius I November 399 to December 401
St. Innocent I December 401 to March 417
St. Zosimus March 417 to December 418
St. Boniface I December 418 to September 422
St. Celestine I September 422 to July 432
430 Death of St. Augustine
431 Third ecumenical council (Ephesus)
432 St. Patrick begins conversion of Ireland.
St. Sixtus III July 432 to August 440
St. Leo I, the Great September 440 to November 461
451 Fourth ecumenical council (Chalcedon)
452 Pope Leo turns back Attila and the Huns from Rome.
St. Hilarus November 461 to February 468
St. Simplicius March 468 to March 483
St. Felix III (II) March 483 to March 492
484 Pope Felix excommunicates the Monophysite Patriarch of Constantinople.
St. Gelasius I March 492 to November 496
494 Pope Gelasius teaches that the emperor, in spiritual matters, must obey the Pope.
496 Franks converted to Catholicism.
Anastasius II November 496 to November 498
St. Symmachus November 498 to July 514
St. Hormisdas July 514 to August 523
519 Formula of Hormisdas (asserting papal supremacy) signed by bishops of the Eastern Church.
St. John I (M) August 523 to May 526
St. Felix IV (III) July 526 to September 530
529 St. Benedict founds monastery of Monte Cassino
Boniface II September 530 to October 532
John II January 533 to May 535
St. Agapitus I May 535 to April 536
St. Silverius June 536 to November 537
Vigilius March 537 to June 655
545 Death of Dionysius Exiguus, who introduced the practice of dividing history into pre-Christian (B.C.) and Christian (A.D.) eras.
553 Fifth ecumenical council (Constantinople II)
Pelagius I April 556 to March 561
John III July 561 to July 574
565 St. Columba founds the monastery of Iona, in Scotland.
Benedict I June 575 to July 579
Pelagius II November 579 to February 590
589 Arian Visigoths converted to Catholicism.
St. Gregory I, the Great September 590 to March 604
597 St. Augustine of Canterbury begins conversion of England.
598 Pope Gregory concludes peace with king of the Lombards.

Sabinianus September 604 to February 606
Boniface III February 607 to November 607
St. Boniface IV August 608 to May 615
St. Adeodatus I October 615 to November 618
Boniface V December 619 to October 625
Honorius I October 625 to October 638
629 Emperor Heraclius recovers the True Cross from the Persians.
Severinus May 640 to August 640
640 Moslems conquer Christian Syria.
John IV December 640 to October 642
642 Moslems conquer Christian Egypt.
Theodore I November 642 to May 649
St. Martin I (M) July 649 to September 655
649 Pope Martin upholds the truth (denied by Eastern bishops) that in Christ are both a human and a divine will.
St. Eugene I[3] August 654 to June 657
St. Vitalian July 657 to January 672
Adeodatus II April 672 to June 676
Donus November 676 to April 678
St. Agatho June 678 to January 681
680 Sixth ecumenical council (Constantinople III)
St. Leo II August 682 to July 683
St. Benedict II June 684 to May 685
John V July 685 to August 686
Cono October 686 to September 687
St. Sergius I December 687 to September 701
692 Council of Greek bishops condemns practices in the Roman Church.
698 Moslems conquer Christian North Africa.
John VI October 701 to January 705
John VII March 705 to October 707
Sisinnius January 708 to February 708
Constantine March 708 to April 715
711 Moslems begin conquest of Catholic Spain.
St. Gregory II May 715 to February 731
726 Byzantine Emperor Leo III forbids veneration of images (iconoclasm).
St. Gregory III March 731 to November 741
732 Charles Martel turns back the Moors at Poitiers.
St. Zachary December 741 to March 752
751 Pope Zachary recognizes Pepin as king of the Franks.
Stephen II March 23, 752, to March 25, 752
Stephen III March 752 to April 757
754 Pope Stephen crowns Pepin king of the Franks.
755 Martyrdom of St. Boniface by the Frisians.
756 Donation of Pepin: founding of the Papal States.

---

[3] When St. Martin was captured and deported, St. Eugene was named as his successor (hence overlapping).

St. Paul I April 757 to June 767
Stephen IV August 768 to January 772
Adrian I February 772 to December 795
  787 Seventh ecumenical council (Nicaea II) condemns iconoclasm.
St. Leo III December 795 to June 816
  800 Pope Leo crowns Charlemagne emperor.
  813 Revival of iconoclasm in Constantinople
Stephen V June 816 to January 817
St. Paschal I January 817 to February 824
Eugene II February 824 to August 827
Valentine August 827 to September 827
Gregory IV 827 to January 844
  842 Council at Constantinople condemns iconoclasm.
Sergius II January 844 to January 847
  846 Moslems attack Rome.
St. Leo IV January 847 to July 855
Benedict III July 855 to April 858
St. Nicholas I April 858 to November 867
  863 Pope Nicholas condemns King Lothair's unlawful marriage.
  863 Pope Nicholas condemns Photius, unlawful Patriarch of Constantinople.
  864 Baptism of King Boris of Bulgaria.
  865 Death of St. Ansgar, Apostle of Scandinavia
Adrian II December 867 to December 872
  868 SS. Cyril and Methodius, apostles of the Slavs, consecrated bishops by Pope Adrian.
  869 Eighth ecumenical council (Constantinople IV) restores the rightful Patriarch of Constantinople, condemns iconoclasm, and recognizes papal supremacy.
John VIII December 872 to December 882
Marinus I December 882 to May 884
St. Adrian III May 884 to September 885
Stephen VI September 885 to September 891
Formosus October 891 to April 896
Boniface VI April 896
Stephen VII May 896 to August 897
Romanus August 897 to November 897
Theodore II December 897
John IX January 898 to January 900
Benedict IV January 900 to July 903
  900 Establishment of Catholic bishoprics in Moravia
Leo V July 903 to September 903
Sergius III January 904 to April 911
  904 Papacy comes under domination of Roman political factions.
  910 Foundation of the monastery of Cluny.
Anastasius III April 911 to June 913
  911 Conversion of the Normans in France
Lando July 913 to February 914
John X March 914 to May 928
  915 Pope John defeats Moslems in southern Italy.

Leo VI May 928 to December 928
Stephen VIII December 928 to February 931
John XI February 931 to December 935
Leo VII January 936 to July 939
Stephen IX July 939 to October 942
Marinus II October 942 to May 946
Agapitus II May 946 to December 955
John XII[4] December 955 to May 964
  962 Pope John crowns Otto I Holy Roman Emperor.
Leo VIII December 963 to March 965
Benedict V May 964 to July 966
  966 Baptism of Mieszko, Duke of Poland.
John XIII October 965 to September 972
Benedict VI January 973 to June 974
Benedict VII October 974 to July 983
John XIV December 983 to August 984
John XV August 985 to March 996
  989 Baptism of Vladimir, Prince of Kiev
  993 Pope John begins system of canonizing saints to be venerated by the entire Church (as distinct from popular or local canonization).
Gregory V May 996 to February 999
Sylvester II April 999 to May 1003
  1000 Pope Sylvester confers on St. Stephen of Hungary the title of "Apostolic King."
John XVII June 1003 to December 1003
John XVIII January 1004 to July 1009
Sergius IV July 1009 to May 1012
Benedict VIII May 1012 to April 1024
John XIX April 1024 to 1032
Benedict IX 1032 to 1044
Sylvester III January 1045 to March 1045
Benedict IX April 1045 to May 1045
Gregory VI May 1045 to December 1046
  1046 Synod of Sutri puts an end to papal disorders.
Clement II December 1046 to October 1047
Benedict IX[5] November 1047 to July 1048
Damasus II July 1048 to August 1048
St. Leo IX February 1049 to April 1054
  1054 Beginning of the Greek Schism
Victor II April 1055 to July 1057
Stephen X August 1057 to March 1058
Nicholas II January 1059 to July 1061
  1059 Lateran Decree and the Treaty of Melfi
Alexander II October 1061 to April 1073

---

[4] John XII was deposed at the Roman Council under the Emperor Otto I, and Leo VIII elected to succeed him. If Leo VIII was a lawful Pope, then Benedict V, who was deposed by him, is an anti-pope.
[5] Elected for the third time. If the removals of Benedict IX (1044, 1046) were not lawful—and this should be certain for Sylvester III—Gregory VI and Clement II were anti-popes.

Gregory VII April 1073 to May 1085
1075 Decree against lay investiture.
1077 Canossa
1084 St. Bruno of Cologne founds the Carthusians.
1085 Spanish Christians take Toledo from Moors.
Blessed Victor III May 1086 to September 1087
Blessed Urban II March 1088 to July 1099
1095 Pope Urban preaches the First Crusade.
1099 Crusaders capture Jerusalem.
1098 St. Robert of Molesme founds the Cistercians.
Paschal II August 1099 to January 1118
1115 Death of St. Anselm; St. Bernard becomes Abbot of Clairvaux.
Gelasius II January 1118 to January 1119
Callistus II February 1119 to December 1124
1122 The Concordat of Worms.
1123 Ninth ecumenical council (Lateran I)
Honorius II December 1124 to February 1130
Innocent II February 1130 to September 1143
1139 Tenth ecumenical council (Lateran II)
1142 Death of Abelard
Celestine II September 1143 to March 1144
Lucius II March 1144 to February 1145
Blessed Eugene III February 1145 to July 1153
1147 St. Bernard preaches the Second Crusade.
Anastasius IV July 1153 to December 1154
Adrian IV December 1154 to September 1159
Alexander III September 1159 to August 1181
1160 Death of Gratian and Peter Lombard
1170 Martyrdom of St. Thomas à Becket
1176 Battle of Legnano
1179 Eleventh ecumenical council (Lateran III)
Lucius III September 1181 to September 1185
1184 Pope Lucius excommunicates the Waldensians.
Urban III November 1185 to October 1187
1187 Saladin captures Jerusalem.
Gregory VIII October 1187 to December 1187
Clement III December 1187 to March 1191
1189–1192 Third Crusade fails to recover Jerusalem.
Celestine III March 1191 to January 1198
Innocent III January 1198 to July 1216
1204 Fourth Crusade captures Constantinople.
1209 St. Francis and the early Franciscans
1208 England under interdict
1209 The Albigensian Crusade
1213 England becomes a papal fief
1215 Twelfth ecumenical council (Lateran IV)
Honorius III July 1216 to March 1227
1216 St. Dominic and the early Dominicans
Gregory IX March 1227 to August 1241
1227 Pope Gregory excommunicates Emperor Frederick II.
1233 Pope Gregory establishes the Inquisition.

Celestine IV October 1241 to November 1241
Innocent IV June 1243 to December 1254
1245 Thirteenth ecumenical council (Lyon I)
1248–1254 St. Louis' crusade to Egypt and the Holy Land
Alexander IV December 1254 to May 1261
Urban IV August 1261 to October 1264
Clement IV February 1265 to November 1268
Blessed Gregory X September 1271 to January 1276
1274 Fourteenth ecumenical council (Lyon II); death of St. Thomas Aquinas and St. Bonaventure
Blessed Innocent V January 1276 to June 1276
Adrian V July 1276 to August 1276
John XXI September 1276 to May 1277
Nicholas III November 1277 to August 1280
Martin IV February 1281 to March 1285
1282 The Sicilian Vespers
Honorius IV April 1285 to April 1287
Nicholas IV February 1288 to April 1292
1291 Fall of Acre; end of the crusades
St. Celestine V July 1294 to December 1294
Boniface VIII December 1294 to October 1303
1296 The bull *Clericis laicos*
1300 The first Holy Year
1303 The Crime of Anagni
Blessed Benedict XI October 1303 to July 1304
Clement V June 1305 to April 1314
1309 Pope Clement establishes the papal residence at Avignon.
1311–1312 Fifteenth ecumenical council (Vienna); suppression of the Templars
John XXII August 1316 to December 1334
1326 Marsiglio of Padua's *Defensor pacis*
Benedict XII December 1334 to April 1342
Clement VI May 1342 to December 1352
Innocent VI December 1352 to September 1362
1353 Statute of Praemunire
Blessed Urban V September 1362 to December 1370
Gregory XI December 1370 to March 1378
Urban VI April 1378 to October 1389
1378 Beginning of Great Western Schism
1381 John Wycliffe denies basic teachings of the Church.
Boniface IX November 1389 to October 1404
Innocent VIII October 1404 to November 1406
Gregory XII November 1406 to July 1415[6]
1409 Council of Pisa produces a Triple Schism.
1414–1418 The sixteenth ecumenical council (Constance)
1415 End of Great Western Schism; burning of John Hus

---

[6] Date of his resignation; he died in October 1417.

Martin V November 1417 to February 1431
Eugene IV March 1431 to February 1447
1431 Burning of Joan of Arc
1431–1443 Seventeenth ecumenical council (Basel-Ferrara-Florence)
Nicholas V March 1447 to March 1455
Callistus III April 1455 to August 1458
Pius II August 1458 to August 1464
Paul II September 1464 to July 1471
Sixtus IV August 1471 to August 1484
Innocent VIII August 1484 to July 1492
Alexander VI August 1492 to August 1503
1493 Bull of Demarcation
Pius III September 1503 to October 1503
Julius II November 1503 to February 1513
1512–1517 Eighteenth ecumenical council (Lateran V)
Leo X March 1513 to December 1521
1517 Luther's ninety-five theses
1520 Excommunication of Luther
Adrian VI August 1522 to September 1523
Clement VII November 1523 to September 1534
1529 Virtual destruction of the Catholic Church in Sweden
1531 Death of Zwingli
1533 Excommunication of King Henry VIII
Paul III October 1534 to November 1549
1535 Martyrdom of St. John Fisher and St. Thomas More
1536 John Calvin's *Institutes of the Christian Religion*
1540 Founding of the Society of Jesus
1545–1563 Nineteenth ecumenical council (Trent)
1546 Virtual destruction of the Catholic Church in Denmark
Julius III February 1550 to March 1555
1552 Death of St. Francis Xavier
1553 Restoration of the Catholic Church in England
1555 The Peace of Augsburg
Marcellus II April 1555 to May 1555
Paul IV May 1555 to August 1559
Pius IV December 1559 to December 1565
1560 Triumph of Protestantism in Scotland
1563 The Thirty-nine Articles and re-passage of the Act of Supremacy
St. Pius V January 1566 to May 1572
1571 Battle of Lepanto
Gregory XIII May 1572 to April 1585
1582 Death of St. Teresa of Avila; adoption of Gregorian Calendar
Sixtus V April 1585 to August 1590
Urban VII September 15, 1590, to September 27, 1590
Gregory XIV December 1590 to October 1591
Innocent IX October 1591 to December 1591

Clement VIII January 1592 to March 1605
1601 Matteo Ricci's mission to China
Leo XI April 1, 1605, to April 27, 1605
Paul V May 1605 to January 1621
Gregory XV February 1621 to July 1623
Urban VIII August 1623 to July 1644
Innocent X September 1644 to January 1655
1649 Cromwell in Ireland
1653 Condemnation of Jansenism
Alexander VII April 1655 to May 1667
Clement IX June 1667 to December 1669
Clement X April 1670 to July 1676
Innocent XI September 1676 to August 1689
1682 Gallican Articles
Alexander VIII October 1689 to February 1691
1690 Condemnation of the Gallican Articles
Innocent XII August 1691 to September 1700
Clement XI November 1700 to March 1721
Innocent XIII May 1721 to March 1724
Benedict XIII May 1724 to February 1730
Clement XII July 1730 to February 1740
Benedict XIV August 1740 to May 1758
Clement XIII July 1758 to February 1769
Clement XIV May 1769 to September 1774
1773 Suppression of the Jesuits
Pius VI February 1775 to August 1799
1790 *Civil Constitution of the Clergy*
1798 The French occupy Rome and carry the Pope a prisoner to France.
Pius VII March 1800 to August 1823
1801 Concordat with France
1809 Pope Pius becomes a prisoner of Napoleon.
1814 Restoration of the Jesuits
Leo XII September 1823 to February 1829
Pius VIII March 1829 to November 1830
1829 Catholic Emancipation in Great Britain and Ireland
Gregory XVI February 1831 to June 1846
1845 Conversion of John Henry Newman (later Cardinal); Norway grants toleration to Catholics
Pius IX June 1846 to February 1878
1849 Denmark grants toleration to Catholics
1850 Catholic hierarchy re-established in Great Britain
1854 Proclamation of the dogma of the Immaculate Conception
1858 Apparition of the Blessed Virgin Mary to Bernadette at Lourdes
1864 The *Syllabus of Errors*
1870 Twentieth ecumenical council (Vatican); loss of the Papal States
Leo XIII February 1878 to July 1903
1879 Revival of Thomistic philosophy
1891 The encyclical *Rerum novarum*
1903 Expulsion of the religious orders from France

St. Pius X August 1903 to August 1914
1907 Encyclical on modernism
Benedict XV September 1914 to January 1922
1917 Apparition of the Blessed Virgin Mary at Fatima; Pope Benedict XV's Peace Plan
Pius XI February 1922 to February 1939
1929 The Lateran Treaty; encyclical on Christian education
1931 The encyclical *Quadragesimo anno*
1937 The encyclical *Divini redemptoris*

Pius XII March 1939 to
1949 Excommunication of all who willingly adhere to communism
1950 The Holy Year; proclamation of the dogma of the Assumption
1954 The Marian Year; canonization of St. Pius X
1957 New Code of Canon Law for Eastern Rite Churches
1958 The 100th anniversary of Lourdes

Glossary

Abbot. Head of a monastery, usually elected for life by the monks.

Absolutism. Rule of a dictator or of a king who recognizes no limits to his power.

Anarchy. Absence of any form of government. Anarchists are those who believe that all government is evil and should be destroyed.

Anti-Clericalism. Hostility to the clergy or to the activity of the Church; may or may not include opposition to religion itself.

Aristocracy. Group that claims special privileges in society because of its birth.

Autocracy. State ruled by one man in accordance with his own desires or judgment.

Autonomy. Right of self-government of a minority group or of a province or part of a country or empire.

Balance of Power. Policy of European powers to align themselves in such a manner as to prevent any one country from endangering the safety of others.

Barbarians. Uncivilized peoples or tribes; a term applied by the Romans to persons living beyond the limits of their empire.

Belligerent. Country at war.

Benefice. Ecclesiastical position which ensures its holder a steady, annual income.

Bishop. Priest who, through powers first conferred by Christ on the Apostles and passed down through the centuries, has the power to ordain priests and bishops and has spiritual authority over the clergy and laymen of a specified area (a diocese).

Borough. In medieval England, a town having the right to elect its own officials, pass local laws, and hold its own courts. On the Continent, a borough was known as a commune.

Bourgeoisie. Originally the merchants and artisans of the towns; later those persons who were socially between the gentry and the peasants; for Communists the term signifies the profit-making as opposed to the wage-earning class.

Buffer State. Small state that separates two larger and rival countries.

Bull. Formerly all important papal letters, now a formal letter or edict used by the Pope on solemn occasions and so called because of the seals attached to it (*bullae*).

Bureaucracy. Centralized government organized in departments and bureaus and administered according to rigid rules and routines and often unresponsive to popular control.

Burgess. A middle-class citizen of a borough.

Caliphate. Office of the successors of Mohammed or the leader of the faithful.

Canon. (1) Ecclesiastical law or decree. The Church's law is called Canon Law.
(2) Member of the cathedral staff of clergymen.

Capitalism. Economic system under which the ownership of capital is in private hands.

Carolingian. Dynasty of the kings of France who descended from Charles (Carolus in Latin) Martel and Charlemagne.

Caste. One of the four unchangeable classes into which ancient Hindu society was divided; the highest caste, the Brahmans, performed religious services, while the lowest or Sudras performed menial labor. Those who belonged to no caste were outcastes or pariahs (untouchables).

Chancellor. Government official in charge of the office (chancery) which handled the king's correspondence; the chancellor was often the equivalent of a prime minister.

Chapter. Assembly of monks or of cathedral canons.

Chartists. Persons who signed the Great Charter or petition that was presented to the British Parliament in 1848, demanding annual elections, equal electoral districts, etc.

Christendom. Christian world, peoples, beliefs, and institutions.

Christian Democracy. According to Pope Leo XIII, Christian democracy is built on the "basic principles of divine faith, and it must provide better conditions for the masses, with the ulterior object of promoting the perfection of souls made for things eternal." Christian democracy means "the beneficent Christian action in behalf of the people."

Citizen. Person who is subject to a government, owes it allegiance, and is entitled to the government's protection.

City-State. Self-governing communities of antiquity consisting of a city and its surrounding countryside governed by free citizens. (See also **Polis.**)

Civilization. State of society characterized by social peace and by advances in social culture.

Clan. Group of families claiming descent from a common ancestry. Several clans claiming descent from a common ancestry are called a tribe.

Class. Loose term to cover all those who might be thought of as engaged in the same general economic activity, as workers, farmers, or professional people.

College of Cardinals, Sacred. Corporate body of the Pope's counselors and adjutants, which, when complete, numbers 70.

Commerce. Buying and selling of goods.

Common Law. Customary law that grew up from judges' decisions in medieval England and became the basis for our own law.

Commons. Lower house of the British Parliament.

Commonwealth of Nations, British. United Kingdom and several former British colonies that are now self-governing nations, united in sentiment and by formal, voluntary agreement into an international, economic, and political association.

Communism. Philosophy formulated by Marx and developed in the U. S. S. R. by Lenin and Stalin. It is purely materialistic and militantly atheistic. It denies the right to private property and placed absolute control of the community in the hands of the Communist Party. Communism holds that history is a constant revolution and, as a result, justifies violence and disregards the sacredness of the human person.

Compurgation. Swearing by several persons that an accused person is of good character and therefore should be acquitted of the crime with which he is charged.

Concordat. Treaty between the Pope and government for the regulation of certain matters in dispute.

Confederate Government. Political system in which member states retain sovereignty and delegate only certain powers to the central government, which is their agent.

Conservatism. Attitude that favors slow, organic growth and change in the political and social structure in order to preserve the best of the past.

Constitution. Basic set of rules by which a people or an association is governed.

Consul. In the Roman Republic the two chief magistrates who ruled jointly; also the three executives who governed France from 1799 to 1804. (Napoleon was the First Consul.)

Corporation. In the Middle Ages a group of persons such as teachers, recognized as a legal entity, distinct from the persons composing it; in modern times a form of business organization.

Cortes. Spanish equivalent of parliament.

County. (1) Feudal district ruled by a count.
(2) In England a political, administrative, and judicial district.

Coup D'État. Sudden overthrow of a government.

Culture. Certain pattern of human activity that is shared by a whole group and has been fixed for some length of time.

Curia. Papal court that assists the Pope in the government of the Church, consisting of departments which handle such matters as papal correspondence, appointments to ecclesiastical office, dispensations, etc.

Custom. Unwritten rule for conduct that is accepted by a group.

Czar (or Tsar). Russian equivalent for Caesar, hence the emperor of Russia.

Dauphin. Title for the eldest son and heir of the King of France.

Deductive Method of Reasoning. Reasoning from the general truth to the particular, as opposed to the inductive method, which reasons from the particular to the general.

Deism. "Natural religion" of the Enlightenment that rejected the Christian revelation. It worshiped God as a master engineer and scientist Who created the universe but Who does not intervene in the world.

Democracy. As a *form of government,* democracy involves the direct control of government by the people, within the restrictions of constitutional law. As a *philosophy of government,* much more is implied: the recognition of the authority of the government and the political and legal equality of all citizens before this authority.

Depression. Period in the business cycle following a recession and characterized by a continuing low level of industrial activity, unemployment, and lack of confidence.

Dictator. In ancient Rome the military person who assumed supreme power for six months during a dangerous period; in modern times a person who seizes control of the government and permits no opposition.

Diet. Formal assembly of the member states and princes of the Holy Roman Empire.

Diocese. Church district and its people over which a bishop has jurisdiction.

Diplomatic Revolution. Sudden reversal of long-standing friendships and enmities among nations; viz., the alliance in 1756 of age-old rivals Austria and France.

Divine Right. Rule of a prince or king who acknowledges no responsibility to people or legislatures but to God alone.

Dominion. One of the self-governing countries, such as Canada and Australia, in the (British) Commonwealth of Nations, dominion status being defined in 1931 by the British Parliament.

Dynasty. A succession of kings (and queens) belonging to the same family.

Eastern Question. Political and international problems raised by the weakening and impending fall of the Polish and Turkish empires in the eighteenth and nineteenth centuries.

Economy. Productive facilities and the characteristics of how people satisfy their economic wants.

Ecumenical (or General) Council. Convening of the bishops of the universal Church by the Pope, presided over either by him or his legates. Decrees of ecumenical councils approved by the Pope are infallible.

Elector. One of the princes who had a voice in the selection of the Holy Roman Emperor.

Embassy. Official duties or official residence of a nation's ambassador in a foreign capital city. An ambassador is the highest-ranking ordinary representative of a nation.

Empire. Government organized over extended territories, once separate, but united by colonization, federation, or military conquest under one monarch (emperor).

Enclosure. Process from the end of the Middle Ages to modern times of replacing the large open fields in England by smaller, individually owned farms.

Encyclical. A letter of the Pope addressed to *all* the Church and containing official teaching on questions of current interest. Encyclical *epistle* is addressed to a specific country or region.

Entente. Agreement or an understanding between nations, such as the Entente Cordiale of 1904 between Britain and France.

Escheat. Feudal practice whereby a fief reverted to the original grantor when the lord of the fief died without heirs.

Established Church. One supported directly by the state through funds and other special privileges denied to other churches.

Estates-General. The assembly in France of the representatives of the three orders, the nobility, the clergy, and middle and peasant classes.

Excommunication. A form of censure by which one is deprived of the sacraments.

Extraterritoriality. Right of a country to exercise jurisdiction over its citizens on the territory of another country.

Factory. In early modern times a European trading station in foreign lands where European factors, or agents, lived and did business with the natives; later, the building where production took place.

Fascism. Totalitarian organization of society in Italy under Mussolini, characterized by an all-powerful state, exaggerated nationalism, and the reign of a dictator and a single party.

Federalism. System of dividing political power and ultimate authority between the central government and the various states into which the country is divided.

Feudalism. Political system of the Middle Ages, characterized by the personal relation of lord and vassal and the conditional possession of land and/or an office by the vassal; the term is generally associated with weak central government and strong landed classes.

Fief. Land or some form of income or office held of a lord by a vassal subject to performance of his duties.

Forfeiture. Feudal practice whereby a fief reverted to its original grantor when the lord of the fief broke his oath of loyalty to his own lord (the original grantor).

Franchise. The right to vote.

Free Trade. System of permitting the easy flow of goods across national boundaries by eliminating or lowering duties on foreign exports; opposed to protectionism.

Gallicanism. Attempt to place the Catholic Church in France under the control of the King of France and not the Pope; the term now signifies a national church free of papal control.

Genesis. First book of the Old Testament, which narrates the creation by God of the universe and man.

Glorious Revolution. Replacement of the Catholic King of England, James II, by his Protestant son-in-law and daughter, William and Mary, in 1688 and the end of divine-right monarchy.

Gold Standard. Monetary standard that defines the unit of value in terms of a fixed quantity of gold and into which all forms of legal tender may be converted.

Grand Jury. Group of citizens selected to examine the case of an accused person to see whether he should be brought to trial.

Guild. Association of craftsmen or merchants for the purpose of regulating their business.

Heresy. Denial of one or more Church doctrines; also, an explicit teaching that goes contrary to Church teaching.

Hierarchy. Sacred rule or government of the Catholic Church in successive ranks from priests to bishops to Pope.

Homage. Feudal ceremony in which the vassal formally acknowledged his lord.

Individualism. (1) Doctrine that the government has negative function of maintaining order, enforcing legal contracts, and protecting individual freedom, leaving individuals to pursue their respective interests.
(2) Tendency to exaggerate individual liberty at the expense of church, state, or a society; individual action against community activity.

Industrial Revolution. Series of inventions and events that led to the replacement of production in the home by hand or simple tools to production in the factory by machines.

Inquisition. Ecclesiastical court of justice in the Middle Ages to investigate and punish heretics.

Institution. Established and accepted way in which a human group satisfies one of its basic needs.

Interdict. Suspension by the Pope of liturgical services and some of the sacraments within a certain area or country.

Interregnum. Interval between two reigns, such as the period between the execution of Charles I of England in 1649 and the restoration of Charles II in 1660.

Islam. Religion preached by Mohammed; literally, submission to God.

Isolationism. Conviction that a country ought to look only to its own interests and avoid international responsibilities that might involve it in conflict.

Jacobinism. Political doctrines of the most radical of the political clubs of the French Revolution; the term is now applied to persons who are extreme radicals.

Jansenism. Heretical beliefs taught by the French bishop, Cornelius Jansen, concerning grace and predestination.

Khan. Formerly the ruler of a Mongol state; now a title assumed by high military and religious officials in Iran, Afghanistan, India, etc.

Knight. In feudal times a mounted warrior, obliged to follow the code of chivalry in warfare.

Koran. Mohammedan holy book containing the teachings of Mohammed; for Islam the final authority in religious, social, and legal matters.

Laissez-Faire. French term that means "let alone" and refers to the theory that government should not interfere in any way in economic activity.

Lay Investiture. The conferring on a cleric of the insignia of a church office, such as the ring and staff of a bishop, by a layman.

Leftist. In politics those who tend to favor sweeping changes, especially the elimination or drastic reduction of established institutions.

Legate. Papal envoy authorized by the Pope to act in his name.

Liberalism. In early nineteenth century it meant a political system inspired by the ideals of the French Revolution and held that man ought to be liberated from religious and political authority; in nineteenth-century England it stood for reform of government and extension of liberty; and in the twentieth century, a loose term that stood for social legislation and a willingness to reject old institutions in favor of new ones.

Liturgy. Public ceremonies of the Church, especially the Mass.

Lords, House of. Upper house of the British Parliament; its members sit there by virtue of their hereditary titles.

Magistrate. Official empowered to administer and enforce the law.

Mandate. In international law, an agreement by which a major world power supervises and protects a weaker or less developed nation.

Manor. Medieval estate, consisting of the lands worked by serfs and tenants, one or more villages, and the lands specially set aside for the lord's use.

Mercantilism. Theory of political economy of the sixteenth to eighteenth century that held that a nation should seek a greater supply of gold for itself by developing its home industries through international trade; if the nation held colonies, these were to function as suppliers of raw materials and markets for manufactured goods.

Mercenary. Professional soldier who fights solely for pay.

Middle Passage. Trip of a slave ship from the African coast to the American colonies.

Military Order. Religious order whose members took the usual vows of poverty, chastity, and obedience but who were distinguished from other monks in that they waged war against the heathen.

Mogul. Or Mongol, the descendant(s) and successor(s) of Tamerlane, the ruler(s) of India from the sixteenth to the eighteenth century.

Monarchy. Form of government with hereditary head of state.

Monasticism. Way of life of monks, who seclude themselves from the world and who practice self-denial and asceticism, according to a Rule (e.g. the Rule of St. Benedict) and religious vows for the purpose of perfecting themselves and of serving God and the Church.

Moslem. Person who embraces Islam.

Mystery Religion. Any one of ancient pagan religions characterized by secret ceremonies and the promise of salvation to the initiated.

Nation. A group of people who, through their common interests (cultural, religious, economic, linguistic, etc.), feel themselves to be a *single* people.

Nationalism. A feeling that one belongs to a group with a common history and certain common traits, which is thereby entitled to have its own independent government; also,·strong attachment and interest in the glory and honor of one's own country.

National Socialism. Doctrines of Adolf Hitler and his Nazis, based on racial nationalism, force, and the fusion of the German people and state into a living organism that would be directed and inspired by the leader or Führer.

Nativism. The practice of discriminating against those who are not natives (i.e. against naturalized citizens or aliens).

Natural Frontiers. Those boundaries which a nation thinks it should have in order to be geographically unified.

Neutral. A nation that takes no direct part in a war.

Oath. Solemn declaration calling God to witness that what one says is true or that one will carry out a certain promise, etc.

Old Regime. Traditional way of life in Europe before the French Revolution that included absolute monarchy, privileged classes, established churches, and age-old customs.

Open Door. Free and equal opportunity for all nations to trade with a given nation, without any restrictions such as tariffs and customs duties.

Ordeal. Primitive method of trial in which the accused sought to clear himself by successfully undergoing some dangerous physical test.

Orthodox Church. The Eastern Church in schism with Rome since 1054. This church calls itself the Orthodox Church and, as a matter of courtesy, is generally called by that name by Catholics. The Eastern Church is, indeed, orthodox in the sense that it accepts all the dogmas issued by the Catholic Church before 1054 and has not *explicitly* rejected any of the dogmas issued since that time.

Parlement. A high court of justice in France during the Old Regime; especially the Parlement of Paris, the highest court of justice in France, which had the right to register the king's laws (Ordonnances) before they could take effect.

Parliament. The legislature of Great Britain, which controls most executive and judicial activity. The term is often used for other countries' legislatures.

Patrician. A member of the ancient Roman nobility.

Pax Romana. State of internal peace which existed within the Roman Empire from the reign of Augustus to the death of Commodus (27 B.C.–A.D. 192).

People's Democracy. Term used by Communists to designate a Communist-controlled state.

Philosophe. An eighteenth-century author who, through the effect of his writings, hoped to remake society so that it would conform to his own notion of reasonableness.

Physiocrats. An economic school that taught that the only true source of wealth was the land and its products (agricultural produce, dairying, metals, etc.) and hence that only the land should be taxed. They further taught that government should neither tax nor interfere with commerce and industry.

Plebeian. Any Roman citizen who was not a patrician.

Plebiscite. Direct election in which citizens determine their form of government or attachment to a particular nation.

Polis. The Greek community or city-state, the focus of religious, political, social, cultural, and intellectual life in Hellas.

Polytheism. Belief in many gods.

Pope. The Bishop of Rome who, as the successor of St. Peter and the Vicar of Christ on earth, holds the supreme governing and teaching authority in the Catholic Church.

Praetor. Annually elected Roman magistrate in charge of the judicial system.

Pragmatism. System of thinking that denies any "absolute truth" and that subjects all reality or all "facts" to a test of utility, determining the truth and goodness of such reality by the degree of practicality and workability shown. Pragmatism makes truth a relative matter that can be distinguished from error by the test of efficaciousness. The entire philosophy is opposed to the teachings of the Catholic Church, since without any "absolute truth" there can be no objective standard of law and morality.

Prehistoric. Pertaining to a period of history from which no written records have survived.

Prince of Wales. The male heir to the British throne.

Proconsul. Roman magistrate who acted in the place of a consul; he was usually appointed to command an army or govern a province.

Proletariat. Word used to describe all those who make their living by receiving wages for labor and who have no other source of support.

Propaganda. The dissemination, in a very organized manner, of ideas, information, doctrine, etc.

Prophet. One who is specially appointed by God to make known His will to men.

Proprietors. Owners of property, especially of real estate.

Protectorate. A state which is protected, and whose affairs are to a great extent directed, by another state; also, the relationship between two such states.

Puritans. A group in England and the American colonies who, in the sixteenth and seventeenth centuries, wanted a greater reformation of the Church of England than that established by Elizabeth I.

Radical. One who is discontented with society as it exists and works to bring about sweeping changes as quickly as possible.

Rationalism. The belief that the only valid ideas and actions are those that can be demonstrated to be valid by reason alone.

Reactionary. A term used to describe those who wish to uphold the old way at all costs and who oppose all change in government or society.

Renaissance. From the fourteenth to sixteenth century, the artistic and literary movement which took as its models the masterpieces of ancient Greece and Rome.

Reparations. Payments made by a defeated nation for damages which it, in the course of a war, inflicted on non-military objectives (civilians, property, etc.) of the victor.

Republic. Form of government in which the governing authority rests in the body of citizens who enjoy the suffrage; in which the executive is elected or nominated (not hereditary) and those responsible for the exercise of government represent directly or indirectly their constituents. The term *republic* has been applied to describe forms of government ranging from the early Roman republic, which was ruled by the patrician class, to the modern republic of the United States, an essentially democratic form of government in which the majority of the adult population makes up the electorate and in which there are the restrictions of constitutional law.

Restoration. The re-establishment of a monarchy after a period when it had ceased to function.

Revolution. An overthrow, by the use of force, of a form of government or society.

Rightist. In politics, those who tend to be more conservative and who dislike changing established customs.

Rite. A prescribed form of conducting a religious ceremony. In the Catholic Church the Mass is celebrated according to several different rites, Roman, Greek, Slavonic, Armenian, Syrian, etc.

Romanticism. In the late eighteenth and the nineteenth centuries, a literary and artistic movement which turned its back on the Enlightenment and stressed the importance of faith, tradition, sentiment, individualism, nationality, imagination, and folkways.

Royal Domain. In the Middle Ages, that part of France whose immediate lord was not a duke or count but the king himself.

Satellite. A state which, though technically independent, is controlled politically, economically, and culturally by a larger state.

Schism. Division within the Church, especially a division resulting from the refusal to regard the Pope as the head of the Church.

Scholasticism. Philosophy characteristic of the Middle Ages, especially of St. Thomas Aquinas; it lays great stress on arriving at truth through the use of reason.

Secession. Act of separation or withdrawal from a federation of states. In the United States, a theory that a state may voluntarily leave the Union; term is also used to indicate a formal statement by a state that it has withdrawn from the Union.

Secularism. Belief that religion is purely a private affair and should be kept out of education, business affairs, public affairs, and all organizations and affairs that are not specifically dedicated to a religious cause.

Sedition. Action that leads to rebellion or treason by tending to incite others to overthrow a lawfully established government.

Senate. In broad usage, an assembly that determines a country's policies through its deliberations and legislation.

Serf. A peasant who, in return for land which he could neither leave nor be dispossessed from, rendered a lord certain services, usually of an agricultural nature.

Sheriff. In medieval England a royal official assigned to a specific county in order to look after the king's interests in that county, enforce the king's law, and preside over the county court.

Sinn Fein. An Irish party, founded in 1905, for the purpose of establishing Irish independence from Great Britain.

Social Contract. Theory that government is based on an original contract between men whereby each man who was a party to the contract voluntarily surrendered, for the common good, his unlimited right to govern himself, thereby establishing government; consequently any government that does not ensure the common good (that is, violates the original contract) may be changed or overthrown by the governed and another put in its place.

Socialism. Theory that the production and distribution of goods should be owned and controlled by the community rather than by private individuals, with all members of the community sharing the work and products.

Sovereignty. Full power and dominion of a self-governing and independent state. Used before the American Civil War to indicate full power of settlers to determine whether they would have slavery in their territory.

Soviet. In Russia, any governing council; its members, all of whom must be Communists in good standing, are elected by the people.

Sphere of Influence. Area comprising countries whose actions, especially political, are influenced by a great power.

State (the). That governing organization within a society which has the authority and the means to govern that society with a view to the common good. The state has its law and its government, both necessary to its existence and the good of society. Whatever authority the state has comes from the source of all authority, God.

Status Quo. Term used to indicate a continuation of existing arrangements or of arrangements that existed before a war or controversy.

Sultan. Moslem prince or sovereign.

Syllabus of Errors. Section of the encyclical *Quanta Cura,* issued by Pope Pius IX in 1864; it is a list of certain false teachings current in the mid-nineteenth century.

Tariff. Tax placed by a government upon exports or, especially, imports.

Tories. In England those who favored allowing the king to play a large role in the affairs of the kingdom and who were characterized, on the whole, by conservative principles.

Totalitarianism. Form of government in which one political party has complete control and allows no opposition.

Tradition. (1) Unwritten teachings of Christ and the Apostles. (2) Beliefs and customs passed down by word of mouth and example from generation to generation.

Treaty. Formal agreement between two or more nations, relating to peace, alliance, trade, etc.

Tribune. Annually elected Roman official entrusted with looking after the interests of the plebeians.

Triple Alliance. Alliance, founded in 1882, of Germany, Austria, and Italy.

Triple Entente. Military "understanding" reached by Great Britain, France, and Russia to counterbalance the Triple Alliance.

Tyranny. In ancient Greece a political situation wherein the machinery of government was controlled by a single man.

Ultimatum. Terms offered by one government to another, the rejection of which leads to a break in diplomatic relations and sometimes to war.

Utilitarianism. Belief that the value of something is determined solely by its usefulness.

Vassal. One who, in return for a fief (usually land), rendered the grantor of the fief military and other honorable services.

Viceroy. One who is appointed by a king to rule a certain country in the king's name.

Virtual Representation. The theory of representative government that holds that every representative (member of parliament) represents the interests of the whole nation, not solely those of his constituents.

Whigs. In England those who favored curbing the king's role in national affairs, increasing the power of Parliament and allowing greater rights to the common people.

Writ. An order issued by a court commanding an individual or individuals to do or abstain from doing a certain act. In the Middle Ages writs were commonly issued by the king's court, ordering that property disputes be settled by trial by jury.

Zollverein. A customs union consisting of all the German states except Austria. Its members imposed no tariffs on one another and adopted uniform tariff rates against the rest of the world.

Index

British Empire, decline of, 699
British North American Act of 1867, 531
British Royal Niger Company, 552
Brittany, settlement of, 187
Bronze, use of, *47, 73*
Bronze Age, 42
Brown, Arthur, 644
Brown, John, execution of, 532
Broz, Joseph. *See* Tito
Bruce, Robert, victory of at Bannockburn, 277
Bruening, Chancellor Heinrich, 654
Brunswick, Duke of, 452
Brunswicks, as British rulers, 418
Brusilov, Gen. Alexei, 605
Brutus, and murder of Caesar, 144
Bucharest, Treaty of, 597
Buddhism, theories of, 65–66
Budget, French, inequality of, 447
Buffon, classification system of, 407
Bulgaria, autonomy of, 544; effect of Neuilly treaty upon, 625; joins Central Powers, 604; offensive against, 605
Bulge, Battle of the, 688–89
Bund, the, 522
Burgoyne, Gen, John, surrender of, *436*
Burgundians, kingdom of, 175; Frankish conquest of, 178, 196
Burke, Edmund, *451;* on French Revolution, 451; influence of on romantics, 492; on religion, 493; on responsibility of governor, 440
Burma, British liberation of, 692
Burns, Robert, 491
Burton, Richard, 551
Byblos, 54
Byrd, Capt. Richard E., 645
Byron, Lord, *491, 493*
Byzantine Empire, civilization of, 186, 218, 219; and Fourth Crusade, 265
Byzantium, founding of, 76. *See also* Constantinople; Istanbul

Cabinet, early English, 431
Cabots, exploration of the, 360
Cabral, Pedro, journeys of, 360
Cadavers, use of, 373
Cadorna, Gen. Luigi, 611
Caesar, Julius Gaius, *142;* conquests of, 142–44; death of, 144; history of the wars of, 147; as member of First Triumvirate, 142; reforms of, 144
Cahiers, 447
Cairo, Allies meet Chiang Kai-shek at, 686
Calendar, Gregorian, 374; origin of, 43–44
Calixtines, demand of, 323
Calixtus II, Pope, 242
Calles, Plutarco, 641
Calvin, John, *338;* doctrines of, 338–39
Calvinism, spread of, 339
Cambrai, League of, 330
Cambyses, reign of, 58
Cameroons, German claim to, 552
Campion, Edmund, 344
Campo Formio, Treaty of, 457

Canaan, 45, 52; Israelites in, 53
Canada, development of, 428; dominion status of, 531; effect of American Revolution on 439–40; French cede to Britain, 428; granted home rule, 531
Canada Reunion Act of 1840, 485
Cannae, Roman defeat at; 136
Canning, George, and Pres. Monroe, 487
Canons, duties of, 242
Canterbury, Archbishop of, and Henry VIII, 340
Canterbury, dispute over archbishopric of, 263
Canute, king of the Danes, 229
Capet, Hugh, dynasty of, 205
Capillaries, discovery of, 373
Capitalists, international co-operation between, 542
Caporetto, Italian defeat at, 611
Cappadocia, kingdom of, 113
Capuchins, work of the, 341
Carbonari, the, 477, 510–11
Caribbean, British ambition in, 362; U.S. interest in, 557–58, 560
Carlyle, Thomas, on French Revolution, 449
Carpini, John, attempt of to convert Mongols, 285
Carthage, 54; civilization of, 134–35; ruin of, 137
Carthusians, the, 243
Cartier, Jacques, explorations of, 360–61
Cartwright, Edmund, invention of, 498
Casablanca, Allied meeting at, 685
Casimir IV, King of Poland, annexes West Prussia, 310
Caste system, beginnings of, 64; influence of Buddhism on, 65
Castlereagh, Viscount Robert, at Congress of Vienna, 471
Castles, purpose of, 210
Catacombs, the, *161*
Catechism, as Napoleonic propaganda, 462–63
Catharine the Great, Czarina of Russia, ambitions of, 435–36; effect of Enlightenment on, 414–15; "Grand Design" of, 438
Catharsis, 103
Catherine of Aragon, 303, 339
Catholic Association, influence of, 495–96
Catholic Church: in the Far East, 286; growth of, 715–16; influence of political changes on, 647. *See also* Catholicism; Catholics; Church; Papacy; Papal States; Religion
Catholic Evidence Guild, 648
Catholicism, English, 647–48; liturgies of, 220; post-World War I, 646–47
Catholic revival, 494
Catholics, persecution of during Glorious Revolution, 394–95
Catholic Social Guild, 648
Catholic Truth Society, 648
Catiline, conspiracy of, 147–48
Catullus, Caius, poetry of, 147
Cauchon, Bishop Pierre, at trial of Joan of Arc, 300
Caudillos, seize power, 488

Cavaignac, Gen. 513
Cavalry, Charles Martel's use of, 197–98
Cavendish, Henry, 406
Cavour, Camillo di, *522;* and unification of Italy, 522–25
Celestine I, Pope, 180
Celestine III, Pope, 255
Center Party, German Catholics form, 539
Centuriate Assembly, 128
Cerularius, Michael, and Great Schism, 221–22
Ceylon, Portuguese interests in, 352
Chaeronea, battle of, 99
Chalcedon, Council of, 180
Chaldean Empire. *See* Neo-Babylonian Empire
Châlons, battle of, 175
Chamberlain, Neville, *670;* appeasement policy of, 670–71
Champlain, Samuel, 362
Charlemagne, Holy Roman Emperor, *198, 199;* and the Church, 200; converts the Saxons, 199; crowned emperor of the Romans, 199; as King of the Lombards, 199; other conquests of, 199
Charles I, Emperor of Austria, peace negotiations of, 606
Charles I, King of England, 383, *384;* conflict of with Parliament, 384–85
Charles I, King of Spain. *See* Charles V, Holy Roman Emperor
Charles II, King of England, religious tension during reign of, 393
Charles II, King of Spain, and emergence of political parties, 393–94; succession to, 396
Charles III, King of Spain, as Benevolent Despot, 415
Charles V, King of France, 294–95
Charles V, Holy Roman Emperor, 304, 334–35, 340
Charles VI, King of France, 297, 299–300
Charles VI, Holy Roman Emperor, Pragmatic Sanction of, 417–18; and partition of Spanish Empire, 397
Charles VIII, King of France, annexes Brittany, 302; invades Italy, 329
Charles X, King of France, and July Ordinances, 481
Charles XII, King of Sweden, *399;* and Great Northern War, 398–99
Charles Albert, King of Sardinia-Piedmont, defeat of, 515–16; nationalism of, 511
Charles of Anjou, King of Sicily, 272–73
Charles the Bald, kingdom of, 202–3
Charles the Bold, Duke of Burgundy, 301
Charles Martel, *197;* cavalry force of, 197–98; defeats Arabs, 198; halts Arab expansion, 195
Chartered company, development of, 366–67
Chartism, 507
Chateaubriand, René de, on Christianity, 494
Chaumont Alliance, the, 464
"Cheka," 626
Cheops. *See* Khufu
Chesterton, Gilbert K., *648*

Chiang Kai-shek, flees to Formosa, 704–5; meets Allies at Cairo, 686; turns against communists, 639
Child labor, *505;* legislation against, 505
Chile, and War of the Pacific, 561
China: under Chinese Republic, 632–33; communists seize power in, 704–5; early civilization in, 66; effect of Sino-Japanese War on, 567–68; and emigrants to Southeast Asia, 564–65; European contact with, 352–54; falls under European economic influence, 565; reaction of to Europeans, 353; relations of with Japan, 661–62; republic and chaos in, 573; Western influence in, 565, 572–73
Choiseul, Duke of, and seizure of Corsica, 434
Christ, Jesus, advent of, 156
Christ of the Andes, *561, 562*
Christendom, Holy Roman Emperor as political chief of, 376
Christian IV, King of Denmark, war of with Ferdinand II, 381
Christian X, King of Denmark, 676
Christian education, Pope Pius on, 649
Christianity, reintroduction into the East, 353
Christians, persecution of, 161–62, 165
Church, the: call for reform in, 215–16; Charlemagne's control of, 200; demand for reform in, 341; in the feudal system, 214; Jesus founds, 159–60; relation of to French Third Republic, 541; role of in Old Regime, 446; spread of, 160. *See also* Catholic Church
Churchill, Sir Winston, *677,* and Atlantic Charter, 681; on Britain, 677; Dardanelles, plan of, 603; on League of Nations, 640; at Potsdam Conference, *691–92*
Cicero, Marcus Tullius, *147;* orations of, 148; public life of, 148; works of, 147–48
Circuit judges, introduced into England, 259
Cistercians, the, 243
Cities, effect of industrial revolution on, 504–5
Citizenship, basis of in Hellenic Greece, 74
Citizenship, Roman, 155; changes in status of, 39; rights of, 130
City of God, The (St. Augustine), 171
City-states: end of the age of, 99; Phoenician, 54; political changes in, 76; rise of, 74–75
Civic religion, Greek, 82
Civil Constitution of the Clergy, 450
Civilization: basic principles of, 638; beginnings of, 31–32; Carthaginian, 134–35; of China, 66–68; definition of, 30; derivation of, 30; early, 41–45; Etruscan, 124–25; Hellenistic, 115–21; Roman, 125 ff.; spread of, 45–46
Civil service, power of in 16th and 17th centuries, 377; Roman, 152
Civil war, in Rome, 163; in U.S., 533–34
Clans, development of, 30
Clare, Richard de, Earl of Pembroke, 258
Clarendon, Assize of, 259
Classicism, definition of, 490–91
Cleisthenes, reforms of, 80
Clemenceau, Georges, *622;* at Paris Peace Conference, 621–22

Edward IV, King of England, reign of, 302

Edward VI, King of England, and rise of Protestantism, 341

Edward the Black Prince, 294, 295

Edward the Confessor, King of England. *See* St. Edward the Confessor

Egypt, agriculture in, 42; Alexander conquers, 111–12; Arab conquest of, 194; art and architecture in, 42–*43;* British recognition of independence of, 633; British protectorate in, 592; civilization of, 37–38, *39;* construction of Suez Canal in, 521–22; early government of, 37–28, 41–42; early writing in, 37; economic life of, 42; and idea of afterlife, 62; kingdom of after Alexander, 113, 114–15; mathematics in, 44; Middle Kingdom of, 40–41; Old Kingdom of, 37–38, 39–40; religion in, 60–61; science in, 43–44; social life in, 42; temple-states in, 36–37

Egyptian Church, orthodoxy of, 180; heresy in, 180

Egyptian empire, rise of, 46–48; weapons of, *47*

Eisenhower, Dwight David, *713;* directs Allied North African invasion, 684–85; elected President, 707; and Normandy invasion, 687–88

Eisenhower Doctrine, 709

El Alamein, British victory at, 684

Elam, and beginnings of Persian empire, 58; kingdom of, 45

Eleanor of Aquitaine, 258

Elements (Euclid), 118

Elizabeth I, Queen of England, *346–47*

Elizabeth II, Queen of England, *713*

Elizabeth, Czarina of Russia, 428

Elizabeth of York, 303

Emerson, Ralph Waldo, romanticism of, 492

Emile (Rousseau), 410

Emirs, 226

Empedocles, theory of, 99

Empire, Alexander's plan of, 112–13

Encyclopedia (Diderot), 413

Engels, Friedrich, *585;* theories of, 584

England, as chief maritime power, 386; civil war in, 385; common law of, 258–59; conquests of, 229; conversion of, 191; Danish invasion of, 205; effect of War of Spanish Succession on, 397; friction of with Spain, 419–20; gains of by treaties of Utrecht and Rastadt, 397–98; Norman influence in, 257; political reforms in, 479–81; Protestant Revolt in, 339–41; restores Catholic hierarchy, 581; united with Scotland, 397, *398;* Viking destruction of, 204; at war with France, 424–28; war of with Spain, 428. *See also* Britain; Great Britain

English East India Company, *358;* and control of India, 357–58

Enlightened Despots, 414–15

Enlightenment: in America, 412; and the Catholic Church, 405; influence of on *Declaration of Rights of Man,* 449; influence of on government, 414–15; influence of on religion, 412–14; and reverence for ancient culture, 405–6; and "useful knowledge," 407–8. *See also* Age of Reason

Entente Cordiale, 592–93

Ephesus, Council of, 180

Epicureanism, 120–21; in Rome, 146–47

Epicurus, *120;* philosophy of, 120–21

Erasmus, *335*

Eratosthenes of Cyrene, 118

Eretria, aids Asian Greeks, 86; destroyed by Persians, 87

Ericsson, John, 504

Erie Canal, opening of, 500

Escheat, custom of, 307

Esdras, 60

Estates-General, and Charles V, 294–95; and King John the Good, 293, 294; Louis XVI convenes, 447

Ethiopia, attacked by Italy, 665; independence of restored, 680

Etruscans, civilization of, 124–*25,* 145; influence of on Romans, 126

Euboea, island of, 86–87

Eucharist, Lanfranc on true nature of, 246; Luther's belief concerning, 337; Zwingli's belief concerning, 337

Eucharistic Congresses, *715;* beginning of, 541

Euclid of Alexandria, *118;* geometry of, 118

Eugene IV, Pope, 322–24

Eugene, Prince of Savoy, drives Turks from Hungary, 390; victory of at Blenheim, *396,* 397

Euripides, *104;* works of, 104

Europe, commercial expansion of, 350–51; communist uprising in, 626; international co-operation in, 541–42; political disunion of, 376 ff.

Europeans, Chinese reaction to, 353; in India, 357–58; in Japan, 354, 356

Evolution, theory of, 578

Excommunication, punishment of, 241

Fables (La Fontaine), 386

Falkland Islands, Spanish seizure of, 434

Family Pact, renewal of, 428

Faraday, Michael, 406

Farms, Roman: reform of, 139–40; ruin of, 139

Farnese, Elizabeth, Queen of Spain, *418*

Fascists, methods of, 658; rise of, 630

Fathers of the Church, works of, 169

Fealty, definition of, 209

Febronius, attacks the Papacy, 413

Feisal, King of the Hejaz, 633

Felix V, antipope, 324

Female deity, origin of, 35

Ferdinand I, Emperor of Austria, abdication of, 516; forced to flee, 513

Ferdinand I, Holy Roman Emperor, 344

Ferdinand I, King of Naples, grants constitution, 477

Ferdinand II, Holy Roman Emperor, squashes Bohemian revolt, 381

Ferdinand II, King of Aragon, 303; aids Columbus, 358; and unification of Spain, 304

Ferdinand VII, King of Spain, *477;* throne restored, 478

Habeas Corpus Bill, 394; suspended in England, 477

Hadrian, Roman emperor, 154–*155*

Hague Conference (1899), 590

Hague Conference (1907), Latin-American participation in, 562; purpose of, 590

Hales, Stephen, 406

Hamilcar Barca, 135

Hammurabi, *41;* code of laws of, 40, 44

Hannibal, *137;* defeat of at Zama, 137; and Second Punic War, 135–36

Hanseatic League, 251, 308–9

Hapsburg dynasty, marriages of, 307; territories of, 419

Harding, Pres. Warren G., calls disarmament conference, 641; election of, 631

Hardrada, Harold, King of Norway, 256

Hart, Major Liddell, on modern defense, 602

Harvey, Sir William, and circulation of the blood, 118, 370, 373

Hastings, battle of, 256–57

Hastings, Warren, 438; trial of, 440

Hattushilish III, 49

Hawaii, annexation of, 557

Hay, John, and Chinese "Open-Door" policy, 568

Hegira, the, 193

Helen, Queen of Sparta, 73

Hellenistic civilization, age of, 115, *116,* 117–21; influence of on Rome, 146; philosophies of, 119–21; role of religion in, 119

Henry I (the Fowler), Holy Roman Emperor, 206

Henry II, King of England, *257*–58

Henry III, Holy Roman Emperor, and Council of Sutri, 229–30

Henry III, King of England, and Provisions of Oxford, 275

Henry IV, King of France, 230; fails in promises, 232; and Edict of Nantes, 344; excommunication and deposition of, 231; penance of at Canossa, 231–32; reign of, 344; and religious toleration, 379–80

Henry IV, King of England, 297

Henry V, Holy Roman Emperor, 242; and Concordat of Worms, 254

Henry V, King of England, *298;* invades France, 297–98

Henry VI, Holy Roman Emperor, 262; succeeds to throne of Sicily, 255

Henry VI, King of England, deposition of, 302

Henry VII, King of England, founds Tudor dynasty, 302–4

Henry VIII, King of England, marriage of to Anne Boleyn, 340; marriage of to Catherine of Aragon, 303; schismatic church of, 340

Henry the Navigator, Prince of Portugal, *352*

Herder, Johann, 491, 511

Heresies: in Greek Church, 179; Innocent III and problem of, 266–68. *See also* names of individual heresies

Herod, King of the Jews, 158

Herodotus, *105*

Herophilus of Chalcedon, discoveries of, 118

Herschel, William, scientific work of, 406

Herzegovina, Austrian annexation of, 594–95

Hesiod, works of, 84

Hieroglyphics, 37

Hildebrand. *See* Pope Gregory VII

Hincmar, Archbishop of Reims, and Pope Nicholas I, 212–13

Hindenburg, disaster of, 645

Hindenburg, Gen. Paul von, 601, *602,* 606; as German president, 629–30

Hindenburg Line, 609

Hinduism, 65

Hippocrates, *108;* oath of, 108; theories of, 107–8

Hirohito, Emperor of Japan, *693*

Hiroshima, atomic attack on, 693

Hitler, Adolf, Blood Purge of, 664; and Nazi party, 629–30; suicide of, 691

Hittites, conquests of, 48–49; kingdom of, 45

Höetzendorff, Gen. Conrad von, 602

Hohenstaufen, destruction of, 272

Hohenzollerns, importance of, 418–19

Holland, French conquest of, 454. *See also* Dutch Republic; Netherlands, the

Holy Alliance, 473–74

Holy Lands, Turks' control of, 226

Holy League, 330; formation of, 390

Holy Roman Emperor, title of, 274

Holy Roman Empire, founding of, 206–7; 262–63

Holy Sepulcher, crusade to rescue, 233–35

Homer, life of, 73

Home rule, in British colonies, 531

Homestead Act, 557

Honorius, Roman emperor, and the Visigoths, 175

Hoover, Pres. Herbert, and moratorium, 654

Horace, poetry of, 153

Horthy, Admiral Nicholas, 626

Hospitalers. *See* Knights of the Hospital

Howe, Elias, 498

Hubertusburg, Peace of, 428

Hugo, Victor, 493

Huguenots, 344; Louis XIV's persecution of, 389

Hundred Years' War, beginnings of, 292–93; end of, 301

Hungary, conversion of, 216–17; effect of Trianon Treaty on, 624; failure of revolution in, 516; Mongol destruction of, 284; October revolution in, 708–9; truce of with Turks, 387; Turkish conquest of, 335; Turks driven from, 390; wins national autonomy, 514

Huns, conquests of, 173–74; invade Roman empire, 175; raids of, 218

Hus, John, *320;* condemnation of, 322; heresy of, 320

Hussey, Obed, 503

Huygens, Christian, 370

Hyder Ali, and Mahratta Confederacy, 438

Hyksos, destruction of, 46; Egyptian conquest of, 41

Ideology, definition of, 657
Iliad, 73, 84
Illyria, 155; Roman annexation of, 137
Immortality, Egyptian idea of, *37–38*
Imperialism, Assyrian, 57, 59; Athenian, 91; forms of, 548; meaning of, 548; Persian, 59; purpose of new, 548; Roman, 134–39; Russian, 569–70
Inchon, 706
India, Alexander's troops mutiny in, 112; British effort to maintain authority in, 661; changes in rule of, 562; civilization of, 64; effect of American Revolution on, 440; geography of, 64; importance of, 562; independence of, 699; mutiny in, 562; religion in, 64–66; rise of nationalism in, 563–64; struggle of for self-government, 632
Indian National Congress, formation of, 563
Indians, civilization of, *363;* significance of, 364
Indo-China, French lose power over, 697; French occupation of, 564
Indus River, early civilization near, 39, 64
Industrial consolidation, rise of, 577
Industrialism, evils of, 505
Industrial revolution, "new," 575
Industrial society, and the state, 713
Industry, Athenian, 78, 79
Inflation, definition of, 642
Influence of Seapower on History, The (Mahan), 556
Ingeborg, Queen of France, 261–62
Innocent III, Pope, *262;* 267–68; and crusade in Spain, 265; and Fourth Crusade, 264–65; and Fourth Lateran Council, 269; and Frederick II of Sicily, 263, 271; and Holy Roman Empire, 262–63; and King John, 263; and new religious orders, 268–69, and Philip Augustus, 261–62; and problem of heresies, 266–68
Innocent IV, Pope, 272, 285
Innocent XI, Pope, *389*
Institutes of the Christian Religion (Calvin), 338
Insulin, development of, 645
Interdict, use of, 241
International Cooperation Administration, *714*
International trade, barriers to, 715; restrictions on as cause of depression, 653
Intolerable Acts of 1774, 433
Iran, formation of, 635. *See also* Persia
Iraq, kingdom of, 634. *See also* Mesopotamia
Ireland, conversion of, 189; effect of American Revolution on, 439; European missionary work of, 189–90; and Henry II, 258; home rule of, 631–32; independence of, 632; Viking destruction of, 204–5
Irish Pale, 258
Isaac Angelus, Byzantine emperor, and Fourth Crusade, 264–65
Isabella, Queen of Spain, 303; and unification of Spain, 304
Ishtar, 60
Isis, 60–*61*
Islam, cities of, 223; civilization of, *223, 224–25;*

conquests of, 223; Five Pillars of, 193; spread of, 191 ff.; teachings of, 193; Turkish "modernization" of, 646
Israel, Assyrian domination of, 55; "children of," 53; and conquest of Canaan, 45; creation of, 702; God of, 62; importance of, 52; kingdom of, 53–54; twelve tribes of, 53
Issus, battle of, 111
Istanbul, Archeological Museum at, *22*
Italian confederation, formation of, 523
Italian War of 1859, effects of, 524–25
Italy, African designs of, 553; alliance of with Prussia, 536; Allies capture, 685; Allied invasion of, 685; attacks Ethiopia, 665; attacks Turkey, 595–96; Austro-German alliance of, 546; barbarism of, 124; declares war against Austria, 604; French invasion of, 456; importance of towns in, 250; lack of unity in, 228; nobles' authority in, 205; at odds with Allies, 630; as part of Holy Roman Empire, 207; post-World War II losses of, 699; reverses of, 679; revolts in, 482, 510–11; seizes Albania, 673; states of, 329
Ivan III, Czar of Russia, *391;* ends Mongol domination, 314
Ivan IV, Czar of Russia, reign of, 391–92

Jacob, exodus of, 52–53
Jacobins, 449; seize power, 452–53
Jadwiga, Queen of Poland, 310
Jagiello, King of Lithuania, 310
James I, King of England, *378,* and divine right of kings, 378; at war with Parliament, 383–84
James II, King of England, *394;* and Glorious Revolution, 394–95
James III, Pretender to throne of England, 398
James IV, King of Scotland, 303
Jameson, Dr. Leander, raid of, 554–55
Jamestown, settlement of, 362
Janissaries, 311
Jansen, Bishop Cornelius, heresy of, 389
Janssen, Zacharias, microscope of, 373
Japan, acquisitions of under Versailles treaty, 625; aggression of in China, 670; aggressive designs of, 682; atomic bombs on, 692–93; attacks Pearl Harbor, 682–*83;* declares war on Germany, 600; defeat of off Solomon Islands, 685; interests of at Paris Peace Conference, 622; isolation of, 565–66; last campaign against, 692; occupies French Indo-China, 682; opening of, 566–67; post-war, 697; prestige of, 571–72; quits League of Nations, 662; relations of with China, 661–62; surrender of, 693; and Western culture, 567; wins Pacific islands, 683
Jellachich, Gen. Josef, 516
Jena, battle of, *461*
Jenkins' Ear, War of, 420
Jenner, Edward, and vaccination, 407
Jerusalem, 53; crusaders liberate, 235; kingdom of, 235; Saladin's capture of, 264
Jesuits, achievements of, 343–44; founding of, 342–43. *See also* Society of Jesus

Lay investiture, condemnation of, 230–31; practice of, 214–15

League Mandates Commission, 623

League of Nations, covenant of, 621–22; Churchill on, 640; Council of, 622; failures of, 662, 663, 665; Germany resigns from, 663; Japan quits, 662; members of, 622; provisions of, 622–24; purpose of, 622; secretariat of, 622; U.S.S.R. joins, 664; work of, 639–40

Leagues, city, 251

Lebensraum, Hitler's theory of, 664

Le Cid (Corneille), 386

Ledru-Rollin, Alexandre, 513

Leeuwenhoeck, Anton van, work of, 373

Legion, Roman, *130*

Legislative Assembly, French, 451

Legnano, Frederick's defeat at, 255

Lend-Lease Act, the, 680–81; and Russia, 682

Lenin, Nikolai, *610*

Leo I (the Great), Pope, *176;* and Attila, 175; condemns Monophysite heresy, 180

Leo III, Pope, 199

Leo X, Pope, *334, 341*; condemns Luther's heresies, 333

Leo XIII, Pope, *582;* pontificate of, 581–82

Leonidas, King of Sparta, 87–88

Leopold I, Holy Roman Emperor, 388

Leopold I, King of Belgium, 482

Leopold II, King of Belgium, *552*

Leopold, King of Hungary, 390

Lepanto, battle of, 345

Lesczynski, Stanislaus, 419

Lesseps, Ferdinand de, *531, 541*

Liberalism, Catholic, 494; Christian, 475; definition of, 474; and democracy, 474–75; economic, 505–6; Pope Leo XIII on, 582; Pope Pius IX on, 580–81; reaction against, 517; triumphs of, 482–83

Liberius I, Pope, 168

Licinian-Sextian laws, 132

Licinius, and Edict of Milan, 166

Liebknecht, Karl, 626

Liebnitz, Gottfried, 369

Lincoln, Abraham, *533*

Lindbergh, Charles A., 644

Linnaeus, classification system of, 407

Lister, Joseph, *579*

Lithuania, conversion of, 310; united with Poland, 310

Little America, 645

Livingstone, David, *551*

Livy, history of, 153

Llewelyn, Prince of Wales, 277

Lloyd George, David, *605–6, 622;* at Paris Peace Conference, 621–22

Locarno Treaty, 640; Germany violates, 666

Locke, John, *409;* theory of, 404, 409

Lollards, movement of, 319–20

Lombard, Peter, *Sentences* of, *247*

Lombard League, 251, 255

Lombards, Charlemagne becomes king of, 199; conquests of, 219; kingdom of conquered, 196; threat of to Papacy, 198–99

London, disarmament conferences in, 641; Treaty of, 597, 604

London Hanse, 251

Longbow, use of, 293, *294*

Lopez, Francisco Solano, 561

Lord, dependence of on serf, 211

Lords, House of, 295

Lorraine, Duchy of, 419

Lothair, kingdom of, 202–3

Lothair II, and Pope Nicholas I, 212

Louis IX, King of France, *278;* sanctity of, 277–78; crusade of, 278

Louis XI, King of France (Spider King), *302;* reign of, 301–2

Louis XII, King of France, *330;* attempts of to rule Naples, 329–30

Louis XIII, King of France, *380*

Louis XIV, King of France, and Catholicism, 388–89; court of, 386–*87;* and Dutch War, 387–88; natural frontier policy of, 387–88; reign of, 385–89; revokes Edict of Nantes, 389

Louis XV, King of France, *445*

Louis XVI, King of France, execution of, 452; flight of, *450;* reign of, 445

Louis XVIII, *471*

Louis the German, kingdom of, 202–3

Louisiana, ceded to Spain, 428; sold to U.S., 460

Louis Philippe, King of France, *482;* July Monarchy of, 481; revolutionary demands during reign of, 512

Louis the Pious, emperor, 202

L'Ouverture, Toussaint, revolt of, 460

Louvois, François, and reorganization of French army, 386

Lower Paleolithic Age, 26

Loyalists, the, 433

Lucretius, poetry of, 147

Ludendorff, Gen. Erich von, 601, 606

Lugalzaggizi, King, 36

Lugard, Capt. Frederick, 552

Luneville, Treaty of, 458

Lusitania, sinking of, 604

Luther, Martin, *333,* doctrines of, 332–37

Lutheran (Evangelical) Church, 336

Lützen, battle of, 382

Luxembourg, Germany occupies, 600; Spain surrenders, 388

Luxemburg, Rosa, 626

Lyceum, Aristotle's, 102

Lydia, civilization of, 54; rule of, 86

Lyons, council at, 272

MacArthur, Gen. Douglas, *685;* aids South Koreans, 706; and Japanese occupation, 693; returns to Philippines, 689–90, 692; South Pacific tactics of, 685–86

Maccabees, revolt of, 157

McCormick, Cyrus, *503*

Macedon, dominates Greek city-states, 98–99; kingdom of after Alexander, 113; rise of, 98; Roman conquest of, 137

Machine, importance of, 497–98
MacMurrough, Dermot, King of Leinster, 258
Madras, capture of, 423
Magellan, Ferdinand, *356*
Magenta, battle of, *523*
Maginot Line, 675
Magna Carta, *274–75*
Magyars, raids of, 205
Mahan, Capt. Alfred, 556
Mahratta Confederacy, 438
Maistre, Joseph de, *494;* on religion, 494; romanticism of, 492
Malacca, Portuguese interest in, 352
Malay States, as British protectorate, 564
Malmaison, battle of, 611
Malpighi, Marcello, capillaries discovered by, 373
Malta, ceded to French, 458; Napoleon conquers, 457
Manchuria, Japanese seizure of, 662
Mandarins, 67
Manfred, defeat of at Benevento, 272
Manifest destiny, theory of, 484
Manin, Daniele, and Venetian Republic, 515
Manning, Cardinal, 496
Manorialism, decline of, 253–54
Manzoni, Alessandro, 492
Mao Tse-tung, 704–5
Marathon, battle of, 58, 87
Marchand, Capt., 554
Marconi, Guglielmo, *577*
Marcus Aurelius, *154,* 162
Marengo, battle of, 458
Margaret, Queen of Scotland, 303
Maria Theresa, Empress of Austria, *423;* signs peace with Frederick the Great, 428; and War of Austrian Succession, 421–23
Marie Antoinette, Queen of France, 449
Marius, *140;* volunteer army of, 141
Mark Antony, rule of, 144–45
Marlborough, Duke of, at Blenheim, *396*–97
Marne River, battle of, *601*
Marseillaise, the, 452
Marseilles, founding of, 76; rise of, 237
Marshall, Gen. George, on Normandy attack, 687; plan of, 703
Marsiglio of Padua, counciliarism of, 317–18
Martin IV, Pope, 273
Martin V, Pope, 322
Marx, Karl, *585;* theories of, 584–86
Mary, Queen of England, Catholic restoration of, 341
Mary, Queen of Scots, 346–47
Mary of Burgundy, 301
Masaryk, Thomas, *672*
Mathematics, advances in, 371; al-Khwarizmi on, 248; early evidences of, 44; Moslem contribution to, 225
Mather, Cotton, 407
Maximian, empire of, 164
Maximilian I, Holy Roman Emperor, 330
Maximilian, Archduke, 537
Maximilian of Hapsburg, 301

Mayans, civilization of, 68
Maynooth College, founding of, 496
Mayors of the palace, 197
Mazarin, Jules Cardinal, 385–86
Mazzini, Giuseppe, *515;* and Italian nationalism, 511; and Roman Republic, 516
Meaux, Treaty of, 268
Mecca, as holy city, 192, 194
Medes, and overthrow of Assyrians, 57–58
Media, 58; Darius' assassination at, 112; Israelites' refuge in, 57
Medici family, 329
Medicine: Avicenna on, 248; Moslem contribution to, 225; Indian discoveries in, 66; progress in, 578–79; Roman knowledge of, *127*
Medina, Mohammed's flight to, 193
Mediterranean, unity of, 156
Megara, Athenian blockade of, 96
Melfi, Treaty of, 230
Mendel, Gregor, 580
Mendelssohn, Felix, 492
Menelik, Emperor of Abyssinia, *553*
Menes, Pharaoh, 37
Mercantilism, rise of, 365; weakening of influence of, 441
Mesopotamia, agriculture in, 42; art and architecture in, 42–*43;* astronomy in, 44; British surrender in, 605; earliest civilization in, 31–32; early government of, 42; early law codes in, 44; economic life of, 42; religion in, 60; Roman conquest of, 154; rule of law in, 42; science in, 43–44; social classes in, 42; trades of, 42
Messina, 134
Metamorphoses (Ovid), 153
Methodism, direction of, 494
Metics, role of, 94
Metternich, Clemens, Prince of Austria, at Congress of Vienna, 471; fall of, 513; against liberalism, 510–11; spy system of, 477
Metternich System, 511
Mexican War, 484–85
Mexico, relations of with U.S., 641
Michelangelo, 327
Microscope, invention of, 373
Midas, King, 54
Middle East, crisis in, 707–8
Middle Kingdom, disappearance of, 203
Middlemen, function of, 252
Midway Islands, U.S. naval success at, 683; U.S. occupation of, 557
Mikado, devotion to, 566
Milan, Edict of, 166
Milan, expels Austrian garrison, 515
Military science, beginnings of, 55
Miltiades, 87
Milton, John, and support of Cromwell, 385
Milvian Bridge, battle of, 166
Ming dynasty, 353
Minoan civilization, 38–39, *73*
Minos, King, 39
Mirabeau, Count Honoré, 447

Miranda, Francisco, 486
Missions: activity of, 581; in New France, 362–63; in Spanish New World empire, 359–60
Mitanni, diplomatic contacts of, 47–48; kingdom of, 45
Mogul Empire, rise and decline of, 356–57
Mohammed, life of, 192–94
Mohammed II, Sultan, conquests of, 312–13
Mohammed Ali, ruler of Egypt, 518
Moldavia, attacked, 519; autonomy of, 521. *See also* Rumania
Molière, Jean Baptiste, 386–87
Molotov, Vyacheslav, 680
Moltke, Gen. Helmuth von, *536*
Monarchial absolutism, age of, 377
Monarchy, absolute, 37–38; French, 278–79
Monasteries, destruction of, 213–14
Monasticism, rebirth of, 215–16; rise of, 171
Mongols, 283–86
Monitor, 504
Monophysite Church, 180–81
Monophysitism, heresy of, 180
Monroe, Pres. James, *486*
Monroe Doctrine, application of, 558–59; issuance of, 487
Montalembert, Count Charles, Catholic liberalism of, 494
Montcalm, Louis, and defense of Quebec, *426–27*
Monte Cassino, abbey of, *214*
Montesquieu, Baron Charles, 409
Montfort, Simon de, Earl of Leicester, 275–76
Montgomery, Gen. Bernard, in Africa, 684; and plan for German invasion, 688
Moors, conversion of Spanish, 304; driven from Spain, 225–26, 265
More, Sir Thomas, *340*
Morgan, J. Pierpont, 577
Moroccan crisis of 1911, 595
Morocco, Allied conquest of, 685; French protectorate in, 592
Morrow, Dwight, 641
Morse, Samuel, 499, *532*
Mortimer, Edmund, claims of to English throne, 297
Mosaic Law, 62
Moscow, German attack on, 681–82; Grand Dukes of, 313–14
Moses, 62; exodus of, 53
Moslems, civilization of, 219, 222–23; conquests of, 219; raids of, 205; religion of, 195–96. *See also* Islam; Mohammed
Motorcar industry, expansion of, 643–44
"Mountain, the," 451
Munich Conference, the, 672
Murad II, Sultan, 312
Mussolini, Benito, on American capital, 643; attempts escape, 691; and Italian puppet government, 685; and Lateran Treaty, 650; rise of, 630
Mycenaean Greeks, civilization of, 72–74; Dorian invasion of, 74

Mysore, attack of on East India Company, 457–58
Mystery religions, 82, 146

Nantes, Edict of, 344, 380
Napier, John, 370
Naples, Austria quells revolt in, 478; founding of, 76; French driven from, 329; Kingdom of, 273
Napoleon (Bonaparte), code of laws of, 459; defeat of at Waterloo, *472;* as emperor, 458–64; and Moscow retreat, 464–65; religious concordat of, 459; returns to rule, 472. *See also* Bonaparte, N.
Napoleon III, *518, 538;* Mexican venture of, 537; defeat of by Bismarck, 538; Second Empire of, 517–18
Narva, battle of, 398
Nasser, Pres., aggressions of, 708
National Assembly (French), and Constitution of 1791, 450; issues Civil Constitution, 450; issues *Declaration of Rights of Man,* 449; Third Estate declares itself a, 447
Nationalism: definition of, 474; German, 511–12; growth of, 476–77; influence of industrial revolution on, 504; reaction against, 517
Nationalists, Spanish, and civil war, 666–67
Nationalities, influence of Italian war on principle of, 524
Nationality, definition of, 475–76
National self-determination, Wilson's theory of, 616
Nations: battle of, 465; beginnings of, 30; derivation of, 475; new, 701–2
Natural frontiers, Louis XIV efforts to gain, 387
Natural law, Stoics' belief concerning, 121
Natural science, beginnings of, 44
Navarre, conquest of, 304
Navigation Acts, English, 365
Naxos, island state of, 89
Nazi party, power of, 659
Neanderthal man, 26–*27*
Nebuchadnezzar, *58*–59
Necker, Jacques, 448
Nefertiti, Queen of Egypt, *47*
Neo-Babylonian empire, 57–58
Neolithic Age, 28–33
Nero, Roman emperor, *160*–62
Nerva, Roman emperor, 153–54
Nestorianism, 180
Nestorius, Archbishop of Constantinople, 180
Netherlands, revolt of, 345
Neuilly, Treaty of, 624–25
Neutrality Act of 1935, 670
New Deal, 659
New France, founding of, 362–63
Newman, John Henry Cardinal, *496*
New Netherlands, settlement of, 362
Newton, Sir Isaac, *369,* 372–73
New World, international rivalry in, 360–61
New Zealand, settlement of, 486
Nicaea, Council of, 167

Nice, ceded to France, 524
Nicene Creed, 168, 169
Nicholas I, Czar of Russia, *479;* Balkan ambitions of, 518–19; routs Hungarian revolutionists, 516
Nicholas II, Czar of Russia, abdication of, 610; murder of, 616
Nicias, 97
Nicholas I, Pope, 212–13
Nicholas II, Pope, issues Lateran Decree, 230
Nicopolis, battle of, 311
Nightingale, Florence, *519*–20
Nimwegen, treaties of, 388
Nineveh, Assyrian capital at, 57
Nirvana, 65
Nobles, duties of to king, 208; growing power of, 205
Normandy, invasion of, *687*
Normans, aid Pope Gregory, 232; conquests of, 229–30
North Africa, Arab conquest of, 194–95
North Atlantic Treaty Organization (NATO), 703–04
Northern Renaissance, 327–28
North German Confederation, 537
Northmen. *See* Vikings
Norway, conversion of, 217
Novara, battle of, 516
Nova Scotia, annexed by England, 398
November Insurrection, Polish, 482
Novgorod, princedom of, 220
Nubia, Egyptian conquest of, 47

Oates, Titus, *393*
O'Connell, Daniel, *495;* election of to Parliament, 495–96
O'Connor, Rory, King of Connaught, 258
Octavian, authority of, 151; rule of, 144–45; titles of, 151–52. *See also* Augustus
Odoacer, 176–77
Odysseus (Ulysses), 73
Odyssey, 73–74, 84
Oedipus Rex (Sophocles), 104, *105*
Ogodai, son of Genghis Khan, 284
O'Higgins, Bernardo, 486
Okinawa, battle of, 692
Old Regime, in France, 444–45
Old Stone Age, 26–28
Old Testament, 52
Olney, Richard, 558
Olympic games, 82
Omar, caliphate of, 194
Ommiads, 195
One World (Willkie), 709–12
On the Nature of Things (Lucretius), 147
"Open-Door" policy, the, 568
Opium War, 565
Orange Free State, independence of, 554; settlement of, 486
Orestes, 81
Origin of the Species, The (Darwin), 578
Orkham, Sultan, 311

Orlando, Vittorio, *622;* at Paris Peace Conference, 621–22
Orleanists, defeat of at Agincourt, 298
Orleans, Joan of Arc saves, 299
Osiris, 60–*61*
Ostracism, *92;* introduction of, 80
Ostrogoths, destruction of, 196; Hunnish conquest of, 174; invade Italy, 177
Otto I (the Great), Holy Roman Emperor, 206–7; concern of for welfare of Papacy, 213
Otto III, Holy Roman Emperor, *207*
Otto of Brunswick, 262–63
Ottoman Empire, decline of, 386, 616; expansion of, 310–11; Franco-Russian conflict over, 464; repulse of, 389–90; and Russia, 518–19; state of, 518; truce of with Hungary, 387. *See also* Turkey; Turks
Ottoman Turks. *See* Ottoman Empire
Ovid, works of, 153
Owen, Robert, 507
Oxford, Provisions of, 275
Oxford Movement, influence of, 496
Ozanam, Frederick, 496

Pacific islands, American naval successes in, 692
Paez, José, 486
Pago Pago, annexation of, 557
Pahlevi, Riza, and Persian nationalism, 634–35
Paine, Thomas, opposes Burke, 451; writings of, 434
Pakistan, independence of, 699
Palaeologus, Michael, 265
Paleolithic man, 26–28. *See also* Old Stone Age
Palestine, British capture, 612; seized by Egypt, 518. *See also* Canaan; Israel
Panama, declares itself a republic, 559; French swindle over proposed canal in, 541
Panama Canal, construction of, 559
Panay, sinking of, 670
Pan-Slav Congress, 514
Papacy: Avignon residence of, 316–17; decline of, 213, 273; in the Feudal Age, 212–13; influence of Renaissance on, 327; post-World War I influence of, 646–47; power of, 233; reform of, 229–30
Papal infallibility, dogma of, 581
Papal States, founding of, 198–99; French invasion of, 458; Napoleon annexes, 463; reforms in, 511; Sardinia invades, 524
Paracelsus, Philippus, 373
Paradise Lost (Milton), 385
Paraguayan War, 561
Paré, Ambroise, 373
Paris, prince of Troy, 73
Paris, as capital of revolution, 483; Pact of, 641–42; revolt in, 512; Treaty of, 428, 438, 520–21; world peace conference at, 621–22
Parliament: development of, 282; English, 276, 295–96, 303, 383–85; medieval, 282
Parthenon, *91,* 106–7
Parthian kingdom, 113–14
Pascal, Blaise, *369, 370*

Richelieu, Armand Cardinal, *380*
Rickenbacker, Capt. Eddie, *617*
Riga, Treaty of, 627
Rigueda, 64
Rivera, Primo de, 658
Rivers: civilizing influence of, 29; importance of to civilization, 31–32
Roads, Roman network of, 156, *157*
Robespierre, Maximilien, dictatorship of, 453–54
Rocket bombs, introduction of, 688–89
Roentgen, William, *579*
Roman Confederation, 129
Romanov, Michael, dynasty of, 392
Romanticism, characteristics of, 491–93; definition of, 491; derivation of, 490
Rome, Allied capture of, 687; coinage of, *162;* civil wars in, 163; conquests of, 154; court procedure in, 149; eastward expansion of, 137; effects of empire on, 137; expansion, 129–31; French troops seize, 463; Italians seize, 538; republic of, 515–16; role of in Western economy, 179; violence in, 141–42; westward expansion of, 135–37
Rome-Berlin Axis, *666, 667*
Rommel, Gen. Erwin, African defeat of, 680, 684
Romulus, and founding of Rome, 126
Romulus Augustus, 176
Roosevelt, Pres. Franklin D., *660, 681;* and Atlantic Charter, 681; New Deal of, 659–60; and Lend-Lease Act, 681
Roosevelt, Pres. Theodore, *560;* and Monroe Doctrine, 558–59; and Panama Canal, 559, 562
Rosetta Stone, *33*
Rossi, Count Pellegrino, and Roman Republic, 515–16
Rossini, Gioacchino, 492
Rotten boroughs, 479
Roum, Sultan of, 310
Rousseau, Jean Jacques, *410*–11; influence of on romanticism, 491–92
Royal Domain, growth of, 277; influence of, 256; Toulouse annexed to, 268
Rudolf of Hapsburg, King of Germany, 274
Ruhr Valley, 629
Ruler worship, 151–52. *See also* King worship
Rumania, allied with Russia, 605; acquires Hungarian portion, 615; Germany controls, 680; growth of, 597; joins Triple Alliance, 546
Russia, abolition of serfdom in, 521; alliance of with France, 461; Asiatic expansion of, 399; Austrian offensive of, 605; Balkan designs of, 543; Chinese sphere of influence of, 567–68; civil war in, 625–26; conversion of, 220; and Crimean War, 520–21; and Crisis of 1908, 594–95; diplomatic recognition of, 639; effects of Crimean War on, 521; expansion of, 569–70; five-year plans of, 639; founding of, 219–20; and Great Northern War, 398–99; as heir of Byzantine Empire, 390–91; in-

ternal troubles of, 392; invades Poland, 454; Mongol conquest of, 284; Napoleon's invasion of, 464; and Ottoman Empire, 518–19; plight of, 616; Polish revolt against, 482; relations of with Austria, 521; revolution in, 570–71, 609–11; rise of, 386, 390; Spanish intervention blocked, 478; war of with Turkey, 419; withdraws from Allied cause, 612–13. *See also* U.S.S.R.
Russo-Finnish War, 675–76
Russo-Japanese War, 570
Russo-Turk War, 435, 544–45
Ryswick, Treaty of, 395–96

Saar region, 664
Sacrosancta, 322
St. Alphonsus Liguori, 413
St. Ambrose, Bishop of Milan, *170*
St. Anselm, *247;* on faith and reason, 246
St. Athanasius, *170;* exile of, 167–68
St. Augustine, Bishop of Hippo, 170–71; on creation, 578
St. Basil, 170; Rule of, 171
St. Benedict, *171;* Rule of, 171; Cistercian variation of, 243; Irish monks follow, 189; as practiced at Cluny, 215
St. Bernard, Abbot of Clairvaux, *244;* works of, 243–44
St. Bruno, 243
St. Catherine of Siena, *321*
St. Cryil, Archbishop of Alexandria, 180; alphabet of, 219
St. Dominic, *268;* new religious order of, 268–69
St. Edward the Confessor, King of England, 229; tomb of, *229*
St. Francis of Assisi, *267;* new religious order of, 268–69
St. Francis Xavier, missionary work of, *353*–54
St. Germain, Treaty of, 624
St. Ignatius Loyola, *343*–44
St. Jerome, *170;* on Arianism, 168; and translation of Bible, 170
St. John Chrysostom, 170
St. Louis of France. *See* Louis IX of France
St. Margaret Alacoque, 413
St. Norbert, 243
St. Patrick, *190;* and conversion of Ireland, 189–90
St. Paul, works of, 160
St. Paul of the Cross, *413*
St. Petersburg, foundation of, 399
St. Robert Bellarmine, and philosophy of Christian democracy, 379
St. Robert of Molesme, 243
St. Rose of Lima, 360
Saint Simon, Count de, 508
St. Thomas Aquinas, 225, *287*–88; revival of philosophy of, 582
St. Vincent de Paul, Society of, 496
St. Vincent Ferrer, 321
Saladin, and capture of Jerusalem, 264
Salamis, Greek naval victory at, 88

Salazar, Antonio de Oliveira, 658
Sallust, history of, 147
Salons, during Enlightenment, 408
Samnites, 130
Samogitia, ceded to Lithuania, 310
Sanders, Liman von, 598
San Francisco, U.N. conference at, 693–95
San Martin, 486
San Stefano, Treaty of, 544
Santa Sophia, *182*
Santos-Dumont, 576
Sarajevo, 598–99
Saratoga, battle of, *436*
Sardinia, joins anti-Russian alliance, 520, 522; Napoleon's defeat of, 457; Roman seizure of, 135; at war with Austria, 523–25
Sargon I, empire of, 36
Sargon II, and conquest of Israelites, 55, 57
Saul, King, 53
Saul of Tarsus. *See* St. Paul
Savannah, the, 500
Savoy, ceded to France, 524; gains of by treaties of Utrecht and Rastadt, 397
Saxe, Marshal Maurice de, 422
Saxons, invade Roman territory, 163; settle in Britain, 176
Saxony, problem of, 471, 472
Sazonov, Baron, 598
Scandinavia, conversion of, 208; Protestant Revolt in, 337; vitality of, 228–29
Schism, the final, 221–22; Great Western, 320–21, 322
Schleswig-Holstein, conflict over, 535–36
Schubert, Franz, 492
Schuschnigg, Chancellor Kurt, 666; and fall of Austria, 671
Schwarzenbert, Count Felix, 516–17
Science: advancements in, 716; in Age of Reason, 406–7; applications of discoveries in, 373–74; beginnings of, 43–44; definition of, 43; early Greek, 83; experimental, 288–89; Hellenistic, *117;* natural foundation of, 30; recovery of, 248–49; role of in Hellenistic civilization, 118–19; seventeenth- and eighteenth-century progress in, 367–74; specialization in, 578
Scientific academies, *370*
Scientific medicine, Hippocrates as founder of, 107–8
Scipio, Publius Cornelius, *137*
Scotland, alliance of with France, 277; restores Catholic hierarchy, 581; united with England, 397, *398*
Scott, Sir Walter, 492
Sculpture, Greek, *107*
Sedan, battle of, *538*
Seeley, Sir John, 549
Selencus, King of Syria, 113–14
Semitic race, beginnings of, 35
Senate, Roman, 126, *128;* and Augustine, 152; power of, 127–28; as a reactionary force, 140–41
Sennacherib, palace of, *57;* reign of, 57

Sentences (Lombard), 247
Separation of powers, Montesquieu on, 409–10
September Massacres, 452
Septimius Severus, 162–63
Serbia, Austrian annexation of, 594–95; autonomy of, 521; expansion of, 597; joins Triple Alliance, 546; occupation of, 604
Serf, dependence of on lord, 211
Serfdom: abolition of in Russia, 521; decline of, 253–54; origin of, 210–11
Servetus, Michael, 373; heresy of, 338
Sevastopol, siege of, 520
Seven Years' War, 423–28
Severi, dynasty of, 163
Sèvres, Treaty of, 625
Seymour, Jane, 341
Sforza family, 329
Shalmaneser III, *55*
Shamash, *41;* laws of, 40, 44
Shelley, Percy B., 493
Shi'ites, beliefs of, 195
Shimonoseki, Treaty of, 567
Shintoism, revival of, 566
Shubbiluliu, King, 49
Sic et Non (Abelard), 247
Sicilian Vespers, 272–73
Sicilies, Kingdom of the Two, 524
Sicily, Allies conquer, 685; capture of Athenian fleet at, 96–97; Norman conquest of, 230; splitting of kingdom of, 273
Sidon, 54
Siegfried Line, Hitler builds, 666
Siéyès, Abbé, 447
Sigismund, King of Hungary, 311
Silesia, dispute over, 421–22
Simony, definition of, 215
Sino-Japanese War, 567–68
Sirius, 43–44
Slavery: and American Revolution, 441; Athenian, 94–95; development of, 366, *367;* importance of, 425; question of in U.S., 532–33
Slavs, Charlemagne's wars with, 199; conversion of, 219; language of, 219; liturgy of, 219; raids of, 205, 218
Smith, Adam, 411–12
Sobieski, John, King of Poland, 390
Social Contract (Rousseau), 410–11
Socialism: beginnings of, 507–8; conservative reaction to, 714; in early Egyptian civilization, 41–42; in England, 643; in Germany, 540; Marxian, 584–86; national, 659; trend toward, 657–58
Social reform, 506–7
Social Revolutionary Party, 610
Society of Jesus, suppression of, 413. *See also* Jesuits
Socrates, *100*–1
Solar Monarchy, Egypt as, 61
Solferino, battle of, 523
Solomon, King, 53
Solomon Islands, 683
Solon, *79*

Somme Valley, 605
Song of Roland, The, 199, 245
Sophist school, 99
Sophocles, *105;* works of, 104
Soto, Hernando de, journeys of, 359
South, U.S., self-determination of, 533
South Africa, British rule in, 486; Dutch settlers leave, 485–86; imperialism in, 554
Southeast Asia, under European control, 564; Chinese in, 564–65
Southeast Asia Treaty Organization (SEATO), 707
Souza, Martin Alfonso de, 360
Souza, Thomé de, 360
Space, investigations in outer, 716
Spain, Arab conquest of, 195; Charlemagne's expedition to, 199; civil war in, 666–67, 674; colonies of in revolt, 486–88; crusade in, 265; under dictatorship, 658; empire of partitioned, 397; European empire of dissolved, 386; friction of with England, 419–20; Moslem culture in, 225–26; New World empire of, 359–60; *Reconquista* in, 225–26, 228; refuses to join Hitler, 679; surrendered to Rome, 137; uprising in against Bonapartes, 463; at war with England, 428
Spanish-American War, 558
Spanish Succession, War of the, *396*–98
Sparta, civilization of, 77; refuses to aid Athens, 87; system of, 78; war of with Athens, 96–98; war strategy of, 96
Spartacists, 626
Speke, John Hanning, 551
Spencer, Herbert, 543
Spengler, Oswald, 646
Speyer, Diet of, 337
Sphere of influence, definition of, 549
Sphinx, *39*
Spice Islands, Portuguese interest in, 352
Spirit of the Laws (Montesquieu), 410
Spirit of St. Louis, The, 644
Stalin, Josef, 611; character of, 686; defeats Trotzky, 639; at Potsdam Conference, *691*–92
Stalingrad, Germans surrender at, 685
Stamford Bridge, battle of, 256
Stamp Act of 1765, 432
Stanley, Henry M., *551*–52
Star Chamber, Court of the, 303
State: early form of in China, 67; emergence of modern, 377–78; Locke's ideas on, 409; origin of territorial, 30; power of, 714; socialism of, 540
Steam engine, invention of, 498
Stein, Baron Heinrich von, 493
Stephen I (St. Stephen), King of Hungary, 217
Stephen II, Pope, and Pepin the Short, 198–99
Steuben, Baron Friedrich von, 437
Stock market speculation, as cause of depression, 653
Stoicism, philosophy of, 121; in Rome, 146
Stonehenge, *31*
Stralsund, Treaty of, 309
Strong, Josiah, 549–50

Stuart dynasty, belief of in divine right of kings, 383; rebellion of supporters of, 422
Suárez, Francisco, and philosophy of Christian democracy, 379
Sucre, Antonio de, 486
Sudan, subjugation of, 554
Suez Canal, construction of, 521–22; Egyptians seize, 708; influence of on imperialism, 551–52
Suleiman the Magnificent, Sultan, 313; invades Hungary, 335
Sulla, attack of on Rome, 141–42
Sumerians, civilization of, 35–36; disappearance of, 40; language of, 47–48
Summa Contra Gentiles (Aquinas), 287
Summa Theologiae (Aquinas), 287–88
Sun Yat-sen, and Chinese Republic, 573; policies of, 632–33
Sutri, Council of, 229–30
Suvorov, Gen. Alexander, 458
Sweden, conversion of, 217; and Great Northern War, 398–99; as principal military power of Northern Europe, 381–82; rise and decline of, 386
Swiss Confederation, independence of, 308
Swiss Guards, Louis' massacre of, 452
Switzerland, civil war in, 512; Protestant Revolt in, 337
Syagrius, defeat of, 177–78
Syllabus of errors, 581
Sylvester II, Pope, and King Stephen of Hungary, 217
Syndicalists, 586
Syracuse, Athenian attack on, 97; founding of, 76
Syria, Arab conquest of, 194; befriends U.S.S.R., 708; kingdom of under Selencus, 113–14; Monophysitism in, 180; Pompey destroys kingdom of, 142; seized by Egypt, 518

Taborites, beliefs of, 323
Tacitus, 161–62
Taft, Pres. William H., interest of in Caribbean, 560
Taille, 445
Taiping Rebellion, 565
Talleyrand, Duke Charles, at Congress of Vienna, 471–72; advice of, 465
Tamerlane, attack of on Golden Horde, 314; conquests of, 311–12
Tammuz, 60
Tank, introduction of, 605
Tannenberg, battle of, 310, 601
Taoism, 67
Taranto, destruction of Italian ships at, 679
Tarentum, 131
Tarquin the Proud, King of Rome, 126
"Taxation without representation," 432–33
Teheran, Allies meet at, 686
Telegraph Union, European, 541
Tell el Amarna, 47–48
Templars. *See* Knights of the Temple
Temples, as early scientific centers, 43–44

Temple-states: in Egypt, 36–37; in Mesopotamia, 35–36; origins of, 35; degree of civilization in society of, 44
Terence, *147*
Terrain, relation of to civilization, 31–32
Tetzel, John, 333
Teutonic Knights, Baltic conquests of, 309
Textile industry, improvements in, 498
Thales of Miletus, philosophy of, 83
Theatines, work of, 341
Thebes, relations of with Macedon, 98–99; destruction of, 110
Themistocles, *88;* on Athenian navy, 87
Theodoric, king of the Ostrogoths, 177
Theodosius, Roman emperor, outlaws Adrianism, 168–69; public penance of, 170
Theogany, 84
Thermopolae, battle of, 87–88
Thessaly, 98
Thiers, Adolph, 481
Third Estate, injustices against, 445; meets as National Assembly, 447
Thirty-nine Articles, 346
Thirty Years' War, *381;* cause of, 380–81; results of, 382–83
Thoreau, Henry, 492
Thorn, Treaty of, 310
Three Emperors' League, 545
Thucydides, 105–6
Thurii, 131
Thutmose III, empire of, 47
Tiglathpileser I, King of Babylon, 54–55
Tiglathpileser III, King of Babylon, 55
Tilly, Gen. Jan, 381
Tirpitz, Adm. Alfred von, 556
Tito, and Yugoslav partisans, 688
Tordesillas, Treaty of, 359
Tories, platform of, 393
Toulouse, Count of, 267–68
Toulouse, as part of Royal Domain, 268
Towns, revolt in, 249–50
Townshend, Viscount Charles, 502
Trade: beginnings of, 30; European international, 541–42; in Mesopotamia, 42; under the empire, 59
Trade-union movement, progress of, 586
Trafalgar, battle of, *460*
Trajan, Roman emperor, 154, *155*
Transportation, progress in, 576
Transvaal, autonomy of, 554; settlement of, 486
Travels of Marco Polo, The, 286
Trent, Council of, *342*
Trianon, Treaty of, 624
Tribal Assembly, 132; and Roman theory of government, 140
Tribes, development of, 30
Tribunes, Roman, 131
Triple Alliance, *545*–46; result of, 591
Triple Entente, German reaction to, 594
Triumvirate, First, 142
Trojan War, 73
Troppau, Concert of Europe convenes at, 477–78

Trotzky, Leon, 611
Troubadours, 245
Troy, importance of in Roman legends, 126
Troyes, Treaty of, 298
Truman, Pres. Harry S., *691;* at Potsdam Conference, 691–92; and atom bomb, 692–93
Truman Doctrine, 703
Tsar. *See* Czar
Tull, Jethro, 502
Tunisia, Allied conquest of, 685; Franco-Italian conflict over, 546
Turkey, effect of Sèvres Treaty on, 625; intervenes in World War I, 603; nationalist movement in, 634; refuses to enter war, 680; and Russo-Austrian war on, 419. *See also* Ottoman Empire; Turks
Turks, Byzantine conquests of, 222; defeat of at Lepanto, 345; lose rule of Greece, 478–79; take over western Asia, 226
Twelve Tables of the Roman Law, 132
Two Sicilies, Kingdom of the, 273
Tyranny, rise of, 76
Tyre, 54, 111

U-boats, German threat of, 604, *606*
Ukraine, German conquest of, 681–82
Ultramontanes, 494
Ulysses. *See* Odysseus
Unam sanctam, papal bull, 280
Union army, victory of, 534
Union of Combat, 630
Union of Soviet Socialist Republics (U.S.S.R.), alliance of with France, 665; annexes Baltic states, 678; army of advances to Berlin, 690; army of advances into Europe, 688; foreign-aid program of, 715; foreign policy of, 628; formation of, 628; German tactics in, 681–82; Hungary revolts against, 708–*9;* industrial progress in, 656–57; invades Poland, 675; joins League of Nations, 664; post-World War II, 700–1; purges in, 674; treaty of with Germany, 674. *See also* Russia; Stalin; Trotzky
Unitarianism, doctrines of, 338
United East India Company, 354
United Irishmen, influence of, 495
United Nations (U.N.), *712;* Assembly of, 693; beginnings of, 683; Charter of, 693–95; Economic and Social Council of, 694; and Korean War, 706; limitations of, 711–12; Secretariat of, 694; Security Council of, 694; and Suez Canal crisis, 708; Trusteeship Council of, 694
United Provinces, founding of, 345–46
United States (U.S.), after the American Revolution, 441; after World War I, 700–1; agricultural progress in, 502–3; aid of to Britain, 678–79; Caribbean interests of, 557–58; Catholic revival in, 648–49; declares war on Germany, 609; declares war on Japan, 683; expansion of, *483,* 556–57; foreign-aid program of, 714–15; growth of Catholic Church in, 581; industrial expansion in, 501,

557; neutrality of, 608, 670; Pacific acquisitions of, 557; population growth in, 483; raises tariffs, 655; refuses to join League of Nations, 630; refuses to sign Versailles Treaty, 630; relations of with Latin America, 562, 641; relations of with Mexico, 641; return of to normalcy, 631; role of in Versailles Treaty, 625

Universal suffrage, *584*

Universities, the first, 248–49

Upper Paleolithic Age, 26–27

Urban II, Pope, 232

Urban IV, Pope, 272

Urban VI, Pope, 320

Utica, 54

Utrecht, Treaty of, 397–98

Valens, Roman emperor, and the Visigoths, 174

Valmy, battle of, 452

Van, Assyrian conquest of, 55

Vandals, conquests of, 175; destruction of the kingdom of, 196; kingdom of, 54

Varna, battle of, 312

Vassalage, definition of, 208–9

Vatican City, formation of, 650

Vatican Council, definition of, 581

Venetia, ceded to Italy, 536

Venice, *235, 236;* "power politics" of, 330; rise of, 235–36; republic of, 515

Verdun, battle of, 604–5; second battle of, *611;* Treaty of, 202–4

Vergennes, Count Charles, and freedom of seas, 437

Vergil, *153*

Verrazzano, John, 360

Versailles, march of women to, 449; palace of, 386, *387;* treaty of, 624, 664, 665, 666

Vesalius, Andreas, 373

Vestal Virgins, college of, 146

Veuillot, Louis, 581

Victor III, Pope, 232

Victor IV, as antipope, 255

Victor Emmanuel I, King of Sardinia, 470

Victor Emmanuel II, King of Italy, 524

Victor Emmanuel II, King of Sardinia, 516

Victor Emmanuel III, King of Italy, *630;* dismisses Mussolini, 685

Victoria, Queen of England, *529;* reign of, 529–33

Vienna, National Library at, *23;* siege of, 389–90; Treaty of, 472–73

Vikings, raids of, 203–5; ships of, *203;* in Russia, 219–20

Villa, Francisco, 641

Villafranca, Franco-Austrian armistice at, 523

Vinci, Leonardo da, *326*

Visconti family, 329

Visigoths, defeat of Valens by, 174; destruction of kingdom of, 196; Frankish conquest of, 178; and sacking of Rome, 174–75

Viviani, René, 600

Vladimir, Grand Prince of Kiev, conversion of, 220

Vladislav V. *See* Jagiello

Vladislav VI, King of Poland, 312

Volta, Alessandro, 406, *407*

Voltaire, François, 410

Volunteers, Irish, 439

Wafd Party, the, 633

Wainwright, Jonathan, 686

Waldemar IV, King of Denmark, 309

Waldensianism, heresy of, 266–67

Wales, annexed to England, 277

Wales, Prince of, title of, 277

Wallace, William, 277

Wallachia, attack on, 519; autonomy of, 521. *See also* Rumania

Wallenstein, Gen. Albrecht, 381

Walpole, Robert, 420; as first modern Prime Minister, *431*

War: effect of industrial revolution on, 503–4; importance of in feudal age, *209*–11; influence of on Old Regime, 446

War debts, payment of, 639

War of 1812, 465

War of the Pacific, 561

Ward, Wilfred, 581

Wars of the Roses, 302

Washington, Declaration of, 683

Washington, George, and American Revolution, 438–41; British commission of, 426

Washington Conference, 641

Washington Treaty, Japan violates, 662

Water clock, *117*

Waterloo, battle of, 472

Watt, James, *497*

Wealth of Nations, The (Smith), 411

Week, origin of the, 44

Weimar Republic, 628–29

Wellesley, Gen. Arthur, 463. *See also* Wellington, Duke of

Wellington, Duke of, aids Spanish uprising, 463; and Catholic Emancipation Bill, 496; at Waterloo, 472

Wesley, John, 494

West, decline of, 178–79; under barbarians, 186–87

West Indies, importance of, 425

Westinghouse, George, 499, 557

Westminster, Statute of, 640

Westphalia, Peace of, 382

Wettins, dynasty of, 419

Weygand, Gen. Maxime, 627

Wheel, development of, 28

Whigs, British, on parliamentary government, 510; power of, 431; platform of, 393–94

White Man's Burden, The (Kipling), 550

Whitney, Eli, 504

William I, King of Prussia, 400; and Bismarck, *535;* proclaimed German emperor, 538, *540*

William II, German emperor, *593;* and German-Russian relations, 593–94; Holland exile of, 615

William III, Prince of Orange, 388
William the Conqueror, Duke of Normandy, 299; authority of, 257; victory of at Hastings, *256–57*
William of Orange, ascends English throne, 394; and founding of Dutch Republic, 345
William of Rubruck, 285
Willkie, Wendell, 709
Wilson, Pres. Woodrow, 609; and American intervention in World War I, 608–9; Fourteen Points of, 613; as mediator in war aims, 605; at Paris Peace Conference, 621–*22*
Wiseman, Cardinal, 496
Woermann, Adolf, 549
Wolfe, Gen. James, storms Quebec, *426–27*
Women, equal rights for, *584*
Wordsworth, William, *491, 493*
Works and Days, 84
World capitalism, breakdown of, 652–54
World Court of International Justice, 694
World Economic Conference (1933), 656
World War I, beginnings of, 591; death and sufferings in, 618; economy of, 617; emotional derangement of, 618–19; use of propaganda in, 618; weapons of, 617
World War II, lack of peace treaties following, 695
Worms, Concordat, 242, 254
Worms, Diet of, Luther before, 335
Would-Be Gentleman (Molière), 387
Wright, Orville, 576, *577*
Wright, Wilbur, 576, *577*
Writs, system of introduced into England, 258–59

Wycliffe, John, *318*

Xenophon, *106*
Xerxes, Greeks defeat forces of, 87–88

Yahweh, 62
Yalta Conference, 690
York, House of, 302, *303*
Yorktown, British surrender at, 438
Young, Arthur, 502
Young China, 573
Young Europe, 511
Young Ireland, 517
Young Italy, 511
Young Turks, 594–95
Ypres, battle of, 601
Yugoslavia, Axis control of, 680; beginnings of state of, 615; as dictatorship, 658; partisans in, 688

Zachary, Pope, 198
Zama, battle of, 137
Zemstvos, 521
Zeno, Roman emperor, 176–77
Zeppelin, Count Ferdinand von, 576, 645
Zeppelin airships, German war use of, 617
Zhukov, Marshal, and German surrender, 691
Zionism, conflict of with Arabs, 634
Zionist movement, aim of, 612
Zollverein, 506
Zoroaster, 63–64
Zoroastrianism, 63–64; influence of on Albigensians, 267
Zwingli, Huldreich, 337–38